Tom's Hardware Guide

Dr. Thomas Pabst
with
Michael Desmond
Larry Barber
Frederick Gross

SAMS
PUBLISHING
201 West 103rd Street
Indianapolis, IN 46290

Tom's Hardware Guide

Copyright © 1998 by Que Corporation

International Standard Book Number: 0-7897-1686-0

Library of Congress Catalog Card Number: 89716860

Printed in the United States of America

First Printing: August, 1998

00   99   98   4   3   2   1

Trademarks

Warning and Disclaimer

Executive Editor
Brad Koch

Acquisitions Editor
Dustin Sullivan

Development Editor
Steve Schafer

Project Editor
Kevin Laseau

Copy Editor
Bart Reed

Indexer
CJ East

Technical Editors
Loyd Case
Michael Brown
Phil Croucher

Production
Marcia Deboy
Jennifer Earhart
Cynthia Fields
Susan Geiselman

Overview

Contents

Part II On Board

Part VI   Completing Your System

Foreword

This book was written to satisfy all my readers who were asking for some kind of paper hard copy of my Web site, Tom's Hardware Guide, `http://www.tomshardware.com`. The guide started out as a hobby more than two years ago when I saw the need for up-to-date PC hardware information on the Internet. At the time I was working as a junior medical doctor in the United Kingdom. To my own surprise, Tom's Hardware Guide has become one of the largest Web sites world wide, and is read in more than 150 different countries.

This book is designed to be a reference covering basic knowledge of high-performance PC hardware components. It acts as a complement to the Web site, but it does not replace it. This book is for people who want to choose the right computer system, as well as for people who want to make intelligent and informed upgrade decisions. As on my Web site, I prefer to let readers make decisions themselves instead of me making decisions for them. Once you are informed well enough, you should be able to withstand the marketing hype in the PC market and pick what's right for you and only you. This book also serves as a tremendous resource if you simply want to increase your background knowledge of PC hardware.

About the Author

Dr. Thomas Pabst is the founder and author of *Tom's Hardware Guide* (www.tomshardware.com), the Internet's largest independent source of cutting-edge hardware information and reviews. Tom's reviews and insights into PCs and PC performance are famous for their thoroughness and independence. Tom has consistently delivered information you can't get anywhere else. From information on Intel's future processor plans (see Intel's actual roadmap), to the latest benchmarks for hot processors and video cards, no one delivers better information or advice.

Tom's advice and reviews are so popular and valuable that in a typical month, Tom's site is read by over one and a half million people. Tom lives and practices medicine in London.

Michael Desmond is a contributing editor for *PC World* magazine, the world's largest computer publication with a circulation rate base of over 1.1 million readers. He is also vice-president of the Computer Press Association, an organization dedicated to promoting the computer press and its writers and editors. In 1996, Michael earned a Jesse H. Neal award from the American Business Press for runner-up in the best investigative article category.

Previously executive editor at *Multimedia World* magazine, Michael has an M.S. in journalism from Northwestern University's Medill School of Journalism, and a B.A. in Soviet studies from Middlebury College in Vermont. Michael has also written for other publications, including *Working Woman* and *Video* magazines, and is a contributing author to *Platinum Edition: Using Windows 95* from Que Publishing.

A native of Cleveland, Ohio, Michael is an inveterate Cleveland Indians fan, and will never, ever forgive Art Modell for moving the Cleveland Browns football team to Baltimore.

Larry Barber is the publisher of *Tom's Hardware Guide*. Larry supports Tom in all the business aspects of the company and manages the overall operations of *Tom's Hardware Guide*.

Fredrick Gross (Fredi) is the first and only Webmaster for *Tom's Hardware Guide*. He joined Tom early on and contributes to some of the editorial content on the site.

Dedication

I would like to dedicate this book to my mother, Hildegard Pabst, and my girlfriend, Catriona Egan, the two most important women and thus the two most important people in my life. My mother has been there for me over the years, and without her I wouldn't have been able to attend medical school or move to the UK, which changed my whole life and made me able to start *Tom's Hardware Guide*. Kate's support especially in the early days of the Guide and her understanding for my inability to spend enough time with her deserve to be mentioned here in particular. Her love carried me through the last 27 months.

I would also like to thank the people who have supported me on the Guide and this book. They are Fredi Gross, Webmaster, editorial contributor and particularly a friend and helper from the very first days of *Tom's Hardware Guide*, and Larry Barber, President and Publisher of *Tom's Hardware*. A special thanks to the Macmillan Publishing team of Brad Koch, Michael Desmond, and Dustin Sullivan.

Above all, I have a deep gratitude to my readers and fellow Internet editors for their support and encouragement. I would like to mention all their names but the list would be way too long.

Thomas Pabst

Acknowledgments

We would like to extend a special thanks to Michael Desmond, whose 'will do' attitude and long hours made this book possible. Also many thanks to Loyd Case, Michael Brown, and Phil Croucher for catching our mistakes and offering their own opinions in just the right places. Finally, thanks to Vladimir Svojanovsky of Emko, Alicia Lowe of Micronics, Kannyn MacRae of Belkin, and Traci Renner of ViewSonic for their quick and gracious responses to our requests for images.

Tell Us What You Think!

As the reader of this book, *you* are our most important critic and commentator. We value your opinion and want to know what we're doing right, what we could do better, what areas you'd like to see us publish in, and any other words of wisdom you're willing to pass our way.

As the Executive Editor for the operating systems team at Macmillan Computer Publishing, I welcome your comments. You can fax, email, or write me directly to let me know what you did or didn't like about this book—as well as what we can do to make our books stronger.

Please note that I cannot help you with technical problems related to the topic of this book, and that due to the high volume of mail I receive, I might not be able to reply to every message.

When you write, please be sure to include this book's title and author as well as your name and phone or fax number. I will carefully review your comments and share them with the author and editors who worked on the book.

Fax:
317-817-7070

E-mail:
opsys@mcp.com

Mail:
Executive Editor
Operating Systems
Macmillan Computer Publishing
201 West 103rd Street
Indianapolis, IN 46290 USA

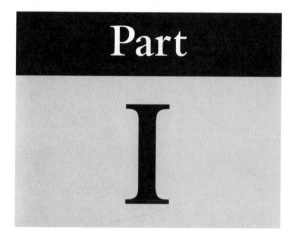

Part

I

Overview

Chapter 1

The Guide Guide

Bloated code. 3D graphics. MPEG-2 video. These are words that strike terror into the hearts of buyers who have forked over $3,000 for a state-of-the-art personal computer. New systems can become relics within scant months after purchase, as emerging technologies, better hardware, and performance-clogging software inexorably grind these investments into dust.

However, it doesn't have to be this way. *Tom's Hardware Guide to High Performance PCs* can help you extend and ensure the useful life of your system by helping you make the critical buying and upgrade decisions that keep your hardware relevant for as long as possible. From in-depth examinations of new memory technologies and CPU architectures to common sense discussions of interface limitations and system bottlenecks, the information you need to get the most out of your PC is here.

1.1 What Is Tom's Hardware

Tom's Hardware Guide(www.tomshardware.com) is one of the most popular sites on the Internet, drawing as many as 200,000 page requests per day and 6,000,000 page requests per month. In a typical month, "The Guide" delivers over 2,000,000 impressions on the front page alone. It's one of the top 50 most-visited Web sites in the world, and it's fourth among all hardware sites (data from www.hot100.com). It has also received numerous awards and accolades in both the computing and general media for its timely, insightful, and critical reviews and analysis of PC-based hardware and technology.

Tom's Hardware is the namesake of its founder and CEO, Dr. Thomas Pabst, M.D. A medical doctor by training and trade, Tom has long held an overriding interest in computing and technology. Tom was born and raised in Hamburg, Germany.

In its nearly three years of existence, Tom's Hardware has reviewed literally hundreds of motherboards, graphics cards, CPUs, and systems. New technologies have been analyzed, lab tested, shaken down, and assessed. Exhaustive benchmarking, long hours of hands-on review, and a commitment to critical reporting have helped Tom's Hardware break stories that other publishers either miss or are unwilling to publish. Whether it's getting the first word on Intel's unannounced Whitney Celeron-class processor or publishing first benchmark results from K6-2 silicon, Tom's Hardware has long led the way.

What started as a hobby has turned into a serious and growing business. Avid readers of the Web site haven't been afraid to speak up. They want more reviews, more breaking news, and greater frequency of updates. The site is growing to meet all these requests, and more. Expect focused subscriber content, a weekly online newsletter, and even more comprehensive and timely coverage of technologies.

1.2 Tom's Hardware Guide to High Performance PCs

This book is part of the Web site's extension. *Tom's Hardware Guide to High Performance PCs* delivers years of experience and technology insights in a single, coherent package. Whether you want to get caught up on PC technologies such as 3D graphics or CPU architectures, or you need a handy reference when making PC buying and upgrade decisions, this book can help you. You'll find useful insights about PC hardware and technology, as well as critical discussions of benchmark suites and methodologies, operating system software, and a host of other topics.

Tom's Hardware Guide to High Performance PCs is broken into eight sections, each addressing a specific area of technology or the industry. Within each section, three to five chapters deliver detailed analysis of specific hardware categories, ranging from CPUs and chipsets to graphics cards and input devices.

1.2.1 Section I: Introductions

This section introduces you to the world of hardware. The first chapter (the one you're currently reading) provides an introduction to the Tom's Hardware Web site, the mission of this book, and its structure. This chapter also provides a useful place to learn about what you'll find elsewhere in the book. Chapter 2, "Hardware Primer," includes a hardware overview that provides a quick, concise, and readable summary of today's PC hardware and technology. Here, you'll gain useful insights into the major issues and bottlenecks that face your performance dollar.

As its title implies, Chapter 3, "Operating Systems," delves into operating systems. You might be asking yourself, "What's a chapter on software doing in a book that calls itself a hardware guide?" Well, the reality is that your choice of operating system plays a crucial role in your hardware performance. This chapter discusses the major OSs and their strengths and weaknesses, as well as provides suggestions for which are best for which applications.

1.2.2 Section II: On Board

It should come as no surprise that our tour of PC technology starts on the motherboard. Chapter 4, "CPU Guide," details the technologies and performance

The Guide Guide

of state-of-the-art *x*86 CPUs. From the fast-fading Pentium MMX to the ultra-pricey Xeon CPUs, you'll get the lowdown on the latest technologies. Chapter 5, "Chipset Guide," looks at system chipsets, perhaps the most important component in your whole system, whereas Chapter 6, "BIOS Guide," gives you detailed insights into the workings (and tweakings) of the PC BIOS. You'll also find chapters covering motherboards and system memory in this section.

Perhaps the most exciting chapter in this section is Chapter 9, "Overclocking Guide." This chapter gives you everything you need to squeeze extra performance out of your new or old PC. You'll learn how to spoof Intel's hardwired overclock protection in Pentium II, and why sometimes you can get faster overall performance by going with a *slower* CPU clock. You'll also see tips on keeping overclocked systems running safely.

1.2.3 Section III: Storage Devices

If you think the CPU market has been hectic with all its advances and product rollouts, take a look at the storage scene. A wildfire of innovation has struck everything from hard disks to tape drives as capacities and performance continue to climb unabated. CD-ROM gives way to DVD-ROM and, soon, rewritable DVD formats. Hard disk drive manufacturers, meanwhile, face the threat of a capacity dead end in the form of the "superparamagnetic limit" and are pitching some very interesting technologies as a solution. All the while, Zip drives are selling and (unfortunately) clicking, even as SyQuest pushes a cheap 1GB drive of its own.

In this section, Chapter 11, "Hard Disk Guide," provides in-depth information about hard disks, and all flavors of CD and DVD drives get attention in Chapter 14, "Optical Storage Guide." To get a look at removable storage options, including the burgeoning class of floppy drive successors, take a look at Chapter 13, "Near-Line Storage Guide." Chapter 12, "Tape Backup Guide," covers tape backup, the slowest but by far more cost effective form of mass storage. However, kicking it all off is Chapter 10, "Disk Controllers," which covers the two preeminent drive interfaces, SCSI and IDE (a.k.a. ATA).

1.2.4 Section IV: Sight and Sound

Many of Tom's Hardware Web site readers spend a lot of time and money playing PC-based games. And as such, they are among the most performance conscious users in the world. They crave visceral 3D realism with 60 frames per second (fps) refresh. They worry about pixel fill rates, triangle draw rates, texture memory ceilings, and Z-buffering capability. However, there are more than just games at stake. A new generation of DVD-equipped PCs are now ready to playback high-fidelity MPEG-2 video, as well as display monster spreadsheets and rich Web pages.

All these tasks require the most from your graphics and audio subsystems, and this section shows you just what is available and what you can expect. Chapter 15, "Graphics Board Guide," shows you why you still need to worry just as much about API support as you do about the menu of 3D accelerated features. Of course, not everyone needs rip-roaring 3D graphics, so we'll also talk about important issues that impact resolutions, refresh rates, and color depths. The graphics board is only half the visual equation; Chapter 16, "Display Guide," gives you the complete lowdown on monitors and displays. Is there a 17-inch flat panel display in your future? Read the chapter and find out. You'll also find out what exactly to look for in a traditional CRT monitor—for example, tube size, refresh rate support, and display controls.

Finally, Chapter 17, "Sound Card Guide," provides an earful on audio, bringing you up to speed on the important changes in this arena over the past 12 months. You'll find out why your next sound board probably *won't* be from Creative Labs, as well as learn to master the new vocabularies of PCI-based audio cards. Positional 3D audio, multichannel support, and even digital AC-3 audio surround sound are all up-and-coming technologies that barely existed just a year ago.

1.2.5 Section V: Getting Connected

You don't need me to tell you how important communications have become in personal computing, and I don't need to tell Tom either. His life has been taken over by the rampant success of his Internet Web site—a testament to the power and popularity of the world-wide network. In this section, you'll learn about PC modems and their digital alternatives. You'll also get the skinny on network technologies, ranging from gigabit Ethernet to home networking products that send Ethernet packets through the electrical wires in your walls.

Chapter 18, "Modem Guide," provides detailed information about various types of wide-area communications hardware. Whether you use 33.6Kbps modems or fast ADSL digital service, this chapter will get you up to speed. Chapter 19, "Network Card Guide," takes a look at the growing importance of networking— not just in business, but in the home as well.

1.2.6 Section VI: Completing Your System

Rounding out the grand tour of PC hardware is this section on input devices and power supplies. Input devices are particularly critical. Like a good large monitor, a comfortable keyboard and mouse can improve your productivity remarkably. For instance, a gamer who flails with the tiny cursor keys on a Microsoft Natural Elite keyboard might prove a worthy opponent on a full-sized Gateway keyboard. Likewise, a scrolling mouse from Microsoft or Logitech can help you browse through long documents and Web pages much more quickly because you don't need to hunt for the onscreen cursor to click a vertical scroll bar.

Chapter 20, "Input Devices," discusses all these issues and more. You'll learn about how new joysticks can boost your game frame rates and why USB could make your PC a viable option to that Sega console. You'll also learn about one of the most important advances in game device technology: force feedback.

Chapter 21, "Cases and Power Supplies," may seem like a tour of the mundane, but it's never a good idea to underestimate the importance of power supplies in your PC. You'll learn to spot one of the many evils of cut-rate PCs—the under-powered electrical supply—as well as ways to avoid overtaxing this vital component. You'll also get a course in self-defense as we look at surge protectors and universal power supply (UPS) units that can save your components and data.

1.2.7 Section VII: Tom's Dream Machine

It all comes together right here. Working with Thomas Pabst, we take two years of experience reviewing and reporting on PC technologies and combine it with the vital overviews in this book to create a vision for the ultimate PC. Chapter 22, "Tom's Dream Machine," represents the best of what's available today—the most powerful processors, the biggest monitors, and the fastest hard disk drives. With our dream budget, we'll stamp out bottlenecks early and often, as well as apply a battery of benchmarks to determine just how fast our dream machine can go.

Returning to planet earth, we tailor our suggestions with your budgets in mind. We pitch viable performance alternatives that can save thousands of dollars, yet still ensure that you enjoy significantly enhanced performance. Savvy readers can pick and choose, pouring extra cash into one subsystem while taking the bargain route on the other.

1.2.8 Section VIII: Appendixes

Some of the most vital material is tucked away in the back of this book. Appendix A, "Benchmarking," includes a discussion of one of the most important elements of hardware evaluation—benchmarking. Few industries have been so impacted and reliant on performance benchmarks, and the results have been decidedly mixed. Rigorous tests can ferret out performance differences and lay bare a lot of suspect vendor claims, but benchmark abuse continues to be rampant. End users, publishers, and vendors alike have misinformed the market by publishing numbers based on poor methodologies, unequal platforms, or optimized code.

This appendix will help you avoid the most common benchmark pitfalls and allow you to enhance the precision of your results. You'll also learn how to spot the classic symptoms of suspect benchmarking, including the dread "missing information" ploy that is a favorite among vendors trying to market based on superior test scores.

Finally, the book finishes on a high note, with a tour of upcoming technologies that promise to extend and transform the PC platform over the next five years. Appendix B, "Future Casting," addresses advanced CPUs, exotic new memory types, and a stampede of attractive removable storage formats all now under development or in planning stage. Of course, we haven't had a chance to lay our hands on any of this hardware yet, but we'll give you the inside track on these developing technologies and their implications for your PC.

1.3 Exploring Each Chapter

Inside each chapter, you'll find consistent coverage of the technologies and issues that are important to you. Each chapter begins with an overview of the technology being discussed. You'll get the "big picture" tour of the hardware as well as a useful introduction to software and driver issues.

Once you get past the initial high-level tour, each chapter offers a performance impact report that lets you assess the relative importance of a particular device class to overall system performance. For example, CPUs play an enormous and obvious role in system performance, and you'll learn why. Also, the monitor chapter reveals the significant gains to be had from large screens.

The next section provides a snapshot of the market, introducing you to the various products available. You'll learn about key product classes and market segments, thus allowing you to better focus on the specific subset of hardware that you need to maximize system performance. The graphics board chapter, for example, breaks out the various markets, including gaming 3D hardware, precision 3D hardware, business 2D accelerators, and even multifunction boards that provide TV broadcast reception and video capture capabilities.

Once you're past this section, you reach the meat of the chapter, where the device class is evaluated. Here, important technologies and components are identified and addressed so that you can weigh the significance of specific features in your decisions. Our CPU coverage, for example, includes in-depth examinations of cache operation and types, instruction set support, floating-point unit design, and MMX capability. By delving into each of these issues, you are able fine-tune your understanding of hardware to your specific needs.

For some chapters, the depth and variety of choices demands that coverage be extended. For example, specific market segments might be drawn out and explained—or, in the case of CPUs, each major product is given its own detailed examination.

We finish up each chapter by presenting a series of useful hardware tips and tricks specific to the device class. These tips might range from troubleshooting ideas to upgrade advice, and they can address everything from system performance to user ergonomics. The goal is to help maximize the effectiveness of your hardware.

Chapter

2

Hardware Primer

The parade of blazing CPUs, cavernous hard disks, and exotic memory technologies never ceases to shock and amaze me. The seemingly endless march of technical advances have turned the PC from a limited (and oft-despised) business tool into the ubiquitous communications, entertainment, and productivity platform of the new society. Behind the transformation are profound achievements in engineering and physics that have quickly found their ways into the general market and onto our desktops.

The numerous technologies that come together in the PC are both broad and deep. Incredible precision combines with flexible connections to turn a sundry collection of subsystems into a powerful, versatile whole. More amazing, these technologies work (more or less) together, even as each and every one evolves along its individual advancement path. Better drive technologies plug into existing motherboards, while new CPUs run code written years, if not decades, ago. And all the while, prices drop at an astounding pace, allowing us to buy more hardware for less money than ever before.

Unfortunately, breakneck advancements can also bring neck-breaking problems. Incompatibilities, obsolete hardware, and burgeoning performance bottlenecks all become a factor as new technologies emerge on the market. The chapters that follow this one will give you the in-depth rundown of each subsystem, enabling you to manage and predict new technologies. This chapter provides an overview that can help you better understand the detailed information and apply the concepts effectively across your system.

2.1 Taking the Tour

Our tour of the PC will run both inside and outside the box. Starting with the motherboard—the backbone of the PC structure—we'll move on to key peripheral technologies and communications. The following subsystems will be addressed:

- Motherboard and components
- Mass storage
- Multimedia
- Modems and networking
- Input devices
- Power

2.1.1 On the Motherboard

The motherboard is where it all starts, defining virtually every aspect of your PC's technology potential. CPU, RAM, disk storage, and graphics and audio adapters are just a few of the critical subsystems that rely on compatible motherboard technologies to run in a system. Older motherboards often lack facilities to support or take full advantage of the latest hardware, creating a technology dead-end that often cannot be circumvented. The finality of motherboard issues—often the only fix is to replace the board entirely—makes this component well worth paying attention to.

In many ways, the motherboard is the backbone of the PC. Virtually all your components connect to it in one manner or another. Likewise, the motherboard is home to a number of electrical and data buses that connect devices to each other. From expansion slots to keyboard ports, CPUs to RAM, the motherboard binds the components and allows them to work together.

Here's a list of the devices you'll find on the motherboard:

- CPU
- RAM and often L2 cache
- System chipset
- Expansion bus slots (ISA, EISA, PCI, AGP)
- Disk interface (ATA, floppy disk, and sometimes SCSI)
- External buses (parallel, serial, PS/2, and more recently USB)
- Power connectors
- Configuration jumpers
- System CMOS
- Realtime clock
- Battery
- LEDs and front-panel electrical connectors

In most cases, these components, connectors, and buses can not be upgraded. Therefore, if you have an older motherboard, for example, you cannot simply add an AGP slot to gain access to the most advanced graphics cards and 3D game features. You'll need either a new motherboard (and new graphics card) or an entirely new system. That's a serious investment.

Hardware Primer

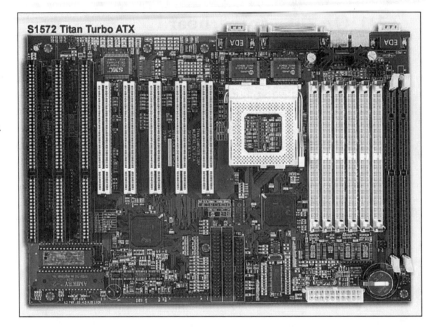

It's worth noting that if your motherboard experiences a problem, your entire system will almost certainly not function. Also, if the problem is an electrical short circuit, it could imperil the working order of expensive components such as the CPU and RAM. For this reason, it is a good idea to approach motherboard interaction with plenty of caution and planning. Don't manhandle the board when installing or removing cards, for instance, and make sure you're well grounded to avoid passing a catastrophic static discharge to the motherboard.

When you buy a new system, make a point to ask about the motherboard specifically. How many PCI and ISA add-in slots does it have? How many will be free when you receive the system as you've configured it? What speed does the motherboard run at and can that speed be adjusted? Is there an AGP slot? What about USB, ATA-33 disk interface, and Advanced Configuration and Power Interface (ACPI) features? Also, check to find out how many IRQs are available on a configured motherboard because too many systems today now ship with no free IRQs, limiting your upgrade options.

Of course, you should inquire about and make note of the manufacturer and model of the motherboard before you buy. Although Intel owns most of the *x*86 motherboard market—particularly with Pentium II systems—many system vendors use models from a variety of Taiwanese companies. Many of these products are very good—in fact, superior to their Intel counterparts—but others may come from unreliable vendors. Once you find out the motherboard model, it makes sense to check with Internet newsgroups and other online communities to get a sense of that vendor's record. You can also find motherboard manuals and documentation online, or you can call the vendor and have the documentation faxed to you. Also check out `www.tomshardware.com` for exhaustive performance and reliability reviews of motherboards from dozens of vendors.

This brings up another point: Don't be swayed by claims of the superior performance of one motherboard over another. Rigorous testing has shown that differences in motherboard performance are virtually nil. The reason: Compliance to well-established standards and the use of identical components (such as CPUs and system chipsets) among vendors means that variations are minimized. In fact, the main areas of concern are features and reliability.

> **NOTE** Beware of buying a motherboard just because it's the only model in stock. Some companies specialize in reselling cheap hardware, often unloading their poorly received product on unsuspecting buyers.

2.1.2 Mass Storage

The explosion of data coming from the Internet, combined with fat file formats, bloated applications, and ever-growing data archives have really turned mass storage into a critical area of concern. Where once the original IBM PC got by on a pair of single-sided 160KB (later dual-sided 320KB) floppy diskette drives—one for running program code, the other for handling files—the typical power desktop today comes endowed with gigabytes of tiered memory: There's a 10GB hard disk, a 7.4GB DVD-ROM, a 100MB Zip drive, a 1.44MB floppy, and maybe a 650MB CD-ROM or rewritable optical. Many systems also include tape backup or removable access to yet more storage in the form of magnetic or MO cartridge media.

Yes, storage has gotten more complicated, and not just because of the variety of media types. There's a veritable barrage of standards activity in almost every corner of this technology, and much of it threatens to make obsolete (or at least minimize) the usefulness of existing hardware. Incompatible tape formats are a dime a dozen, as are formats for near-line and floppy disk successor media. Even the safest format bets, CD and DVD, are beleaguered by tough choices in the rewritable arena. Finally, the emergence of future capacity limitations in hard disks could spur a high-stakes technology standards battle in the next two or three years.

Table 2.1 shows the drive options available for most PCs (in order of declining importance and performance) and their missions.

Hardware Primer

Table 2.1. The hierarchy of mass storage on the PC.

Drive	Storage Range	Mission
Hard disk	4GB to 16GB	Primary application and data storage; primary boot device
CD-ROM	650 MB	Application and file distribution; secondary file access
DVD-ROM	4.7GB to 17GB	Multimedia playback; large application and data file distribution
Near-line	2GB to 5GB	Supplementary file storage; supplementary application and OS execution platform
Rewritable CD/DVD	650MB to 3GB	Data backup and archiving; custom digital publishing and limited content distribution
Floppy disk	1.44MB	Primary file sharing; secondary boot device; very limited backup
Floppy successor	100MB to 1GB	Emerging file sharing; secondary boot device; *ad-hoc* file backup
Tape	4GB to 35GB	System and file backup and archiving

Ubiquitous Storage Devices

Three storage devices appear on virtually every PC sold today: a hard disk, a floppy drive, and a CD-ROM drive. Taken together, they provide a combination of fast mass storage, access to distributed data, and the ability to share files with other PCs. The most critical storage device, however, is the hard disk, which is the primary mass storage and boot device in the system. The hard disk is both large, storing 4GB to 16GB of data, and fast, providing performance that is many times faster than CD-ROM or DVD-ROM, for example. A large hard disk is critical to ensure that your system can handle the enormous installation routines of programs such as Windows 95 and NT, Office suites, Internet browsers, and advanced games and creative applications.

Figure 2.2.
Bigger and faster than ever, hard disks are a main determiner of overall performance.

Two other ubiquitous storage devices complement the hard disk drive on virtually all desktop systems. The venerable floppy disk drive reads and writes 3.5-inch disks that hold up to 1.44MB of data. Old, slow, and short on capacity, the drive technology continues to survive for the simple reason that every system has one. Floppies remain useful for moving small files among systems and for making temporary backups of selected data. However, the 1.44MB limit on the disks is too restrictive for general-purpose use going forward.

The floppy drive also acts as the secondary boot device on most PCs. Therefore, if your hard disk should go bad, you could still boot up the PC to a DOS prompt using a system disk with the critical boot files on it. From there, floppy-based utilities can allow you to assess system status, attempt fixes to the hard disk, and otherwise pursue recovery.

On the other end of the spectrum is the CD-ROM drive, the 650MB optical read-only format that has become the preferred delivery vehicle for application software and titles. Because the 5.25-inch optical media—which is essentially identical to audio CDs—is cheap to publish and distribute, CD-ROM is the preferred method of delivery for most applications and operating systems. However, like floppy disks, CD-ROM drives are slow, making the media inappropriate for directly running applications or even directly accessing some data files.

In between the two are a class of magnetic removable disc media that can best be described as *floppy disk successors*. With capacities ranging from 100MB to 4.7GB and beyond, these devices provide fast, reusable storage that can be used to both store data and run applications. The main problem: Compatibility with other systems—no industry-wide standard has emerged.

As the name implies, CD-ROM drives are unable to write data to the media, thus limiting their application. Still, that hasn't kept CD-ROM drives from becoming required equipment on virtually all PCs, as many applications and operating systems now require a CD-ROM drive for installation. Rewritable CD formats are available, but they cost more and provide slower read performance. More significant, many systems now sell with DVD-ROM drives, an update of the CD-ROM format that can store 4.7GB of data on a side.

Optional Storage Hardware

Once you get past hard disks and floppy and CD-ROM drives, you enter a broad market of removable mass storage devices that are tailored to specific missions and needs. They also come in a variety of noncompatible or semicompatible media formats that can make buying decisions quite difficult.

Perhaps the most established of these technologies is tape backup, a critical drive type for anyone running network or Web server systems. Tape media can store prodigious amounts of data—up to 35GB uncompressed on a single cartridge—allowing you to preserve data from even the most high-powered servers and workstations. Intelligent software eases backup routines, scheduling them for off-hours or kicking off operations on a disciplined rotation that ensures protection of your data.

However, tape has a real problem—it's extremely slow. It usually takes tens of seconds for a tape drive to access a particular stretch of data, if not longer. And while data transfer rates have improved to about 1.5Mbps and beyond in many cases, they still lag well behind the transfer rates of any rotating disk-based media type. Still, you can't find a more cost-effective way to archive or backup hundreds of gigabytes of data.

Less common are so-called *near-line storage devices*, which occupy a middle space between tape backup archiving duties and the fast, mass storage provided by hard disk drives. These "tweener" drives use removable, disk-based media designed around magnetic or magneto-optical (MO) technologies to deliver 2GB to 6GB of data storage on a single cartridge. Very common in art departments and other creative production environments, near-line storage is particularly adept at sharing, storing, and protecting large media file types for applications such as photo editing, 3D and animation design, and video editing.

Figure 2.3.

SyQuest's Sparq drive is among the first to straddle the line between near-line storage and floppy disk successor.

Few standards exist in the near-line market, however, so file sharing typically occurs in the limited office environment. What's more, the cost of both the drives and the cartridges can make near-line storage unattractive to some, although prices are dropping rapidly. Perhaps most intriguing, rewritable CD and (later) DVD formats can play a role in this market, providing both gobs of removable data storage and greatly enhanced compatibility and cost.

On the lower fringe of near-line storage are so-called *floppy drive successors*. These devices (such as the familiar Iomega Zip drive) typically store 100MB to 200MB on a single cartridge, with drives costing less than $200. Newer technologies seem to be pushing this segment toward the 1GB capacity mark; however, it remains to be seen what format, if any, will eventually replace the aged floppy drive.

2.1.3 Multimedia

Numerous technologies come together to allow your PC to process, display, and output complex visual and aural data. 3D games, high-resolution Mpeg-2 Video, and 3D-positional and surround sound audio all demand vast amounts of processing power. In fact, even fast Pentium II PCs cannot keep up with the load posed by these applications, making effective multimedia enhancing hardware an absolute must for most power users.

Here are the three main areas of concern:

- Graphics acceleration

- Display

- Audio

Graphics Acceleration

The graphics accelerator is the most critical coprocessor in any PC. The chip located on your graphics board is tasked with the duty of managing every screen refresh, pixel update, and 3D scene draw. Four, eight, sometimes even sixteen megabytes of memory are needed to handle the enormous flow of visual data coming from applications such as 3D games and design software or Mpeg-2 Video clips. Even simple word processing and other productivity applications call on the graphics chip to make screens snap to attention and allow menus and text to respond instantly onscreen.

Today, most graphics boards accelerate three tasks:

- 2D graphics

- 3D graphics

- Video playback

You will see boards that stress one such task over another. For example, Creative Labs' 3D Blaster Voodoo2 only handles 3D graphics displays. You need a separate graphics display to juggle standard 2D graphics and video playback. Better boards will produce faster system operation, higher video and game play frame rates, and a more appealing visual image. Advanced features smooth out blocky pixels from video, and in 3D games they eliminate annoying shimmer and provide neat transparency effects.

Display

Your CRT monitor is, comparatively speaking, the most mature of the technologies operating in your PC—television. Yet the monitor remains one of the most expensive single components in your system, as more powerful applications and faster hardware have driven tube sizes from 15 inches a few years ago to 19 inches today. One piece of advice: Do not underestimate the importance of the monitor in your computer-buying thought process. It will determine exactly what you can see and how well you see it.

Figure 2.4.
Advanced 3D games demand powerful graphics coprocessors to produce visual effects.

Like their TV cousins, PC monitors are specified by the size of the cathode ray tube (CRT) inside the casing. The diagonal area measures the area of the tubes' front glass, which faces out to the user and provides the visual canvas for all the graphics updates. Unlike TVs, however, PC monitors actually provide slightly less viewable area than the tube size would indicate. In fact, about an inch of diagonal viewable area is lopped off by the monitor's front bezel and the black area just inside it. Why? PC graphics are much, much more demanding than TV, making it extremely difficult to display reasonable fidelity at the outer reaches of the tube face. To prevent distorted pixels and mushy colors, most vendors bring in the graphic edges.

Look for 17-inch and even 19-inch monitors for game play and multitasking productivity applications. A 15-inch monitor might do for undemanding users, but once you've gone to a larger monitor, you simply won't want to go back. The wide field of view lets you display much more information onscreen, thus reducing the amount of scrolling you need to do to view spreadsheets and documents. At the same time, games and video gain an added dimension, more closely achieving the immersing effect you want to achieve.

Audio

It took awhile for PCs to integrate sound, but today the audio facilities inside new systems are taking a quantum leap forward. The advent of DVD-ROM and sophisticated gaming has spurred a raft of intriguing new features while finally placing a focus on reasonable fidelity. What's more, the emergence of Microsoft DirectX as the multimedia standard has helped unseat the Creative Labs Sound Blaster standard as the technology base for soundboards.

The change means that your new soundboard is more likely to run on the PCI bus than it is on ISA. It also means that you'll see advanced features such positional 3D audio, which lets games produce the effect of encompassing sound from a two speaker system. DVD-ROM based Mpeg-2 Video, meanwhile, introduces high-quality, AC-3 surround sound digital audio, which produces true, home theater output.

2.1.4 Modems and Networking

The Internet has proved beyond doubt that one of the greatest benefits of the PC is its ability to communicate. Email, Web surfing, shared scheduling, and even online gaming have become critical applications for personal computers and have helped to change both the working and recreational landscape. Whether you have a PC you need to connect to in the next cube or in the next time zone, you face a dizzying array of connectivity options and choices.

The most common communication device is the analog modem, which connects your PC to a standard phone line, enabling it to talk to other systems over the wire. Today's fastest modems use one or more of three standards—v.90, x2, and K56Flex—and can download information at approximately 53Kbps while uploading at 33.6Kbps. However, actual transfer rates can vary widely depending on the quality of the telephone connection and the interaction among modems of different manufacturers and standards.

Modems are ubiquitous because everybody has access to standard, analog phone lines. However, new digital alternatives are emerging that could make them the choice for future remote connectivity. Unfortunately, all these technologies require big investments from telcos or cable providers, who must upgrade their infrastructures and often lay uncounted miles of new cable and wire to provide advanced services. It will be many months, if not years, before a clear technology path presents itself.

The most attractive options seem to be cable modems and asynchronous digital subscriber line (ADSL) services. Cable modems use the existing coaxial network established by cable broadcast companies (already installed into tens of millions of homes) to deliver high-speed downstream bandwidth. Data rates go as high as

6Mbps, although it will vary depending on local usage and data delivery resources. However, most cable infrastructures lack an upstream path, so users currently need a modem connection to send data to the Internet.

ADSL may be an even better fit. Although downstream data rates are generally a bit lower than cable (1.5Mbps), ADSL provides upstream data rates of 512Kbps over the one connection. ADSL can run over existing copper phone lines, and it even runs concurrently with voice calls, thus making it a terrific option. Unfortunately, a significant fraction of phone lines will not be able to handle ADSL traffic without requiring expensive upgrades, and the telcos face years of upgrading networks. Even then, availability will remain limited in rural areas.

Table 2.2 shows the various connectivity options and their relative performance.

Table 2.2. Digital technologies promise terrific performance but availability remains limited.

Technology	Performance	Comment (Up/Downstream)
Modem	33.6/53Kbps	Cheap and universal; slow
ISDN	128/128Kbps	Available near most cities; established services; only moderately fast and difficult to install
Cable modem	33.6Kbps/5Mbps	Very fast downstream; cable widely installed to homes; often requires modem connection upstream
ADSL	Varies	Very fast and reasonably priced; standards recently set; very limited availability

2.1.5 Input Devices

Of course, you need to somehow communicate with your PC; otherwise, it will live a Seinfeldian existence—ticking away millions of times each second and processing nothing. Your primary means of interacting with your computer are the keyboard and a pointing device (typically a mouse). Both these devices are present on virtually every system, although you can find variations on their design and application.

Device input is one of the few areas where you don't need to worry about incompatibilities or performance obsolescence. These devices are such staples on PCs (and relatively low-tech to boot—after all, they only need to keep up with sluggish human input) that operation is rarely a problem. The biggest issues really have to do with personal comfort and features.

Figure 2.5.

Logitech's MouseMan Plus incorporates the same scrolling wheel design used in Microsoft's IntelliMouse pointing device.

In fact, keyboards have gained a lot of attention for their ability to actually injure those who use them constantly. Lawsuits have been won based on the assertion that no visible warning was made about the potential deleterious effects of typing for hours on end. As a result, you'll see keyboards with sloped and split faces, tweaked key positions, and integrated pointing devices—all with the goal of eliminating the strain from their use.

The one area where pointing becomes a big issue is with game controllers. Here, you'll find a dizzying variety of hardware designed to match up with almost any genre of game software, from flight sims and arcade fighters, to first person shooters and driving games. Virtually all these devices plug into your sound card's Midi/game port, but newer models also use the Universal Serial Bus (USB) for a more convenient connection.

2.2 Mobile Computing

One area of computing that isn't talked about enough is *mobile computing*. Notebooks have been around for a long, long time, yet they remain a much more expensive and problematic proposition than desktop PCs. Your notebook hardware dollar buys less performance, features, and obsolescence protection than does the same dollar spent on a desktop PC. In fact, that reduced return could widen as rampant CPU advancement and new drive and memory technologies all emerge on the desktop.

2.2.1 Notebook Compromises

The problem is that notebook components must be smaller, lighter, and less energy intensive than their desktop counterparts. That kind of advancement requires months of additional development and means that notebooks typically lag 12 to 24 months behind their desktop counterparts in integrating the latest features. Pentium II CPUs are a good example. The first Pentium II notebooks only arrived after Intel was able to perfect its Deschutes technology, which shrank the manufacturing process from .35 microns to .25 microns. Mobile Pentium II processors also use a different packaging design and require lower voltage (2.1 volts versus 2.8 volts) than the desktop version of the Pentium II.

Therefore, when you shop for a notebook, you need to go in with eyes wide open. Realize ahead of time that even the fastest notebook can't keep pace with desktops costing $1,000 less. Also be aware that battery life, among the most critical of notebook computing concerns, will almost certainly suffer on the fastest, high-end systems. Finally, don't expect to add or improve components to extend the life of your notebook—most are unable to accept more than the most basic add-ons to memory.

Table 2.3 provides a list of the most important PC subsystems and the compromise or difference you're likely to see between a desktop and notebook system.

Hardware Primer

Table 2.3. Desktop and notebook components compared.

Component	Assessment Against Desktop Technology
CPU	Lower clock speeds; often one generation behind.
Memory	Comparable performance.
Hard disk	Smaller capacities can be one-half to one-third the size of desktop disks.
CD-ROM drive	Slightly slower spin rates.
Display	Largest LCD screens are 4 to 5 inches smaller than a 19-inch monitor.
Graphics	Negligible 3D graphics acceleration and no Mpeg-2 Video support.
Audio	Abysmal speakers; rudimentary FM synthesis Midi.
Communications	Comparable performance but PC card devices are pricey.
Input devices	Small keyboards and pointing devices can be uncomfortable.

2.2.2 What to Look For

There are many types of portables for a wide variety of uses. Frequent travelers may crave lightweight and rugged design over the fastest CPU. Those who use a notebook primarily as a second machine will value performance and a large screen over portability. Other considerations include the availability of desktop docking stations and multiple-battery operation.

Battery Life

Perhaps the most critical element is battery life because this determines whether or not your notebook will be useful during long meetings or plane flights. Fortunately, almost all current notebooks use lithium ion batteries, which provide about 30 to 40 percent more energy than a same-sized battery using nickel metal hydride (NiMH) technology. What's more, lithium ion batteries do not suffer from an annoying "memory" effect, where repeated charges of a partially discharged battery causes it to store only a portion of its available capacity.

You should also consider a notebook that can handle two batteries simultaneously, effectively doubling the battery life while you're traveling. Just be aware that this type of operation usually means pulling out a CD-ROM or floppy drive module and limiting your ability to use applications or share files when using both batteries. In some models, you can swap out batteries on-the-fly after putting the notebook into suspend mode.

Most notebooks also support advanced power management features for extending the life of their batteries. This feature can slow CPU speed, spin down disk drives, and disable unneeded components in order to reduce the power draw. Of course, these steps will impact performance. A sleeping hard disk will take several seconds to spin up, and an underclocked CPU will drag down overall performance.

One coming Intel technology, code-named *Geyserville*, will enable CPUs to scale up and down in clock rate depending on the power source. If the notebook is running off an AC outlet, the system detects it and runs the CPU at full speed. Go to battery power, however, and the processor is throttled back to a speed that will preserve the battery life. The technology may also engage a powered fan to manage the greater heat dissipation of the fully clocked CPU.

Display Choices

Also critical is the LCD display screen because it cannot be replaced or upgraded. The largest screens today measure 15.1 inches diagonally, offering nearly as much viewable area as a 17-inch CRT monitor. Although the large screens are gorgeous to look at and enable high 1024×768 resolution, they add significantly to the cost of the notebook. In addition, extra-large displays demand a wider notebook form factor, which is generally more prone to damage from impact or torque. Finally, these oversized screens draw a lot of power, thus shortening battery life. If you travel a lot, you might consider reigning in the screen size in favor of greater portability and durability.

If you're looking for a bargain, check out displays based on passive-matrix technology. These produce less contrast and brightness than active-matrix (TFT) displays, but you'll save $500 or more on the cost of the notebook. The main problem with these displays is that sunlight can make them all but unreadable, and viewing from an angle is very difficult as well. Passive screens also do not update as quickly as their active-matrix counterparts, making them inappropriate for games, animation, and video playback.

Form Factor

Notebooks come in lots of shapes and sizes, and you'll have to weigh this in your thinking. So-called *ultrawide* notebooks often feature the largest screens, but they skimp on integrated drives in order to preserve portability. Sub-notebooks, meanwhile, skimp on everything, but they can weigh as little as 2.5 pounds. Systems that integrate the most powerful CPU and other options are often thicker and bulkier than other models, and they can weigh nine pounds or more.

Hardware Primer

Before you buy, you'll want to lug one of these babies around a bit to see if it suits you. If you spend a lot of time running through airports, a power-minded desktop replacement will simply exhaust you on the road. A sub-notebook might be a much better fit, and it will leave more room in your briefcase for papers, appointment books, and other non-computer materials.

In many cases, all you need is simple scheduling capabilities, access to contact lists, and maybe light note-taking and communications capabilities. Here, systems such as the 3Com PalmPilot III or any number of WinCE-based devices come in handy. They are extremely light, enjoy long battery lives, and can fit easily into a shirt pocket. Of course, you won't be handling complex documents or spreadsheets on these little machines.

Chapter 3

Operating Systems

3.1 Understanding Operating Systems

Bill Gates knew it all along. Without software, even the fastest, coolest, most advanced hardware isn't worth much. It's a lesson that fans of the Amiga are certainly familiar with—that once promising gaming and multimedia platform was steamrolled by the Windows market. And to this day, the Macintosh platform struggles for market share in a world where software developers flock to the enormous installed base of Windows PCs. In fact, many businesses have switched from Macs specifically because key business applications are simply not available anywhere else but on Windows-based PCs.

But what really makes or breaks a hardware platform is the operating system. This software is the interface between your PCs hardware and your applications, and it sets all the rules when it comes to establishing performance, feature sets, and behaviors. From disk accesses to icon design, the operating system has the first and last say in how things look and act. Because the OS is so important both in the success and everyday operation of the hardware, a discussion of high-performance hardware is hardly complete without a look at the code it runs under.

3.1.1 What Does the OS Do?

In a word, everything. The operating system runs directly on top of the computer hardware, providing the crucial, operational layer between your applications and the hardware they run on. The OS manages file access, printing tasks, screen updates, and myriad other tasks as they are requested by your applications.

The advent of advanced operating systems has raised the ante considerably over the years, however. Where in the past OSs such as Microsoft's DOS provided basic services and left much of the interface work to individual applications, today's OSs tend to be beefy, one-stop shops that integrate a host of talents. From integrated disk and system monitoring utilities, to built-in Internet browsers and applets, the effective reach of OSs has never been longer. This growing reach has been accompanied by growing code bases. Windows 98 and NT 4.0, for example, both consume well in excess of 150MB of disk space apiece.

More important, the OS determines how applications must be written to interact with the OS and the underlying hardware. The OS sets the rules of play for all applications and their developers, determining exactly how programs must behave to access resources, as well as defining what is allowed and what is not. Where one OS may allow your application to directly access graphics RAM, another OS will strictly require you to make such calls through it. Here are some other critical issues:

- Flexibility

- Access to system resources

- Stability

- Security

- Performance

- Scalability

- Compatibility

- Openness

3.1.2 Performance Impact Report

The operating system plays a big role in system performance—bigger even than many individual hardware components. That's because most commands and data must pass through logical OS structures before they can achieve their desired result. Graphics calls may take much longer in a secure, mission-critical OS such as Windows NT 4.0, whereas DOS's hands-off attitude allows applications to cut out all the fat by taking such actions directly to the hardware.

Unfortunately, trying to precisely benchmark OS differences can prove a very challenging task. For one thing, the tools used to drive benchmarks often create different levels of overhead in different OSs—provided, of course, they support more than one or two. This overhead difference makes it very difficult to tell whether or not you're looking at performance differences or simply variations in the testing software's efficiency.

What's more, the availability of identical applications in multiple OSs may be limited. Also, if the same product is available, it may vary significantly in its actual code base, file formats, or version. Finally, some OSs run only on different hardware platforms—such as MacOS and Windows 98—making it all but impossible to identify performance differences in the OS itself.

With that said, you can draw some conclusions about operating systems that run on a common hardware platform. The $x86$ platform is clearly the most fertile OS ground, despite Microsoft's staggering dominance in this sector. You'll find a wide variety of OSs that will run on top of Intel and Intel-compatible CPUs, including the following:

- Microsoft Windows 95/98

- Microsoft Windows NT 3.51 and 4.0

- Microsoft Windows 3.x

Operating Systems

- Linux

- IBM OS/2

- Microsoft DOS

- DOS compatibles from IBM and Digital

- BeOS

Of these, DOS remains the fastest, yet most feature-limited, of them all. It's utter lack of hardware interface standards in many areas allows games and software to directly access the graphics frame buffer, system RAM, and other resources to maximize performance. However, the stripped-down hot rod doesn't come with rearview mirrors, airbags, or antilock brakes—all very useful for preventing and surviving crashes. What's more, this 16-bit operating system requires tricky extenders to allow efficient access to large amounts of memory.

Among modern operating systems, Microsoft's Windows 98 leads the perfor-mance pack, thanks largely to enhancements from the company's DirectX API set. DirectX essentially instituted a series of shortcuts and acceleration opportunities into a variety of multimedia operations, including graphics handling, video playback, 3D graphics display, audio playback and multichannel audio handling. Enabling some of these features is Windows 95/98's less-than-strenuous security, which allows Ring 0 access to avoid overhead involved in OS oversight.

Windows NT is a terrific server-side OS, but it's strict security and reliability features generally make it slower than its lightweight, 32-bit counterpart. With that said, NT-optimized CPUs such as Intel's P6-cored Pentium II largely eliminate this disadvantage. The true 32-bit code lends itself to the out-of-order execution these processors support, providing a big jump on the execution of NT code over Windows 98 code.

What's more, NT is gaining more and more of the swift DirectX talents of its little brother. Microsoft has tailored DirectDraw, for example, to allow conditional Ring 0 access. The change eliminates sapping processor mode-switching over-head, and Microsoft has tailored the access to prevent any breech of NT's strict security structure. Application code still must hand off to the operating system when accessing system resource, thus preventing reckless consumption of system resources.

3.2 Current State of the Market

As detailed earlier, the *x*86-compatible OS market remains a thriving segment, despite Microsoft's enormous success in squelching its competitors. More to the point, much of the OS activity is, in fact, coming directly from Microsoft. No less than four Microsoft operating systems continue to run on the PC—five if you count NT Workstation and NT Server as separate entities—though both DOS and Windows 3.*x* have since been dropped from the company's active development plans. Rounding out the *x*86 OS scene is IBM's OS/2, which continues to hang in there despite plummeting market share, and the Open Systems Forum's freeware version of Unix, called Linux.

3.2.1 Desktops OSs

Believe it or not, the age of the 16-bit OS on the *x*86 desktop is not yet over. Despite outstanding 32-bit operating system offerings in the form of IBM's OS/2 Warp and Microsoft's Windows NT 4.0, the preeminent *x*86 OSs remain encrusted with 16-bit code. Windows 95/98, the fastest selling and rapidly growing desktop OS, is rife with 16-bit internal code in order to ensure compatibility with the dwindling universe of DOS-based software and games.

Windows 3.*x*, meanwhile, continues to enjoy substantial market share in the corporate arena, where reliability-obsessed IS managers cannot afford to undertake a risky and expensive transition to a true 32-bit OS without total compatibility assurance. In other words, 16-bit drivers for new products will have to cease being available in order to move this conservative market segment, or Microsoft needs to deliver a killer OS to make the move truly worthwhile.

That bright day is already coming. Windows NT 4.0 started breaking up the corporate bottleneck, providing a common interface with Windows 95, as well as DirectX and other similar internal structures. However, NT still lacks Plug and Play, power management, and broad driver support for many devices. Also, technologies such as USB and FireWire, which are natively supported under Windows 98, are not accounted for in NT 4.0. However, with NT 5.0 due around the end of 1998, these missing elements should be addressed. Add the common Windows driver model (WDM) that allows hardware vendors to use a single driver for all Windows OSs, and companies may well push off the Windows 3.*x* dime (that is, if Year 2000 concerns don't freeze all IS purchases and transitions entirely until the end of the millennium).

Win95/98

No, Windows 95/98 is not a true 32-bit operating system, and no, Windows 95/98 does not do away with DOS. In fact, DOS 7.0 is right there for anyone to see simply by booting up to the DOS prompt. Microsoft's early DOS-is-dead assertions were tipped over by some keen investigative work by Andrew Schulman, then of O'Reilly Associates, who proved that both DOS and 16-bit code were alive and kicking in Microsoft's most-heralded OS release.

Operating Systems

The bait and switch aside, Windows 95 has done a terrific job of moving a recalcitrant developer and hardware vendor market to the 32-bit world. Although internal Win95 structures do contain 16-bit code, the application programming interfaces (APIs), device driver interfaces (DDIs), and other developer resources are all 32-bit architectures. The design is perhaps the most critical element of Windows 9x—it introduced protected, 32-bit memory accesses to the desktop PC market. The new scheme ensures that OS code and resources are quarantined from program code and resources, thus reducing many of the stability problems under Windows 3.x.

More than anything, Windows 95's protected mode capability introduced 32-bit computing to the mainstream software market. For over three years, the broad industry of software and hardware development has been focused on 32-bit development, something that a more aggressive—if pure—32-bit OS simply could not have managed. Compatibility was a big reason the OS did as well as it did.

Windows 95 delivered a lot of key improvements over Windows 3.x. Here are some examples:

- Protected 32-bit memory access
- Plug and Play
- Preemptive multitasking of 32-bit applications
- Dynamic device driver loading and unloading
- Integrated peer networking
- Improved interface
- Multimedia acceleration and performance optimizations

Although the 32-bit transition was critical for application and hardware developers, it was Plug and Play (PnP) that really grabbed the end users. Sound cards that once confounded all but the brightest or luckiest of users now found their resource niche in the system. Gone were cryptic `config.sys` and `autoexec.bat` scripts, replaced by graphical and orderly Device Manager menus and rosters.

But PnP was not easy. The operating system must work with PnP-enhanced devices and BIOS to be able to detect and enable hardware. The vast base of non-PnP devices meant that Microsoft had to include a large database of so-called *legacy devices*, which allowed the OS to make reasonable guesses about where these aging device should go.

Another crowd-pleaser was the spiffed up interface. The ubiquitous Start button, customizable desktop, and Mac-like folders all served to fine-tune the interface and ease usage. System setup and troubleshooting was aided by the System

Control Panel, which allowed one-stop access to various hardware devices. Most important, the Device Manager facility made it much easier to ascertain information about installed devices and their status. Underlying the interface was the Windows 95 Registry, a single database of user, hardware, and software information that told Windows everything it needed to operate. Although the Registry has a rudimentary interface—in the form of `REGEDIT.EXE`—the Device Manager is the most used portal for hardware Registry editing.

On the performance side, preemptive multitasking enabled 32-bit applications to actively request and gain system attention for time-critical tasks. The cooperative multitasking of Windows 3.x did little more than switch between competing programs at set intervals, often starting critical tasks for much less important ones. However, older 16-bit apps still only operate under cooperative multitasking. DirectX multimedia extensions added to the performance picture over the years following its release, boosting graphics, video, audio, and networking operation.

Windows 95 claimed to be much more stable than Windows 3.x, and it delivered on that. Its 32-bit operation is much more stable because Windows 95 carves out a dedicated space in memory for the application, preventing other apps from corrupting its session. In addition, the OS itself exists outside the application space, generally preventing bad applications from overwriting system memory and knocking over the OS entirely.

With that said, Windows 95 is hardly bulletproof. In order to allow compatibility with 16-bit Win 3.x drivers and DOS programs, Windows 95 had to provide an open playing field where this code likes to play—the bottom 1MB of memory space. Problems arise because this memory space is also used to access key system resources, essentially opening a soft underbelly to the operating system. What's more, DOS applications in the 1MB space are not segmented from each other, making it easy for them to stomp on each other and cause crashes.

And there's more than just the lower memory problem to deal with. Chronic memory leakage and limited user and GDI heap resources mean that cumulative multitasking can and will rattle Windows 95/98 right down to its colorful bones. As a result, Windows 95/98 is not a terrific choice for business users who need "always on" reliability, or those who want to have a system they can reliably dial into from the road. Over time, stability will likely degrade, forcing reboots or application restarts.

One key advantage of Windows 9x is its advanced power management. Notebooks running Windows 95 or 98 enjoy sophisticated power-saving features for PC card devices, as well as the capability to shut down specific subsystems. As a result, Windows NT is unlikely to play in the notebook market until version 5.0 delivers power-specific features.

Operating Systems

Windows NT (Workstation and Server)

Despite the familiar name and a similar look, Windows NT has little in common with Windows 95/98 in terms of its core structure. In fact, NT was designed from the ground up as a wholly new OS, with a kernel adapted from the Unix-like Mach OS developed at Carnegie Mellon University in Pittsburgh. On the outside, however, NT comes equipped with the familiar Windows-family interface, providing an instant impact in terms of end user perception.

NT provides many of the same features of its 32-bit little brother, including preemptive multithreading, protected 32-bit memory access, and integrated networking. However, NT both adds and omits a variety of other features, making it a somewhat confusing companion to Windows 9x. With that said, the company has transitioned NT over the years to more closely match the Windows 9x feature set, with an eye to eventually making NT its sole OS platform sometime after 2000. One prime example: Windows NT 4.0 adopted the successful Windows 95 interface, making it a virtual look-alike.

So what is NT missing compared to Windows 95? For one, it still lacks the Plug and Play technology that was so critical to Windows 95's initial marketing success. Although users interact with the same Device Manager and individual Control Panel device facilities found in Windows 95, they won't find intelligent device detection and arbitration behind the scenes. It also lacks critical compatibility for older devices, DOS software, and the latest multimedia titles. Unlike Windows 9x, NT presents no friendly 1MB space for 16-bit device drivers and old DOS programs to do their thing. Such a structure—as Windows 9x has proved—is entirely too unstable and subject to compromise to be allowed in a mission-critical OS such as Windows NT. That means older DOS applications and many games won't work at all, although NT DOS includes a DOS emulation mode. Hardware vendors must provide NT-specific device drivers in order to work with the OS.

On the multimedia front, NT lags behind Windows 9x in terms of DirectX technology, the suite of components and APIs that allow for accelerated graphics, game play, audio, and other capabilities. Although Microsoft has been porting its DirectX technology over to NT, the DirectX version generally lags by a version or two behind Windows 9x—a critical shortfall since games support advanced features such as AGP memory texturing, advanced 3D graphics, and DirectMusic MIDI streaming.

However, there is good news on the NT front. With DirectX 6.0, Microsoft intends to draw Windows NT 5.0 into parity with the latest Windows 9x release—Windows 98. Microsoft has had to noodle with the underlying operating system a bit—specifically, a special form of Ring 0 access to the processor had to be provided without undermining NT's critical security features.

However, NT comes well-equipped for the suit-and-tie crowd. Its uncompromising structure may scare off 16-bit software and device drivers, but it ensures that bad code can't get into NT's kitchen and mess up the cooking. Furthermore, DOS emulation is set up to prevent any resource conflicts—though at the expense of overall compatibility. DOS programs run in a so-called *DOS virtual machine*, causing the 16-bit applications to think they reside on their own 16-bit system, blissfully unaware of the NT OS surrounding them. This structure ensures that DOS code never shares space or resources with other applications or drivers. Run two DOS programs, for example, and NT will set up a pair of virtual machines for them, maintaining code quarantines.

Where Windows 9*x* users complain that they must reboot two or more times a day, NT runs literally for months without incident. The stability comes from NT's strenuous segmenting of resources. Each application resides in its own resource space and is never given direct access to system hardware or the OS kernel. In fact, all program calls are handled in relay fashion, with the call being handed over to NT by the application, where it's then translated into NT's internal call structure and passed on by the OS.

This gatekeeping prevents system resource conflicts and gradual destabilization, but it certainly comes at a cost. For one thing, the handoff process takes time, forcing NT to switch from one mode to another for literally every transaction, both inbound and outbound. The result has been significantly slower overall performance than found under Windows 9*x*. Second, whereas NT shares the Win32 API with Windows 9*x*, allowing developers to create one code base for both OSs, the development of DirectX and other peripheral technologies have been impeded by the OS structure. Often, Microsoft has had to take long months of development time to port important Win 9*x* technologies over to NT.

NT does add a raft of key capabilities to the corporate crowd beyond just stability. For example, the NT File System (NTFS) offers useful file monitoring and management capabilities, which are useful for IS managers needing to track down problems. You'll also find more advanced system-monitoring tools bundled with NT than you will with Windows 9*x*, allowing you to track network performance and other critical operational areas. Perhaps most important are the advanced network configuration facilities of NT. Administrators are able to set up user groups, accounts, passwords, and access privileges from a single control panel.

Finally, unlike Windows 9*x*, NT provides multiprocessor support for taking advantage of systems with two or more CPUs. With its two-way symmetric multiprocessing (SMP) in the Workstation version, up to two CPUs can be used to execute program code. NT Server adds to that capability, recognizing eight CPUs.

Operating Systems

OS/2

IBM's OS/2 could go down as the saddest success story in personal computing history. After all, OS/2 was first to market with a true 32-bit operating system, leading Windows NT by nearly five years. IBM did a terrific job providing a powerful, attractive, object-oriented interface that delivered both flexibility and usability to the user desktop.

For years, OS/2 was actually a contender. The OS, which was originally developed as a joint Microsoft-IBM effort to succeed DOS, emerged after the two camps split. Microsoft went on to pursue its fledgling Windows project, whereas IBM pursued OS/2, with a handful of Windows licenses in hand. As the two OSs were developed, an increasingly bitter rivalry developed.

IBM and OS/2 fans (not to mention Microsoft antagonists) will tell you that Windows was a sham and that OS/2 was killed by a conspiracy among the trade press and general media. That's a bit extreme, but the fact is, Microsoft did a vastly superior job of marketing its Windows environment to the user, developer, and media communities. In fact, IBM routinely made things very difficult for press and programmers alike—a critical shortcoming in a market where the most popular product gains a critical and enduring advantage.

However, what really killed OS/2 was timing and development. IBM imbued OS/2 with an aggressive feature set requiring hardware resources that were extreme for the time. With most PCs still using 286 CPUs and RAM being parsed out in 4MB quantities, high system cost limited OS/2's appeal to servers, higher-end workstations, and other demanding applications.

What's more, OS/2 was decidedly difficult to develop for. IBM's API structure and documentation proved a challenge to even committed OS/2 developers, whereas programming tools such as REXX were much less numerous than those available for DOS, and soon, Windows. The result was a double-whammy—a small prospective market and a limited developer base.

The sad thing is, OS/2 was doing what Windows NT only managed to deliver five years later. It has always been a true 32-bit operating system—unlike the Windows 3.x DOS-based environment and even Windows 95's internal structure. What's more, it has been successfully deployed in mission-critical applications such as banking and transaction services, running smoothly for years on end without shutting down or freezing up. Also, OS/2's object-oriented user interface—complete with nesting folders, customizable icons and graphics, and useful file links—remains technically superior to Windows 95 to this day. Finally, versions of OS/2 were offering SMP capabilities years before Microsoft could deliver it in NT 4.0.

Today, OS/2 soldiers on but is essentially limited to vertical markets. At the end of 1997, for example, NetWare held about 51 percent of the server market, whereas

Windows NT had grabbed nearly 33 percent. OS/2? Its share was a paltry 3.2 percent, one-tenth that of its Microsoft rival. Today, in an effort to find living space in the market, IBM is repositioning its upcoming IBM OS/2 Warp OS—code named *Aurora*—for smaller, entry-level networks. A focus on Java and thin client computing, IBM hopes, will allow it to shoulder into an emerging market not already overrun by its competitors.

Linux

This freeware version of Unix—developed by Finnish student Linus Torvalds—features all the classical strengths of the long-fractured Unix platform. Designed from the ground up for a networked, multiuser mission, Linux is well-suited as a Web server platform and as a network server. Fully SMP-capable and armed with the latest directory services technology, Linux scales very well, providing a reach that NT 4.0 still cannot match.

Linux is the little OS that could. Launched by a student, and later taken up and improved by an open group of developers, Linux costs nothing and is owned by no one. Its low cost ($0) makes it a terrific platform for hobbyists and home users who want to set up their own Internet server, for example, as well as for academics, scientists, and others needing Unix-type power under a budget.

However, Linux's biggest advantage is also its major shortfall. Without a corporate sponsor, if you will, the OS lacks a service and support network to ensure that installations will be maintained. For this reason, corporate networks and Web sites typically shy away from the freeware Unix-variant, opting instead for Microsoft Windows NT, SCO Unix, or other Unix variants. Linux also lacks a graphical user interface—though freeware GUIs of varying effectiveness are available—meaning that administration and OS operations are all handled at the command line.

Although hardware device support is a thorny issue, particularly among older hardware models, Linux benefits from a fairly broad offering of applications and utilities. The OS includes a Java runtime engine, for example, and runs major Web server applications such as Apache. It also supports all the Unix protocols, including TCP/IP, NFS, and HTTP. However, client applications such as spreadsheets and word processors are simply not as numerous as they are for Windows 9*x* and NT platforms.

NetWare

Unlike the other OSs mentioned here, NetWare is different in that it's a dedicated network operating system (NOS). There is no "Novell NetWare client" the way there is with Windows NT and OS/2. Nor will you find desktop workstations running this OS, the way you might with Linux. With that said, NetWare is the grand dame of network operating systems, holding over 50 percent of the market at the end of 1997.

NetWare's proven track record, outstanding print and directory services, and well-supported installed base make it a real option for anyone looking to set up a client-server network. Although Microsoft has made swift and significant gains in market share with Windows NT Server over the past three years, many companies are simply unwilling to tip over the platform on which all their server and client PCs rely. Despite furious development in Redmond, NetWare continues to be the best platform for managing a broad range of distributed devices, user accounts, and email address lists over a LAN or WAN.

Not to say that all is rosy at Novell, either. Windows NT is gaining ground fast, in equal parts because of improved technology, relentless marketing, and perceived compatibility with all those Windows-based clients. Just as important, NetWare continues to be a relatively difficult beast to work with.

BeOS

There's a new OS contender in town, and its name is Be. The BeOS is the brainchild of Jean-Louis Gasse, former head of R&D at Apple Computer. Originally designed as an alternative to Apple's MacOS, the BeOS is a modern, compact, multiprocessing operating system that's now available for the x86 architecture. It features a fully preemptive kernel and an elegant graphical interface. With networking built in and good Internet integration, the BeOS is well equipped for today's connected applications. Unfortunately, device driver support on Intel-based systems is limited, meaning that your hardware might not be recognized on systems running the BeOS.

The operating system shines in the area of multimedia authoring, and a few applications are actually beginning to emerge. Although Be probably missed its best window of opportunity several years ago—when Gasse tried to sell the technology to Apple at a stiff price—it's not unlikely that elements of this intriguing technology will end up in mainstream applications and OSs. Whether it will ever be a major factor is open to question, but it's an interesting OS in its own right.

3.3 Evaluating OSs

A lot of factors go into choosing an OS, beginning with the question "Will it run on my hardware?" x86 PC owners won't be thinking about installing the MacOS on their desktops anytime soon. With that said, there are a lot of OSs out there to choose from, each tailored to a different mission, and each boasting a varying set of features, support, and reliability.

3.3.1 Applications

The catch phrase is easy to remember: "The OS with the most applications wins." And the winner here is Windows 95/98 by a long shot. Although NT is well-endowed with the entire range of Win32-developed applications, it's lack of broad DOS compatibility and lagging DirectX facilities make it inappropriate for most home users. Hardware support is also more limited, and you'll find a more active Win95 utility market as well.

Although NT is generally well supported among active developers, game and multimedia title vendors simply cannot make a living under NT's strict security protocols, which sap performance. Microsoft is addressing this flank with NT 5.0; however, the lack of advanced DirectX features under NT means that for the time being the best games and titles will only run well under Windows 95/98.

If you don't care about the latest version of Quake or Incoming, however, NT 4.0 and its successors are well supported and make a terrific platform for business computing. The application selection through the range of productivity, utility, development, and networking applications is simply vast, in large part because NT shares the Win32 API with Windows 95/98.

Once you get past Microsoft's offerings, the field slims considerably. Linux does well in the Web server, network server, and scientific application spaces, but you may often have to find and personally compile freeware applications yourself. OS/2 features its own office application in the form of Lotus SmartSuite and is well served again in the vertical network markets. However, its compatibility with Windows applications only goes as far as Windows 3.x, and developer support for end-user applications has withered markedly.

3.3.2 Hardware Compatibility

Once again, Windows 95/98 excels in its support for the broadest range of hardware devices. The OS's capability to work with both 32- and 16-bit drivers means that even peripherals from the hoary old days of DOS will generally work—though performance and reliability are both likely to take a hit. In addition to the built-in compatibility, hardware vendors generally target the Windows 9x market first, because of its large and growing user base and the vast number of new systems shipping with the OS.

Extending the hardware advantage is the DirectX technologies, which are developed most aggressively for the Windows 9x platform. 3D graphics cards, TV tuners, DVD media decoders, and force feedback joysticks all depend on the presence of DirectX 5 or 6 to operate. Although Microsoft is tailoring its DirectX tools to NT and is slowly making progress in extending its features sets to this corporate OS, the lagging pace and different user base has made this area less compelling.

Operating Systems

In addition, Windows 9x has been first to market with key technology support such as USB, FireWire, DVD, and AGP. As a result, these emergent product sectors have all been focused squarely on the Windows 9x market (most specifically, Windows 98). In fact, in this area, Windows 98 enjoys a distinct advantage over Windows 95, because it fully integrates USB and DVD features into the OS, whereas Windows 95 requires extra driver development work from hardware vendors.

Other operating systems can't even approach the level of support of NT. IBM OS/2 has simply fallen off the development map for many companies, though support continues for the continuing market of OS/2-based servers. Although some areas, such as printers and network devices, enjoy reasonable coverage, support in areas such as DVD, 3D graphics, advanced audio, and other applications is very slim. Linux enjoys a vibrant grass routes driver development effort, but its progress is limited and many older devices simply are not supported at all.

3.3.3 Reliability

Don't look to Windows 9x here. Microsoft made its compromises when it decided that Windows 95 must be compatible with existing DOS code and 16-bit drivers. It has paid the price in the form of the OS's reliability. Windows 95 and 98 are prone to crashing when subject to moderate to heavy multitasking, in part due to the lack of control in the 1MB lower memory space and the effects of memory leakage and resource shortages.

For reliability, you can look to any of the advanced 32-bit operating systems, but your best bet is with Linux and OS/2. Both systems can run for months without a hiccup, resisting even attempts by poorly behaved applications to bring them down. However, Linux is a tough choice here—if things go bad, there's no coherent, corporate service presence to call on. At least with OS/2, you can tell your boss that the service techs are on the way to look into the problem.

Windows NT 4.0, while a significant advancement over Windows 9x, still lags in overall reliability compared to Unix and OS/2. Crashes can occur on occasion— and we're talking about weeks or months between events here—making it important for NT administrators to ensure that proper redundancy is in place. Although Microsoft assures us that their twiddling with Ring 0 access in the DirectX for NT set won't imperil the kernel's security, it may be worth taking a wait-and-see approach before installing the latest multimedia extensions.

Of course, NT has also suffered from some well-publicized security lapses, in both its network server and Web server iterations. ActiveX components, for example, have proved to be a problem that needed addressing, as has integration of IE4 into the package. In virtually all cases, however, Microsoft has been swift and effective in plugging these holes when they came to attention.

3.4 Tom's Pick

So what software should you run? Well, when it comes to OSs, for most of us, the decision is about compromises. Yes, OS/2 and Linux provide better scalability and reliability. And, yes, Windows 9x has proved to be nearly as buggy and crash prone—particularly in its Active Desktop iteration—as the much-despised Windows 3.x. However, you won't find a broader and more attractive selection of software and hardware than you will with Microsoft's Windows 9x and Windows NT.

Whether you run a small office and network or use a PC for playing online games and viewing reference titles, the choice is clear. Microsoft Windows enjoys such a commanding advantage in terms of application and device support that no other OS can come close. From force feedback joysticks and USB scanners to red-hot 3D games and graphics software, Windows 9x and NT can run them. Yes, you'll have to live with crashes, compromises, and the fact that you've helped fill Bill Gates's pockets. But today, no other OS—or even the combination of them all put together—can deliver as much value to your PC as either Windows 9x or NT can.

With that said, Windows 9x is poor enough that I can't live with it alone. For that reason, I dual-boot my current Pentium II-300 system with Windows 98 and NT 4.0 Workstation. Windows 98 allows me to play the latest games and titles, whereas NT gives me rock-solid crash protection, Internet Information Server Web serving software, and advanced network administration features. The two OSs live comfortably side by side, accessing common application code from a FAT 16 partition.

Will Windows NT 5.0 knock Windows 98 off my desktop? I certainly hope so, but I'm not expecting it. Although Microsoft has high hopes and big promises for this next version, we'll have to wait and see. The common driver model, for example, may not effectively extend to critical devices such as 3D graphics cards, though NT will make big gains with DirectX 6.0, which should bring NT's multimedia talents in synch with Windows 98. The addition of ACPI-compliant Plug and Play will be welcome, as will be the much-improved suite of directory services.

Operating Systems

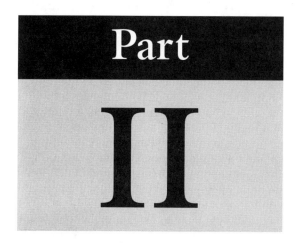

Part

II

On Board

Chapter

4

CPU Guide

If you expect top performance from your system, you have to accept that it all starts and ends with the CPU. Whiz-bang graphics cards and oceans of RAM won't fix a system that's dragged down by a pokey processor. Whether you're crunching numbers in Excel or rendering dimly lit hallways in Quake, the capability of your system to get the job done relies first and foremost on its CPU.

In this chapter, I'll get into the nitty-gritty of CPU operation and behavior. You'll see why even the fastest AMD K6 will fall behind any Pentium II when running MMX-enhanced software and how you can avoid buying a system with a CPU that already has one foot in the grave. I'll also take you on a tour of virtually every major PC CPU on the market, allowing you to fathom the intricacies of these critical components.

4.1 Understanding CPUs

It's a testament to the importance of PCs in society that Moore's Law is as well known as it is. True to Gordon Moore's assertion, CPUs have continued to double in performance approximately every 18 months. However, Moore's Law doesn't come without a price. The growth in performance has been matched by the growing complexity of the processors themselves, requiring billions of dollars of investment to create fabrication plants(or *fabs*) to build these tiny constructs (see Figure 4.1).

Figure 4.1.

The complex core of modern CPUs often contain 8 million individual transistors. (Figure courtesy of AMD Corp.)

How much more complex are we talking about? When the Pentium emerged on the market in March, 1993, it had an astonishing 3.1 million transistors built on a .8-micron process. Today, the mainstream CPU processor of choice is Intel's Pentium II, which weighs in with 7.5 million transistors built on a .25 micron process. At the same time, clock speeds went from 66MHz to 450MHz, a seven-fold increase.

> **NOTE** The compactness of CPU transistors is a critical component of processor design and a factor in the chip's clock speed. Better CPUs have smaller transistors, which are measured in microns, with one micron equaling 1/100th the width of a human hair. Today's Pentium II CPUs are built using a .25 micron process (1/400th of a human hair), whereas most 486 CPUs were built using one micron transistor. The smaller sizes allow electrical charges to move more efficiently through the semiconductive medium, enabling higher clock rates while reducing heat output that can damage the chip.

The task of building such intricate, complex products is daunting. At .25 microns, the traces within the CPU are a mere 1/400th the width of a human hair, requiring rigorous precision in manufacture and testing. As the complexity has increased, CPU competitors such as AMD and Cyrix have struggled with high failure rates for products coming off the line. With a CPU fabrication plant costing up to $10 billion to build, the risk associated with CPU manufacturing is enormous.

4.1.1 The Internal Workings

To understand how a CPU works, it helps to think of a CPU as a tiny assembly line, where incoming bits are shuffled through a series of pipes and stages until they come out at the other end as a complete product. CPUs process data and instructions in stages, much the way a factory floor might work, prepping bits in one area so that they might be sent onto the next.

The work happens on an atomic level, with individual 1s and 0s moving through the CPU's structure. By conducting millions of these individual operations each second, processors can assemble everything from mathematical results to annual reports to frames of high-quality MPEG-2 video.

CPU Clock Speeds

Today, Intel's fastest Pentium II CPU runs at a staggering 450MHz, or 450 million ticks per second. That's 55 times faster than the 8MHz CPU found in the original IBM PC, and twice the speed of the fastest Intel CPU from the generation before—the Pentium Pro.

Surely a 386- or 486-based PC would benefit from a CPU running at 300 or 400MHz, so why didn't they run at higher clock rates? Here's a simple answer: They can't. The bits moving through a CPU are a series of discreet electrical charges, high voltage for a 1 value and low voltage for a 0 value. As they move through the semiconductive silicon medium of the processor, they encounter resistance—resistance that is expressed as heat.

Heat is the waste product of CPU operation, and it effectively limits clock speed. Generate too much heat, and the semiconductive silicon is not so "semi" anymore—electrical charges stop moving altogether. By shrinking the size of the transistors (the objects that store electrical values at each stage of the assembly line) in the CPU, companies such as Intel and Motorola have managed to reduce the amount of resistance produced by the medium, thus lowering the thermal output. The result? CPU designers could step on the gas and boost clock rates.

The higher clock rates demand CPU designs tailored to the job. Because the clock is moving things forward very quickly, a segmented architecture that keeps bits moving helps to avoid blockages that can sap performance. Called a *pipeline*, this structure closely resembles an assembly line in that a small operation is conducted at each point and then the value is moved on. As the CPU gets faster, pipelines need to become deeper to maintain efficient movement.

Clock speed hardly tells the story of CPU advancement. In fact, the speed of the CPU clock can be more deceptive than almost any other spec you read about. However, it is one spec that nearly everyone can understand—even marketing folk—so it tends to be overworked in advertising and press accounts. Advanced CPU architectures are able to do more in a single clock tick than older designs, acting as a performance multiplier that simply doesn't show up in the megahertz hype. This is known as *superscalar* processing. A complex CPU can conduct multiple operations simultaneously and can work on incomplete data by making educated bets about what types of bits are coming next. Older designs may only have one or two independent pipes and must often wait idle while requested data makes its way to the process.

CPU Size and Voltages

Building long, fast pipelines is complex business. The number of transistors required to build a Pentium II CPU is seven or eight times that used in a 486. However, if the CPU were to be proportionally larger, you'd end up with an enormous, liquid cooled processor that would cost thousands to build and maintain.

Today, Intel's fastest Pentium II processors are built on a .25-micron process, with .18 micron CPUs expected by the end of 1998. Shrinking the transistor size allows designers to build more complexity and features into a similar-sized package, yielding the critical performance gain. The more compact package also drives down manufacturing costs by increasing the number of CPUs produced on each circular die and helping increase the relative proportion of "good" CPUs that roll off the production line.

At the same time as transistors are getting smaller, the amount of voltage needed to express 1s and 0s is decreasing. The more efficient operation again reduces heat and allows for higher clock rates. So where the original 486 ran at 5 volts, most Pentiums in use today run at 3.3 volts. Pentium MMX runs at 2.8 volts, whereas newer Deschutes-class Pentium II CPUs draw a meager 2.0 volts.

The next step down in size is to .18 microns. At this level, Intel CPUs should be able to run well above 500MHz, perhaps as high as 700 or 800MHz. Although Intel has discussed gigahertz (1,000MHz) clock rates for its Merced IA-64 CPU, it's unclear whether this is expected on the current .18 micron process or perhaps on a smaller process (around .13 microns).

One other notable advancement promises to kick CPU clocks toward 1GHz: the use of copper in the CPU material. In the past, aluminum has been used in the CPU traces because it was the most efficient affordable conductive material available. Although copper is much more efficient electrically, the material has the undesired side-effect of destroying the properties of the silicon around it. When IBM discovered a way to safely use copper in their CPU designs, the efficiency of the inner workings improved immensely. Intel, AMD, and others are expected to adopt similar copper technologies over the next three years.

4.1.2 The Role of Instruction Sets

The *instruction set* defines the specific operations a CPU can recognize. At the broadest level, the instruction set determines compatibility—programs written to the *x*86 instruction set cannot run natively on PowerPC CPUs, just as PowerPC-coded programs won't run on a Pentium II system. The instruction set is also a major determiner of CPU performance.

Intel and compatible CPUs all use the so-called *x86 instruction set*, which consists of 147 individual operations. In most cases, programmers don't actually write to the low-level instruction, rather they use a programming language (such as C++ or Visual Basic) that provides a structured syntax. The programming environment then compiles the code into the intricate, tiny instructions recognized by the target processor.

Puzzling out the RISC versus CISC Debate

For years, the performance debate revolved around two philosophies of computing: Reduced Instruction Set Computing (RISC) and Complex Instruction Set Computing (CISC). The difference boils down to the size of the instruction set used by the CPU. A larger inventory of instructions requires additional transistors and microcode to execute, thus slowing CPU performance.

The *x*86 instruction set is of the CISC variety. Intel went with the complex set because, at the time, it allowed the CPU to do more in each clock tick, helping

CPU Guide

offset the limitation of the 8MHz clock rate. As CPU speeds increased, however, the CISC design became a burden. The complex CISC microcode and circuitry made it more difficult to operate at high clock rates than streamlined RISC type processors such as PowerPC.

What's more, Intel couldn't do much to change things. The strength of its *x*86 processors was in the widespread software written for it. Change the underpinnings of the CPU, and you not only threaten compatibility with existing programs but some developers might even jump to the Macintosh 680*x*0 and PowerPC architectures. Instead, Intel did the pragmatic thing and went about the hard work of building RISC characteristics into its CPUs—an effort that has paid off handsomely in the P6 architectures of the Pentium Pro and Pentium II.

Today, there's not a lot of argument about the merits of CISC versus RISC computing. The fact that Pentium II CPUs run at 400MHz is ample testament to Intel's success in streamlining its CPU designs. Competitors such as AMD and Cyrix, meanwhile, have done much the same thing.

MMX, Katmai, and 3D-Now

The *x*86 instruction set continues to grow. In 1996, Intel launched the Pentium MMX processor, an enhanced version of the Pentium. In addition to a larger L1 cache that helped boost overall performance, the Pentium MMX featured an extended instruction set targeted at multimedia operations, including image manipulation, audio, and video playback.

The introduction of the MMX instruction set represented the first major retrofit of the *x*86 architecture since the 386, when Intel moved from a 16-bit to 32-bit addressing model. MMX adds 57 instructions to the existing 147 found in the original *x*86 set. Many of these instructions do in one step what took numerous *x*86 instructions to complete. In effect, MMX instructions are a kind of multimedia speed dial for *x*86 processors, yielding higher video frame rates, better 3D graphics, and greater all around performance.

The catch? Developers must tune their software to use the new MMX instructions or else they will never get used. Companies, such as Microsoft, reworked their programming languages so that compilers would take advantage of MMX. Similarly, the DirectX components in the Windows family of operating systems was updated to take advantage of MMX. It's worth noting that the additional instructions add to the Pentium MMX transistor count, making the CPU more complex and power hungry than its Pentium predecessor. Intel's solution: shrink the CPU die and run the Pentium MMX at 2.8 volts internally (Pentium runs at 3.3 volts).

Intel is not done tinkering with the internal rules of its CPUs. In 1999, the company expects to introduce Katmai New Instructions, which will add instructions to further enhance 3D graphics and video playback. Expect Katmai NI instruction set–enabled CPUs to appear with the Merced AI-64 CPUs in 1999 or 2000.

AMD has also cooked up its own extended instruction set for the upcoming new K6-2 processor, which will reduce the need for separate graphics coprocessors for realistic 3D game play. Fellow CPU competitors Cyrix and IDT have agreed to adopt the AMD instructions, whereas Microsoft has incorporated 3D-Now support into its DirectX 6.0 software. The combination should help motivate at least some publishers to tune their applications and games for the new instructions, although it could be some time before development cycles make such support ubiquitous.

4.1.3 Performance Impact Report

So how important is the CPU to your system's performance. Obviously, it plays a critical role in almost every area of system performance. If you have plenty of RAM, a fast graphics bus with advanced acceleration, and decent response and throughput on your hard disk and CD-ROM drive, a fast CPU will be able to deliver optimal performance. However, if your PC is rife with performance bottlenecks, you'll find that upgrading to a faster CPU will have a limited impact.

In my experience, diminishing returns makes CPU upgrades questionable for performance-minded users. New systems have faster buses, memory, cache, graphics, and hard disks. They also boast more efficient BIOS designs. The result: Dropping a faster CPU into an aging system *never* yields performance equal to that of a brand new PC (see Figure 4.2).

The question that always begs answering is what speed version of a CPU to get. Do you stretch for the fastest and greatest processor, or do you buy its little brother and save $300 or more in the process. For business users, it makes good sense to take a step back from the cutting edge. Absent any improvements in the CPU bus or cache, a 15 percent clock speed increase usually yields a system performance boost of just three to seven percent.

Finally, keep in mind that gamers face a very specific set of performance needs. Even a fast CPU with a bulked up L1 and L2 cache will not perform well in Quake II if its floating-point (FP) performance is subpar. 3D graphics require that the CPU core provide efficient, superscalar FP capability for top performance.

CPU Guide

Figure 4.2.

Evergreen Technologies' 200-MHz MX Pro uses an IDT WinChip C6 CPU to provide boost to aging Pentium-75 to Pentium-166 systems, but overall performance will likely be held back by other aging subsystems. (Figure courtesy of Evergreen Technologies.)

4.2 State of the CPU Market

In case you haven't noticed, there are a lot of CPUs out there. Intel produces about a dozen active desktop CPUs across four processor families, and it also produces another half dozen for portables. AMD and K6 both market Intel-compatible processors at a variety of clock speeds, while newcomer IDT's WinChip looks like a possible contender in the market. All of them take different approaches to the task of crunching data and code, resulting in varying levels of performance depending on the applications being run.

Next, we'll step through the products to give you a brief overview of the market.

4.2.1 Intel CPUs

Intel owns 90 percent of the desktop CPU market, thanks in large part to the enormous success of the company's Pentium processor, introduced in 1993. The company has since defended its position by ramping up clock speeds, introducing new CPUs, and keeping prices low on its older models.

The result is a dizzying selection of processors that vary widely in architecture, clock, speed, instruction set, and cache.

Pentium: The Granddaddy

Intel was a successful company back in the days of the 386 and 486, but the Pentium CPU was what helped turn the Santa Clara chipmaker into a titan. When the Pentium was introduced in 1993, companies such as AMD and Cyrix both had a small but healthy portion of the CPU market, producing 486 knockoffs at low prices for both systems and upgrades. However, when the Pentium hit, neither company could counter. For five years, Intel would face negligible competition in the desktop CPU market. Today, the classic Pentium is a fading star in the Intel constellation, yet it still can be found in tens of millions of desktop PCs.

Packed with more than 3 million transistors, the Pentium more than doubled the transistor count of the 486. Early models, which ran at 60 and 66MHz, suffered from chronic overheating—a result of their fairly large .8-micron production process. It wasn't until the debut of the .6-micron Pentium-90, nearly a year later, that this concern was addressed (see Figure 4.3).

Figure 4.3.

Intel's Pentium is fast becoming a part of computing history, but its impact on the personal computing market is difficult to overstate. (Figure courtesy of Tom's Hardware.)

The Pentium was the first Intel CPU to take aim at the CISC problem by employing multiple execution pipelines—allowing more than one instruction to complete in each clock tick—and using tricks to line up instructions to reduce stalls in the pipelines. Behind the dual pipelines was a trick called *branch prediction*, which allowed the Pentium to intuit the correct path to take when multiple results were presented.

CPU Guide

Intel also widened the pipes and beefed up fast memory in the Pentium, making a clean break from the past. The internal L1 cache was doubled to 16KB, while the external I/O bus was widened from 32 bits to 64 bits. Inside, a pair of 32-bit pipelines (named U and V) kept the 64-bit I/O bus running at full tilt (see Figure 4.4). The first Pentiums ran at motherboard clock speeds of 60 and 66MHz (up to twice that 486 motherboards), with later versions employing integer and noninteger clock multiplication to ramp internal CPU speeds up to 200MHz.

Figure 4.4.
This schematic shows how instructions are shared among the Pentium's multiple pipelines.

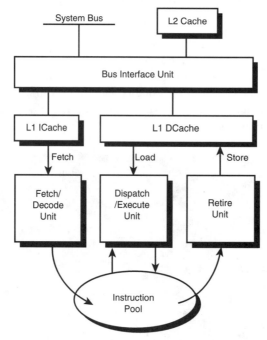

Sometimes overlooked was Intel's decision to fix the floating-point unit, or FPU. The FPU in the 486 was woefully underpowered—in fact, it was the first Intel processor with a built-in FPU. Pentium more than doubled FP performance, creating a market for FP-aware software on x86-compatible systems. CAD/CAM, 3D gaming and design, and statistical software all enjoyed an enormous boost from the beefed up FPU. Still, FP performance on Pentium and Pentium MMX processors lags well behind that of competing RISC CPUs such as Motorola's PowerPC and Sun's MIPS CPU lines. This failing has made fifth-generation Pentium-class CPUs inappropriate for many workstation-type applications.

Multiple Personalities

Something that seemed overlooked was the fact that Pentiums of the same clock speed can be *very* different. For example, some Pentium models are not capable of multiprocessing (SMP) operations. Others must use a higher voltage to run correctly even in single processor mode. You can tell what kind of chip you have by looking at the bottom of it. You'll see letters stenciled into the bottom, such as SK 106 SSS.

SSS: standard 3.3 volt operation

> **NOTE**   If you want to overclock a Pentium, make sure you have an SSS model, because it should be able to run at an inflated voltage and allow for pushed operation. A VRE Pentium running at 3.6 volts will quite likely fail if pushed any higher.

Why the different clocks? It comes down to the manufacturing process. You see, the Pentium-133 and the Pentium-200 are built on the same line using the same process. The clock speed is determined at the testing phase. If a CPU does well, it's rated for faster operation and is designated a Pentium-200. Those that do poorly are set to a lower clock speed, such as 133MHz. However, some chips only work at a specified clock rate when run at a higher voltage. Rather than discard the chip, Intel sells this subset of Pentium chips using the higher voltage level. Although most users never realize the difference, those intending to overclock a system will do best to check the voltage before pushing the chip. Otherwise, the higher voltage level could result in rapid overheating.

Beware of Faked Clock Rate Markings

Early Pentiums lacked markings on the bottom side that indicated the rated clock speed. Unscrupulous vendors simply ground off the etching and printed a new number. This changed a Pentium-75 into a Pentium-90 or 100, so the vendor could turn a few extra bucks on the sale. The only way to verify the clock type is to actually measure the thickness of the ceramic body to the tenths of a millimeter (2.8mm is the correct thickness for a Pentium-90). A faked CPU would measure slightly thinner.

Today, vendors spoof the bottom-side printing by putting real-looking black stickers on the bottom of the chip. You can try to verify your chip purchase by seeing if there's a black label on the bottom. Peal it off, and you should see the official marking. My advice: Only buy in shops that you trust.

Pentium MMX: The Next Generation Pentium

Introduced in January, 1997, Pentium MMX extended the Pentium franchise by adding multimedia-specific instructions, a larger L1 cache, and some welcome

CPU Guide

pipeline improvements to the familiar P5 core. The results were impressive. Our tests of the Pentium MMX-200 showed a 16 percent improvement over the Pentium Classic-200 in standard Windows application performance. The lead gets even bigger when MMX-tuned software is involved. Here, we saw improvements as high as 50 percent or more in popular applications such as Adobe Photoshop.

The big news is the addition of 57 instructions to the venerable x86 instruction set. Targeting video, audio, and graphics operations, the MMX instructions can significantly speed the performance of multimedia software. The Pentium MMX also uses a single instruction, multiple data (SIMD) scheme that speeds work on the large data sets common with media applications. What's more, MMX instructions can be paired up to execute simultaneously, allowing two SIMD instructions with 16 bytes of data to be processed in one clock cycle (see Figure 4.5).

Figure 4.5.

A lower internal voltage and .35-micron process enabled Pentium MMX to incorporate more transistors and run at higher clock speeds than Pentium Classic. (Figure courtesy of Intel Corp.)

Table 4.1 shows how the Pentium MMX compares against our benchmark Pentium-90 CPU.

Table 4.1. The technical advantages of the Pentium MMX over the Pentium Classic.

Spec	Pentium Classic-90	Pentium MMX-200
Clock speed	90MHz	166MHz to 233MHz
Transistors	3.1 million	4.4 million
Process	.6-micron BiCMOS	.35-micron CMOS
L1 cache	8KB data/8KB instructions	16KB data/16KB instructions
Int/ext bus	32 bit/64 bit	32 bit/64 bit

Spec	Pentium Classic-90	Pentium MMX-200
Connector type	Socket 5	Socket 7
Data cache scheme	Two-way set associative	Four-way set associative
Write buffers	2	4

Intel also borrowed enhancements from other CPUs to make the Pentium MMX a superior performer. A new branch prediction unit was taken from the Pentium Pro, and Intel implemented a return stack similar to the one found on the Cyrix/IBM 6x86 processors. The two integer execution pipelines were also extended by one step to allow incremental clock increases, and the parallel processing ability of the two pipelines was improved.

It's no surprise that the additional instructions, bulked-up L1 cache, and tweaked pipeline logic all added to the transistor count of the Pentium MMX. To accommodate the additional complexity and allow higher speed operation, Intel adopted a split voltage design for Pentium MMX. Whereas the external I/O continued to run at 3.3 volts (the same as Pentium), the CPU's insides ran at a lower and cooler 2.8 volts. The change required voltage regulation on motherboards, which most Socket 7 designs provided, whereas older motherboards required a separate voltage regulator be attached to the new CPU in order to work.

After MMX's tremendous success, it's easy to forget that Intel took a risk with the new instruction set. Adding 57 instructions, which occur in their own processor state, could have resulted in a bulked-up CPU prone to overheating problems. As it was, Pentium MMX carried 1.3 million transistors more than the Pentium-90.

However, Intel managed the transition by mapping the MMX execution pipeline over the existing eight-register FP pipeline. The decision minimized the transistor count and eased the work of software and compiler developers by keeping the instructions within a known resource. Still, the approach does have its dangers. The shared register set invites lengthy stalls when programs switch directly between FP and MMX operation, because the registers have to be flushed and reset in such a situation.

However, Intel's own profiling and the CPU's behavior in real-world applications have shown that such juxtapositions are rare, because programs tend to stress MMX or FP in a batch. Thrashing back and forth rarely occurs. Likewise, OS-based task switching does not pose a register reset problem, because the delay involved in switching tasks is much greater than that associated with resetting the MMX/FP registers.

CPU Guide

Today, both Cyrix and AMD have adopted MMX in their CPU designs (with K6 and 6x86MX) and a significant number of multimedia titles now ship with MMX support built in. Microsoft boosted Intel's MMX appeal by adding support for MMX to version 3 of the DirectX components, although the lack of MMX-savvy compilers initially forced a lot of time-consuming hand-coding to take full advantage of the instructions.

Pentium Pro: The Big Daddy

When the Pentium Pro shipped in 1996, it was a monstrosity. Counting the L2 cache, the Pentium Pro package included 15.5 million transistors—five times that found in the original Pentium—in two separate dies. Even without the 10 million cache-related transistors, the Pentium Pro's core was much more complex than that of the Pentium. Included inside the CPU was an architecture tuned for 32-bit code, allowing Pentium Pro to do several things at once (see Figure 4.6).

Figure 4.6.

The unique dual-cavity PGA packaging of the Pentium Pro includes a 256KB or 512KB L2 cache running at the speed of the CPU core. (Photo courtesy of Tom's Hardware.)

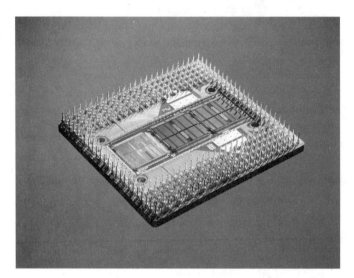

In fact, Pentium Pro breaks in many ways from its predecessors in that is uses elements of Reduced Instruction Set Computing (RISC) to enhance performance. RISC designs use fewer, equal-sized instructions that can be executed both quickly and efficiently. This is in contrast to Complex Instruction Set Computing (CISC) processors, which leverage a large number of nonuniform instructions to execute code. As clock rates go higher and CPUs attempt to do more and more in a single cycle, RISC has proven to be at an advantage.

With Pentium Pro, Intel extended the five-stage pipeline in the Pentium to 12 stages, allowing individual tasks to be broken down into more manageable segments. The longer pipe also allowed higher clock rates. The RISC approach comes in the pipeline, where incoming *x*86 instructions are actually translated into RISC format before being sent down one of the three execution pipes. By breaking unwieldy CISC instructions into micro-operations, the pipeline is able to run much more quickly and smoothly. However, the Pentium Pro threw off prodigious amounts of heat—about 16 watts, three times that of Pentium—and its integrated 256KB L2 cache made it expensive to build. What's more, Intel mistimed the arrival of true 32-bit computing environment, as Microsoft's Windows NT was still just a market sliver. When Pentium Pro's highly optimized core ran across the 16-bit code found in Windows 95 and Windows 3.*x*, its ability to conduct out-of-order execution failed, causing drastic performance losses. In fact, Pentium CPUs of the same speed often matched or even beat Pentium Pro when running 16-bit applications.

Still, the Pentium Pro is quite a feat. The integrated L2 cache runs at the speed of the CPU—66MHz—making the Pentium Pro perfect for database and server applications, where large data sets bog down the CPU in cache and memory fetches. Most important, when the Pentium Pro does get a chance to have at 32-bit code, it excels. Our tests under Windows NT show that the Pentium Pro-200 enjoys a significant performance advantage over the Pentium-200 (see Table 4.2).

Table 4.2. The technical advantages of the Pentium Pro over the Pentium Classic.

Spec	Pentium Classic-90	Pentium Pro-200
Clock speed	90MHz	150MHz to 200MHz
Transistors in core)	3.1 million	15.5 million (5.5 million
Process	.6-micron BiCMOS	.35-micron CMOS
L1 cache	8KB data/8KB instruction	8KB data/8KB instructions
Int/ext bus	32 bit/64 bit	32 bit/64 bit
Connector type	Socket 5	Socket 8
Data cache scheme	Two-way set associative	Four-way set associative
Write buffers	2	4

CPU Guide

Out-of-Order Execution

The real secret behind Pentium Pro is its highly superscalar architecture. Intel added pipelines and buffers to allow this beefy CPU to do many things at once. The Pentium Pro employs three integer pipelines, versus two for Pentium and Pentium MMX. In addition, it extends the five-stage Pentium pipelines to 12 stages. Among the stages: A decode unit at the front of the pipelines that turns unwieldy, variable-length *x*86 instructions into standard-size RISC-like instructions (called *micro-ops* by Intel). This design allows the CPU core to chew through instructions fast, much the way PowerPC and other RISC-style CPUs do.

Of course, with many pipelines, you invite many stalls. Data dependencies that stall the pipeline can cost tens of CPU cycles at a crack, mounting into a real performance drag. To resolve this, Intel focused on *out-of-order execution*, which allows processing to continue even though a dependent piece of data has yet to be delivered. Pentium Pro speculatively executes instructions, making educated guesses about the bits to come and storing the results in an instruction pool. Although a bad guess results in a penalty, Intel's engineers have managed to make sure that Pentium Pro is rarely wrong.

Usually, any 16-bit code confounds the Pentium Pro's out-of-order execution. As a result, the CPU cannot run at peak efficiency when running Windows 3.*x* and Windows 95 applications, thus limiting the CPU's appeal outside of server applications.

Too Heavy

Weak 16-bit performance isn't Pentium Pro's only problem. At 15.5 million transistors, the CPU is simply enormous. Ten million transistors worth of L2 cache sit inside the second of the Pentium Pro's dual cavities, adding bulk, heat, and yield problems to all the usual processor manufacturing challenges. Even with its .35-micron CMOS process, the Pentium Pro still throws out an unbelievable 16 watts of heat.

It's no surprise that clock speeds are limited. The Pentium Pro hits its ceiling at 200MHz; overclockers are advised to respect this limit. The CPU runs very hot, inviting catastrophic breakdown by pushing the CPU beyond its limits. That said, the integrated L2 cache does make an inviting performance target, because overclocking the chip also yields a linear increase in L2 cache speed.

Today, Pentium Pro has been thoroughly niched by Pentium II. Still, it brings impressive symmetric multiprocessing (SMP) capabilities, allowing up to four CPUs to be hooked together without requiring extensive support. Also, 16-way SMP boxes are not uncommon.

Pentium II: Now We're Talking

Pentium Pro was not a failed experiment, but it was a risk (so to speak). With Pentium II, Intel combined the best aspects of Pentium Pro with the best of Pentium MMX. From the Pro, the Pentium II gets its superscalar design and out-of-order processing. Pentium MMX, meanwhile, lends its enhance instruction set, a boosted L1 cache, and an efficient design (see Figure 4.7). Most important, Intel fixed the 16-bit problem, making the Pentium II an effective mainstream processor (see Table 4.3).

Figure 4.7.

Inside the SEC cartridge you'll find a small circuit board with the Pentium II CPU and its attendant L2 cache chips. (Photo courtesy of Tom's Hardware.)

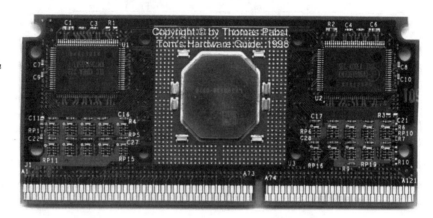

Table 4.3. The technical advantages of the Pentium II over the Pentium Classic.

Spec	Pentium Classic-90	Pentium II-300
Clock speed	90MHz	233MHz to 400MHz
Transistors	3.1 million	7.5 million
Process	.6-micron BiCMOS	.35/.25-micron CMOS
L1 cache	8KB data/8KB instruction	16KB data/16KB instructions
Int/ext bus	32 bit/64 bit	32 bit/64 bit
Connector type	Socket 5	Slot 1
Data cache scheme	Two-way set associative	4-way set associative
Write buffers	2	4

Don't think that Pentium II is on a diet: At 7.5 million transistors, the CPU is more than double the size of Pentium and has a larger core than Pentium Pro. However, moving the L2 cache back outside of the processor package enables higher clock rates—currently at 400MHz—and cooler operation. The result: An affordable, high-performance CPU design that has been a runaway success.

Packaging Power Plays

The most noticeable thing about Pentium II is its unique packaging, known as the *single-edge connector (SEC) cartridge*. The CPU actually sits inside of a standard cartridge assembly, which also includes a discreet L2 cache (512KB) and supporting logic. The cartridge features an edge connector similar to that found on add-in cards—a departure from the pin grid arrays of all CPUs since the 286. The motherboard component of this connection is called Slot 1.

Things get interesting inside the black cartridge. The L2 cache inside runs at one-half the CPU speed, much faster than the 66MHz motherboard speed limit that rules Socket 7 caches of Pentium and Pentium MMX. A 300MHz Pentium II, therefore, enjoys L2 cache operation of 150MHz, which is 225 percent faster than that of a motherboard-bound cache. The newest Pentium II CPUs, based on the modified Slot 2 design, can actually run the L2 cache at full CPU speed.

The marketing staff at Intel refer to this design as a *dual independent bus (DIB)*, because the L2 bus is decoupled from the motherboard bus. The design makes good engineering sense. Pentium II CPUs *are*, after all, cheaper to make than Pentium Pro. Also, the move to a slotted design makes damage to pins much less likely than with earlier Socket 7 and Socket 8 designs.

Intel also enjoys a competitive edge with Pentium II. Both the P6 CPU bus and the new Slot 1 architecture are surrounded by patent and trade secret protection. By moving off the widely licensed Socket 7 architecture, Intel makes it much more difficult for competitors to produce knockoff CPUs that fit into Pentium II's Slot 1 or Slot 2 connector. The enhanced L2 cache operation, meanwhile, helps provide Intel with a real performance edge that's designed to woo users and OEMs away from the Socket 7 architecture. However, Intel's intellection shield may be crumbling. National Semiconductor enjoys a cross-license that gives it access to the P6 bus design—access that it can share with its new Cyrix subsidiary. Cyrix plans to introduce a Slot 1–based CPU (code-named *Jalapeno*) in 1999.

Malleable Design

The Pentium II is certainly the most versatile CPU Intel has produced. Already, the original process has been shrunk to .25-micron CMOS, enabling clock rates to move up from 300MHz to 400MHz. Code-named *Deschutes*, Pentium II's tighter design is being moved into notebooks. The Deschutes line also adds new talents that promise to greatly enhance performance. The Pentium II-350 CPUs are the first to support the 100MHz system bus (based on the 440BX chipset).

Further up the food chain, we find the so-called *Xeon processor*, which is a Pentium II core goosed up for high-end workstation and server applications. The 512KB L2 cache is boosted to 1MB or even 2MB, and it runs at the speed of the CPU itself (rather than at one-half CPU speed as is the case with Pentium II). As no surprise for a server product, SMP support gets a jump, improving from two-way to four-way SMP. This last improvement finally makes the new P6 CPU a match for Pentium Pro in the network and Web server marketplace.

The Pentium II family is also extending downward to low-cost PCs. The so-called *Covington CPU* does away with the L2 cache, enabling Intel to place its Pentium II CPU into the increasingly popular class of sub-$1000 PCs. The design enables Intel to bring the benefits of superscalar processing to even the lowest part of the market. However, our tests show that all the pipelining magic is wasted because the lack of an L2 cache forces the CPU to wait around for bits coming in from the motherboard.

Celeron: Pentium II Lite

Intel wasn't about to leave the sub-$1000 PC market to Cyrix and AMD, but it was becoming clear that Pentium MMX lacked the guns to stop the competition. What's more, as long as Intel kept marketing CPUs for the Socket 7 motherboard platform, its competitors enjoyed a viable platform for their compatible products. Therefore, Intel shaved the L2 cache off its Pentium II, slashed the price, and voilá, it created a serious low-cost contender.

Figure 4.8.
Despite the different name, Celeron uses the same Pentium II CPU core. The difference is in the packaging, where Celeron lacks L2 cache, as seen in this photo. (Photo courtesy of Tom's Hardware.)

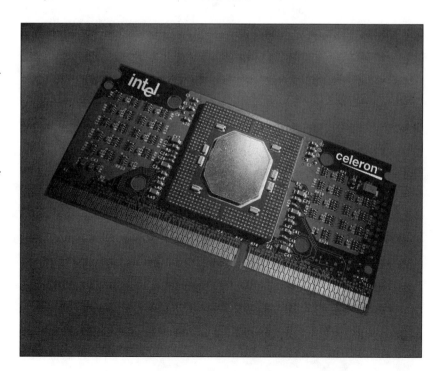

Originally code-named Covington, the Celeron CPU line is basically a Pentium II Lite CPU that uses a modified Slot 1 connector and comes packaged in the familiar SEC cartridge (see Figure 4.8). The line starts at 233MHz and moves up from there. The chip cuts costs by losing the 512KB L2 cache built into Pentium II SEC cartridges.

Pentium II Lite has been mated with the new 440EX chipset, a stripped down version of the 440LX chipset found in most Pentium II systems before 1998. The 440EX chipset includes support for the AGP 2X bus specification for graphics, but it only runs at 66MHz (versus 100MHz for the newest Intel motherboards). The EX has only four RAS lines, thus limiting the DIMM socket count to two. Also, only three PCI slots are supported. Unlike the LX, EX only supports a single CPU (which is not a problem for the sub-$1000 market).

Testing in business applications shows Celeron to be a real disappointment. Virtually all the Socket 7 CPUs, including Intel's own Pentium MMX, provide better Windows application performance than Celeron. It's no surprise that the missing cache is the culprit—the CPU is stuck in low gear making main memory accesses while K6 and its ilk are cruising along in the L2 cache.

Gaming is another matter. The Celeron uses the same P6 core in Pentium II, including the impressive FPU and MMX instruction pipeline, which is clearly superior to its rivals. In games such as Quake II, the P6 core enables Celeron to execute geometry and setup tasks more quickly than K6 or 6x86MX. If you want a low-cost machine for the kids to play games on, Celeron is a better buy than you might think.

Down the road, Intel is looking at Celeron derivatives as it continues to fight a rear-guard action against Socket 7/Super 7 CPU designs. The Mendocino CPU is to put an L2 cache inside the Celeron—at time of this book's publication, it's expected to be 128KB—that should yield significant gains in performance. Further down the road, the Whitney CPU pulls the i740 2D/3D graphics processor into the CPU, creating a powerful all-in-one CPU that could spell doom for Cyrix's Media GX line. Both these CPUs are designed to pull the most rapidly growing segment of the PC market—sub-$1000 desktops—into the Slot 1 camp.

Xeon: The High End

In many ways, the Xeon is an unexciting processor. Essentially, the Xeon CPU is a Pentium II pumped up with additional L2 cache and a few critical tweaks for the server market. It uses the same .25 micron process found in the Deschutes-class Pentium II, and even runs at similar 400 and 450 MHz clock speeds. But it would be a mistake to discount this high-end processor, because it promises to shake up the market for workstations and sever systems. In fact, it is the first new CPU from Intel since the venerable Pentium Pro to really serve this high-end market.

What's special about Xeon? The most obvious change is the L2 cache, which as with Pentium II is housed inside a single edge connector (SEC) cartridge. Xeon boosts the speed of this L2 cache memory from 1/2 CPU speed to full clock speed, using custom SRAM (CSRAM) chips manufactured by Intel. Getting a couple megabytes of memory to run at 400+ MHz is not a trivial matter, and is one of the reasons the price of the Xeon CPU is so much higher than that of Pentium II. The fast cache is also the reason for the extremely large Xeon SEC cartridge, which stands more than twice as high as the Pentium II module in order to dissipate all the extra heat thrown off by the high-speed silicon.

Figure 4.9:
The massive Xeon cartridge provides additional thermal conduction to transfer heat produced by the high-speed L2 cache.

In addition, Xeon can support much more L2 cache than the 512KB limit imposed by Pentium II. 512KB, 1MB, and even 2MB cache versions of Xeon are available to serve a variety of applications. While more cache is almost always better, at these levels you can expect little or no impact on typical desktop applications. Rather, the large and fast L2 memory is intended to speed the enormous data sets and multithreaded operation of server and workstation software.

CPU Guide

If cache were the whole story, the Xeon would be a non-starter. One significant shortcoming of the Pentium II architecture is its dual-processing limitation—a critical concern for servers. Despite the fact that Pentium II could run at 333-MHz and above, many shops continued to buy old 200-MHz Pentium Pro systems because they could be outfitted with four or more CPUs. Xeon fixes this problem by allowing four or even eight CPUs to be linked together in a symmetric multiprocessing configuration (SMP).

Xeon also steps up memory support. Using a 36-bit memory address scheme (up from 32 bits for Pentium II), the Xeon CPUs can address and cache as much as 64GB of RAM. Enabling the vast memory access pool is a new PSE36 mode that is part of Intel's Extended Server Memory Architecture. Keep in mind that not all Xeon systems will provide this 64GB capability, but the architecture is there for server system makers who need to push the limits of their designs.

This kind of high-end SMP capability doesn't happen alone—an advanced system chipset is needed to link the CPUs together, enable multi-cache coherency, and allow for efficient multi-processor memory accesses. Enter the Intel 450NX, which provides 4-way SMP on its own, or 8-way operation when coupled with a cluster controller. Tailored for servers, the chipset lacks AGP support, but allows up to 8GB of main memory, and can support a pair of 64-bit PCI buses or four 32-bit PCI buses.

Finally, Xeon adds a couple bells and whistles that are useful for system management and troubleshooting. An integrated thermal sensor, for example, sits on the Xeon PCB and alerts the system should heat buildup become a threat. Also added is a Processor Information ROM (PIROM), which provides—in the words of Intel—"robust addressing headers to allow for flexible programming and forward compatibility, core and L2 cache electrical specifications, processor part and S-spec numbers, and a unique electronic signature."

The upshot is that counterfeiting a Xeon CPU should be much more difficult than it is with Pentium II today. Overclocking becomes highly unlikely too, but that's hardly an issue for the server crowd, who value stability and reliability over all other things. There is also a special EEPROM chip within the Xeon cartridge that system vendors can program. Called a scratch EEPROM, this resource can host information like (again, Intel talking) "system specifications, inventory and service tracking, installation defaults, environment monitoring, and usage data. Its contents can be write-protected by the system, as well."

When we ran Xeon through our tests, there were few surprises. Single-tasking on a Windows 98 desktop produces virtually no performance advantage for a dual-CPU Xeon-400 system over its clock-mate CPU, a pair of Pentium II-400s. All that additional high-speed cache and SMP capability is frankly wasted on a tinker toy operating system like Windows 9x. When we did some ad-hoc multitasking tests under Windows NT, however, we began to see differences. We saw Xeon pull away when we ran a gigantic WinZip session (compressing a 1.2GB file), played a looped AVI video clip, and executed ZD's High-End WinStone 98. The combination of tasks maxed out the Pentium II memory bus and allowed the Xeon system to gain a 16 percent advantage over the similarly-configured Pentium II PC.

It's worth noting that even this test is a relatively limited display of multitasking capability. Network and Web servers must handle enormous streams of data, multiple threads, and a multitude of applications. In this environment, the more robust Xeon architecture allows for significant boosts in performance, particularly when you put four CPUs on task.

Given Xeon's high-end pedigree, should you consider one (or two) for your NT workstation? Almost certainly not. Even the most avid desktop user will gain little from the pricey Xeon CPU, unless it involves working with extremely challenging 3D graphics and design environments, such as those present in Autodesk's 3D Studio MAX. Even in many of these cases, the Xeon decision needs to be made carefully. A Xeon CPU starts at about two to three times the price of same-clock speed Pentium II parts, making them a relatively poor price-performance choice for the desktop. Unless you know you need the multiprocessing muscle that Xeon can bring to bear, you are almost certainly better off with a fast Pentium II loaded with top-notch coprocessors and storage and display hardware.

4.2.2 Cyrix CPUs

Once a powerful supplier of 486-class clone CPUs, Cyrix all but disappeared from the performance range of the market when Intel's Pentium hit stride. However, in 1996, the company made something of a comeback with its 6x86 and 6x86MX (since renamed M II) CPUs. In 1997, National Semiconductor purchased Cyrix, intending to focus on the company's successful GX system-on-a-chip CPU for the sub-$1000 market. Today, only two CPUs are produced by Cyrix: the 6x86MX and the GX.

CPU Guide

Cx6*x*86

It's Cx6*x*86 CPU turned a lot of heads by dishing out better-than-Pentium performance at a low price. The 150MHz Cx6*x*86 outpaced 200MHz Pentium systems in virtually all benchmarks and promised to be a credible challenge to Intel's franchise CPU. Instead, the product got held up in manufacturing shortages, heat problems, and the competitive MMX rollout.

Figure 4.9.
The Cyrix 6x86 provided better-than-Pentium performance but was plagued by heat problems. (Photo courtesy of Cyrix Corp.)

Originally built on a .6-micron CMOS process, the chip was soon shrunk to .5 microns, where it ran at speeds up to 150MHz. Like the Pentium, the 6*x*86 features two integer pipelines and uses the Socket 7 connector. Its 16KB unified L1 cache, however, provided an advantage because the design allowed greater amounts of data to be cached than was possible with the Pentium's 8KB data L1 cache (see Table 4.4).

Table 4.4. The technical advantages of the Cyrix 6x86 over the Pentium Classic.

Spec	Pentium Classic-90	Cyrix 6x86
Clock speed	90MHz	100MHz to 150MHz
Transistors	3.1 million	8 million
Process	.6-micron BiCMOS	.5-micron CMOS
L1 cache	8KB data/8KB instruction	16KB unified

Spec	Pentium Classic-90	Cyrix 6x86
Int/ext bus	32 bit/64 bit	32 bit/32 bit
Connector type	Socket 5	Socket 7
Data cache scheme	Two-way set associative	Four-way set associative

The 6x86 also provides support for 75MHz external bus operation, an attractive upside that could allow greater amounts of data to get into and out of the CPU. Unfortunately, Cyrix had a hard time moving the market to its 75MHz bus, and the majority of 6x86 systems ran at standard 66MHz external clock rates. What's more, the 6x86 lacks a noninteger clock multiplier, limiting the internal CPU speeds to either 2× or 3× the motherboard bus. The result, the fastest 66MHz motherboard variant of the 6x86 ran at 133MHz—twice the speed of the motherboard bus.

The company eventually released an updated version of the CPU, the 6x86L, which offered a split-voltage design. Running at 2.8 volts internally and 3.3 volts at the external I/O, the 6x86L finally put to rest the chronic heat problems of the original chip.

However, Cyrix still had problems to deal with. The CPU is very sensitive to reflections on buses, causing instability under Windows NT 4.0. Cyrix disabled write-back cache mode on the L1 cache, yielding a 15 percent or so performance penalty. (The company will replace these older CPUs to registered Windows NT 4.0 owners.) If your CPU is of revision 2.7 or higher, you're not affected by this problem and can use the optimized write-back cache scheme.

One problem it can't fix is the slower-than-Pentium FPU. Although the majority of users won't notice a difference, those doing CAD or playing FPU-intensive games such Quake will see a pretty significant performance degradation. In addition, some games and software failed to recognized the 6x86 as a Pentium-class CPU, mistaking it for a Cyrix 486-class unit, and sometimes aborting installations as a result. Updates to Windows 95 and to software titles have broadened recognition of the CPU.

Cyrix M II

Cyrix's follow up to the 6x86 has fared better. The M II, previously known as 6x86MX, adds full MMX instruction set support to the 6x86 core (see Figure 4.10). In addition, the company enhanced the architecture by enhancing its

CPU Guide

superscalar operation, enabling multiple instructions to execute in each clock tick. Perhaps most important, M II employs a huge 64KB unified L2 cache (up from 16KB in the 6x86).

Figure 4.10.

Based on the 6x86 core, M II bulks up the L2 cache, adds MMX instructions, and tweaks the internal design to provide strong business application performance. (Photo courtesy of Cyrix Corp.)

The M II also fixes a lot of problems in the 6x86 (see Table 4.5). Gone is the integer-only bus multiplier—a 2.5× internal clock allows the 150/60MHz and 166/66MHz operation. Better still, fast 150/75MHz and 225/75MHz versions of the chip are also included in the specs. The low 2.8-volt operation (with 3.3 volt I/O) eliminates the thermal problems that plagued the 6x86.

Table 4.5. The M II compared to the original Pentium CPU.

Spec	Pentium Classic-90	Cyrix M II
Clock speed	90MHz	150MHz to 225MHz
Transistors	3.1 million	8 million

Spec	Pentium Classic-90	Cyrix M II
Process	.6-micron BiCMOS	.35-micron CMOS
L1 cache	8KB data/8KB instruction	64KB unified
Int/ext bus	32 bit/64 bit	32 bit/64 bit
Connector type	Socket 5	Socket 7
Data cache scheme	Two-way set associative	Four-way set associative

The M II proved its mettle in our performance tests. Running at 187.5/75MHz, the M II nearly matched the performance of the Pentium II-233 in the Business Winstone benchmark under Windows 95. The more common 166/66MHz version was close behind, running nearly 10 percent faster than the Pentium MMX-200. However, FPU and MMX performance lag significantly behind Pentium II-233 levels and also trail Pentium MMX-200 by a slight margin.

The reason for the big performance gains in standard applications is the M II's massive 64KB unified L1 cache. The cache is four times the size of that in the 6x86 and still twice that of Pentium MMX. The external bus has also been widened to 64 bits, matching that of the Pentium and Pentium MMX, further improving throughput. Still, the FPU lags seriously behind that of Intel's designs, and MMX performance is weaker than both Pentium MMX and K6.

Cyrix has plans to improve M II, particularly in the area of MMX performance, where the single execution pipeline and lower real clock speeds hinder performance. The Cayenne CPU, expected in the second half of 1998, adds a second MMX/FP pipeline, which should provide an immediate boost to optimized applications. In addition, it will add support for the 3D-Now instructions, thus promising to boost 3D graphics performance. Based on a .25-micron process and slated for performance ratings of PR300 to PR400, Cyrix hopes to keep pace with the midrange computing market.

4.2.3 AMD

Cyrix isn't the only Intel competitor who has fallen on hard times. Advanced Micro Devices enjoyed a healthy business selling 386 and 486–class CPUs to first-tier system vendors; however, like Cyrix, the company was unable to mount a defense against Intel's Pentium CPU. After floundering with the K5 CPU (a Pentium competitor), the company's fortunes finally improved with the release of the K6 processor in 1997.

CPU Guide

AMD K5

The K5 was a classic case of "too little, too late." Intended to compete head to head with Intel's Pentium, K5 uses an innovative superscalar architecture that yields better-than-Pentium performance (see Figure 4.11). However, K5 parts were not available in quantity until the end of 1996—just prior to the Pentium MMX rollout (see Table 4.7).

Figure 4.11.
AMD's ill-fated K5 delivered decent performance at a low price, but manufacturing problems and delays kept this CPU out of the mainstream market. (Photo courtesy of AMD.)

Table 4.7. AMD K5 compared to Pentium Classic.

Spec	Pentium Classic-90	AMD K5
Clock speed	90MHz	75MHz to 116.66MHz
Transistors	3.1 million	4.3 million
Process	.6-micron BiCMOS	.35-micron CMOS
L1 cache	8KB data/8KB instruction	16KB data/8KB instruction
Int/ext bus	32 bit/64 bit	32 bit/32 bit
Connector type	Socket 5	Socket 7
Data cache scheme	Two-way set associative	Four-way set associative

Early versions of the K5 performed about on par with Pentium CPUs of the same clock speed. However, midway through the product's life, AMD updated the CPU's core, thus yielding more efficient performance. The result: CPUs of the same internal clock speed were marketed—and, indeed, proved to perform—at higher levels than their predecessors. The K5 PR120, PR133, and PR166 all featured improved integer processing efficiency: A 90MHz K5 PR120, for example, ran close to the performance of a 120MHz Pentium.

Unlike the 6x86, K5 used a split L2 cache with a larger data cache for handling multimedia and big data sets. However, it did use the same slimmed-down 32-bit external bus found on the 6x86. Despite its brief performance edge, K5 remains little more than a footnote in the CPU market, having been made obsolete by Pentium MMX. Fortunately, AMD's next foray into the market fared better.

AMD K6

When AMD bought NexGen Corp., a small CPU company with some big ideas, it breathed new life into the company's faltering CPU efforts. After all, the much-hyped K6 project was stalled, and AMD was being rocked by defections from large customers such as Compaq, who had tired of waiting for K5. However, K6, despite some missteps, delivered. At the core of the new design is a decoding unit that breaks complex x86 instructions into streamlined, RISC-like code.

When the K6 arrived in May 1997, it proved worth the wait. Our tests showed integer performance to be superior to anything on the market at the time. The fastest K6, running at 233MHz, outperformed the 233MHz Pentium II in the WinBench applications test. With K6 CPUs priced at a fraction the cost of Pentium II CPUs, the processor is a credible alternative to Intel-based systems (see Table 4.7).

Table 4.7. AMD K6 compared to Pentium Classic.

Spec	Pentium Classic-90	AMD K6
Clock speed	90MHz	233MHz to 300MHz
Transistors	3.1 million	8 million
Process	.6-micron BiCMOS	.35/.25-micron CMOS
L1 cache	8KB data/8KB instruction	32KB data/32KB instruction
Int/ext bus	32 bit/64 bit	32 bit/32 bit
Connector type	Socket 5	Socket 7
Data cache scheme	Two-way set associative	Four-way set associative

CPU Guide

Despite its clock-equivalent performance edge, AMD has not been able to produce K6 CPUs with clock speeds matching that of the fastest Pentium IIs, leaving the lucrative high end of the market to Intel. In addition, the K6's MMX and FP performances both lag significantly behind its Pentium II competition.

Like the Cyrix 6x86MX, the K6 features a large, unified L1 cache that is 32KB. With 8 million transistors built on a .35-micron process, the original K6 was limited to 233MHz clock operation. AMD recently shrunk the K6 to a .25-micron process, reducing the die size from 162mm2 to 68mm2. This version runs at 2.5 volts internally, enabling clock rates of 300MHz and higher.

AMD K6-2

Now we're talking! AMD may have had a hit with its K6 CPU, but the follow up on looks to pose an even bigger challenge to the Intel gorilla. The K6-2 adds 21 3D graphics–specific instructions to the existing *x*86/MMX instruction set (see Figure 4.12). The addition to single instruction, multiple data (SIMD) operation to the 3D-Now pipeline enables the processor to execute complex operations at top efficiency. A superscalar MMX processing unit also addresses one of K6's biggest shortfalls compared to Pentium II.

Figure 4.12
AMD's K6-2 provides big improvements i 3D graphics performance fo applications tuned for the 3D-Now instruction set. (Photo courtes) of AMD.)

The original K6 fared well in integer performance with Pentium II, but it got pasted in MMX tests because the Pentium II offers dual MMX pipelines. Now K6-2 offers dual decode and execution pipelines for MMX (see Table 4.8). Also, K6-2 maintains the K6 advantage of low execution latencies—there are no decode pairing restrictions and only a one-cycle misalignment penalty on memory accesses.

Table 4.8. AMD K6-2 compared to Pentium Classic.

Spec	*Pentium Classic-90*	*AMD K6-2*
Clock speed	90MHz	300MHz+
Transistors	3.1 million	9.8 million
Process	.6-micron BiCMOS	.25-micron CMOS
L1 cache	8KB data/8KB instruction	16KB data/8KB instruction
Int/ext bus	32 bit/64 bit	32 bit/32 bit
Connector type	Socket 5	Socket 7
Data cache scheme	Two-way set associative	Four-way set associative

Like Pentium II, the K6-2 will be able to run on a 100-MHz front bus, thus offering a 50 percent increase over K6. That means it will be able to take advantage of the coming wave of motherboards, chipsets, and RAM designed to run at the higher speeds. We won't see any Classic K6 CPUs designed for 100-MHz external operation, so expect K6-2 to take over as the flagship CPU at AMD. The K6-2 also supports SIMD operation, which should further break the MMX bottleneck.

K6-2 is being built on a .25-micron process and runs at 2.5 volts internally. That should allow K6 engineers to run the chip at clock speeds well above 300MHz, which is the opening clock rate for the CPU. The K6-2 packs 9.8 million transistors—about 20 percent more than in the K6—into a die that is 81mm2. The CPU runs on "Super 7" motherboards (100MHz system boards that use the familiar Socket 7 connector). The fast motherboard definitely helps, but even with the boost the K6-2's L2 cache still runs at half the speed of a Pentium II-400.

The K6-2 gets a further boost due to the fact that both Cyrix and IDT have agreed to support the extensions in the K6-2's instruction set. This agreement makes it more likely that at least some software vendors will tune their code for K6-2. Perhaps most critical, Microsoft has said that DirectX 6.0 will support K6-2. Of course, software that is not written for, or does not require, 3D-Now

CPU Guide

instructions will enjoy no benefit from this feature. In fact, our tests show that K6-2's performance in business applications is identical to that of the K6 running at the same clock speed and on the same motherboard bus.

If vendors do decide to make use of 3D-Now, whether it's through DirectX 6.0 or via hand-tuning the instructions, the payoff looks significant. Early tests under 3D WinBench 98, which uses Direct3D 6.0 as its API, shows that a K6-2-333 CPU nearly matches the performance of a Pentium II-400.

4.2.4 IDT

When integrated circuit maker IDT formed its CPU-centric Centaur division in 1995, the odds looked long indeed. After all, Intel was pummeling Cyrix and AMD with its Pentium processor as well as building an enormous lead in marketing and manufacturing infrastructure that seemed to prohibit new entries into the market. However, two years later, the company's WinChip C6 processor managed to turn heads with its adequate performance, efficient design, and extremely low cost. The result: a new, competitive entry in the burgeoning sub-$1000 PC market (the one place where Intel is weakest).

IDT's WinChip C6 targets the Intel Pentium MMX in the sub-$1000 PC marketplace (see Figure 4.13). Working for this CPU is its small die size (about half that of Pentium MMX) and low thermal output, which could allow the chip to run at 400MHz despite running at a relatively high 3.52 volts. If IDT can get voltages down to 2 volts or so, the WinChip could be a blockbuster low-cost CPU for notebooks.

The architecture of the C6 is much less sophisticated than the architecture of its competitors AMD K6 and IBM/Cyrix 6x86MX (see Table 4.9). No register renaming or out-of-order execution is used here for reaching Pentium MMX performance. Rather, a single execution pipeline is bolstered by large 32KB data and instruction L1 caches.

Table 4.9. IDT's WinChip C6 compared to the Pentium Classic.

Spec	Pentium Classic-90	IDT WinChip C6
Clock speed	90MHz	150MHz to 225MHz+
Transistors	3.1 million	5.4 million
Process	.6-micron BiCMOS	.35-micron CMOS
L1 cache	8KB data/8KB instruction	32KB data/32KB instruction

Spec	Pentium Classic-90	IDT WinChip C6
Int/ext bus	32-bit/64-bit	32-bit/32-bit
Connector type	Socket 5	Socket 7
Data cache scheme	Two-way set associative	Four-way set associative

Figure 4.13.
IDT's WinChip lacks the aggressive superscalar designs of its competitors but provides adequate performance for the low-cost PC market. (Photo courtesy of IDT.)

Current C6 CPUs actually run at a high 3.5 volts yet use only 10 watts of power. Therefore, not only is the C6 a viable alternative for older motherboards that can't accept Pentium MMX, K6, or Cyrix 6x86MX CPUs, but it seems destined to provide lower power consumption down the road. Another compatibility edge: The C6 requires no BIOS update to work. You may find some weird BIOS reporting, but the chip runs fine.

CPU Guide

We tested the C6 in the FIC PA-2007 board, one of the fastest Socket 7 boards available. It also offers *linear burst* to enable full performance of the 6x86MX CPU. The WinChip C6 turned in decent integer performance under Windows 95, but faltered under Windows NT. Floating-point performance is much weaker than any Intel CPU, making the WinChip C6 an unlikely choice for 3D gaming and mathematically intensive applications.

The upcoming WinChip 2+ should improve FP performance, which the company expects to be as fast as that in the Pentium MMX. A version called WinChip 2 3D will add the 3D-Now instruction extensions for speeding 3D graphics. These new instructions—which are identical to those introduced in AMD's K6-2 CPU—will be supported in Microsoft's Direct3D 6.0 release. Introduced at 266MHz, both WinChip versions will be built on .35- and .25-micron processes and run at 2.5 volts. By late 1998, 300-MHz WinChip 2 and WinChip 2 3D CPUs will be available.

Further down the road, IDT has plans to extend and broaden its line of WinChip CPUs. The WinChip 2+ will integrate a 256KB on-chip L2 cache, whereas the WinChip 2+NB will integrate part of the system chipset directly into the processor. Further out, WinChip 3 will feature a new processor core and much higher clock rates, ranging from 400MHz to 600MHz.

4.2.5 Upgrade Products

A healthy market of processor upgrade products exists for updating aging PCs. These retail kits usually consist of an *x*86-compatible CPU, an attached fan or heat sink, BIOS detection software, and documentation. Pentium MMX, K6, and 6x86MX based upgrade products also include an attached voltage regulator, which allows older motherboards to work with the dual-plan voltage used by these CPUs. Upgrade products for 486 systems might a tool for removing the CPU from the motherboard as well.

If this description sounds like a dressed up CPU, you're right. For many users, there's no need to go to the extra expense of a retail upgrade kit—buying the CPU itself will suffice. That said, upgrading a CPU can be serious business, and the retail kits can help you work through BIOS incompatibilities and difficult physical installations.

Here's a list of some of the companies that sell upgrade products:

- Evergreen Technologies: www.evertech.com

- Gainbery Computer Products: www.gainbery.com

- Intel Corp.: www.intel.com

- Kingston Technology Corp.: www.kingston.com

Intel sells Pentium MMX upgrade processors as part of its OverDrive line. You can upgrade a Pentium-100 system using Pentium's MMX-200 OverDrive or Evergreen's MxPro-200, which uses IDT's WinChip C6 CPU. Both will give you a 30 percent (or so) speed improvement, while costing about $300.

Depending on your existing hardware and preferred applications, CPU upgrades can have a big impact. Evergreen's MxPro, for example, can add a lot of kick to an old Pentium PC by putting a fast 200-MHz CPU in its place. That's a 2× increase in internal CPU clock performance. You also get more efficient processing from the advanced superscalar execution engine, an enlarged 64KB of L1 cache (up from 16KB on Pentium), and MMX support. In fact, MMX support may be one of the most compelling reasons to upgrade for some users.

Our tests show that enhancements such as enlarged caches or more advanced CPU cores are critical to adequate upgrade performance. The boost from clock speed upgrades tends to get flattened out by the unchanged system bus speed and bottlenecks from older hard disks, chipsets, and RAM. A large L1 cache, however, helps move transactions off the old hardware and directly onto the chip, which really helps overall performance. When shopping for a CPU upgrade, make a point to review the L1 cache size.

That said, in most cases, CPU upgrades provide only limited returns. Even a large L1 cache can't overcome pokey 80ns system RAM, old asynchronous L2 cache memory, or a hard disk drive that takes 15ms to access date. In general, it's best to think of a CPU upgrade as a great way to extend the life of your PC so that you can wait out the next great technology on the horizon, whether it's Intel's upcoming Katmai New Instructions or four-way SMP Xeon-class CPUs.

The real problem is that CPU upgrades aren't cheap: $300 is about double what you would pay for a decent 3D graphics card or for another 64MB of RAM, for example. Also, a new CPU won't resolve your RAM, hard disk, or system chipset bottlenecks. You need to be careful not to spend money on a CPU upgrade when your system is already pinched by too little system RAM (anything under 32MB for Windows 95) or an underpowered graphics card. Still, a CPU upgrade can deliver a welcome performance boost if you have the right mix of hardware and applications.

Of course, the ultimate upgrade solution is to replace the entire motherboard. This lets you wipe clean the RAM, cache, CPU, and system chipset bottlenecks and can also bring you up to speed on the latest in bus technologies, including AGP and USB. Now, however, you're paying for both the CPU and the surrounding motherboard. Expect to pay $600 or more for a brand new motherboard with a Pentium II CPU.

CPU Guide

4.3 Buying Considerations

Comparing CPUs can be tricky business. CPU makers often spin the market by producing custom benchmarks designed to show big leaps for their architectures. Also, differences in internal designs can yield big performance variances among different types of processes, ranging from integer and floating-point arithmetic to the handling of MMX-optimized code. Of course, a chip that is fast under Windows NT—such as Intel's Pentium Pro—may flag when running the 16-bit code of Windows 95.

Other factors come into play. Many CPUs run quite hot, making them poor overclocking candidates. Also, some non-Intel processors may spoof software detection schemes, causing some applications to fail to load. This section will help you get a sense of the landscape and adjust your buying decisions to suit.

4.3.1 Clock Speed

Clock speed is the most simple and obvious metric of CPU performance, but it's also the most abused. Even CPUs within the same family may deliver very different performance on a per-clock-tick basis. AMD's K5 PR-90 and K5 PR-120, for instance, both run at 90/60MHz; yet the K5 PR 120 provides better performance in our tests. Why? AMD tweaked the internal architecture of the K5 in midlife, resulting in a CPU that got more from less.

One problem is the fact that Cyrix and AMD decided to market based upon perceived performance instead of clock speeds. Cyrix's M II-PR200, for example, only runs at 150MHz internally but provides performance similar to the Pentium MMX-200. Although integer performance does fall in line with the PR rating, MMX and FP performance often lag well behind, because Cyrix is unable to apply the same amount of optimization to these important pipelines. The result: Games often run much slower on the Cyrix CPU than you might expect. AMD used similar performance rating schemes in its K5 line but has since dropped this nomenclature.

Once you cross CPU families, of course, the situation gets foggier still. Clock speed is of little value when comparing Pentium MMX and Pentium II CPUs, since the internal workings of the two chips are so different. L1 and L2 cache configurations, CPU I/O, pipeline designs, and a host of other issues come into play.

All that said, we know that a faster clock will, by definition, make a CPU go faster. Push a Pentium II-233 to 266MHz and your machine will go faster—so clearly the smart buy is to reach for the faster CPU. What is not so clear is how much of a benefit an incremental clock boost will deliver, particularly at higher rates where the CPU is running as much as five times the rate of the 66MHz system bus. If you're trying to keep to a budget, you may find the extra cost of the fastest CPU not worth the relatively meager performance boost in most applications.

4.3.2 Internal vs. External Clock

Since the introduction of the 486DX/2, CPUs have run faster inside the chip than outside. The microscopic scale of CPU connections allows them to run much, much faster than motherboard bus connections that are millimeters long. However, clock multiplying poses a problem—push the internal clock too fast, and your performance returns diminish.

We see it with the current Pentium II-333, which runs at 333/66MHz, or 5× multiplier. Despite an 11 percent internal CPU boost over the Pentium II-300, our tests show a meager five percent increase in overall system performance. In fact, as clock multipliers have risen, we've seen a general flattening of overall performance impact.

The internal/external clock equation comes into play when your CPU choices span different motherboard bus speeds. For example, the Pentium-150 CPU provides little if any benefit over the supposedly slower Pentium-133. The reason: The Pentium-150 runs on a 60MHz motherboard bus (at a 2.5× multiplier), whereas the Pentium-133 runs on a faster 66-MHz bus (at a less extreme 2× multiplier).

A similar effect occurs when you overclock a motherboard. That Pentium-150 running at 150/60MHz will get a pretty nifty boost if its pushed to 166/66MHz. Although the clock multiplier remains at 2.5×, the 10 percent gain in the motherboard bus speed makes the most of the increase in the internal clock. Similarly, pushing the system bus to 75MHz and 83MHz yields CPU clock speeds, in this case, of 187MHz and 207MHz.

A good rule of thumb: Always buy a CPU that keeps the internal-to-external clock multiplier as low as possible. Our tests show that once you get past a 3× internal/external clock split, CPU performance starts to degrade. For this reason, the Intel 440BX chipset—which allows 100MHz motherboard bus speeds—is a critical buy. Although the 400/100MHz clocks of the Pentium II-400 run at a higher multiplier than we would like, the impact of the fast motherboard is enormous. Also, the fast L2 cache (running at 200MHz) eases the pinch at the CPU I/O.

4.3.3 Cache Size and Type

Whether it's internal or external CPU cache, bigger is always better. AMD's K6 and Cyrix's 6x86MX both get a good deal of their integer performance from

CPU Guide

their extra-heavy L1 caches. In fact, the 6x86MX runs at internal clock speeds well below its PR rating, thanks in large part to the massive 64KB L1 cache.

The L1 cache is a super-fast store of memory internal to the CPU. Running at the speed of the CPU clock, the cache employs predictive algorithms to intelligently grab data that is likely to be needed next. The problem with L1 cache is that it requires real estate, thus boosting transistor counts, increasing complexity, and adding to the thermal output of the chip.

L1 caches comes in two flavors—unified and split data cache. Unified caches excel in multimedia playback and other applications where large data chunks are moving through the CPU, because a large percentage of the unified cache can be dedicated to data retrieval. A segmented data/instruction cache design, on the other hand, will run more efficiently when a relatively even mix of data and instructions are moving over the bus.

The first Intel CPU to use an L1 cache was the 486, which employed an 8KB unified cache. Both the Pentium and Pentium Pro employ separate 8KB data and instruction caches, whereas Pentium MMX doubles that to 16KB each for data and instruction caches. AMD's K6 and Cyrix's 6x86MX go even further, employing 64KB of L1 cache—an unfathomable amount just a few years ago.

Because L1 cache is so limited by the CPU manufacturing process, virtually all systems use a larger L2 cache to serve as an intermediary between system RAM and the processor. With the Pentium Pro CPU, Intel moved the L2 cache into the CPU package, allowing a 256KB or 512KB store of memory to run at full CPU clock speed. The problem: The large L2 cache significantly complicates the manufacturing process. For this reason, Pentium II moves the L2 cache back outside while employing a tight dedicated bus to allow for high L2 clock speeds.

4.3.4 Thermal Characteristics

Anyone who buys a system or separate CPU needs to worry about heat. Aggressive CPU designers are constantly playing chicken with the thermal envelope, inviting problems by packing more and more transistors into larger and larger CPU dies. You need to look no farther than the massive heat-sink assembly on the Pentium II SEC cartridge to see proof of this challenge.

Although shrinking processes alleviate much of the problem, vendors are always under pressure (whether from Wall Street or their customers) to get that faster CPU version shipping sooner. In 1996, Cyrix pushed out red-hot 6x86 PR166 CPUs and paid the price when systems began failing. Cyrix claimed that the systems themselves were poorly designed and lacked airflow to keep their chips cool, which was in fact true. Also true was the fact that 6x86 CPUs were running too close to the thermal edge, inviting disaster in all but the most rigorously designed PCs. Similar tales have arisen around AMD's early K6-233 CPU (itself a victim of poor manufacturing yields).

Right now, the fastest CPUs are being built on a .25-micron process and running at speeds up to 450MHz. Older designs built on a .35-micron process are generally restricted to speeds of 233 to 300MHz, depending on the efficiency of the CPU design. The .35-micron Pentium II reaches 300MHz, whereas AMD's .35-micron K6 tops out at 233MHz. Where possible, you should buy a CPU built on a smaller process, because the cooler operating temperature will likely allow a longer useful life.

Another measure of thermal output is *heat dissipation*, measured in watts. The Pentium Pro shocked the press when the massive 15.5-million transistor die proved to dissipate 16 watts of heat during normal operation. The Pentium II-300, a .35-micron CPU, throws off 12 watts, whereas its .25-micron sibling running at 333MHz only gives off 8 watts. As you can see, higher clocks do not mean more heat if the CPU properly designed.

If overheating is a concern, make sure the CPU has an effective CPU fan installed. If the existing fan is faltering or does not provide adequate airflow, you can purchase a replacement from companies such as PC Power and Cooling. Another useful item is a thermal sensor inside your PC. The 110 Alert sensor from PC Power and Cooling costs $20, and it sounds an alarm whenever the temperature inside the case rises above 110 degrees Fahrenheit.

4.3.5 SMP

Web servers, network servers, and CAD and 3D design workstations can all benefit from multiprocessor designs. However, don't be fooled—there's little to be gained from piling more CPUs onto most application tasks. In fact, even the most CPU-intensive operations run under a fairly steep curve of diminishing returns as processors are added. The reason? Bus I/O and management overhead cut into the advantage served by raw processing power.

Today, the Pentium II has assumed the role as the preeminent *x*86-compatible SMP processor, supplanting the Pentium Pro. Until this year, Pentium Pro was the most scalable *x*86 CPU, able to support four-way SMP without modification. However, the newest Pentium II variant—designed for the Slot 2 connector—ratcheted up the Pentium II's SMP capabilities from two-way to four-way, matching that of Pentium Pro. Additional CPUs can be run on a single motherboard, but it takes significant customization to make the additional CPU caches and memory management work together.

SMP is no mean trick due to the complexity involved in having multiple CPUs accessing a common pool of memory. What's more, you must be running a multiprocessor-aware operating system; otherwise, only a single CPU will be utilized. Windows NT Workstation can employ two CPUs, whereas NT Server recognizes up to four CPUs. Linux, OS/2, the BeOS, and various forms of Unix all provide SMP support.

Applications must also be tuned to take advantage of SMP using a process called *multithreading*. Multithreaded applications break program operations into distinct components (or threads) that can be parsed readily among multiple CPUs. Without multithreading, only a single processor is able to work on application tasks at any one time.

4.4 Tom's Pick:

For high-performance computing, no CPU family outpaces the Pentium II. While Xeon performs great in symmetric multiprocessing (SMP) settings, the premium Intel demands for the faster and larger L2 cache is simply too much. For my money, the CPU to own is the Pentium II-450.

Why? For one, the PII-450 offers all the advantages of Pentium II: Great integer performance, unrivaled x86 floating point performance, and the best MMX processing you can find. And the highly-tuned superscalar P6 architecture really gets its legs when running 32-bit applications under Windows NT. Here, the Pentium II's out-of-order execution capability enables the CPU to widen the performance margin against other models.

But perhaps most important, PII-450 is priced sell in the desktop computing world. Whether you are running demanding office applications, hot, new 3D games, or desktop publishing and CAD software, the PII-450 makes a great choice. And because the PII-450 is coupled with a fast 100-MHz front side motherboard bus, memory accesses and overall system performance benefit across the board.

Can't afford to spend $3000 on a new PC? If you seek bargains, the CPU to buy is the AMD K6-2. Early tests of this new processor show it to be a capable successor to the K6. While straight up integer performance is unchanged from K6, the 300-MHz K6-2 nonetheless delivers office application performance that is on par with Pentium II systems of the same CPU clock speed. What's more, AMD has incorporated its 3D-Now instruction set extensions, which help speed the setup of 3D scenes in games and software. Combine that with enhanced MMX and FPU performance, and the K6-2 makes a fine choice for a CPU in systems costing about $1700.

Chapter

5

Chipset Guide

Every computer purchase, every motherboard upgrade, every CPU buying decision comes back to the same thing: the system chipset. If the CPU is the brain of your PC, the chipset is its heart. It controls the flow of bits that travel between the CPU, system memory, and the motherboard bus. Efficient data transfers, fast expansion bus support, and advanced power management features are just a few of the things the system chipset is responsible for.

A funny thing about chipsets is that they can't be upgraded (see Figure 5.1). You can add new memory, swap out graphics cards, and even replace an aging CPU, but system chipsets are soldered to the motherboard and are intricately entwined with the motherboard environment. If the chipset in your motherboard won't recognize SDRAM memory, you'll need a whole new motherboard to add that capability.

Figure 5.1.

The two-chip Intel chipset is clearly visible at the center of this Pentium MMX motherboard from Tyan.

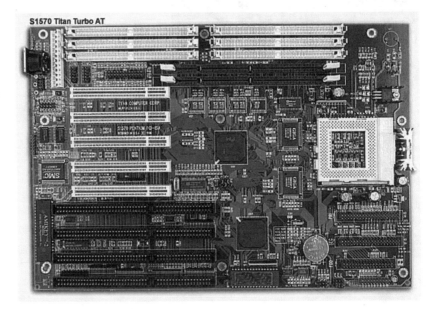

This chapter will help you understand how a system chipset can impact performance as well as what you can do to wring a little more out of the hardware you've got. Of course, we'll also show you what to look for in a chipset when making a system buying or motherboard upgrade decision.

5.1 Chipset Mission and Workings

Chipsets are the traffic cops of the PC, and as such, play a critical role in overall performance. The chipset connects directly to the CPU, system memory, and bus subsystems, serving as the waypoint for all bits moving between these three points. Figure 5.2 shows a typical map of chipset interconnections.

Figure 5.2.

As the communications hub of your motherboard, the chipset determines how quickly and efficiently the CPU, memory, and bus I/O subsystems can talk to each other.

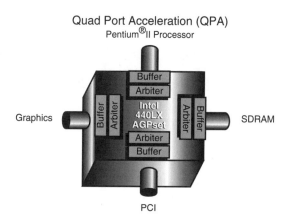

Physically speaking, the chipset can be found on the motherboard in proximity with the CPU socket, expansion bus slots, and main memory. This is no accident: The timings involved in the high-speed communications between the chipset and its clients, if you will, is very tight. Short, direct electrical pathways ensure that signal reflection and cross-talk don't degrade performance or result in break-downs.

The chipset operates at the speed of the motherboard bus, which in most PCs sold today is 66MHz. The new 440BX chipset from Intel runs at a higher 100MHz, as do the MPV3 from Via and the Aladdin V from ALI. The spate of 100MHz chipsets should in particular boost performance on PCs using the Socket 7 interface employed on Pentium MMX and competing CPUs, because the speed of the processor's secondary (or L2) cache will get a 50 percent clock increase. The L2 cache on Pentium II systems, by contrast, will not speed up at all, because they already run at half processor speed within the single-edge connector (SEC) cartridge used to package the CPU, cache, and supporting logic.

Essentially, the chipset is a collection of individual controllers that manage and interface with subsystems ranging from CPU and memory to disk drives and mice. Here's a list of some of the specific functionality provided by the chipset:

- CMOS SRAM: A tiny storage area used to store critical system data.

- DMA controller: Manages direct accesses to memory without CPU intervention. Provides critical efficiencies for data transactions.

- EIDE controller: Controls transactions with the Enhanced IDE bus used to interface with hard disks and CD-ROM drives.

- IrDA controller: Supports industry-standard infrared communication devices.

- Keyboard controller: Interfaces with the keyboard.

- L2 cache controller: Determines the type, amount, and performance of L2 cache.

- Memory controller: Determines the type and maximum amount of system RAM that may be used in a motherboard. The design of this unit also impacts the efficiency of memory operation.

- PCI bridge: Serves as the interconnection between the PCI expansion bus and other system components, including the ISA bus.

- PS/2 mouse controller: Interfaces with the mouse or other pointing device connected to the PS/2 port.

- RTC (real-time clock): Keeps track of the time and date, even when the PC is shut off. The clock is usually powered by a small lithium battery located on the motherboard.

The chipset itself is generally split into two logical sections—the *north bridge* and the *south bridge*. The north bridge is where the hard work happens, including the interfaces to the cache, RAM, CPU, and buses. The south bridge contains the peripheral I/O operation, including IDE controllers as well as the serial, parallel, USB, and other ports. The north bridge sometimes consists of more than one chip, whereas the south bridge is generally a single, smaller chip in the set.

Even as chipset makers pile more features into their devices, the packages themselves grow smaller and smaller. Intel's 440LX, for example, cuts the chipset count from three chips (found in the 440FX) to two. Chipsets from VIA and ALI provide similar economies. The smaller packaging saves both money and motherboard space, helping reduce the cost of new systems.

5.2 Performance Impact Report

The chipset is absolutely critical to system performance, even if its role is frequently overlooked by both end users and the computer media. Two motherboards of the same design, clock rate, CPU, and system RAM can return very different performances based on the chipset. For example, one chipset may lack efficiency in working with SDRAM memory, whereas the other shaves precious clock ticks off each new memory access. Likewise, an older chipset may fail to cache system RAM beyond 64MB, whereas a newer model can support and cache 128MB, 256MB, or even more system memory.

Unfortunately, one-to-one chipset performance comparisons are difficult to do because you can't plug competing chipsets into a reference motherboard. Also, new chipset designs are often mated with different motherboard models, RAM types, and other enhancements. These variables prevent effective, across-the-board benchmarks.

Still, a chipset's impact can be seen across the platform of PCs on which it's installed. The original Triton chipset, Intel's 430FX, had a huge impact on Pentium motherboard performance thanks to its support for EDO DRAM and other welcome tweaks. The 430TX, likewise, provided a boost for Pentium MMX systems, whereas the 440BX has upped the ante significantly in the Pentium II arena.

5.3 Available Chipsets

The chipset market has changed drastically over the past five or six years. A bevy of semiconductor companies have vied for chipset market share—Opti, SiS, VIA, ALI, UMC, and others all supplied chipsets for motherboards running Intel, AMD, Cyrix, and IBM processors. Today, Intel owns a large portion of the x86 chipset market, leaving the others to compete in a shrinking segment. Because Intel now makes the majority of motherboards found on PCs, it's no surprise that its chipsets are used on them.

The following are chipset manufacturers active in the x86 market:

- Intel
- Via
- ALI
- Opti
- AMD

Perhaps the best way to demarcate chipsets is by the CPU classes they support. Because the CPU interfaces of the P5 and P6 architectures differ so much, the same chipset can not be used for both processors. Intel's 430 line of chipsets, for example, services Pentium and Pentium MMX processor system, whereas the 440 line appears in Pentium Pro and Pentium II systems.

It's worth noting that even chipsets within the same product line are not created equal. All manufacturers "step" their chipsets, introducing updated silicon under the same chipset name. Often, the stepping is used to smooth out bugs, tweak performance, or introduce a more efficient manufacturing process. This can address major points of functionality.

For example, the Intel 430HX chipset did not initially support the USB ports found on systems based on the chipset. Only later did Intel update the HX to service the USB ports. As a result, early 430HX-based Pentium MMX PCs were unable to support USB peripherals despite the fact that two USB connectors appear on the motherboard.

5.3.1 Intel's Pentium and Pentium MMX Chipsets

The line of Pentium-class Intel chipsets is long and distinguished, a regular alphanumeric smorgasbord of advancing features and performance. Table 5.1 shows the Pentium-class chipsets.

Table 5.1. Intel's march of P5 chipsets have helped it dominate the industry.

Chipset	Introduced	Socket Type
430LX	1992	Socket 4
430NX	1992	Socket 5
430FX	1994	Socket 7
430HX	1996	Socket 7
430VX	1996	Socket 7
430TX	1997	Socket 7

Surprisingly, the first Pentium chipsets—the 430LX and 430NX—were quite impressive. Both the 430LX and 430NX supported parity memory, with the LX able to manage 192MB of RAM, and then the NX upped that figure to 512MB. It's no surprise that time has passed these early Pentium chipsets by. Neither chipset could work with EDO DRAM and bus speeds that top out at 133MHz.

The 430FX (code-named *Triton*) was a breakthrough; it added support for fast EDO DRAM (though only 128MB) and pipeline-burst SRAM L2 cache memory. It also delivered an updated PCI bus interface that improved bus mastering capabilities. Pentium systems with the new chipset enjoyed an immediate and significant performance boost, helping Intel break out of the once-competitive chipset pack.

The next CPU in the food chain, the 430HX, bulked up with dual-processor support and the ability to address 512MB of parity- or ECC-enabled EDO DRAM, as well as 512KB of L2 cache. It also added support for USB, enhanced IDE, and PCI bus version 2.1.

While the 430HX served in high-end *x*86 Pentium systems of the time, the 430VX made a play for the consumer market. As a single-processor chipset, it introduced support for SDRAM and USB—two critical forward-looking technologies. However, the VX only addresses 128MB of RAM, only 64MB of which can be cached, thus effectively limiting installed RAM to 64MB. What's more, its SDRAM performance is poor, with a 7-1-1-1 burst cycle that adds two cycles to the setup of SDRAM's potential 5-1-1-1 burst operation.

As it turned out, the 430VX never stood much of a chance in the market. Intel launched the 430TX in January of 1997 and it immediately overran all but the highest segments of the market (see Figure 5.3). The 430TX behaved in many ways like the VX predecessor, with the onerous 64MB SDRAM caching limitation, single processor capability, and USB support. However, the 430TX introduced the fast ATA-33 IDE interface, boosting hard disk performance and throughput, and it fixed SDRAM support by providing 5-1-1-1 burst operation. The 430TX is also the first chipset designed for both notebooks (it appears in Pentium MMX notebooks) and desktops, adding support for the Advanced Configuration and Power Interface (ACPI).

Figure 5.3.
Intel's 430TX, despite a host of compromises, turned up the heat on the Pentium MMX platform by delivering cheap SDRAM support, working USB, and ATA-33 capability.

5.3.2 Non–Intel Chipsets for Socket 7

Intel has made it no secret that it intends to move the market to Pentium II. After all, AMD and Cyrix have made good livings making CPUs to fit into the Socket 7 connectors used by Pentium MMX. However, with Intel discontinuing chipsets for Pentium MMX motherboards, competing CPU companies face a dead end. Enter companies such as VIA and ALI, which have rolled out important new chipsets that promise to extend the Viability of the Socket 7 platform. Here are some of the most important chipsets:

- ALI Aladdin V

- ALI Aladdin IV

- Via MVP3

- Via VP3

- Via VP2

The ALI Aladdin V is remarkable in that it kicked off the critical Super 7 motherboard market. This chipset features a fast 100MHz front bus that pushes the speed of system memory, L2 cache, and CPU interface to 100MHz (50 percent faster than the 66MHz standard before it). In addition, Aladdin V provides an AGP implementation and ultra DMA support for faster IDE hard disk operation. The result: Socket 7 motherboards that carry all the feature richness of Intel's Pentium II offerings but at a much lower price.

In order to carry off a 100MHz front bus, the Aladdin V provides more detailed timing division of the system bus clock. Whereas 66MHz motherboards simply divide the bus clock by two to get the 33MHz clock of PCI, the Aladdin V divides the 100MHz clock by one-third to keep PCI within spec. This is an important distinction, because most PCI boards simply will not work once the bus is pushed to 40MHz or higher. In fact, PCI bus failure is a common ailment of overclocked systems. The Aladdin V will run at 66, 75, 83, and 100MHz.

One area where Aladdin V falls short is AGP, as the implementation is only of the 1X variety. Although AGP 2X cards like ATI's Rage Pro will work in Aladdin V motherboards, they will only provide 1X features. Note that the loss of 2X operation is really only a concern for heavily-optimized AGP games and software, where tens of megabytes of texture data are being piped directly from system memory. To date, few if any such programs exist, but future software may make AGP 2X support important to consider.

Like the Aladdin V, the Via MVP3 is a Socket 7 chipset that features a 100MHz front bus and AGP support. However, the MVP3 enhances AGP support with AGP 2X capability, which pushes throughput of main memory to the graphics card from 256MBps to 512MBps. Otherwise, the feature set is competitive, including ATA-33 IDE capability, USB, ACPI power management, and the ability to address up to 1GB of system memory. The MVP3, shown in Figure 5.4, also supports DDR SDRAM, which can double the effective clock rate by working on both the rising and falling edges of the clock.

Figure 5.4.
VIA's MVP3 chipset extends the Socket 7 market by introducing AGP and the 100MHz front bus to AMD- and Cyrix-based PCs.

The other active chipset maker on the market is SiS, which recently came out with its SiS5591 chipset. Like Aladdin V and MVP3, the SiS5591 provides AGP, SDRAM, and ATA-33 on the existing Socket 7 motherboard platform. Up to 256MB of SDRAM memory can be addressed, whereas the L2 cache tops out at 1MB. The SiS5591 includes ACPI compliance for power management and enhanced on/off/sleep control. Most important, SiS5591 offers high front bus clock speeds, with 66, 75, 83, and 100MHz settings. An asynchronous PCI bus interface means that PCI devices continue to hum along at their specified 33MHz regardless of the clock setting of the motherboard bus itself.

The SiS5591 supports ECC memory and features six RAS lines, which is enough for three DIMM sockets. The three DIMM sockets is a reasonable number considering the 5591's relatively low 256MB memory ceiling. One drawback: The chipset does not support 133MHz AGP operation, which means that only AGP 1X mode is available to graphics cards.

Older competing chipsets abound. VIA's VPX/97 played a key role in legitimizing Cyrix's 75MHz front bus 6*x*86 and 6*x*86Mx CPUs. The chipset can run at both 66 and 76MHz, and it uses an asynchronous PCI bus to keep PCI clock rates within spec. Otherwise, a 75MHz motherboard would push the PCI rate to 37.5MHz, similar to what occurs when you overclock an Intel motherboard. Although some devices will continue to work, many graphics and network cards will fail at the higher data rate.

Prior to the VPX/97, the VIA VP2/97 offered competitive features to the popular 430TX, including excellent memory support. The VP2/97 can address up to 512MB of SDRAM memory, including ECC type memory, and it can support a large 2MB L2 cache. However, VP2 lacks an asynchronous PCI bus. So while VIA specs the chipset for 75MHz operation to support the fastest Cyrix chips, system memory and PCI devices will not run reliably on VP2 motherboards clocked at 75MHz.

With its memory support and ATA-33 disk I/O, the VP2/97 became a popular platform for other chipsets. AMD's 640 chipset, launched in an effort to jump-start its aggressive K6 and K6-2 efforts, is essentially a remarked VP2/97. The VP2 follows, the VP3/97, adds AGP capability to the existing VP2 platform. Table 5.2 provides a summary of P5-class motherboards available from third-party vendors.

Table 5.2. The new P5-class chipsets' advanced features.

Chipset	System clock	RAM type	Max. cached DRAM
SiS5591	66/75/83/100	SDRAM	512
MVP3	66/75/83/100	SDRAM/DDR/SDRAM	1024
AMD 640	66	SDRAM	512
ALI Aladdin V	66/75/83/100	SDRAM	512
430TX	66	SDRAM	64
VP3	66	SDRAM	1024
430HX	66	EDO	512
430VX	66	SDRAM	64
VPX/97	75	SDRAM	512
VP2/97	66	SDRAM	512

Legend: System clock in MHz
             RAM: Maximum RAM cached (MB)
             ECC: ECC/parity support (Y/N)
             L2: Maximum L2 cache size (Kb)
             AGP: AGP type supported (1/2)
             USB: USB support (Y/N)
             ATA: ATA-33 support (Y/N)
             CPU: Number of CPUs supported
             ACPI: ACPI support (Y/N)
             Chips: Number of chips in chipset

5.3.3 P6-Class Chipsets

The line of P6-class Intel chipsets may not be as long as that of the P5, but recent introductions have made the message clear—Intel is focusing squarely on P6. The release of the 440LX in 1997 finally brought fast SDRAM to Pentium Pro and Pentium II PCs, whereas the addition of the AGP bus provided a trump card in Intel's fight against Pentium clone makers. Before that, Pentium Pro and early Pentium II buyers were frustrated by P6 platform lag. Although the 440 line of chipsets delivered enhanced data integrity, greater memory capacities, and multiprocessing capability, performance-enhancing features found on the P5 platform often took a year or more to reach Pentium Pro buyers. Table 5.3 shows the lineage of P6-class chipsets.

ECC	L2	AGP	USB	ATA	CPU	ACPI	Chips
Y	1024	1X	Y	Y	1	Y	2
Y	2048	2X	Y	Y	1	Y	2
Y	2048	N	Y	Y	1	Y	2
Y	1024	2X	Y	Y	1	Y	2
N	512	N	Y	Y	1	Y?	2
Y	2048	1X	Y	Y	1	Y	2
Y	512	N	Y	N	2	N	2
N	512	N	N	N	1	N	4
N	2048	N	Y	Y	1	Y	4
Y	2048	N	Y	Y	1	Y	2

Table 5.3. P6-class Chipset Lineage

Chipset	Introduced	Socket Type
450GX	1995	Socket 8
450KX	1995	Socket 8
440FX	1996	Socket 8
440LX	1997	Socket 8/Slot 1
440BX	1998	Slot I/Slot II
440EX	1998	Slot I

What's more, Intel's dominance in the P6-class chipset market is even more pronounced than it is in the P5 arena, because cross-licenses for the P6 bus and connectors have been much harder to come buy (although Cyrix now enjoys access thanks to its purchase by National Semiconductor).

Pentium Pro Chipsets

The Intel 440FX Natoma chipset was the second Pentium Pro chipset, and it turned into the workhorse for Socket 8 motherboards. The most cost effective of Pentium Pro chipsets, the 440FX provided limited dual-processor SMP. It could, however, serve up as much as 1GB of ECC memory. Although it lacked support for SDRAM, USB, and other incoming features, its affordability made it a mainstay on desktop workstations.

On the server side, Intel delivered the 450GX (Orion) and 450KX (Mars). The KX ended up being an unhappy stepchild. With its dual-processor support and 1GB memory ceiling, it lacked the way-out features needed for serious NT servers. What's more, the less-expensive 440FX soon arrived and matched its features.

The 450GX, therefore, became the chipset for the server savvy. It runs four Pentium Pro CPUs and can address 4GB of ECC memory (but not SDRAM). However, like the 450KX and 440FX, this chipset lacks ATA-33 IDE support for ultra DMA hard disks (it uses the PIIX3 IDE controller). Still, the 450GX remains the chipset of choice for four-way SMP servers—at least until four-way capability gets built into upcoming Pentium II CPUs and chipsets.

Pentium II Chipsets

When the Pentium II first arrived, the only chipset for it was the 440FX, which limited the appeal of this new CPU in the mass market. Lacking were key (and imminent) features such as SDRAM, AGP, and ATA-33. Smart shoppers waited for the 440LX chipset, which was introduced in September, 1997 and fixed a lot of problems. Presumably, Intel wanted to lockstep the Pentium II introduction with 440LX (it would have made a lot more sense), but heat from AMD's K6 and Cyrix' 6x86Mx (now called M II) forced Intel to roll its Pentium IIs as soon as they were ready.

The 440LX did for Pentium II what the 430TX Triton chipset did for the Pentium—it raised the platform enough to turn the CPU into a mass-market hit (see Figure 5.5). The list of additional features is quite impressive, most notable among them being support for faster SDRAM memory and the new Accelerated Graphics Port (AGP) bus. AGP quadruples the bandwidth available to PCI graphics cards—though little real-world impact has resulted—while also enabling system memory to store large amounts of texture data for enhanced realism in 3D graphics.

Figure 5.5.

Intel's 440LX chipset finally brought SDRAM and power management to the Pentium II scene, and it delivered a haymaker in the form of AGP graphics capability.

Less touted, but nearly as important, was the inclusion of the updated PIIX4 IDE controller, which enabled ATA-33 (also called *ultra DMA*) enhanced IDE hard drives. The chipset also provided ACPI support for power management and instant "on" capability. And talk about your slam dunks, the 440LX employed a compact two-chip design that reduced the motherboard footprint compared to the three-chip 440FX. The 440LX retained the dual-processor capability and the 1GB memory ceiling of the 440FX.

The Pentium II platform took a major performance leap in April 1998, with the introduction of the 440BX chipset. With its 100MHz front bus, the BX enables a 50 percent increase in motherboard bus clock speeds. The enhancement is critical for AGP, because AGP cards must share memory bandwidth with the CPU, in effect taking what's left of the 528MBps once the CPU is done with it. The 440BX expands the bandwidth pie to 824MBps, providing more headroom for AGP graphics data transfers. The enhancement also benefits all noncached memory accesses. However, neither the PCI nor AGP buses budge from their 33MHz and 66MHz specifications.

The 440BX delivers an enhanced IDE controller (PIIX6) that adds support for the fast IEEE 1394 (a.k.a. *Firewire*) bus. Able to transfer up to 400MBps, 1394 is an external, plug-and-play expansion bus that bears a resemblance to USB. However, it's targeted for high-performance applications such as video capture, data storage, and networking.

Even as it tunes the Pentium II for top performance, Intel continues to ply the lowball market. The 440EX chipset was introduced in March 1998, for the

Celeron (code-named *Covington*) CPU. Essentially a Pentium II stripped of its L2 cache, the Celeron takes the P6 architecture into the sub-$1000 PC market. The 440EX is a stripped down LX chipset that lacks multiprocessor support and uses a 66MHz front bus. Expansion is limited to three PCI slots and two DIMM sockets, although AGP remains in the picture. Future chipsets will offer AGP 4X capability, support for faster and larger L2 caches, and IEEE 1394 capability.

Non-Intel vendors are finally getting into the P6 fray. The only shipping Pentium II chipset at the time of this writing is ALI's Aladdin Pro II, which consists of the M1621 north bridge chip and the M1533 or M1533 south bridge chip. Like the 440BX, the Aladdin Pro II provides a 100MHz front bus—a critical feature in the market. Notable is the optimized memory access architecture, which pipelines memory cycling to reduce time lost to latency and recharging. The Aladdin Pro II also supports a fast 66MHz PCI bus and AGP 1× and 2×, as well as provides deep buffers for PCI bus mastering operations. Otherwise, Aladdin Pro II is competitive with ATA-33, USB, and ACPI capabilities.

SiS has plans for the SiS5601 AGP chipset, but no details were available at the time of this writing. Table 5.4 provides a helpful breakdown of P6-class chipsets.

Table 5.4. New P6 class chipsets add updated memory support, SMP, and advanced I/O in found earlier Pentium-class offerings.

Chipset	System clock	RAM type	RAM	ECC	L2
450GX	66	FPM DRAM	8GB	Y	1024
450KX	66	FPM DRAM	1GB	Y	1024
440FX	66	EDO DRAM	1GB	Y	1024
440LX	66	SDRAM	512MB (1GB EDO)	Y	512
440BX	100	SDRAM	1GB	Y	512
440EX	66	SDRAM	1GB	Y	512
Aladdin Pro II	100	SDRAM	???	Y	???

Legend: System clock in MHz
              RAM: Maximum RAM cached (MB)
              ECC: ECC/parity support (Y/N)
              L2: Maximum L2 cache size (Kb)
              AGP: AGP type supported (1/2)
              USB: USB support (Y/N)
              ATA: ATA-33 support (Y/N)
              CPU: Number of CPUs supported
              ACPI: ACPI support (Y/N)
              Chips: Number of chips in chipset

5.4 Evaluating Chipsets

The previous description of chipsets gives you a pretty good idea of what to look for in a chipset. Manufacturers are constantly making tradeoffs in their designs, weighing features and performance against price and timeliness. Historically, the first chipset serving a new CPU has been woefully inadequate. For example, inefficient memory handling, limited feature sets, and slow bus speeds plagued front-line chipsets such as the 430LX and 440FX. Even if you do buy into a third-generation chipset design, you can expect the march of progress to move past you within a year or two.

You should keep in mind that chipsets are a key standards-building tool for Intel. If Intel wants to implement AGP on the Pentium II platform in order to clobber pesky Socket 7 competition, it just forms a standards body, rolls AGP into its chipsets, and gets the market moving. Four hundred days later, your Pentium II system is obsolete.

	AGP	USB	ATA	CPU	ACPI	Chips
	N	Y	N	4	N	4
	N	Y	N	2	N	4
	N	Y	N	2	N	4
	Y	Y	Y	2	Y	2
	Y	Y	Y	2	Y	2
	Y	Y	Y	1	Y	2
	Y	Y	Y	???	Y	2

This is why it pays to look at the larger market before committing to a chipset. If you bought into the 440LX in the fall (as I did) you would have been well served to think hard about the relatively low 528MBps throughput ceiling that AGP must share with system RAM. Rumors of AGP 4× and 100MHz SDRAMs were pretty much the writing on the wall for the LX—a good chipset that essentially ran point in the Pentium II advance. When you buy, don't just consider the chipset itself, look at the environment it occupies.

5.4.1 Bus Bandwidth and Speed

The lessons of the 440BX are quite fresh here. The 100MHz front bus on the newest Pentium II chipset really opens the flood gates, particularly for AGP transactions. These kinds of changes don't happen all that often—once every three to five years—but when they do, they invariably have a major performance impact. That impact is even greater on the Socket 7 platform, because the L2 cache is tied to the motherboard clock (the Pentium II places L2 cache in the module, running at one-half CPU speed).

Because chipsets are closely tailored for the CPUs they serve, the bus bandwidths and clocks will match up with their processor. Even the earliest Pentium chipset employed a 64-bit data bus and a 60/66MHz clock. Likewise, the first AGP-aware chipset—the 440LX—added a port for the 64-bit, 66MHz AGP bus so that data from main memory could flow directly to the graphics subsystem.

With chipsets now running at 100MHz, the width and speed of the front bus is reaching its logical limits for current memory designs. Fat SDRAM interfaces are replete with signal and timing issues at high speeds. Doubling the bus width (to 128 bits) means doubling the pins, an expensive proposition that is untenable. However, double data rate (DDR) SDRAM promises to increase the bandwidth available to memory by two times (though once again chipset support is required). In the long term, expect the memory architecture to change before speeds or bus widths change again.

Although Intel has not made any announcements yet, a 200MHz system bus is the likely next stop. Such bus speeds are probably mandated to optimize performance for processors running in the gigahertz range targeted by IA-64 Merced and other CPUs. However, major design issues stand in front of such a 2× improvement.

5.4.2 Memory Handling

Clearly, memory handling is a big deal. Not only must chipsets be designed to recognize enhanced memory types, but they must be well designed to avoid wasting clock ticks at every access. The 430VX chipset for Pentiums was first to market with SDRAM support, yet its seven-tick setup (versus five ticks optimal) dragged down performance considerably. It wasn't until the 430TX showed up a year later that memory accesses reached their 5-1-1-1 potential.

Main Memory Support

If you're buying into a chipset, make every effort to get one that addresses SDRAM memory. Although 66MHz is fine for most applications, it's worth stretching for the 100MHz front bus. Virtually all aspects of operation will improve, and AGP-enabled systems could see big benefits as AGP-optimized applications start to fill the wide pipes opened between the memory and graphics subsystems.

Beyond speed, you need to worry about how memory is supported. Pentium chipsets provided a confusing array of memory quantity support. The 430TX could address 256MB of SDRAM, but few buyers realized that only the first 64MB of that amount was covered by the L2 cache. Load up on memory beyond this limit, and performance would degrade significantly—on the order of 25 to 30 percent! Because Windows 95 loads itself into the highest reaches of memory (leaving the lower area free for DOS compatibility), the OS and all its critical I/O operations are certain to be hamstrung by the dumbed-down cache support.

What's more, the chipset determines the number and type of memory expansion sockets. Many SDRAM motherboards use just two or three DIMM sockets, which can get a bit cramped if you upgrade down the road. (Figure 5.6 shows the best of both worlds.) Likewise, many Pentium MMX motherboards actually included both SIMMs and DIMMs, in order to provide adequate support in a transitioning market.

Figure 5.6.

The Tyan Tacoma motherboard provides six SIMM and two DIMM sockets, which is generous support for memory. In addition, the chipset allows five PCI add-in slots, whereas chipsets such as Intel's 440EX allow only three.

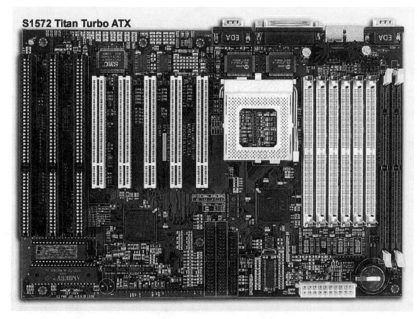

The memory support picture will get more complicated before it gets simpler. The arrival of Double Date Rate (DDR) SDRAM extends the Viability of the SDRAM memory type significantly, clouding Intel's plans to introduce Rambus

DRAM (RDRAM) as the system memory of choice for future desktops. Although DDR SDRAM will require incremental tweaks to existing chipset designs, RDRAM changes all the memory interface rules.

Basically, the wide SDRAM interface delivers data like a canon shot. Large clumps of data roll in at a moderate clip (66 or 100MHz). RDRAM, on the other hand, works like a machine gun. Its 8-bit interface is just one-eighth that of SDRAM, but it clicks off at a staggering 800MHz. Because the chipset talks directly to the memory subsystem, the move to RDRAM will entail major changes to existing designs.

Cache Memory Support

A related issue is the chipset's support for L2 cache memory. Although virtually all chipsets on new motherboards now support fast pipeline-burst SRAM (PB SRAM), they differ widely in the amount of cache they can address. What's more, chipsets may place limits on your main memory performance based on the L2 cache installed in the PC. This is a slippery area of chipset "specmanship" that can result in big disappointments down the road. Be sure to keep a close eye out for cache support.

Today, full-featured chipsets address 1MB or 2MB of L2 cache, more than most desktop systems are likely to need. Some lower-cost desktop-oriented chipsets top out at 512KB, which is a realistic number for today's affordable Pentium II, Pentium MMX, and compatible CPUs. Any less than 512KB, however, should not be considered, because today's large programs and multitasking operating systems need a larger pool of fast cache memory.

Some chipsets limit the amount of memory you can install or use optimally based on the cache present in the system. Intel's 430TX imposes an abominable 64MB limit to the RAM that can be cached, even though the chipset will address a total of 256MB. That means any system with the full RAM amount will be running cacheless for most operating system transactions.

Other caches will scale the amount of cached main memory based on the size of the L2 cache present on the motherboard. Therefore, if you have a 256KB L2 cache and want to upgrade to 128MB of RAM, you may once again be walking into a cache trap where only 64MB gets serviced by the fast SRAM. You may have to boost L2 cache (presuming you even can) to 512KB in order to enable optimal 128MB system memory operation. Even this may not allow you to reach the top cached memory capacity of your chipset and motherboard, however. If your additional memory lacks sufficient TAG RAM to provide indexing to the chipset, you could end up with a larger cache and the same 64MB restriction. Make sure to check both the required L2 cache amount and the TAG RAM configuration required to boost memory should you face this issue.

These things vary by the individual chipset product, so you need to look closely at the specs on the motherboard. In some cases, you may not be able to find the cache-to-RAM relationship, so you'll need to ask questions of the vendor and perhaps other users. In any case, if you have a system you intend to boost to 128MB of RAM, you should pay very close attention to the L2 cache addressing capability of the chipset. Otherwise, you'll end up with a purchase that's nearly useless.

5.4.3 CPU Handling

Chipsets are made to serve their CPU masters. As such, the bus interfaces, clock rates, and cache support are all designed to meet the needs of a specific processor. With that said, Intel chipsets have served multiple processor variants. The 430VX appeared on both Pentium and Pentium MMX CPUs (a minor difference really), whereas the 440FX served both Pentium Pro and Pentium II. In both cases, the chipsets served within the same platform (P5 and P6), which means that issues of bus interface remain fixed.

Aside from the usual updates to introduce emerging capabilities, different chipsets serving a CPU model enable task-specific features. The 440FX and 450GX both work with Pentium Pro CPUs, but their missions are quite different. The 450GX is tailored to the server market, with its four-way SMP support and 4GB memory ceiling. The 440FX, on the other hand, is limited to two-way SMP and 1GB of RAM. Likewise, the 440EX is basically the 440LX chipset, but it supports only a single processor and drives fewer RAM and PCI slots.

An important element of CPU handling is the capability to accommodate multiprocessor motherboards. The Pentium II can run in dual-processor configurations by design, whereas Pentium Pro scales to four-way SMP. The chipset needs to handle the interaction of the CPUs, including the tricky job of keeping different L2 caches in lockstep. If one CPU changes data in its cache and the same data in the second CPU's cache is not changed to match, the results can be disastrous.

One solution would be to simply have all writes sent directly to main memory, but the performance drag of such an approach—particularly on an SMP system—is untenable. Therefore, the chipset must be able to identify cache data as being shared, changed, or invalid. The chipset then makes sure that the two or four L2 caches are in synch, thus avoiding conflicts while maintaining performance.

5.4.4 Ins and Outs

Chipsets play a critical role in enabling I/O. For years, all Intel chipsets have had built-in controllers for PCI, IDE, keyboard, and PS/2 mouse. More recently, USB and AGP have become standard issue on Pentium II–class chipsets. Integrated

Chipset Guide

support is critical for gaining access to emerging I/O technologies such as USB and AGP. It also plays a critical role in enabling emerging standards, because support for a bus type in a popular chipset means that vendors can count on an established market.

Enhanced Disk Operation

Once an I/O interface is added, things don't sit still. The IDE bus controller seems to be enhanced every few months. The PIIX3 controller, for example, delivered enhanced IDE capabilities for disk drives—a critical improvement that boosted both performance and capacity. The PIIX4 controller found in the 440LX, in turn, brought fast ultra DMA (a.k.a. ATA-33) hard disks to the market, and a tweaked version (the PIIX4e) is already built into new chipsets. Next up for the IDE controller is the PIIX6, which adds the IEEE 1394 bus to the mix.

ATA-33 is a critical feature because large, enhanced IDE hard disks have become so appealing from a price standpoint. Earlier chipsets only supported program-mable I/O operation (called *PIO*), which requires CPU involvement in every hard disk transaction. As a result, older ATA drives were poor multitaskers, because they tended to tie up system resources. ATA-33 drives use direct memory access (DMA) to transact without processor intervention, thus enabling efficient multitasking and enhancing throughput.

Why didn't chipsets come up with this attractive DMA support earlier? For one thing, DMA is a tricky proposition on a hard disk, because the IDE bus often splits its time among multiple devices. Disk makers must provide custom drivers in order to deal with all the variables. Poor DMA implementations can lead to fatal drive errors—hardly the type of thing you want rolled into a platform before it's ready.

If you're buying a motherboard, ATA-33 support is crucial. The feature not only doubles the top data rate of earlier enhanced IDE drives (from 16MBps to 33MBps), but it frees the CPU and other components to do work while the hard disk is busy. Virtually all new P5 and P6 class chipsets support ATA-33. Down the road, look for IEEE 1394 support in the chipset, because future disk drives may transition to the fast 1394 bus.

AGP's Enhanced Graphics

AGP is undergoing a similar transition to the IDE bus. The 440LX delivered AGP 1× and AGP 2× support, enabling throughputs of 264MBps and 528MBps, respectively. By allowing the graphics card to tap directly into system memory, 3D games could use the extra capacity to serve up megabytes of realistic-looking textures. The result: Enhanced game play. Although we've yet to see compelling implementations of AGP software, the promise remains a strong one. However, the AGP interface is not sitting still. While 440LX provides AGP 2×, the VIA VP3 chipset is limited to AGP 1× operation. That's not a big deal on the slower 66MHz front bus, but anyone buying a 100MHz motherboard will want the 528MBps of bandwidth that AGP 2× can deliver.

Intel, meanwhile, is gearing up to introduce AGP 4×, also referred to as *AGP Pro*. This specification doubles up the bandwidth again, delivering a full gigabyte per second (1GBps or 1,024MBps) of data from main memory to the graphics subsystem. Intel is targeting graphics workstations for this technology, but gaming PCs will certainly enjoy the benefit. The simple rule of thumb is "the more bandwidth, the better."

Other I/O Features

Other areas to look at include support for infrared communications (IrDA), USB, and different PCI variants, including 66MHz PCI. Make sure at the very least that the PCI 2.1 specification is provided in the chipset. Also, if you intend to upgrade to non-Intel CPUs, the system chipset should have the capability to recognize other products.

5.4.5 Power Management Features

An area of recent focus in chipset products is power and system management. The ACPI specification, which stands for *Advanced Configuration Power Interface*, provides an industry standard for power-saving modes, instant "on" operation, and other features. ACPI was critical in the development of Intel's 430TX, for example, the first chipset to be designed for use in both desktop and notebook PCs.

ACPI support in your chipset yields one very visible benefit to desktop users of recent Windows 95 versions. When you shut down your PC, you don't have to wait around for the all-clear screen to manually shut off the power. Once the system gets to a shut-down state, the chipset turns off the power automatically, as has been typical for notebook PCs for years. Also, the Windows 95 Shutdown menu includes a sleep mode option that allows you to keep the PC on but in a low-power state.

IS managers also gain the ability to turn systems on remotely through this chipset feature. This enables them to perform tasks such as overnight system upgrades and software installations without having to manually boot up every PC individually.

More advanced chipsets add security and additional management features to the mix. Again, IS managers want client PCs they can maintain from a central site in order to save time and money. Working with Microsoft, Compaq, and others, Intel and other chipset makers are rolling a growing suite of management tweaks into their chipset designs. For the individual desktop, many of these features may seem like overkill, but it's likely your future motherboard purchases will include management intelligence. One benefit: Those seeking remote access from the road will find more reliable and responsive means of dialing into the home PC.

5.5 Tom's Pick

Picking the best chipset is a little like picking the Best Director in the Academy Awards. The CPU and graphics card may hog all the glory, but the chipset provides the critical glue that makes everything work together. The conflicting demands of memory, cache, CPU, disk devices, and various system buses all come to a head at the system chipset. Better chipsets improve performance by smoothing over inevitable resource clashes, allowing your hard disk to move data efficiently, for example, or enabling PCI peripherals to transact gobs of data without bothering the CPU.

More visible are the basic elements of device support wrapped into every chipset. The ability to recognize and work well with SDRAM system memories and multiple CPUs plays a critical role in performance. Most recently, 100-MHz system chipsets help deliver a 50 percent clock boost to the CPU's front-side bus and to RAM, while support for USB and—soon—FireWire buses open doors to future peripherals.

So what chipset is our top pick? At the time of this writing, no one has matched Intel's impressive 440BX, which runs on Pentium II motherboards. The only 100-MHz Pentium II chipset, the 440BX improves on the advances delivered by its direct predecessor—the 440LX's SDRAM support and better IDE interface—while boosting the front side bus speed by 50 percent. Advanced Configuration and Power Interface (ACPI) adds extended management and power saving resources. No, this chipset won't run four or eight CPUs, and L2 cache is limited to a relatively-paltry 512KB, but these shortcomings are more of a concern for network administrators and graphics professionals who are willing to spend a $5000 premium for a slightly fast Xeon-based system.

If you are shopping in the Socket 7 world, your choices grow narrower. Intel's 430 line of chipsets is at a dead end, as the company tries to coax the world to its Slot 1 designs. So it falls to third parties to come up with fast 100-MHz designs that offer support for crucial technologies like AGP, ACPI, and Firewire.

Right now, the best option is ALi's Aladdin V chipset. The only 100-MHz chipset shipping at the time of this writing, the ALi provides almost all the features of 440BX, but does it for the cost-effective Socket 7 platform. The fast 100-MHz front bus means that L2 cache will gain a welcome 50 percent boost, while AGP 2X support means that your graphics card choices will be wide open for motherboards implementing this feature.

Unfortunately, ALi has had a heckuva time getting the Aladdin V to market—it went through what seemed like countless revisions before finally shipping. So users are warned to take their time and look hard at the chipset's record of compatibility. And unstable chipset, after all, can spell curtains for users seeking to make use of new technologies.

Chipset Guide

BIOS Guide

Adapted from *The BIOS Survival Guide, version 5.1*, by Jean-Paul Rodrigue and Phil Croucher.

6.1 Understanding the BIOS

As the lowest level of software in your PC, the basic input/output system (BIOS) performs the most basic housekeeping chores required to keep your software and hardware running. When you first start up your PC, it's the BIOS, not the operating system, that takes stock of your hardware and starts loading the OS from the hard disk drive. Once things are running, the BIOS determines how the operating system may interface with the hard disk, the timing of system and cache memory, and the configuration of various ports and interfaces, including IDE, parallel, and serial.

Just as the PC has gotten more sophisticated over the years, the BIOS that serves it has become more flexible, intelligent, and capable. The introduction of Plug and Play concurrent with the release of Windows 95 added crucial dynamic hardware recognition and initialization capabilities to PnP-compliant BIOSs. Likewise, advanced power management features and improved automatic detection capabilities have reduced the amount of time users need to spend messing around with inscrutable BIOS settings.

The problem is, the even the best, most recent BIOS can't anticipate or correctly detect everything. A wrong setting here or an unoptimized switch there can result in dreaded BIOS bottlenecks. Worse still, older BIOSs or undercooked new versions can lead to compatibility problems and mysterious crashes. In other words, if you want to get the most performance out of your PC, you'll have to go through your BIOS to get it.

6.1.1 How the BIOS Works

As mentioned earlier, the BIOS gives the computer a built-in starter kit to run the rest of the software from floppy disks and hard disks. It's also responsible for booting the computer by providing a basic set of instructions. It performs all the tasks that need to be done at startup time, including POST (power-on self-test). Furthermore, it provides an interface to the underlying hardware for the operating system in the form of a library of interrupt handlers. For instance, each time a key is pressed, the CPU (central processing unit) performs an interrupt to read that key. This is similar for other input/output devices (serial and parallel ports, video cards, sound cards, hard disk controllers, and so on).

Some older PCs cannot cooperate with all the modern hardware because their BIOSs don't support them. If your operating system can't call a BIOS routine to use it, this problem can be solved by replacing your BIOS with a newer one that does support the new hardware or by installing a device driver for the hardware.

Singling Out CMOS

CMOS stands for *Complementary Metal Oxide Semiconductor* and is the little piece of RAM (64 bytes) used to store BIOS settings so that the PC doesn't forget them every time it's switched off. A small battery keeps the CMOS contents active. In earlier systems, this memory was part of the clock chip, but it now resides in a highly integrated circuit (IC). CMOS describes the low-power technology used in the RAM to enable battery life (measured in years).

Newer boards actually use a Nickel Cadmium (NiCad) accumulator—rather than a battery—which recharges every time the computer is turned on. If your CMOS is powered by external batteries, be sure they're in good operating condition and that they don't leak (this will damage the motherboard); otherwise, your CMOS may suddenly "forget" its configuration, and you may be looking for a problem elsewhere. Some new motherboards include a technology named the *Dallas Nov-Ram*. It eliminates the need for an onboard battery by using a 10-year lithium cell glued into the chip itself.

BIOS Setup

The BIOS setup is the set of procedures that enables you to configure a computer according to its hardware characteristics. It allows you to change the parameters with which the BIOS configures your chipset. The original IBM PC was configured by means of DIP switches buried on the motherboard. Setting PC and XT DIP switches properly was something of an arcane art. DIP switches/jumpers are still used for memory configuration and clock speed selection. When the PC-AT was introduced, it included battery-powered CMOS memory that contained configuration information. CMOS was originally set by a program on the diagnostic disk; however later clones incorporated routines in the BIOS that allowed the CMOS to be configured (or reconfigured) if certain magic keystrokes were used.

Unfortunately, as the chipsets controlling modern CPUs have become more complex, the variety of parameters specified in setup has grown. Moreover, there has been little standardization of terminology among the half-dozen BIOS vendors, three dozen chipset makers, and the large number of motherboard vendors. Complaints about poor motherboard documentation of setup parameters are very common.

To exacerbate matters, some parameters are defined by BIOS vendors, others by chipset designers, others by motherboard designers, and still others by various combinations of all of these. Parameters intended for use in design and development are intermixed with parameters intended to be adjusted by technicians—who are frequently just as baffled by this stuff as everyone else is. No one person or organization seems to understand all the parameters available for any given setup, although Jean-Paul Rodrigue and Phil Croucher have compiled an

BIOS Guide

extensive list in their *BIOS Companion* (http://www.lemig.umontreal.ca/bios/bios_sg.htm).

6.1.2 Microsoft's Fast BIOS Specification

More changes are coming. Specifically, Microsoft is pushing its so-called *Fast BIOS specification*, which seeks to radically reduce the startup time of PCs. Today, much of the time spent during startup is dedicated to BIOS activity. Detection and initialization of devices, the power-on self-test, and memory checking all take precious seconds.

The Fast BIOS specification takes aim at sluggish startups by replacing the labor-intensive initializations with a series of compact boot flags. These flags, which are stored in CMOS, instantly tell the BIOS everything it needs to know. If a change has occurred, the discrepancy will be noted when the boot flag value is invoked, and the BIOS will double back to handle the change.

Fast BIOS operation is more than a simple convenience issue for home and office PCs. Microsoft sees it as critical to enabling convergence PCs that offer the same instant-on experience we see in televisions and stereos. Likewise, remote access products that turn on the PC when a call comes in will benefit greatly from the reduced startup time.

6.2 Basic Optimization Tricks

This section is intended for users who have a limited knowledge of BIOS setup. It provides four fundamental procedures that may help improve the performance of your system:

- Make sure all standard settings correspond to the installed components of your system. For instance, you should verify the date, time, available memory, hard disks, and floppy disks.

- Make sure your cache memory (internal and external) is enabled. Of course, you must have internal (L1) and external (L2) cache memory present, which is always the case for recent systems (less than five years old). Recently, some motherboards have been found that contain fake cache memory. Some unscrupulous manufacturers are using solid plastic chips that contain no memory to lure vendors and customers in order to gain extra profits in an highly competitive semiconductors market. Buyer beware.

- Make sure your "wait state" values are at the minimum possible. You must, however, be careful—if these values are too low, your system may freeze (hang up).

- Make sure to shadow your video and system ROM. On older systems, this may improve performance significantly.

6.2.1 Clearing BIOS Memory

Three alternatives for clearing BIOS memory are available, depending on your type of motherboard:

- Enter BIOS setup and change to settings to their power-on defaults.

- Disconnect the battery.

- Insert the appropriate jumper on the motherboard and wait until the BIOS memory is cleared. (See main board documentation; the jumper is often located near the battery).

Sometimes this is possible with DIP switches on the motherboard. If not, you'll have to remove the battery. Otherwise, if there are no DIPs and no removable battery (and you're not willing to unsolder the battery), you may be able to short the battery with a resistor in order to lower the current available for the CMOS.

This is only recommended as a very last option. The NiCad cells usually employed have a very low internal resistance, so the resistor will have to be of a very low value for the voltage to drop significantly. The corresponding current would be quite high, which is not very good for battery life. A better option would be to use a resistor to discharge the battery. Obviously, this only makes sense when you have a NiCad cell (which will be recharged every time you turn the computer on) as opposed to a lithium cell (which cannot be recharged). In the former case, a 39-Ohm resistor will discharge the battery in under half an hour relatively safely.

Another good way to discharge the NiCad is to put a 6-volt lantern lamp across it and let it discharge completely. Not only does this provide an effective load, it also gives a visual indication of the charge state. It's a good way to prevent "ghost memory" that's so common with NiCads. Once the NiCad is discharged, turning the system on will restore a flow of energy to the rechargeable cell, allowing you to reassert data stored in the CMOS. Nickel Metal Hydride (NiMH) batteries, which eliminate this problem (albeit at additional expense), are used in some systems.

6.2.2 Upgrading a BIOS

When it comes to upgrading a BIOS, everything boils down to two camps: flash and non-flash. Most systems sold over the past three years use a flash BIOS, which can be easily updated using software. To perform a flash update, you simply

BIOS Guide

download the updated BIOS code from the BIOS vendor's Web site and save it to a formatted disk. The flash BIOS code includes a special file that enables the BIOS flashing routine when you boot your system with the disk in the drive. You just follow the text prompts in the flash interface to overwrite your old BIOS with the new one.

Of course, updating a BIOS is not a simple step. A BIOS change impacts every aspect of system performance, and it can introduce unexpected problems that may range from a few lost hours of tweaking to a complete meltdown of your PC. Therefore, a BIOS update is an action to be taken only after you've made thorough backups of your data and applications. Also, it pays to backup your existing flash BIOS settings, as well, because you may need these should your "upgrade" go badly.

Before you do anything, however, you should check your BIOS version, which appears onscreen every time you boot the system. The display goes by fast, so keep a sharp eye out for the information. Even better, enter the BIOS interface by pushing the magic key sequence (often the Delete or Esc key or some other combination) during boot up. Your system documentation will specify how to launch the BIOS utility. You'll be able to see the specific BIOS make and version in the utility. Just remember: PC vendors sometimes tailor BIOS code for their PCs, so the AMI BIOS in a Gateway system may be different from an AMI BIOS found in another system.

If you don't have a flash BIOS, you're probably out of luck. Older BIOSs require that you physically replace the BIOS chip, a component that's specifically de-signed for a specific motherboard and its chipset. It's no surprise that BIOS chip upgrades are a rare find from BIOS vendors. In fact, your only option may be a motherboard upgrade if you have a non-flash BIOS.

6.3 The Grand Tour

Our exploration of the BIOS and its CMOS storage facilities is just beginning. In this section, you'll learn about the operation of the power-on self-test (POST) and how to update BIOS settings. Step-by-step explanations and instructions will help demystify this most critical—yet least understood—aspect of system operation.

6.3.1 POST and Entering Setup

When the system is powered on, the BIOS will perform diagnostics and initialize system components, including the video system. (This is self-evident when the screen first flicks before the video card header is displayed). This is commonly referred as POST. Afterward, the computer will proceed to its final bootup stage by calling the operating system. Just before that, the user may interrupt to have access to Setup.

To allow the user to alter the CMOS settings, the BIOS provides a little program called Setup. Usually, Setup can be entered by pressing a special key combination (Del, Esc, Ctrl+Esc, or Crtl+Alt+Esc) at boot time. The popular AMI BIOS is generally accessed by pressing the Del key during power up. You can bypass the extended CMOS settings by holding the Ins key down during bootup. This is helpful for recovering after you've managed to bend the CMOS settings out of shape, causing the computer to no longer boot properly. This is also a handy tip for people who play with the older AMI BIOSs with the XCMOS setup. It allows changes directly to the chip registers with very little technical explanation.

Typical BIOS POST Sequence

Most BIOS POST sequences occur along four stages:

1. Some basic information about the video card such as its brand, video BIOS version, and video memory available is displayed. This information actually comes directly from the BIOS located on the video card. The video card is the first of various system peripherals to "check in" during the POST.

2. The BIOS version and copyright notice is displayed in upper-middle screen. This information is helpful for identifying BIOS-specific conflicts, because it provides the precise version information of the BIOS code.

3. Memory count is displayed. You'll also hear tick sounds if you have enabled them (see the "Advanced CMOS Setup" section).

4. Once the POST has succeeded and the BIOS is ready to call the operating system (DOS, OS/2, NT, Win95, and so on), you'll see a basic table of the system's configurations.

System Configuration Items

The following are standard configuration items listed in most BIOS versions:

- **Main processor**

   The type of CPU identified by the BIOS. Usually Cx386DX, Cx486DX, and so on.

- **Numeric processor**

   Present if you have a FPU or None if you have no FPU. If you have a FPU and the BIOS does not recognize it, see the "Advanced CMOS Setup" section for more information on the numeric processor.

BIOS Guide

- **Floppy drive A**

  The drive A type. See the section "Standard CMOS Setup" to alter this setting.

- **Floppy drive B**

  Essentially the same as floppy drive A.

- **Display type**

  See the "Standard CMOS Setup" section for information on the primary display.

- **AMI or AWARD BIOS date**

  The revision date of your BIOS. Useful to mention when you have compatibility problems with adapter cards.

- **Base memory size**

  The number of KBs of base memory (usually 640KB).

- **Ext. memory size**

  The number of KBs of extended memory.

  In the majority of cases, the summation of base memory and extended memory does not equal the total system memory. For instance, in a 4,096 KB (4MB) system, you'll have 640KB of base memory and 3,072KB of extended memory—a total of 3,712KB. The missing 384KB is reserved by the BIOS for a variety of uses, including addressing peripherals, providing shadow memory for ROM, and enabling access to higher memory areas.

- **Hard disk C**

  Type: Identifies the hard disk as IDE, ESDI, or other format types.

  The master HDD number. See hard disk C type information in the "Standard CMOS Setup" section.

- **Hard disk D**

  Type: Identifies the hard disk as IDE, ESDI, or other format types.

  The slave HDD number. See hard disk D type information in the "Standard CMOS Setup" section.

- **Serial port(s)**

  This is usually the hex address of your COM ports (3F8 and 2F8 for COM1 and COM2). Occasionally, these fields are set by the number of the port controlling both address and IRQ settings.

- **Parallel port(s)**

  The hex address of your LTP ports (378 for LPT1). Occasionally, this field is set by the number of the port controlling both address and IRQ settings.

- **Other information**

  Under this table, BIOS usually displays the size of cache memory. Common sizes are 64KB, 128KB, and 256KB. You'll find external cache memory information in "Advanced CMOS Setup."

AMI BIOS POST Errors

During the POST routines, which are performed each time the system is powered on, errors may occur. Nonfatal errors are those that, in most cases, allow the system to continue the boot up process. The error messages normally appear on the screen. Fatal errors are those that will not allow the system to continue the bootup procedure.

If a fatal error occurs, it's time to start troubleshooting. Errors are usually communicated through a series of audible beeps. Your system or motherboard should include documentation that defines the meaning of different beep patterns, allowing you to focus on the misbehaving component or subsystem. All the errors you'll find listed, with the exception of #8, are fatal errors. All errors found by the BIOS will be forwarded to the I/O port 80h. The following are explanations of common beep patterns:

- **One beep**

  DRAM refresh failure. The memory refresh circuitry on the motherboard is faulty.

- **Two beeps**

  Parity circuit failure. A parity error was detected in the base memory (first 64KB block) of the system.

- **Three beeps**

  Base 64KB RAM failure. A memory failure occurred within the first 64KB of memory.

- **Four beeps**

  System timer failure. Timer #1 on the system board has failed to function properly.

- **Five beeps**

  Processor failure. The CPU on the system board has generated an error.

- **Six beeps**

   Keyboard controller 8042–gate A20 error. The keyboard controller (8042)
   contains the gate A20 switch that allows the computer to operate in
   virtual mode. This error message means that the BIOS is not able to
   switch the CPU into protected mode.

- **Seven beeps**

   Virtual mode (processor) exception error. The CPU on the motherboard
   has generated an Interrupt Failure exception interrupt.

- **Eight beeps**

   Display memory R/W test failure. The system video adapter is either
   missing or its memory is faulty. This is not a fatal error.

- **Nine beeps**

   ROM-BIOS checksum failure. The ROM checksum value does not
   match the value encoded in the BIOS. This is good indication that the
   BIOS ROMs went bad.

- **Ten beeps**

   CMOS shutdown register. The shutdown register for the CMOS memory
   Read/Write error has failed.

- **Eleven beeps**

   Cache error/external cache bad. The external cache is faulty.

Still More AMI BIOS POST Codes

Wait, there's more. To provide further troubleshooting information, the AMI
BIOS can combine patterns of short and long beeps. The result is a virtual Morse
code of troubleshooting information:

- **Two short beeps**

   POST failed. This is caused by a failure of one of the hardware testing
   procedures.

- **One long and two short beeps**

   Video failure. This is caused by one of two possible hardware faults:

   - Video BIOS ROM failure. Checksum error encountered.

   - The video adapter installed has a horizontal retrace failure.

■ **One long and three short beeps**

Video failure. This is caused by one of three possible hardware problems:

- ■ The video DAC has failed.
- ■ The monitor detection process has failed.
- ■ The video RAM has failed.

■ **One long beep**

POST successful. This indicates that all hardware tests were completed without encountering errors.

BIOS Error Messages

This is a short list of most frequent onscreen BIOS error messages. Your system may show them in a different manner. When you see any of these, you're usually in real trouble:

■ **8042 gate – A20 error**

Gate A20 on the keyboard controller (8042) is not working.

■ **Address line short!**

Error in the address decoding circuitry.

■ **Cache memory bad, do not enable cache!**

Cache memory is defective.

■ **CH-2 timer error**

There is an error in timer 2. Several systems have two timers.

■ **CMOS battery state low**

The battery power is getting low. It would be a good idea to replace the battery.

■ **CMOS checksum failure**

After CMOS RAM values are saved, a checksum value is generated for error checking. The previous value is different from the current value.

■ **CMOS system options not set**

The values stored in CMOS RAM are either corrupt or nonexistent.

■ **CMOS display type mismatch**

The video type in CMOS RAM is not the one detected by the BIOS.

- **CMOS memory size mismatch**

  The physical amount of memory on the motherboard is different than the amount in CMOS RAM.

- **CMOS time and date not set**

  Self-evident.

- **Diskette boot failure**

  The boot disk in floppy drive A is corrupted (virus?). Is an operating system present?

- **Display switch not proper**

  A video switch on the motherboard must be set to either color or monochrome.

- **DMA error**

  Error in the DMA (Direct Memory Access) controller.

- **DMA #1 error**

  Error in the first DMA channel.

- **DMA #2 error**

  Error in the second DMA channel.

- **FDD controller failure**

  The BIOS cannot communicate with the floppy disk drive controller.

- **HDD controller failure**

  The BIOS cannot communicate with the hard disk drive controller.

- **INTR #1 error**

  Interrupt channel 1 failed POST.

- **INTR #2 error**

  Interrupt channel 2 failed POST.

- **Keyboard error**

  There's a timing problem with the keyboard.

- **KB/interface error**

  There's an error in the keyboard connector.

- **Parity error ????**

  Parity error in system memory at an unknown address.

- **Memory parity error at XXXXX**

  Memory failed at the XXXXX address.

- **I/O card parity error at XXXXX**

  An expansion card failed at the XXXXX address.

- **DMA bus time-out**

  A device has used the bus signal for more than allocated time (around 8 microseconds).

If you encounter a POST error, there's a good chance it's a hardware problem. You should at least verify whether adapter cards or other removable components (SIMMs, DRAMs, and so on) are properly inserted before calling for help. You could save yourself a lot of lost time and aggravation.

6.3.2 BIOS Identification Line

There may be up to three identification lines in the BIOS startup screen.

BIOS Guide

First Identification Line

1. Processor Type

   - ? 8088 or 8086
   - ? 80286
   - ? 80386
   - X 80386SX
   - 4 80486
   - 5 Pentium

2. Size of BIOS

   - 0: 64KB
   - 1: 128KB

4–5. Major version number

6–7. Minor version number

9–14. Reference number

16. Halt on POST error

   ■ 0: Off

   ■ 1: On

17. Initialize CMOS in every boot

   ■ 0: Off

   ■ 1: On

18. Block pins 22 and 23 of the keyboard controller

   ■ 0: Off

   ■ 1: On

19. Mouse support in BIOS/keyboard controller

   ■ 0: Off

   ■ 1: On

20. Wait for F1 if error found

   ■ 0: Off

   ■ 1: On

21. Display floppy error during POST

   ■ 0: Off

   ■ 1: On

22. Display video error during POST

   ■ 0: Off

   ■ 1: On

23. Display keyboard error during POST

   ■ 0: Off

   ■ 1: On

25–26. BIOS date month

27–28. BIOS date day

29–30. BIOS date year

32–39. Chipset identification/BIOS name

41. Keyboard controller version number

Second Identification Line

1–2. Pin number for clock switching through keyboard controller

3. Indicates high signal on pin—switches clock speed to high or low

- H: High
- L: Low

5. Clock switching through chipset registers

- 0: Off
- 1: On

7–10. Port address to switch clock to high

12–13. Data value to switch clock to high

15–16. Mask value to switch clock to high

18–21. Port address to switch clock to low

23–24. Data value to switch clock to low

29–31. Pin number for turbo switch

26–27. Mask value to switch clock to low

Third Identification Line

1–2. Keyboard controller pin for cache control

3. Indicates whether high signal on cache control pin enables or disables cache

- H: Enable
- L: Disable

5. Indicates if the high signal is used on the keyboard controller pin

- 0: False
- 1: True

7–9. Cache control through chipset registers

- 0: Cache control off

- 1: Cache control on

11–12. Port address to enable cache through a special port

14–15. Data value to enable cache through a special port

17–20. Mask value to enable cache through a special port

22–23. Port address to disable cache through a special port

25–26. Data value to disable cache through a special port

28–29. Mask value to disable cache through a special port

31. Pin number for resetting the 82335 memory controller

33. BIOS modified flag (incremented each time BIOS is modified)

6.3.3 Standard CMOS Setup

Always, always, always write your current setup options down on paper. Better yet, take that sheet and tape it to the inside or the outside of the case. CMOS memory has a tendency to get erased as the battery gets old, or it becomes inaccessible if you forget the password. Especially remember the hard disk settings; they are the most important.

If you have warm-booted the computer (via Ctrl+Alt+Del) to go into the CMOS setup, the BIOS routine to handle the Print Screen key will probably be installed. You can display each screen of the CMOS setup and press Shift+Print Screen to get a printed copy directly. There are several good CMOS saver programs out on the market, including the PC-Tools and Norton recovery programs. These programs allow you to save a copy of the CMOS registers to a file in case the battery dies, or if they messed around with the settings, and so on.

Here's a rundown of the settings stored in your system CMOS:

- **Date (mon/day/year) and time**

    Used to change the date and time of the system clock. Do not expect your computer to keep track of time as accurately as an atomic clock, or even a wrist watch! Depending of the quality of the motherboard, you can expect to lose (or gain) several seconds per month. Only rarely will you need to set the clock in the BIOS because all operating systems allow you to change this setting within their environments.

■ **Daylight savings**

Allows the clock to automatically adapt to the daylight savings scheme, which removes one hour on the last Sunday of October and adds one hour on the last Sunday of April.

■ **Hard disk C type**

The number of your primary (master) hard drive. Most of the time this number is 47, which means that you must specify the drive specs according to your hard drive manual.

> **NOTE**   Newer drives and BIOSs take the pain out of setup by auto-detecting drive hardware. In most cases, you'll never have to worry about setting up the specific geometry of the drive. The BIOS will detect it, map the geometry, and then abstract it into a linear format using the Logical Block Addressing (LBA) scheme.

■ **Cyln**

The number of cylinders on your hard disk.

■ **Head**

The number of heads.

■ **WPcom**

Write precompensation. Older hard drives have the same number of sectors per track at the innermost tracks as at the outermost tracks. This means that the data density at the innermost tracks is higher; therefore, the bits lie closer together. Starting with this Cyln number until the end of Cyln numbers, the writing starts earlier on the disk. In modern hard drives (all AT-BUS and SCSI), this entry is useless. Set it either to -1 or max Cyln (a common value is 65,535). For IDE (Integrated Device Electronics) hard drives, it's not necessary to enter a WP cylinder. The IDE HDD will ignore it in favor of its own parameters stored onboard.

■ **LZone**

The address of the landing zone. Same as WPcom. Used in old hard drives without an auto-parking feature—MFM (Modified Frequency Modulated) or RLL (Run Length Limited). Set it to 0 or max Cyln#.

■ **Sect**

The number of sectors per track. It's often 17 for MFM and 26 for RLL HDD. On other types of drives, it will vary.

BIOS Guide

■ **Size**

This is automatically calculated according the number of cylinders, heads, and sectors. This setting is in megabytes and applies the following formula:

(Hds * Cyln * Sect * 512) / 1048

With the growing capacity of hard disks on desktop computers, a redefinition of IDE specifications 'was necessary. The old IDE specification only supported drives up to 528MB, which is the Normal partition setting. In 1994, the EIDE (Extended IDE) protocol was designed and now all new motherboards support it. This newer protocol uses the LBA (Logic Block Addressing) system, which considers logic blocks instead of heads, cylinders, and sectors. If your BIOS does not support LBA, several hard disk manufacturers provide drivers to trick the BIOS. You'll also find a Large partition setting that can accommodate drives up to 1,024 cylinders (1GB) but does not support LBA.

■ **Hard disk D type**

The number of your secondary (slave) hard drive. Same procedure as above. Jumpers must be set for a hard drive to perform as slave. Refer to your hard drive manual. You might also want to refer to the hard disk data file frequently posted to.

Most new PCI motherboards can accommodate up to four IDE drives: primary master, primary slave, secondary master and secondary slave.

■ **Floppy drive A**

The type of floppy drive installed for drive A. Frequent configurations are 1.44MB (3 $\frac{1}{2}$ inches) and 1.2MB (5 $\frac{1}{4}$). Newer systems also have a 2.88MB (3 $\frac{1}{2}$) setting.

■ **Floppy drive B**

The type of floppy drive installed for drive B.

■ **Primary display**

The type of displaying standard you're using, or, in the case of systems with two video adapters, the primary one. The most frequent is VGA/PGA/EGA. Modern computers have VGA (Video Graphics Array). If you have an older black-and-white display, select Mono or Hercules. If your video adapter card is text only, select MDA.

■ **Keyboard**

Installed. If "not installed," this option sets the BIOS to pass the keyboard test in the POST, allowing the PC to reset without a keyboard (file server, printer server, and so on), without the BIOS producing a keyboard error. As a system administrator, you can uninstall the keyboard as a supplementary security procedure to prevent people from messing with the server.

6.3.4 Changing Your Password

BIOS-level password protection is the most stringent security you can provide on your desktop PC. Unlike other password routines, BIOS security runs straight from the lowest-level hardware (CMOS) and software (BIOS) on your motherboard. Lose that password and you're simply out of luck. No system administrator can come by and make it better. Write it down somewhere, or better yet, ask yourself if you really need a password-protected BIOS.

If security is a minor concern to you, you should disable the password. Otherwise, if you lose your password, you'll have to erase your CMOS memory to gain access to the PC again. Some systems allow you to choose when the password is needed to change the CMOS settings—for example, to boot the machine.

6.3.5 Auto-Configuration

All recent motherboards now have an auto-configuration setting, leaving much of the BIOS setup problems, such as bus clock speed and wait states, out of the user's hands. In the majority of cases, it will do just fine. However, you must remember that it's not an optimization of your system's performances but rather a set of efficient settings that will ensure a good result. You'll have to disable this setting if you want to alter the BIOS yourself; otherwise, your settings will be ignored. On some systems, you may get supplementary performance by improving the auto-configuration settings, but on others auto-configuration is all you'll ever need.

Auto-Configuration with BIOS Defaults

The BIOS defaults may not be tuned for your motherboard/chipset, but they have a reasonable chance of getting into the POST. Usually these settings are a good start for fine-tuning your system. If you did something wrong and don't know what, select this option. It will replace your BIOS settings with default values, and you'll have to start all over again. Be sure you know your system's configuration. This option does *not* alter the date, hard disk, and floppy disk configurations in the standard CMOS setup, so, in general, you can expect your system to boot without problems after selecting this option.

Auto-Configuration with Power-on Defaults

When powering on, the BIOS puts the system in the most conservative state you can think of. Turbo off, all caches disabled, all wait states to maximum, and so on.

This is to make sure you can always enter BIOS setup and is useful if the settings obtained by selecting Auto-Configuration with BIOS Defaults fail. If the system does not work with these values, you're almost certainly looking at a hardware problem such as a fried component.

6.3.6 Exiting BIOS

There are two ways to exit BIOS settings:

- **Write to CMOS and exit**

  Saves the changes you made in the CMOS. You must do this to permanently keep your configuration. Users often change the CMOS setup but forget to exit with this option. This is a common error.

- **Do not write to CMOS and exit**

  If you're not sure of the changes you made in the CMOS settings, use this option to exit safely.

6.3.7 Advanced CMOS Setup

Available configuration options will vary according to your system, BIOS version, and brand. Some functions might not be present, or the order and name may be different (particularly for different BIOS brands). Make a point to know *exactly* what you're doing. In addition to describing each function, this section provides recommended settings that will work best for most—but not all—users.

Switch the power off. Turn your computer on while keeping the Del key pressed. This is supposed to erase the BIOS memory. If it still doesn't boot, consult your motherboard manual. Look for a "forget CMOS RAM" jumper. Set it. Try booting again. If your computer still doesn't boot, ask a friend to post a query to a computer hardware newsgroup (because your machine is obviously out of operation).

- **Typematic rate programming**

  Disabled recommended. This feature enables the typematic rate programming of the keyboard. Not all keyboards support this. The following two entries specify how the keyboard is programmed if this feature is enabled.

- **Typematic rate delay (msec)**

  500ms recommended. The rate delay defines how long you must press a key before it starts repeatedly inputting the pressed value.

■ **Typematic rate (chars/sec)**

15 characters per second. This defines the frequency of the auto-repeat—that is, how fast a pressed key repeats.

■ **Above 1MB memory test**

If you want the system to check the memory above 1MB for errors, enable this feature. Otherwise, disabled it to get faster boot operation. The `HIMEM.SYS` driver for DOS 6.2 now verifies the XMS (Extended Memory Specification), making this test redundant. `HIMEM.SYS` also operates in the real environment, thus making it a superior test.

■ **Memory test tick sound**

Enabled recommended. This feature provides an audible record that the boot sequence is working properly as well as confirmation that your CPU clock speed/Turbo switch setting is set properly. An experimented user can hear if something is wrong with the system just by the memory test tick sound. What's more, if you have a display problem, the ticking sound confirms that the boot process is working and that your system memory is *not* the problem.

■ **Memory parity error check**

Enabled recommended. This is an additional feature to test bit errors in the memory. Many PCs check their memory during operation, using a ninth bit dedicated to confirming the value in the other eight. With every write access, the ninth bit is set in such way that the parity of all bytes is odd. With every read access, the parity of a byte is checked for this odd parity. If a parity error occurs, the NMI (Non-Maskable Interrupt) is issued, stopping computer operation to display a RAM failure message that usually looks like this:

```
PARITY ERROR AT 0AB5:00BE SYSTEM HALTED.
```

On some motherboards, you can disable parity checking with standard memory. Most Pentium and Pentium MMX systems, for example, use nonparity RAM. However, because the price advantage for nonparity memory has largely evaporated, most new systems support this data security feature.

■ **Hard disk type 47 RAM area**

The BIOS has to place the HD type 47 data in an unused area of interrupt vector address space in lower system RAM. The RAM area can be verified by checking the addresses of int41h and int46h. These are fixed-disk parameters blocks. If they point to the BIOS area, BIOS made a modification of the parameters before mapping the RAM there.

BIOS Guide

- **Wait for F1 if any error**

  Enabled recommended. When the boot sequence encounters a nonfatal error, it asks you to press F1 to continue the bootup. If this feature is disabled, the system displays a warning and continues to boot without waiting for you to press any keys. If you want your PC to operate as a server without a keyboard, you'll need to disabled this function.

- **System bootup Num Lock**

  Specify if you want the Num Lock key to be activated at bootup. Some users like it, some do not. MS-DOS (starting with 6.0, maybe earlier) allows a NUMLOCK= directive in CONFIG.SYS that overrides a conflicting setting in the BIOS.

- **Numeric processor test**

  Enabled is highly recommended if you have a math coprocessor (built in for the 486DX, 486DX2, 486DX3 and all Pentium and newer CPUs). If you have a very old system without an FPU (386SX, 386DX, 486SX, 486SLC, and 486DLC), you should disable this function. Disabling the numeric processor test means that the CPU's floating-point unit will not be recognized as present and may significantly decrease the performance of your system, particularly in 3D graphics and mathematical applications.

- **Weitek coprocessor**

  If you have Weitek FPU for a 386 or 486 system, you should enable this feature. If not, disable the setting. This high-performance FPU has two to three times the performance of the Intel FPU. Weitek uses some RAM address space, so memory from this region must be remapped elsewhere.

- **Floppy drive seek at boot**

  Disabled is recommended for a faster boot sequence and reduced damage to heads. This feature powers up your A floppy drive at bootup. Disabling the floppy drive, changing the system boot sequence, and setting a BIOS password are good techniques for adding security to a PC.

- **System boot sequence**

  Recommended that you set this function to A, C. This function tells the system which drive letter to check first for an operating system. To get faster boot times, set this function to C, A. This will avoid time consuming A floppy drive accesses at each startup, while allowing the floppy to serve as a rescue drive should the C become corrupt. For additional security, you can disable A boot access altogether—thus eliminating the ability to boot from an outside configuration—but you run the risk of being stuck without an easy way to run from a floppy disk in the event of hard disk failure.

■ System bootup CPU speed

The High setting is recommended. This specifies which processor speed the system will boot from. Usual settings are High and Low. If you encounter booting problems, you can try Low. You can also change the CPU speed with Ctrl, Alt, + key combination.

■ External cache memory

Enabled if you have external cache memory (better known as L2 cache memory). A common error is to have the L2 cache disabled in CMOS setup, which decreases system performance significantly. If the system does not have cache memory but this BIOS function is enabled, the system will likely freeze up.

■ Internal cache memory

Enabled for all 486 and newer CPUs. With this setting, you can enable or disable the internal cache memory of the CPU (better known as L1 cache memory). Enabling this function on a CPU without L1 cache will likely freeze the system. In many AMI and AWARD BIOSs, this option and the pervious one are implemented either as separate internal and external enable/disable options or as a single option (Cache Memory Disabled/ Internal/Both).

■ CPU internal cache

Same as "internal cache memory" described previously.

■ Fast gate A20 option

A20 refers to the first 64KB of extended memory (A0 to A19), known as the *high memory area*. This option uses the fast gate A20 line, supported in some chipsets, to access memory above 1MB. Normally, all RAM access above 1MB is handled through the keyboard controller chip (8042 or 8742). Using this option will make the access faster than the normal method. This option is very useful in networking and multitasking operating systems.

■ Turbo switch function

Disabled recommended. This setting enables or disables the turbo switch.

■ Shadow memory cacheable

Yes recommended. You can increase system performance by copying BIOS code from slow ROM to fast system RAM. To further boost speed, you can set up a cache for the BIOS. Just be aware that Linux and other Unix-like operating systems will not use the cached ROM and will benefit from the additional available memory if it is not cached. Be aware that AWARD usually disables this function first if there's trouble, because caching occurs in the L1 cache, which is always very busy.

■ **Password checking option**

The setup password for access to the system and/or the setup menu. This is recommended if the computer is to be shared with several users and you don't want anyone (friends, sister, and so on) to mess with the BIOS. The default password is AMI (if you have AMI BIOS) and AWARD BIOSTAR or AWARD_SW for newer versions. (Believe it or not, I know a computer store that kept the standard AWARD BIOS configuration for its systems because nobody knew what the default password was!)

■ **Video ROM shadow C000, 32KB**

Enabled recommended. Memory hidden under the "I/O hole" (from 0x0A0000 to 0x0FFFFF) may be used to "shadow" ROM. This function copies the contents of ROM into the faster RAM, thus significantly enhancing performance. The video BIOS is stored in slow 120ns to 150ns EPROM (Erasable Programmable Read-Only Memory) chips that are a meager 8 or 16 bits wide (whereas RAM is 32 bits wide).

If you have flash BIOS (EEPROM), you can disable this feature. Flash BIOS enables access at speeds similar to memory access so that you can use the memory elsewhere. However, flash BIOS can still only perform accesses at the speed of the bus (ISA, EISA, or VLB). On systems where the BIOS automatically steals 384KB of RAM anyway, it shouldn't hurt to enable shadowing even on flash ROM. One side effect is that you'll not be able to modify the contents of flash ROM when the chip is shadowed. If you reconfigure an adapter you think might have flash ROM and your changes are ignored (or, of course, if you're given an error message when you try to change it), you'll need to temporarily disable shadowing for that adapter.

On VGA and SVGA, you should enable both video shadows. Some video cards may use different addresses than C000 and C400. If this is the case, you should use supplied utilities that will shadow the video BIOS, while disabling this setting in the CMOS. Video BIOS shadowing can cause software such as XFree86 (the free X Window System) to hang. This should probably be disabled if you run any of the 386 Unix operating systems.

Some cards map BIOS or other memory in the usual a0000-fffff address range as well as just below the 16MB border (or at other places). On the PCI bus, the BIOS can use a hole in the address range where the card sits.

- **Adapter ROM shadow C800, 16KB**

  Disabled. These addresses (C800 to EC00) are for special cards, such as network and controllers cards. This option should only be enabled if you've got an adapter card with ROM in one of these areas. Keep in mind that it's a *bad* idea to use shadow RAM for memory areas that aren't really ROM, such as the buffers on network cards or other memory-mapped devices. To intelligently set these options, you need to know which cards use which addresses.

- **Adapter ROM shadow CC00, 16KB**

  Disabled. Some hard drive adapters use this address.

- **Adapter ROM shadow D000, 16KB**

  Disabled. D000 is the default address for most network interface cards.

- **Adapter ROM shadow D400, 16KB**

  Disabled. Some special controllers for four floppy drives have a BIOS ROM at D400..D7FF.

- **Adapter ROM shadow D800, 16KB**

  Disabled.

- **Adapter ROM Shadow DC00, 16KB**

  Disabled.

- **Adapter ROM shadow E000, 16KB**

  Disabled. However, E000 is a good "out of the way" place to put the EMS page frame, if necessary.

- **Adapter ROM shadow E400, 16KB**

  Disabled.

- **Adapter ROM shadow E800, 16KB**

  Disabled.

- **Adapter ROM shadow EC00, 16KB**

  Disabled. SCSI controller cards with their own BIOS could be accelerated by using shadow RAM; however, some SCSI controllers have some RAM areas as well, so it depends on the brand.

BIOS Guide

Some SCSI adapters do not use I/O addresses. The BIOS address range contains writeable addresses that, in fact, are the I/O ports, which means this address must not be shadowed or even cached.

■ **System ROM shadow F000, 64KB**

Enabled recommended. Like video shadowing, this function copies BIOS ROM to RAM for improved performance. Note that system BIOS shadowing and caching should be disabled to run anything but DOS and Windows.

On older BIOS versions, the shadow choices are in 400(hex)-byte increments. For instance, instead of one video ROM shadow segment of 32KB, you have two 16KB segments (C400 and C800). Same thing for adapter ROM shadow segments.

■ **Boot sector virus protection**

Disabled recommended. This feature tells you whenever your boot sector is accessed for writing, allowing you to disable the access or continue. This function protects against boot sector viruses and can be extremely annoying if you use a program such as OS/2 Boot Manager, which writes to the boot sector. Also, because SCSI drives use their own BIOS, this function won't detect boot sector writes on these drives. Therefore, if you want virus protection, use an antivirus program.

6.3.8 Advanced Chipset Setup

■ **Automatic configuration**

Allows the BIOS to automatically set several important items, such as clock divider, wait states, and so on). Very useful for newbies. Disable this option if you want to play around with the settings. Also, if you have some special adapter cards, you'll have to disable this option.

■ **Keyboard reset control**

Enables Ctrl+Alt+Del warm reboot. Enabled is recommended for more control over your system.

6.3.9 Memory Refresh Settings

■ **Hidden refresh**

Enabled recommended. Allows the RAM refresh memory cycles to take place in memory banks not used by your CPU at this time, instead of together with the normal refresh cycles, which are executed every time a certain interrupt (DRQ0) is called every 15ms. Every refresh takes 2 to 4ms, so hiding refreshes can slightly boost performance. Not all RAM supports hidden refresh.

There are typically three types of refresh schemes: cycle steal, cycle stretch, and hidden refresh. Cycle steal actually steals a clock cycle from the CPU to perform the refresh. Cycle stretch delays a cycle from the processor to perform the refresh. (Because refresh only occurs every 4ms or so, it's an improvement from cycle steal.) Hidden refresh typically doesn't stretch or steal anything. It's usually tied to DTACK (Data acknowledge) or ALE (Address Latch Enable) or some other signal relating to memory access. Because memory is accessed all the time, it's easy to synchronize the refresh on the falling edge of this event. Of course, the system performance is at its optimum efficiency refresh-wise because clock cycles are not being taken away from the CPU.ß

■ **Slow refresh**

Enabled recommended. Causes RAM refresh to happen less often than usual, thus increasing performance slightly by reducing contention between the CPU and refresh circuitry. Not all memories support reduced refresh rates, however. The function also saves power.

■ **Concurrent refresh**

Enabled recommended. Both the processor and the refresh hardware have access to the memory at the same time. If you switch this off, the processor has to wait until the refresh hardware has finished, thus slowing performance.

■ **Burst refresh**

Performs several refresh cycles at once, thus increasing system performance.

■ **DRAM burst at four refresh**

Refreshes occur in bursts of four, thus increasing system performance.

■ **High-speed refresh**

Refreshes occur at a higher frequency, thus improving system performance. Not all memories support high-speed refresh.

■ **Staggered refresh**

Refreshes are performed on memory banks sequentially, thus consuming less power consumption and creating less interference between memory banks.

■ **Slow memory refresh divider**

The AT refresh cycle occurs normally every 16ns, thus straining the CPU. If you can select a higher value, such as 64ns, you can increase the performance of your system.

■ **Decoupled refresh option**

Enables the ISA bus and the RAM to refresh separately. Because refreshing the ISA bus is slower, this causes less strain on the CPU.

■ **Refresh value**

The lower this value, the better overall performance.

■ **Refresh RAS active time**

The amount of active time needed for Row Address Strobe during refresh. The lower, the better.

6.3.10 Data Bus Settings

■ **Single ALE enable**

Disabled recommended. Address Latch Enable (ALE) is an ISA bus signal (pin B28) that indicates whether a valid address is posted on the bus. Some chipsets have the capability to support an enhanced mode in which multiple ALE assertions may be made during a single bus cycle. This setting enables this capability and may slow the video bus speed.

■ **AT bus clock selection (or AT bus clock source)**

Determines the clock divider used on the CPU clock to achieve appropriate ISA-EISA bus clock operation. An improper setting may cause a significant decrease in performance or result in system crashes. The settings are in terms of CLK/x, (or CLKIN/x and CLK2/x), where x may have values such as 2, 3, 4, 5, and so on. CLK represents the processor speed (with the exception that clock-multiple processors need to use the external clock rate, so 486DX33, 486DX2/66, and 486DX3/99 all count as 33 and should have a divider value of 4). For 286 and 386 processors, CLK is half the speed of the CPU. You should try to reach 8.33MHz (that's the old bus clock of IBM AT; there may be cards that could do higher, but it's not highly recommended). On some motherboards, the AT bus speed is 7.15MHz. On new BIOS versions, there's an Auto setting that will look at the clock frequency and determine the proper divider.

■ **ISA bus speed**

Same as previous but for PCI.

■ **Bus mode**

Can be set in synchronous or asynchronous mode. In synchronous mode, the CPU clock is used; in asynchronous mode, the ATCLK is used.

■ **AT cycle wait state**

Whenever an operation is performed with the AT bus, it indicates the number of wait states inserted. Older ISA cards may need additional wait states inserted to provide reliable operation on fast systems.

■ **16-bit memory, I/O wait state**

The number of wait states before 16-bit memory and I/O operations.

■ **8-bit memory, I/O wait state**

Same as previous except that this setting is for 8-bit operations.

■ **16-bit I/O recovery time**

The additional delay time inserted after every 16-bit operation. This value is added to the minimum delay inserted after every AT cycle.

■ **Fast AT cycle**

If this option is enabled, it may speed up transfer rates with ISA cards (most notably video).

■ **ISA IRQ**

Informs the PCI cards of the IRQs used by ISA cards so that PCI assignments can be made accordingly.

■ **DMA wait states**

The number of wait states inserted before direct memory access (DMA). The lower the number, the better.

■ **DMA clock source**

The source of the DMA clock that some peripheral controllers (such as floppy, tape, network and SCSI adapters) use to address memory (which is 5MHz maximum).

 ■ **Memory remapping**

Remaps the memory used by the BIOS (A0000 to FFFF, 384KB) above the 1MB limit. If this option is enabled, you cannot shadow video and system BIOS. (Disabled recommended.)

■ **Fast decode enable**

Refers to hardware that monitors the commands sent to the keyboard controller chip. The original AT used special codes not processed by the keyboard itself to control the switching of the 286 processor from protected mode to real mode. The 286 had no hardware to do this, so the CPU actually had to be set to switch back. This was not a speedy operation in the original AT—IBM never expected that an OS might need to jump back and forth between real and protected modes.

Clone makers added a few PLD chips to monitor the commands sent to the keyboard controller chip, and when the "reset CPU" code was seen, the PLD chips performed an immediate reset rather than wait for the keyboard controller chip to poll its input, recognize the reset code, and then shut down the CPU for a short period. This "fast decode" of the keyboard reset command allowed OS/2 and Windows to switch between real and protected mode faster, thus providing much better performance. (Early 286 clones with Phoenix 286 BIOS had this setting for enabling/disabling the fast decode logic.)

On 386 and newer processors, fast decode is not needed because these CPUs have hardware instructions for switching between modes. However, there's another possible definition of the "fast decode enable" command. The design of the original AT bus made it very difficult to mix 8-bit and 16-bit RAM or ROM within the same 128KB block of high address space. Therefore, an 8-bit BIOS ROM on a VGA card forced all other peripherals using the C000-Dfff range to also use 8 bits. By performing an "early decode" of the high address lines along with the 8/16-bit select flag, the I/O bus could then use mixed 8- and 16-bit peripherals. It's possible that on later systems this BIOS flag will control the "fast decode" on these address lines.

- **Extended I/O decode**

  The normal range of I/O addresses is 0-0x3ff (10 bits of I/O address space). Extended I/O decode enables a wider I/O address bus. The CPU supports a 64KB I/O space and 16 address lines. Most motherboards or I/O adapters can be decoded only by 10 address bits.

- **I/O recovery time**

  I/O recovery time is the number of wait states to be inserted between two consecutive I/O operations. It's generally specified as a two-number pair—for example, 5/3. The first number is the number of wait states to insert on an 8-bit operation and the second is the number of waits on a 16-bit operation. A few BIOSs specify an I/O setup time—AT bus (I/O) command delay—which is specified similar to I/O recovery time; however, it's a delay before *starting* an I/O operation rather than a delay *between* I/O operations.

5/3 has been recommended as a value that yields a good combination of performance and reliability. When this feature is enabled, more I/O wait states are inserted. A transfer from IDE hard drive to memory happens without any handshaking, meaning the data has to be present (in the cache of the hard disk) when the CPU wants to read it from an I/O port. This is called PIO (Programmed I/O) and works with a REP INSW assembler instruction. Enabling I/O recovery time adds wait states to this instruction. Disabling this function speeds up the hard drive.

Note that there's a connection between I/O recovery time and AT bus clock selection. For example, if the AT bus clock is set to 8MHz and you have a normal hard disk, I/O recovery time can be turned off, thus resulting in a higher transfer rate from the hard disk.

■ IDE multiblock mode

This function enables IDE drives to transfer several sectors at a time. According to the hard drive cache size, six modes are possible. Mode 0 (standard mode transferring a single sector at a time), Mode 1 (no interrupts), Mode 2 (sectors are transferred in a single burst), Mode 3 (32-bit instructions with speeds up to 11.1MB/sec), Mode 4 (up to 16.7MB/sec) and Mode 5 (up to 20MB/sec). If this setting is not set properly, communication with COM ports might not work as expected.

■ IDE DMA transfer mode

The settings are Disabled, Type B (for EISA), and Standard (for PCI). Standard is the fastest setting, but it may cause problems with IDE CD-ROMs.

■ IDE multiple-sector mode

When IDE DMA transfer mode is enabled, this feature sets the number of sectors per burst (with a maximum of 64). However, problems may occur with COM port operation.

■ IDE block mode

Enables multiple-sector transfers.

■ IDE 32-bit transfer

When this feature is enabled, the read/write rate of the hard disk is faster. When it's disabled, only 16-bit data transfers are possible.

■ Extended DMA registers

This function extends access to DMA transfers from the first 16MB of system RAM to the entire 4GB range addressable by 32-bit processors.

BIOS Guide

6.3.11 Caching Commands

■ **Cache read option**

This is often referred to as "SRAM (Static Random Access Memory) read wait state" or "cache read hit burst." It's a specification of the number of clocks needed to load four 32-bit words into a CPU internal cache and is typically specified as "clocks per word." 2-1-1-1 indicates five clocks needed to load the four words (this is the theoretical minimum for current high-end CPUs).

Conceptually, the m-n-n-n notation is narrowly limited to CPUs supporting burst mode, with caches organized as four-word "lines." However, it would not be surprising to see this extended to other CPU architectures. Simple integer values, such as 2-1-1-1, 3-1-1-1, and 3-2-2-2, are used. This determines the number of wait states for the cache RAM in normal and burst transfers (the latter for 486 only). The lower the number your computer can support, the better (4-1-1-1 is usually recommended).

■ **Cache write option**

Same thing as memory wait states but this represents cache instead.

■ **Fast cache read/write**

Enable this option if you have two banks of cache—64KB or 256KB.

■ **Cache wait state**

Just as with conventional memory, the lower the wait states for your cache, the better. A wait state of 0 provides optimal performance, but a wait state of 1 may be required for bus speeds higher than 33MHz.

■ **Tag RAM includes dirty**

Enabling this feature will cause an increase in performance because the cache is not replaced during cycles but is rather simply written over.

■ **Noncacheable block-1 Size**

Disabled. The noncacheable region is intended for a memory-mapped I/O device that isn't supposed to be cached. For example, some video cards can present all video memory at 15MB to 16MB so that software doesn't have to bank-switch. If the noncacheable region covers the actual RAM memory you're using, expect a significant performance decrease for accesses to that area.

If the noncacheable region covers only nonexistent memory addresses, don't worry about it. If you don't want to cache some memory, you can exclude two regions of memory. There are good reasons not to cache some memory areas. For example, if the memory area corresponds to some kind of buffer memory on a card so that the card may alter the contents of the buffer without warning. Some BIOSs take more options than enabled/disabled—namely nonlocal/noncache/disabled (VLB only).

■ **Noncacheable block-1 base**

0KB recommended. Enter the base address of the area you don't want to cache. It must be a multiple of the noncacheable block-1 size selected.

■ **Noncacheable block-2 size**

Disabled.

■ **Noncacheable block-2 base**

0KB recommended.

■ **Cacheable RAM address range**

This function limits the number of bits per memory address that need to be saved in the cache. If you only have 4MB of RAM, select 4MB here. The lower, the better. Also, don't enter 16MB if you only have 8MB installed.

■ **Video BIOS area cacheable**

You'll need to play with settings here to see whether video BIOS area caching is a good idea. Enabling this function speeds video access, but graphics accelerators may make changes to the video RAM region. In this case, you'll want to disable caching so that the CPU can see changes in the graphics frame buffer from the drawing engine.

6.3.12 Memory Settings

■ **Memory read wait state (often referred as DRAM wait states)**

The CPU is typically much faster than system memory. Wait states allow memory to fall into step with the fast CPU, thus eliminating parity errors, but at the expense of performance. This really is dependent on the chipset, motherboard and cache design, CPU type, and whether you're talking about reads or writes.

■ **Memory write wait state**

Same as previous but for memory writes. In some BIOSs, these two options are combined as "DRAM wait state." In that case, the number of read and write wait states is necessarily equal.

BIOS Guide

■ **DRAM CAS timing delay**

The default is no CAS (Column Access Strobe) delay. DRAM is organized by rows and columns and accessed through strobes. Then a memory read/write operation is performed and the CPU activates RAS (Row Access Strobe) to find the row containing the required data. Afterwards, a CAS specifies the column. RAS and CAS are used to identify a location in a DRAM chip. RAS access is the speed of the chip, whereas CAS is half the speed. When you have slow DRAM, you should use a state delay of 1.

■ **DRAM refresh method**

Selects the timing pulse width of RAS, either from "RAS only" or from "CAS before RAS." A RAS-only refresh occurs when a row address is put on the address line and RAS is dropped, resulting in that row being refreshed. CAS before RAS (CBR), on the other hand, provides power savings. CAS is dropped first and then RAS, with one refresh cycle being performed each time RAS falls. The power savings occur because an internal counter is used (not an external address) and the address buffers are powered down.

■ **RAS precharge time**

Technically, this is the duration of the time interval during which the Row Address Strobe signal to a DRAM is held low during normal read and write cycles. This is the minimum interval between completing one read or write and starting another from the same (nonpage mode) DRAM. Techniques such as memory interleaving or the use of page mode DRAM are often used to avoid this delay.

Some chipsets require this parameter in order to set up the memory configuration properly. The RAS precharge value is typically about the same as the RAM access (data read/write) time. The latter can be used as an estimate if the actual value is unavailable. At least one BIOS describes the precharge and access times as RAS Low and RAS High times.

■ **RAS active time**

The amount of time an RAS can be kept open for multiple accesses. High figures will improve performance.

■ **RAS to CAS delay time**

The amount of time a CAS is performed after an RAS. The lower, the better; however, some DRAMs will not support low figures.

■ **CAS before RAS**

Reduces refresh cycles and power consumption.

■ **CAS width in read cycle**

The number of wait states for the CPU to read DRAM. The lower, the better.

■ **Interleave mode**

Controls how the CPU accesses different DRAM banks.

■ **Fast page mode DRAM**

This speeds up memory access for DRAMs capable of handling it (most do). When access occurs in the same memory area, RAS and CAS are not necessary.

6.3.13 Hard Disk Utility

■ **Hard disk format**

Formats your hard disk so it can receive new partitions. This feature will destroy all data on your hard disk, so use it with caution. A lot of inexperienced users have lost their sanity with this one. There's no need to perform this unless you experience errors or if you want to change the interleave.

More important, do not touch this setting if you have an IDE hard disk drive. It will perform a low-level format and probably destroy the drive. The drives actually don't perform the low-level format, but some old AT bus (IDE) drives can be scratched with this.

If normal (high-level) hard disk formatting is required, you can use FDISK.EXE to first erase and create partitions and then use the FORMAT command. This is also a good idea when your hard disk becomes inaccessible to see if it is just the system files that are corrupted. Several packages (PC-Tools, Norton, and so on) provide utilities for repairing "damaged" drives as well. Therefore, low-level formatting is always a last resort when you encounter HDD problems.

■ **Auto-detect hard disk**

This is handy when you forget the specs of your hard drive. The BIOS will detect the number of cylinders, heads, and sectors on your hard disk. In some BIOS versions, this option is in the main Setup menu.

■ **Auto-interleave**

Determines the optimum interleave factor for older hard disks. Some controllers are faster than others, and you want sectors laid out so that consecutive addresses are accessible without the disk having to spin around an extra time. On new drives, the interleave setting is always 1:1.

Interleaving is specified in a ratio of n:1, where n stands for small positive integers. Basically, it means that the next sector on the track is located n positions after the current sector. The idea is that data on a hard drive might spin past the heads faster than the adapter can feed it to the host. If it takes more than a certain amount of time to read a sector, then when it's time for the next sector, the heads will have passed it already, thus requiring the disk to rotate once more to bring the sector back under the head. In this case, the interleave is said to be "too tight." The converse is when the CPU spends more time than necessary waiting for the next sector to spin under the head, which is called "too loose." Clearly, it's better for an interleave to be too loose than too tight; however, the proper interleave is best, especially because any controller with read-ahead caching can pull the whole track into its buffer, no matter how slow the CPU is in fetching the data.

The 1:1 interleave arranges the sectors on a track as follows:

```
0 1 2 3 4 5 6 7 8 9 a b c d e f g
```

There are 17 sectors, using base 17 for convenience. This is clearly the in-order arrangement (one after another).

Here is 2:1 interleaving:

```
0 9 1 a 2 b 3 c 4 d 5 e 6 f 7 g 8
```

The CPU has a whole sector's worth of time to get a sector's data taken care of before the next sector arrives. It shows which logical sector goes in each physical sector.

Only ancient MFM, RLL, and maybe ESDI, as well as floppy drives require and offer interleaving.

■ **Media analysis**

This performs selective low-level formatting on damaged portions of the disk. Therefore, this function should not be used on IDE, SCSI, or ESDI type drives. When a bad block is found, the formatting is used to recover the affected area. In the case of newer drives, the drives themselves store bad block data. Recommendation: Use a media analysis program provided by a utility package or your hard drive manufacturer.

6.3.14 Power Management

This menu appears on computers having the "Green PC" specification, which minimizes power usage when the system is inactive. In most cases, the power management strategies are incremental, meaning that the longer a system stays inactive, the more parts will close down.

There are three power management schemes: APM (Advanced Power Management) proposed by Intel and Microsoft, ATA (AT Attachment) for IDE drives, and DPMS (Display Power Management Signaling), which matches video monitors and video cards so they may simultaneously shut down.

■ **Green timer of main board**

Allows you to set the time after which the CPU of an idle system will shut down. Disabled or a time interval ranging from 1 to 15 minutes are the usual options. (5 to 10 minutes recommended.)

■ **Doze timer**

Amount of time before the system will fall to 80 percent of its activity.

■ **Standby timer**

Amount of time before the system will fall to 92 percent of its activity. At this level of power management, network connections will be lost.

■ **Suspend timer**

Amount of time after the system goes in the most inactive state possible, which is 99 percent of its activity. After this state, the system will require a warm-up period so that the CPU, hard disk, and monitor can go online.

■ **HDD standby timer**

Allows the user to set the time after which the hard disk of an idle system will shut down. There are some reports that this option may cause problems with slave hard drives (AMI BIOS only).

6.4 Updating Your BIOS

Updating the BIOS is a relatively simple but extremely critical operation. If you have the bad luck of experiencing a power outage during the upgrade, for example, you may corrupt the BIOS code and make your motherboard unbootable. A bad BIOS can do much the same thing. For this reason, a good deal of caution is advised anytime you're considering a BIOS update.

BIOS update steps can vary depending on the vendor and your system. Of course, older non–flash BIOSs must be upgraded by physically replacing the chip. In some cases, this may mean that no upgrade is available; therefore, a show-stopping BIOS problem could mean you must upgrade your motherboard. For a flash BIOS, the steps involved are pretty simple. The following sections detail the instructions provided by Intel for updating the flash BIOS on Intel motherboards.

BIOS Guide

6.4.1 Getting Ready to Upgrade the BIOS

Before you do anything, you need to prepare your system for a flash BIOS upgrade. The following steps outline these setup steps. Of course, different BIOSs require different steps, so your specific experience may vary from the instructions given here:

1. Place an unformatted floppy disk in the floppy drive and format the floppy using the /S option (for example, `format a: /s`). Alternatively, place a formatted floppy in the floppy drive and use the `sys` command (for example, `sys a:`)

2. Enter BIOS setup by rebooting the system and pressing the appropriate key during boot (F1 for an AMI BIOS, and F2 for a Phoenix BIOS). Carefully write down all your current CMOS settings. You'll need to reset these settings after you have upgraded to the latest BIOS.

6.4.2 Upgrading the BIOS

Next, you need to get the BIOS software and prepare to install the new BIOS onto your system. Then, you'll launch the automatic flash software to update the BIOS:

1. Download the correct BIOS file via FTP.

2. Insert the bootable floppy disk into drive A.

3. The file you downloaded will be a self-extracting compressed archive that includes other files that need to be extracted. Put the file in a temporary directory; then from within this directory, type the filename of the downloaded BIOS and press Enter. This will cause the file to self-extract.

4. If the extracted files contain files named `LICENSE.TXT` and `BIOS.EXE`, you should read the software license covering the BIOS file. After this, you can extract the contents of the `BIOS.EXE` file to the bootable floppy you created.

5. Use this DOS command `BIOS A:`.

6. If the extracted files do not contain the file named `BIOS.EXE`, you must extract the original file you downloaded to the bootable floppy in drive A. Use the DOS command `[filename] A:`. (For example, if the BIOS filename is `10005CV2.EXE`, you would type `10005CV2 A:` and then press Enter.)

7. Place the bootable floppy containing the BIOS into drive A of the system you want to upgrade; then boot the system while the floppy disk is in the drive.

8. Press Enter to go to the main menu.

9. Select the option that reads "Update flash memory from a file."

10. Select the option that reads "Update system BIOS."

11. At the screen that asks you to enter the path and name of the file, press Enter, press Tab, and then press Enter again.

12. Once the BIOS has been successfully loaded, remove the floppy disk from the drive and reboot the system.

6.4.3 Resetting CMOS after the Upgrade

Once you've completed the BIOS upgrade, you'll need to reset the information stored in CMOS:

1. As the system reboots, watch the BIOS identifier to make sure the new BIOS version was properly installed.

2. During bootup, press the appropriate key (F1 for an AMI BIOS and F2 for a Phoenix BIOS) to enter the Setup utility.

3. Return the CMOS settings to the factory defaults by pressing the appropriate key (F5 for an AMI BIOS and F9 for a Phoenix BIOS).

4. Go through each screen of options and return the CMOS settings to the values you wrote down prior to upgrading the BIOS.

5. Press F10 to save the settings; then press Enter to accept the changes.

6. Turn the Machine off and reboot.

6.4.4 BIOS Recovery

In the unlikely event that a flash upgrade is interrupted catastrophically, it's possible that the BIOS may be left in an unusable state. Recovering from this condition requires the following steps be taken (make sure a power supply and a speaker have been attached to the board and a floppy drive is connected as drive A):

1. Change the "flash recovery" jumper to the recovery mode position.

2. Install the bootable upgrade disk into drive A.

3. Reboot the system.

4. Because of the small amount of code available in the nonerasable boot block area, no video is available to direct the procedure. The procedure can be monitored by listening to the speaker and looking at the floppy

drive LED. When the system beeps and the floppy drive LED is lit, the system is copying the recovery code into the flash device. As soon as the drive LED goes off, the recovery is complete.

5. Turn the system off.

6. Change the flash recovery jumper back to the default position.

7. Leave the upgrade floppy in drive A and turn the system on.

8. Continue with the original upgrade.

9. Jumper locations can be found in the Technical Product Specification or on the "Jumpers" page for each individual product.

Not all standard Intel products support the flash BIOS recovery feature. If your motherboard (for example, the Advanced/AS) does not have the recovery feature, make sure you don't power down your system during a BIOS upgrade. This could corrupt the BIOS code. If your BIOS is left in an unusable or unrecoverable state, it will be necessary to contact the place of purchase.

Chapter

7

Motherboards

The motherboard is the foundation of any PC. All the critical subsystems, including the CPU, system chipset, memory, system I/O, expansion bus, and other critical components run directly off the motherboard. Likewise, the interconnections among these components are laid into the motherboard itself.

The motherboard is actually a large printed circuit board (PCB) that is made up of several layers. Each layer contains its own network of traces, enabling engineers to run thousands of connections among the components on the surface of the board. There's a stunning variety of motherboard designs serving everything from low-cost home PCs to compact corporate workstations to multiprocessor network servers.

Figure 7.1.

Intel's NLX-based motherboards include advanced features like Pentium II-300 CPUs, AGP graphics, power management, and USB and IrDA ports

Perhaps most important, the motherboard serves as host to the system chipset, which provides key housekeeping services for the PC. Because the chipset is soldered directly to the motherboard, it cannot be upgraded. Any limitation in a motherboard's chipset, therefore, extends to the motherboard itself. If the chipset lacks support for SDRAM, the motherboard won't be able to support that memory type—in fact, it will likely lack the 168-pin DIMMs needed to plug in SDRAM modules. You need to check the specs for the matching chipset on your motherboard in Chapter 5, "Chipset Guide."

7.1 Components of the Motherboard

The motherboard consists of a number of subsystems, all of which are critical to defining the performance and capabilities of your PC. Among the subsystems on the motherboard are the following:

- CPU socket
- System chipset
- Memory sockets
- Expansion bus slots
- BIOS
- IDE connectors
- Floppy disk drive connector
- Serial and parallel ports
- Keyboard and mouse ports
- USB ports
- System clock
- Battery
- Power cable connectors
- Connectors for front panel LEDs and buttons
- Jumpers for adjusting system settings

Motherboards

7.2 Performance Impact Report

The performance profile of motherboards is something of a paradox. No single component of a PC impacts performance as greatly as the motherboard type, because it defines the CPU, memory, and I/O speed employed by the system. However, by the same token, two similarly configured motherboards from two vendors will usually provide very similar performance. The reason: Motherboards are essentially collections of industry standard parts connected using industry standard buses. This conformity ensures that everything will work together and has the additional effect of leveling the performance playing field.

Still, differences can emerge. A motherboard with a newer version of a system chipset and an updated expansion bus can deliver enhanced performance and features. Also, some SMP motherboards employ complex custom circuitry that can have a real impact on relative performance.

The single biggest factor on motherboard performance is the front bus speed. Newer Intel Pentium II motherboards run at 100MHz, 50 percent faster than older models. With main memory running at higher speeds, the CPU spends less time sitting idle when the system must go beyond fast cache to main memory. 100MHz Socket 7 motherboards provide an even bigger performance upside than do their Slot 1 cousins, because the faster clock also speeds up the L2 cache next to the processor, thus greatly increasing the percentage of accesses affected by faster clock rates.

7.3 Currently Available Motherboards

Intel controls the vast majority of the x86 motherboard market—up to 90 percent by some accounts. Whether you buy a PC from Gateway or Dell, NEC or Packard Bell, it's very likely that an Intel motherboard is hard at work inside. Naturally, Intel uses its own system chipsets and CPUs in its motherboards, which means that much of the critical performance aspects of your system are in the hands of a single vendor.

Still, motherboard competitors continue to survive. There's a host of Taiwanese players, including Abit, Asus, FIC, Tyan, and Micronics. These manufacturers make motherboards for everything from low-cost motherboards for old K5 and 6x86 CPUs to high-end, multiprocessor boards for servers and workstations.

The market for motherboards runs roughly along CPU family lines. The reason is that the CPU, chipset, and the motherboard must all be tailored to each other. Therefore, when Intel introduces a new CPU type with an updated bus, a new generation of motherboards tailored to the CPU must arrive to make systems available.

Here's a list of the major motherboard categories:

- Pentium-class motherboards

- Pentium MMX–class motherboards

- Pentium Pro motherboards

- Pentium II motherboards

7.3.1 Pentium-Class Motherboards

Pentium-class motherboards are those designed to work with the 3.3-volt Pentium CPU (75 to 200MHz versions) and its clones, including AMD's K5 and Cyrix's 6*x*86. These motherboards hearken back to the introduction of the Triton chipset in 1994. Most employ a Socket 5 or Socket 7 CPU design and use a single-voltage 3.3-volt I/O bus. On the majority of these boards, you'll find Intel's aging 430HX, 430VX, and 430FX chipsets, although competing chipsets from SiS, Opti, and others can be found.

One thing to look out for is the ability of your motherboard to handle all Pentium CPUs. Although most Pentiums run at a standard 3.3 volts (the S*xx* series), Intel actually sold a minority of Pentium CPUs set to run at a higher 3.53 volts. These V*xx* type Pentium CPUs suffered from flawed manufacturing that require higher voltage in order to run reliably. However, your motherboard may not be able to provide 3.53 volt I/O if you happen to have an V*xx*-type CPU.

Performance on these boards is limited in part by the CPU (because none of the MMX-enhanced processors will work natively in the single-voltage architecture) as well as by aging memory and I/O subsystems. System RAM is limited to EDO DRAM or poorly supported SDRAM (7-1-1-1 cycles). You won't find ultra DMA support, USB ports, or other enhancements on the bus. L2 caches are often COAST-formatted modules, ranging from poor asynchronous SRAM to fast pipeline burst synchronous SRAM.

All these motherboards support 60 and 66MHz front bus speeds. Pushing many of these boards is not advisable. The EDO DRAM won't scale past 66MHz, whereas the relatively hot 3.3-volt CPUs tend to overheat when clocked beyond their specified rate.

7.3.2 Pentium MMX–Class Motherboards

The introduction of Pentium MMX in January, 1997 ushered in a few critical motherboard advancements. Based exclusively on the Socket 7 architecture, the MMX-class motherboards employ a split-voltage bus that runs at 3.3 volts externally and a low 2.8 volts internal to the CPU. The lower voltage accommodates higher CPU speeds in the Pentium MMX CPU line, but requires the addition of a voltage regulator at the CPU module to manage the step down.

In addition to Pentium MMX CPUs, these motherboards generally support AMD K6 and Cyrix 6*x*86Mx processors. Like the Pentium MMX, the K6 and 6*x*86Mx run at a lower internal voltage (actually 2.9 volts, instead of 2.8 volts). Not all motherboard BIOSs recognize the non-Intel CPUs, however, so you must check to see if you might need to update the BIOS before installing one of these CPUs in the motherboard.

Soon after the arrival of Pentium MMX, Intel's cost-effective 430TX chipset took over the consumer desktop market. 430TX-based motherboards add effective SDRAM support (optimal 5-1-1-1 cycle operation) as well as ultra DMA IDE hard disk access and enhanced power management features. Virtually all these motherboards provide PCI 2.1 bus support, which ensures bus-mastering features on every PCI expansion slot. USB is also a standard feature on most of these boards.

Figure 7.2.
Tyan's S1572 motherboard uses the ATX form factor and Intel's 430TX chipset.

S1572 Titan Turbo ATX

Today, the Pentium MMX-class Socket 7 motherboard is the battleground for CPU competition. Even as Intel attempts to move the market to its Slot 1 architecture, AMD and Cyrix are tuning their CPUs and attendant chipsets to maximize the value and performance of the older platform. 100MHz Socket 7 motherboards, for example, boost both system memory and L2 cache performance, and new designs also include features such as AGP and ACPI (Advanced Configuration and Power Interface).

7.3.3 Pentium Pro Motherboards

Pentium Pro motherboards are characterized by their large Socket 8 CPU modules and the lack of L2 cache on the motherboard plane. Although Pentium Pro motherboards run at the same 60 and 66MHz speeds of Pentium and Pentium MMX models, the P6 CPU bus that mates the processor to the motherboard is heavily patented. Whereas you'll find Pentium Pro motherboards from other vendors, you'll not find non-Intel CPUs designed to plug into the Socket 8 connector.

As with Pentium and Pentium MMX, a variety of chipsets—including non-Intel ones—can be found on Pentium Pro motherboards. Newer chipsets offer support for fast SDRAM memory, USB support, and ultra DMA hard disk interface. Also, because Pentium Pro specifically targets servers, there's a wide variety of multi-processor motherboards. Standard SMP is supported in both two-way and four-way configurations; however, custom designs exist that extend the CPU count to six and beyond.

7.3.4 Pentium II Motherboards

Pentium II motherboards diverge from the familiar CPU socket designs of past models and instead employ Intel's proprietary Slot 1 architecture. The Pentium II CPU, which fits into the edge-on Slot 1 connector, is packaged in a single-edge connector (SEC) cartridge. Inside the cartridge is the CPU, the L2 cache, and supporting circuitry. Despite the obvious visual difference with the Socket 8 architecture, the Pentium II uses the same P6 bus architecture introduced with the Pentium Pro.

Figure 7.3.
Micronics' Tigercat motherboard uses the 440LX chipset to include fast SDRAM and AGP graphics with the Pentium II CPU.

Motherboards

Today, Pentium II motherboards lead the way in technical design. The 440LX and 440BX chipsets pushed these motherboards past both Pentium MMX– and Pentium Pro–class products. The 100MHz front bus of the 440BX, for example, provides significant performance upside for virtually all applications. It also unleashes the potential of the AGP bus, by raising the memory bandwidth ceiling from 524MBps to 826MBps.

Single- and dual-processor Pentium II motherboards populate the market, whereas newer four-way Pentium II SMP is just making its entrance. Behind the four-way SMP is the enhanced Slot 2 connector, which also bolsters performance by allowing for L2 caches that are both larger (up to 2MB) and faster (up to full CPU speed).

7.4 Evaluating Motherboards

No matter what class of motherboard you're buying—whether it's an upgrade or part of a new system—there are a lot of factors to consider. Remember, the motherboard defines both the existing and potential capabilities of your PC. Underbuying could mean facing a tricky motherboard upgrade just a year or two down the road.

7.4.1 Think Before You Buy

Before you start reviewing specs, counting expansion slots, and sizing up form factors, consider the source. There are a lot of companies making motherboards out there, but only a few enjoy a significant presence on the market. Although a very small vendor can make motherboards vastly superior in quality and performance to that of an Intel or Tyan product, you need to make sure the company has resources for supporting your investment.

At the very least, make sure the vendor you buy from has a Web presence. A decent Web site will give you instant access to all sorts of critical services and features, including the following:

- Downloadable flash BIOS upgrades.

- Downloadable device driver upgrades for fixing bugs, enabling advanced features, and improving performance.

- In-depth documentation, including lists of POST beep codes and other references that sometimes (unfortunately) are omitted from the printed manuals.

- Up-to-date information regarding compatibility with new CPUs, processor upgrade products, and RAM types.

- Access to online tech support, FAQs, and announcements about product problems or fixes.

Of course, anyone can put up a Web site, so you'll also want to consider how long the company has been around and whether it's doing well in the marketplace. Also, look for decent warranty coverage on your purchases, as well as a 30-day, unconditional money-back guarantee so that you can return a bad motherboard without hassle. Just be sure to check the fine print—many vendors will charge a restocking fee on these returns that can run up to 15 percent of the purchase price.

You can also avoid trouble by checking out the latest motherboard reviews at the Tom's Hardware Web site (`www.tomshardware.com`). The recently expanded test suite includes compatibility tests in addition to the usual performance benchmarks, which provide insight into Plug and Play compliance and resource management. You'll also find valuable information from Internet newsgroups.

Finally, when you buy a motherboard, avoid paying with cash or check. Using a credit card enables you to dispute payment should a problem develop with the product (or if it's never delivered at all). Some credit cards will even provide extended warranties and coverage on your purchase, providing another level of protection should the motherboard show up defective.

Table 7.1 is a list of prominent motherboard manufacturers, and it includes Web sites where you can find more information about specific products.

Table 7.1. A quick look at major motherboard vendors and their related Web page addresses.

Manufacturer	Web address
Intel Corp.	www.intel.com/design/motherbd/
Abit Computer	www.abit.com.tw
ASUS	www.asus.com
Elitegroup Computer Systems	www.ecs.com.tw/ecs/ecs/ mainboard.htm
First International Computer	www.fic.com.tw
Gigabyte	www.giga-byte.com
Micronics Computer	www.micronics.com/micronics
Supermicro	www.supermicro.com
Tyan	www.tyan.com

Motherboards

7.4.2 Understanding Chipsets

The most critical element of any motherboard is the chipset. This collection of two or more chips defines many of the features and capabilities of your motherboard. From CPU support to RAM capacities to the hard disk interface, the system chipset determines what your motherboard can and cannot do with its hardware. You can't underestimate the importance of this component in the motherboard, because it literally defines the performance range of the product.

Making things more critical still is the fact that chipsets cannot be upgraded or replaced. These devices are soldered onto the motherboard. If you need access to technology not supported in your motherboard's chipset—such as PCI bus-mastering or ATA-33 hard disk interface—your only option is to buy a new system or replace the motherboard.

When buying a motherboard, it's a good idea to draw up a list of the devices and technologies you want to support. For example, if you want to play the latest 3D games, you'll certainly want AGP 2× support—something that many Socket 7 motherboards lack. Likewise, an ATA-33 IDE interface for the largest hard disk drives is a good idea. For convenient remote access, features such as Wake-on-Ring and Wake-on-LAN let you power up the computer remotely, whereas ACPI offers fast shutdown, quiet sleep modes, and other useful options. Finally, take stock of your hardware and figure out how many PCI and ISA slots you'll need.

You can identify the chipset easily. Aside from the CPU, the chips of the chipset are the largest on the motherboard. They are placed near the center of the motherboard, often sitting between the CPU and expansion bus slots. Silk-screening on the top of the chips reveals the manufacturer as well as the model. For example, the north bridge chip of the Intel 430TX chipset carries the designation 82439TX.

When buying a motherboard, you should take a close look at the chipset. Make sure it provides support for the newest memory types and CPU, can handle fast motherboard speeds, and includes advanced disk and external I/O. Otherwise, no amount of upgrading will undo the bottlenecks that the chipset presents.

7.4.3 Processor Support

One of the most critical aspects of any motherboard is its CPU support. Of course, choosing a motherboard is in large part a question of what CPU you want to run. Some motherboards, such as Socket 7 models from numerous vendors, can play host to a variety of CPUs, including Pentium, Pentium MMX, Cyrix 6x86 and 6x86Mx, and AMD K5 and K6. Others designed for Intel's patent-protected Pentium Pro and Pentium II CPU buses won't offer such a wide range of options. In general, it's a very good idea to decide on which CPU you want to run your applications before taking on the larger task of selecting a motherboard.

Processor speed is also an issue. Pentium II motherboards based on the 440LX chipset only provide 60 and 66MHz front bus operation, with the CPU maxing out at 333MHz (a 5× CPU clock multiplier). If you want a faster Pentium II, you either need to go with a 440BX-equipped motherboard with the 100MHz front bus or look into pushing the CPU above its rated limit. However, for .35-micron Pentium II chips (those running at 300MHz and lower), overclocking does present the danger of overheating the chip. You'll need to carefully assess the thermal design of your PC and make sure that enough cooling air is travelling through the chassis.

CPU Modules

Today, you have four basic CPU connector types to choose from, as shown in Table 7.2.

Table 7.2. CPU modules and their compatible processors.

Connector	CPU Models	CPU Speeds
Socket 7	Pentium, Pentium MMX, K5, K6, 6x86, 6x86Mx, WinChip	75MHz to 233MHz
Socket 8	Pentium Pro	166MHz to 200MHz
Slot 1	Pentium II, Celeron	233MHz to 450MHz
Slot 2	Xeon	400MHz to 500MHZ+

If you want cutting-edge performance for the desktop, Slot 1 is your best choice. Coupled with a 100MHz front bus and the 440BX chipset, these motherboards can support Pentium II speeds as high as 450MHz. The L2 cache runs at half CPU speed, but at 225MHz, it's still extremely fast. Network and Web servers may be best off with Slot 2 motherboards, because these allow CPU-speed L2 cache operations (up to 450MHz) and double the two-way SMP of Slot 1 designs to support four-way SMP. Expect to pay a lot of money for a loaded four-way SMP Pentium II motherboard with fast L2 cache. The emergence of Slot 2 and the fast L2 cache makes Socket 8 Pentium Pro motherboards a marginal choice.

Bargain hunters will find lots of choices in the Socket 7 market, where Cyrix and AMD continue to press their fight against Intel. Although Pentium MMX tops out at 66/233MHz, AMD has released its 300MHz K6 running on 66MHz Socket 7 motherboards. Cyrix is pushing the clock speeds on its 6x86Mx line as well. However, all these CPUs are hamstrung by the slow 66MHz clock governing the motherboard-bound L2 cache.

Look for AMD K6 3D to provide a partial fix for the L2 cache bottleneck by supporting faster 100MHz motherboard speeds. Soon after, AMD's K6 3D+ will actually move the L2 cache into the CPU itself, meaning that motherboards supporting it will not have L2 cache (like current Pentium II motherboards). In addition, Cyrix has already introduced 75MHz system bus operation to the market with its CPUs, and 100MHz Socket 7 buses are the next stop.

Motherboards

> **NOTE** Even if your motherboard has the right socket to host a CPU, your BIOS needs to be able to recognize the hardware. Older Socket 7 motherboards may need a BIOS upgrade to recognize AMD's K6 and Cyrix's 6x86Mx CPUs, for example.

Symmetric Multiprocessing Support

With Windows NT Workstation supporting dual-processor operation right out of the box, there's a lot of talk about SMP. First, you should realize that your operating system must be SMP aware. DOS, Windows 3.*x*, and Windows 95/98 will *not* recognize any more than one CPU. Windows NT Workstation recognizes two CPUs, whereas NT Server can juggle four. OS/2, Linux, BeOS, and various flavors of Unix all support multiple CPUs as well.

Figure 7.4.

The Dual Fortress motherboard from Micronics delivers a pair of Pentium II CPUs in side-by-side Slot 1 connectors.

SMP motherboards are easy to spot by the two or more CPU sockets laid into the motherboard. On Pentium Pro systems, in particular, SMP can pose a space problem, because the Socket 8 connectors are so large. Likewise, Pentium II SMP motherboards can be jammed up with the massive SEC cartridges, possibly cutting down airflow. Motherboard and system designers need to be careful to provide adequate airflow and proper channeling of air in order to avoid potential thermal damage to internal components.

Our testing shows that SMP doesn't draw a straight performance line compared to single processor operation. In fact, some applications show little improvement at all, because they are not CPU bound and the presence of SMP actually produces overhead that drags performance a bit. Heavy-duty CAD, 3D rendering, and mathematical applications are the ones that gain the most from additional CPUs. 3D Studio Max, for example, shows a 44 percent performance increase with two instead of one Pentium CPUs. Likewise, network and Web servers enjoy a benefit from SMP.

In order for SMP to be fully utilized, the software must be multithreaded, which allows a number of coherent, individual processes to be processed independently of each other. Without multithreading, the application would be unable to have its tasks split up efficiently among multiple CPUs, thus limiting the advantage of SMP operation.

> **NOTE** When adding a CPU to an SMP motherboard, you must be sure that the stepping number of the CPU matches that of the original. CPUs based on different steps, or revisions, might not work reliably together, if at all. You can generally find the stepping designation on the ceramic topside packaging of the CPU or etched along the bottom.

7.4.4 Voltage Issues

Okay, so your BIOS and connectors check out. However, you may run into problems with voltage regulation. When Intel moved from the early 5-volt Pentium to a 3.3-volt setup, it was a big step. Memory, chipsets, and other interfaces had to be reengineered so they could recognize high and low signals at the lower voltage. With Pentium MMX, Intel once again dropped the voltage, but this time only internally. The Pentium MMX runs at 3.3 volts outside of the chip, so existing memory and chipsets work fine, but it runs at a lower 2.8 volts internally to keep CPU temperature cool.

The so-called *split voltage*, or *dual-plan voltage*, requires that a voltage regulator be present on the motherboard to step the current down to the appropriate level. Otherwise, you run the risk of frying your chip. You need to pay attention to this little appendage, however, because it can cause big problems.

Any regulator will produce some heat (hey, the excess voltage has got to go somewhere), so the motherboard and chassis should be designed such that the component is well cooled. The regulator must also be able to supply a good current, even when mated with the cheap power supplies that get used in some systems.

Whenever possible, go with a switching-voltage regulator rather than a less-expensive passive regulator. Switching-voltage regulators intelligently convert current, so when none is needed, the regulator isn't sitting there throwing off excess heat. Switching models also tend to work better with low-quality power supplies—a key advantage, in particular, with current-hungry CPUs such as AMD's K6-233.

Finally, you'll want a regulator that can vary its voltage delivery. Although Pentium MMX and the 6x86 run at 2.8 volts, the K6-166, K6-200, and 6x86Mx run at a slightly higher 2.9 volts. Also, the fast K6-233 actually runs at 3.2 volts,

Motherboards

just a tenth of a volt less than the 3.3-volt motherboard bus. If your motherboard can't handle different voltage settings, you'll be unable to install some CPUs—that is, unless you purchase a separate voltage regulator.

7.4.5 RAM Support

The parallel rows of RAM sockets are among the more prominent features on the motherboard. These sockets are designed to physically hold 72-pin SIMM or 168-pin DIMM modules. The number and type of sockets can determine how much memory you can install in the motherboard. Most Pentium and many Pentium MMX motherboards top out with EDO DRAM support, and they use 72-pin single inline memory module (SIMM) sockets for hosting RAM. In order to provide 64-bit accesses, SIMMs must be installed in pairs, which means you may have to sometimes discard old memory in order to find room for new memory modules. Most motherboards offer between four and eight SIMM sockets—the more sockets, the more better.

The dual-inline memory module (DIMM) form factor used by SDRAM can be installed singly, ending the onerous SIMM pair requirement. Most motherboards offer two to four DIMM sockets. In addition, many Pentium MMX motherboards actually include both SIMM and DIMM sockets—reflecting the transition from EDO DRAM to SDRAM, when availability of the new memory could not be guaranteed. A typical configuration is four SIMM and two DIMM sockets.

There are lots of weird quirks to worry about with motherboards, and vendors don't often go out of their way to tell you about them. For example, how many system makers touted the fact that their 430TX-based Pentium MMX systems could only cache 64MB of system RAM? Not a whole lot. In fact, most show 128MB of RAM as the maximum supported amount, even though installing anything over 64MB meant you would experience severe performance degradation.

Generally, the amount and type of RAM are defined by the system chipset (as was the case with the 430TX). You'll want to check right away for the maximum amount of supported RAM, because many motherboards limit you to 128MB or sometimes even 64MB amounts. As mentioned earlier, the majority of Pentium MMX systems only cache 64MB of RAM, effectively lowering the ceiling to that amount despite the physical 128MB RAM capacity. Another wrinkle: Some motherboards won't recognize modules with more than 32MB capacity, making it difficult to load up memory without discarding existing RAM.

Of course, you also face the usual issues of matching up SIMM capacities. Older 8MB SIMMs, for example, often cannot coexist with 32MB SIMMs, forcing upgraders to actually throw away that memory. Likewise, if all your slots are filled, the only way to boost the memory amount is to discard the lower density parts for higher densities RAM.

You'll also want to check out the RAM type. In general, SDRAM is superior to EDO DRAM, although some chipsets provide such poor support for SDRAM that a good EDO DRAM motherboard is a better choice. At 60 and 66MHz front bus operation, the two memory types are pretty evenly matched—you'll see perhaps a five percent system performance boost from the SDRAM memory. However, if you plan to overclock the front bus to 75 or 83MHz, you'll definitely want to go with an SDRAM motherboard. EDO DRAM simply lacks the ability to keep pace with speeds above 66MHz.

Also keep in mind cache support. Some Pentium and Pentium MMX motherboards comply with the COAST (which stands for cache on a stick) cache module. This allows you to insert cache much the way you add memory. This can be useful if you have a motherboard with no or little cache and want to be able to push it up to 512KB down the road. Many newer motherboards have the cache solder down on the board, whereas Pentium II and Pentium Pro CPUs actually contain the L2 cache inside the processor packaging itself, making upgrades impossible. In these cases, you need to make sure the CPU you purchase comes with the amount of cache you'll need for the life of that product; otherwise, an expensive CPU upgrade lurks in your future.

Motherboards also vary by the type of L2 cache they can support. The best cache technology is pipeline burst SRAM (PB SRAM); it's the only one you should consider for a new motherboard. This SRAM cuts time off of burst reads by multitasking operations, thus allowing the system to request data from the cache even as the cache is serving up bits from the previous request. If you have asynchronous SRAM (asynch SRAM) cache in your PC, your performance will likely be severely limited. As with other motherboard characteristics, cache support is largely a function of the chipset, so it pays to research the chipset very carefully.

Motherboards

7.4.6 Buses

The motherboard connects all the various subsystems of the PC. Expansion buses, I/O, and disk operation all go through the motherboard. Some motherboards provide plenty of expansion and features, whereas others may limit your upgrade options. You need to keep a sharp eye out for this.

Here are some of the buses to look for:

- PCI slots
- AGP slot
- ISA slots

- Enhanced IDE interface

- USB ports

- Serial ports

- Parallel port

- Mouse and keyboard ports

- Infrared port

Of these technologies, the most important to look for are AGP, USB, and infrared (IrDA), because they do not appear on all motherboards. For AGP, be sure the motherboard at least provides AGP 2× capability, and check for AGP 4× if you intend to do demanding 3D applications such as mechanical engineering. USB should be present on most motherboards; however, if you're buying a Socket 7 system, you should try to make sure that a pair of USB ports are provided on the back of the motherboard.

Finally, infrared capability is widely supported in the chipset, but the actual port itself is often left off. If you work a lot with notebook PCs, you should look for ready-made IR solutions. The facility makes transferring files much more convenient. It also allows you to print to IR-equipped printers without having to plug in a cable. Otherwise, you'll have to buy an add-on module that plugs into the PC's serial port.

Expansion Bus

PCI, AGP, and ISA fall into this category. These are the slots mounted on the motherboard that accept add-in cards for video, audio, communications, and drive support (among other things). Although the buses themselves all conform to industry standards, different versions can exist. For example, the current PCI 2.1 specification allows for bus mastering in all slots but may not be supported in older Pentium motherboards. Likewise, AGP is expected to move to a 4× specification, which will be unavailable in current systems.

The biggest concern with expansion bus support is availability of slots. Pentium II motherboards, in particular, suffer from a shortage of ISA slots—Intel's AL440LX motherboard only includes two. If you intend to use an internal modem, sound card, and another ISA device (such as a NIC, scanner, or dedicated comm card), you may be out of luck.

In fact, the PC 98 and PC 99 specifications call for ISA to be phased out entirely. Eliminating this old 16-bit, 8MHz bus will go a long way toward improving the reliability of Plug and Play, reducing system costs, and boosting overall performance. However, there are so many ISA cards out there that an ISA-less motherboard is unlikely to be a big hit until ISA peripherals are phased out. If you have ISA cards that you want to move to your new motherboard, you should make sure that enough slots are available for them; otherwise, you'll need to buy new PCI or AGP devices.

With new sound cards and NICs moving to PCI, you also must worry about availability of PCI slots. Whenever possible, look for a motherboard with at least four PCI slots (some only offer three). Also be aware that older motherboards did not provide uniform bus-mastering support in the PCI bus. In some cases, you must designate which slot or slots are bus masters using a setting in the BIOS interface; in other cases, you might not have access to that feature at all. Without bus-mastering, you'll lose the ability to run many devices, such as 3D accelerating add-in cards and video capture cards.

> NOTE
>
> Keep a look out for the shared ISA/PCI slot. Most motherboards feature at least one expansion slot space that allows for either an ISA card or a PCI card—but not both. Often, the shared slot will be reported as two available slots, effectively inflating the slot count. If you intend to load up a system with hardware, then failing to take into account the shared slot could leave you with some tough choices.

Pentium II systems with AGP offer some headroom, because the graphics card will presumably plug into the ultra-fast AGP slot, thus freeing a PCI connector. Don't bother looking for multiple AGP slots—the spec allows for only one along the high-speed connection to the chipset. However, make sure a slot is present. If an AGP graphics card is soldered into the motherboard, you won't be able to upgrade the graphics. With AGP cards evolving so quickly, that poses a serious dead end for your system performance.

Another big concern is motherboard layout. Poorly placed resisters, heat sinks, CPUs, and RAM modules will prevent installation of full-sized and even three-quarter-sized add-in cards, thus limiting your upgrade options. Newer motherboards based on the standard ATX form factor ensure that each expansion slot enjoys free access across the width of the motherboard so that full-length cards may be installed.

If you are buying a slimline system, be aware that all the slots on the motherboard may not be available to you. Often, the lowest-most slot on a vertical riser board will be unable to accommodate standard-size cards because components on the motherboard are in the way. CPU heat sinks, RAM modules, and L2 COAST cache modules are common obstacles. My advice: Avoid these tight motherboard design—or at least examine the layout before you buy.

Standard size motherboards often cannot accept full-length cards in one or more of the expansion slots. CPU and RAM assemblies often only leave room for one-half- or three-quarter-length cards. Newer motherboards conforming to the ATX

Motherboards

form factor specification fix this problem while at the same time improve airflow and component accessibility. Whenever possible, you should buy a motherboard that provides space for full-length add-in cards in all slots.

External I/O

The back of any PC is littered with ports—serial, parallel, keyboard, mouse, USB, IrDA, and so on. Support for all these ports must be present on the motherboard, both in terms of the circuitry and the mechanical connector that pops out of a hole in the back of the chassis.

Sorting out Serial and Parallel

With almost all motherboards, you can assume that parallel, serial, and keyboard and mouse ports will be present. However, some motherboards provide two parallel ports, whereas most limit you to a single such port. Older motherboards often used different-sized serial ports—one the familiar 9-pin connector and the other a not-so-common 25-pin connector. Depending on the port form factors, you may have to use serial port converters to get your device cables to match up. Just be aware that converters may cause compatibility problems.

Also worth looking into is support for enhanced parallel port operation. Two flavors of parallel port exist beyond the vanilla Centronics standard—Enhanced Parallel Port (EPP) and Enhanced Capabilities Port (ECP). Both boost data rates from about 500KBps to over 1MBps, and both add bi-directional capability for allowing printers and other devices to interact and send status messages with the PC. However, again, not all cables and devices are compatible with the extended standards—look for cables that adhere to the IEEE 1284 specification. Also, be aware that parallel port pass-through connectors—often used to let external video capture, audio playback, and other devices coexist with a printer—can cause incompatibilities.

The PS/2 mouse and keyboard connectors have long ridden the back of the board, although sometimes in different shapes and sizes. Newer boards use the more compact miniDIN6 connector—a form factor that is identical to that found on notebook PCs. If you have an older motherboard, you may have a larger DIN5 connector type. If your existing mouse and keyboard don't match up, you can purchase inexpensive adapters to make your hardware fit. In some cases, however, back ports on new motherboards will not fit into the spaces left for them in the back of an old case. You'll need to make sure that these ports line up properly.

The New Buses

Most motherboards sold over the past two years have included a pair of USB ports—never mind that USB-compatible peripherals are only now reaching the market. If you buy a new motherboard, make sure at least two USB ports are present on the back of the machine. You might not use them now, but you should consider building a collection of USB peripherals.

What's the big deal? USB lets you hot-swap devices and use a single connector type for everything from modems to mice and keyboards to cameras. Scanners, printers, joysticks, speakers, and many other low- to medium-bandwidth devices can run off the USB wire (up to 127, theoretically). Because you can hot-swap peripherals, you no longer need to worry about loading drivers or shutting down the system to plug in or remove a device.

USB provides 12Mbps of throughput, about a dozen times faster than that provided by a standard parallel port. Although that bandwidth is shared by a number of devices, it should be more than enough for even fully loaded USB configurations. However, don't expect additional performance from USB versions of peripherals, because most devices that use the bus are not affected by bandwidth.

The other addition to most motherboards is IrDA, a standard for infrared communication. Useful for moving data between notebook and desktop PCs, IrDA can transfer up to 4Mbps of data (although older ports are limited to just 115kbps). Be aware that even if an IrDA port is present on your motherboard, you'll still need to get an IR transceiver to let you send and receive infrared signals.

Other Developments

We haven't seen it yet, but expect IEEE 1394 (a.k.a. Firewire) to begin popping up on high-end motherboards. Firewire resembles USB in that it's an external, Plug and Play, daisy-chainable expansion bus. However, where USB tops out at 12Mbps of bandwidth, Firewire can achieve 400Mbps (and soon, 800Mbps) data rates. If you want to capture video or connect to consumer electronics components, Firewire may be an option to look for.

Firewire may get its PC introduction thanks to the long-suffering Device Bay specification, which has been championed by Microsoft, Intel, and Compaq as a way to allow for readily removable mass storage. Device Bay essentially puts USB and Firewire connectors into an industry standard externally accessible bay. Users with Device Bay–compliant PCs could buy compatible drives and CD-ROMs and be able to swap them without opening the case. The plugs on the drives would simply fit into the appropriate bus slot in the back of the Device Bay interface.

Device Bay has gotten off to a slow start, in part because the Firewire technology needed to enable compliant hard disks drives, which has been expensive and poorly supported. The superfast Firewire bus costs much more to implement than

Motherboards

USB, and Microsoft has yet to put Firewire support into its operating systems, although it promises to do so in the future. For now, Device Bay is not likely a feature you need to wait for, but you should keep an eye out for it.

> **NOTE** New bus developments won't chase away the jumble of ports on the back of PCs. Support must continue for the millions of existing modems, printers, scanners, mice, keyboards, and other devices. That means serial, parallel, keyboard, and mouse ports will continue to grace the back plane.

7.4.7 BIOS

The Basic Input/Output System, or *BIOS*, is the lowest-level software that controls the basic operation of your PC. The BIOS conducts critical start up functions prior to the activation of the operating system, and it provides basic services that occur even below the OS level. The best BIOSs provide stable operation, automated configuration capabilities, and easy upgrades. Critical system configuration data is stored in the NV RAM (nonvolatile RAM) of the BIOS. This RAM does not require refreshing and only changes its data state when subject to electrical charge.

Over the past three years, most motherboards have adopted BIOSs that comply to the Plug and Play specification. A PnP BIOS features 13 new function calls that enable the BIOS to detect, enumerate, and manage hardware devices installed into the PC. The critical role is played during bootup, when the BIOS takes stock of PnP-compliant hardware and determines appropriate resource assignments.

Most important, any motherboard you buy should use a flash BIOS. BIOS code is stored on a chip on the motherboard. Older BIOS types can only be updated by replacing the chip, because the code is actually burned into the chip. A flash BIOS can be upgraded via software using a special utility to access the BIOS code. This means you can readily download enhanced BIOS code and update your motherboard. The ability to update a BIOS via software is an important one, because older BIOSs can lack features and pose incompatibilities that can limit functionality.

Just keep in mind that updating a BIOS can be an extremely risky proposition. Mismatched or buggy BIOS code can disable your motherboard and leave you with an unbootable system. At that point, your only option is to replace the BIOS chip itself, something that may not be possible on some flash BIOS systems.

When it comes to BIOS features, key resources are supported for Plug and Play, ACPI, and Logical Block Addressing, or *LBA* (used for supporting large hard disks over 2GB in size). Most recently, FastBoot BIOSs can shave tens of seconds off the bootup process by using readily detected boot flags to set system configuration during startup. Note that you may need to flash update your BIOS to gain access to this intriguing feature (which is part of Windows 98).

7.4.8 The Motherboard Clock

People are used to thinking in terms of CPU clock rates, but the device that controls the CPU rate actually resides on the motherboard. The motherboard clock consists of a chip of quartz that resonates in response to an electric charge. Changing the electrical input alters the frequency of the clock resonance. You can see the clock near the edge of most motherboards in a black rectangular housing. Dallas Semiconductor is the largest maker of clocks, but other manufacturers exist.

Most motherboards run at 60 or 66MHz, by default; however, new motherboards can run as fast as 100MHz. Adjusting the clock rate is a matter of setting jumpers on the motherboard itself. These control the electrical flow, thus controlling the resonance of the crystal to push the clock to the desired rate.

The operation of the clock allows users to push the speed of their PCs, a practice known as *overclocking*. By setting jumpers or changing BIOS settings, you can often change the electrical input to the quartz crystal in the clock and push the motherboard speed from, say, 66MHz to 75 or even 83MHz. Because the CPU simply multiplies the system clock to get its internal clock rate, the speed of the processor will likewise increase by a proportional amount.

Keep in mind that all system elements work in time with this clock. The PCI bus, for example, gets its 33MHz pace by dividing the system clock speed by two. If you push the motherboard to 75MHz, then your PCI cards are operating out of spec at 37.5MHz, which can lead to crashes and other problems. Main memory, likewise, is tuned for the rated motherboard speed. Going to 75 or 83MHz will pose a problem for 66MHz SDRAM and particularly for EDO DRAM—you may actually experience a slow down if wait states begin to pile up in memory accesses.

7.4.9 Motherboard Battery

The battery is an often overlooked but absolutely critical component of system operation. This tiny lithium battery usually looks like a silver circle connected to a metal attachment. The battery is the reason your PC knows the time and date despite the fact that the system has been powered down. It also allows flash BIOSs to keep their data stored safely, even after years of not operating.

How long does a motherboard battery last? That depends, because the battery receives a slight charge whenever your PC is on. Long periods of downtime (and we're talking years, here) will slowly drain the battery to the point that it can no longer provide the charge needed for the BIOS. If you run your PC on a daily or even weekly basis, it's very likely that the PC itself will become utterly obsolete before the battery inside fails.

Motherboards

If you need to replace the unit, it's a simple procedure. You just disconnect the unit and replace it with a compatible one. Of course, you need to make sure you're well grounded and that the PC is disconnected from the power cord to avoid potentially catastrophic damage. However, that's a practice you should always consider. In any case, an easily accessible battery will add convenience should you have to replace the unit down the road.

7.4.10 Form Factors

There's a motherboard for every system size, or so it seems. That's good news if you are upgrading, because you need to match the motherboard form factor to the specific dimensions and layout of your case. For years, the majority of desktop systems used so-called *AT* and *Baby-AT* form factor motherboards. If you have an old 486 or Pentium system that needs upgrading, you'll want to shop in this area.

Newer systems, over the past two years, have hewed to the Intel-driven ATX form factor. The boards are quite a bit more convenient because they allow full-length add-in cards in every slot and provide clear access to RAM and the CPU. They also provide built-in plugs for the I/O ports, thus eliminating messy wires. Essentially, ATX is Baby-AT rotated 90 degrees, with added enhancements for positioning of the power supply and treatment of I/O connectors.

There's a functional upside, too. ATX places the CPU directly in front of the power supply, thus enhancing the airflow around hot-headed Pentium MMX, Pentium II, and other powerhouse chips. This is also worth thinking about if you intend to overclock your PC. Unlike most AT boards, the ATX power supply features a shaped motherboard plug, so even if you get an ATX motherboard to fit in your older case, the power supply may not match the board.

The potential for mismatches continues at the back of the motherboard. ATX motherboards line the ports up along the edge of the motherboard itself, too low for the openings found in older cases. If you purchase a motherboard to upgrade your system, you need to make sure that the openings in the case line up; otherwise, the upgrade won't work.

Again, avoid slimline systems if possible. These PCs not only hamper upgradability—sometimes severely—but you'll often find yourself saddled with proprietary power supplies (meaning *expensive*) and soldered-in graphics and audio. Until recently, these systems used custom motherboard designs, meaning your ability to upgrade the motherboard could be severely limited.

Table 7.3 shows the rundown of standard form factor types.

Table 7.3. A look at standard motherboard form factors.

Board type	Dimensions	Application
AT	12"w × 13"d	The early *de facto* standard, AT motherboards offer plenty of slots for expansion.
Baby-AT	8.5"w × 13"d	The progenitor of ATX, Baby-AT largely replaced the AT form factor because of its more-economical design.
ATX	12"w × 9.6"d	The standard for new motherboards over past two years. Excellent expansion and airflow characteristics. MiniATX and MicroATX variants also exist.
NLX	9"w × 13.6"d	Compact motherboard for slimline systems. Uses a riser card for expansion cards.
LPX	9"w × 13"d	Compact and integrated design for corporate PCs (with riser card optional).

7.4.11 Bus Clocking

Last but not least, consider the motherboard bus clock. The vast majority of motherboards run at either 60 or 66MHz, with the CPU running at some multiple of these speeds. Therefore, a Pentium MMX-233 runs at 3.5× the speed of the 66MHz motherboard, whereas the Pentium MMX-200 runs at 3×.

Push the bus clock, and you'll see a proportional increase in the CPU. That 200MHz CPU will run at 225MHz on a 75MHz system bus (75 × 3 = 225) and at an even faster 249MHz on an 83MHz system bus (83 × 3 = 249). Of course, higher CPU speeds means more heat, and that can lead to intermittent failure and even damage. You need to make sure you provide adequate cooling if you intend to push your system clock.

If you're looking to overclock a motherboard, you need to shop carefully. Not all motherboards allow for easy overclocking; those that do are not equal in their ability to handle the stress of fast clock speeds. The two overclocking speeds you'll want to consider are 75MHz and 83MHz (respectively a 12 percent and 20 percent increase over the 66MHz standard).

Motherboards

Realistically, implementing PLLs for higher bus speeds isn't a big deal, but some vendors (rightly) fear a flood of returns due to malfunctions at the higher bus speeds. As a result, many products don't even allow overclocking. When you buy a motherboard, ask specifically about the ability to boost the system bus to 75 and 83MHz. The settings are often changed on the motherboard using jumpers located near the CPU module.

Overclocking introduces some risks, but the payoff is significant. Boosting the front bus speed from 66 to 83MHz means that your memory and L2 cache (on Socket 7 systems) is running 20 percent faster than normal. This can really boost performance on fast CPUs that often wait idly for data.

> **NOTE**   Be aware that when you increase the motherboard speed, the clock on the 33MHz PCI bus will also increase. Because PCI runs at half the bus speed, an 83MHz overclock will have your graphics and other cards popping along at 41.5MHz. The faster timings can cause problems on some cards.

7.4.12 Sundry Connectors

In addition to all the sexy, performance-impacting stuff, there are plenty of workaday connectors and plugs on your motherboard. Many of these are arrayed along the edges of the board, far from the lightning-fast electrical communications that occur among the CPU, chipsets, RAM, and expansion slots.

The most prominent of these connectors are the power plugs found near the back of the motherboard. On an ATX motherboard, these are located at the corner nearest to the CPU and feature a beveled shape to avoid misplugging the power cable. Because some motherboard form factors use different plug types, you need to make sure your power supply has compatible connectors.

You'll also see series of very small ports along the front edge of the motherboard. These provide power to your hard disk activity, power-on and turbo (if present) LEDs, as well as to the on/off, sleep, and reset buttons. If you're upgrading, you'll want to make sure you have marked the individual wires before you disconnect them from their respective ports, because you need to correctly reconnect them to the new motherboard. Otherwise, you may disable your system because the power switch and other front panel controls will not work.

You'll also find a number of jumpers near the CPU and other components. These are used to adjust the system clock, set the CPU type, and other low-level functions. You'll want to work closely with your motherboard documentation when working with jumper settings, because an incorrect setting can disable your PC—for example, a wrong CPU recognition setting will make it impossible to boot up. Before changing settings, it's a good idea to make detailed notes of the original jumper states so that you can quickly return to a working configuration should your new adjustments not work out.

Also make a point to confirm the settings in the manual against the silk-screened notes on the motherboard (if present). Poor and inaccurate documentation is not uncommon among motherboard products (particularly due to mismatched product revisions) and can result in a lot of lost time when things go wrong. Often, the correct settings will be printed directly on the board.

7.5 Tom's Pick

The best motherboard needs to successfully bring together a lot of subsystems and components. Established technologies such as the venerable ISA bus must operate side-by-side with AGP, USB, and advanced power management. What's more, the layout of the board needs to be well designed in order to avoid blocking access to critical components, while at the same time ensuring adequate airflow over the processor and other heat-producing components.

One thing your shouldn't fret over too much is performance. Once you've found a motherboard that suits your processor, memory, and functional needs, you're likely to enjoy performance parity with other motherboards in its class. The reason? Many motherboards use the same chipsets, supporting logic, and memory designs, thus limiting the possible range of differentiation in performance. What you put into that motherboard will affect performance, however. So be sure to think hard about what hard disk, CD-ROM drive, CPU, and graphics board you'll put into your system.

Which motherboard stands out from the rest? Our pick is the Microstar MS-6119, a 440BX-based motherboard that supports a single Pentium II CPU in a Slot 1 connector. Notable with the MS-6119 are its jumperless controls, which let you change clock speeds and other critical features without having to work pins on the motherboard surface. The MS-6119 supports a wide range of clock rates, including 66, 75, 83, 100, and even 133MHz. That means you can push a Pentium II-350 or Pentium II-400 CPU up a notch by moving the system bus to the 133MHz setting.

The MS-6119 tested well in Tom's labs, providing performance that was just a half-step behind the fastest 440BX-based motherboard tested to date. More important, the board provides system management features such as Wake-on-LAN and Wake-on-Ring, as well as tweaks such as a CPU fan suspend mode for cutting down noise. The one caveat: The MS-6119 had some trouble making a network card work when configured to IRQ5, although operation was otherwise flawless.

Motherboards

Chapter

8

RAM GUIDE

Three years ago, there wasn't much to say about system RAM. Almost all PCs came with fast page mode (FPM) DRAM, which ran at speeds between 100ns and 80ns. However, escalating CPU and motherboard bus speeds outstripped the ability of FPM DRAM to deliver data in a timely manner.

The developing bottleneck spurred a flurry of RAM advancements. Enhanced data out (EDO) DRAM, burst EDO DRAM, and synchronous DRAM (SDRAM) began appearing in systems. Each memory design not only increased the memory speed but provided more efficient operation. The result has been incremental enhancements to system performance that, taken together, have allowed overall system performance to scale along with advancing CPU clock rates and architectures.

The bottleneck has reached a decision point, however. No matter how fast your RAM is, it's limited by the system bus (or *front bus*) on which it resides. The system bus of virtually all Pentium and newer PCs runs at 60 or 66MHz, as little as one-fifth the speed of the CPU itself. For a couple years now, Cyrix has tried to budge the system clock to 75MHz, whereas technically-savvy users sometimes overclock their motherboards to 75 or even 83MHz. The 10 to 20 percent speed increase can make a big difference because both RAM and L2 cache (on Socket 7 motherboards) run at the higher speed. Our tests show that overclocking a 66MHz bus to 75MHz and 83MHz delivers some real results (see Figure 8.1). For more on overclocking your system, go to Chapter 9, "Overclocking Guide."

Figure 8.1.

Pushing both the system and CPU clock delivers a greater performance delta than when only the CPU clock is increased. Faster memory operation allows the CPU to keep up with software demands, enabling higher frame rates.

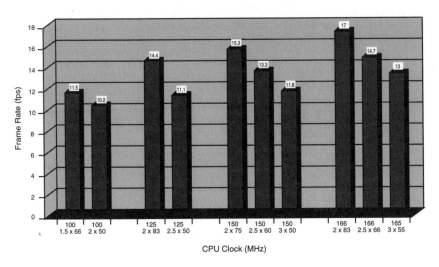

Help is on the way in the form of a standard 100MHz motherboard bus. It should come as no surprise that the market giant Intel is behind the new clock rate, which enables this performance with its 440BX chipset for Pentium II system boards. In order for the faster bus to work, however, faster RAM is needed because current SDRAM simply can't keep pace. Enter 100MHz SDRAM memory, which delivers a 50 percent bandwidth gain over the previous 66MHz technologies.

Even this advance is a stopgap. Vendors are tinkering with their SDRAM designs to deliver yet more performance, and Intel seeks to transition to an entirely new memory architecture called Rambus DRAM, or *RDRAM*. The reason: Fast AGP graphics—specifically, texture data—threatens to soak up all the bandwidth that 100MHz SDRAM can deliver, and more.

Of course, the issue of how much RAM you need continues to be of primary concern. Windows 95 pushed the entire desktop market to 16MB, whereas the advent of big, fat Web browsers and Office applications has motivated a push to 32MB. With Windows NT growing fast in market share, and all applications consuming more memory than ever before, 64MB has become a common profile. At the same time, main system memory is being used for both AGP textures in 3D games and Midi sound samples for PCI sound cards. Behind the memory capacity gains is a glut of RAM that has depressed prices and made consumers very, very happy.

8.1 How RAM Works Inside the System

RAM is the short-term memory of your PC, and as such, it's called upon to quickly serve up data to the CPU. Although L1 and L2 caches can speed performance by making small amounts of data ready for retrieval, they can't cover for slow system memory. In fact, the large data sets involved in today's complex programs, operating systems, and multimedia file types often outstrip the caches altogether. The only way to ensure smooth delivery of Mpeg-2 Video and 3D textures, for example, is to have system RAM installed that can keep pace—and that pace is blistering.

System memory connects directly to the system chipset (or PCIset in Intel parlance), traveling along a wide 64-bit bus running at 66 or 100MHz. The CPU sits on the other side of the chipset, enabling theoretical data throughputs of 528MBps or 800MBps, as shown in Figure 8.2. Chipset advancements and caching make the most of the pipe, but the emergence of AGP (Accelerated Graphics Port) means that main memory will be called on to deliver tens of megabytes of realtime 3D texture data.

RAM Guide

Figure 8.2.

Connecting directly to the system chipset, system RAM on a 66MHz front bus enjoys a 528MBps path to the processor and cache. That number jumps to 800MBps on new 100MHz motherboards.

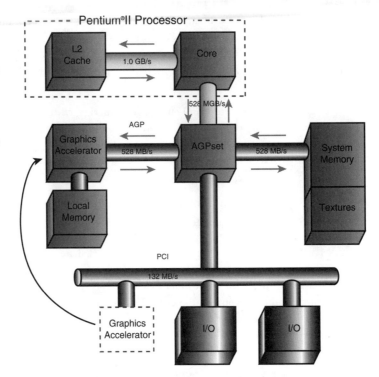

The RAM itself is usually packaged as a number of silicon chips mounted on a small PCB, either a dual-inline memory module (DIMM) for SDRAM and some EDO memory or on a single inline memory module (SIMM) for older DRAM types. The modules plug into sockets on the motherboard and are arrayed in parallel rows. The system BIOS automatically detects the presence of additional memory.

Of course, RAM chips are not able to store memory indefinitely. Rather, the silicon must be periodically refreshed to ensure that the stored electrical states are maintained. The swiftness with which memory can be refreshed (measured in nanoseconds) determines how quickly it can be ready to accept system reads or writes. Today, fast SDRAM is rated for 50ns operation, whereas older EDO DRAM may run at 60ns or 70ns. A few years back, 80ns and even 100ns memory was common. By contrast, static cache memory (which does not require refreshing but is much more expensive) is typically rated for 8ns to 15ns operation.

8.2 Performance Impact Report

System RAM can be a defining performance component of your PC. The two primary issues are the amount of RAM and the design of the RAM. The quantity of RAM becomes an issue when operating systems use the hard disk to store inactive data when the available pool of RAM is exhausted. This so-called *virtual memory* lets users multitask without inviting system crashes and out-of-memory errors, but the performance penalty for going to the hard disk is severe. When your system runs short of RAM, everything grinds to a crawl, or sometimes even to a dead stop as the system pages to and from the disk.

With RAM prices where they are today, virtually all PCs should be outfitted with at least 64MB of system RAM. This is enough memory to handle Windows 98, Windows NT, and Office applications without going to disk. The additional RAM serves a second benefit because operating systems can use excess RAM to act as a fast hard disk cache. Suddenly, virtual memory—that bane of performance hounds everywhere—starts working in reverse. Your hard disk with a 10MB or 20MB RAM cache will work a lot faster than without—and your overall performance will improve.

Faster DRAM speeds and enhanced architectures can improve performance. For the most part, these improvements have been incremental—on the order of 5 to 10 percent for each advancement—but the introduction of 100MHz SDRAM has proved an exception. Expect a Pentium II-350 with 100MHz SDRAM to run TK percent faster than an identical Pentium II-300 with 66MHz SDRAM. Further down the road, Rambus DRAM will improve performance further, particularly for bandwidth-hungry multimedia applications.

8.3 RAM Choices

The range of RAM types and choices is nothing less than stunning. No less than four major types currently populate the market—fast page mode, extended data out, burst extended data out, and synchronous. And more is coming. Intel is pushing Rambus DRAM for its next-generation motherboards due in 1999, and memory makers have gotten together to agree on double data rate SDRAM, which extends the life of current SDRAM designs.

You won't get an argument from me about the introduction of faster RAM. It's all good news. However, the different architectures put a burden on buyers and system makers alike. Motherboards must be specifically designed to accept new RAM types, which can get expensive. What's more, if a RAM type is not quite there, manufacturers may need to actually build in sockets for more than one

RAM type—as was the case with many Pentium MMX systems that include both SIMMs for EDO DRAM and DIMMs for SDRAM. Of course, the redundant sockets consume space and add cost.

For buyers, advancing RAM technology is closely tied to every system purchase. Those who bought early Pentium II systems based on the 440FX chipset are probably kicking themselves now. Not only did they miss out on AGP—a marginal benefit unless you're a 3D gaming addict—but they're stuck with older EDO DRAM. The 440FX doesn't know from SDRAM, and the sockets on most FX-based motherboards are strictly of the SIMM variety. A more recent wave of anguish surrounds the 100MHz 440BX and the 100MHz SDRAM that works with it.

Your system RAM works very closely with the L2 cache that keeps your processor up to speed. Even the best RAM and fastest processor can't help a system devoid of L2 cache or hampered by slow cache memory. Again, there are a few varieties to choose from, and you need to keep an eye on them when you buy your motherboard. In many cases, you'll not be able to upgrade the L2 cache.

8.3.1 A Look at System RAM

We'll look at the various system RAM architectures available on the market and give you a profile of how they work. Later in this chapter, we'll also delve into critical buying decisions, ranging from error handling properties to the pin material.

It's helpful to understand first how memory is accessed. Data is read from and written to RAM at set intervals, corresponding to the motherboard clock. The memory is logically set up in a matrix of rows and columns, with each individual bit address expressed as the intersection of a row and a column. When a program needs a particular piece of information, signals from the system chipset reach out to activate the required combination of row and column to retrieve the bit.

First, the row address is set up with the chipset sending a row access strobe (RAS) to activate the desired section in memory. Next, a column access strobe (CAS) activates a vertical column of memory that intersects the activated row at the point where the initial bit resides. By toggling RAS and CAS from Low to High, or vice versa, the system is able to start and complete a transaction in a particular area of memory. As you can see, accessing a point in memory is a multistep operation, which is why the initial stage in any memory transaction takes quite long—as much as five to seven CPU clock cycles.

To speed things, numerous data points can be grabbed in a single transaction. As before, the address row and initial column must be set up, but because most memory accesses involve contiguous bits, subsequent accesses can happen quickly.

Instead of repeating the lengthy addressing process for the next bit, the chipset simply lights the desired number of contiguous columns, grabbing bits along the row. The result: Subsequent data can be grabbed in one or two clock ticks.

Fast Page Mode RAM (FPM RAM)

This is where it all started. Fast Page Mode (FPM) RAM, better known as just DRAM, is found today on aging Pentium PCs and those creaking 486 boxes that are still out there. The fastest FPM DRAM refreshes at a fairly tepid rate of 70ns to 60ns—the 60ns variety requires a 66MHz I/O bus to make the timings work right. FPM DRAM also gets employed on older graphics cards, though it's sometimes run at a faster 48ns access time.

The Fast Page Mode moniker refers to the fact that the RAM logic hopes that the next access will be in the same row, allowing the RAM to save time on the subsequent access. Despite this optimization, FPM DRAM has a pretty dismal clock-efficiency cycle: Even the fastest FPM DRAM will turn five CPU cycles for the first access, and three cycles for each access thereafter. Today, 5-3-3-3 for a four data (Byte/Word/Dword) burst read is no great shakes.

Okay, here's how it works. The FPM read access starts with the activation of a row in the DRAM array, providing a row address and bringing RAS Low. Then, multiple-column accesses may be executed by cycling CAS. Each CAS cycle includes application of a column address, bringing CAS Low, waiting for valid data coming out, latching data in the system, and then bringing CAS High to prepare for the next cycle. The sequence is shown in Figure 8.3. Note that CAS going High disables the data outputs, so it must occur after the valid data is latched by the system.

Figure 8.3.
FPM DRAM requires a separate access for each individual address, resulting in slow performance.

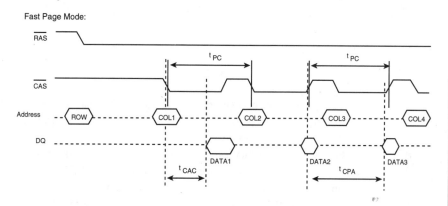

Extended Data Output RAM (EDO RAM)

Extended Data Out (or EDO) DRAM arrived in 1994 and provided a quick kick in the pants for Pentium CPUs starved for data. With EDO DRAM, data comes

RAM Guide

out more frequently than with FPM, making for much quicker sequential reads, which are common in large multimedia and other types of data sets.

The change comes down to a variation of the CAS# and data output timing from that of FPM DRAM, as you can see by comparing Figure 8.4 with Figure 8.3. The CAS# timing can be condensed to crank more data out in a given period of time, enabling clock cycles on the order of x-2-2-2 (versus x-3-3-3 with FPM DRAM). Still, EDO DRAM does not solve the five-cycle setup, which is the same as that of FPM DRAM; however, subsequent reads do move 33 percent more quickly.

EDO DRAM is available in three flavors—70ns, 60ns, and 50ns—with 60ns required for 66MHz bus operation. Starting with the Triton HX or VX chipsets, 50ns EDO DRAM is supported, which can provide an incremental boost over 60ns operation.

For all the good it did Pentium systems, EDO DRAM is on its way out. The design can't deal with fast 75MHz and 100MHz bus clocks, and it lacks the advantages of synchronous clock operation provided by SDRAM. The fastest access speed of EDO RAM in CPU cycles is 5-2-2-2 for a four-data (Byte/Word/Dword) burst read.

Figure 8.4.
*EDO DRAM
cuts the fat out
of memory reads.*

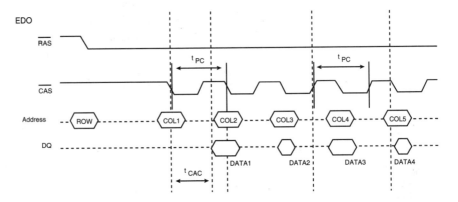

Although EDO page-mode read accesses are similar to those of FPM, it's worth noting that CAS going HIGH does not disable the data outputs. The data latch is used to guarantee that valid data is held until CAS goes LOW again. Our simple functional representation shows that the data latch (which is already available) is now controlled during page-mode accesses by CAS. Data is effectively captured in the latch as a result of CAS going HIGH. A new address can then be applied and new data accessed in the array without corrupting the output data from the previous access. In effect, EDO cuts a corner to cut a cycle out of subsequent reads.

Burst Extended Data Output RAM (BEDO RAM)

This EDO variant never really caught on, despite Micron's best efforts. Simply put, SDRAM came along and made the tweaked design irrelevant. As the name implies, Burst Extended Data Out (BEDO) DRAM reads data in a burst—once the address has been provided, the next three data accesses are read in a single clock cycle for each. The result is a streamlined 5-1-1-1 CPU cycle burst. Despite the 50 percent improvement over the subsequent read rate of EDO DRAM, chipset support has been limited. Intel's 430HX and a variety of other chipsets, including the 580VP, 590VP, 680VP, were the only ones to support this technology.

In addition, BEDO DRAM creates a pipeline that allows operations to process more quickly. The main downside of this technology is its inability to cope with bus speeds faster than 66MHz. Like EDO DRAM, it faces extinction once motherboard bus speeds all transition to 100MHz.

BEDO read accesses differ from those of EDO in two ways. First, because the data latch is replaced by a pipeline containing a register (that is, an additional latch stage is added), data can appear initially in a shorter amount of time than for regular EDO DRAM, thus activating CAS edge in the second cycle. Second, BEDO devices include an internal address counter so that only the initial address in a burst of four needs to be provided externally. This burst mechanism optimizes transfers of contiguous memory. A simplified representation of BEDO DRAM and the sequence of events is shown in Figure 8.5. As you can see, BEDO DRAM's pipelined architecture compresses the memory access cycle, both on the initial access as well as on subsequent accesses. Note that the first CAS cycle for BEDO, which loads the internal pipeline, does not cause additional delay in receiving the first data element, because the time it takes to access from the RAS limits how quickly the first data item may be accessed.

Figure 8.5.
BEDO DRAM is the first mainstream RAM to deliver single-cycle burst reads.

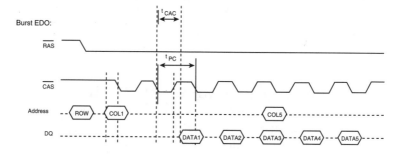

Synchronous Dynamic RAM (SDRAM)

Today, SDRAM is the memory of choice in Pentium MMX, Pentium Pro, Pentium II, and Intel-competitive systems. With ubiquitous chipset support and a technology road map that embraces 100MHz operation, SDRAM is finally enjoying its time in the limelight. As the name implies, Synchronous DRAM (SDRAM) handles all input and output signals in synch with the system clock. Given that a couple years ago only Static Cache RAM was able to achieve this feat, SDRAM is a notable technical achievement.

Like BEDO DRAM, SDRAM employs a burst mode to achieve a CPU cycle profile of 5-1-1-1 for a four-data (Byte/Word/Dword) burst read. But unlike BEDO DRAM, SDRAM scales to 100MHz, opening the pipes for AGP graphics, video playback, and other demanding applications. So where even BEDO DRAM tops out at 528MBps along with a 66MHz, 64-bit motherboard bus, 100MHz SDRAM can push 800MBps.

Coming soon is a new type of SDRAM, called Double Data Rate SDRAM, or *DDR SDRAM*. DDR SDRAM is able to deliver data on both the rising and falling edge of the bus signal, effectively doubling the bandwidth of a 100MHz system from 800MBps to 1.6GB/sec. The new flavor otherwise works identically to SDRAM, with the same 5-1-1-1 clock profile and timing structures. Table 8.1 shows the advancing memory types that improve burst accesses.

Table 8.1. Advancing memory types improve burst accesses.

Memory type	Bit1	Bit2	Bit3	Bit4
SDRAM	5	1	1	1
BEDO DRAM5	1	1	1	
EDO DRAM5	2	2	2	
FPM DRAM5	3	3	3	
Synch-burst SRAM2	1	1	1	
PB SRAM3	1	1	1	

Rambus Dynamic RAM (RDRAM)

If Intel has its druthers—and it frequently does—the industry will soon abandon the incrementally improved DRAM scheme and adopt Rambus DRAM, or *RDRAM*. Rambus, the company, has been around for a few years now, preaching the benefits of a narrow-but-blindingly-fast memory bus design to all who would listen. RDRAM is found in graphics cards using the Cirrus Logic Lagune graphics controller and is part of Microsoft's Talisman plans. It's also used in the Nintendo 64 game console and Chromatic's Mpact media processor.

RDRAM uses a narrow 8-bit bus running at a torrid 400MHz. By synchronizing both edges of the clock (as DDR SDRAM does), RDRAM runs at an effective 800MHz along the memory bus—rates unachievable by SDRAM architectures. The architecture is slated to move up to 500/1000MHz soon thereafter. The fast clock is possible because the serialized bus does not suffer from timing degradation, signal reflection, and other issues involved with loading on the complex SDRAM memory bus.

RDRAM operates in channels, each 8-bits wide. A single-channel 800MHz RDRAM system can push 0.8GBps (about on par with 100MHz SDRAM), whereas a dual-channel system running at the same speed doubles that rate to 1.6GBps. Not surprisingly, at four channels, system throughput goes, well, through the roof—3.2GBps.

With widespread manufacturing commitments from memory makers, existing RDRAM designs on the market, and behemoths such as Intel and Microsoft firmly behind the technology, the writing is certainly on the wall—and it spells *Rambus*.

Will you need to worry about RDRAM support in your upcoming purchases? For the time being, no. RDRAM is likely to make its Intel debut on motherboards using the Merced processor, the 64-bit CPU being developed jointly with Hewlett Packard. Targeted specifically at the workstation CPU market owned by Sun, HP, and IBM, it's likely to be 2000 before the IA-64 family migrates to mainstream desktops.

8.3.2 Cache RAM

Cache RAM is that fast-but-pricey store of memory that holds data close to the CPU for quick access. Fast cache memory, mated with an effective logical design, can result in big performance jumps. Today, even low-end PCs ship with 512KB of L2 cache, with 1MB and 2MB cache configurations supported in Intel's newest Pentium II CPUs. This section covers key performance-related areas of cache technology, including the following:

- Capacities
- Write policies
- Memory mapping schemes
- Physical memory types

The memory involved is static RAM (SRAM), the main advantage of which is that it does not need to be refreshed. By eliminating the time drag of refreshing the electrical state of the RAM, chip operation can occur as fast as the system bus

RAM Guide

allows it—66 million times per second in most cases. In order to keep pace with the 66MHz system bus, cache must operate at 15ns cycle times, which is more than four times faster than the swiftest 50ns SDRAM.

Critical to cache operation is the concept of *hit rate*, expressed as the percentage of CPU memory accesses that do not need to go beyond the L2 cache. Generally, hit rates vary from 92 to 97 percent, though heavy multitasking and some multimedia operations can lower that number because they outstrip the capacity of the cache memory. These lofty numbers are possible because memory accesses are not random. Usually, when a CPU calls for a certain address, it's more likely than not to want to call on data contiguous to that address. Taking advantage of this known behavior, caches are able to reliably pre-fetch bits from main memory so that they are ready and waiting when the CPU gets around to the next access.

Even at a 95 percent hit rate, the CPU accesses main memory once every 20 accesses or so. Unfortunately, in these cases, the cache actually poses a drag on performance because time is spent on the cache miss before the CPU can get around to the slower task of hauling bits out of main memory.

Cache Size

How much cache is enough? Certainly, large 32-bit, multitasking operating systems and applications put a strain on the cache pool. At one time, 256KB was more than adequate, but today most Pentium MMX and faster PCs use at least 512KB. However, even that amount is not sufficient for caching streaming multimedia data types (Mpeg-2 Video and 3D textures) or large databases.

For servers, 1MB or 2MB of L2 cache is often warranted.

The larger size and greater demands of both the network OS (NOS) and the applications puts a premium on cache size. In some cases, a third-level cache, or *tertiary cache*, may be called for.

Cache-Writing Policies

There are two major caching schemes:

- Write-back
- Write-through

The simpler of the two schemes, write-back cache, is essentially a one-way road. The CPU can read data directly from a write-back cache, but when it writes data, it must write directly to system memory. At the same time, the CPU writes data back to the L2 cache, ensuring that the data in the L2 cache and system memory stay in sync.

Write-through caching improves performance by caching both read and write operations. When the CPU needs to write data back to system memory currently stored in the L2 cache, all it does is write to the cache. The cache holds the updated data until the cache memory must be made available for another data set, at which point the previously written bits are transferred back to main memory without CPU involvement. The CPU is freed of time-consuming writes to system memory.

To get the best performance out of your system, you must make sure your cache is set for write-through operation. In some cases, this capability may be disabled or unavailable. Check your system BIOS to access write policy controls of your L2 cache.

Cache Memory Mapping Schemes

Managing cache memory in an efficient manner is a real challenge. A large, highly flexible memory store may boast high cache hit rates, but it will take so long to search out the cached bits that the performance impact is lost. Likewise, a highly indexed mapping scheme reduces the effective hit rate to the point that quick access loses its value.

At issue are the address lines running from the cache to main memory. On a 512KB cache, 16,384 address lines need to be managed (32 bits per address line). If you leave all these open to any memory address in main memory, it becomes extremely difficult for the CPU to quickly find the location in the cache holding the desired bits, and performance, therefore, suffers.

There are three approaches to cache mapping:

- Direct mapped
- Fully associative
- n-way set associative

The simplest approach is to use a *direct mapped cache*, where the entire pool of system memory is divided so that an equal amount is dedicated to each of the cache lines. However, only one address may occupy the cache line at any time. As a result, hit rates for this type of cache tend to be lower than for cache schemes that split the cache into sections.

At the other extreme is *fully associative cache*, which allows any memory location to be served by any cache line. This wide-open approach is flexible and allows for high hit rates because open cache lines are almost always available. However, ferreting out data in the cache requires sophisticated algorithms and can take so long that the benefit of cache hits is lost.

RAM Guide

The approach seen in motherboards today use a two-, four-, or eight-way set associative cache. The number describes how many cache lines are contained in each set. Therefore, a four-way set associative cache takes the pile of 16,386 cache lines and divides it into 4,096 sets of four cache lines each. That provides four cache lines to be shared for each segment of memory, thus improving hit rates while keeping the search size manageable enough for efficiency.

Asynchronous SRAM Cache

The oldest and slowest cache memory is asynchronous SRAM, or *async SRAM*, which appeared on the first system to employ L2 cache, the 386. There are no tricks here. Async SRAM's only advantage is that it runs faster than the main memory it supports, working at 20ns, 15ns, or 12ns. However, the lack of synchronous operation means that the CPU must wait for this cache RAM (though for a shorter period than for DRAM), thus exacting a performance penalty.

Synchronous Burst SRAM (Sync-Burst SRAM) Cache

With sync-burst SRAM, things get interesting. By working synchronously with the CPU clock, sync-burst SRAM can deliver data in lightning-quick 2-1-1-1 burst cycles. The memory also provides quick turnaround times, ranging from 12ns to 8.5ns. The problem? Sync-burst SRAM tops out at 66MHz. Move to a 75MHz or 100MHz bus, and the cache drops to a clock cycle profile of 3-2-2-2.

Pipeline-Burst SRAM (PB SRAM) Cache

Pipeline-burst SRAM, or *PB SRAM*, populates most machines sold today. Like synchronous burst SRAM, PB SRAM employs synchronous operation. However, PB SRAM improves on burst performance by using input and output registers that create a pipeline in the cache memory. The additional circuitry lets the memory initiate an address access even as the previous transaction is still underway. In effect, PB SRAM can do two things at once.

However, loading the extra registers exacts a penalty, requiring an extra leadoff cycle for each access. Subsequent accesses occur in a single clock tick. Most important, PB SRAM stays effective at speeds up to 133MHz, well above the 100MHz bus rate of new Pentium II motherboards. On 66MHz motherboards, PB SRAM lags on the setup, with a 3-1-1-1 burst cycle. However, address/data times are even lower than sync-burst SRAM, at just 4.5ns to 8ns (see Table 8.2).

Table 8.2. The performance sweet spot of Pipeline burst SRAM extends out to 100MHz and beyond, making it the only cache memory appropriate for fast motherboards.

Bus Speed	Async SRAM	Sync Burst SRAM	Pipelined Burst SRAM
33	2-1-1-1	2-1-1-1	3-1-1-1
50	3-2-2-2	2-1-1-1	3-1-1-1
60	3-2-2-2	2-1-1-1	3-1-1-1
66	3-2-2-2	2-1-1-1	3-1-1-1
75	3-2-2-2	3-2-2-2	3-1-1-1
83	3-2-2-2	3-2-2-2	3-1-1-1
100	3-2-2-2	3-2-2-2	3-1-1-1
125	3-2-2-2	3-2-2-2	3-1-1-1

8.4 Evaluating RAM

Your system performance depends on you making the right choices about the amount, type, and configuration of the RAM in your system. Purchase an early Pentium II motherboard, and you'll be stuck with 66MHz EDO DRAM that puts you firmly in the back of the Pentium II performance heap (you'll also miss out on AGP graphics, but that's another story). Wait for the 100MHz Pentium II motherboards with the 440BX chipset, however, and you'll see big gains in performance across the board.

Depending on your system, you'll also have to worry about a host of other issues, such as error-handling circuitry, pin composition, module capacities, and rated speeds. If you're upgrading RAM, these issues are extremely important because mismatching RAM can actually hamper performance, if not crash your PC entirely.

8.4.1 How Much Is Enough?

The most critical question is how much RAM is enough? The answer I usually give is, "As much as you can afford." If you do any sort of multitasking or run Microsoft Office applications, 32MB is a bare minimum for acceptable performance—any less, and you'll be waiting while your hard disk grinds away on

RAM Guide

virtual memory accesses. Serious business users—those running Windows NT, Lotus Notes, and Microsoft Access, for example—should jump right on to 64MB. The same goes for serious gamers.

With RAM prices lower than ever, some mainstream power desktops now ship with 128MB of RAM standard. However, most applications won't see a real benefit at this level, though the extra capacity can be useful when multitasking large applications and documents. However, if you use CAD/CAM, 3D design, or video editing applications, 128MB of RAM is actually a good minimum. The same goes for Web and network servers. Otherwise, that last 64MB ends up being little more than a really nice hard disk caching resource. You're betting off spending those dollars for a top-notch processor or graphics acceleration.

Table 8.3 is a good guide of what you should consider.

Table 8.3. Assessing RAM amounts.

Applications	Minimum	Optimum
Basic business	16MB	16MB
Mainstream business	16MB	32MB
Mixed home use	32MB	32MB
Gaming/multimedia	64MB	64MB
Windows NT	32MB	64MB
3D design/video	64MB	128MB
Servers	64MB	512MB

When More Is Less

Keep in mind that you must be aware of your system chipset before you install any more than 64MB of RAM into any system. Chipsets such as the popular 430TX found on Pentium MMX and compatible-CPU systems will not provide cache support for any more than 64MB of RAM. Although the chipset will recognize and work with 256MB of RAM, only the lower 64MB of that amount will benefit from the critical performance enhancement of L2 cache.

The result is a severe loss of overall performance. Because Windows NT and Windows 95/98 both load into the uppermost reaches of system memory, all OS transactions and operations will occur in uncached memory. In fact, the only time your system will enjoy a cache benefit in these situations is when more than 64MB of code is loaded into main memory—a relatively rare situation for many users. Even then, the OS itself will remain uncached.

Also, some chipsets provide differing memory caching profiles depending on the amount of L2 cache installed. Therefore, a system with a 256KB L2 cache, for instance, may only cache the first 64MB of RAM. In order to cache 128MB, the L2 cache must be boosted to 512KB. Consult your system, motherboard, and chipset documentation closely to avoid an accidental "downgrade."

Assessing Memory Impact

Provided caching is in place, how does memory amount affect performance? We tested different memory profiles on a variety of systems in order glean the impact delivered in different scenarios. Windows 95/98, for instance, generally ran smoothly at 32MB, though heavy multitasking showed a benefit at 64MB. Windows NT, meanwhile, really needs a minimum of 64MB, particularly when multiple applications are used.

Of course, a lot depends on the applications and the surrounding subsystems. Cranking up the RAM amounts will make a big difference in Quake II, causing frame rates to jump as the processor is freed from delays caused by hard disk accesses. However, simple word processing and business applications only get a marginal boost at 32MB—unless, of course, they are being multitasked.

In fact, our tests show that multitasking is probably the key argument for more RAM. If you run multiple applications at once, consider installing at least 32MB and preferably 64MB of RAM. Otherwise, the system goes to disk for virtual memory, yielding frequent slow downs in performance.

Table 8.4 shows how much memory typical applications need when running. These numbers vary depending on the document loaded, the tasks being performed, and the software version.

Table 8.4. Multitasking adds up.

Application	Memory
Windows 95	12MB
Internet Explorer 4.0	12MB
Microsoft Word 97	8MB
Microsoft Excel 97	8MB

8.4.2 Getting the Most of Your Memory

Looking beyond the amount of RAM, you need to make sure your system is using the most advanced RAM it's designed to handle. In general, this is a function of the chipset and the RAM sockets installed on the motherboard.

RAM Guide

Neither of these items can be updated or modified (at least, not significantly), so if you find that you absolutely must get access to the latest RAM, a motherboard upgrade may be in the cards. Here's the optimal RAM type supported by key Intel chipsets:

- EDO DRAM: 430FX, 430HX, 430TX, 430VX, 440FX

- SDRAM: 430TX, 430VX, 440LX

- 100MHz SDRAM: 440BX

If you want to add RAM to your existing PC, you need to worry about a number of things in order to make the upgrade work. What kind of RAM is installed in your system and how much? Is the RAM a parity, ECC, or nonparity design? What speed is the RAM rated for? These and other questions must be answered before you attempt any upgrade.

Check Your Chipset and SIMM/DIMM Sockets

Most Pentium MMX and Pentium II systems use SDRAM memory, which is packaged in 168-pin DIMMs. The key advantage here is that the 64-bit DIMM interface allows modules to be installed singly. Generally, 168-pin SDRAM DIMMs come in capacities of 32MB, 64MB, and even 128MB. Although many SDRAM motherboards only contain two or three DIMMs, it's not difficult to reach high memory capacities in the small number of sockets.

Many 486 and Pentium systems use familiar 72-pin SIMMs, which are common among both EDO DRAM and FPM DRAM. Because SIMMs present a 32-bit interface to the motherboard, they must be installed in pairs in order to provide a full 64-bit path. Two SIMMs make up a bank of RAM, with the processor interleaving accesses within the bank (hitting one module while the other refreshes) to create 64-bit operation. Most motherboards provide six or eight SIMM sockets (logically arrayed in three or four banks), whereas typical SIMMs modules contain 1MB to 32MB of RAM. Be aware that some motherboards may not support the highest capacities because these SIMMs are double sided and protrude over the second slot in the bank, thus preventing the installation of a second SIMM.

The oldest type of memory module still present in systems is the 30-pin SIMM. Like the 72-pin variety, this is a single-sided module that must be installed in pairs. However, 30-pin SIMMs present a 16-bit interface to the system, with the paired SIMMs providing 32-bit access using an interleaved access scheme. The 32-bit path matches up with the 32-bit external bus found on 386 and 486 PCs. Capacities for 30-pin SIMMs are typically from 1MB to 16MB. If your system is using this type of memory, you should really consider a new PC if you want to achieve reasonable performance for games and complex applications.

Fortunately, it's easy to tell what memory form factor your PC uses. Although all the memory PCBs are about one inch in height (actually, 30-pin SIMMs are three-quarters of an inch high), they differ in width as follows (also see Figure 8.6):

- 30-pin SIMM: 3.5 inches wide

- 72-pin SIMM: 4.25 inches wide

- 168-pin DIMM: 5.375 inches wide

Figure 8.6.
The different types of common RAM modules are easy to tell apart. (Photos courtesy of Crucial Technology.)

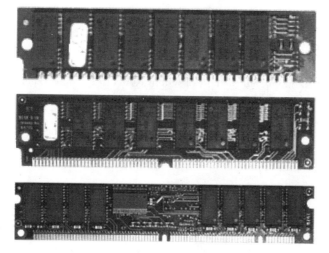

In some cases, your PC may be able to accept both 72-pin DIMMs and 168-pin DIMMS. Many Pentium MMX motherboards included modules for both form factors, anticipating the arrival of SDRAM memory before manufacturers were able to deliver the memory to market in quantity. Although some motherboards let you mix these memory types, my advice is to steer clear of such a practice. Timings of mixed memories can get tricky, and you'll be dragging your SDRAM memory down to the performance of the slower EDO DRAM plugged into the SIMM sockets.

In either case, you should match the data speed of the new modules with those of the old. Therefore, if you have 70ns SIMMs already installed, buy 70ns SIMMs when you upgrade. Although you can certainly put in faster memory (say 60ns), the new SIMMs will not yield any performance difference—accesses are constrained by the slower parts. Also, be careful not to end up with slower memory because this can disrupt timings from the chipset and cause your system to crash.

> **WARNING**   Unscrupulous vendors may remark slower, less valuable SIMMs and
> sell them as faster parts in order to get a better price. This practice can
> degrade performance and cause system crashes. You should always check new SIMMs
> carefully to see if the silk screening and other identifying marks look in order. You can
> also test memory using a SIMM tester, which can be found at many computer stores.

Error Handling and Memory

Another important distinction among memory types is the existing error-handling circuitry. Initially, PC-based RAM provided parity checking, in which an extra bit of memory was dedicated to tracking the contents of eight other bits. Intel helped kill this type of memory with its Pentium chipsets, which only supported the simplest nonparity memory.

Economics also certainly came into play here. Not only was a nonparity chipset easier to design, but the cost of system RAM (then quite expensive) could be slimmed down by losing the extra bit. Today, most Pentium and Pentium MMX systems do not support any sort of error handling, though the price delta between nonparity and parity RAM has long since closed. The good news: RAM errors are infrequent enough that most users have not noticed the lack of error handling in their memory.

There are actually two types of error handling in RAM:

- Parity
- Error-correcting code (ECC)

Parity Memory Explained

Parity memory is the simpler of the two schemes, employing a single bit for every eight bits of memory. The system chipset detects the 1s and 0s in the eight bits in the memory, and then sets the parity bit so that the total of the nine bits comes up odd. Therefore, if the eight-bit range contains four 1s and four 0s, the parity bit would be set to 1 to keep the sum of nine bits odd. If there are five 1s and three 0s, the parity bit would be set to 0, again resulting in an odd result.

If a bit value gets switched along the way, the nine bits will likely add up to an even value—a sure sign of trouble. At this point, the system chipset issues a nonmaskable interrupt, which halts processing and displays a message on the screen declaring a parity error. Depending on your BIOS, you may be given the option of restarting the system or continuing on. Of course, there's a chance that *two* bits may be off kilter, in which case the end value would still be odd. Still, it's unlikely that more than a couple such errors would occur before a single-bit error is detected.

Because parity memory works in conjunction with the logic located in the system chipset, parity must be supported in the chipset itself. A system without parity logic will generally accept and work with nonparity memory (you have to turn off parity checking in the BIOS); however, the reverse is not true. Also, it's worth noting that parity checking does not pose any drag on system performance.

Error-Correcting Code Memory

Parity memory helps protect you against corrupted RAM; however, it won't reconstitute lost data, and it can be spoofed by double-bit errors. A more robust form of error handling is provided by error-correcting code (ECC) memory, which is found in most Pentium II and Pentium Pro systems.

Like parity RAM, ECC RAM adds a single check bit to every eight bits of data storing memory. However, ECC aggregates the check bits across a wider range, combining nine check bits to track the value of 72 bits of data. The amount of error-checking data is enough that the ECC circuitry is able to identify a single-bit error and correct it on-the-fly. As far as the system knows, nothing ever happened. Multiple bit errors cannot be fixed and will generate a nonmasking interrupt and parity error message.

Again, the system chipset and memory must be specifically tailored for ECC operation. The Intel 440BX and 440FX chipsets all require ECC memory—you cannot use nonparity or parity memory in systems using these chipsets.

Reading SIMMs and DIMMs

If you're upgrading a system with new RAM, you may find yourself puzzling through a lot of obscure memory details. You can glean a lot of information just by observing. Memory modules feature some cryptic markings on the top of the chips, such as 1M×9 or 4M×8. These markings and others indicate the capacity of the memory, its speed, and information about its make. Printed batch numbers may help you track down a problem if one is caused by a known bad run of SIMMs, for example.

Speed

You can tell the data/address rate of the RAM by looking for a marking such as "-7" or "-5". In some cases, this may read "-70" or "-50". This number identifies the speed, in nanoseconds, of the chip. A -7 or -70 indicates 70ns RAM, whereas a -5 or -50 indicates faster 50ns RAM. Older RAM with speeds of 100ns will often be marked -10.

Capacity

RAM is marketed using some fairly cryptic codes. For example, memory capacities are expressed not in simple megabyte values, but rather in terms such as 4×32, 4×36, or 4×72. The format reflects the make up of the RAM itself, where the first number is the depth of the module, in millions of bits. The second number refers to the data width of the module.

That second number is an important one because it determines whether or not the RAM will work with your existing RAM sockets. A RAM module marked with a value of 32 or 36 will have a data bus 32- or 36-bits wide, which corresponds to the 32-bit interface of a 72-pin SIMM socket. Likewise, a module with a second value of 64 or 72 is designed for DIMMs, which use a wider 64-bit data bus.

That second number also identifies the presence of parity or ECC capability. If the number is divisible by eight (32, 64), the memory is of nonparity design. If the number is divisible by nine (36, 72), the memory is parity or ECC memory. The higher value for parity/ECC memory reflects the fact that an extra check bit is added to every eight bits. Because a 32-bit RAM interface consists of four sets of eight, four additional check bits are added to allow a check bit to be associated with each of the four sets. Add those four to 32 and you get 36 bits.

The first number refers to the density of the memory—that is, for every data line going to the RAM (32, 64) how many millions of bits are present. Therefore, 4×32 memory (or 4MB×32 memory) contains 16MB of memory. Don't believe me? Do the math: 4 million times 32 equals 128 million. Divide that by 8 (to convert bits to bytes) and you get 16 million bytes, or 16MB.

If the memory is parity/ECC, you need to alter the equation slightly to account for the check bit. Let's say you have memory marked 4MB×72. Rather than divide 288 million (4 million times 72) by 8, you would divide by 9. The result is 32 million, or 32MB, of data capacity.

Data Protection

As mentioned earlier, parity and ECC circuitry require an extra bit be associated with every eight bits of data. This bit is used to provide a flag to the system should a value in RAM be changed unexpectedly. Of course, that extra bit needs to be accessed by the system, so parity and ECC memory use a slightly wider connection than does nonparity memory.

You can quickly tell if your RAM features error-handling circuitry by dividing the second value in the RAM designation format by either eight or nine. Whichever of the two divisors comes up with a result that is a factor of two is the one that matches your RAM. Divide by eight for nonparity RAM and nine for parity/ECC RAM.

For example, let's say you're trying to determine if RAM marked as 4MB×72 will work in your nonparity Pentium MMX system: 72 divided by 8 equals 9, which is not a factor of 2. However, 72 divided by 9 equals 8, which is a factor of 2. This means that nine bits are used for each byte of data and that the memory includes parity or ECC capability.

Another example might be SIMMs marked 2MB×32. Divide this value by 9 and you get something like 3.5555—clearly not a factor of 2 and, therefore, not a parity/ECC-enabled component. Divide that 32 by 8, however, and the result is a nice round number—4. Because 4 is a factor of 2, the memory is of nonparity design.

Data protection in RAM is something that puts many folks in a tizzy; however, there really aren't many options from a buyer's perspective. Either the system you own supports data-protected memory or it doesn't. If you feel that this protection is important, you should stay away from Pentium and Pentium MMX systems, whose chipsets usually support only nonparity memory. Pentium Pro and Pentium II chipsets, on the other hand, generally (but not always) require parity or ECC memory for the system to operate.

Memory Pin Makeup

If you're upgrading your memory, you need to think about the pin material used in the SIMMs or DIMMs. In the past, almost all SIMMs and SIMM sockets used gold-plated leads and pins to provide electrical contact between the memory and the system. Gold is a very efficient and reliable conductor of electricity, and it is not prone to corrosion or breakdown, which is why it was widely used.

The problem? Gold is obviously expensive, and with SIMMs shipping in the millions and billions of units, manufacturers were anxious to reduce costs. For this reason, most newer SIMMs and DIMMs use tin leads, which are silver colored. Likewise, the sockets in most newer motherboards are also tin.

When you buy memory, match the material of the RAM pins to that of the motherboard socket leads. If the leads are silver colored, buy memory with tin pins. If the leads are gold colored, make sure to purchase memory with gold-plated pins. The reason: When tin and gold are placed in direct contact, a slow but sure chemical process begins that will eventually degrade the contact. This process is accelerated by heat and humidity(so you need to be extra careful if you're computing in a balmy environment).

This is not to say that mixing lead types will result in tragedy. In a climate-controlled environment, mixed leads will likely work flawlessly for years—you may never notice a problem. However, if you find yourself encountering mysterious RAM errors, you might check to see if the lead types are mixed. If so, the cause may be corrosion of the contact material. You can wipe the leads on the

RAM Guide

SIMMs or DIMMs easily enough, but getting at the sockets can be a bit trickier. Blowing compressed air into the socket could loosen things sufficiently, or you might use a thin bit of cloth to rub inside the sockets.

Another, somewhat related issue, is the phenomenon of *chip creep*. Creep is what happens after months and years of alternate heating and cooling of components. As the motherboard, SIMMs, and sockets expand and contract slightly with each heating/cooling cycle, the contact between the SIMM and the socket may be lost or degraded.

If you experience intermittent memory errors or a wholesale failure of memory, don't jump to conclusions. Often just reseating the RAM modules or wiping clean the module leads can fix the problem completely.

Memory Strategies

So you've figured out the type, speed, capacity, and even the lead material in the RAM you need to buy. You still need to make the right decision about how it goes into your system. SIMMs, for example, require that you install modules in equal-capacity pairs. Also, you need to consider where certain modules go in the row of sockets to avoid problems.

Figure 8.7 shows a RAM table from a Micronics Pentium MMX motherboard. As you can see, users of this—as well as many other motherboards—must follow a rigid order to achieve memory capacities.

If you're using SIMM-type memory, you need to keep three rules in mind, regardless of what your documentation says.

- RAM must be arrayed in banks of two modules each to provide a full 64-bit interface to the system chipset.

- You must make sure that the first bank (Bank 0) in the row of SIMMs is always populated.

- Always make sure that bank capacities are arrayed in order of most capacity to least, so if Bank 1 contains 16MB of RAM, Bank 0 should contain at least 16MB.

Of course, the 64-bit interface provided by DIMM-style memory means that each module forms a complete bank of RAM. Still, you need to make sure that the first bank (Bank 0) is always populated and that Bank 0 contains as much or more memory than each of the following banks.

Figure 8.7.

To avoid poor performance or RAM-related errors, make sure your system memory is installed as specified in the motherboard documentation.

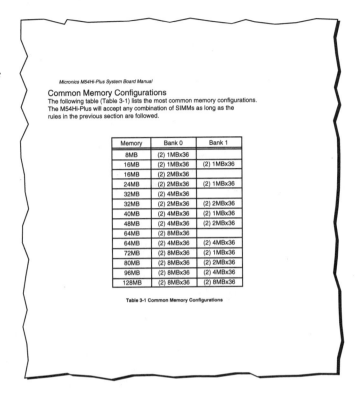

Micronics M54Hi-Plus System Board Manual

Common Memory Configurations
The following table (Table 3-1) lists the most common memory configurations. The M54Hi-Plus will accept any combination of SIMMs as long as the rules in the previous section are followed.

Memory	Bank 0	Bank 1
8MB	(2) 1MBx36	
16MB	(2) 1MBx36	(2) 1MBx36
16MB	(2) 2MBx36	
24MB	(2) 2MBx36	(2) 1MBx36
32MB	(2) 4MBx36	
32MB	(2) 2MBx36	(2) 2MBx36
40MB	(2) 4MBx36	(2) 1MBx36
48MB	(2) 4MBx36	(2) 2MBx36
64MB	(2) 8MBx36	
64MB	(2) 4MBx36	(2) 4MBx36
72MB	(2) 8MBx36	(2) 1MBx36
80MB	(2) 8MBx36	(2) 2MBx36
96MB	(2) 8MBx36	(2) 4MBx36
128MB	(2) 8MBx36	(2) 8MBx36

Table 3-1 Common Memory Configurations

8.5 Tom's Pick

Much as memory makers like Toshiba, Samsung, Micron, and others hate to admit it, PC memory is a commodity. The silicon they make adheres to well-documented standards, provides roughly equal performance, and is generally reliable. In fact, competing memory products of the same class are often indistinguishable from each other except by price.

So rather than pick a specific RAM product from a single vendor, I'll recommend a best memory technology. And certainly, there are a few to choose from. Since the arrival of EDO DRAM, the range of memory choices has continued to increase. And performance has increased with the choices. More efficient operation, faster response, and greater reliability have all arrived with each new generation.

If you are a buying a system today, the best system RAM is so called synchronous DRAM (SDRAM) that conforms to Intel's PC100 specification. These memories, mounted on efficient 168-pin dual inline memory modules (DIMMs), are fast enough to run synchronously with the fast 100-MHz front side bus found on 440BX Pentium II systems, as well as on 100-MHz Super 7 systems running Cyrix or AMD CPUs.

RAM Guide

Our testing has shown that PC100 SDRAM is not the only show in town. Older 66MHz SDRAM modules, when tested on motherboards running at 100MHz, can often keep pace with the faster motherboard clock. The result: True 100MHz performance using lower cost memory. But given the importance memory plays in reliable system performance, I recommend buying properly spec'd memory.

Future systems will make use of even better memory types. Right now, so-called Double Data Rate (DDR) SDRAM is the likely successor. DDR SDRAM reads accesses on the rising and falling edges of the clock to effectively double the available bandwidth. Key memory suppliers have already crafted a DDR SDRAM standard—a critical watershed in the adoption of this technology in future chipsets and motherboards.

A more radical advancement is coming in the form of Rambus DRAM (RDRAM). This new memory uses a very fast serial interface to move bits on and off a dedicated memory bus at high speed. RDRAM's claim to fame is the fact that Intel has committed to the technology for its next-generation systems. Expect RDRAM-equipped motherboards and chipsets to appear in 1999.

No matter what memory technology you use, the quality of the supplier remains critical. Vendors such as Samsung and Micron have good reputations in the industry and generally build reliable parts. Where possible, you should try to ensure that the memory you use comes from reliable sources. Also try to make sure that the memory you buy is from a trusted vendor, since unscrupulous companies may remark chips at higher-than-rated speeds in order to make a quick profit.

Chapter

9

Overclocking Guide

9.1 Overclocking Explained

The term *overclocking* describes the process of running a CPU and/or motherboard at a clock speed higher than what it was originally specified for. Boosting the clock is the cheapest way to increase performance—turning a Pentium-166 system, for example, into the equivalent of a Pentium-200. However, this budget-minded upgrade isn't without its risks and difficulties.

In fact, most users don't even know that you can increase the speed of the motherboard and CPU at all. This is hardly a surprise, really. Intel makes its living by selling the exact same chips at different clock speeds, charging more for those chips that happen to be marked at a faster speed. The controls for adjusting motherboard settings are also difficult to find, because Intel and major system vendors don't publish them in their documentation.

9.1.1 What Is Overclocking

The tempting idea behind overclocking is that it lets you increase system performance at very little or even no cost. In many cases, you only need to change a few settings on your motherboard to make your system run anywhere from 5 to 20 percent faster. In other cases, you may have to add a few components to adequately cool the CPU when running at the higher speed.

In the past, overclocking usually meant increasing the CPU clock speed to that of the next higher model—say, from a Pentium-120 to a Pentium-133. Now with many motherboards supporting faster bus speeds, both the CPU clock and the motherboard clock can be changed to values that don't officially exist. The result is a multiplier effect on performance— the CPU and system memory and bus run at higher speeds. In addition, you can increase the performance of the fastest model of a particular CPU line—pushing a Pentium MMX-233 to 266MHz, or a Pentium Pro-200 to 233MHz.

CPU Manufacturing Issues

Overclocking is possible because of the way CPUs are built. You see, when Intel manufactures a Pentium MMX processor, it doesn't necessarily know what speed it will be run at. Rather, before the CPU is bonded to its protective ceramic cover and pin array, it's tested to determine the quality of the material. If the tested CPU performs well, it's generally marked as a higher-speed part. If the CPU material shows impurities, it's either rated at a lower clock rate or discarded as unsaleable.

It's worth noting that in many cases, lower-rated CPUs actually test very well at this end-of-run evaluation. When a company such as Intel irons the kinks out of the manufacturing process, the percentage of CPUs that can handle high CPU speeds approaches 90 percent or more. Yet the market often still wants the lower cost, lower speed versions of the processor. As a result, the only difference between many Pentium MMX-200 CPUs and their faster 233MHz siblings are the markings etched on the CPU.

Of course, it's impossible to tell how any specific CPU tested in its evaluation, so you have to assume that the processor won't run efficiently at higher speeds than it's rated for. As a general rule, though, your chances of getting a clocked-down processor increase if you buy into a mature product line. The first Pentium CPUs ran so hot, for example, that they often suffered from early failure even at their rated speeds. However, later Pentiums used a smaller process (from .6 micron to .35 micron) and better manufacturing techniques. Those later products could run as fast as 200MHz, yet many were sold at speeds 166MHz or 150MHz, leaving plenty of headroom for overclocking.

> **NOTE** A word of warning: Non-Intel CPUs traditionally have not enjoyed much thermal headroom. In order to keep up with Intel's rapid-fire CPU introductions, Cyrix, IBM, and AMD often release CPUs that run significantly hotter than their Intel counterparts—the first generation of Cyrix 6x86 CPUs, for example, was hamstrung by overheating problems. You must take extra care to keep these CPUs cool in overclocked conditions.

Clock Multiplication

Because CPUs are not built to run at a specific clock speed, the speed is controlled by the system motherboard. The speed at which the CPU operates is actually slaved to the motherboard clock, which on most Pentium MMX and many Pentium II systems is 66MHz. A clock multiplier is used to set the CPU speed.

Therefore, a Pentium MMX-233 runs 3.5 times faster than its 66MHz motherboard, whereas a Pentium MMX-166 runs just 2.5 times faster than the same 66MHz clock. By the same token, a 450MHz Pentium II runs at 4.5 times the 100MHz motherboard clock, whereas the Pentium II-350 runs at a 3.5× multiplier.

Because motherboards are designed to work with a variety of CPU speeds, families, and even manufacturers, they include controls for adjusting clock speeds. All you need to do is adjust the multiplier factor using jumpers or sometimes BIOS software. Increasing the multiplier setting on a Pentium MMX motherboard from 2.5× to 3.5× effectively turns that 166MHz CPU into a 233MHz model. Of course, the additional signals moving through the CPU increase thermal output—a major challenge to reliable overclocking.

Bus Speed Increases

Clock multiplication has its limits. As the CPU runs faster and faster than the motherboard, performance increases are flattened out by the lack of improvement to memory access. We've already seen this in the diminishing returns of Pentium II-333 processors, which fail to deliver much of an overall performance gain over Pentium II-300 systems. The reason: The CPU is waiting for system memory and other components to move data off the 66MHz motherboard bus.

Overclockers can push past the motherboard bus bottleneck by increasing the speed of the system bus. Many new non-Intel motherboards offer this intriguing option. So rather than running at a standard 66MHz, your Pentium MMX motherboard can run at 75MHz—an increase of nearly 15 percent. In fact, a few motherboards actually allow for operation at 83MHz. That's a serious 25 percent increase in clock speed, which translates into a 25 percent improvement in memory and L2 cache speeds.

The problem with running at these high bus speeds is that some system components can't keep up. Most FPM and EDO DRAM system memories simply poop out at anything higher than 66MHz. Likewise, most motherboards can't keep the PCI bus running at its specified rate (33MHz), thus leading to possible failures in graphics and other PCI-based adapters.

9.1.2 Overclocking Goals

The goals of overclocking are pretty simple. Three basic tenants must be adhered to when deciding to overclock a PC:

- Improved performance

- Reliable operation

- Sustainable performance

There's no surprise on the first point—everyone wants faster performance. Because faster CPU and system bus operations are surefire ways to improve every aspect of system operation, overclocking is a great way to meet this first goal.

Of course, system stability and reliability can't be sacrificed for enhanced operation. After all, if your system becomes unstable, you'll lose more time in troubleshooting than you could ever gain in operational performance. To ensure reliable operation, it's important to put a newly overclocked PC through a rigorous shake-down test, running it through a sustained suite of benchmarks that will introduce your system to a stressful environment while under supervision.

Finally, overclocking must not come at the expense of CPU life. Chronic overheating poses a very real danger to solid-state components, and you need to manage thermal stress in order to avoid shortened CPU life. That means ensuring proper cooling and airflow, and possibly even installing monitoring hardware to warn you when case temperatures go above 110 degrees F.

One thing you might not know is that increasing bus speed can have a greater impact on performance than boosting the CPU. If you can't boost the bus—either because the motherboard doesn't support higher bus speeds or your RAM or PCI devices aren't up to it—you can change the CPU multiplier. Again, expect the law of diminishing returns to make a show.

Also, be careful not to inadvertently decrease the motherboard bus speed when boosting the CPU multiplier—you'll actually degrade performance. An example of this is changing a Pentium CPU from 166 to 180MHz. The 166MHz mode runs at 2.5× the 66MHz motherboard clock, whereas the 180MHz mode runs at 3× the slower (by 10 percent) 60MHz bus clock. The same issue applies when changing the Pentium-133 (2× 66MHz motherboard) to a Pentium-150 (3× 50MHz bus).

In order to stay within the three basic tenants, owners of 6x86 CPUs should not attempt to overclock their CPUs beyond a slightly higher speed than the original. You see, the 6x86 only has multiplier options for 2× and 3× bus clock multiplication, which limits your options. The big jump is enough to fry the already-hot 6x86 processor. Your best bet is to settle for a moderate increase by moving the motherboard from 60MHz to 66MHz.

9.1.3 Full Disclosure: Limitations and Dangers

So you want to overclock your CPU? In order to achieve the three goals (performance, reliability, sustainability), you need to know about the risks. Running your CPU at higher-than-rated speeds invites all sorts of mayhem if you don't plan to manage the new configuration. Done properly, however, overclocking doesn't need to put your hardware or data at peril. The following subsection provide a few points to consider.

Electromigration

One of the most likely causes of damage to an overclocked CPU is from *electromigration*. This takes place in the CPU's silicon in areas that operate at very high temperatures. Over time, overheating the semiconductive material causes the silicon to lose its conductivity.

Before you panic, you should realize that CPUs are designed to run at temperatures between −25 and 80 degrees Celsius. To give you an idea, 80 degrees Celsius is a temperature that nobody is able to touch for longer than one-tenth of a second. I have never come across a CPU at this temperature, and there are plenty of ways to keep the air inside the CPU case at less than 50 degrees C, thus increasing the probability of keeping the chip inside at less than 80 degrees C.

In addition, electromigration is not a sudden event; rather, it's a process that takes place over time. In fact, the net effect is to shorten the life of the CPU. A normal CPU is meant to live for about 10 years—well beyond the useful life of any chip—so even a 50 percent shortening in CPU life will have no effect on your system. Of course, if the overheating is severe, electromigration will occur more quickly, which can lead to failure in short order.

To avoid a breakdown in conductivity, you need to make sure the overclocked CPU runs cool. Large heat sinks, CPU fans, and even active cooling devices can all allow the CPU to throw off heat more efficiently, thus keeping the part below the critical 80 degree C mark.

Timing Failures

Another problem associated with overclocking is systems crashes or failures caused by timing problems. The CPU and motherboard components talk to each other at very high speeds using very fine tolerances. Speeding up the rate at which these components speak can violate the expected timings. In effect, components may talk to each other faster than they are designed to listen, thus causing system shut downs, data loss, and crashes.

This problem is particularly true of peripherals sitting on the PCI and IDE buses. The PCI bus, which is rated to run at speeds of 25, 30, and 33MHz, uses a clock divider to run at exactly one half the motherboard speed. If you nudge your motherboard to 75MHz, your PCI components will run at 37.5MHz, about 10 percent faster than their rated speed. Although some components will work just fine at this rate, you should be on the lookout for lockups, reboots, and other symptoms of bad timing. If this does occur, you'll have to back off the bus clock.

Even if your components can keep talking, they may not be able to recognize the data that's going by. As clock speeds ramp up, the CPU and components have less and less time to distinguish digital 1s from 0s. These values are indicated by the presence or absence of a specific electrical charge. However, if the charge rises and falls to quickly, the component simply may not have time to register the value. The symptoms are the same as those for bad timings.

9.1.4 Performance Impact Report

Our tests show that overclocking can deliver big returns in the right situations. Socket 7–based PCs, in particular, can benefit from the combination of higher motherboard bus and CPU clock speed operation. However, a lot depends on where your original PC is clocked and where it can go to.

The biggest returns come to those with 60MHz motherboards, because they can immediately boost clock rates by 10 percent without any fear of impacting PCI bus timings. The CPU will get a similar nudge even if the multiplier settings aren't touched. If the multiplication is pushed by another 0.5, an additional benefit will be seen.

The best results in terms of improvement come when you head for the sky. A 60MHz motherboard running at 75MHz is realizing a 25 percent speed gain. If you have SDRAM (or very good EDO DRAM) memory in your motherboard, the results can be astonishing. L2 cache runs at the same speed as the motherboard, so the CPU enjoys must faster service from this critical performance component. Unfortunately, 83MHz operation—possible on some motherboards—is generally untenable. Although CPUs can be cooled to handle the clock, and SDRAM is capable of keeping pace, most PCI devices will balk when faced with a 41.5MHz clock rate. The only real way to get an 83MHz clock to work reliably is if the motherboard supports asynchronous PCI clock operation, where the PCI bus can maintain 33MHz no matter what the system bus speed is.

9.2 Overclocking Your PC

Overclocking can be satisfying yet somewhat risky work. To reduce the risk and to ensure you get maximum impact from your changes, you need to consider a lot of factors in pushing the speed of the system and CPU clocks. This section will provide step-by-step instructions and tips for effectively getting more performance out of your existing hardware.

9.2.1 Overclocking Basics

When you overclock a CPU, three variables come into play:

- System bus speed
- CPU clock multiplier
- CPU supply voltage

In the following subsections, you'll get a quick introduction to these issues and how they are controlled.

Changing the System Bus Speed

To understand how you can overclock a Pentium, Pentium Pro, 6x86, or K5 CPU, it helps to realize that the internal clock in these CPUs runs at a different speed than the external clock or bus speed. The external clock is the speed at which the cache and the main memory run, and when divided by 2, it yields the speed of the PCI bus. There are only three different official bus speeds used by the Intel Pentium, Pentium Pro, and the AMD K5 CPUs: 50, 60, and 66MHz. The 6x86 uses five bus speeds: 50, 55, 60, 66, and 75MHz. There are also new boards available that support the unofficial bus speed of 83MHz.

To change the bus speed, look in your motherboard manual for a section titled something like "CPU External (BUS) Frequency Selection." This will discuss the jumpers you must change. If you're lucky and happen to have a motherboard with the new SoftMenu BIOS technology, you can change these settings from the BIOS setup menu.

Remember to always take it slow. Increase the bus speed one step at a time (say, from 60MHz to 66MHz, not 60MHz to 75MHz). Then try using the system for a few days, or even a week, to ensure you're getting reliable operation. If you don't have that kind of patience, consider loading and running a large benchmarking application, such as ZD Bop's WinBench, several times over. For best results, you'll want to run application-based tests, because these tend to run longer and use real-world data sets, thus helping ferret out problems caused by overclocking.

Changing the Multiplier

The internal CPU clock is controlled by a clock multiplier in each CPU. The multiplier is programmed via CPU pins, with options based on the CPU design. Multiplier support varies by product and manufacturer; it can be an important factor in defining your overclock options.

The multipliers for popular CPUs break out as shown in Table 9.1.

Table 9.1. A look at multiplier settings available on popular CPUs.

CPU	Multiplier settings
Intel Pentium II	3.5, 4, 4.5, 5
Intel Pentium and MMX	1.5, 2, 2.5, 3, 3.5
Intel Pentium Pro	2.5, 3, 3.5, 4
Cyrix M II	2, 2.5, 3, 3.5
Cyrix 6x86	2, 3
AMD K6	2.5, 3, 3.5, 4, 4.5
AMD K5 (PR75 to PR133)	1.5
AMD K5 (PR150 to PR200)	1.5, 2

To change the multiplier setting, find a section titled something along the lines of "CPU-to-Bus Frequency Ratio Selection" in your motherboard manual. There are usually two jumpers used to change these settings. Again, you can do all of this in the BIOS setup menu if you have a SoftMenu motherboard, such as the new Abit motherboard.

Changing the CPU Supply Voltage

You might not like it, but you may need to noodle with the voltage going to your CPU in order to get it to run more reliably. I should stress that the Intel Pentium and Pentium Pro CPUs can run at a supply voltage of up to 4.6 volts. Of course, you need to do some serious cooling, because the additional voltage will produce more heat. However, long-term use on a Pentium-166 CPU (running at 208MHz) shows that it works well.

More often than not, the trick is switching between two Intel-specified voltages: STD and VRE. The 3.4 VRE voltage widens the gap between the digital High and Low conditions, resulting in "cleaner" signals for the CPU and other motherboard devices to latch onto. If you can't run your CPU reliably at one particular clock speed, it's always worth considering a change to a higher supply voltage before discarding the change.

The silicon in STD and VRE CPUs is identical, so pushing the voltage to VRE levels won't damage your Intel CPU. However, the chip will run a little hotter, so you should *always* verify that you have adequate cooling in place. Note that the Abit IT5 motherboards offer a voltage that's even higher than VRE (at 3.6 volts) that can be selected in the SoftMenu BIOS CPU setup. I'm currently running my CPU at this voltage and it runs completely stable at 205MHz on a 68MHz bus (2.5× multiplier).

9.2.2 Overclocking Requirements

Four things come together when overclocking your motherboard and CPU. In order to get best results, you need to address all four:

- CPU
- Motherboard
- Memory
- Cooling hardware

The CPU

As a general rule, you'll have the most success overclocking Intel CPUs. These products tend to run cooler and more reliably than competing products in the same performance category. With that said, it's not all smooth sailing. Early dies in a CPU generation may lack the level of material purity found in later runs. Your only way to tell if your CPU is handling the transition gracefully is by observing your system behavior.

The Motherboard

The quality of the motherboard is absolutely crucial for successful overclocking. Because overclocked CPUs produce fewer "clean" signals, reflections and other flaws on the bus can cause the system to crash or hang. The reverse situation is also true—in overclocked mode, the CPU is more sensitive to unstable signals from the bus and will crash if the motherboard can't deliver clean signals. Always go for a branded motherboard, because these tend to avoid the design shortcuts and cut-rate components that can fail when even mildly stressed.

When you decide to overclock, you face a choice. Do you go for a higher bus speed or do you stick to a maximum of 66MHz? Motherboards with 75MHz bus speed support are hard to find, and those offering 83MHz bus speed are more rare still. Remember that boosting bus speed can impact reliability, so you need to test your new configuration.

Your motherboard should support a wide range of CPU supply voltages, because these are critical to managing both the thermal output and the signal quality in the CPU. At the very least, you need support for voltages of 3.3 volts (also known as *STD*) and 3.45 volts (known as *VRE*).

If you want to use an MMX-class processor, your board must support *split-voltage operation*. This means that the core of the CPU runs at a lower voltage than the I/O ports of the CPU. The latest boards all support a range of voltages from 2.5 volts to 2.9 volts, in convenient 0.1 volt increments. If your board happens to offer voltages higher than 3.45, you enjoy an expanded option. Sometimes, boosting the voltage can get a reluctant CPU to successfully overclock (although you'll face greater risks from overheating).

The RAM

Decent RAM is critical if you want to run your system bus at speeds higher than 66MHz. If you want to run a 430HX motherboard, such as the Asus P/I-P55T2P4, at 83MHz bus speed, you'll require high-end EDO DRAM. In my experience, the marking on the RAM is less important than it's brand. Try to stick with name brand memory whenever possible. Be careful, however, that you don't get second-rate chips from the manufacturers being sold in some stores. These chips have brand names etched on them, but their quality won't live up to your expectations.

Better still, if your motherboard supports SDRAM, go with it. The synchronous SDRAM architecture is much better equipped to run at 75, 83, and even 100MHz, running flawlessly where EDO DRAM may balk.

Cooling

I can't stress this enough: Cooling the CPU is absolutely critical. If you're able to boot your system with an overclocked CPU, but find that it crashes within the first few minutes, you most likely don't have sufficient cooling in place. The typical small heat sink and fan simply can't do the job if your CPU tends to run hot.

Where do you find a decent heat sink or fan? You can discern the efficiency of a heat sink by its K/W value (which stands for degrees Kelvin per watt of power dissipation). K/W tells how hot the heat sink gets for each watt of heating power produced by the CPU. The smaller the K/W value, the better the heat sink. My advice: Look for a heat sink with a rating below 1K/W.

If you're shopping for heat sinks, avoid the usual computer shops. You'll find professional heat sinks only in shops that sell electronic equipment such as transistors, resistors, chips, and the like.

Installing the heat sink is just as critical as finding the right one. Botch the installation, and the sink will fail to draw heat away from the CPU, thus inviting disaster. Here are some CPU heat sink installation tips:

- The contact surface of the heat sink must match the size of the CPU—if necessary, see if an electronics shop will cut it for you.

- Be careful that the contact surface stays completely flat on the CPU. Gaps between the heat sink and the CPU surface will reduce the thermal exchange.

- Always use a thermal compound (also available in any electronics shop) to affix the heat sink to the CPU. This special glue will ensure that heat is exchanged efficiently from the CPU to the heat sink. In a pinch, you can use super glue, but it should be applied very sparingly to avoid insulating the CPU surface from the heat sink. Also, be aware that you might not be able to remove the heat sink if the super glue is good stuff.

- Finally, consider some form of active heat management. A good fan placed on top of the heat sink can help actively draw heat out of the CPU. You'll want a fan that is both powerful and quiet.

Does this stuff work? In my experience, yes. My overclocked Pentium-133 runs at 180MHz and has a temperature of about 30 degrees C, which is well within Intel's specs for thermal stress. If you achieve this cooling effect, you can be sure that any crashes that do occur are not a result of overheating.

> **NOTE** The best way to ensure safe operation is to monitor the temperature inside the case. PC Power and Cooling's Alarm 110 unit costs about $20; it sounds an audible alarm when interior temperature goes above 110 degrees F. You can also find units that display the interior temperature on an external LCD, so you can see changes in the thermal load over time.

9.2.3 Step-by-Step Guide to Overclocking

Pushing the clock on your CPU or motherboard isn't as straightforward as many other operations on your PC. You'll need to have your complete motherboard and system documentation on hand for reference, and you'll also want to take detailed notes of system settings before and after you start. Although you may have to do a little digging to get all the information you need, any reasonably accomplished PC user should be able to run through these overclocking steps without too much trouble:

1. Turn off your computer, open it up, and get your motherboard manual.

2. Check the CPU markings on the top and bottom of the CPU. Write them down and put your CPU back in again.

3. Check the current clock speed and multiplier jumper settings on your motherboard. Compare them with your manual and write them down.

4. Check the supply voltage jumper settings on your motherboard and compare them with manual and your CPU markings. Write them down.

5. Have you arranged for decent cooling for your CPU? If so, apply it now.

6. Change the jumper settings for clock speed and/or multiplier according to your manual.

7. Check to make sure all your new settings and changes are okay. Recheck those jumper settings.

8. Start the computer and watch it like a hawk.

9. Does the PC reach BIOS setup? If so, go to step 12.

10. Turn off the computer and change the jumper to a higher supply voltage according to manual, if possible.

11. If you still can't reach BIOS setup, you can forget about overclocking to this speed.

12. Change the BIOS setup settings to the appropriate clock values. Save the settings and continue with the boot operation.

13. Does the PC complete its boot up process and seem to behave normally?

14. Start the testing phase by running Winstone, the BAPCo Suite, or other extended automated benchmarks.

15. If your PC fails in the benchmark test or does not reach full operation, check your cooling setup or try changing the voltage as per Step 10. You might also try more conservative memory timings in the BIOS setup, increasing the wait states or the read/write cycles. Just make sure to check to see if you're gaining speed in your benchmarks—there's no point in overclocking if your memory access slows you down!

16. If everything works well, congratulations! You just achieved a nifty system upgrade.

This sounds simple enough, but you must remember to keep your documentation close by, take detailed written notes, and keep a keen eye on system operation. Failure to do any of these things can stymie your efforts and can even leave you stranded, because you may not have the information you need to return to your original settings.

Finally, here are a few more tips:

- If you encounter trouble, check your cooling setup. Perhaps contact was lost on the heat sink, or the fan was not plugged in properly and is not running. Also look for blocked air vents and other problems.

- If you can't get things to work, you can try boosting the voltage to the CPU. This makes the 1s and 0s more prominent, thus allowing the CPU to see them despite their faster pace.

- If you do noodle with the voltage, be aware that the chip will get hotter still.

- If you're running Windows 95, be aware that it's much more picky about overclocking than DOS or Windows 3.x. Therefore, don't assume that if things work well under DOS that they will continue under Windows 95. Test all your operating systems.

9.2.4 Working with Specific CPUs

This general rundown draws a fairly straightforward picture. The reality is, of course, less clear. Different motherboards and CPUs offer different controls, features, and capabilities. Some CPUs are also more prone to trouble when overclocked than others—an important issue you should not overlook.

This section guides you through some instructions for specific CPU models to enable you to make good decisions before you turn on the gas.

Overclocking the Intel Pentium II

When Intel unleashed its Pentium II CPU, it not only shook up the desktop CPU market, it also changed the rules of overclocking for end users. Unlike previous CPUs, Pentium II is housed in a coherent module called a *single-edge cartridge (SEC)*, which contains the CPU, L2 cache, and associated control circuitry on a small PCB. The Pentium II was also the only CPU architecture at the time to run off both 66MHz and 100MHz motherboards.

The problem is, older Pentium II CPUs were intended only to run on the slower 66MHz front side bus. To enjoy the performance of a fast 100MHz motherboard, you need to shell out a lot more bucks for a Pentium II-350 or Pentium II-400 CPU. However, our examinations have shown essentially no difference between Deschutes-class Pentium II CPUs running on the 66MHz bus (Pentium II-333) and those running on the 100MHz bus (Pentium II-350 and 400). The only question, then, is how do you get your PII-333 to run like a PII-350 or even PII-400.

Here's how to do it: Essentially, every Pentium II includes a single pin that identifies the CPU to the chipset. This pin (B21) toggles the clock on 440BX-based motherboards to either 66MHz or 100MHz operation. On the PII-333 CPU, B21 is set to High (with the High signal indicating that the motherboard must run at 66MHz). On PII-350 and PII-400 CPUs, B21 is set to Low, and the chipset responds by running the motherboard at the faster 100MHz.

The only question is, how do you fool the Intel chipset into thinking pin B21 is set to Low, thus toggling the motherboard to 100MHz and providing a swift kick in the pants to your pokey PII-333 CPU? Here's how:

1. Shut down your system, unplug the power cord, and remove the case. Be sure to ground yourself by touching a metal object (or using a grounding wrist strap and pad) before handling the motherboard components.

2. Remove the Pentium CPU SEC cartridge from the motherboard by releasing the tabs and pulling the module straight up.

3. Turn the front of the CPU module toward you and, counting from the right on the lower row of pins, find the seventh pin from the edge. This is pin B21, the magic arbiter of bus speeds.

4. To trick the 440BX into thinking it's seeing a Low signal value, you need to mask the pin from its contact in the connector. There are a number of ways to do this (more on that later), but perhaps the best way is to use a small tab of electrical tape.

5. Cut out a small length of tape that matches the width of the pin. Starting from the front, affix the top edge of the tape just above the point where the B21 pin widens out. Don't worry if you partially cover the adjacent top row pins—they have plenty of contact area available to them provided you don't obscure their main parts too much.

6. Draw the tape against the pin surface and then pull it around the bottom edge of the connector, being careful to keep the tape in line.

7. Pull the tape up and press it against the pin surface. Measure where the top of the tape will just cover the B21 pin and make a clean cut at that point.

8. Inspection time. Press the tape home. Work the tape to make sure no bubbles or wrinkles will invite kinks or partially expose the B21 pin.

9. If everything looks good, insert the Pentium II SEC cartridge into the Slot 1 module.

10. Plug in the power cord and restart your system. Watch the screen carefully for signs of trouble. If you've covered other pins, the system will not boot. You'll have to power down, remove the CPU, and start over.

11. If everything checks out, your 440BX motherboard should now be running at a crisp 100MHz using an inexpensive PII-333 or slower CPU.

12. You can now tweak processor speed by setting the clock divider. Remember, clock increments for CPUs on the 100MHz front bus move in 50MHz jumps (0.5×100MHz is 50MHz). Keep a very close eye on heat accumulation if you intend to push a non-Deschutes Pentium II over the 100MHz front bus.

Although this description suggests using electrical tape to obscure pin B21, there are a variety of materials that can do the job. The main concerns are convenience—that is, how easy or difficult it is to precisely position the blocking material on the small pin surface—and durability. This second aspect is a somewhat scary question, because the adhesives used in many tapes can degrade or seep, inviting corrosion of the contact leads or migration of electrical signals across pins. The possible result could be a CPU that's rendered temporarily or permanently inoperable.

If you intend to keep your system around for a good long time and work in a hot and humid environment where corrosion and adhesive breakdown is a concern, it's worth the effort to get specialized tape. Your best bet is Teflon electrical tape, which provides a rock-solid surface as well as an electronics-friendly adhesive.

Overclocking the Intel Pentium and Pentium MMX

The Intel Pentium processor enjoys the distinction of being the most "overclockable" CPU ever made. That qualification extends to the Pentium MMX product family; in fact, MMX may be even better at handling the stresses of overclocking than its predecessor. The reason is that Pentium MMX runs at a cool 2.8 volts, whereas many motherboards that support this voltage also offer 2.9- or 2.93-volt modes.

The slightly higher voltage is just the thing for overclocking reluctant Pentium MMX CPUs. At 2.9 volts, the electrical difference between 1 and 0 becomes more clear, without overstressing the silicon. For example, a Pentium MMX-200 that we've been running does just fine with 2.8 volts at 208/83MHz and 225/75MHz. To get it to run at 250/83MHz, however, we had to step up the voltage to 2.9 volts, which works smoothly.

In some CPUs, Intel has built in so-called *overclock protection*, which prevents the CPU from running at higher multipliers. About 50 percent of the Pentium MMX CPUs marked "SY022" and perhaps 10 percent of those marked "SU073" have been governed. Although the multipliers are frozen, you can still boost the system bus to cause the CPU to run faster. Therefore, a Pentium-133 can run at 166MHz if you boost the 66MHz bus to 83MHz.

This overclock protection is more to defend against fraudulent chips than it is to stop people from overclocking their hardware. The problem is that there's a burgeoning market in remarked chips. Unscrupulous vendors can increase their take by purchasing low-cost Pentium MMX-166 CPUs, for example, and remarking them at Pentium MMX-233. Slap a sticker on the bottom to conceal the etching and the consumer is none the wiser.

Whenever you decide to overclock a Pentium or Pentium MMX CPU, you should check first to make sure the chip is not remarked. This is particularly a problem in Europe and Asia, but it's a threat in North America as well. If you can peel off a black sticker underneath the CPU, it has definitely been remarked. In this case, your CPU is most likely already overclocked and you should avoid pushing it any further.

If you can, make a point to avoid the Pentium-133 of the SY022 and SU073 varieties. About 33 percent of the Pentium-133s with this S spec have been disabled for multiplier settings of more than 2×. A small number of the SU073s also seem to suffer from the same problem.

Here's a list of the most overclockable Pentium CPUs:

- Pentium-150: This is the big winner. The Pentium-150 is really nothing but a Pentium-166 in disguise. This chip will run flawlessly when pushed to 166MHz operation.

- Pentium-166 (Classic and MMX; hence the P150): These clock mates are excellent for 187.5MHz operation on a 75MHz system bus (2.5× multiplier). They generally run fine at 200MHz on a 66MHz system bus as well (at 3× multiplier).

- Pentium-133: This one-time workhorse CPU runs great at 150MHz on a 75MHz bus (2× multiplier) as well as at 166MHz on an 83MHz bus (also a 2× multiplier). However, avoid higher multiplier settings with this CPU.

- Pentium-75: Most of these run flawlessly at 90MHz using the standard 60MHz bus at 1.5× multiplier. You should also have good luck at 100MHz, using the same multiplier on a 66MHz bus.

- Pentium-200 (Classic and MMX): These clock mates are superb at 208MHz (which is 2.5× an 83MHz bus) and can even run at 250MHz by tripling up the 83MHz system bus. In between, you'll find 225MHz on a 75MHz bus (at 3× multiplication) may work well for motherboards that can't handle these higher speeds.

Table 9.2. A rundown of available settings for Pentium-class CPUs.

Pentium	1st Choice	2nd Choice	3rd Choice	4th Choice
75MHz	112.5MHz @ 1.5× 75MHz	100MHz @ 1.5× 66MHz	90MHz @ 1.5× 60MHz	83MHz @ 1.5× 55MHz
90MHz	125MHz @ 1.5× 83MHz	112.5MHz @ 1.5× 75MHz	100MHz @ 1.5× 66MHz	
100MHz	125MHz @ 1.5× 83MHz	112.5MHz @ 1.5× 75MHz		
120MHz	125MHz @ 1.5× 83MHz	133MHz @ 2× 66MHz	112.5MHz @ 1.5× 75MHz	
133MHz	166MHz @ 2× 83MHz	150MHz @ 2× 75MHz	166MHz @ 2.5× 66MHz	
150MHz	166MHz @ 2× 83MHz	187.5MHz @ 2.5× 75MHz	200MHz @ 3× 66MHz	150MHz @ 2× 75MHz
166MHz	208MHz @ 2.5× 83MHz	166MHz @ 2× 83MHz	187.5MHz @ 2.5× 75MHz	200MHz @ 3× 66MHz
166MHz MMX	266MHz @ 3.5× 75MHz	250MHz @ 3× 83MHz	225MHz @ 3× 75MHz	208MHz @ 2.5× 83MHz
200MHz	250MHz @ 3× 83MHz	225MHz @ 3× 75MHz	208MHz @ 2.5× 83MHz	
200MHz MMX	290MHz @ 3.5× 83MHz	266MHz @ 3.5× 75MHz	250MHz @ 3× 83MHz	225MHz @ 3× 75MHz
233MHz MMX	290MHz @ 3.5× 83MHz	266MHz @ 3.5× 75MHz	250MHz @ 3× 83MHz	

Overclocking the Intel Pentium Pro

The Intel Pentium Pro still doesn't seem to be a popular CPU for overclocking. This may be in part because of the types of applications that Pentium Pro is typically used for—corporate, mission-critical fare that doesn't lend itself to experimentation. Often, these users and organizations value reliability over performance. In addition, the lack of 75- and 83MHz capable motherboards for Pentium Pro CPUs really limits the options.

Although you may not be able to go to higher speeds, you certainly should explore pushing a 50- or 60MHz motherboard to 66MHz. The Pentium Pro-150 and Pentium Pro-180 can both be overclocked to run on a 66MHz bus, delivering a welcome performance increase while maintaining a high level of reliability.

Table 9.3. Pentium Pro presents fewer alternatives, but you can still realize serious gains.

Pentium Pro	1st choice	2nd choice
150MHz	166MHz @ 2.5× 66MHz	
180MHz	233MHz @ 3.5× 66MHz	200MHz @ 3× 66MHz
200MHz	266MHz @ 4× 66MHz	233MHz @ 3.5× 66MHz

Pushing a Pentium Pro-180 to 233MHz, or a Pentium Pro-200 to 266MHz, is no picnic. However, it may be worth a try. The second choices work well in most instances, and they still provide a real performance boost.

Also, keep in mind that the integrated L2 cache of the Pentium Pro changes the performance equation a bit. When you turn up the speed on the CPU, the L2 cache will run faster as well, regardless of what happens on the motherboard. For this reason, Pentium Pro systems are not as reliant on motherboard overclocking to receive a performance increase. With that said, access to main memory will be stuck at 66MHz, so at least some of that bottleneck remains.

The main problem with the Pentium Pro is that it's difficult to adjust. Here, the SoftMenu BIOS technology is a letdown, because it doesn't let you choose 233 or 266MHz. Also, you can't tweak the voltage because the levels are automatically handled by the motherboard.

Overclocking the Cyrix/IBM 6x86

Due to the massive heat production of the older versions of the 6x86 CPU (steppings of less than 2.7) and the still-high heat production of the latest versions, this CPU is not as flexible as the Pentium for overclocking. You can indeed kill your 6x86 by overclocking it. Although I've never heard of an Intel CPU getting cooked by a pushed clock, I have heard several stories of fried 6*x*86 CPUs. As a result, I recommend against overclocking the 6*x*86 CPU at all.

Even if you do choose to take your chances, you'll find tweaking this CPU a good deal more restrictive than overclocking a Pentium. In addition to thermal issues, the 6*x*86 uses a simple integer multiplier that limits you to 2× and 3× operation (and 3× mode is nearly useless, because the only viable scenario is for 3× 50MHz operation, a pathetically low bus speed that can only hamper performance).

If you really want to overclock your 6*x*86, only do so in small steps. That means limiting yourself to a single clock increment on the CPU, as shown in Table 9.4.

Table 9.4. Know your limitations: The 6*x*86 doesn't leave you much room to roam.

6x86 P-Rating	Original MHz	Pushed MHz
P120+	100MHz	110MHz
P133+	110MHz	120MHz
P150+	120MHz	133MHz

The step from the P166+ (133MHz) to the P200+ (150MHz) seems to be too big and has a fairly low success rate. The risk of losing the CPU is quite high, making it an inadvisable option. In general, you'll get the most success with the 2.7 or 3.7 stepping of the 6*x*86 CPU. These versions run more stable and produce less heat than earlier runs.

No matter what the case, cooling is paramount for the overclocking 6*x*86 CPUs. You'll need a very large heat sink and possibly a powered peltier.

Overclocking the AMD K5

Late to market, but priced to move, the AMD K5 has a split personality when it comes to overclocking. The earlier PR75, PR90, and PR100 versions of the K5 were poor targets for overclocking. Most of the time, K5 systems would go dead after moving up only one clock increment. What's more, these CPUs share the same serious heat problems that plague the 6*x*86.

Life gets much better with the K5 PR120 and PR133 CPUs, however. Despite their higher P-ratings, these two chips actually run at the same external and internal speed as the PR90 and PR100. The internals of the CPU were improved significantly, thus enabling better performance at the same clock speed. What's more, the thermal output was reduced markedly, thus enhancing the overclocking outlook. The new PR150 and PR166 (at 120 and 133MHz) seem to be of the same design.

9.2.5 Protecting Against Failure

Nobody likes system crashes or hangs, but in a professional business environment, avoiding breakdowns is absolutely critical. Overclocking, by definition, increases your odds of experiencing trouble, which makes it a questionable practice in these environments. Still, done right, overclocking can prove to be a reliable and pain-free practice. Your task is to manage the risks.

The following points outline things you must do to avoid serious trouble:

- Cool the CPU: Before you push the clock, beef up the heat sink, add a strong fan, and even consider a powered peltier to draw heat away from the CPU.

- Monitor the chassis: For mission-critical work, consider a thermal alarm, such as the PC Alert 110. This device sits inside your case and sounds an alarm when the temperature inside rises above 110 degrees F.

- Evaluate the new settings: You should run through a complete set of Winstone, BAPCo, or other benchmark suites. The routine should be something that takes at least half an hour or so in order to expose the CPU to heat. Run the test immediately after overclocking; then run it again after eight hours of operation to ensure that you don't fall victim to creeping heat stress.

- Be observant: If you notice strange lockups or crashes, you should suspect a heat problem.

- Maintain your PC: Don't let vents get blocked by dust or papers. Also, periodically check on the operation of the fans to make sure they're not getting gummed up.

9.3 Expert Overclocking

You may be wondering how can you find out which bus speed your motherboard supports.

To be honest, the easiest and most sensible answer is to try it out. Switch the multiplier to the lowest setting and then put the bus speed jumpers in all the different configurations. For non-mathematical people, these are two to the power of the number of jumper configurations. Therefore, there are four configurations for two jumpers, eight configurations for three jumpers, and so on.

Once you've done this, boot up to the DOS prompt and run `CTCM.EXE` or a similar program that will report CPU speed. You then only have to divide it by the multiplier setting to find your bus speed. Again, if your motherboard uses the SoftMenu BIOS, you only have to look in your BIOS setup menu to find all of the different bus speed settings from which you can choose.

The following sections rundown the jumper settings for specific bus speeds.

9.3.1 PLL52C59-14

Note that motherboards with the PLL chip PLL52C59-14 can run at up to 75MHz. They also support the "turbo frequency" feature, which increases the bus speed by 2.5 percent (officially approved by Intel's CPU specifications).

75MHz Operation

Pin 8 via 2.2 K Ohm to 0 V ("0 V" means "ground," not "disconnected"!)

Pin 12 via 10 K Ohm to 5 V

Pin 13 via 10 K Ohm to 5 V

68MHz Operation (Turbo Frequency for 66MHz Bus)

Pin 8 via 2.2 K Ohm to 0 V

Pin 12 via 10 K Ohm to 0 V

Pin 13 via 10 K Ohm to 5 V

61.5MHz (Turbo Frequency for 60MHz Bus)

Pin 8 via 2.2 K Ohm to 0 V

Pin 12 via 10 K Ohm to 5 V

Pin 13 via 10 K Ohm to 0 V

This is measured on the Abit boards IT5H, IT5V, PR5, which all use the PLL52C59-14. The PR5 also comes in a version with the PLL52C61-01; however, the setting shown in the next section seems to set the board at 61.5MHz instead of 83MHz.

9.3.2 PLL52C61-01

Motherboards with the PLL chip PLL52C61-01 can run at 83MHz bus speed as well and also theoretically support the "turbo frequency" feature. Note that some motherboards eliminate the 83MHz mode, which may limit your options.

83MHz operation or 61.5MHz (Turbo Frequency for 60MHz Bus)

Unfortunately, this depends on the circuitry on the motherboards.

Pin 5 via 10 K Ohm to 0 V ("0 V" means "ground," not "disconnected"!)

Pin 12 via 10 K Ohm to 5 V

Pin 13 via 10 K Ohm to 5 V

75MHz

Pin 5 via 10 K Ohm to 5 V

Pin 12 via 10 K Ohm to 0 V

Pin 13 via 10 K Ohm to 5 V

For 68MHz (Turbo Frequency for 66MHz Bus)

Pin 5 via 10 K Ohm to 5 V

Pin 12 via 10 K Ohm to 5 V

Pin 13 via 10 K Ohm to 5 V

I have measured this on the Asus P/I-P55T2P4 rev. 3 board and was able to verify the exact same settings on the FIC PA-2006 board. The FKI SL586VT II or Magic Pro MP-586VIP board also uses this chip, but you can't get it to 83MHz. Instead, you get the pathetic speed of 61.5MHz.

In terms of jumpers, this means you'll have to find out which of the three jumpers is connected to the particular pins. It's circuited via the pull up/down resistor of 10 K Ohm. In case you only have jumpers with On/Off positions instead of 1-2/2-3 positions, the On condition is the condition for 0 V, and the Off or open condition is for 5 V.

Keep in mind that this information is for the real freaks who want to get their boards to 75 or maybe even 83MHz no matter what. This approach allows you to get to higher bus speeds on boards that only present four bus speeds. That is, as long as the board uses one of these PLL chips. You'll need to do the necessary soldering at your own risk and should only attempt this if you know exactly what you're doing!

There are several motherboards that use one of the two PLL chips, depending on what was available when the motherboard was assembled. The Abit PR5 is such a fellow (of course, I was unlucky enough to receive a board with the PLL52C59-14) and it seems that the shuttle HOT 557 is another. There are a few reports of 83MHz bus speeds with these boards, but most simply can't run at this faster bus speed.

9.3.3 Special Precautions for 75 and 83MHz Bus Speed

Using higher bus speeds includes some important restrictions you should be aware of.

The PCI Bus Runs at 37.5 or Even 41.6MHz

Speeding the PCI bus can lead to trouble, particularly with SCSI controllers and network cards. Some video cards may also balk at the higher speed and will tend to run a good deal hotter than normal. This can be a real concern with high-end graphics cards, whose controllers often run quite hot.

EIDE Interface

The speed of the EIDE interface included in the system chipset is determined not only by the PIO or DMA modes, but also by the PCI clock. This is one reason why the EIDE interface—and the hard disks and CD-ROMs that run off it—are always slower in systems with 60MHz bus speed. Speeding the motherboard to 75 or 83MHz can boost EIDE performance.

Unfortunately, either the interface or, in most cases, the hard disk are not up to the quicker pace. Although hard drives may work fine on a 75MHz motherboard, at 83MHz they start to fail. You either have to back off the clock or reduce the EIDE interface to the slow PIO mode 2.

ISA Issues

The Asus P/I-P55T2P4 is an example of a motherboard with an ISA bus slaved to the system clock. The fixed divider works from the PCI clock, causing peripherals such as sound cards to run into trouble if they can't handle faster ISA bus operation. If you run into this problem, increase the ISA wait states in the BIOS setup as a potential fix.

RAM Issues

As stated earlier, the type and quality of your system RAM is a major factor in successful overclocking. Most 60ns EDO DRAM chips will run fine at 75MHz, but for 83MHz operation you'll need either high-end EDO DRAM or, better yet, good SDRAM.

One pleasant surprise is the behavior of many SDRAM products and motherboards at the higher clock operation. Although Intel and others recommend that you shell out a bit more for PC100 SDRAM designed for operation on a 100MHz memory bus, you may be able to use RAM from your existing 66MHz Pentium II motherboard. In our tests, SDRAM modules from Samsung proved particularly reliable at the higher clock. Therefore, not only can you push your CPU, you can push your memory as well. What a deal!

Of course, pushing memory adds yet another variable to the overclocking equation. You'll want to keep a real sharp eye on system behavior regardless, but even more so if you're running your SDRAM modules at speeds 50 percent higher than their rated limit.

9.4 Tom's Pick

When it comes to overclocking, no CPU is more adept than the Pentium MMX. Late versions of this CPU were built well within the performance envelope, making it possible to push both clock rates and voltages with reasonable certainty that the part would still operate. What's more, the flexibility of the Socket 7 motherboard platform allows users to push front bus speeds from 66MHz to 75MHz and even 83MHz.

All this flexibility means that the Pentium MMX can be overclocked in more ways than any other CPU I can think of. Sure, the Pentium II Pin B21 trick is neat, but the 50MHz clock increments on the 100MHz front side bus really raise the stakes when it comes to overheating. However, if you bought a late-model Pentium MMX-200 CPU on a reliable motherboard with an asynchronous PCI clock, there's a good chance you can really light things up. At 83MHz, a pushed Socket 7 front bus is running 26 percent faster than its original 66MHz rating. If you have a 200MHz Pentium MMX CPU running at its typical 3X clock rate, the resulting CPU speed is 252MHz—again, 26 percent faster than before. Perhaps most important, the L2 cache of the Pentium MMX CPU (as with other Socket 7 motherboards) enjoys the same clock increase. If you own a Pentium MMX system, you might want to explore your overclocking options, because they are many.

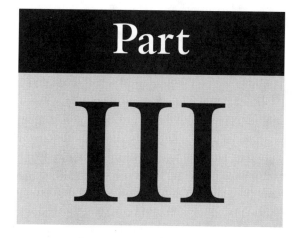

Part

III

Storage Devices

Chapter 10

Disk Controllers

When it comes to PC storage, one of the most critical issues is the interface used to connect the device to the PC. After all, a fast hard disk is of little benefit if the connection to the PC is slow and inefficient. For years there have been two main choices when it comes to the disk storage interface on the PC—the Small Computer System Interface (SCSI) and the Integrated Drive Electronics (IDE) standard.

The two technologies are very different in both scope and implementation, but they've followed similar paths through the years. Both have advanced in features and performance to keep pace with the growing demands of PC hardware and applications, and both have provided the flexibility to serve as much more than just a connection for hard disks. However, where SCSI has remained a niche technology in desktop PCs, IDE has become a ubiquitous—and critical—element of the PC platform.

Even though an IDE connector comes built into the vast majority of motherboards, users face an important decision when choosing between SCSI and IDE. Although purchasing a system with a built-in SCSI adapter and drives will cost more, you'll find that the hard disks provide better throughputs and superior operation in multitasking situations, such as when working with two or more disk drives. The benefits extend to a variety of peripherals such as scanners, CD-ROM and DVD-ROM drives, as well as recordable media (ranging from CD-R to tape backup to DVD-RAM).

This chapter will help you determine the performance and cost benefits of IDE and SCSI controllers so you can balance your system to suit your budget and needs.

10.1 Examining IDE

Created as a disk drive interface to replace the unreliable and slow drives based on ESDI, MFM, and RLL drive technologies, IDE has since become the workhorse storage connection on the PC. Virtually every PC motherboard includes one or more IDE-style controllers and ports, thus ensuring compatibility with a large universe of disk drives and other devices.

10.1.1 Finding IDE Controllers on the Motherboard

You can determine if your PC has an IDE connector by looking for a 40-pin connector (arrayed in 20 pins by two rows, as shown in Figure 10.1) on the motherboard. Usually, the pins are located near the edge of the motherboard and are often identified by silk screening nearby that identifies the bus type. A "1" usually is printed at one corner of the connector to indicate the important pin 1, used for lining up an IDE cable with the pins.

Figure 10.1.
*The twin IDE
connectors are
clearly visible just
in front of the
RAM sockets on
this Micronics
Pentium II
motherboard.*

If you see a pair of these 40-pin ports, you have an enhanced IDE (also called ATA-2 or Fast-ATA) interface. Each port corresponds to an IDE channel, with each channel capable of supporting two peripherals. If only a single 40-pin connector is present, the bus is IDE (or ATA). In this case, both the performance and disk handling capabilities of the motherboard are quite limited, and you may want to use an add-in card to connect hard disks to the motherboard.

Even if you've determined the general flavor of IDE on your systems, don't think you've settled everything yet. There are no less than three varieties of enhanced IDE on the market, delivering significant variances in performance and device support. Unfortunately, there's no way to tell which IDE version you have by looking at the pins. You'll want to check your system documentation to make sure of the IDE type.

10.1.2 The Many Faces of IDE

The IDE standard actually embraces a number of different specifications because the standard has evolved over the years. In fact, the term "Enhanced IDE" is something of a misnomer itself, because this is the phrase that Western Digital coined for its ATA-2 disk drives. The following is a list of the various IDE-related interface standards for the PC:

- ST-506/ST-412 interface
- ESDI
- IDE
- ATA-2
- ATA-3
- ATA-4

The Beginning: ST-506/ST-412

Like the hard disk interface used on the IMB PC XT platform, drives using the ST-506/ST-412 were dumb as a stump, with all the controller intelligence located on a separate controller card. The technology was usually referred to as *RLL* or *MFM*, which is actually the names of the encoding schemes used on these types of drives. The RLL/MFM drive interface was not long for this world, because the lack of onboard electronics limited reliability—data was often lost on its way from the drive to the controller card that handled the processing.

Compared to modern IDE and SCSI interfaces, this standard was both slow and difficult to work with. Throughputs were limited to 5Mbps, whereas separate drive and electronics packages meant that users had to manually configure low-level access settings. Incompatibilities between components were not uncommon.

A Short Life: Enhanced Small Device Interface

When ESDI arrived in the mid 1980s, it seemed poised to take over the hard disk market. The interface resolved many issues by moving controller resources from a separate card and onto the drive, thus improving performance, convenience, and reliability. Data throughput improved by two to three times over that of ST-506/ST-412, ranging from 10Mbps to 15Mbps. However, the standard was soon pushed out of the market by the arrival of IDE, which was simpler, cheaper, and more powerful than ESDI.

The Dawn of a New Age: ATA/IDE

The AT Attachment interface, called *ATA* or *IDE*, emerged in the late 1980s and quickly became the *de facto* market standard. The IDE moniker stands for *integrated drive electronics*, which refers to the fact that ATA drives incorporate all the drive controller electronics into the drive itself, thus eliminating expensive and persnickety controller cards.

The original IDE interface introduced a standard protocol for drive communications called *programmable input/output (PIO)*. PIO modes defined how IDE drives talked to the system chipset, with higher modes enabling more efficient—and therefore faster—communication. Table 10.1 shows the IDE PIO modes and their throughputs.

Table 10.1. Advancing PIO modes allow later IDE versions to boost performance over the original ATA specification.

Mode	Transfer Rate (MBps)
Mode 0	3.3
Mode 1	5.2
Mode 2	8.3
Mode 3	11.1
Mode 4	16.6

Original ATA/IDE disk drives were able to support PIO modes 0, 1, and 2, yielding maximum throughputs of 3.3MBps, 5.2MBps, and 8.3MBps, respectively. However, the drives themselves always fell short of these ceilings, which are based on best-case performance during burst-mode transfers. PIO modes require that both the disk drive and the system chipset (or controller card) support the mode being used, which means that newer drives will have to drop to lower PIO mode operation when installed into an old system.

The original IDE specification also delivered direct memory access (DMA) operation to the disk interface. DMA enables transfers to happen without CPU involvement, thus enhancing overall system performance. As with PIO modes, there are several flavors of advanced DMA for the IDE interface (see Table 10.2).

Table 10.2. IDE's support for DMA eventually opened the door to much faster performance.

Mode	Transfer Rate (MBps)
Single-word 0	2.1
Single-word 1	4.2
Single-word 2	8.3
Multiword 0	4.2
Multiword 1	13.3
Multiword 2	16.6
Multiword 3	33.3

The original ATA/IDE specification included support for all three single-word DMA modes as well as for multiword DMA mode 0. However, instability in

Disk Controllers

disk based DMA transfers essentially meant that few IDE hard disks made use of the DMA facility.

The original ATA specification provided support for two hard disk drives on a single channel. In order to share the channel, one drive must be configured as a master and the other as a slave. This setup continues to be used in more advanced IDE versions today. It's worth noting that older ATA drives often failed to comply to the ATA standard, and that two drives from different manufacturers often failed to work together when sharing an IDE channel.

IDE remains an internal device interface, just as it was at its inception. Cable lengths are limited to 18 inches, and the spec lacks provisions for the grounding and signal control necessary for external operation. This is one of the main reasons that IDE is less expensive than SCSI.

The Big Jump: ATA-2

ATA-2 represented a big jump in disk performance and capabilities. For the first time, IDE drives could support more than 504MB, whereas peak performance moved from 8.3MBps to 16.6MBps. Alongside ATA-2, a separate but critical standard called ATAPI (ATA Packet Interface) was adopted that enabled the ATA interface to support CD-ROM drives and other non–hard disk devices. However, BIOS limitations would limit drives to 504MB until the advent of logical block addressing (LBA), which allowed BIOSs to recognize drives as large as 2GB.

ATA-2 was ratified as an ANSI standard in an effort to improve the performance of hard disks. New to ATA-2 were PIO modes 3 and 4, which delivered through-puts of 11.1MBps and 13.3MBps, respectively. DMA support was extended to include multiword 1 (13.3MBps) and multiword 2 (16.6MBps). The addition of *block transfers* allowed ATA-2 hard disks to move multiple reads or writes using a single processor interrupt. By lumping batches of transfers together, disk transactions occurred more quickly and the CPU was subject to less frequent interruption.

A critical functional enhancement came in the form of logical block addressing, or *LBA*. Combined with an LBA-aware BIOS, ATA-2 hard disks are able to do away with the slow and inefficient Cylinder, Head, Sector (CHS) addressing scheme, where bits are located by specifying the cylinder number, the head number, and the sector number. By assigning every sector on the disk a unique value, LBA-enabled transfers over the ATA-2 connection are able to happen more efficiently.

The LBA scheme also helped resolve the once-crippling 504MB hard disk capacity barrier. This limitation arose because of the interaction between the ATA/IDE spec and the BIOS 13h interrupt used to control disk accesses. The ATA specification can theoretically address 128GB across 65,536 cylinders, 16 heads, and 256 sectors. However, the 13h interrupt only allows for 7.88GB across 1,024 cylinders, 256 heads, and just 63 sectors. Because disk transfers require the least common denominator from the interrupt and ATA interface be employed, the available addressable disk space is limited to a meager 504MB.

To get around this, the enhanced CHS addressing scheme was employed to trick the BIOS 13h interrupt into supporting drives with more than 1,024 cylinders. To do this, addressing is remapped so that the extra cylinders are expressed to the 13h interrupt as heads, thus keeping the transaction within the limits. Just before the bits go to the drive, the BIOS translates the data to the actual disk geometry, which often features 6,000 or more cylinders—well above the 13h limitation.

LBA requires support from the BIOS to work. If your BIOS is not LBA aware, you may not be able to get optimal performance results from your disk drive, though translation should still be enabled. ATA-2 helps matters in this regard since it provides for improved device recognition over the connection. This allows the OS and BIOS to query disk drives and other devices for specific information about issues such as disk geometry.

It's worth noting that the following specifications (marketed by individual disk drive vendors) are essentially ATA-2. However, should you find yourself purchasing a drive with one of these monikers, you should confirm that it complies with the ATA-2 specification:

- Fast ATA

- Fast ATA-2

- Enhanced IDE

Tweaking: ATA-3

The ATA-3 specification does nothing for performance of IDE drives. Rather, it specifies the use of a diagnostic scheme called Self-Monitoring Analysis and Reporting Technology (SMART, naturally) to detect and report impending disk problems. System utilities are able to report on drive status using SMART. ATA-3 also tweaks the newer transfer modes (PIO and DMA) to enhance reliability over the standard IDE cable.

The Next Big Thing: ATA-4

The world of IDE hard disks got another big boost with the adoption of ATA-4, also called *ultra DMA*. In fact, ATA-4 has a lot of aliases. Here are a few:

- Ultra ATA

- Ultra DMA

Disk Controllers

- ATA-33

- DMA-33

ATA-4 introduces fast, multiword DMA mode 3 transfers to the IDE connection. This facility enables 33.3MBps burst mode transfers free of CPU intervention, twice the data rate of ATA-2. In order to work, both the system BIOS and the hard disk must be ATA-4 compliant—if you want to use a fast ATA-4 hard disk in your PC, you may want to purchase a PCI add-in card such as the Ultra33 from Promise Technology. The specification includes error detection and correction technology to enable reliable high-speed operation over the standard IDE cable.

If you intend to buy an IDE drive, you should make sure it provides ATA-4 compliance. The same advice goes for any new motherboard or IDE controller card, because ATA-4's 2× data rate advantage makes it a compelling buy.

Beyond Hard Disks: ATAPI

The ATA Packet Interface welcomed the IDE interface to the growing zoology of mass storage. Although CD-ROM drives were the first and are by far the most common ATAPI devices, everything from tape backup drives to DVD-RAM drives have found on a home using the ATAPI protocol (see Figure 10.2). The ATAPI specification did away with the abundant number of propriety CD-ROM interfaces and provided the first reasonable alternative to SCSI for these and other devices.

Figure 10.2.

The standard ATAPI interface made possible inexpensive DVD-ROM drives, such as the PC-DVD Encore Dxr-2 from Creative Labs.

In fact, ATAPI is entirely separate from the ATA standards, although it does share the same connector and cabling resources used by ATA. The operating system loads ATAPI drivers to enable access to the non–hard disk devices; however, support for PIO and DMA mode operations can vary widely among products. ATAPI devices work side-by-side with ATA hard disks, using the same master/ slave relationship employed when using two or more hard disk drives.

ATAPI is not part of any of the ATA specs, so you don't need to confirm compatibility when you purchase a motherboard or system. In almost all cases, however, current motherboards include ATAPI support in their IDE channels, making the technology another critical common element in the platform.

10.1.3 Performance Impact Report

There's no question that ATA-4, despite its many, many names, is the protocol of choice over the IDE interface. If you're buying a new hard disk or system, make sure it provides support for ATA-4 (a.k.a. ultra DMA, ultra ATA, Ultra33, and DMA-33). The enhanced DMA capability doubles the potential throughput of the IDE bus to over 33MBps, enabling a fast hard disk to burst data effectively. Putting ATA-4 in your new system will also ensure that you enjoy full compatibility with upcoming devices.

Fortunately, you won't need to worry much about ATAPI support—it's part and parcel of every chipset, BIOS, and IDE interface on the market. ATAPI drivers are also included in major operating systems, thus enhancing the Plug and Play experience of these drives. The recent innovation of a scheme called *independent channel timing* has also enhanced CD-ROM installation.

In the past, devices on an IDE channel dropped to the timing of the slowest device on that channel. Therefore, a CD-ROM drive set up as a slave on Channel 1 would kill the performance of a hard disk drive set up as a master on the same channel. To avoid this, users had to think hard before pairing up devices on the IDE interface. Newer IDE connections allow slow and fast devices to coexist on the same channel without impacting each other's performance, thus enhancing flexibility.

IDE has its limitations, and they are very real. External operation is simply not an option—you'll need to consider alternatives such as SCSI, USB, parallel/serial, or even FireWire if you want to run devices out of the box. Also, IDE still lacks the robustness of a true bus, which means multiple devices will behave more efficiently on a good SCSI controller than they will on an IDE controller.

10.2 Examining SCSI

Since its beginnings in the graphics workstation market, the Small Computer System Interface (SCSI) has proved itself a versatile, performance-minded technology able to fulfill a variety of missions. Unlike IDE, which started as a hard disk interface and grew modestly from there, SCSI is a feature-rich data bus designed for a variety of uses. Scanners, recordable optical drives, video capture modules, and networking devices frequently use SCSI because of its excellent throughput, flexible layouts, and strong multitasking.

Disk Controllers

Also unlike IDE, which only services internal devices, SCSI lets you run both external and internal peripherals. SCSI devices can be set up in a daisy chain—one device hooked to the next—with as many as 15 devices running off a single adapter. Therefore, a single SCSI host adapter can support multiple hard disks, for example, as well as a mix of other devices. Multiple SCSI controllers can be set up in a system, extending system expansion even further. Also, unlike IDE, SCSI doesn't require a separate interrupt request (IRQ) line for each device. A single IRQ services the entire SCSI chain, making SCSI an efficient solution for the resource crunch in many PCs.

Despite its many talents, SCSI hasn't made a big mark on the PC platform. For one thing, SCSI controllers have often been expensive, typically running $100 to $300, depending on the feature set. In addition, PC-based SCSI has been rife with problems, ranging from driver snafus to tricky termination and SCSI ID setup.

10.2.1 Finding SCSI

You won't find SCSI controllers in most of today's motherboards. Although motherboards a few years back sometimes included integrated controllers, rapid changes in SCSI specifications made it more economical to leave the controller on separate add-in boards. Also, the added cost of the SCSI circuitry meant that that motherboard could only be sold to the small portion of the market seeking SCSI. Today, if you want SCSI for your PC, you'll almost certainly need to purchase a SCSI card or have one included in the system when you buy it.

To add SCSI to your system, you'll need to purchase a SCSI controller card from companies such as Adaptec and Diamond Multimedia. These cards include the SCSI bus circuitry as well as ports for internal and/or external SCSI devices. Most new SCSI boards use the PCI bus to take advantage of its superior performance and its built-in support for Plug and Play.

Figure 10.3.

Diamond Multimedia's Fireport 20 SCSI Fast Wide SCSI adapter delivers 20MBps data transfers over a PCI add-in card.

The best products include SCSI management software for configuring and maintaining the bus and its peripherals. Included with the board is driver software, which is needed to allow the operating system to see the devices in your SCSI chain. Adaptec's EasySCSI and Corel's SCSI can also be purchased separately.

10.2.2 The Many Faces of SCSI

Like IDE, there are a whole lot of SCSI standards out there. Advancements have yielded big gains in performance as well as welcome improvements in features. The following SCSI standards are out on the market:

- SCSI-1

- SCSI-2: Fast SCSI, FastWide SCSI

- SCSI-3: Ultra SCSI, UltraWide SCSI, UltraWide Low Voltage Differential SCSI

In fact, SCSI cards and devices are rarely referred to by the standards, such as SCSI-2 or SCSI-3, to which they adhere. More often, you'll hear devices referred to by the width and type of SCSI connection employed. Therefore, a fast hard disk would use the UltraWide SCSI connection, and cards are called Fast SCSI, FastWide SCSI, UltraWide SCSI, and the like.

The naming refers to the fact that a particular SCSI specification can embrace more than one connection type. SCSI-2 devices, for example, can push anywhere from 10MBps to 20MBps, depending on the flavor of SCSI-2 connection employed. Knowing the connection type is critical not just for optimizing performance, but also to ensure that you can get your SCSI hardware to fit together. The various SCSI connections use differing pinouts, as shown in Figure 10.4, which may require you to buy specific cables or adapter modules to make everything fit together. As with IDE, SCSI specifications are backward compatible—faster SCSI cards and hardware can recognize and communicate with slower devices.

Even as standards developed over time, innovations have served to extend the architecture. Low-voltage designs reduced the amount of voltage needed to define 1s and 0s along the bus, thus reducing crosstalk and pushing maximum cable lengths to 12 meters. The introduction of *differential technology* enhanced reliability by sending verifying signals for every bit. Differential requires more lines, but it pays off by significantly reducing errors in transmission. Differential SCSI designs can run over as much as 25 meters of cable.

Disk Controllers

Figure 10.4.

Mixing devices based on different SCSI transfer protocols can really confuse installation. These incompatible connectors are used for Narrow SCSI, Fast SCSI, Fast Wide SCSI, and Ultra SCSI, respectively.

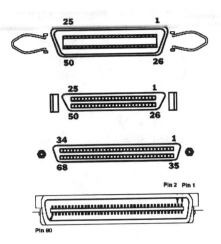

The Old Guard: SCSI-1

The initial SCSI specification, called *SCSI-1*, uses an 8-bit-wide bus running at a tepid 5MHz to provide a maximum data rate of 5MBps. Today, the 8-bit connection is called *Narrow SCSI* and is the standard bus width in SCSI parlance. If the bus is an 8-bit type, you won't see mention of width in the name, whereas a wider 16-bit bus will be called *Wide SCSI*. External SCSI devices can operate over cable lengths as great as six meters.

Crafted in the mid 1980s, the specification suffers from varying levels of support in the market, leading to many problems beyond just slow performance. Still, SCSI-1 supports both internal and external devices, although its device support is essentially limited to hard disk drives. Up to eight devices can run off a single SCSI-1 daisy chain. (Note that this number includes the host adapter itself, so seven SCSI peripherals may be hooked to the adapter.)

The Big Jump: SCSI-2

Like the ATA-2 specification, the second time was a charm for SCSI. SCSI-2 introduced two key concepts to the SCSI universe: Fast and Wide. The Fast SCSI transfer protocol boosts the clock on the 8-bit bus to 10MHz, doubling SCSI-2 data rates to 10MBps. Wide SCSI delivers the same results using a wider-but-slower 16-bit, 5MHz bus. Combining these two characteristics results in the so-called *Fast Wide SCSI transfer protocol*, which delivers 20MBps throughput over a 16-bit, 10MHz bus.

To support the faster and wider bus operation, the cabling on SCSI-2 was improved. However, the increased number of pins and wires on the new wide connections meant that SCSI cabling options proliferated, leading to complexity in the buying market. Also, Fast SCSI operation requires shorter cable lengths to operate properly—down to three meters from six meters.

SCSI-2 adds support for a variety of devices, including CD-ROM drives, scanners, and removable media drive. Wide SCSI controllers also extend the number of devices it can support, to a total of 16. Improved bus termination—often by way of those external modules you plug into the last device in a SCSI chain—enhance reliability, whereas performance gets a welcome boost from a technology called *command queuing*. This scheme enables multiple SCSI instructions to travel the bus at one time, thus breaking open bottlenecks on loaded SCSI chains.

Moving On Up: SCSI-3

SCSI-3 further boosts data rates by introducing the world to Ultra SCSI, which defines an even faster 20MHz bus clock that is double that of the 10MHz Fast SCSI clock. An Ultra Wide SCSI connection therefore runs 16-bits wide by 20MHz fast, thus yielding 40MBps operation. Today, most SCSI hard disk drives use an UltraWide SCSI connection.

Once again, the cabling has been enhanced to support faster operation, and once again, buyers are asked to contend with more confusing choices. As with the introduction of Fast SCSI, doubling the clock also requires a halving of the maximum cable length. Ultra SCSI devices can be separated by no more than 1.5 meters of cable (versus 3 meters for Fast SCSI and 6 meters for Narrow SCSI).

Most recently introduced was Ultra2 SCSI, which further increases data rates by taking advantage of the specified—but little used—32-bit bus width in the SCSI-2 standard. Narrow Ultra2 SCSI (generally called just *Ultra2 SCSI*) provides 40MBps data rates, whereas Wide Ultra2 SCSI delivers 80MBps. That's double the 40MBps throughput of UltraWide SCSI. Ultra2 happens to be the end of the line for SCSI performance, because boosting clock speeds along the wide, external cable is all but impossible to do at an affordable cost.

Disk Controllers

Ultra2 takes advantage of both low-voltage and differential technologies to achieve its impressive throughputs. Because of this, it uses very specific cabling and connectors, which may not be compatible with other devices installed on the bus. You'll need an adapter to connect the disparate cable types, as shown in Figure 10.5.

Figure 10.5.

The Diamond Multimedia Fireport 40 upgrade kit includes cables and adapters to let the Ultra Wide SCSI card attach to devices using the 8-bit Narrow SCSI interface.

Here is a summary of your SCSI options:

- SCSI-1: The original SCSI features an 8-bit bus and 5MBps data transfer rates, but it can only support a single peripheral.

- SCSI-2: The maturation of the SCSI spec, SCSI-2 provides support for up to seven devices, including peripherals such as scanners and optical drives. SCSI-2 uses a 50-pin connector.

- Wide SCSI: A flavor of SCSI that offers a 16-bit bus over a wider 168-pin cable, thus doubling transfer rates to 10MBps.

- Fast SCSI: A flavor of SCSI that doubles the interface clock on the 8-bit bus to 10 MHz, thus yielding a 10MBps data rate over an 8-bit bus. Fast SCSI interfaces can only run half the cable length of standard implementations.

- Fast Wide SCSI: Provides 20MBps performance from a wide (16-bit) bus and fast SCSI interface.

- Ultra SCSI: Uses an 8-bit bus and a faster 20MHz clock to achieve data rates of 20MBps.

- SCSI-3: Generally known as Ultra Wide SCSI, SCSI-3 employs a 16-bit bus and can push 40MBps of data.

- Ultra2 SCSI: Ultra2 doubles the clock once again to 40MHz, thus pushing 40MBps of data over a narrow 8-bit bus.

- Wide Ultra2 SCSI: As the fastest SCSI variant, Wide Ultra2 employs a 16-bit bus and the fast 40MHz clock for data rates of 80MBps.

10.2.3 Performance Impact Report

If you demand top performance, you can't do better than SCSI. With the latest controllers supporting astounding data rates of 80MBps, there's plenty of head-room for demanding applications such as video capture and high-speed transfers. Even at the more common 40MBps throughput found in Ultra Wide SCSI controllers, hard disks enjoy 20 percent more bandwidth than the fastest ATA specification (ATA-33). More important, SCSI's bus-specific talents enable effective multitasking over the bus.

Of course, if you need an external device, IDE is no option at all. Although the fastest SCSI implementations are limited to about four feet of cable, that's four feet more than you get with IDE. The ability to daisy chain devices means that you can conveniently array your SCSI peripherals along the desktop. This kind of convenience and performance makes SCSI attractive to performance-minded buyers.

Of course, you pay for these capabilities. SCSI cards run $100 to $200, and SCSI versions of peripherals generally command a stiff premium over their IDE counterparts. Where an IDE drive might cost $250, you can expect to pay $350 for a SCSI drive of the same capacity. Given that most applications won't gain a performance benefit from a SCSI drive, the expense is simply not worth it for large segments of the market.

Also, despite improvements in reliability and convenience, SCSI remains persnick-ety. Users must remember to terminate their daisy chains, which can get confus-ing if both internal and external SCSI devices reside on the bus. Also, users must set ID numbers for their devices, often having to contend with hardware that wants specific settings in order to work optimally. Although these issues are getting resolved with newer products, the cable/connector mess remains. A confusing mix of Wide, Fast, and Ultra SCSI devices means that your daisy chain could present three or more separate connector types. You'll need to do a good survey of your bus to figure out which cables and adapters you need to make the whole thing fit together.

10.3 Adding a Controller

The market for ATA controllers is predictably small. Every PC motherboard sold over the last four years or so has included an IDE connector. What's more, the

Disk Controllers

most advanced form of ATA—ATA-33—has been resident since the introduction of Intel's 430TX chipset at the beginning of 1997—in other words, for nearly two years, ATA-33 controllers have been flowing into the market.

If you have an older system that you want to upgrade to ATA-33, consider products such as the ATA-33 from Promise Technology. This PCI add-in card provides two ATA-4-compliant IDE connectors, each capable of supporting a master and a slave device. This card will allow older Pentium MMX and Pentium PCs to gain the full benefit of the fastest ATA-33 hard disk drives. What's more, the original motherboard-based IDE connectors remain available, so you can run up to eight internal devices—provided you have space for them all—over your IDE interfaces. However, most systems will run out of interrupt request (IRQ) lines to support the drives before physical space becomes an issue.

If you want to use SCSI hard disk drives and other peripherals, you'll probably have to use a SCSI controller that plugs into an ISA or PCI expansion slot. Most current motherboards do not included a built-in SCSI adapter, but fast PCI models provide excellent performance, with low latencies, full bus mastering, and plenty of bandwidth. Whether you need to add SCSI to your PC or update the aging SCSI adapter that's already there, you can buy the hardware from a number of vendors.

Fortunately, SCSI standards compliance has improved vastly since the late 1980s, and you can feel confident that the controller will work with your hardware. Adaptec, Promise Technology, Diamond Multimedia are just a few of the companies that sell SCSI host adapters for the PC market. These products include both the hardware and cabling needed for SCSI connections, as well as the SCSI management software and drivers.

10.4 Performance Tips and Tweaks

Because IDE and SCSI controllers work with a variety of device types, the relative performance you see over these interfaces can vary widely. Certainly, a fast, new hard disk is going to challenge the performance capabilities of IDE or SCSI more than a CD-ROM or tape backup drive. Still, there are things you can do to boost the performance of your existing IDE or SCSI controller.

10.4.1 IDE Tips

Here are a few tips to keep in mind when you're working with IDE controllers:

- If you have just two IDE devices, make sure to install them on separate IDE channels as master devices. On older motherboards, the built-in IDE controller is unable to provide concurrent access to two devices on the same channel, thus blocking access to the second (slave) device. By using two channels, you eliminate the possibility of blocked transfers.

- Consider a flash BIOS update if your system is more than a couple years old. An updated BIOS can enable hard disk geometry translation for addressing hard disks larger than 504MB. It can also allow access to more efficient LBA operation.

- If you have two hard disks and a CD-ROM drive on the ATA interface, set the two hard disks as the master devices on each channel. This ensures priority to the fast, magnetic disks. Then, place the CD-ROM drive as the slave device on the channel supporting the hard disk that's less performance critical. This will help minimize the possibility of slow downs on your primary hard disk drive.

- Get an ATA-4 controller. If your system doesn't support 33.3MBps burst mode, consider a product such as the Promise Technology DMA33, a PCI add-in card that complies to the ATA-4 specification.

- If you intend to upgrade to a hard disk larger than 8.4GB, make sure your system BIOS is capable of supporting the large-capacity device first. Older BIOSs lack the INT13 extensions that allow them to address capacity beyond 8.4GB. If this is your case, you'll need a third-party disk management utility to gain access to capacity beyond the 8.4GB limit.

10.4.2 SCSI Tips

Here are a few tips to keep in mind when you're working with SCSI controllers:

- Order your SCSI daisy chains such that the most performance-sensitive devices are placed closer to the controller. Also provide the lowest available ID numbers to these devices, because peripherals with lower ID numbers are accessed faster on the bus.

- Check for SCSI driver updates on occasion to make sure you're enjoying maximum benefit.

- If you're experiencing trouble or slow performance, try limiting your cable lengths. This can help reduce corrupted bits that can cause failures or require data to be sent multiple times.

- Speaking of cables, don't try to save too much money by going with cheap SCSI cables. Poor cables suffer from crosstalk, signal attenuation, and other problems that impact the performance and reliability of SCSI devices. Look for high-quality cables that will ensure consistent operation.

Disk Controllers

■ Lose IDE devices. If you have a SCSI controller installed, don't hesitate to dump your IDE devices. You're just asking for confusion by having two controllers running because they'll both want to tie up your PCI bus.

10.5 Tom's Pick

It's a funny position to be in, trying to pick a top controller when virtually all the IDE controller devices you'll ever see are built right into the motherboard and chipset. So this section will actually address two areas. I'll pick an IDE add-in controller (as opposed to the one that comes with the system), and I'll pick a SCSI controller.

Picking an Interface

But before I even do that, I do want to pick the best interface. And no surprise, it's SCSI. Despite the additional expense and somewhat smaller selection of peripherals, SCSI offers enough advantages over IDE that it remains the clear choice for power-minded users. No, IDE doesn't choke on multiple devices the way it used to. New ATA-33 compliant disks and interfaces, meanwhile, open the pipes for streaming media types like MPEG video. But SCSI still enjoys several important edges.

For one, SCSI's ability to reorder commands and data along the bus helps clear out logjams that can otherwise cause IDE processes to stall. And of course, SCSI offers a measure of flexibility and device support that IDE can't touch. External SCSI devices can be laid out in an easy-to-configure daisy chain, allowing users to run scanners, printers, hard disks, tape backup drives, and a variety of other drives from a single controller. Perhaps most important, SCSI helps relieve the resource crunch in your PC, since individual SCSI devices don't need a separate IRQ or DMA line to operation. Rather, the devices work within the SCSI bus structure, and allow the SCSI controller itself to interact with the PC.

Of course, not all types of SCSI are created equal. If you intend to use SCSI to run your hard disk drives, my recommendation is to go with at least an Ultra-Wide SCSI controller that is able to push 40 MBps of data. Anything slower than that, and you are limiting your PC's ability to efficiently transfer large files and rich media data. Better yet, check out the latest 80-MBps SCSI standard, sometimes called Ultra-Wide low voltage differential SCSI. Now you'll have bandwidth to spare for multiple hard disks and other drive types, though the limited cable lengths mandated by the faster SCSI clock may crimp your desktop layout.

Picking an IDE Controller

So which controllers are best? If you need to add an ATA-33 compliant controller to an aging PC, or if you simply wish to add more drives than the four allowed by your motherboard, consider a PCI-based controller add-in card. Promise Technology makes an intriguing ATA-33 adapter that costs just $79 and can put up to four ATA-33 compliant drives on a single card. The Ultra33 works side-by-side with your existing IDE interface to double the number of available IDE drives, terrific if you want to run tape drives and various CD-format drives off your system.

Promise also offers an intriguing IDE controller for RAID operation. The FastTrack IDE RAID adapter is a PCI card that allows you to run a pair of disks in a RAID configuration. At $149, the FastTrack is the least expensive RAID controller you can find, though performance won't match that of good SCSI RAID controllers. The controller supports a pair of ATA-33 hard disks and provides RAID Level 0 and RAID Level 1 capability.

Picking a SCSI Controller

When it comes to getting SCSI, you can't do better than with Adaptec. This company offers a wide array of SCSI controllers, ranging from simple ISA-based SCSI cards to sophisticated combo adapters that role SCSI, ethernet, and modems into a single PCB. But for a simple, effective, performance-ready SCSI controller, the Adaptec AHA-2940 Ultra Wide fits the bill. This $220 PCI controller moves 40 MBps of data over a fast and wide SCSI interface, allowing you to connect up to 15 devices.

Like all other Adaptec SCSI products, it comes with the company's EZ-SCSI management software, a useful suite of utilities for managing devices on the daisy chain. The board not only provides superior SCSI throughput. It supports efficient transfers of data and instructions through the use of features such as command queuing and scatter/gather DMA.

40MBps not enough for ya? Adaptec sells an Ultra2 version of the AHA-2940, called the AHA-2940U2W. This PCI boards costs about $410, but doubles the available bandwidth to 80MBps. Quite honestly, most people won't be able to find a use for this device, since few Ultra2 drives are out yet. But those who need certain bandwidth, such as video editors and 3D graphics designers and animators, will love the extra boost.

Chapter 11

Hard Disk Guide

The press goes on and on about Moore's Law and the continued multiplication of CPU processing power, but not much is said about hard disks. Yet, without the inexpensive and fast mass storage provided by these new hard disks, the personal computing revolution would be a flop. Superscalar 400MHz processors and advanced burst-mode RAM would be sucking air, limited to tiny data sets and simple programs that fit on smaller drives.

Fortunately, the folks at companies such as IBM, Seagate, Quantum, and Maxtor have been every bit as busy as those at Intel (if not as profitable). When Intel shipped its 486 CPU in 1989, the typical PC hard disk could hold 100MB and deliver average seek times several times slower than today's 9ms drives. Today, with Pentium II CPUs on systems large and small, 9GB drives—90 times the size of those old products—are standard issue. What's more, 18GB hard disks are already on the market, and even bigger units are on the way.

Most important, your hard disk can have a huge impact on the performance of your PC: The fact is that the rotating magnetic media of the hard disk is one of the severest performance bottlenecks, causing seconds-long delays while fat programs spin off the disk and into RAM. Whereas disk access times are measured in milliseconds, system RAM performance is counted in nanoseconds. Under-standing hard disk operation—and optimizing it—can eliminate teeth-grinding delays.

11.1 How Magnetic Hard Disks Work

The hard disk works a little like an old record player. Inside the drive, a series of platters are mounted one atop the other on a spindle. A motor on the spindle spins the platters so that a read/write head can detect or change patterns in the magnetic media of these platters. The head itself is positioned over the platters using an actuator. In most cases, the platters are made of a ceramic media—to avoid deformation during heating and cooling—with data stored in a layer of magnetic coating on the disk surface.

As you can tell, the term hard *disk* is somewhat misleading, because most hard disk drives really incorporate a number of disks. There are often two, three, or more platters in a disk drive, each with a pair of read/write heads—one posi-tioned above and one below—to access data. Although the operating system and applications see the collection of platters as a single logical drive, your data is actually spread across multiple physical disks.

Figure 11.1.

The read/write head and platter assemblies resemble a record player, but the drive components are designed to exacting tolerances.

The disk media rotates at a constant velocity, which is measured in revolutions per minute (rpm). A higher rpm yields the potential for higher data throughput and faster seek times, although a host of other issues—including drive interface, cache memory, and areal density—come into play. The read/write head, held by the actuator arm, floats just two to three microinches off the media and writes and reads data on the disk, sensing polarity changes in the magnetic layer to interpret 1 and 0 values. To write data, an electrical current is pushed through the head to create a recognizable pattern in magnetic media—again corresponding to a 1 or 0 value.

In the past, a step motor was used to position the read/write head over the desired section of the disk. Today, a servo motor moves the actuator arm, providing quicker response and, thus, faster performance. To retrieve or write data, the head is moved to the appropriate position on the disk, and then it waits for the specific bits to move under it as the disk rotates. The time spent moving the arm and waiting for data is called *latency* and is a key performance bottleneck in drive performance.

11.1.1 Disk Geometry

In order to enable quick access to data, hard disk drives are rigidly laid out into four types of segments: platters, cylinders, tracks, and sectors (see Figure 11.2).

Hard Disk Guide

Figure 11.2.

*Hard disk drives
actually consist of
a series of
vertically stacked
platters that are
segmented to
enable quick
access.*

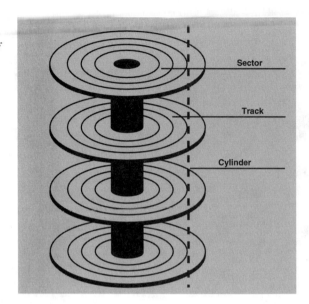

As discussed earlier, the platter is the component that contains the spinning media,
and it may be one of several platters mounted on the spindle inside the drive
casing. The platters are broken into cylinders, which are a series of concentric
rings that run vertically through all the disks. On each platter itself are thousands
of tracks. These concentric rings, which fall in line with the cylinder layout, play
an important role in finding data. When a piece of data is called for, the track
number allows the head to move to the point that will line it up with the
requested bits.

Each track on the disk is broken into a number of sectors, which vary in size
depending on where the track is located along the arc of the platter. This breakdown allows the read/write head to quickly move to the portion of the disk
containing the desired data, while at the same time presents a standard interface
readily addressable by the system BIOS and operating system.

Because the outer tracks are longer than the inner tracks, more sectors are found
to the outside of the disk than to the inside. The process of varying the number of
sectors on a track is called *zoned bit recording*, and it enables drives to take advantage of the fact that the outside of the disk travels faster than the inside. Because
sectors move more quickly beneath the read/write head along the outside edge,
you'll see better overall performance from programs and data loaded there.

By default, files are written first to the outer edge of the disk to take advantage of
this phenomenon. Windows 98 includes intelligent disk management that actually
reorders disk data based on usage patterns, moving the most-accessed data to the
outer edge. Likewise, program files and related data are placed contiguously to cut
down on excess head travel (which can cause throughput rates to plummet).

How much faster do things move on the outside edge of a disk? Well, that depends entirely on the disk geometry, areal density, spin rate, and a variety of other factors. However, you can expect the rate of data transfers to be nearly twice as fast at the outer edge of the disk than they are at the inside.

11.1.2 Disk Capacities

Today, most desktop hard drives use 3.5-inch platters, whereas notebooks use drives with 2.5- or even 1.8-inch platters. Although larger 5.25-inch platters can hold more data, the broader media presents a number of challenges. Larger disks are less reliable than smaller ones, in part because of stresses incurred on the expanded media space, as well as due to greater amounts of power required to spin the drive, which results in more heat. Larger platters also consume more space inside the PC. It's generally much more efficient for a drive maker to add platters than it is to use wider disk media—although additional platters do add to the cost and push the vertical height of the drive.

Figure 11.3.
Mobile hard disks, such as the Seagate Marathon, use smaller platters to fit within the space and power limitations of notebook PCs.

The key driver of disk capacity has been *areal density*, which defines the closeness of bits on the hard disk. Drive makers have made stunning advancements in their manufacturing processes, creating more sensitive media and read/write heads that can pack bits closely together. Read/write heads also must operate closer to (but not touch) the surface in order to read the tiny bits stored using ever-weaker electrical charges.

The payoff is two-fold. The dense bit structure increases capacity without adding to the number of platters, and it increases performance to boot. By putting more bits on the platter, more bits can move past the read/write head in the same amount of time. Because the bits are closer together, the head can get to locations on the disk more quickly.

Areal density is expressed in terms of *bits per square inch (bpsi)*. This figure is the product of two factors:

- Tracks per inch: The number of tracks—or concentric rings—found on one inch of disk media.

- Bits per inch: The number of individual bits found in one inch of track.

Multiply the number of tracks per inch by the number of bits per inch on a track, and you get the number of bits per square inch. All other things being equal, the drive with a higher bit density will provide higher throughput and better response than a drive with its bits placed farther apart.

Today, affordable IDE hard disks provide capacities of 9GB and higher. These drives use magneto-resistive (MR) heads to enable much tighter bit densities than possible with ferrite-style read/write heads. IBM's giant magneto-resistive (GMR) process will push those numbers up further still, with 16GB drives already hitting the market.

11.2 Performance Impact Report

Despite advances in performance and capacity, the hard disk continues to be a critical bottleneck in system performance. Operating systems and applications must often load tens of megabytes of data into RAM, which can take many seconds to complete, depending on the design of the drive and the location of the data. In addition, multitasking operating systems rely on the hard disk to hold inactive programs and data in virtual memory. When these bits are needed, there can be significant delays while data is retrieved from disk and placed into RAM.

In general, you'll get the best results from SCSI-based hard disks. Although various SCSI interface flavors can provide throughput ranging from 20MBps to 80MBps, the real benefit comes in multitasking. Unlike IDE, which can get bogged down when multiple IDE drives (CD-ROM, hard disk, tape, and high capacity floppy replacements) are being accessed, SCSI is able to multitask cleanly. The higher potential throughput rates of SCSI also raise the performance ceiling.

With that said, new IDE-based drives—specifically those based on ATA-33 (a.k.a. ultra DMA)—deliver the bits nearly as quickly as the fastest SCSI interfaces. Not only are throughputs higher (from 16MBps to 33MBps) due to the use of direct memory access, but the elimination of CPU involvement in transactions improves the multitasking capability of these drives. ATA-33 drives remain less expensive than their SCSI cousins, due to the use of integrated electronics.

Within a general drive class, however, you're unlikely to see big differences in system performance. A pair of ATA-33 drives in the same price range and class, for example, will result in system performance within a percentage point of each other. Therefore, once you decide on a drive type and capacity, you're usually best off going with the vendor you're most comfortable with. Price, service, warranty, and perceived reliability should all weigh heavily in your decision-making once you've narrowed your technology options down.

11.3 Currently Available Hard Disks

When picking a hard disk, you can choose from among several general categories. In addition to the IDE and SCSI interfaces, so-called *A/V hard disks* can optimize throughputs for video capture and other intensive streaming media operations. RAID drive arrays, meanwhile, provide critical redundancy for network servers, as well as the ability to cut down latency. Finally, solid-state drives—essentially super-charged flash memory devices—can hold upward of a gigabyte of data on superfast, silicon-based media.

11.3.1 Enhanced IDE

The most popular disk drives today are those that use integrated drive electronics, or *IDE*. The vast majority of disk drives are so-called *ATA-3 enhanced IDE drives*, which can move up to 16MBps of data, or *ATA-33 ultra DMA drives*, which can transfer 33MBps. Both these drive types integrate the controlling electronics directly on the drive, thus reducing cost and obviating the need for a separate adapter card. As shown in Figure 11.4, these drives plug into the enhanced IDE connector found on most motherboards, making installation and support extremely easy.

Hard Disk Guide

Figure 11.4.

The standard pinout and jumper configurations for IDE drives is shown in this schematic of the Seagate ST9051 drive.

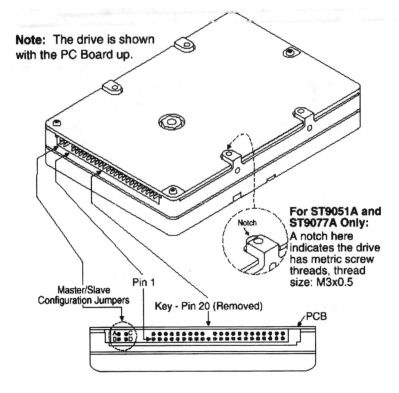

Note: The drive is shown with the PC Board up.

For ST9051A and ST9077A Only:
A notch here indicates the drive has metric screw threads, thread size: M3x0.5

Notch

Master/Slave Configuration Jumpers

Pin 1

Key - Pin 20 (Removed)

PCB

::	Drive is Master, no Slave drive present
:▪	Drive is Master, Seagate Slave drive present
▪:	Drive is Slave to another ST9144 Family Master
⠿	Reserved Positions (Do Not Use)

The main drawbacks of IDE are the relatively low throughput ceiling and their inability to multitask drives. This second problem is becoming more of a concern as different drive types start to pile on the IDE bus. CD-ROM, DVD-ROM, tape backup, and floppy drives all use the integrated IDE facilities found on most motherboards, thus increasing the chance that your critical hard disk data could get caught in a data traffic jam.

New ATA-33 (or ultra DMA) drives limit many of these concerns. ATA-33 data rates are competitive with all but the fastest SCSI implementations, and the DMA capability reduces CPU overhead. Advancements in system BIOS and IDE logic have also reduced limitations imposed by multiple drives on the IDE bus, further enhancing the attractiveness of these drives.

Of course, the integrated IDEs connected on older motherboards lack ATA-33 capability. You'll either have to upgrade the motherboard to one that supports this technology or purchase a PCI add-in card, such as the TK Promise Ultra33 TK, which provides an ATA-33 interface for your devices. Note that an ATA-33 drive plugged into an ATA-3 enhanced IDE connector will still work, but it will drop down to the PIO mode 4 support, which limits data rates to 16MBps.

11.3.2 SCSI

If you need to break a hard disk bottleneck, SCSI (which stands for *Small Computer System Interface*) is the way to do it. With 40MBps and now 80MBps data throughputs becoming common, SCSI drives can ably serve up data for video, network access, and other multimedia applications. SCSI's multitasking talents also make it well suited for users accessing multiple media types, because the bus is able to maintain effective performance where IDE falls flat. This is most critical in multiple hard disk situations, because each hard disk is capable of flooding the bus with data.

Unfortunately, you pay for SCSI. The discreet electronics and generally higher-end nature of SCSI drives serve to drive up the price on these units. Expect to pay $150 to $400 more for a SCSI drive than for an equal-capacity IDE model. For many users, the extra money will not deliver a significant performance impact, particularly because ultra DMA has helped to close the throughput gap between SCSI and IDE.

What's more, SCSI can spell trouble for less adept users, as shown in Figure 11.5. First, few motherboards include a built-in SCSI port, in part because of rapid-fire updates of the specification. You'll probably have to purchase a PCI add-in card with an internal and an external back plane SCSI port. Second, configuring and managing SCSI devices can be difficult, particularly if you have a mix of internal and external peripherals running off a SCSI daisy chain. Device termination, ID assignments, SCSI drivers, and other issues can all complicate matters.

Hard Disk Guide

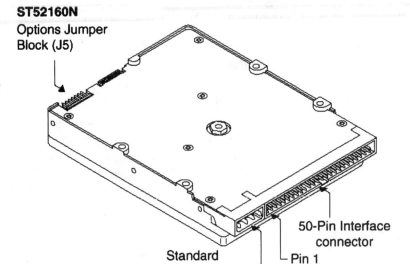

ST52160N
Options Jumper
Block (J5)

Standard
power connector

50-Pin Interface
connector

Pin 1

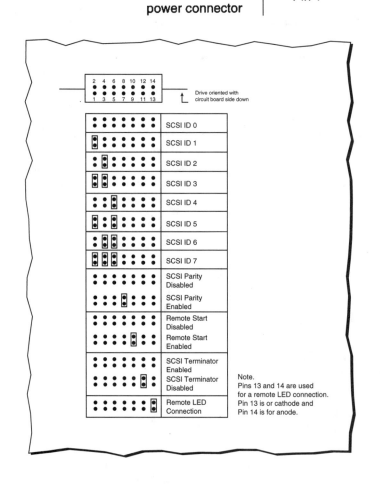

Multimedia professionals, software engineers, and network administrators will all want SCSI hard disks. Also, anyone who wants to gets maximum performance out of multiple hard disks should consider going the SCSI route. Also, SCSI is your only performance-minded drive alternative if you want to use external hard disk drives, because the IDE specification does not address grounding and other electrical issues encountered with external devices.

Keep in mind that if you decide to install a SCSI hard disk, you are best off avoiding the IDE bus altogether. That means you may want to also purchase SCSI versions of CD-ROM drives and other products whenever possible.

11.3.3 A/V Models

A/V hard disks get their name because they're widely used by video editors for capturing analog video to disk. Video capture is an extremely demanding task, requiring an uncompromised stream of data through the bus and to the disk. For this reason, all A/V hard disks are SCSI-based models—IDE simply cannot ensure this type of data delivery.

An A/V disk differs from a standard SCSI disk in that the internal housekeeping mechanism of the device has been shut off. Most notably, all standard drives pause occasionally to conduct *thermal calibration*, a process by which the drive measures the media area in order to compensate for disk expansion that occurs due to heating during operation. Thermal calibration ensures that the drive head can still find addressed data even when the media has shifted enough to otherwise throw it off. In addition, these drives ship with SCSI mode page parameters that are optimized for recording long, sequential files, which results in degraded random access performance. The result: A/V drives are subpar general-purpose storage devices.

A/V drives take a calculated risk by switching off thermal calibration, because an overheated drive could expand enough to confuse the drive head. In effect, the head might have a correct address, but when it gets to the proper neighborhood, it finds that all the streets have moved. This can result in loss of data—sometimes just temporarily, until the disk cools down and the head can get its bearings again.

A/V drive performance can vary depending on the configuration set by the manufacturer. Also, the drives are not recommended for use for normal data operations, because the data on the drive itself could become compromised. It's generally a good idea to keep your operating system, applications, and crucial data on a second, non-A/V drive and use the A/V model only for capture tasks.

Hard Disk Guide

11.3.4 RAID Drive Arrays

RAID is an industry standard that stands for *redundant array of inexpensive disks*. There are five RAID specifications, which, in no particular order, address issues of data integrity and performance. Although RAID products are sold as a unit, the disks themselves are simply standard SCSI disks partnered using dedicated RAID electronics.

There are several elements to raid operation. *Disk striping* enhances performance by distributing data reads and writes across several disks, thus reducing the impact seek time delays when transferring data. *Disk mirroring* and *duplexing* provide data protection by writing redundant data to separate disks—in other words, if a disk should fail, the same data is available on another disk in the array. *Error-correcting code (ECC)*, on the other hand, provides data protection by creating a checksum based on the data on the disk. The checksum detects errors immediately and can even serve to restore limited amounts of lost data.

Here are the six levels of RAID operation:

- RAID 0: Disk striping without parity

- RAID 1: Disk mirroring or duplexing

- RAID 2: Disk striping with error-correcting code (ECC)

- RAID 3: Disk ECC stored as parity

- RAID 4: Disk striping with large blocks

- RAID 5: Disk striping with parity

Historically, the problem with RAID is that it has been expensive—an array often costs $10,000 or more. However, for network servers, Web servers, and mission-critical workstations, the technology is a vital defense against data loss. Disk striping, meanwhile, helps boost performance for disk-bound applications. More recently, low-cost RAID hardware provides RAID 0 and RAID 1 operation for under $1,000. These products allow you to boost performance using RAID 0 striping to cut down on delays due to seek times and rotational latency. You can even get a RAID controller for IDE drives in the form of the Promise FastTrack, which costs just $149.

11.3.5 A Word about Floppy Disk Drives

The 1.44MB floppy disk drive has been a staple on *x*86-compatible PCs for nearly a decade. However, the dwindling utility of the disk capacity, coupled with glacial performance, has prompted a spate of floppy wannabes. This transition could take years, though, as vendors jostle for position and market share.

Inside the Floppy Drive

The floppy drive works similarly to a hard disk drive in that a read/write head is positioned above a spinning, magnetically charged medium to interpret 1s and 0s into meaningful data. However, where hard disk read/write heads float just above the surface of the disk, floppy drives use a pair of spring-loaded read/write heads that grip the disk surface on both sides. The constant contact results in a good deal of wear and tear, and it exacerbates the reliability problems floppies suffer from due to exposure to dirt and other contaminants.

Floppy drive performance is truly abysmal. The controller itself is limited to no more than 1Mbps in the case of newer devices, whereas those sold before about 1995 can support 500Kbps. However, the fact is, neither of these limits really bottleneck floppy disk throughput, because mechanically the media just can't deliver bits that fast. However, performance does become an issue with tape backup drives that use the floppy disk controller—a handy cost saving measure, particularly because every PC has a floppy controller. In these cases, the controllers have a hard time enabling quick backups.

Performance is further limited by huge latencies in accessing data on floppy disks. It can take a second or longer for a floppy drive to respond to a simple directory update, and the update itself can take several seconds. In fact, floppy disk access is orders of magnitude slower than hard disk access.

Of course, the floppy drive plays an important role as a bootable device on any system. During system conflicts, the ability to boot from a floppy is critical. The boot characteristics are typically accessed from the BIOS, where you'll find floppy-centric controls such as these:

- Boot sequence control: Lets you change the order of drives accessed during bootup. Useful for avoiding accidental infection by viruses resident in the floppy boot sector.

- Floppy drive seek: Turning this option off will cause the system not to access the floppy during boot time—effectively eliminating its use as a boot device. This can help eliminate virus infection.

- Swap floppy drives: On systems with two floppy drives, this switches the A and B designation between the two.

Floppy Drive Alternatives

With their abysmal performance, low capacities, and legendary unreliability, 3.5-inch floppy disks and drives are a fading breed. Already, Iomega's 100MB Zip format has emerged on many systems as the successor to the floppy disk. It's performance is many times that of floppies, and the capacity is enough even for spot backup duty. Perhaps most important, key system vendors such as Dell, Gateway, and Micron all sell Iomega Zip drives as standard or optional equipment on their higher-end PCs.

However, other options are out there. Sony's HiFD specification employs larger and faster 200MB cartridges and costs about the same as Zip. What's more, HiFD drives can read current 3.5-inch floppies, something that Zip won't do. Because Sony helped establish the current 3.5-inch diskette standard, you have to like this format's chances for becoming a market standard. The main issue? HiFD arrives two years after Iomega Zip.

Longer on the market is the LS-120 format, now commonly called *SuperDisk*. Promoted by Compaq, Matsushita, 3M, and others, SuperDisk drives have appeared in Compaq and HP systems. They pack 120MB of data on a disk, and the drives can read and write floppy diskettes just like HiFD can. However, Compaq's involvement in the SuperDisk effort seems to have scared away competing system vendors.

More recently, cheap gigabyte drives have emerged. SyQuest's Sparq packs one gig of data on a removable cartridge and provides superior performance to competing formats. At $299, the drive is a bit expensive; however, SyQuest is a proven name in the storage business, which should help. Newer still is the Orb drive from Castlewood Systems, which, at 2GB, promises fast, cheap, and plentiful storage, although drives were unavailable at the time of this writing.

In all cases, you'll need to make sure that the drive you select to succeed your floppy can take over boot operation. Otherwise, you could be without a way to restart your system should your hard disk go south. It's a good idea to check your BIOS version to make sure it supports bootable IDE devices before you rip out that floppy drive.

11.4 Evaluating Hard Disks

A lot of factors impact hard disk performance, and you need to consider them all when looking for optimal performance. Perhaps most important, you need to buy not just for your current storage needs, but for what you think you'll need a year or so down the line. With hard disk capacities growing so quickly, and applications and file sizes growing to match, it's not unusual to run out of space within 18 months of a hard disk purchase.

Of course, you want to get as much performance out of the disk subsystem as you can, but you'll have to balance that benefit with price. A striped RAID drive, for example, will deliver great results but at a cost of thousands of dollars. An 8GB ATA-33 hard disk, meanwhile, can be had for $299 and will deliver perfectly good performance for the vast majority of users.

What should you look for when buying a new hard disk? This section will provide insights to help you avoid trouble.

11.4.1 Size, Size, Size

Without question, data capacity is the overriding concern of any hard disk purchase. With programs, files, and operating systems growing every year, and Web-based data pouring in at an unchecked clip, a large hard disk is the only defense against quick obsolescence. You'll find the most bits for the buck with enhanced IDE drives, but large-capacity SCSI drives can be had for a couple hundred dollars more.

Disk capacity is determined by several key criteria: Disk area, areal density, and the number of platters. The disk area is simply the size of the media surface. Although most desktop drives are 3.5 inches across—down from 5.25 inches in early drives—the use of multiple platters within the drive housing more than makes up for the lost area. Why not just use multiple, 5.25-inch platters? The extreme precision of current drives makes the larger platters inefficient, because they require more power and are more subject to failure than more compact drives.

As mentioned earlier, increases in areal density is the driving force behind higher hard disk capacities. Lighter, quicker, and more sensitive read and write heads allow for magnetic points to be pushed closer together on the media. Both the number of bits in a linear inch and the number of tracks in a linear inch have increased, yielding big jumps in capacity.

Today's high-end drives feature areal densities in excess of 7,000 megabits per square inch, allowing 1GB of data to be stored on a single platter. By the year 2000, a single 3.5-inch platter is expected to hold over 4.3GB of data, thus enabling a typical hard disk to provide 16GB of storage.

The number of platters simply refers to the number of disks built inside the drive. Although notebook computers, with their compact form factors, are often limited to hard drives with a single disk inside, desktop models can afford the room to use multidisk hard drives. In effect, the multiple disks increase the available surface area, enabling higher data capacities.

So, how much hard disk do you need? As much as you can get, really. I bought a 486 system with a 345MB hard disk and figured that was the end of it. Surely, no reasonable mix of applications and operating systems could fill up that vast storage resource. However, I hadn't counted on Windows 95, Office 95, Office 97, 20MB Web browsers, and all that Internet data. I was young, foolish, and it was 1994. Today, 8GB hard disks are cheap, fast, and a good minimum for any serious computer user.

Hard Disk Guide

BIOS Limitations

Just because a 10GB IDE hard disk costs $300, don't assume you can use it. Older BIOSs often won't recognize more than the first 2GB, or sometimes even the first 512MB, of the disk. Try to install a gargantuan disk into your aging PC and you could be wasting a lot of money (as well as bits).

There are three capacity barriers to worry about:

- 504MB

- 2GB

- 8GB

The 8GB Limitation

The problem arises from the Int13h software interrupt used by the BIOS to handle all disk accesses. This interrupt allocates 24 bits to map out the hard disk's physical geometry. Unfortunately, when the resources for Int13h were minted, no one considered multigigabyte hard disks as even a remote possibility, and as a result, there are far to few bits to address larger drives.

Geometry Element	Bits Used	Number Recognized
Cylinders	10	1,024
Heads	256	8
Sectors	63	6

Do the math and you'll find that multiplying the number of sectors by the number of heads and then cylinders yields a little more than 16.5 million available sectors. Each sector holds 512KB of data; multiply again and you'll find that Int13h can't address more than about 8GB of data. Windows 95 gets around this by bypassing Int13h altogether, using its own 32-bit protected-mode access scheme. Extensions for the Int13h resource are being developed to enable full BIOS-level access to larger hard disks.

The 504MB Limitation

The 504MB limit also occurs because of the BIOS, but the situation is exacerbated by interaction with the IDE specification. IDE specifies resources for the same cylinder, head, and sector elements found in the BIOS, but it uses different maximums. The problem is that IDE allows for only 16 heads (versus Int13h's 256), effectively cutting available disk space by a factor of 16.

Obviously, some solution was worked out, because 500MB hard disks are utterly obsolete. In fact, a scheme called *BIOS translation* is used to play a shell game with the cylinder, head, and sector resources. This approach tricks the operating system into thinking the disk has more heads and fewer cylinders than it actually does. When a disk transaction comes in, the BIOS translates the juggled resources so that they fit within the Int13h limits. The software knows no better, and the overhead involved is minor.

Most BIOSs that employ translation use the Logical Block Addressing (LBA) scheme to map sectors. Rather than track separate cylinders, heads, and sectors, the disk is expressed in terms of sector addresses only, with each sector having a unique number ID.

The 2GB Limitation

As if all the BIOS problems weren't enough, disk makers had to contend with the limitations of the mainstream file system of the day—FAT16. Used for Windows 95, Windows 3.*x*, and DOS, FAT16 is unable to address more than 2GB of data in a single drive letter. Larger drives must be broken into drive letter partitions, each of less than 2GB in capacity, in order to gain access to the entire volume.

The FAT32 file system used in Windows 98 and OSR 2.1 and later versions of Windows 95 addresses this limitation. Although Microsoft talks about faster application load times with FAT32, the real reason for its creation was to break the capacity bottleneck. Microsoft's other file system, NTFS (used with Windows NT), also does not suffer from the 2GB limitation.

Actual Space

Here's a final note to keep in mind: The specific capacity of a hard disk can be a very slippery number. Vendors sometimes overstate capacities by marketing disks on the assumption that there are one million bytes in a megabyte and one billion bytes in a gigabyte. In fact, there are 1,048,576 bytes in a megabyte and 1,073,741,824 bytes in a gigabyte. On a drive marketed at 4.3GB, you may find that the vendor means that there are 4.3 billion bytes of capacity, when in fact there should be 4.617 billion bytes. That's nearly 300MB of lost space.

The slipperiness continues when you format a drive, because system files, cluster slack, and other variables can all reduce the available space. What's more, use three different utilities to read hard disk capacity, and you'll likely get three different answers.

11.4.2 Performance Specs

When researching a disk drive purchase, you'll encounter an impressive array of performance specifications that define everything from the speed of disk rotation to the relative quickness of a bit access. These numbers can certainly be helpful in your search, although you need to consider that even a highly rated drive can't make up for a cumbersome file system or an aging interface to the system.

Hard Disk Guide

Here are the major specifications to look for:

- Rotation speed
- Seek time
- Head switch time
- Cylinder switch time
- Rotational latency
- Data access time

One interesting note is that the specifications can be affected as much by the design of the drive as they are by the layout of data on the disk. Even the fastest disk won't provide optimal performance if related files are scattered in bits and chunks across several tracks, sectors, and platters. Windows 95 and 98 include the Disk Defragmenter utility, which lets you push data together on the media in order to reduce the amount of time the read/write head spends traveling.

What's more, Windows 98 takes a cue from acceleration programs such as Dtime95 and DiskSpeed by optimizing application launches. The OS profiles application launches and events as well as arrays data on the disk to optimize accesses to files needed during the setup. The results can be impressive—launch files are lined up contiguously, eliminating slack time accrued when the read/write head dances around for needed files. Be aware that only application launches are affected—the optimization in no way improves general disk performance.

Rotation Speed

Rotation speed is critical to the transfer rate of a hard drive. The faster the media spins, the quicker bits traverse beneath the read/write head, and the faster data can be accessed or written. Typical hard disks have a rotation speed ranging between 4,500rpm to 7,200rpm, and drives as fast as 10,000rpm exist on the market.

Although the rotation speed of hard disks is constant—known as *constant linear velocity*—the rate at which data is read at different points on the disk changes, because the outside of the disk is always moving faster than the inside. As a result, transfer rates along the outer edge will always be higher than along the inner edge. To take advantage of this behavior, programs and data are always written first to the outermost tracks and then filled in from there.

> **TIP** Windows 98 lets you optimize disk performance by moving the most often accessed data to the outer portion of the media. The Disk Performance utility tracks your usage and then reshuffles the data on disk accordingly. Moving program application code to the outer rim of the disk can yield significant decreases in application launch times, because a lot of time is spent waiting for data to move from the hard disk to RAM.

High rotation speeds do present a problem, because they run both louder and hotter than a typical hard drive. You may need to cool a 7,200rpm disk with an extra fan to prevent chronic thermal stress from shortening its operating life. Because current hard drives read all sectors of a track in a single turn (called, *interleave 1:1*), a faster rotating drive is able to move to and read or write data more quickly. However, fast-rotation speed disks also draw more power, making them inadvisable for notebooks.

High rotation speeds do not translate into better overall performance. Seek times, by far the most critical element of hard disk performance, is only marginally affected by the speed of rotation (in effect, bits can race get under the head more quickly). Quicker response demands better performance from the drive head and its actuator arm. Still, all other things being equal, you should look for a drive with the highest rotation speed you can get, because it will have the potential to provide the best throughput.

Seek Time, Head Switch Time, and Cylinder Switch Time

A lot of things can affect seek time, but the most critical is the positioning of data on the disk. Moving from one track to the next produces the quickest seek time (as low as 2ms), whereas a so-called *full stroke*—where the head must traverse the distance between the outermost and innermost tracks—results in seek times of about 20ms. Because data on hard disks is almost always scattered across tracks, the ability of your drive to quickly get to a specific point on the media is critical. Good hard drive designs can cut seek times and boost performance.

The seek time spec you see most often is the average seek time, which measures the time (in milliseconds) it takes to position the drive's heads for a randomly located request. A typical enhanced IDE hard drive might boast a seek time of 9ms, although some can manage times as low as 6ms. It doesn't sound like much, but we're talking about a difference of 30 percent! Add up millions and billions of individual seek operations, and the quicker drive can make a difference. Note that the performance gap is narrowing, and that today's affordable IDE drives provide a much better performance value than those available five years ago.

Another important spec is *head switch time*. This measures the average time it takes to switch between two heads when reading or writing data. This specification is critical because most desktop hard drives include multiple disk platters, each of which is usually served by a pair of heads (one on top and one on bottom). It's not at all unusual for data reads and writes to jump across platters, so any delays in this operation can mount into a performance drag.

Finally, *cylinder switch time* is the average time it takes to move the heads to the next track when reading or writing data. All these times are measured in milliseconds (ms).

Rotational Latency

Rotational latency combines the two ideas we've just discussed—disk rotation speed and average seek time. Latency measures the time the read/write head must wait for the right sector to arrive after the head has positioned itself over the desired track. Therefore, the faster the spin rate, the quicker sectors will come around, and the shorter the rotational latency (in ms). The average rotational latency is defined as the time the disk needs to turn half way around, usually about 4ms on a 7200rpm drive and 6ms on a 5400rpm drive.

One trick that disk drive makers employ is *head skewing*, where contiguous data is arrayed on different platters in such a way that the beginning of the second data set is located behind in the rotation from the end of the first data set. Therefore, when the read/write head on one platter is done reading, the head on the other platter is in position to pick up the needed data just as it arrives underneath. By intelligently arraying data on the disk this way, the drive cuts down on the amount of time spent waiting for the media to spin beneath the heads.

Data Access Time

Combine seek, head switch, and rotational latency times, and you end up with the data access time, measured in milliseconds. As you now know, seek time only tells you about how fast the head is positioned over a wanted cylinder. Until data is read or written, you'll have to add the head switch time for finding the track and also the rotational latency time for finding the wanted sector. In general, data access time is the best measure of expected disk/head performance, because it accounts for variables such as drive size (3.5 or 5.25 inches), multiple platters, and read/write head performance. The best drives offer access times below 7ms.

11.4.3 IDE Specifications

Performance specs, such as the ones discussed earlier, mainly dwell on the ability of the read/write head to locate and retrieve data from the spinning media. However, the interface between the drive and the system is a critical one; it affects the ability of the drive to move chunks of data quickly to system RAM.

With IDE drives dominating the market, manufacturers have looked for ways to break through the severe limitations IDE imposes on performance. CPU overhead, for example, dragged down both disk and overall system performance on IDE drives. Likewise, low data rates meant that video playback and large file transfers took much more time than might be expected based on areal densities and disk rotation speeds.

The IDE interface has undergone a steady and impressive run of enhancements, culminating with the ATA-33 (or ultra DMA) specification that's now employed on most new disk drives. As a result, SCSI drives have been pushed to a more marginal segment of the market. Unless you're into multimedia producing, need to use a RAID drive array, or want to use external disk drives, chances are a new IDE disk drive, such as the one shown in Figure 11.6, is up to the task.

Figure 11.6.
Seagate's IDE-based Medallist drive includes documentation for setting IDE channel and master/slave settings on the drive housing.

There are several flavors of disk drive access with hard disks. To learn more about the ATA/IDE specifications, see Chapter 10, "Disk Controllers." Table 11.1 shows the various standards for PC-centric hard disks.

Table 11.1. PC-centric hard disk interface standards have grown to meet the performance and affordability demands of the market.

Standard	Description
ST-506/ST-412	Used in the early 1980s; sometimes called *RLL* or *MFM*. ST-506/ST412 suffered from slow performance and reliability problems and is now obsolete.
ESDI	Enhanced Small Device Interface. Used in mid 1980s, ESDI is now obsolete.
IDE/ATA	First Integrated Drive Electronics standard; performance limited to 5MBps.
ATA-2 (enhanced IDE)	Added multiple channels, better performance, and extensions for other internal storage devices via ATAPI specification.
ATA-3	Added reliability and diagnostic tweaks to ATA-2.
ATA-33 (ultra DMA)	Introduced in 1997. DMA transfers increased throughput from 16MBps to 33MBps.

11.4.4 Cache

Like CPUs, hard drives employ their own cache, or *buffer*, which speeds performance by storing frequently used data in a small amount of fast memory. Also like CPUs, it's not simply the cache size that matters, but rather the organization of the cache itself (*write/read cache* or *look-ahead cache*).

On SCSI hard drives, you may have to enable write caching, because vendors often disable it, by default, reducing the performance upside of the fast memory. You can check the hard drive cache status with a program such as ASPIID from Seagate. Most SCSI hard drives ship with a minimum of 512KB (although some of that may be used for the "firmware"). Some SCSI drives ship with 1,024KB or more. Most IDE drives, meanwhile, usually come with only 128KB of cache memory onboard, although the better ones have 256KB or 512KB of cache.

Of course, many operating systems dedicate system RAM to act as a hard disk cache. Windows 95 dynamically allocates RAM to store frequently requested disk data, often consuming tens of megabytes of RAM to this purpose. The payoff can be significant, particularly in systems with 32MB or 64MB of RAM. RAM accesses are tens or even hundreds of times faster than hard disk accesses, resulting in big performance gains.

With most enhanced IDE drives, the PC's system memory is also used to store the hard drive's firmware (the software that defines the drive's basic interactions and operation). When the drive powers up, the firmware code is read from special sectors and transferred to system RAM. Manufacturers save money by eliminating the need for separate ROM chips to store the firmware code. In addition, it allows you to easily update the drive "BIOS," if necessary. For example, some Western Digital drives experienced conflicts with certain motherboards, resulting in head crashes. A quick software-based firmware update fixed the problem.

11.4.5 Read/Write Head Technology

The type of read/write head used on a hard disk drive can have a huge impact on both performance and capacity. Five major technologies exist in the market:

- Ferrite heads

- Metal-in-gap (MIG) heads

- Thin film (TF) heads

- Magneto-resistive (MR) heads

- Giant magneto-resistive (GMR) heads

Ferrite read/write heads are obsolete today. Based on a U-shaped iron core, a ferrite head uses opposing charges in the two ends to read and write data to and from disk. Ferrite heads have the disadvantage of being heavy and bulky, making them hard to move quickly. They must also travel relatively far from the disk media, thus impairing their ability to read tightly packed bits. Metal-in-gap heads improve upon ferrite heads by using an alloy that greatly enhances the magnetic sensitivity of the read/write head.

Disk drive performance and capacities got a real boost with the arrival of thin film heads, which consist of coated wafers similar in design to semiconductors. The patterned alloy coating on the head enables extremely sensitive detection of magnetic fields on a compact and lightweight device. Disk drives of up to 1GB capacities and beyond use thin film heads.

Today, the most popular head technology is the magneto-resistive (MR) head, which is actually a dedicated read-only head that requires a separate thin film mechanism for handling writing duties. The MR head is charged with a constant current that reacts to magnetic fields in the disk media. The head detects changes in resistance by fluctuations in the amperage of the current, which are interpreted as 1 and 0 values. MR heads are extremely light and fast, enabling much higher areal densities. This is in part a benefit of the dedicated read-only design.

Most recently, IBM announced its giant magneto-resistive (GMR) technology. Improved detection in the read head enables lower magnetization of the disk media, in turn, enabling more closely packed bits. GMR head disks can pack 16GB of data or more.

11.4.6 Organization of Data

As you know, a hard disk includes cylinders, heads, and sectors. If you look in your BIOS, you'll find these three values listed for each hard disk in your computer. Unlike early drives, these are not fixed values.

Today, these values are only used for compatibility with DOS, because they have nothing to do with the physical geometry of the drive. The hard disk calculates these values into a logical block address (LBA); then this LBA value is converted into the real cylinder, head, and sector values. Modern BIOSs are able to use LBA, so limitations such as the 504MB barrier have been eliminated.

Cylinder, head, and sector addresses are still used in IDE drives in DOS environments, whereas SCSI drives have always used LBA to access data on the hard disk. Modern operating systems access data via LBA directly without using the BIOS, thus reducing incompatibilities.

One critical issue that can impact drive performance is the mapping scheme used when writing data on disk. There are three approaches:

- Vertical mapping: Data is written to the outermost cylinder first, writing from the top track to the bottom, before moving inward to the next cylinder.

- Horizontal mapping: Data is written first to the outermost track of the top platter and then to contiguous tracks moving inward. When the platter is full, the drive drops to the next platter and writes from the inside out.

- Combination mapping: Within the sector zone of each cylinder (a subset of tracks with same-sized sectors), the drive uses the vertical mapping technique. Between sector zones, it moves back to the top platter of the next sector zone and resumes vertical mapping.

Vertical mapping is the most common approach among hard drives, because it attempts to keep as much data as possible pushed to the outer edge of the disk (where data rates are highest). This approach is best for video playback and large file operations. Some drives combine horizontal and vertical mapping to try to boost seek times, because these operations take longer at this largest area of the disk. Mapping schemes are designed into disks, so you may want to inquire about this issue when comparing disks.

Figure 11.7.
The various mapping techniques impact performance in different ways.

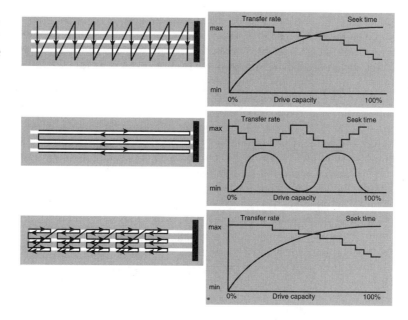

11.4.7 Media Reliability

High-capacity hard disks rely on precision manufacturing to deliver performance and storage. The read/write head on new disk typically rides a scant one to three microinches above the disk surface. Even a slight deviation in the head's flight path can result in a catastrophic crash, because the impact of the head into the disk surface would likely gouge out a portion of the media, resulting in lost data.

Despite the precise tolerances, disk drives are more reliable than ever before. Early PCs suffered from frequent disk crashes and data loses, and the drives often failed after just a few years of operation. Today's drives, by contrast, generally run until they're simply obsolete due to growing performance and capacity needs.

A popular measure of projected reliability is *mean time between failure (MTBF)*. This specification, expressed in hours of operation, is determined by taking the total number of hours of disk operation observed by the manufacturer and dividing that by the number of failures that occurred. A few years back, a typical drive was rated for 100,000 hours of active operation, whereas many new drives are rated to run for 300,000 hours—that's 34 *years* of nonstop operation.

Keep in mind that the MTBF spec in no way implies a warranty on the device. By definition, the mean time specification indicates that half the drives in the field will fail *before* the determined number of hours. Still, a higher MTBF number can be taken as an indicator of greater reliability—just don't weigh it too heavily.

Hard Disk Guide

A far more relevant measure of probable reliability is the vendor's warranty policy. A high MTBF doesn't mean much if the vendor won't back it up with a long three-year warranty and 30-day money-back guarantee. This is your best assurance that a drive will work for as long as you need it.

Of course, no drive will work long if it's abused. Moving or knocking your system while the drive is working can cause the read/write head to crash into the media surface, destroying data and disabling your PC. One thing to avoid is sliding a PC across a surface, because the resonant vibration of pushing the rubber feet causes the read/write head to pitch wildly. This is virtually a surefire way to destroy a working hard disk drive.

11.4.8 Focus on File Systems

Regardless of what kind of hard disk you have, you'll need to face the file system question. Microsoft's dueling OSs—Windows 95/98 and Windows NT—use different schemes for accessing data on hard disks, which means you have to make some decisions. The file system is the scheme used to turn the magnetic media of the hard disk into a navigable space that can hold data. Without a file system in place, the operating system would be unable to tell where files begin or end, not to mention being unable to find specific tracks or sectors.

There are three primary Windows-based file systems:

- FAT16

- FAT32

- NTFS

FAT16

FAT16 is the same file system used for DOS and Windows 3.x. It's also the only file system that's recognized by all versions of Windows, as well as by OS/2. For this reason, FAT16 is often used on dual-boot computers—such as my Windows 98/Windows NT dual-bootable Pentium II-300.

Unfortunately, FAT16 is getting long in the tooth and is unable to easily recognize the large hard disks common even on low-cost systems these days. Specifically, FAT16 can only address a maximum of 2GB of data on each logical drive. If you have a 4GB hard drive, you must partition the drive (using FDISK or some other utility) into two separate, logical drives in order to access the entire 4GB. With hard disks heading toward 11GB and 12GB sizes, before long we'll simply run out of letters to use for our drive assignments!

What's worse, the sectoring scheme that FAT16 employs can waste a lot of real estate. You see, FAT16 breaks drive sectors into clusters, which range in size from an efficient 2KB to a wasteful 32KB as the partition size grows. The problem is that files must be assigned an entire cluster, so even the smallest 1-bit file will consume anywhere from 2KB to 32KB of disk space. Larger files consume as many whole clusters as is needed to contain the data, with the last cluster possibly containing unused, or *slack*, disk space. Table 11.2 shows the breakdown of cluster sizes based on the size of the disk partition.

Table 11.2. FAT16 serves up the slack when drive sizes move to a gigabyte and beyond.

Partition size	Cluster size
16MB to 128MB	2KB
128MB to 256MB	4KB
256MB to 512MB	8KB
512MB to 1GB	16KB
1GB to 2GB	32KB

If you have a lot of small files on your disk, a good deal of the magnetic media is actually being used to store, well, nothing. With hard disks so large, slack becomes a growing problem on systems using the FAT32 file system.

FAT32

Enter FAT32. Introduced with Windows 95 OSR2, the FAT32 file system is able to address disk partitions up to 4TB in size. Although you can certainly still partition your drive as you wish—whether you host another OS or create a logical division for data and application files—you're able to see the entire drive on a single drive letter. FAT32 also addresses the slack problem, by reducing the minimum cluster size from 32KB to 16KB.

FAT32 provides a few other key advantages to Windows 95 and Windows 98 users. For one thing, the file system is intelligent; it tracks file accesses to determine optimal performance. The file system will move frequently accessed data to the outer tracks of the disk, where it will enjoy the greatest throughput because of the higher relative speed of travel. Likewise, the file system optimizes positioning of application data, such that application launches require less read/write head movement.

However, FAT32 poses a real problem. Windows NT cannot read FAT32 formatted drives, nor can FAT16-based Windows 3.x, DOS, and Windows 95. Likewise, your FAT32 Windows 95 or 98 OS cannot recognize Windows NT disk partitions formatted using the NT file system (NTFS). Before you decide to move one or more partitions to FAT32, make sure you're not creating a tower of Babel that will cause coexisting OSs to stop talking to each other.

NTFS

The NT file system (NTFS) is the most complex of Microsoft's disk file systems. Like FAT32, it can recognize large hard disks and reduce slack by limiting cluster sizes. It can also recognize FAT16 partitions, thus allowing NT to read and write FAT16 disk partitions. However, operating systems running on a FAT16 or FAT32 partition will be unable to make sense of the NTFS-formatted partition.

NTFS is a useful file system for networks, because it tracks more information about files than does its FAT cousins. Windows NT administrators can see file-level security settings and other useful information, because NTFS reserves bits for such data.

11.5 Tom's Pick

The hard disk is perhaps the most critical element in efficient system performance. After all, every program, document, and even the operating system must first be dragged off the hard disk before the CPU and RAM can begin working. As applications grow larger and multitasking more common, hard disks also must spend more and more time swapping virtual memory, providing a place for that Excel session to stay while you work with Lotus Notes and Netscape Navigator. A slow disk can turn virtual memory into a spinning jail sentence, robbing you of critical moments of productivity at every turn.

The vast majority of systems today ship with big and reasonably fast IDE hard disks. These devices employ the ATA-33 technology to burst up to 33MBps of data, while reducing overhead and inefficiencies carried in older versions of the IDE bus. But for top performance, you can't do without a SCSI drive. SCSI provides efficiencies in data and instruction handling that IDE simply can't match, and the bus robs less CPU time than does ATA-33.

Our pick for a drive, therefore, uses a SCSI interface. The **IBM UltraStar 9ZX** runs off an ultra-wide SCSI interface to enjoy 40 MBps of data throughput—enough for even the most outlandish video-centric tasks. (It's also available in a 200MBps Fibre Channel format.) The 9ZX's platters spin at 10,000 rpm to reduce latencies caused when the read/write head must wait for the proper area of the disk to spin around underneath. Of course, quickness is a key component of drive performance, and the Ultra 9ZX delivers, with 6.7ms access times that are among the best you can find. Sustained data transfers measure out at about 17 MBps, thanks in part to a large 1MB cache.

Beyond performance, the 9ZX goes the extra mile to keep your data safe. The Self-Monitoring Analysis and Reporting Technology (SMART) integrated into the drive provide real-time data on drive parameters. IBM's Predictive Failure Analysis (PFA) detects bit-level problems that allow you to see drive issues developing before they become actual crashes. An thermal sensor catches over-heating problems early, as well.

If you are determined to go IDE, stick with IBM. The DeskStar 16 uses IBM's Giant Magneto Resistive (GMR) head technology to hold 16GB of data in a single drive. At $399, DeskStar 16 is affordable for its size, while the ATA-33 IDE interface provides burst transfers of 33 MBps—enough for heavy desktop use.

Hard Disk Guide

Chapter

12

Tape
Backup
Guide

12.1 Understanding Tape Backup

This is a book about high-performance computing, so what's a discussion of tape backup drives doing here? After all, tape is the slowest, most restrictive, and least applicable form of mass storage you'll find for the PC. The drives almost always take several seconds (tens of them, in fact) to find data, making them orders of magnitude slower than even your creaky, old floppy disk drive. Then, once they find data, their transfer rates—while vastly improved—are still paltry compared to the fast action of hard disks and even CD-ROM drives.

However, tape backup drives do one thing better than any other storage option out there: They hold tons of data dirt cheap. From single desktops outfitted with 10GB ATA hard disks, to bulked up, multiprocessor servers running a RAID disk array, tape backup is the only option that can serve them all. With more and more of our vital documents and data now sitting inside of PCs, rather than on paper, a tape backup drive becomes an important insurance policy against disaster.

After all, personal computing is all about data. Your spreadsheets and correspondences, tax files and contact lists, email archives and Web layouts—all are vitally important, and all reside on hard disks that can, at any time, fall victim to a hard disk crash, severe power spike, or undetected virus.

Certainly, the Iomega Zip drives aren't up to the task. At 100MB a piece, they are woefully overmatched by today's 14GB and 16GB ATA hard disk drives. Even 2GB Jaz drives now on the market may be unable to handle all the data on those gargantuan disks. If you're relying on floppies to keep your data safe, well, good luck.

12.1.1 Why Tape?

Removable magnetic and even MO drives are faster, and CD-R and CD-RW media are more universally recognized. So why would anyone want to use cassette tapes, a technology that harkens back to the early 1980s and the TRS-80? Three words: Cost per megabyte.

No media can match the economy that tape delivers to the desktop. Although there are a variety of tape backup technologies (more on that in a minute), all deliver outstanding value for the amount of storage. Low-cost QIC-format cassettes (most of which now comply with the Travan standard), typically cost below a penny per megabyte. In fact, the numbers are getting so small that a better metric now is probably "megabytes per penny." Table 12.1 provides a quick round up of storage options and their relative megabytes-per-penny value.

Table 12.1. A megabytes-per-penny comparison.

Drive Type	Capacity	Cost	MB Per Penny
Tape (Travan TR-4)	4GB	$30	136.5MB
CD-RW	640MB	$12	42.67MB
SyQuest Sparq	1GB	$30	34.1MB
Hard disk	6.4GB	$299	21.9MB
Iomega Zip	100MB	$13	7.69MB

As you can see, no current spinning media type even comes close to the value offered by a typical 4GB Travan tape drive (see Figure 12.1). Although larger Travan cassettes and more heavy-duty formats are more expensive, the megabytes-per-penny ratio actually improves. A 7GB DAT cartridge costs only about $12 per unit, for an incredible value of 597.3MB per penny. That's half a gig for each penny you spend. Of course, DAT drives are expensive, so you face big up-front costs, but clearly the storage punch offered by tape is unmatched.

Figure 12.1.

Seagate's TapeStor Travan line of QIC/ Travan external tape backup drives is available in both SCSI and IDE versions and can store up to 4GB of data (uncompressed).

Of course, tape is not for everyone. In fact, it's only appropriate for a very small portion of your general storage needs. The problem is that tape—unlike hard disks, CD-ROMs, and other spinning media—is linear. The drive can't simply jump to the spot on the media where the desired bits are located. Rather it must spool through yards and yards of tape to find the portion of the media it needs. The result: Access times that can take tens of seconds, if not minutes. The average access time for a typical tape backup drive is orders of magnitude slower than for that of a hard disk or even CD-ROM drive. In a word, tape is too slow to act as general data storage, but it serves well for restoring large amounts of data.

12.1.2 How It Works

Tape backup drives work on the same principles that made eight-track tape players popular back in the 1970s. A drive head makes contact with a magnetic-coated, flexible medium that confers or detects magnetic charges as the material passes under it. Fluctuations in the charge are interpreted by the drive to indicate a change in value, from 1 to 0 (or vice versa). A pair of drive spools pull and feed the tape along a path that move through the read/write head assembly (see Figure 12.2).

Figure 12.2.

Travan tape drives use mechanisms similar to those found in VCRs and eight-track tape players to read and write tape media.

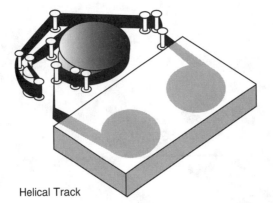

Helical Track

We're Talking Tracks

The eight-track analogy comes into play in the way the tape itself is physically divided. When writing and reading data, the head does not access the entire width of the tape. Rather, numerous tracks run in parallel along the width of the tape material. The first track might run along the top one-eighth of the media material. At the end of the tape where the first track ends, the second track picks up on the one-eighth space of media directly below it. This track runs in the opposite direction of the first, starting where the first track ended. The third track, then, sits below the second track and runs opposite of it.

This snake-like string of data tracks increases the effective length of the tape many-fold. It also serves a number of advantages. First, this layout cuts down on seek times, because a longer tape would take even longer to spool through. Second, it allows for a tape wide enough to hold up under the strain of being pulled by a spindle, without simply throwing away valuable surface area.

A typical cassette can contain 740 feet of media, which is divided into 72 tracks of data (see Figure 12.3). That yields an effective recording surface area of 53,000 feet, or just over 10 miles! Not bad for a little 3.5-inch cassette that weighs about an ounce or two.

Figure 12.3.
Parallel tracks of data on the tape media extend the effective length of the data string to just over 10 miles. This DLT-format tape extends that further by orienting the head diagonally along each track to fit more bits per inch.

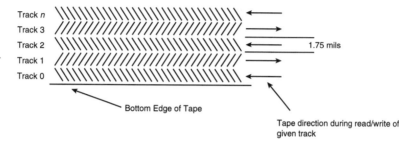

Track *n*
Track 3
Track 2 — 1.75 mils
Track 1
Track 0

Bottom Edge of Tape

Tape direction during read/write of given track

Storing Bits on Tape

Like any storage media, the tape is logically segmented to allow the drive and software to make assumptions about where data will be located and how to read and write it. Spaces called *bit cells* are used to compartmentalize magnetic charges, so if the drive detects a change in charge between two bit cells, it interprets that as a digital 1. If the bit cells are of the same charge, a 0 is identified. These changes in values are called *flux transitions* and are the smallest component of the tape geography.

Of course, different tape formats will take different approaches to laying bits onto their flexible magnetic media. In general, the bit cells are contained within larger sectors called *frames*. The sectors are more than just logical aggregations of data bits; they also contain error-correction data to ensure the integrity of stored data. In addition, every sector and frame includes a little extra space to allow the drive head to start and stop without losing its place on the tape. This feature keeps things going smoothly when the data stream to the tape gets interrupted, for example, which requires the drive to pause while the processor catches up.

Tape Backup Guide

The buffer zones in the sectors enable the drive to stop and then start the tape and not miss the beginning of the next sector. Otherwise, the tape would roll past the necessary point before the head could start effectively reading or writing data, much the way a VCR doesn't start displaying the video until after a couple seconds of tape motion have already passed.

The capacity of a tape is determined by the following issues:

- Length of the tape
- Number of tracks
- Flux transitions per square inch

Flux transitions per inch (FTPI) define the number of individual magnetic charges packed into a linear inch of tape. The more transitions per inch, the greater the data density of the media. Similar to area density in hard disk drives, flux transitions per inch have been increasing steadily as drive makers improve the process of recording to magnetic tape.

Compression is an integral, and somewhat thorny, issue in tape backup hardware. Tape drive vendors almost always spec cassette capacities based on the amount of compressed data the tape can hold, usually assuming a 2-to-1 compression ratio. However, as anyone knows, the actual effectiveness of compression can vary widely and is usually lower than 2-to-1. Although text files compress very nicely, you're likely to see ratios of 1.7-to-1 or lower for the kind of mixed file formats found on most hard disk drives. If you have a lot of already-compressed media files, including graphics and video, your compression ratio is likely to be closer to 1-to-1 than 2-to-1. My advice is to always make a point to find out the uncompressed capacity of a tape drive and media when you're considering storage.

12.1.3 Performance Impact Report

Tape backup drives are not going to impact the performance of your games or applications. However, the speed at which these devices can find and transfer data does vary significantly, making some unsuitable for even backup tasks. Travan type drives generally offer low drive price points, reasonably affordable media, and acceptable performance. DAT and DLT tapes, however will both improve throughputs, with DAT data rates peaking at 1.2MBps and DLT taking that figure to 5MBps.

Keep in mind that even the fastest accessing media type and drive cannot promise anything better than averages of tens of seconds. The differences can be important if you tend to frequently pull data off tapes for some reason, but in no case are they fast enough to make tape a cheap alternative to near-line disk storage such as MO drives or removable magnetic media.

The interface type can impact performance. Drives based on the SCSI bus will run best, if only because SCSI has features that ensure acceptable data rates and low latencies. IDE-type drives can get held up in general hard disk and CD-ROM traffic, whereas floppy-based drives are held back by the slow interface. Parallel port drives suffer similar problems.

12.2 Currently Available Tape Backup

Despite years of standards jockeying and advancement, the tape backup market remains a confusing one from a format standpoint. Although a few standards do exist and own significant portions of the market, a variety of proprietary schemes continue to complicate buying decisions. In addition, totally incompatible types of tape standards are playing in the low, mid, and high ends of the market, forcing buyers to make tough choices. This is particularly true if your needs lie in the gray area between market segments.

Here are the most popular types of tape backup drives available:

- QIC-format Travan
- DAT: Digital Analog Tape
- DLT: Digital Linear Tape
- 8mm cartridge, AIT, others

Of these, only the QIC-format tape is designed for use on single desktops. The others are priced for larger network duty and can handle capacities of 10 to 35GB. DAT is often found in the mid range of the market, providing lower media costs but burdening buyers with high drive costs. DLT has a tight hold on the highest portions of the market thanks to its large capacities.

12.2.1 Quarter-Inch Tape (QIC)

QIC gets its name from the quarter-inch tape width it employs. Established in 1987, QIC has proved to be an affordable, resilient, and effective standard for standalone systems and small offices. Originally started at 400MB with the QIC-40 specification, today new Travan versions of QIC can store as much as 4GB of data, uncompressed. The new NS-20 specification promises to move that figure to 10GB, making it an effective competitor to DAT drives.

Travan was an important milestone in the QIC evolution. Crafted in 1992 by 3M (now Imation) and several hardware vendors, the technology boosted the relative density of magnetic charge changes that could be laid down on each portion of the tape. Expressed as flux transitions, this bit-carrying density has allowed Travan drives and media to store more and more data on the same 750-foot long tape strip (see Table 12.2).

Table 12.2. Travan flavors defined.

Travan Type	Capacity	Flux Transitions Per Inch
TR-1	400MB	14,700
TR-2	800MB	22,125
TR-3	1.6GB	44,250
TR-4	4GB	50,800

How much greater densities are we talking about? The TR-1 specification allows 14,700 flux transitions per inch, which yields 400MB of data stored in 36 tracks. By comparison, the TR-4 employs 50,800 flux transitions per inch on 72 tracks, for a total of 4GB (see Figure 12.4).

Figure 12.4.
These portable TR-4 cassettes are available from a variety of different vendors, but they cost more per megabyte than DAT cassettes.

QIC/Travan drives are enormously popular for single desktop PCs because of the low cost of the drives and the very good tape capacities. However, QIC/Travan cassettes contain tracking controls in the cartridge, which make the media somewhat more expensive than some other standard choices.

12.2.2 Digital Analog Tape (DAT)

As the name connotes, the Digital Analog Tape (DAT) format uses the same media and structure found in digital audio cassettes of the same name. DAT drives are an excellent option for those with larger storage needs, with capacities of 12GB available at the highest end with the DDS-3 specification.

Two flavors of DAT are available on the market, and they are distinguished by the width of the tape. DDS-3-compliant DAT drives can store up to 12GB of uncompressed data, and they provide complete compatibility with earlier DDS-format DAT tapes. DAT uses a *helical scan approach* to laying data down on the tracks. In this scheme, data is not positioned linearly along the track (as it is with QIC/Travan), but rather the head positions itself so that data is written along the track diagonally. To do this, the head describes the motion of a partial helix as it travels along the tape—thus the name of the scheme. The approach provides significantly higher data densities on the tape; however, the more complex drive mechanisms come at a higher price.

DAT cassettes carry no tracking controls inside the removable media cartridge; instead, all this logic resides in the drive itself. This makes DAT cassettes significantly less expensive than their QIC/Travan counterparts, but it adds cost to the drives. In fact, DAT drives can cost $2000 or more, five to ten times the cost of affordable Travan models.

Growing QIC/Travan capacities have eaten into DAT's high-capacity market. For this reason, the decision between DAT and QIC/Travan may come down to the number of individual cassettes you intend to use on each drive. If you use a large number of cassettes, DAT may actually be a better deal despite the fact that the drive itself costs so much more.

12.2.3 Digital Linear Tape (DLT)

Digital Linear Tape (DLT) is the highest-end standard tape format, with cassette capacities as high as 35GB per tape—an unmatched capacity among the popular standard formats (see Figure 12.5). Perhaps most important, DLT delivers the best performance, with transfer rates that can go to 5MBps or higher—a critical concern if you have only a limited amount of time to push backup data off a busy workstation or over a congested network.

Most important, DLT allows the drive to both write and read data on the tape at the same time. Because data should usually be verified before a backup is considered complete, this technology enables the drive to eliminate the time-consuming step of scanning through the entire tape a second time to check for errors. Rather, the head simply reads and confirms the data immediately after it is written.

However, drive costs are exorbitant, making DLT an option limited to professionals. Expect to pay $5000 or more for a 35GB DLT drive. Media costs are not as low as those found for DAT drives (see Figure 12.6). For network applications, a six-drive DAT switcher makes an excellent option, because you can automatically back up hundreds of gigabytes without having to stop the process to load a new tape.

Tape Backup Guide

Figure 12.5.

High-performance DLT drives integrate a tape reel directly into the drive housing, thus enabling better control and higher speeds than allowed by formats that have two tape reels inside the cartridge.

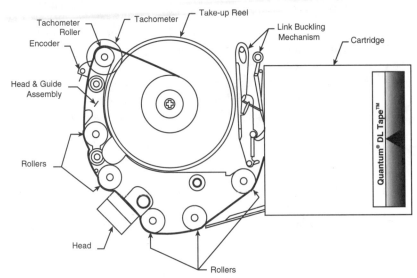

Figure 12.6.

This auto-loading DAT drive holds as many as four DDS-3 cassettes.

12.3 Evaluating Tape Backup

When looking at tape backup drives, you need to consider your likely needs. A tiny 800MB Iomega Ditto drive running over a parallel port just doesn't cut it on a dual-processor graphics workstation with a pair of 15GB hard disk drives. Of course, a 35GB DLT drive is probably a bit much for a $999 PC your mom might buy.

Of course, the capacity of your current hard disk drive or drives is the overriding factor, but issues of performance, interface, and media cost all come into play. Among the issues to consider when buying are the following:

- Capacity

- Performance and interface

- Compatibility

- Software capabilities

12.3.1 Capacity

No one wants to pay more than he needs to, and that goes double for tape backup hardware. After all, these devices don't add anything to the performance or application capabilities of your PC. The money you spend on backup hardware could go toward a hefty RAM upgrade, cutting-edge 3D graphics card, or faster CPU. So it's important to figure out how much data you're likely to need to back up, and then you tailor your plans to suit.

Of course, if it's likely that you'll be adding a second drive or upgrading your current hard disk, you need to keep that in mind as well. Do you want to be able to capture all the data on all your drives to a single cassette? If so, you'll need to go with a much higher-capacity format. If you're content-saving individual drives to separate tapes, you'll be able to save some bucks by going with a lower-capacity model.

Tape vendors don't make it easy, though. Virtually without exception, all vendors market their cassettes and drives based on compressed data amounts, and they always assuming an optimistic compression ratio of 2-to-1. As a result, a 10GB drive that you think can hold the contents of your 9GB hard disk drive may, in fact, come up short by as much as 30 percent.

Always buy drives based on their uncompressed data capacities. If you want an idea of what to expect from compression, consider using a more realistic figure, such as 1.7-to-1. Even better, play it a bit conservatively and go with a ratio such as 1.5-to-1, particularly if you intend to backup large amounts of already compressed media data, such as MPEG video and JPEG graphic files.

The relative costs and capacities of the three standard drive types are broken down in Table 12.3. Included in this table are the megabytes per penny, which gives you a sense of the relative value of the media cost. Of course, terrific megsto-money ratios don't mean a lot if you have a small disk that needs to be backed up. However for larger backups, such as those for network servers, this consideration becomes vital. Over the life of a drive, it's likely that you'll spend many times the drive's cost on the media used to store the data. Remember, media must be periodically retired to avoid the probability of backing data up to a compromised tape.

Table 12.3. Data capacities of standard tape backup formats.

Format	Format Capacity	Low End Cost	High End MB Per Penny
Travan TR-4	4GB	$30	136.5MB
DAT DDS-3	12GB	$25	492MB
DLT	35GB	$120	228MB

12.3.2 Performance and Interface

Tape is dog-slow in comparison to hard disks and CD-ROM drives, but big differences exist among the tape backup drive types. DLT, for example, uses significantly more expensive drive mechanics and logic to enable simultaneous reading and writing of data. The sensitive heads also use schemes borrowed from hard disk drive technology to read closely packed magnetic charges that frequently overlap each other. The result: Higher densities that allow data to pass more quickly beneath the head at any given tape speed.

Random access performance is a lost cause with tape drives, but some DLT models give you a jump by storing index information in onboard RAM. This eliminates the need for the drive to rewind all the way to the beginning of the tape to read the directory index in order to find specified data. Even with this innovation, however, access times will never come close to those of even the slowest floppy disk drive.

Throughput is another story. Large backups are purely sequential operations. A system or systems stream data from disk to the tape in an uninterrupted transaction, with bits being laid down on the tape media in the order they're received. The critical specification here is sustained data rate, which defines exactly how much data the tape drive can reliably write to the media per second, every second.

In this respect, DLT technology wins hands down with 5MBps transfer rates (nearly five times that of competing DAT models, which max out at data rates of about 1.2MBps). Keep in mind that these are raw transfer rates. Compression can nearly double these numbers, because files are scrunched in real time before being written to the media.

Also critical to performance is the device interface. You'll want to consider whether you want an internal or external model, because this might determine which interface you use. Tape drives are sold with interfaces for the following bus types:

- SCSI

- Parallel port

- Enhanced IDE

- Floppy drive

- USB (soon)

Heavy-duty backups will go best over a SCSI bus. In fact, you'll have a hard time finding non-SCSI versions of the most powerful DLT and even DAT drives. SCSI provides superior multitasking to both IDE and parallel port interfaces, enabling the PC's other storage devices to stay busy with their own tasks while the backup goes on.

This is particularly true if you already have external SCSI peripherals installed, because the host controller is already in place. You just have to add the tape drive to the daisy chain. If you do not have a SCSI controller on your system, consider your habits. Frequent large backups will go more quickly and smoothly over a SCSI bus, particularly if you want to work with your PC while backups are underway.

At the low end, you'll find QIC/Travan drives built to run over the parallel port. These drives are typically low cost, come with consumer-oriented software, and take forever to back up significant amounts of data. Still, these external devices can be shared with virtually any desktop or notebook PC (the parallel port being a universal commodity), thus providing an unequaled measure of flexibility. They are also easier to install than IDE or SCSI models.

Tape Backup Guide

At the same low-end occupied by parallel port devices are even less expensive tape drives that talk over the floppy disk controller. They use the second connection long since abandoned by the 5.25-inch floppy drive, again ensuring complete compatibility with the installed market. Because these drives are internal and need no special controller or cabling, they are dirt cheap (see Figure 12.7). Of course, they cannot be easily shared and are captive to the slow floppy drive interface.

Figure 12.7.

The Seagate TapeStor TR-3 external drive is stylish, but the parallel port interface will bog down large backup routines.

More recently, enhanced IDE-based drives have taken over the segment served by floppy-based units. All aspects of IDE performance are much improved, and IDE is another sure thing in every system you buy. These drives are also very cheap because of the lack of external housing, power supply, and cable. However, the IDE interface is getting awfully crowded with CD-ROM, hard disk, and other drives creating the prospect of data traffic jams on the bus.

One thing to look for is a drive based on the Universal Serial Bus. With its 12MBps data rates, USB is faster than the parallel port, and it provides terrific Plug and Play features such as hot swapping, automatic device detection, and dynamic driver loading and unloading. Of course, your PC will need to be outfitted with USB ports to work with these types of drives.

Also, it's not clear whether USB drivers will be available for Windows 95 and Windows NT systems, or if support will be limited to Windows 98. The problem is that the USB implementation under Windows 95 OSR 2.1 requires hardware vendors to provide device drivers that can be somewhat tricky to write. Unwilling to take on the risk of product returns or heavy technical support, many vendors are only implementing devices for Windows 98. The new operating system provides much more streamlined support for USB devices.

12.3.3 Compatibility

No doubt about it, compatibility is a big deal. Tape formats get revised every year or so as new schemes and drive types emerge to increase capacities and performance. If you buy a drive and have existing tapes, your best bet is to buy within the same technology family. Generally, you'll enjoy some level of backward compatibility when moving from, say, a Travan TR-2 model drive to a TR-4 drive. Likewise, DDS-3 DAT drives can read and write your old DDS-1 tapes as well as provide triple the data storage for the new DDS-3 tapes you buy.

If you decide to leap over to a new technology family, say from Travan to DAT or DLT, you'll have to start over in your media buying and backup efforts. The existing tape will not be readable in those different format drives. This concern is most relevant in office situations, where numerous systems must be backed up using numerous drives. Creating a mismatch of media and drives can lead to confusion and problems down the road.

12.3.4 Software Capabilities

Just as important as the hardware is the software you use to drive your backup operations. In order to be effective, backups must occur on schedule, using regimented methodologies that ensure you know the location and disposition of your data. Backup software ensures that everything happens on schedule, by automating the time and type of backup operations.

In general, when you buy a tape backup drive, you'll get a bundled package with it. What you won't find is an enormous market of competing tape backup products. Microsoft's Backup applet comes as part of Windows 95 and includes rudimentary controls for scheduling and targeting backups. However, for serious work, you'll want to go with a third-party package such as Seagate's Back It package.

Here are some of the critical capabilities of backup software:

- Can schedule backups to occur at specific intervals (daily, weekly, twice weekly, monthly, and so on).

- Can target specific drives and directories for backup to avoid storing unneeded information.

- Can schedule different backup routines. For example, full disk backups might occur once a week, whereas smaller incremental data backups might occur daily.

- Includes verification routines that read over a just-written tape to ensure that the media is good.

Tape Backup Guide

12.4 Understanding Backup Routines

Unlike other forms of storage, tape backup is guided by orderly management and rigid methodology. Proper maintenance of drives, storage of tapes, and rotation of backup media are critical to ensure that the data you write to tape will be there when you finally need it. This section addresses strategies and tactics for making tape backup work for your system.

12.4.1 Making Backups

Backing up data is a time-consuming process despite major advances in the speed with which these drives can transfer data to tape. Today's hard disk drives are 16 times larger than they were a scant three years ago, and the explosion of Internet use has invited enormous amounts of data onto virtually everyone's desktop.

Fast tape drives can move data at up to 500KBps, enough to actually play back video files directly from tape. However, there is simply no fix for the dreadfully long access times, making tape inappropriate for all but archiving duties. In fact, spinning media types may compete effectively in the traditional tape market thanks to the introduction to Terastor technology, which promises to increase magnetic and MO storage capacities by orders of magnitude over those viable today. This technology is still being worked out, but Terastor-based drives could appear within the next few years, which means that tape may be headed for retirement in the PC storage hierarchy.

Until then, users who need to protect their data will be juggling little cassette tapes. Fortunately, intuitive software packages that provide graphical controls and powerful optimizations are available. Better software allows you to schedule backups using detailed settings, tweak data verification settings, and otherwise make the most of your hardware.

Three different types of backups can be used. (These are often used together to find the best balance of timeliness and security.) For example, you can choose to save all the selected data on a disk or only back up the data that has changed since the last backup routine. Here are the three categories of backups:

- Full backup: Writes everything on the disk to tape

- Incremental backup: Writes to tape anything that has changed since the last incremental backup

- Differential backup: Writes to tape anything that has changed since the last full backup

Full backups write everything you select to the tape, regardless of whether that data has changed since the last backup. This type of session takes the longest time and consumes the most media, but you can't beat it for protecting your data. Even in the case of a total disaster, you know that you have a mirror of all your needed data on a tape, allowing you to quickly reassert it on another system or drive.

More problematic are incremental backups, which only write to tape that data which has changed since the last backup, whether it is a full or incremental backup. To make incremental backup routines work, you must keep both the original full backup and all subsequent incremental backups handy. Otherwise, you'll have gaping holes in your media history that will stop a recovery in its tracks. Of course, recovering data in this way will take longer, because you'll be swapping tapes during restoration. However, incremental backups save both time and money—lots of it—by reducing the sheer number of cassettes needed to keep a secure copy of your data on hand.

In between incremental and full backups are differential backups. This type of backup routine saves to tape all the data that has changed since the last full backup. Although you repeat the work of earlier incremental or differential backups, you won't find yourself juggling half a dozen cassettes in order to put all your data back together. At most, you'll have two tapes—one of the first backup and the other of everything that has changed since—to deal with. Usually, you'll find yourself using a combination of these three approaches to efficiently secure your data.

Just remember, backups can and do go bad. Tape media are more prone to failure than most people suspect, posing a real threat to both your data and your sanity. You can tilt the odds in your favor by taking the extra time to conduct a full verification of the tape after your backup is finished. The drive will go through the entire tape, comparing the bits on the media to that taken from the hard disk, thus ensuring that every bit the drive thought it wrote did, in fact, end up on the tape.

More important, you should consider doing test restores of your tape data every once in a while. Although it's time-consuming, you may end up catching an unnoticed problem with your media or drives. You'll also become more familiar with the restoration routine before you must perform it in a do-or-die situation.

12.4.2 Tape Management: Handling with Care

Dealing with backup drives can get tricky. The cassettes, themselves, are sensitive to environmental stress, and the physical logistics of juggling backup media can get complicated. In both cases, it makes sense to have a strategy to avoid trouble down the road.

Tape Backup Guide

Before you get started backing up data, establish a routine. Decide how often you need to back up your data and how thorough you want to be. Usually, you can avoid burning too much time (and money on tapes) by establishing a set of incremental backups between full backups.

Hewlett-Packard recommends the following practices for weekly backups, depending on your usage pattern:

- Three-tape rotation

- Six-tape rotation

- Ten-tape rotation

Three-Tape Rotation

If your files don't change much from day to day, a three-tape rotation strategy may be adequate. Here, you do a total backup on Monday night using tape 1. Then you perform modified backups daily using tape 2. On the next Monday, you use tape 3 for a total backup and remove tape 1 to offsite storage. Then, after erasing the previous backups from tape 2, you repeat the daily modified backups (see Figure 12.8).

Figure 12.8.

A typical three-tape backup system.

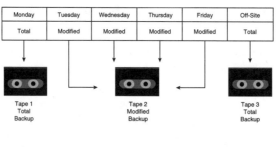

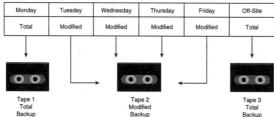

Six-Tape Rotation

If your files change daily, consider a six-tape rotation. Simply label five of the tapes "Monday" through "Friday" and then label the sixth "Offsite." On Monday, you perform a total backup on the "Monday" tape. For Tuesday through Friday, you perform modified backups of each day's tape. At the end of the week, you perform a total backup on the "Offsite" tape (see Figure 12.9).

Figure 12.9.
A typical six-tape backup system.

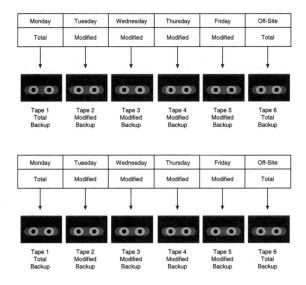

Ten-Tape Rotation

If you need to preserve weeks or months worth of data, use the ten-tape rotation method. This is similar to the six-tape rotation method except you add four tapes to perform separate total backups at the end of each week and retain them for a month's worth of data.

12.4.3 Backup Tips

I've heard just too many horror stories from users who have gone to the trouble to faithfully back up their data, only to find that the media was corrupted when they actually needed to restore a disk drive. This kind of failure can be absolutely devastating. Fortunately, there are a number of things you can do to avoid making backups to tapes that have gone bad weeks before. This section contains tips that will help ensure the reliability and effectiveness of your backup practices.

Set Aside an Archive Tape

No matter which backup strategy you use, you should always have one or more archive tapes. By moving files to an archive tape, you can save those time-intensive reports and presentations (or anything else on the disk that you'd like to remove but still have access to, including programs).

Archiving is easy with the Selective Backup function in Colorado Backup for DOS or with the Move function in Colorado Backup for Windows.

Archiving files on tape not only gives you economical near-line storage, it can also speed disk access. You also save money by eliminating the need to add more disk space.

Tape Backup Guide

Backup Strategy Guidelines

Here are guidelines you should follow for performing backups:

- Perform a total backup weekly and modify backups daily.

- Label tape cartridges so you know which tape to restore if the need arises.

- Tapes wear out. Rotate new tapes into your schedule. Keep at least one new tape on hand.

- Store tapes in cases or caddies. Keep them away from magnetic fields (such as power supplies, telephones, and monitors).

- Never attempt to clean the heads of the HP Colorado 5GB, T3000, 4000s/es, or the HP SureStore T4i&e; they are self-cleaning and you're likely to damage them irreparably. Clean the tape heads of older products (e.g., Jumbo and Trakker ranges) after about 20 backups or restores. You should periodically retension the tape.

- Store a weekly total backup offsite in case of fire, flood, or theft.

- Archive seldom-used files to tape to make efficient use of your hard disk.

- Automate backups with scheduler and batch files.

- Perform regular compare operations to verify proper tape drive function.

12.4.4 Care and Feeding of Backup Tapes

You should by now be aware that tape is a vulnerable media. Dirt, heat, humidity, and other factors can all impact the ability of the media to reliably hold a magnetic charge. What's more, the media is constantly exposed to the stress of being pulled and stretched as drives move the tape through their internal mechanisms. As a result, you should make a point to care for your tapes.

There are a lot of factors that impact tapes—many of them originate from the environment in which they operate. The following subsections describe some things to look out for to extend and ensure the useful life of your media.

Thermal Stresses

Like any material, tape media expands and contracts when heated and cooled. This can affect the spacing of bits and cause problems during operation—particularly if expansion and contraction is happening in the middle of a routine. If tapes are being brought in from outside, give them at least eight hours to heat or cool to the temperature of the room they are to be used in. As a general rule, it's a good idea to keep your media in the same place where they will be used. Be aware that the more thermal stress tapes are exposed to, the shorter their useful lives will be.

Dirt and Dust

Because tape drives are not sealed, exposure to dirt is a factor. Dust that gathers on tape heads can end up on the media, thus impairing the drive's ability to read and write. The problem is exacerbated by the fact that tape heads must actually make contact with the media, unlike disk drive heads, which float above the disk surface. If dust or other particles block this contact, the device can't operate properly.

Your best course of action is to keep a clean work area, because this will drastically reduce problems caused by dust and dirt. Also make a point to periodically clean the drive heads and motor assembly using a cleaning media tape. This cassette fits into the drive like any other data cassette, but it's designed to clear the internal components of dirt.

Retensioning Slipping Tapes

As mentioned earlier, tape is unique in that the media is physically pulled when in operation. This action can loosen the tape on the spools, resulting in decreased precision as the tape slips. To eliminate this problem, make a point to periodically run the tape from beginning to end in a single run. This is a process known as *retensioning*. This will restore the tightness of the tape around the spools and alleviate slack that can cause slippage. Some backup software actually includes a retension command that performs this operation automatically. Note that if a tape is subject to extreme temperature changes, the tape should be retensioned.

Tips on Taking Care of Tapes

To get the longest life out of your tapes and to avoid nasty surprises during restore operations, keep the following tips in mind:

- Remove cassettes from the tape drive when they're not in use.

- When you're finished using a tape, reset it to the very beginning or the very end.

- Store cassettes in the same room where they will be used and keep them in their protective covers.

- Keep tapes away from destructive exposures such as magnetic fields and sunlight.

Tape Backup Guide

12.5 Tom's Pick

A couple years ago, a QIC/Travan tape drive was a toy. Iomega's 800MB parallel port Ditto offering was typical of this segment, with low capacities, dog-slow backup performance, and overly loud operation. However, Travan has grown up, and new TR-4 drives will put 4GB of uncompressed data onto a tape (and about 7GB or 8GB after compression). With 300KBps data transfer rates, these drives are not a match for the much more expensive DAT-type drives, but they are still adequate for most low- and mid-range backup jobs. Also, you'll still want an IDE or floppy-based Travan model to enjoy the transfer rate—parallel port drives can't keep pace with the sustained transfer rate.

If you need to get a handle on more than 10GB of data, DAT is the best option for small or home offices. DLT tape drives are unmatched in performance, but they are so expensive that they really are limited to the network crowd. DAT DDS-3 tapes hold gobs of data (12GB uncompressed and about 20GB or so compressed), are four times as fast as Travan at 1.2MBps transfer rates, and provide the lowest media cost of the bunch. If you find yourself living outside the reaches of Travan technology, consider a DAT DDS-3 backup drive.

Finally, if you use a lot of media, you may actually want to take a hard look at DLT. Despite the thousands of dollars you'll spend on DLT tape drives, the media itself is significantly cheaper than DAT tapes. The result: If you cycle through scores of tapes, the cost savings of the DLT media will more than pay for the premium of the DLT drive—and you'll get better performance to boot.

Chapter

13

Near-Disk Storage Guide

13.1 Understanding Near-Line Storage

As the data demands on desktop PCs get larger and more intense, you can expect to see more and more levels of storage serving your desktop. The first IBM PCs often came with little more than a floppy disk drive or two. The XTs and ATs expanded on that by adding a 10MB or maybe even a 40MB hard disk drive. By 1993, CD-ROM drives were beginning to find their way inside PCs, adding yet another level to the data-storage hierarchy.

Each of these devices serves a specific (though sometimes changing) purpose in the storage food chain. Today, that chain of data stretches past your CD-ROM drive, even through tape drives, out your modem and onto the Internet. People are sending data backups over the public network or relying on the Internet to access data and services they would otherwise store on disk.

Somewhere in between your tape drive and your hard disk lurks a category of devices often referred to as near-line storage. These products vary in their media types and applications, but they have a few things in common:

- Rewritable, disc-based media

- Removable cartridges

- Relatively fast access and high data rates

- Capacities above 100MB

It's a broad swath of territory, to be sure, but it's one that's becoming quite important. Near-line products include Iomega's Zip and Jaz drives, SyQuest's Sparq and SyJet drives, and Compaq/Matsushita's LS-120 drive. Many of these devices are vying to become the successor to the venerable floppy disk—perhaps one of the most important standards battles being waged today. At the same time, multigigabyte formats enable you to become a true data hog, practice frequent and fast backups, and exchange enormous files with other PCs.

The term *near-line* comes from the fact that these drives are actually fast enough to run application code directly from the removable media—allowing them to provide a level of storage that's much more accessible than that available from CD-ROM media, for example. They can also quickly transfer large data files, such as graphics and video, between disk and the PC. Near-line reflects this "almost there" character of these drives.

13.1.1 Applications

Near-line storage is an application catch-all that stretches the gamut of competing drive types. If you can do something with a floppy disk, hard disk, CD-ROM, DVD-ROM, CD-RW, DVD-RAM, or tape cartridge, there's a near-line alternative that can do the same thing. In fact, near-line storage can often do more applications more quickly than other formats. The problem? The lack of format standards means that near-line products operate in their own universe, unable to read or write to cartridges from other manufacturers, or even other products from the same manufacturer.

Among the key applications for these devices are the following:

- Archiving and backup

- Large file sharing and distribution

- Hard disk offloading

- Media playback platform

- Effective second hard disk

The applications for these products is growing as the need for a high-capacity floppy drive alternative becomes critical. Most of these products range from 100MB to 250MB in capacity, with drive prices of $100 to $200 dollars each. However, it will take system manufacturers making a common decision to go with a single drive type to actually make a floppy disk replacement real. Until there's a ubiquitous base of these products, it's difficult to favor one over the other.

The higher-end models are less constrained by compatibility. In this range, the devices are being called on to do the work of hard disks, tape backup drives, and rewritable CD/DVD media. Often, these drives never encounter media originating from another PC—rather, they're used to store and access data found solely on a host system.

13.1.2 How It Works

Near-line storage devices work very much like their fixed-disk counterpart: the hard disk drive. The difference is that the spinning, magnetic media is contained in a cartridge housing that may be inserted and removed. Like floppies, these cartridges include a siding window that protects the media when the cartridge is in the open but allows access to the read/write head when it's in the drive.

These drives differ from floppies in an important way, however. At no point does the drive mechanism actually clamp down on the media. Rather, the read/write head floats above the surface of the spinning disk, detecting and changing the alternating magnetic fields laid onto the surface coating. The read/write head, drive spindle, and electronics never leave the drive housing. Rather, the cartridge slides into place among the components, allowing the drive to spin the disk and then access its surface.

For magnetic-only media, the read/write head very much resembles that of a hard disk drive. Newer products even use the same magneto-resistive (MR) head employed by current hard disk drives. The head flies just microinches above the surface of the spinning media, sensing changes in the magnetic field that it interprets into 1s and 0s. To write data onto the surface, a magnetic charge is applied to the desired point by passing an electric current through coils in the head.

Because removable disks are not as precise and stable as fixed hard disks, the capacities of these products do not compare to that of hard disks. In order to avoid making contact with the spinning media, the drive head must fly further from the surface, impeding its ability to detect weak magnetic fields. This limitation means that each bit must be larger than those found on hard disks. The net effect is that fewer bits are found on each square inch of removable media (a measurement known as *areal density*) than are found on a fixed hard disk. For more on areal density, see Chapter 11, "Hard Disk Guide."

13.1.3 Performance Impact Report

Near-line products won't make or break your system performance. In virtually all cases, you won't even notice that they are there. However, the relative speed with which they can access, transfer, and write files does vary significantly. If you need lightning-quick response for running program code off a near-line drive, your options are both limited and expensive. However, if you want occasional backups, archiving, and file swapping, there's a broad selection of products that provide workmanlike performance for the job.

As a general rule, don't expect these drives to give your hard disk a run for its performance money. In almost all cases, access times lag behind those of fixed, magnetic media. For best performance, large-capacity magnetic drives usually fare best, with seek times approaching 12ms.

Next in line are small-capacity magnetic drives, such as Iomega Zip. At this point, however, you're getting far enough away from hard disk–level performance that it's unlikely these devices can serve as a surrogate hard disk. Zip drives, for example, typically deliver random access times of about 25ms, nearly three times slower than the best hard disks.

At bottom of the performance heap? Magneto-optical drives, which use a laser to prep the media for writing data. The two stage optical-magnetic writing process is a comparatively lengthy one, resulting in dog-slow write access and transfer times. Reads can be fairly snappy but still lag behind those of large-capacity magnetic devices.

In almost all cases, however, performance is superior to CD-ROM and DVD-ROM drives. The media cartridges these drives use allow for more precision and tighter operation with the drive than do CD-ROMs, eliminating the need for time-consuming initialization, for example. Although data rates can be well in excess of the 1,800 to 4,800kbps that the fastest CD-ROMs deliver, this aspect of performance is generally unnoticeable—there are simply too few operations where transfer rates get completely soaked.

13.2 Currently Available Near-Line Storage

Near-line storage options can be broken into three (relatively) neat categories:

- Floppy disk successors

- Large-capacity magnetic

- Large-capacity magneto-optical (MO)

Products in different categories can often serve the same applications. Both a large-capacity magnetic and a large-capacity MO drive are suitable for backing up and archiving data. However, you'll find differences in the drive and media cost that may tip the balance in favor of one technology over the other. Even floppy disk follow-ups, with their 100MB to 200MB capacities, can serve as selective backup devices.

The near-line storage market is unique in that absolutely no standard formats exist to allow a drive from one company to read media from another. Iomega, SyQuest, Matsushita, and Pinnacle Micro all have their own proprietary media formats. Consider the direct opposite, the CD-ROM/DVD-ROM arena, where media formats are carefully sculpted to ensure that the 5.25-inch discs will play in any current drive.

13.2.1 Floppy Disk Successors

The least expensive, most pervasive, and potentially most important segment of the market is that of the floppy disk successor. These drives aim to supplant the aging and despised 3.5-inch floppy drives that sit in every single desktop PC sold over the last seven years. With capacities of 100MB to about 250MB, these drives lack the capacity to act as a near-line hard disk or to be used for mass backup. However, they are well suited to take over tasks from the overmatched and undersized floppy drive. In fact, many are able to both read and write existing 1.44MB floppy disks.

The numbers tell the story. When the 1.44MB floppy disk format first took hold, the typical PC had a 100MB hard disk drive. That meant you needed 65 or so floppies to store the contents of a full hard disk—and about half that with compression. Today's 100MB+ media deliver a similar disk-to-disk ratio on a typical 6.4GB hard drive. Therefore, 65 Iomega Zip drives will hold 6.5GB of data, returning us to the 65-to-1 ratio.

Of course, time marches on, and questions arise about whether 100MB is really enough for a long-term floppy disk successor. Sony, Teac, and others have gotten behind the HiFD format, a 200MB floppy-wannabe format that's about the same price as Zip. SyQuest, meanwhile, is breaking some of the rules in this segment. It has weighed in with a longer term solution, in the form of the SyQuest Sparq, which puts 1GB of data onto a removable disk. However, drives cost just $199— the same as the Iomega Zip. Although the media is about three times more costly than Zip disks, the actual cost per megabyte is much lower. A 1GB bundle of Zip discs will cost you $100 to $150 retail, whereas the same $100 will buy you three 1GB Sparq cartridges.

The following is a list of the existing floppy successor formats on or nearing the market. All these drives cost less than $200 retail and, with the exception of the SyQuest Sparq, offer media capacities of 250MB or less.

- Iomega Zip

- LS-120 SuperDisk drives (Imation, Compaq, Matsushita, others)

- Sony/Teac HiFD

- SyQuest EZFlyer 230

- SyQuest Sparq

If you want a true floppy disk replacement, you need other users to have the drive as well. Otherwise, there's no one to share the disks with. Although Iomega has an early jump on the market with Zip, the price of the drives and the media will ultimately tell the tale. In order for a drive to take off, penny-cautious system vendors need to find an option that fits their budgets.

One critical issue is compatibility with existing floppy disks. Both the LS-120 SuperDisk and HiFD drives are able to accept 1.44MB disks, eliminating the need to keep a second floppy disk drive handy for this still-common media type. In addition, SuperDisk drives are common in notebooks—something that only

Iomega's Zip has even begun to address. Recently, most of these drives became available for the IDE interface, adding to the SCSI and parallel port options offered by most vendors.

Table 13.1. A look at existing floppy alternative options.

Drive	Capacity	Cost	Cartridge Cost	Assessment
Teac floppy drive	1.44MB	$19.95	$0.25	Old, slow, but everywhere.
Iomega Zip	100MB	$150	$15	Established and growing install base, good performance, but at 100MB, it's the smallest of the contenders.
LS-120	120MB	$110–$150	$15	Compatible with floppies, some install base, and 20 percent more storage than Zip.
Sony/Teac HiFD	200MB	$150	TBD	Faster and bigger than Zip. Compatible with current floppies, but late to market and costly. Still, Sony knows how to craft standards.
SyQuest EZ Flyer	230MB	$150	$20	Good technology from SyQuest. Compatible with EZFlyer 135 media.
SyQuest Sparq	1GB	$200	$30	Could be *the* one. Ten times the capacity of Zip and quicker, too; however, no system OEMs have signed on.

Of course, even the cheapest, fastest, most capacious drive isn't going to catch on if the media costs a bundle. Table 13.2 provides a breakdown of the media costs for the contending technologies. A good metric for balancing out the relative costs of different capacity media is to look at the cost per megabyte. As you can see, today's floppy disks are by far the worst deal, costing about 35 cents for each megabyte of storage.

Table 13.2. Media cost comparison.

Drive	Media Cost (Per Unit)	Cost Per Megabyte
Teac floppy drive	$0.50	$0.35
Iomega Zip	$13	$0.13
LS-120	$15	$.12
Sony/Teac HiFD	TBD	TBD
SyQuest EZ Flyer 230	$20	$0.9
SyQuest Sparq 1GB	$30	$0.03

Not yet available at the time of this writing is the intriguing Orb product from Castlewood Systems. This drive uses the same magneto-resistive (MR) head technology used in today's hard disk drives, and it advances the low-cost magnetic media drive market toward and beyond the standard set by SyQuest's Sparq. Orb disks store 2.16GB of data on a 3.5-inch magnetic disk. Drive prices are expected just below $200—right in line with Zip and Sparq. Orb says the media will retail for about $30, for a cost per megabyte approaching a penny. We'll see.

It's worth noting here that the CD-RW drive and media are, in fact, a credible contender for floppy disk successor. The media is based on an industry standard and is compatible with tens of millions of already installed drives. However, CD-RW drives still cost close to $500—too much for system vendors to consider populating in their mainstream desktops—and the media remains somewhat expensive at about $15 per unit. By contrast, write-once CD-R media cost about $1 per disc.

13.2.2 Magnetic Large Capacity

You won't find better performance in a removable drive than that available from this class of magnetic media-based products. All these drives work on the same principals as your hard disk—and they deliver similarly swift access and high transfer rates. This is a drive segment on the rise, emerging from the shadow of magneto-optical (MO) drives that have long served as the primary choice for large-capacity, near-line data storage.

In fact, part of the reason why these drives are on the rise is the fact that floppy-class devices are starting to poke up into this stratosphere. SyQuest Sparq and Castlewood's Orb both carry floppy-class prices (under $200), yet provide respective media capacities of 1GB and 2.2GB. If these two drive manage to squelch the Zip movement and halt Sony's HiFD before it starts rolling, it's very likely that the next floppy standard will emerge from this large-capacity segment.

Today, large-capacity near-line storage is defined by big media (over a gig), fast access and throughput, and often high drive prices. These drives are perfect for a wide range of applications, including the following:

- Rapid-fire, full-disk backups

- Multimedia capture and playback

- Execution of applications

- Alternate boot device and operating system host

A number of drives serve this market now. Among the current and future offerings are the following:

- Iomega Jaz 2GB

- SyQuest SyJet 1.5GB

- SyQuest Sparq

- SyQuest Quest 4.7GB

- Castlewood Orb

SyQuest is really gunning for this segment of the market, with three different drives addressing different shades of removable mass storage needs. Ultimately, the SyJet is likely to get squeezed out of the picture, but it remains a known and respected brand name—a big deal in a fickle market.

One thing you won't see here are drives that use the pathetically slow parallel port interface. The parallel interface can muster only 1.2MBps transfer rates, robbing drives of up to 90 percent of their throughput potential. Although parallel connections are useful for notebooks and drive sharing, the performance hit on these higher capacity drives is devastating. Moving 1GB to 2GB worth of data from your system onto one of these drives will take a long time if you try to do it over a parallel connection.

For most of these units, consider a SCSI connection if you want to share the drive and enjoy the best balance of performance with other peripherals. If cost is a concern, shop for an IDE interface model. Of course, this means you'll have to find room inside your PC for the drive.

Table 13.3. Emerging near-line hard disk products.

Drive	Capacity	Drive Cost	Assessment
Western Digital 6.34GB hard disk	6.4GB	$280	Fast, faithful, and fixed.
Iomega Jaz 2GB	2GB	$500	Large capacity and affordable media, but sluggish performance for a magnetic drive.
SyQuest SyJet 1.5GB	1.5GB	$299	Another good SyQuest technology eclipsed by Sparq; provides fast performance.
SyQuest Quest 4.7GB	4.7GB	$500	Sparq won't succeed this one. Largest available magnetic data storage, fast performance, and a proven vendor.
SyQuest Sparq	1GB	$200	The only shipping cross-over contender in the near-line storage segment. Cheap drives, low-cost media, relatively quick.
Castlewood Orb	2.2GB	$200	Blockbuster prices and media capacities, but Orb remains unproven in the market.

When you get to the higher levels, the cost of media is certainly a factor. Although cost per megabyte is generally much lower than on floppy-class drives, the direct cost of the media is always much higher, because even if the cost per meg is half that of a Zip drive, the media holds 20 times as much data. That means you shell out 10 times more for a single disk than you do for a single (albeit smaller) Zip disk.

13.2.3 Magneto-Optical

In the past, the only way to get big storage was to go MO—magneto-optical, that is. These hybrid drives combine the talents of your hard disk and CD-ROM drive to deliver very large capacity removable media. These drives suffer from two serious problems, however. One, they are expensive; two, they are slow.

Figure 13.1.
The Maxoptix T6-5200 MO drive stores up to 5.2GB of data on a single 5.25-inch disk

So why do these drives exist at all? Until recently, you had no option but an MO drive if you wanted to be able to store more than 1GB of data on a removable disk. Magnetic removable drives were not yet available at those capacities, yet graphics professionals and others had an absolute need to safely store and share large image and media files.

MO drives have another critical advantage—data integrity. Magnetic media such as hard disks, floppy disks, and removable cartridges are written to by placing a magnetic charge on a disk's coating. Should a stray magnetic field come into contact with the disk, it's possible that the stored charges will be altered, thus corrupting the data. If you need to permanently archive information, the potential volatility of magnetic media is a concern. If your disks happen to get stored next to a magnetic source—such as a PC monitor, stereo speakers, or a speakerphone—prolonged exposure to the fields could silently wipe out your data.

MO disks eliminate this concern, because the drives use a combination of heat and magnetic fields to lay data on the disk. Although the coating on the disk is magnetic—and stores charges just like hard disks do—the media will not alter the polarity unless heated to a threshold temperature (called the *Curie point*). MO media can be placed directly against a magnetic source for long periods of time and not suffer any adverse consequences—unless, of course, it happens to be sitting in a 570-degree (F) room.

Figure 13.2.

MO disks, like this 2.6GB cartridge, are rated for 100 years of usable storage life.

The MO drive's laser does the cooking, prepping the media to receive a new magnetic charge. When the disk comes around again, the magnetic write head transfers the desired magnetic charge to the disk coating in the same way your hard disk does. The two-stage process slows things down dreadfully when writing data to disk—a real problem for multimedia capture (as well as impatient users). The dual-head technology also boosts the price to $2000 and beyond for models with 5GB capacities.

There are simply too many MO drives and vendors to list here. In fact, MO has little bearing on the mainstream performance area of the market, which is now very well served by magnetic media. Still, the high data capacities and relatively secure media makes these drives good for a number of applications, including the following:

- Hard disk backup

- Long-term data archiving

- Media and graphic file access and storage

- Medical imaging and other vertical imaging applications

An MO variant currently in development could give this technology a real shot in the arm. Near-field recording, developed by Terastor, promises to deliver 20GB capacities at near hard disk speeds. The technology, which is to be licensed to drive vendors, uses a flying head to read magnetic data, and a specially focused laser enables writing onto amazingly tiny spots on the disk. The result is areal densities unmatched by current magnetic drives, with a roadmap for serious improvements.

Terastor plans to introduce this technology into the mainstream hard disk market as well, thus enabling disks to continue their explosive capacity growth. Until then, however, the MO segment will benefit from removable media disks that will likely store five times the data available on a single-sided, single-layered DVD-ROM disc.

13.3 Evaluating Near-Line Storage

Before deciding on a specific product or even a particular drive technology, you should pay a lot of attention to your current and future needs. The decision-making process is a good deal more complicated than that for, say, hard disk drives because the formats keep changing. A bad decision will imperil your ability to share drives with others, not to mention prohibit you from having enough storage to make for a useful solution.

Here are some things to ask yourself before buying:

> Do I need to share these disks with other users and systems?
>
> Will I use and buy a lot of disks?
>
> Is performance critical?
>
> Am I looking for secure, long-term archiving?

We'll address these, and other, questions and provide a look at how each of the three near-line media types match up. This will help you think across technology lines, helping you find a drive that's not only fast, but useful, too.

13.3.1 Compatibility/Ubiquity

If you're searching for that elusive floppy drive replacement, the issue of compatibility with other drives is paramount. The only reason we have 3.5-inch floppies today at all is the fact that every system has a drive that will recognize the disks. That includes notebook PCs—an area that poses a bit of trouble for any of the emerging floppy disk successors.

Right now, there's simply no right answer to this issue. Iomega's Zip drive is clearly the farthest along, with millions of the 100MB drives installed in existing systems. Key PC vendors such as Dell, Micron, and Gateway offer Zip drives in many of their higher-end configurations, further seeding the nascent market. Iomega has also done a good job of covering the interface market, selling SCSI, parallel, and, most recently, IDE versions of its drive. In fact, Iomega Zip is as close as there is to a sure bet when dealing with service bureaus.

Compaq and Matsushita's LS-120 drive technology probably comes in second in the popularity contest. These drives have a big edge in the fact that they can read and write 1.44MB floppy disks, which means vendors and users don't have to worry about having a separate floppy drive during the ugly transition period to the new media type. Unfortunately, Compaq's backing seems to have scared off the major system OEMs, and LS-120's heat has really cooled in the market.

Surprisingly, the two drives with the best chance of taking on the Zip freight train are two with virtually no install base at this point. SyQuest's new Sparq drive is a truly revolutionary product that changes all the rules in the floppy-successor market. With 1GB capacities at affordable prices, it's in almost all ways a superior drive to the Zip. SyQuest is a market leader in the removable storage market, which should help it move drives into systems and through retail, but for now, Sparq is very much in its infancy.

The other contender here is HiFD, which is sponsored by Sony, a veteran standard-maker of legendary proportions. Sony pushed through the original 3.5-inch floppy standard, and the company hopes to anoint the successor in the form of the 200MB HiFD format. On the drive side, it has teamed up with Teac—a huge market maker in the floppy and CD-ROM drive business—which should help HiFD's chances. Like LS-120, HiFD drives will read and write floppy disks, easing the pain for users and system vendors alike.

None of the large-capacity near-line alternatives really play here, because they cost of the drives and the media make them inappropriate for the day-to-day file shuffle. Can you imagine dropping off a $50 Jaz disk with a stranger, just in order to hand over a few megabytes of files? Likewise, the high drive costs will cause system vendors to balk (and you need those guys cramming drives into their new PCs if you want a floppy successor to emerge). Still, if you want to share multigigabyte drives with someone, the Iomega Jaz gives you the best chance of success.

Likewise, MO is not a reasonable choice for sharing data. Vendors only build in compatibility for their own media and often supporting media that goes two generations back in the product family.

13.3.2 Capacity and Cost

Not so long ago, this picture was crystal clear. MO drives were way too expensive (and still are), large-capacity magnetic drives were moderately too expensive, and floppy successors were only mildly too expensive. Today, large-capacity drives are getting cheaper, thanks to SyQuest's terrific Sparq drive. This $199 drive delivers 1GB of storage per disk and blows away the competition in drive cost. Expect Sparq and Orb (if it works out) to put some much needed pressure on Iomega and the rest of the market.

The problem is, system vendors are not going to go for a drive that costs $200 retail (figure $100 for them) to install. Floppy disk drives cost a meager $10 or so ($20 to $30 retail), which is exactly why they are so ubiquitous. Although everyone is willing to pay a little more for a high-capacity floppy alternative, a premium of 10 to 20 times over existing floppy drives is probably out of hand.

If drive and media costs are the burning issues, the LS-120 is actually your best bet. Unlike Zip and Sparq, these drives are made by multiple vendors, enabling healthy pricing competition within the format. You can find LS-120 drives for $110, about 40 percent less than the cost of a Zip drive. With per disk media costs running about $13 (based on 10-unit quantities), the disks cost just a smidgen more than Zip, the least expensive media around. Remember, you're getting 20 percent more bits with LS-120 than with Zip, further sweetening the deal.

We can't talk about capacity without gushing about SyQuest Sparq. However, although the $199 drive price is right, the $30 per-disk cost is a bit intimidating if you just want to swap files with others. Do the division, however, and you'll find that you can't beat the Sparq's three-cent-per-megabyte media cost.

For real capacity, SyQuest trumps the Iomega Jaz 2GB. The Quest uses 4.7GB disks—the same capacity found in DVD-ROM discs—making it more than twice the data handler Jaz is. At $500, the drive costs just as much as the Jaz, making it a pretty clear price/capacity winner.

Although MO is no bargain, disk capacities edge out those available on large-capacity magnetic drives. If you need to store really large data files and multimedia clips, an MO drive can give you 5.2GB of storage on a single 5.25-inch disk. However, because the media is proprietary to each vendor, and because these drives sell into a limited market, disk costs can be substantially higher than those for popular magnetic drives.

13.3.3 Performance

When it comes to getting things done fast, the floppy-wannabes fall away. Hard disk–level products such as Jaz and Quest offer access times and transfer rates reasonably close to that of fixed disks. All these drives are available with a SCSI interface, which maximizes performance, particularly when multiple drives are operating at once.

For copying large files, playing back video and animation, and doing disk backups, the key performance issue is transfer rate. SyQuest rates its Quest drive at transfer rates of 10.6MBps, although the write data rate is half that at just over 5MBps. Average seek time is rated at 12ms, about 25 percent slower than the 9ms time rated in a fast IDE hard disk drive. However, that number is 10 to 20 times better than a typical CD-ROM drive, and twice as good as a Zip drive. Jaz offers similar numbers, with an 11ms seek time and about a 7MBps transfer rate.

Some of the floppy contenders flop around in the performance arena. Iomega Zip poops out with a sluggish 29ms seek time, whereas transfer rates are about 1MBps, one-seventh that of Jaz. The real winner here—again—is the Sparq, which matches the performance numbers of the Quest. That makes it by far the swiftest floppy-class drive option.

It's worth noting here that although MO drives are painfully slow at writing data to disk, they can actually approach hard disk speeds during read operations. The reason: The laser mechanism is not involved in reading data, freeing the drive to perform all operations in a single step. This performance disparity makes MO inappropriate for casual use that may involve lots of reading and writing, because the drive will bog down badly when you send data to the disk.

A related technology to MO drives are WORM drives. WORM stands for *write-once, read-many*, and it's a magneto-optical format that only allows for a single write to the cartridged media. Although CD-R and CD-RW have largely taken over this niche, WORM still plays a role in regulated data archiving, where the ability to audit data writes is needed to confirm the integrity of archived data.

13.3.4 Interface

Three decisions face most users: SCSI, IDE, or parallel port. Each has its advantages and drawbacks, which are well covered in other areas of this book. Still, a quick rundown of the relevant issues is called for here. In some cases, drives may not be available in certain interface versions. For example, the Quest only ships for a fast-wide SCSI interface, whereas none of the large-capacity products come equipped for parallel port.

The mainstream market tends to get involved when the letters IDE pop up next to product names. However, this class presents a challenge because the IDE bus is getting very crowded very quickly. Already, most PCs have at least a hard disk and CD-ROM drive running off IDE, which leaves only two available channels. With recordable CD, all DVD-ROM, and tape backup already vying for space on the IDE cable, some users may face a resource crunch.

What's more, the IDE bus could foil the high-performance benefits of drives such as the Iomega Jaz and SyQuest Sparq. Simultaneous drive accesses can block the IDE bus, forcing your busy drives to wait for an opening in the traffic. Of course, if you have that many IDE drives running in your system already, you may be all out of externally accessible drive bays.

If you intend to have a multitude of storage devices running on your PC, it may be time to seriously consider a SCSI adapter. Removable media drives, by definition, are more convenient when the drives are sitting on the desk, rather than between your knees. If you swap disks a lot, you'll appreciate not having to constantly duck and bend to get at the drive in your PC.

Parallel port interfaces appear on many of the floppy-class disk drives, allowing excellent flexibility. A parallel drive can be easily shared between a notebook and desktop PC, or it can provide a solution to a PC that lacks drive bays or IDE connections. You'll pay a price, though, in performance. Parallel throughput is sluggish, and access times will suffer, too. Also, you face the issue of having to probably share the parallel port with a printer and perhaps some other device already installed on the PC.

My advice: If you intend to spend money on a removable drive that you want to be big, flexible, fast, and compatible, don't blow it by putting it onto your parallel port. You'll find that large data transfers will bog down hopelessly, so much so that you may avoid using the drive altogether.

13.3.5 Durability/Shelf Life

You thought we'd never talk about MO, didn't you? Well, here's where the expensive, slow, incompatible, and generally ornery MO drives get their comeuppance. When it comes to safely tucking away bits, you can't do better than one of these products. Yes, CD-R and CD-RW offer similar durability in a distributable medium, but their capacities flame out at a scrawny 650MB. Even the capacities of DVD-RAM/DVD+RW discs—currently stuck at or below 3GB—won't match the 5.2GB and growing capacities of today's MO drives.

MO drive media are generally rated for anywhere from 100 to 300 years of useful life. That means you can save your data, grow old, and die before you have to worry about its integrity. In fact, the biggest problem will be ensuring that you can find a drive to read your aging media, because MO disks are not compatible across vendor lines. With that said, vendors do generally offer at least a generation or two of backward compatibility within their product families, allowing users to at least transition data to new media without too much hassle.

Keep in mind that magnetic media is not made of glass—well, sometimes it is, but you get the idea. A properly stored magnetic cartridge can and usually will keep its data safe and secure for years on end. I have six-year-old floppy disks, for example, that I've pulled out of the bottom of an old box and have had no problem pulling data off them. However, the real danger of losing your data to a stray (and especially persistent) magnetic field does exist.

If you need to do mission-critical backup, archiving, and record keeping, it's best not to do it with a magnetic drive. However, if you want a way to perform occasional data backups that you'll repeat periodically, a fast magnetic drive will allow you to do them quicker and more quietly than you could with a tape drive. Just be sure to take proper care of the written disk.

13.4 Tom's Pick

In such a broad market segment, it's extremely hard to pick a single technology or product. After all, someone looking for the data integrity features provided by WORM drives isn't likely to be considering SuperDisk or Zip drives for the same application. With that said, when it comes to high-performance computing, a single, best option does present itself—SyQuest's Sparq.

Yes, the Iomega Zip drive is more ubiquitous, the SuperDisk drive is more compatible (with 1.44MB floppies), and the Iomega Jaz 2GB is more capacious; however, none of these drives delivers the all-around combination of price, performance, capacity, and utility presented by Sparq. This $199 drive features spacious 1GB 3.5-inch cartridged discs (10 times the size of Zip) and is available for both IDE and SCSI interfaces.

Sparq's performance is also on par with the best large-capacity drives, such as Iomega Jaz and SyQuest SyJet 1.5GB. Its 12ms access times are nearly a match for the newest IDE hard disk drives. The media is affordable, too. Sparq discs offer nearly three times the capacity of Zip discs, at one-third the cost. Finally, SyQuest's proven record in the removable storage arena means that users can feel confident that the company can produce plentiful and reliable drives and media.

Chapter

14

Optical Storage Guide

14.1 Understanding CD-ROM, DVD-ROM, and Writable Drives

It wasn't all that long ago—1994 or 1995—that every PC *didn't* come with a CD-ROM drive. The hard disk stored all the applications and data, and 1.44MB floppy disks were used to move and share data among PCs. Despite growing program and file sizes, floppies were still considered adequate for distributing software and handling files. The emergence of multimedia features, and enormous programs such as Microsoft Office, CorelDRAW, and Windows, changed all that.

A solution arrived in the form of an optical drive and media format called *CD-ROM (Compact Disc-Read Only Memory)*. CD-ROM discs use the same form factor and technology used in popular audio CD discs. However, unlike the magnetic media used in hard drives and floppy drives, the optical CD-ROM drives cannot write data to the media, thus the moniker ROM (for read-only memory).

The familiar-looking CD-ROM discs changed the ecology of PC-based mass storage. The optical CD-ROM discs hold up to 650MB of data, nearly twice the amount held on the 340MB hard disks common when CD-ROMs first emerged. Today, CD-ROMs are the preferred method for mass distribution of software and data, including digital video and audio files that are simply too large to store otherwise.

The success of CD-ROM drives, combined with expanding files sizes, motivated advances in optical drives. Rewritable versions of CD drives allow users to create their own 650MB optical discs, whereas the DVD format pushes mass storage to the next level. This chapter will introduce you to the workings of optical media and their impact on system performance.

14.1.1 How Optical Storage Works

Optical drives such as CD-ROM and DVD-ROM drives are both similar and different from magnetic-based hard disks. Like hard disk drives, optical drives detect variations on the surface of a spinning disk, which are then interpreted as digital 1s and 0s. An actuator arm positions a read head along the surface of the media so that the desired bits travel directly under it to be accessed.

The similarities end there. The read head of a hard disk drive detects changes in the polarity of slight magnetic charges embedded in the disk media. CD-ROM and DVD-ROM drives, on the other hand, focus a beam of light onto the spinning media. A lens detects changes in the reflected light, which indicate the presence or absence of pits burned into the disk surface. Changes in reflection are interpreted as data by a microprocessor inside the CD-ROM drive.

Performance

As a rule, the performance of optical drives lags well behind that of magnetic hard disk drives. Where the typical hard disk can access data in less than 10 milliseconds (ms), a CD-ROM or DVD-ROM drive takes 80 to 200ms to access data. Data rates are much lower as well. A small amount of cache RAM—often 256KB or 512KB—in the drive can help to boost these initial accesses.

A number of issues impact the ability of CD-ROM drives to keep pace with hard disks. For one, CD-ROM (and DVD-ROM) discs are not fixed within a sealed chassis, thus limiting the rotation speed of the media. Where fast hard disks can spin at 7200 or even 10000 revolutions per minute (rpm), CD-ROM drives spin at about 6300rpm. The fastest CD-ROM drives spin at 32× spin rates, at which point vibration in the spinning media becomes a serious issue.

However, disc makers aren't done pushing the specs. A company called Zen Research has now developed technology to read and buffer entire tracks and even multiple tracks of a CD-ROM. The result of the caching is an effective 40× drive speed without inviting stability problems encountered at very high spin rates.

Likewise, access times are impaired by the slower spin-up speeds of optical discs. Because the optical media is not fixed to a spindle the way hard disk platters are, the drive must incrementally increase the spin rate. In fact, you can often hear the CD-ROM drive mechanism spinning up when you first access the disc. The time needed to get up to speed can rob long microseconds from initial accesses.

With hard disks, the density of bits on the media can impact performance. However, the density of pits on CD-ROM media is determined by the format. Therefore, it's not possible to simply squeeze pits closer together in order to boost the amount of data that passes beneath the read head.

The DVD-ROM format improves performance by packing bits closer together. Where CD-ROM drives use a 300nm-wide red-colored laser beam, DVD-ROM drives use a tighter yellow-colored beam that's only 50nm across. The result is greater disc data densities and higher throughput.

Spin Rates Explained

CD-ROM drives are distinguished by their rotation rate, expressed in terms of the number of times faster they spin than audio CD discs. The first CD-ROM drives spun at 1× rate, whereas today's drives operate at spin rates of 24× or 32×. Although the faster spin rate doesn't have much impact on access times, the amount of data that can be read off the disc each second increases in proportion with the spin rate. It's worth noting that the newest drives run 32 times faster

Optical Storage Guide

when reading along the outer edge of the disc. Near the center of the disc, spin rates are typically about 12× to 14×.

The first 1× CD-ROM drives could read 150KBps of data, whereas the first popular CD-ROM drive types—2× models—could move 300KBps. At this rate, the drives were fast enough to play back low-resolution software-based video files, as well as MPEG-1 video. Today's 24× drives can feasibly move 36,000KBps, or 3.5MBps. 32× models up that figure to nearly 4.7MBps, but the overall impact is negligible. In fact, few CD-ROM operations require the full throughput of the drive, because most titles and software are designed to run on a lowest common denominator of 2× or 4× drives. With that said, file copies and program installations do gain significantly.

Until recently, drives spun their discs at a variable rate so that the pits passed beneath the head at a constant rate no matter where on the disc the read head is located. This was done because the outside of the disc always spins faster than the inside. Rather than slow down the entire drive to keep the outer ring of the disc below the read head's threshold, vendors varied the spin speed, spinning the disc faster when the head is at the inside of the disc and slower at the outside.

This scheme is called *constant linear velocity (CLV)* and is employed in virtually all CD-ROM drives of 12× and slower spin rates. As the read head moves toward the outside of the disc, the spin rate slows. The result: Maximum theoretical data throughputs remain fixed.

Newer CD-ROM drives use a *constant angular velocity (CAV)* approach. Here, the drive spins at a single speed at all times, no matter where the read head is positioned. At the outside of the disc, therefore, data can be read much more quickly than it is at the inside. This is similar to the way that hard disks operate and means that data along the outer edges can be read faster than data near the center.

CAV CD-ROM drives are usually rated using two performance speeds, reflecting the relative rate at the inside and the outside of the disc. Today, the fastest drives use CAV and are rated at 12× to 24× or 14× to 32×. The spin rate along the inside is limited to 12× or 14× because at higher speeds the disc begins to vibrate too much to allow for reliable operation. Yet the faster outside access allows CD-ROM drives to take advantage of more advanced electronics easily capable of processing data at the higher rates.

Table 14.1. Data transfer rates vary greatly with CAV drives.

Drive Speed	Minimum	Maximum
1×	150 KBps	150 KBps
2×	300 KBps	300 KBps

Drive Speed	Minimum	Maximum
4×	600 KBps	600 KBps
6×	900 KBps	900 KBps
8×	1200 KBps	1200 KBps
10×	1500 KBps	1500 KBps
12×	1800 KBps	1800 KBps
12× to 20×★	1800 KBps	3000 KBps
12× to 24×★	1800 KBps	3600 KBps
12× to 32×★	1800 KBps	4800 KBps

★ *Uses constant angular velocity (CAV), so effective rotation speed at the center of the disc is lower than at the outside edge.*

Optical Storage Guide

Interface

The vast majority of CD-ROM drives today use the IDE interface provided on the PC motherboard. Both IDE and SCSI have more than enough bandwidth to handle even the fastest CD-ROM drive; however, the two vary greatly in their efficiency. As a general rule, if you crave performance, you should buy a SCSI-based CD-ROM drive or a model that uses the ATA-33 interface.

Why? Because the basic IDE interface requires a lot of CPU hand-holding when conducting PIO (programmed I/O) mode transactions. So when your CD-ROM is reading off data, your CPU is doing little else than passing it along. With large or frequent file transfers, the result can be a lot of lost time. SCSI takes the CPU out of the picture, allowing the CD-ROM to read off data while other things are happening. Although this does not necessarily improve data throughput or access times, it will improve the overall responsiveness of your PC.

Newer systems and CD-ROM drives alleviate this problem by using efficient transfer modes found on the ATA-33 (also known as *ultra DMA* or *ultra ATA*) interface. Access to DMA transfers removes the CPU from the transaction process, and burst-mode operation reduces the amount and frequency of address information moving along the bus.

SCSI drives not only provide superior multitasking to IDE, they offer the additional advantage of allowing external drives. What's more, SCSI is the only interface that's fast enough for CD-to-CD copying. If you're out of space on your PC or prefer the flexibility of an external drive, SCSI is your only choice. The problem: SCSI drives cost significantly more than their IDE counterparts.

14.1.2 Performance Impact Report

As discussed earlier, CD-ROM and even DVD-ROM drives provide significantly slower response and lower data rates than do typical hard disk drives. The main advantage of these media types is that they are portable and can hold a lot of data on a standard disc. With that said, performance varies a lot among the different types.

CD-ROM Drives

CD-ROM performance is best expressed by the spin rate, with the fastest drives using CAV to spin at 12× to 32× rates. For top performance, you'll want to get a SCSI drive, because this will relieve the CPU of processing overhead. Although IDE drives can move and access data every bit as fast as SCSI models, your CPU won't be able to attend to other tasks in the process.

Another thing to look for is a large internal cache, often 256KB or 512KB of RAM. The RAM lets the drive get a jump start on data accesses, but it's too small to help large transfers. For this, you'll want to make sure you have a good disc cache in place, such as that used in Windows 95 and Windows 98. This software reserves space on a fast hard disk for storing CD-ROM directory information and expected data, thus significantly aiding performance.

Drive quality can really have a role in performance. Better drives use superior optics and provide more stable operation to avoid disruptive vibration in the disc. Drives that use disc caddies for loading the media can improve performance by limiting vibration and other unwanted movement of the media during operation.

CD-R and CD-RW Drives

Make no mistake: If you use a CD-R or CD-RW drive as your only CD-ROM device, you *will* sacrifice performance. If you need fast access and data transfers, no CD-R or CD-RW drive will be able to keep pace with even a cheap 14× to 32× CD-ROM drive. Most recordable CD drives play back discs at relatively slow 8× speeds, one-fourth the rate of the fastest CD-ROM drives. If you want reasonable playback performance, consider using a standard CD-ROM drive alongside the CD recorder.

Recording performance is an issue also. Most recorders put information onto the disc while spinning at rates of 2× or 4×. Again, the faster the spin rate, the more quickly data can be laid down on the media. However, as with CD-ROM drives, you'll get better overall performance using a SCSI-based product, because SCSI is able to handle bus overhead asynchronously—that is, allowing commands to be processed without holding up data delivery. As a result, only SCSI will allow you to write from a CD-ROM directly to a recordable CD drive.

DVD-ROM Drives

DVD-ROM drives provide superior data transfer rates to their CD-ROM cousins due to a single factor—greater area densities on the disc. DVD-ROMs are able to store 4.7GB of data in the same space CD-ROMs store 650MB because the data pits are placed much closer together. The tighter wavelength laser does the trick, allowing both individual pits and the concentric tracks to be pushed closer together.

Because the pits are closer together, more pass under the read head in a given period of time. The result is that data rates increase to 2,000KBps despite the fact that the DVD-ROM disc never spins at rates higher than 20×. Like new CD-ROM drives, DVD-ROM drives use a CAV approach to vary disc speed according to the location of the read head.

14.2 Currently Available Optical Storage

One thing's for sure: There's certainly no lack of standards-based optical storage formats. Whether you need a drive to read shrink-wrapped programs and titles, or a device to create archives and multimedia content, there's a drive for you. In fact, deciding what type of drive to go with is the real challenge, because neat new features often come at the expense of straightforward performance.

This section will help you weigh your options by providing in-depth information about each alternative.

14.2.1 CD-ROM

CD-ROM is the workhorse removable media format for PCs, and it has enabled a wide variety of new applications. The familiar 5.25-inch discs, which are identical in appearance to those used in audio CD players, can store 650MB. Today, the format is widely used to distribute software, media files, and other large data sets.

Because of the low cost of both CD-ROM drives and their media, these drives are a near-necessity for any PC. Most major applications now ship standard on CD-ROM—if you need floppy disks, you must often order a special package. Likewise, most games and reference titles require that the CD-ROM be in the drive in order to access the large amounts of data used by the interface. In these cases, there's no floppy alternative.

After years of explosive speed increases, CD-ROM drives have reached the limits of their performance. Drive makers cannot speed up the spin rate of drives any further without running afoul of thorny—and expensive—vibration problems. For this reason, you won't see drives spinning higher than 32X. Even at this level, however, returns on performance have been diminishing, in part because faster spin speeds do nothing to improve data access times.

Finally, the CD-ROM format is running out of gas in terms of data capacity. Many games and applications now require two or more CD-ROMs to store all the program code and related data files—an expensive proposition for vendors. In addition, the current format lacks enough storage to deliver two hours of theater-quality video—a real concern for multimedia publishers looking to bring their titles to the next level.

CD-ROM drives are so ubiquitous and so necessary to PC operation that a wide variety of types has emerged. Where other optical drives are available in only one or two form factor types, CD-ROM drives run an impressive gamut:

- Internal or external
- Tray fed or caddy fed
- Single or jukebox

In or Out

Internal CD-ROM drives are inexpensive, unobtrusive, and secure. However, external devices provide enhanced flexibility and added convenience by placing the drive on the desktop. If you want an external drive, your only real choice is a SCSI model (although you can go with a slow parallel port device, usually used on notebooks). The SCSI bus adds to the expense already incurred in the CD-ROM's external chassis and separate power supply.

Loading Type

Most of today's CD-ROM drives use a tray-fed loading mechanism, for the most part because they're dirt cheap. However, these mechanisms are prone to attracting dirt to the optics and can be easily damaged by an errant kneecap. Caddy-fed drives resolve the dirt and damage issue by forcing the user to insert a caddy into the CD-ROM slot—no component of the drive ever wanders outside of the case. The disc itself is held inside the caddy, which allows for reliable side-mounted operation (some tray models won't do this) and better vibration control.

To use caddies properly though, you really need many that are used to store a specific CD-ROM. That can get expensive. If you choose to swap discs in and out of the caddies, you face additional time wrestling with the cases. One recent introduction among internal drives is the use of slot-fed mechanisms, similar to those found on car CD audio players. These may be the best choice of all, as they combine the error-free design of caddies with the convenience of tray operation.

Single or Jukebox

Most desktops use affordable, single-disc drives, but you may want to consider a jukebox drive if you have a number of discs you need to access frequently. Affordable versions of these drives hold anywhere from four to seven discs and let you switch among discs directly from Windows Explorer. These drives are also popular for shared access over a network, allowing managers to make a variety of reference materials available at all times.

Jukeboxes have some serious drawbacks, though. For one, they're a good deal more expensive than single-disc units, so you really want to have a need for them. Also, they tend to lag behind the latest drive specs, thus limiting performance. Finally, switching among discs in the drive can be a tooth-grinding ordeal, as the mechanism moves discs into place, initializes the disc, and finds the bits. In some cases, flawed drives cause the operating system to initialize all the discs every time you start the system or open Explorer—a process that can take minutes.

14.2.2 CD Writable

People have been talking about these drives for a long time, but they've finally become attractive due to a number of advancements. The most important is price. You can buy a decent recordable CD player for as little as $299, making it an affordable way to write data to a universally recognized format.

There are two types of recordable CD drives:

- CD-Recordable (CD-R)
- CD-Rewritable (CD-RW)

Both drive types use specially designed discs that allow the small laser in the drive to alter the properties of the disc coating. This process changes the reflectivity of the media, allowing CD-ROM drives to interpret 1s and 0s on the media. However, because actual pits are not created on the media, older drives lack the ability to recognize the different reflection signature produced by recordable units. You'll have to make sure that your intended audience is properly equipped before using a CD-R or CD-RW drive to distribute data to others.

CD-R Drives

CD-R drives are able to write data once to special CD-R media recognizable by virtually all CD-ROM drives sold over the last three years. This capability makes CD-R a good choice for archiving valuable data, as well as for distributing software or data to a limited audience. Because the optical media is immune to compromise from stray magnetic fields, the format provides excellent durability— a key consideration for archiving data.

Optical Storage Guide

The write-once capability of CD-R media is a drawback. CD-R drives use a relatively high-powered yellow laser to heat the green-colored chemical coating on the CD-R disc. When heated, this coating reacts with an underlayer of gold-color media, altering the reflectivity of the heated point. The drive creates the illusion of pits and lands on the media, which most CD-ROM drives are able to detect. However, because the change is permanent, it precludes writing to any portion of the disc that already carries data. Also, the chemical pits are not as prominent as on professionally pressed CD-ROMs, which is why older drives may not be able to recognize CD-R media.

CD-RW Drives

More recently, CD-Rewritable drives have become an affordable option. Like CD-R, CD-RW is an optical medium that is immune to stray magnetic fields and fits neatly into any CD-ROM or CD-R drive. These characteristics make CD-RW attractive for backup, archiving, and distribution. At the same time, the rewritable nature means that the CD-RW drive is essentially a super-charged floppy disk drive, able to write vast amounts of data to a universally recognized format.

Or is it? In order to write data to the same portion of the media many times, the drive cannot permanently change the surface. Rather, CD-RW fires laser pulses at a crystalline, phase-changed media, which causes the exposed point to go from being reflective to nonreflective, or vice versa. CD-ROM drives are then able to interpret the presence or absence of a reflection as digital 1s or 0s. Each point on a CD-RW disc can be rewritten about 1,000 times.

Unfortunately, CD-ROM drives have only recently been designed to look for the unique CD-RW created change in reflectivity. Many older drives simply will not recognize these discs. Most CD-RW drives can write to CD-R media, however, which does broaden the potential audience for write-once data.

14.2.3 DVD-ROM

DVD has really started to shake things up. This high-density, high data rate optical media was first designed to replace the venerable laser disc format used for video playback. Recognizing the potential of the format's superior performance and data capacity, computing companies have been quick to support the new specification. Today, DVD-ROM drives have replaced CD-ROM drives in many high-end PCs, and upgrade kits are widely available as well.

DVD-ROM uses the same 5.25-inch form factor disc used by CD-ROM drives, but the media is burned using a tighter pattern of tracks and pits to increase the density of data by about 7.5 times. The result: A single DVD-ROM disc can store 4.7GB of data on a single side, compared to 650MB for CD-ROM drives. The tighter pits also improve performance. Despite not spinning any faster than CD-ROM drives, DVD-ROM drives can move up to 2MBps of data, enough to produce 30-frame-per-second, high-resolution MPEG-2 video.

Although 4.7GB sounds like a lot compared to CD-ROM drives, it's clear that the demands for compact data storage are insatiable. DVD-ROM provides additional storage by using a clever multilayered media that allows the laser to read two sets of data on a single side of the disc. This is done by using a coating that absorbs laser light when shined from straight on, yet becomes transparent when the light strikes at an angle. This property allows the read head to access two layers of data on a single side of the disc. Because of the way the coatings are overlaid, some density is lost in the process. A single-sided, dual-layer disc can hold 8.5GB of data, not 9.4GB (as you might expect).

DVD-ROM is also specified to provide two sides of data storage. These double-sided discs provide a straight 2× increase in the amount of available capacity. Therefore, a single-layer disc with two sides holds 9.4GB of data, whereas a two-sided disc with double-layers will hold 17GB. In virtually all affordable DVD-ROM drives, the user will have to flip the disc to access data on the second side.

Table 14.2 shows how the data capacities break down, based on the layers and sides employed on the media.

Table 14.2. The many faces of DVD-ROM storage.

Media type	Data capacity
Single-sided, single-layer	4.7GB
Single-sided, dual-layer	8.5GB
Double-sided, single-layer	9.4GB
Double-sided, dual-layer	17GB

Early DVD-ROM drives lacked compatibility with CD-R and CD-RW media and could only spin CD-ROMs at the equivalent of 6× spin rates. Be on the lookout for these older drives and avoid them if possible. Otherwise, you'll not be able to play recordable optical media and will suffer from subpar CD-ROM operation. The compatibility issue arises because of the red laser DVD-ROM drives employ to read the media. The green-tinted chemical layer on recordable CD-ROM media absorbs too much of the red laser light, thus preventing adequate reflection to let the drive read data.

Second-generation drives resolved these problems. To read CD-R and CD-RW discs, DVD-ROM drives actually added a second laser that uses the same yellow light used by standard CD-ROM drives. This eliminates the light absorption

Optical Storage Guide

problem and allows for reliable playback. Spin rates were also notched up in these drives, to the equivalent of 20× performance with CD-ROM discs.

14.2.4 DVD Writable

DVD-ROM is a slam dunk, but things get ugly with recordable versions of DVD. Here, a protracted and confusing standards spat has turned this promising technology into a huge risk. The following recordable specifications were still vying for the market at the time of this writing:

- DVD-Recordable (DVD-R)

- DVD-Random Access Memory (DVD-RAM)

- DVD-Rewritable (DVD+RW)

- Divx

- Multimedia Video Format (MMVF)

Each specification has its own set of sponsoring companies, slightly different mission, and varying capacities. All conform to the same, magic 5.25-inch form factor that made the CD-ROM disc such a huge hit. However, none store as much data as a standard DVD-ROM disc, a key differentiation from the CD recordable market, where these formats offer the same 650MB capacities found in the base CD-ROM specification. Ultimately, several of these standards can—and probably will—coexist on the market, fracturing the compatibility and publishing picture.

DVD-R

The first enhancement to the DVD-ROM specification was DVD-R, which acts much like CD-R. Drives are able to write a single time to any portion of the DVD-R media, making the format excellent for permanent and secure archiving of data. However, the write-once capability precludes DVD-R's use as a general-purpose data-sharing media.

A DVD-R disc can hold 3.95GB of data, a bit less than you'll find on a bare bones DVD-ROM disc. Also like CD-R, DVD-R uses an organic dye layer that interacts with the substrate below to create permanent—if illusionary—pits in the media. A laser heats the overlying material, causing the interaction. DVD-R discs are readable by the newest DVD-ROM drives, as well as by DVD-RAM drives. Of course, CD-ROM drives and their variants cannot recognize the high-density media.

DVD-RAM

The first rewritable DVD specification, DVD-RAM became the quick target of most industry players as they passed on the limited DVD-R to focus on this versatile media type. DVD-RAM uses a phase-change media—similar to CD-RW—that toggles between reflective and absorptive when exposed to a laser pulse. This allows the drive to create the illusion of pits on the media, as well as being able to overwrite areas already altered.

DVD-RAM can only hold 2.6GB of data on a side, nearly half the single-side capacity of DVD-ROM discs. This will pose a limitation for those who want to use a DVD-RAM drive to mirror professionally published DVD-ROM media. To extend the capacity, DVD-RAM allows for dual-sided recording, pushing total available capacity to 5.2GB. Of course, the disc will need to be flipped to do this.

A final drawback: The initial DVD-RAM spec called for the media to be used in a cartridged format, similar to that used by many MO and PD drives. Of course, DVD-ROM drives don't generally come equipped to accept cartridges, nullifying the whole point of a compatible media type.

The spec has since been revised to allow for noncartridged use, but only for single-sided discs. If you opt for dual-sided operation, you'll need to use the cartridge for both playback and recording. An enhanced version of DVD-RAM, due in 1999, will also resolve the capacity problem, allowing up to 4.7GB of data to be recorded on a side.

DVD+RW

A group of companies—including Sony, HP, and Philips—split from the DVD Forum and its DVD-RAM specification to create their own rewritable DVD standards. Called *DVD Rewritable*, or *DVD+RW*, this format shares the phase-changed media that's used with the DVD-RAM standard. Like DVD-RAM, the media can be recorded on two sides to effectively double the storage. However, several differences exist, and initial drives will not be compatible with DVD-RAM.

The DVD+RW group pushed up the capacity on their discs to 3GB, adding about 400MB over the capacity offered by DVD-RAM. In addition, DVD+RW does not require a cartridge for recording operation, which is a requirement for DVD-RAM. This bare-disc recording scheme should help reduce the cost of DVD+RW drives and provide a more appealing consumer package.

Divx

This format is aimed straight at the consumer video rental market and therefore has a limited impact on the PC space. Minted by Circuit City and others, Divx is a DVD-based format that enables a pay-per-view scheme for disc content. Divx players will include a modem for calling into a payment center, where users make a credit card payment to gain access to the disc content for a limited period of time. At the end of the time period, the disc becomes unreadable unless the user again pays an incremental viewing fee.

Divx main impact may be to stall the burgeoning DVD player market on the home electronics side. Divx and DVD discs are not compatible, and DVD players (at least as they are made now) cannot make sense of the Divx format. Adding Divx to consumer players is expected to add another $100 to the price of the hardware. Of course, PC-based DVD-ROM drives will be unable to recognize Divx, unless modifications are made.

MMVF

Launched by NEC, the MMVF file format takes the capacity high road. It offers more data storage than any other rewritable specs—up to 5GB per side on a disc. However, the lack of an industry group—and the longish moniker—seem to make MMVF the dark horse in the rewritable DVD race.

14.3 Evaluating Optical Storage

With so many standards, choices, and applications available, choosing an appropriate optical format is a tough decision. All the more so because your choice can really impact your system performance. Buy a CD-RW drive to burn the occasional disc, and you'll find yourself hampered with spin rates and access times several generations behind those of the latest $150 CD-ROM drive. A host of bus issues, compatibility questions, and industry trends come into play.

There are two major flavors of optical storage, which we'll split out to keep things in sync:

- Read-only
- Recordable/rewritable

The following sections run through these two categories, providing comparisons of the drive types and the factors that should be considered when making your purchase.

14.3.1 Read-only Optical Storage

For fast, cheap, reliable data access, you can't beat a good CD-ROM or DVD-ROM drive. Because they lack the additional electronics and optics required to write data to disc, these drives are less expensive, better integrated, and faster than their writing counterparts. If you play games or access and move large files from optical media types, you should make sure a read-only optical drive is in your system.

Performance in Applications

CD-ROM drives are ubiquitous, and by 2001, DVD-ROM drives should be on their way to unseating CD-ROM as the universal standard. Because these drives can—or will (in the case of DVD-ROM drives)—be found on every PC, every application developer assumes they are there.

Of course, this means your PC spends more and more of its time accessing data and code from the optical drive, instead of the hard disk. With optical drives typically offering performance that is 10 times slower than hard disk drives, that can spell trouble. For those particularly dependent on optical data access, therefore, a fast drive and beefed up caching scheme are needed.

When it comes to optical drive usage, applications split into three categories:

- General-purpose applications

- Reference

- Games

General-purpose Applications

General-purpose applications are those that are delivered on CD-ROM (such as any business productivity application or OS) but that do not require the presence of the disc to run. Of course, there may be clipart, templates, and other files on the disc that you may access occasionally, but overall, optical drive performance is not critical to the behavior and performance of these applications.

In these cases, CD-ROM performance becomes a minor issue. Sure, installation can get a big boost from a fast spinning drive, but that's an operation that happens perhaps two or three times in the shelf life of an application. If all you do is run Lotus Notes and Microsoft Office, the dollars you spend doubling your drive speed to 24X will be largely wasted. You'll do much, much better pouring more RAM into a system like this, because both these applications really need 64MB to work well in a multitasked environment.

Reference Titles

Here's where CD-ROM and DVD-ROM performance becomes critical. Programs such as Microsoft Encarta and DeLorme Map N Go rely on the presence of a CD-ROM disc to supply requested data. Although program code executes from the hard disk drive, virtually all the data—hundreds of megabytes of it—come from the optical drive.

Often, programs such as these are utterly CPU bound. The fastest Pentium II with 128MB of RAM can't do a thing, because it's locked up waiting for sluggish CD-ROM I/O. Trying to quickly browse through or find specific data can really get bogged down unless you have a fast CD-ROM drive in place.

The iron rule of optical performance is simple: Fast data rates are easy, but fast access is hard. In fact, most of the time you spend waiting on an optical drive is due to the device trying to find bits on the disc. Once things get moving— provided the data is contiguous, as it often is—transfers can be relatively speedy.

This problem undercuts all the impressive "specmanship" surrounding the latest CD-ROM drive. That 12X to 32X CD-ROM drive you just bought will not double the perceived performance of applications that were running on an old 12X or even 8X drive, because the access times have barely budged. In fact, access times on a good 12X drive can be much lower than those on a $100 32X drive. Unless all you do is pour huge data sets, video, and application loads onto your PC, the thing to look for is access time.

Games

Surprisingly, for many games CD-ROM performance is not that much of an issue. With the exception of interactive movie titles, the CD-ROM drive is rarely accessed in the midst of the action. Rather, data is downloaded at the beginning of a scene, mission, or level, and then accessed directly from the fast hard disk.

Of course, a faster CD-ROM or DVD-ROM drive can deliver a number of benefits. The game will load a lot faster—a welcome benefit, as anyone who has waited breathlessly for the latest game to install well knows. Likewise, cut scenes—some of which are absolutely huge and gorgeous—usually play directly off the CD-ROM, so they'll load and play more quickly and more smoothly. Finally, faster drives will speed up game setup, such as when you start a new mission or level.

If you do play games with interactive video, access time is again the killer issue. Generally, these games keep the video data rates below 300KBps, well within the talents of even the creakiest 4X CD-ROM drive. However, you'll encounter frustrating pauses and stops each time you access a new scene as the drive ferrets out the next portion of contiguous data. A newer drive can smooth things out for you.

One more note about game play: CD-ROM and DVD-ROM drives have a habit of sucking CPU cycles, particularly older models running over an inefficient IDE connection. A more efficient drive can help boost frame rates and responsiveness by freeing more CPU time for the software.

Capacity

This is a standards issue, pure and simple. CD-ROM's 650MB was a lot back when hard disks were 340MB in size. However, now my 14GB ATA-33 IBM hard disk can swallow 20 CD-ROMs and not even get a case of indigestion. Programs and reference titles are feeling the pinch, too—some use as many as seven CD-ROM discs. Anyone who has tried to find the right CorelDRAW disc can attest to the CD-ROM space crunch.

In this case, DVD-ROM is the clear and obvious choice. Initial software only uses a single layer on a single side of the disc—the cheapest option—for 4.7GB of data storage. However, larger titles can boost that all the way to 17GB by using both sides of the disc and putting data on two media layers per side. Of course, DVD-ROM drives can read CD-ROM discs, meaning you get your data storage without sacrificing compatibility.

Interface

The interface you use is a big deal. Not only does it impact performance, but it opens or closes choices about the location of the drive and the ability to share with other devices. The choice boils down to two standards: SCSI and IDE.

To my mind, the choice is pretty easy. Although SCSI drives consistently test better than their IDE counterparts—in terms of access rates, data throughput, and CPU utilization—they cost a bundle. Unless you have a very specific need for SCSI, IDE CD-ROM and DVD-ROM drives are the best—and sometimes the only—way to go.

So who needs SCSI? The biggest factor is SCSI's ability to support external devices, something IDE cannot and will never do. External devices provide greater flexibility, more comfortable access, and the ability to share with other PCs. They are also a big benefit on systems that are running short of 5.25-inch externally accessible drive bays. SCSI drives are the only option in these cases. It's also the best option if you intend to run two or more CD-ROM drives side by side, because you can daisy chain these peripherals.

Of course, SCSI enjoys a performance edge. Although both IDE and SCSI have bandwidth to spare for optical operation, you'll generally get better system responsiveness from SCSI, particularly if you have three or more drives running. Although the ATA-33 interface has resolved performance hits that occur when two IDE devices try to access the interface at the same time, SCSI still does a better job of juggling data and commands at the same time. As a result, SCSI remains a superior multitasking environment for these drives, particularly because commands can be reordered for best response (a feature called *command queuing*). CPU utilization is generally significantly lower on SCSI-based drives as well.

The problem is, you're talking about incremental performance improvements but drastic price jumps. SCSI CD-ROM drives can cost twice or more than their equivalently rated IDE cousins. What's more, you may not even be able to find a SCSI DVD-ROM product at all. With the narrow and pricey selection of products, IDE is the best choice for the mainstream market.

14.3.2 Writable Optical Storage

Writable optical drives are cool technology, no doubt about it. However, enough nagging problems exist that relying on one as your only optical storage device is probably a bad idea. Still, they can be a terrific complement to your drive collection, and they give you a way to throw gigabytes of data at an unsuspecting world.

Of course, expense is always an issue with these drives. Many of these products are only available on the SCSI interface (that's changing though), which inflates prices quite a bit. Not to be overlooked is the cost of the media. Although CD-R media can now be had for less than $1 per disc (provided you buy in quantity, say a 50-disc package), the cost of CD-RW media remains relatively high (at about $15 per disc). If you intend to do mostly archiving and one-off publishing, the additional expense of CD-RW, both in drive and media cost, starts to get prohibitive. DVD-RAM discs, meanwhile, will cost about $50 per disc and will not likely come down much in price for some time.

However, if you want the optical equivalent of a floppy drive with a format that can be read anywhere, CD-RW is cool stuff. Just be aware of the cost of the discs, as well as the fact that a significant percentage of CD-ROM drives (and DVD-ROM drives, for that matter) will not be able to recognize the CD-RW discs. If you know your playback platforms well, though, CD-RW is an attractive option; and it will only get more so over time.

Performance in Application

In virtually all cases, recordable/rewritable drives, be they CD or DVD, require you to make some performance compromises. In the case of some CD-RW drives, the penalty can be severe. Many of these drives will only spin at 8X speeds for playback. So you should at least consider keeping your existing CD-ROM drive and adding a recordable device to the drive mix. A side benefit of having the two optical drives is that it makes it easy to copy data from one CD format to the other.

Faster recordable drives may prove tempting, such as 4×/12× CD-RW drives that can playback at 12× speeds. Still, these drives provide less than half the data transfer capacity of cheap CD-ROM drives, which will impact your large file transfers, application installations, and program load times.

When it comes to recording, you need to be aware that it can take a while to put data onto discs. A full disc copy can take upwards of an hour on slower 2×-write models. Although newer products boost write spin speeds to 4× and even 8× rates, don't expect your write times to be cut in half. Time gains are incremental, with 4× drives doing the job in about 45 minutes, while 8× can get that down to close to 30 minutes. Also keep in mind that you'll need a fast device, such as your hard drive, to be able to feed data to the CD writer when writing at 4× speeds or higher. Of course, if you're not burning full 650MB drives, your write times will be lower.

If you're buying a new drive, make sure it supports *packet writing*, a scheme that lets you start and stop the recording process. In the past, CD-R discs had to be written all in one go, with the PC pouring data at a steady rate while the laser burned its way through the disc. Any interruption in the process—including an unexpected pause in hard disk access or a delay in RAM—resulted in a ruined disc. The way the discs were burned did not allow for file tables that could deal with these hiccups.

Needless to say, then, packet writing is a good thing. It lets you write a little and stop, and then later write again—even on CD-R discs. It also means that a slight pause in system performance doesn't spell curtains for your media. The drive will just mark the miswritten sections of the disc as bad in the final directory table and rewrite the information elsewhere. If you have an older drive that does not support packet writing, you should consider upgrading.

Packet writing isn't suitable for copying very large amounts of data, however. The problem? Packet-writing operations take significantly longer than traditional writes. For example, a 600MB burn using disc-at-once may take less than 20 minutes on a 4× CD burner. However, copy the same data using packet writing, via an intuitive drag-and-drop interface, and the process can take four to five times longer.

Capacity

No variables here. All CD-based drives write the same 650MB to the 5.25-inch media. That means any CD-ROM disc can be transferred to a CD-R or CD-RW media without question. This parity with professionally burned discs is a neat symmetry that doesn't exist in the DVD world.

DVD-RAM only writes 2.6GB to a side, whereas DVD+RW bumps that figure up to 3GB. Both camps expect to release drives capable of burning 4.7GB per side—the same available to DVD-ROM—but you won't see dual-layer writing any time soon. That means only professionally published DVD media can eke out the full 8.5GB-per-side potential of the DVD format.

Despite the asymmetry, the capacities are truly impressive. A single DVD-RAM disc can hold the equivalent of four CD-ROM discs—and that's just writing on one side. Splurge on your writable media, and you can flip the disc over and put the equivalent of four more CD-ROMs on the B side.

Interface

Writable media has been a SCSI universe for quite some time. One reason is that older drives could not allow for any delays in the data stream during operation. However, IDE is subject to all sorts of burps and hiccups, particularly because the hard disk and CD-ROM drives sharing the interface are usually churning away at the same time. As a result, access gets blocked, data flow gets stopped, and the writable media gets wrecked.

Packet-writing standards have fixed this mess and have allowed vendors to release IDE-based drives without fear of truly massive customer returns. You'll probably see some minor differences in write times from the IDE models, but overall the experience should be close to the same.

However, if you want to write discs while doing other tasks, SCSI carries significant advantages. Again, because the CD-R or CD-RW drive exists on the same bus used for your mainline storage, writing operations can and will bog down other drives. SCSI's command queuing and better multitasking talents will ensure that accesses don't stall too much during writing.

14.4 Tom's Pick

No surprise, there are a lot of choices in this area. If you're concerned about straight up performance for playing CD-ROM-based games and multimedia titles or for accessing large databases, you'll want to stay away from all the fancy writable drives and advanced DVD formats. None of these alternatives can match the speed and responsiveness of a good IDE-based CD-ROM drive, much less a SCSI model.

14.4.1 Read-only Media

However, not all CD-ROM drives are created equal. In fact, the vast majority are built for low cost rather than high performance, inviting all sorts of compromises that can degrade performance and lead to problems down the road. Therefore, our pick in this arena is a high-end model from Plextor, one of the standout manufacturers in the CD-ROM drive business.

The Plextor UltraPlex runs at 14× to 32× constant angular velocity so that content in the center of the disc is run at the equivalent of 14× spin rates, whereas data at the outer edges goes by at 32×. Plextor puts a lot of extra work into its read head mechanism, drive cache, and interface, thus squeezing additional performance out of its hardware. Access times are about as low as you'll find, at 80ms. Because the drive uses a SCSI interface, the UltraPlex does not get bogged down with data and command traffic going to and from the PC.

Plextor provides great documentation and builds rock-solid drives. In addition, the company includes intriguing software for optimizing disc performance, as well as an audio CD player utility. If you want top-notch CD-ROM performance, the Plextor UltraPlex is unmatched.

Unfortunately, hardcore gamers face a tough choice, because access to DVD-ROM titles is becoming more critical every month. For this reason alone, it's worth considering taking a step and a half backward in performance, and going with a good DVD-ROM upgrade kit.

My pick here is Creative Labs' DVD Encore Dxr2, which includes a second-generation DVD-ROM drive that can read and write CD-ROM, CD-R, and CD-RW media at 20× spin rates. The kit also includes an MPEG-2/AC-3 decoder board, allowing full-screen, full-frame rate playback of theater-quality video. AC-3 Dolby Digital audio support allows you to set up a six-speaker surround sound set to enjoy the full fidelity of the encoded digital audio signal. Good stuff.

14.4.2. Recordable Media

For data archiving and storing, a CD-RW drive is the way to go. DVD-RAM's multigigabyte capacities may be tempting, but the lack of drives to play the media back on, as well as the expense of individual discs, make DVD-RAM inappropriate for this type of application. What's more, the competing DVD+RW specification may yet knock DVD-RAM off the market. In effect, any DVD recordable format faces the dreaded VHS/Betamax syndrome.

Therefore, if you want to write optical, go with CD-RW. You can still read and write CD-R discs, and you add the considerable versatility of rewritable capability. If the CD-ROM drives on the systems you share data with are new enough, you can essentially use the CD-RW media as a supercapacity floppy drive, rewriting over the disc as needed.

My pick for CD-RW drive is HP's CD-Writer Plus 7200i, a 2× record and 6× playback drive that runs off the SCSI bus. Although slower than most CD-R models, it can write to both CD-R and CD-RW discs for maximum flexibility. However, the low playback speeds mean you'll probably want to keep a second CD-ROM drive handy for performance sake.

Optical Storage Guide

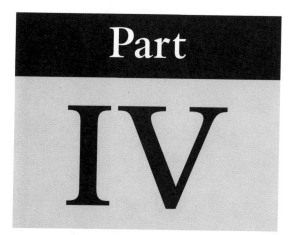

Part

IV

Graphic & Audio Systems

Chapter
15

Graphics
Board
Guide

15.1 Understanding Graphics Boards

No single component of the PC is developing as quickly right now as the graphics subsystem. Graphics chip companies such as Nvidia, ATI, and 3Dfx trump their own products with astonishing swiftness, releasing new chips that more than double the capabilities of the product released just six or nine months before. Behind the surge of new silicon: The emergence of 3D applications programming standards as well as games and applications that use them.

3D is not everywhere—at least, not yet. Word processors, spreadsheets, email, and Web browsing are applications that are largely devoid of complex 3D graphics. However, that may change as Microsoft moves 3D awareness into its Windows 95/98 and NT operating systems, and graphics chip makers provide baseline 3D acceleration in affordable chipsets. Certainly gamers have the 3D religion. Games such as Quake II, Incoming, Forsaken, and G-Police provide an entirely different experience when played with a cutting-edge 3D accelerator.

Of course, there's more to graphics than 3D. The familiar interface elements of Windows—including text, windows, and icons—need to be shuffled around quickly. Also, most graphics cards and chips provide features for boosting video playback, including features for handling high-quality Mpeg-2 Video.

However, there's no doubt that 3D graphics technology has energized a market that had reached a plateau. Today, with heavy competition in CPUs, hard disks, and RAM driving costs down to historically low levels, more and more of the overall system cost is flowing back to the graphics subsystem. That trend is likely to continue until 3D feature sets stabilize enough for manufacturers to leverage mature chip designs that tightly integrate features. The quantum jumps in 3D performance, combined with the growing cost of the hardware, make your graphics board decisions among the most critical in your PC.

15.1.1 Getting Up to Speed

Graphics accelerators speed system performance by taking over tasks that would otherwise pull down CPU performance. The dedicated circuitry in the graphics chip allows accelerators to execute tasks much more quickly than a general-purpose CPU, as well. It's no surprise that Moore's Law is very much in effect in the world of graphics chips. The Voodoo2 3D graphics chip from 3Dfx weighs in with—count 'em—7 million transistors, more than you'll find in a Pentium MMX CPU.

The transistor inflation isn't surprising, given the expanding role that graphics accelerators play in your system. Back in 1992, these devices added oomph to your program windows and scrolling text, shortcutting clumsy GDI (Graphics Device Interface) calls in silicon. Two or three years later, cheap CD-ROM drives enabled multimedia titles filled with video clips—and graphics chips added circuitry to ease the burden. Most recently, the need for 3D graphics acceleration has exploded onto the market.

One reason for the 3D push has been the emergence of standards for programmers creating 3D graphics and games. Acceleration hardware can only speed up operations it understands, but it's simply impossible for chips to work effectively with several different 3D graphics architectures. 2D acceleration became possible under Windows 3.*x* when the GDI became the transport for graphics data. Likewise, Intel's DCI (Display Control Interface) specification, and later Microsoft's DirectDraw, provided standard ways for hardware to accelerate video processes. Today, OpenGL and Microsoft's Direct3D have gained widespread acceptance. The two APIs provide a common development target for chip makers and software vendors.

15.1.2 Graphics Board Basics

The graphics board is really a system unto itself. At the heart of the board is the graphics chip, and memory, bus interfaces, and output converters enable it to move and communicate data. Because of all the variables involved, graphics performance can vary widely.

Here are the key elements to think about:

- Graphics coprocessor

- RAM

- RAMDAC

- Bus

The brains of the operation, the coprocessor, serves as the CPU of your graphics board. Here reside all the whiz-bang acceleration features that boost 2D, video, and 3D graphics. Specifically designed for graphics operation, this chip relieves your general-purpose system CPU of the heavy lifting involved in displaying images. What's more, the graphics chip does it faster than your CPU ever could.

As is the case with a CPU, tradeoffs are often made in order to deliver features at a reasonable price. Low-cost graphics chips that provide 2D, 3D, and video acceleration may not do any of these tasks extremely well—particularly complex 3D work. Really fast 3D chips, meanwhile, may add $100 or more to the cost of your graphics subsystem, which is a steep price for many users. Also, not all chips speak the same 3D language. In fact, some boards, such as those based on 3Dfx's Voodoo and Voodoo2 chips, are dedicated to 3D graphics—you need a separate 2D graphics board for the system to run. Just as CPUs are tuned for their instruction set, graphics chips come tailored for specific 3D APIs, which can limit the selection of applications tuned for your board.

Graphics Board Guide

As the center of attention on the board, the graphics chip talks to everything—the bus interface, graphics memory, and the RAMDAC. A bottleneck in the graphics chip will certainly slow everything down.

You can never be too rich, too thin, or have enough graphics RAM. The amount of RAM on your graphics card determines what number of colors and pixels you can display on the monitor. The emergence of 3D titles makes memory more critical than ever, as effective 3D acceleration demands much more RAM to display a resolution than is needed in 2D mode. What's more, to attain reasonable levels of realism, you need 4MB or more of data available to store texture graphics, which make polygonal 3D shapes look like real-world objects. Newer cards based on Accelerated Graphics Port (AGP) allow you to boost texture realism by making use of system memory for this purpose, thus enabling graphics cards to use less memory and still achieve reasonable visual fidelity.

There's a dizzying array of memory choices out there, both in terms of capacity and type. You need to keep a close eye on these issues before buying because a board with too little memory will be unable to deliver compelling graphics output.

The final piece of the onboard puzzle is the RAMDAC. This chip sends the final video data out to your monitor, converting the digital 1s and 0s into a stream of signals representing the red, blue, and green areas of the spectrum. A simple rule applies: The faster the RAMDAC, the better.

15.1.3 The Basics of 2D and 3D Accelerations

Graphics cards boost performance by accelerating operations in the Windows GDI, the main graphics component of the operating system. Applications send GDI calls to Windows in order to display graphics onscreen. On the graphics board side, the GDI checks with the driver to see what features are present in the hardware. Operations that can be accelerated are sent to the graphics board for handling, whereas those not recognized are handled by the CPU (see Figure 15.1).

Exploring 2D Acceleration

Virtually all graphics boards accelerate a similar set of 2D operations. These operations were largely defined by the original GDI established under Windows 3.x. Today, most boards support a very similar set of 2D operations, although some may provide optimizations for infrequently accessed functions that are common for high-end applications.

Figure 15.1.

Microsoft enables reliable hardware acceleration by establishing functional layers in its operating systems that provide a standard interface to both applications and hardware.

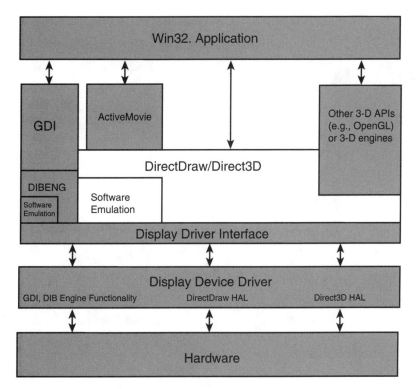

Here's a quick list of the functions your graphics card commonly accelerates in 2D graphics:

- Bit block transfers: Called *bit blits*, these transfers occur anytime a chunk of graphics data is moved from one place onscreen to another. When text is scrolled or an application window is dragged across the screen, GDI performs a bit blit.

- Line drawing: Lines are drawn by defining the two end points and then filling the space in-between—a process that is much faster than filling each pixel individually. Arcs and polygons are handled in a similar manner.

- Color and pattern fills: This is the application of color in a geometric shape such as a circle or polygon. Rather than apply color to pixels individually, the range on the screen to be colored is mapped out, and the area is updated in a single step. A similar process is used to speed gradient fills (see Figure 15.2).

Graphics Board Guide

Figure 15.2.

DeLorme's graphically intensive Map'n'Go application stresses accelerated operations such as line draws, bit blits, and color fills.

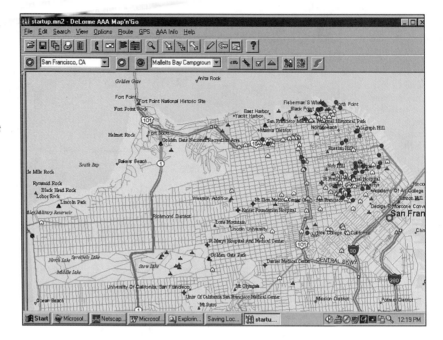

Figure 15.2.

DeLorme's graphically intensive Map'n'Go application stresses accelerated operations such as line draws, bit blits, and color fills.

- Clipping: Enables quick refresh of obscured items, such as when a drop-down menu covers part of a word processing document. The hidden graphics are stored in offscreen memory—essentially cache—so that they can be quickly swapped back when the obscuring element is removed.

- Offscreen memory caching: Many boards make use of unused memory, called *offscreen memory*, to store frequently accessed graphical information. This effective cache is particularly useful for font and icon handling.

Exploring Video Acceleration

Video acceleration became critical around 1994, when affordable CD-ROM drives ushered digital video files into the PC universe. Apple's QuickTime and Microsoft's Video for Windows software delivered the tools for turning the compressed video data into a visual and aural stream of content. Once developers found a common standard or two to develop toward, video became yet another data type for the PC.

There's just one problem. Video is exceedingly hard to do. Digital video playback stresses virtually every subsystem of the PC, demanding realtime or near real-time processing of huge streams of data. Each second of video data is comprised of about 15 to 30 individual snapshots, called *frames*, that are played in rapid succession to form the illusion of motion. Adding to the challenge is the fact that the accompanying audio track must be processed and synched with the video frames. Uncompressed video would require 200MB to be moved every second from the hard disk, through system memory, and out to the graphics card—an impossible amount for even the fastest PCs.

To cut video down to size for both storage and internal processing, clips are heavily compressed. However, the compression itself takes a lot of horsepower to decode back into a video stream. If the processor falls behind, frames get dropped. Smooth 30-frame-per-second video can become a choppy, out-of-synch mess that jerks along at one or two frames per second. Of course, any other applications or operations running alongside the video will suffer as well, as they become starved for processor bandwidth.

Today's graphics boards include hardware for unburdening the CPU of the most common video playback tasks. Although the specifics of video decompression are generally not handled onboard—codecs simply change too quickly to make it economical to burn them into hardware—other operations are addressed:

- Color space conversion

- Pixel interpolation

- Motion estimation

Color Space Conversion

In order to conserve storage space, color data in video clips is stored in a format called *YUV*, the same format used in TV broadcast. YUV represents video as separate color and brightness components. For each pixel, Y represents luminance (or brightness), U represents color, and V represents the saturation value. The problem is that your monitor expects color in RGB (red, green, blue) format. Converting YUV data to RGB is a time-consuming process that hogs CPU cycles during video playback.

Virtually all graphics cards now perform color space conversion on-chip. This feature can save 20 to 30 percent of the execution time involved in processing video—a big gain. Best of all, color space conversion occurs in almost all video file types, from the Windows AVI and QuickTime MOV files, to Mpeg-1 and Mpeg-2 formats. In all cases, color space conversion delivers a real boost in performance.

Pixel Interpolation

In order to manage the size of digital video files, the video is usually captured to a limited resolution. Many QuickTime and AVI video files, for example, are captured to 320×240 pixel resolutions, and then played back in expanded form to fill the screen. Expanding a video file involves creating new pixels where none existed, whether by duplicating pixels or by adding new pixels that represent a midpoint between two originally existing pixels.

Again, computing the location and color of all those extra pixels consumes a lot of CPU cycles. Graphics boards handle pixel interpolation on-chip, relieving your CPU of this onerous burden. In addition to boosting frame rates for expanded video playback, pixel interpolation can markedly improve the appearance of the video.

The best chips average pixel values across several pixels in both the X and Y dimensions, thus yielding smooth transitions. Without the averaging, video appears blocky (and just plain ugly), even if the frame rates stay high.

Just keep in mind that pixel interpolation, no matter how sophisticated, is still creating something out of nothing. The same averaging algorithms that make stretched video look smooth will smudge and blur sharply defined edges. For example, a black-and-white checkered kitchen floor will be marred by unwanted grays along the edges where the highly contrasting pixels meet (see Figure 15.3).

Figure 15.3.
You can see the effects of scaling in this video. Note the stair-step effect along the edges of the jet's wings and tail.

Motion Estimation

Just as CD-ROM drives invited digital video into the PC party, the arrival of affordable DVD-ROM drives has opened the door for even higher quality video in the form of Mpeg-2. Mpeg-2 Video is a high-resolution (740×480 pixels), high-quality video format identical to the one used by direct broadcast satellite providers such as DirecTV and PrimeStar. Mpeg-2 provides video quality that is vastly superior to that of earlier digital video formats and even makes Super VHS tape look bad.

The problem is, Mpeg-2 is too much data for even the fastest Pentium II systems to handle without a good deal of help. Most DVD-ROM kits feature a dedicated card for decoding Mpeg-2 Video data streams for this very reason. However, if your graphics card adds motion estimation to its laundry list of video features, faster Pentium II PCs can play back Mpeg-2 Video without expensive, dedicated hardware (see Figure 15.4). Just be aware that decoding the complex Mpeg-2 Video stream will likely max out even a fast Pentium II CPU, resulting in slowdowns in system performance.

Figure 15.4.
What a difference a few megabits makes. The eye-popping quality of Mpeg-2 Video will make everyone forget all about those chunky AVI files of our youth—but you'll need serious hardware.

On-chip motion compensation relieves the system CPU of the burden of noticing differences among frames of video. When little action happens among frames, the chip is able to update automatically the unchanged parts of the frame, leaving only a small subset of the frame for the CPU to assemble. This capability to compare among frames is a critical component of Mpeg compression because small file sizes are achieved by throwing out redundant information. By moving the reincorporating of this repeated data to the graphics board, a large part of the work is done without processor involvement.

Exploring 3D Acceleration

Certainly the most explosive and most important area of graphics hardware development has been in 3D. Everything from Microsoft Flight Simulator to Quake II makes use of true three-dimensional graphics to produce interactive worlds of unprecedented realism. However, like earlier advances in 2D graphics and video, 3D operations completely swamp the system CPU, bogging down performance and reducing visual fidelity.

Graphics Board Guide

At the center of 3D graphics acceleration is the 3D pipeline, a linear series of steps and functions that graphics cards can tap into and take over from the processor. This pipeline is defined by the 3D software API on your system—say, Direct3D or OpenGL—and defines how 3D scenes and objects are put together. In almost all cases, 3D scenes consist of thousands or even millions of triangles, which are stitched together to form worlds, objects, people, and so on. In essence, it's a massive, interactive lesson in geometry, which your 3D graphics card blazes through millions of times each second.

These triangles are manipulated to create motion, visual realism, and all manner of effects. Moving groups of triangles creates motion, and covering them with color and bitmap images makes shapes appear like real-world objects. Light sources can be defined, oriented, and manipulated for effect, with light reflecting off objects according to their position and makeup. Likewise, fog and haze can limit visibility and add realism (see Figure 15.5).

Figure 15.5.
Sophisticated 3D hardware can produce compelling effects such as smoke, lens flare, and realistic-looking texture maps in realtime.

However, not all cards accelerate all things. In fact, some less-expensive 2D/3D graphics cards—sometimes called free-D cards—only accelerate a small portion of the pipeline, resulting in limited performance and realism. Even more confusing, the vocabulary of 3D acceleration is daunting. Here's a rundown of what you need to know:

- Geometry: The CPU computes the position of triangle vertexes and assigns effects such as texturing, lighting, atmospherics, and other elements.

No graphics rendering is involved at this stage; this work generally occurs on the CPU. The exception is with high-end accelerators such as those based on the 3D Labs Glint chip.

- Setup: The line edges of the triangles are positioned so that they form the desired scene and objects. Again, the CPU is responsible for most of the work at this stage.

- Texture mapping: Creates the illusion of realistic objects by placing two-dimensional images, called *bitmaps*, atop the 3D shapes. Images are mapped onto the physical geometry or formed by the assembled triangles to create a realistic appearance. Instead of solid-colored triangles, you now see objects that look like real cars, trains, people, rocks, and so on. Video and animation may also be laid onto objects as texture maps.

- Bilinear and trilinear filtering: Provides more realism, this time by smoothing out blockiness in the texture-mapped graphics. Trilinear filtering offers a superior effect because it averages color data across more pixels than does bilinear filtering.

- Flat or gouraud shading: Flat shading yields cartoonish graphics, such as those seen in Falcon Gold and Hornet flight sims, that are easy for "unaccelerated" PCs to draw quickly. Gouraud shading blands the color values in triangles to smooth out transitions and enhance realism.

- Alpha blending: Haze, fog, and smoke are all examples of atmospheric effects known collectively as *alpha blending*. Better graphics cards can accelerate the process where the user sees objects through a medium with appropriate distortion, fading, and lighting applied.

- Lighting: Real-looking scenes must have light sources, be they universal sources such as the sun, or focused sources such as spotlights. The color, intensity, direction, type, and reflection of light can all be accelerated to enhance realism.

- Z-buffering: This technology uses graphics memory to map triangles along the Z-axis, which runs toward and away from the user. Z-buffering eliminates the need for time-consuming processing to determine which pixels will block others in a 3D scene.

- MIP mapping: Enhances realism of texture mapping by storing down-sampled versions of texture map files. These smaller versions are used to maintain visual fidelity when you move close to a texture-mapped object, avoiding the blockiness that would otherwise occur. What does the "MIP" in MIP mapping stand for? It's Latin for *multum in parvum* (many in one).

The list goes on and on and on, but this is a good introduction to the features you should look for in any graphics card. Just remember, more features don't always need higher frame rates. Many acceleration resources focus on visual fidelity. What's more, the results in your actual applications will depend also on the 3D application programming interface (API) the game is running under.

15.1.4 Performance Impact Report

Next to the CPU and perhaps hard disk, the graphics board delivers the most impact on overall system performance of any component in the PC. If you play 3D games or use 3D design programs, a powerful graphics accelerator is simply crucial. Without it, even the fastest Pentium II system will be hamstrung and may not even be able to display some software at all.

Benchmarking of graphics boards shows that 2D graphics performance has reached a relative plateau, with cards in a similar price range often delivering very similar results. The reason: Most board makers now provide largely similar feature sets in these areas of graphics handling, whereas fast CPUs, combined with PCI and AGP buses, have relieved bottlenecks that really made graphics acceleration critical in the first place. With that said, support for resolutions, refresh rates, and video-specific visual fidelity enhancements are not universal. Some boards provide much higher refresh rates at 1600×1200 resolution, for example, just as some produce much better-looking video.

The real performance battle is being fought over 3D, and it's a pitched battle indeed. Acceleration features, developer APIs, and memory amounts are advancing so quickly that 12 months can bring a doubling of effective performance. As the hardware picks up features, titles are being developed to leverage them, thus resulting in better gameplay and realism.

15.2 Currently Available Boards

The explosion of 3D graphics has fueled a lot of activity in the graphics board market. As a result, buyers face a wide range of choices from numerous vendors. Although a graphics board from Diamond may be a near twin of one from STB, enough graphics chip manufacturers maintain that the selection of boards is truly daunting. As a result, a board maker such as Diamond Multimedia may market over a dozen different brands, each with a different type of graphics coprocessor and intended market.

This section will walk you through the available boards and their intended use. There are essentially three segments to the graphics boards market:

- 2D graphics boards
- 3D graphics boards
- Multifunction graphics boards

15.2.1 2D Boards

When I say 2D graphics boards, I actually mean boards that provide 2D graphics and video acceleration. Over the past two years, virtually every chip maker has rolled video enhancing features directly into the coprocessor, if for no other reason than it was cheap to do.

Business 2D

This area of the market is dominated by business-oriented graphics acceleration, including tasks such as word processing, spreadsheets, Web browsing, and email. Because the graphics technology behind these operations has not changed significantly since the introduction of DirectDraw in 1996, the silicon used to enhance them can be made cheaply. In fact, $99 will buy you a very good business–class 2D graphics card with 4MB or even 8MB of graphics memory and rudimentary 3D graphics acceleration, as shown in Figure 15.6.

Figure 15.6.
The $99 Matrox Productiva G100 is a good example of a consumer-level graphics board.

You'll face sacrifices in this area of the 2D market, however. To cut costs, vendors often sell boards with a meager 2MB of RAM (enough for 24-bit color at 800×600 resolution) expandable to 4MB. However, keep in mind that you generally have to buy pricey, proprietary memory modules directly from the board vendor. Perhaps more critical, some boards provide minimal refresh rate support at higher resolutions, a function of a slow and cost-conscious RAMDAC. If you intend to run your graphics at 1024×768 resolution, you need to take a close look at refresh rate support.

Professional 2D

Of course, some serious 2D work is happening out there. Graphic designers, software developers, and other professionals need quick graphics response, fast refresh rates, and high resolution and color modes. Here, more sophisticated graphics chips are mated with faster and larger stores of RAM to open the pipes for this kind of work.

A typical high-end graphics board will use 8MB of dual-ported RAM, such as VRAM or WRAM. Unlike SGRAM, SDRAM, and EDO DRAM, these memory types use one port to interface with the graphics chip and a separate port to move bits out to the RAMDAC. Because of this, the memory can go about refreshing the display 90 or more times per second without clogging up the busy data path to and from the chip. As a result, VRAM- and WRAM-based boards have much more potential bandwidth available to them, which translates into higher refresh rates.

Matrox's Millennium II is a good example of a high-end 2D graphics board. With 8MB of WRAM and a fast 250MHz RAMDAC, it can produce TK-Hz refresh rates at 1600×1200 resolution, as shown in Figure 15.7. What's more, memory can be boosted to an incredible 16MB for displaying up to 1920×1200 pixels in 24-bit color. However, its 3D acceleration features are rudimentary at best and pale in comparison to the talents of newer engines such as 3Dfx's Voodoo2 or Nvidia's Riva 128ZX.

15.2.2 3D Boards

New graphics cards outfitted with 3D features boost performance of popular games and design software by taking over critical areas of the 3D graphics workload. Of course, an interface for these features must be available—something that Microsoft has been providing and improving with its Direct3D API. With both hardware and standards evolving, the range of 3D performance varies widely, making it critical that you explore 3D options to suit your needs. There are three different types of 3D boards to consider, as shown in Table 15.1.

Figure 15.7.

The Matrox Millennium II uses 8MB or more of dual-ported WRAM to deliver top refresh rates and 2D graphics capability.

Table 15.1. 3D graphics chips serve a wide variety of markets.

Accelerator type	Chips	Applications
General 2D/3D	S3 Virge VX, ATI Rage Pro	Office applications 3D games
Game-centric 3D accelerators	3Dfx Voodoo2, Nvidia RIVA 128	High-end 3D games
Professional 3D accelerators	3D Labs Glint GMX	CAD/CAM, 3D design and animation

These different types of products bring different levels of acceleration and API support to the market.

General-Purpose 3D

Low-end 3D products—sometimes called *free-D* because they're 2D accelerators with 3D added on for little or no extra cost—really fall close to the 2D category discussed earlier. The 3D feature set is usually quite limited in both coverage and performance, whereas memory amounts are too limited to allow for high-resolution 3D display.

These boards appeal to the business set looking to prepare its desktops for VRML and other 3D environments that it may need to support. Web browsing, PC-based presentations, and nifty spreadsheet graphs are the main drivers of 3D in the corporate space. All of these applications are adequately served by these low-cost accelerators.

Gaming 3D

The market is really popping in the gaming arena, where a host of board and chip makers are duking it out in this exploding market. Advancing APIs and much-improved silicon are driving quantum leaps in 3D performance and realism. The main problem is that advances are occurring so quickly that boards are becoming obsolete within months after being purchased.

Perhaps more troubling is the ongoing API situation in 3D gaming. Microsoft's Direct3D is oh-so-slowly establishing itself as the standard in the market, but only after several early versions of the API were ignored by developers as too slow, too feature-poor, or too difficult to use. The best 3D graphics engine on the market at the time of this writing—3Dfx's Voodoo2 chip—works best with games written for its own Glide API (see Figure 15.8). The Nvidia RIVA, meanwhile, is tuned to support Microsoft's Direct3D API. The result: Board buyers must place a bet on which API they think will attract the best games and titles.

Figure 15.8.

The Creative Labs 3D Blaster Voodoo2 uses the 3Dfx Voodoo2 chip for uncompromised game play. However, you need a second graphics board for displaying 2D graphics.

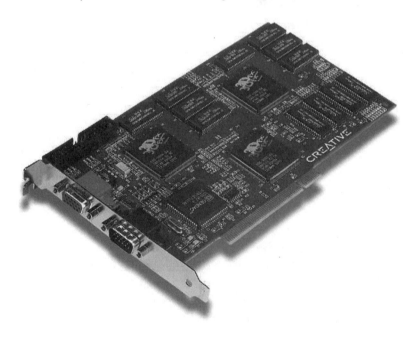

Better 3D gaming boards need to bulk up on memory in order to handle the multiple levels of display, management, and texture data that occur in realtime 3D. It's not unusual for high-end gaming boards to ship with 12MB of RAM—4MB is used to allow 800×600 3D graphics at 16-bit resolutions, and the additional memory is kept to store realistic-looking bitmap images for object textures. In most cases, single-ported SGRAM or SDRAM are used to keep the large memory pools affordable.

15.2.3 Multifunction Graphics Boards

This class of boards has been around for awhile but keeps improving as components get less expensive. ATI's All-in-Wonder Pro, for example, provides 2D and 3D graphics acceleration, a TV tuner, and S-video ports for video capture on a single PCI card. The board is targeted mainly at the home market; however, stock brokers and others often use this type of hardware to monitor CNN or other broadcasts while they work.

In fact, most of these boards appeal to home users who want to noodle with their camcorder video or watch basketball games while working in the home office. These added features don't impact the memory or graphics acceleration picture in any way—most ship with 2MB or 4MB of single-ported RAM. It's worth noting that video capture quality is quite basic, with no onboard compression or sophisticated filtering for allowing high-resolution, high frame rate capture. For that, you need a dedicated board such as the miro DC30 or TruVision Targa 2000.

Windows 98 includes a TV-viewing facility called *WebTV* among its multimedia applets. This should add to the appeal of these hybrid boards. You can download TV broadcast schedules from Starsite Networks and set the PC to display the TV viewer when a programmed show is broadcast. Also supported are data-handling features that let broadcasters send text, closed captioning, stats, and HTML content alongside the normal broadcast. However, support for this technology is not widespread.

Graphics Board Guide

15.3 Evaluating Graphics Boards

If there are so many choices, technologies, and APIs out there, how do you narrow down the selection of graphics boards? The first thing is to decide what you want the board for and to make a realistic assessment of your PC. No graphics board, no matter how good, will make your aged Pentium-75 go fast. Once you've got a handle on your needs and your situation, you can look at what features and performance levels will work for you. Of course, keep in mind that items such as exotic chips, tons of memory, and fast RAMDACs all serve to boost the price.

Here are the main components of the graphics board:

- System bus interface
- Graphics chip
- RAM
- RAMDAC

When looking at boards, it helps to understand how they work. The fast and efficient flow of bits to the board and through its components is critical in avoiding delays and other problems. As soon as graphics data leaves the system CPU, it goes through four steps before it gets to the monitor:

1. Data flows from the bus into the graphics chip, where it is processed.

2. From the chip, the data is sent to graphics memory.

3. From graphics RAM, the bits then go to the digital-to-analog converter (or RAMDAC), which converts the digital signal to the analog signal that the monitor can understand.

4. The RAMDAC fires an analog signal out over the 15-pin VGA connector to the monitor, where the signal is used to drive an electron gun in the monitor that lights pixels onscreen. By scanning across each line of the display 70 times or more per second, the monitor creates the illusion of a stable image.

15.3.1 The System Bus

Any bottleneck in the digital portion of the process will hold up performance. For this reason, it's imperative that wide and fast buses be used both outside and inside the graphics board. The flow starts with the system expansion bus, which connects the board to the CPU. Here, two main buses exist: PCI and AGP (see Table 15.2).

Table 15.2. A comparison of the prominent PC system buses, including the forthcoming AGP 4× specification.

Bus	Width	Clock	Data Rate
PCI	32 bits	33MHz	132MBps
AGP 1X	32 bits	66MHz	264MBps
AGP 2X	32 bits	133MHz	528MBps
AGP 4X	32 bits	266MHz	1024MBps

The PCI Bus

The PCI bus is present on virtually all Pentium and faster PCs and is fast and wide enough for all but the most extreme graphics applications. It can burst up to 132MBps of data and provide full bus mastering to allow data transfers to happen without CPU involvement. Up to five PCI slots sit on many motherboards, with the majority of graphics boards being designed for PCI.

Be aware that in some cases, PCI only runs at 25 or 30MHz. This is true of 60MHz system bus operation, which is found with systems using the Pentium-75, -90, -120, and -150 processors. Data rates will decrease proportionately. Although AGP ups the ante significantly, tests have shown that it really doesn't improve performance in 2D operations. At this point, PCI is not the bottleneck.

There are different PCI specs, but the vast majority of PCI buses run at 33MHz and 32-bits wide. A 66MHz PCI and a 64-bit PCI bus are both spec'd out, but they are limited to niche server applications for RAID disk arrays and other such applications. For graphics, any PCI board should work in any PCI slot.

AGP

New to the game is the Accelerated Graphics Port, a dedicated graphics-only bus that doubles or even quadruples PCI performance. Enabled by Intel's 440LX and 440BX chipsets found in Pentium II motherboards and the 440EX chipset that's designed to work with Intel's Celeron, AGP can move data as high as 528MBps. Two AGP flavors are available on the market now: 1× and 2×. AGP 1× has an effective clock rate of 66MHz and moves data at 264MBps, whereas AGP 2× doubles the clock to 133MHz and pushes data at 528MBps.

Tests show that AGP fails to enhance 2D performance, indicating that PCI already provides more than enough bandwidth for even demanding graphics operations. However, AGP's ace in the hole is its ability to let graphics cards make use of main system memory. 3D applications tailored for AGP can store texture map data in extra system RAM, thus allowing developers to use tens of megabytes of visual data to enhance the realism of 3D scenes. AGP's prodigious bandwidth also provides the potential for better software-based Mpeg-2 Video playback, particularly on PCs with 100MHz motherboards.

There's a catch, however, and potentially a big one. Intel doesn't require AGP graphics cards to actually support this neat memory-sharing feature. Therefore, don't assume the AGP board you buy will be able to make use of enhanced texture memory—a process called *AGP texturing*—until you've confirmed it.

There are several elements of AGP you'll want to look for, including the following:

- AGP texturing

- AGP version support

- Sideband addressing

- Pipelining

AGP Texturing

The technical term is *direct memory execute (DIME) mode*, but *AGP texturing* is a more understandable term. Essentially, this feature lets your graphics chip reach into the system's main memory and grab textures from there. It's here that the fast AGP bus pays off, because any delays in moving textures over the system bus will result in frame loss.

Be aware that not many games have made much use of this feature, and it could be some time before compelling AGP-optimized games arrive. Microsoft is doing its part, having added AGP awareness to its DirectX 5.0 suite so that developers have the tools they need to make AGP texturing happen. However, until AGP is ubiquitous on PCs, support will remain somewhat spotty.

To get AGP features to work on your system, you'll need to make sure you're running Windows 98 or Windows 95 OSR 2.1. Windows 95 users will also need the program **USBSUPP.EXE** from Microsoft, which includes the USB supplement and a new memory manager (**VMM32.VXD**) needed for the AGP DIME feature. You also need DirectX 5 because it's the first DirectX version that supports AGP's DIME capability.

The graphics card vendor should supply you with a virtual device manager called **VGARTD.VXD**, which usually will be installed in the installation procedure of the Windows 95 card driver. This virtual device manager is the key to the DIME feature; without it your AGP card is unable to use DIME. VGART stands for *virtual graphics address remapping table*. After you've set up Windows 95 with these items, your system is ready to take advantage of AGP's DIME feature.

AGP Version Support (1×, 2×, and 4×)

As mentioned earlier, there are three AGP flavors. Intel's current 440LX and 440BX chipsets handle AGP 1× and AGP 2× modes, and any graphics board you buy should do the same. Ask specifically about this support because most early AGP boards only provided AGP 1× support. Although the distinction isn't critical in 2D applications—in fact, there is no performance difference at all—the extra 264MBps of bandwidth becomes crucial in 3D texturing situations. If developers do jump onto the AGP bandwagon, you'll regret having only AGP 1× capability.

Coming soon is AGP 4×, which doubles the data rate once again to 1,024MBps (or 1GBps). This is major bandwidth, which Intel is positioning initially at the professional market of CAD/CAM and 3D design workstations.

With a 100MHz system bus in place, AGP 4× enables the graphics bus to outstrip the 800MBps main memory interface, which should help ensure timely delivery of textures to your AGP-optimized software.

Sideband Addressing

Sideband addressing takes instruction and address traffic off the AGP data highway. This conserves some of the ample bandwidth for textures and helps ensure that address bits don't get held up in a data bottleneck.

Pipelining

This is another enhanced feature not found on many early AGP cards. Pipelining reduces downtime on the bus by allowing the graphics card to issue multiple commands without waiting for a response from the system CPU.

15.3.2 The Graphics Chip

The graphics chip is the most critical component of any graphics board. In addition, it defines the board's features and performance. Boards based on the same graphics chip generally provide very similar levels of performance and features. For example, Diamond's Monster 3D II and Creative Labs' 3D Blaster Voodoo2—both based on the 3Dfx Voodoo II chip—deliver similar results in benchmark tests and provide identical 3D acceleration features.

The graphics chip includes an interface to local memory, which often determines exactly what type of memory the board can use. Most higher-end gaming-oriented graphics chips use SDRAM, SGRAM, or RDRAM memory types because the memory is both fast and affordable enough to be installed in quantity. Professional 2D graphics chips often support dual-ported VRAM or WRAM memory because these can deliver higher refresh rates and uncompromised performance at the highest resolutions and color depths. Finally, value-oriented boards often use slower EDO DRAM because this memory is the least expensive to acquire.

The interface to main memory usually runs 32, 64, or 128 bits wide. Wider buses offer better potential for higher throughput between the graphics chip and memory, although the internal design of the chip itself plays a big role in maintaining optimal data flow. However, wide 128-bit buses do require that memory be installed in 4MB increments in order to take advantage of the full width of the bus. It's worth noting, however, that some boards run 128 bits wide in the chip but use narrower (and less expensive) 64-bit connections to local memory. Obviously, you lose some of the bandwidth benefit with these narrowed memory pipes. Also, keep in mind that before you purchase any board, it's a good idea to make sure your preferred software is compatible with the hardware. A low-end

Graphics Board Guide

Rendition Verite–based card will almost surely disappoint you because few games work directly with its hardware. However, you can't go wrong with a 3Dfx Voodoo2. Of course, the market can change fast, and Intel's i740, Nvidia's Riva 128ZX, or some other graphics chip could emerge with the hot hand.

15.3.3 A Look at Graphics Memory

Memory plays a critical role in graphics performance. It must be fast to keep up with the huge amounts of graphics data flowing through the board, and there must be lots of it to address the million-plus pixels on the screen. Growing demands on the graphics subsystem has resulted in a good deal of innovation. As a result, graphics boards use any one of a half-dozen memory types to store graphics data.

RAM Amounts

When it comes to 2D graphics, the RAM equation is pretty darn simple. You multiply the horizontal resolution by the vertical resolution, and then you multiply the product by the number of bits in the color depth. How much RAM is enough? Table 15.3 shows the breakdown of available resolutions using specific RAM amounts.

Table 15.3. A look at RAM capacities and the supported resolutions.

Resolution	Megabytes at 24-bit Color	Megabytes at 16-bit Color
640×480	.88MB	.59MB
800×600	1.37MB	.91MB
1024×768	2.25MB	1.5MB
1280×1024	3.75MB	2.5MB
1600×1200	5.5MB	3.67MB

With most boards today shipping with 4MB of RAM, all but the highest resolutions are available at 24-bit color. However, working out resolution support with 3D graphics is a more complicated matter because 3D graphics require a front, a back, and a Z-buffer store of memory. The front buffer holds what you see, the back buffer holds the next picture while it's being processed, and the Z-buffer holds the third dimension (depth) value.

That's why a card with 4MB of memory can offer 2D graphics resolution of 1600×1200 at 16-bit color. However, the same 4MB board when running a 3D game using Z-buffer data can only produce 16-bit color at 800×600 resolution. Here's the reason: For every pixel, additional bits are being dedicated to nondisplay tasks, including a 16-bit Z-buffer and additional bits in the front and back buffers. As a result, that 800×600 by 16-bit 3D scene requires 2.74MB, whereas a 1024×768 scene needs 4.5MB.

Memory Types

A major bottleneck beckons between the memory and the graphics chip and RAMDAC. Performance declines when poor graphics memory sits between two very busy devices that must be served simultaneously. Each time the screen changes, the graphics chip alters the data in memory. At the same time, the RAMDAC must read out the graphics memory continuously in order to refresh the screen 70 or more times each second. Caught in the middle is the graphics RAM.

With higher screen and color resolutions, more data has to be transferred from the video chipset to the video memory. Also, the data has to be read faster by the RAMDAC to be sent to the monitor. In order to handle all these demands, graphics vendors have turned to enhanced RAM designs optimized for graphics operation.

Dual-Ported Memory

The best memory uses two ports to allow access: one for the graphics chip and the other for the RAMDAC. This way, board components can access memory from two directions at once and not have to split precious bandwidth between screen refreshes and graphics updates. The graphics chip doesn't have to wait for the RAMDAC, and the RAMDAC is freed from waiting for the graphics chip. In other words, everybody's happy—except the buyer. Dual ported RAM is expensive compared to even fast single-ported SDRAM and SGRAM.

VRAM is the most popular dual-ported memory type, although boards from both Matrox and Number Nine employ WRAM-type memory in their high-end graphics cards. WRAM incorporates some graphics-specific tweaks that provide more efficient access to data laid out for display. Both memories can sustain significantly higher refresh rates at top resolutions than can single-ported RAM amounts.

How big of a challenge are refresh rates? An 8-bit 1024×768 display consists of 786,432 bytes, which must be read by the RAMDAC 70 or more times per second. The same screen at 24-bit color consumes 2,359,296 bytes—nearly three times as much. The additional data takes more time to access. Without the second port, graphics performance would suffer because the chip is forced to wait for the RAMDAC.

Wider Buses

AGP speeds up the outside bus, but things are happening inside as well. In 1994, most cards used 32-bit memory buses to move data internally on the board, whereas most today use 64-bit buses. Some 128-bit designs, such as those from Tseng Labs' ET-6000 and Nvidia's RIVA 128, double the pipes up yet again. Some products actually take a split approach with wide 128-bit buses inside the chip and narrower 64-bit connections to local memory, thus allowing for affordable pricing.

Just be aware that the wider the bus, the more memory you need onboard to take advantage of it—the standard 8×1MB memory chip presents a 32-bit interface, so you need two modules to aggregate an effective 64-bit bus. 128-bit chips need to double this again, up to 4MB. If you fail to match the graphics chip with a wide enough memory bus, your performance will drop like a rock. Fortunately, plummeting RAM prices have made 4MB graphics cards very affordable.

Faster Clocks

The third way—and to us maybe most obvious way—to get the graphics RAM accessed faster is to increase the clock speed of the graphics chip and RAMDAC. Years back, the graphics chip ran at clock speeds well above that of the mainboard memory bus clock. Currently, SGRAM is running at a 100MHz clock, and some graphics chip manufacturers are already talking of a 125 or even 133MHz graphics RAM clock using 7ns SGRAM. SGRAM is nothing more than a special graphics version of SDRAM (synchronous DRAM); therefore, it's able to run at clock speeds up to 133MHz.

15.3.4 The RAMDAC

The RAMDAC converts the digital image data to analog form and pumps it to the monitor. Two factors are important in the RAMDAC: the quality and the maximum pixel frequency (measured in MHz). All other things being equal, a 220MHz RAMDAC is better than one running at 135MHz. The faster clock allows the graphics board to produce higher refresh rates. In the past, RAMDACs were discreet components on the graphics board, but now most are integrated directly into the coprocessor. However, high-quality boards with high refresh rates, such as Matrox Millennium and Number Nine Revolution 3D, often use an external RAMDAC running at very high clock rates.

15.4 3D Graphics in Depth

3D is a particularly important and complex area of graphics acceleration. The first thing to consider is whether the 3D graphics are for professional work or mainly for games. The two approaches to 3D are very different, making gaming cards poor matches for CAD/CAM work, and vice versa.

15.4.1 Gaming Graphics

The most pervasive form of 3D graphics is found in gaming software. Titles such as Id's Quake II and Rage Software's Incoming have helped make powerful 3D graphics acceleration a must-have feature for serious gamers. These games have very specific needs when it comes to 3D graphics display, including fast frame rates, realtime rendering, and the capability to run effectively on a broad range of machines. However, even though faster and more powerful silicon has helped significantly boost the realism of games over the past two years, serious concerns about compatibility remain.

Dueling APIs

The first question to answer is whether you want a card tailored for Microsoft's Direct3D API or one that uses a proprietary 3D scheme. This is a tough question because it means you have to decide what kind of games are important to you. Currently, many of the best games are designed for a specific graphics chip or work best on a specific chip. Currently, the 3Dfx Voodoo II chip—and its Glide engine—is enjoying the best level of support among proprietary 3D APIs. However, Microsoft's Direct3D enjoys the broadest support, if only because software vendors can be assured of almost all hardware being able to run their games.

At the same time, many new games are using the Direct3D API to run on a wide selection of graphics chips and boards. Although games written to the specific API of a particular board—say, 3Dfx's Glide API—can look stunning and run quickly, they won't run on other products. However, when they are written to Direct3D, both visual quality and performance will suffer because the boards are not finely tuned to the Microsoft API. What's more, incompatibilities can crop up in the Direct3D interface. Therefore, although PowerVR's PCX1 and PCX2 chips are quite powerful, some cards that use them seem to have trouble running games. However, if the PCX engine is written to directly, the games can look stunning. Some 3D chips forego a proprietary API entirely, using Direct3D exclusively for 3D acceleration. Examples include Nvidia's RIVA 128, 3D Labs Permedia, and S3's Virge, which all natively support Microsoft Direct3D.

Assessing 3D Performance

It's not easy to measure 3D graphics performance because there are so many different ways a 3D engine can be used. Most official benchmarks—such as ZD's 3D WinBench or VNU's Final Reality—use Microsoft's Direct3D. These benchmarks can only show you the card's Direct3D performance; they do nothing to show how well the driver translates Direct3D into the chip's own 3D engine. Nvidia's RIVA 128 doesn't need this "translator"; it uses Direct3D as its own API, which is one reason why the RIVA scores best in Direct3D benchmarks.

However, some games written specifically to a chip can run much faster than the 3D WinBench score would lead you to expect. VQuake for Rendition's Verite 1000 is a good example—the Verite 1000 doesn't score well in 3D WinBench, yet VQuake looks good and runs fast on-chip.

Assessing 3D Quality

It can be easy to overlook the quality of graphics produced by 3D accelerator boards. The latest version of Direct3D in DirectX 5 offers a strong set of features, but even more are coming in DirectX 6. No matter what the API, no 3D chip can support all the various 3D operations, requiring drivers to emulate these features in the software. The best overall feature support comes in the 3Dfx Voodoo2 chip.

In any case, you need to look for extensive 3D acceleration features in order to avoid poor-looking graphics. Support for trilinear filtering, MIP mapping, and complex lighting and shading effects can all help to smooth out jagged pixels and banded colors.

How Powerful Is Your CPU?

Some 3D chips are taking a lot of workload from the CPU, whereas others need decent CPU performance for their operation. PowerVR's PCX chips want at least a Pentium MMX 166 for decent quality, for example, whereas 3Dfx's Voodoo lets games run fast even on systems with weak CPUs. Rendition's Verite 2100/2200 chip gives a huge improvement to slow CPUs, but fast CPUs are reaching its limit and don't really benefit from this chip. Nvidia's RIVA 128 chip seems to scale directly from 6x86 CPUs up to Pentium II CPUs.

15.4.2 Considerations for Professionals

Although gaming and professional 3D graphics hardware can both produce stunningly realistic three-dimensional scenes and objects, the two classes of products are very different. Applications such as CAD/CAM software, animation packages, and other specialized graphics fare demand levels of precision far beyond that of Quake II. Mechanical engineering software, for example, must be able to reproduce three-dimensional representations of architectural models based on extremely large and precise data sets. By contrast, the capability to render scenes in realtime is not an issue.

Picture Quality

Image quality is absolutely essential for professional graphics applications. A high-quality and fast RAMDAC—such as those found on Matrox Millennium II and Number Nine Revolution 3D—produce the sharpest and cleanest picture on the screen. They also support very high refresh rates at top resolutions, which is critical if you spend long hours doing detailed graphics work.

2D Performance

2D performance used to define the quality of a graphic card, but today 2D acceleration seems to be reaching its limit, with almost all cards offering good 2D performance. In this area of the market, driver support under the Windows NT and Unix operating systems becomes critical because Windows 95 is not an appropriate platform for these applications.

Professional APIs: OpenGL and Heidi

For people who use a real graphic workstation with CAD or 3D rendering, the APIs to look for are OpenGL and Heidi. 3D Labs does great work in the OpenGL space, with its Glint line of processors and its terrific Permedia 2 chip, which crosses over between the professional and consumer market.

15.4.3 The CPU

The CPU plays an enormous role in the effectiveness of 3D graphics hardware. A mismatch between a slow CPU and fast 3D accelerator often results in the graphics card waiting for the data it needs to draw scenes. On the flip side, a fast CPU and slow graphics card can result in delays in the drawing stage, with the CPU sitting idle while the card strains to move pixels onto the screen.

Also, keep in mind that 3D chips don't necessarily scale linearly with CPU performance. A 3D graphics chip has a maximum polygon and pixel fill rate, which limits its performance. On the other side, a CPU is limited by its own capability to execute 3D geometry setup, which is determined primarily by the FPU.

If the CPU lacks FP performance, delays in geometry setup mean that the graphics chip must wait—and frame rate will be determined by the CPU. If the graphics chip reaches its top pixel fill rate or polygon rate, then the CPU cannot push frame rates any higher by sending geometry data more quickly. In this case, the frame rate is not determined by the CPU at all; the graphic chip is what limits it.

If you want to buy a 3D graphic card, you must consider the 3D geometry performance of your system. Intel still rules in the critical FP performance area, with Pentium II providing, by far, the fastest geometry execution of any $x86$ CPU. Pentium MMX follows, with AMD's K6 just behind it. Cyrix's $6x86$Mx lags in FP execution, due in part to its lower clock rates, whereas IDT's WinChip is the worst of the bunch.

If you intend to play Quake, Quake II, or any other game that uses the FPU, you'll want to consider an Intel CPU. The Quake/Quake II engines are the most FP dependent in 3D gaming, whereas many Direct3D games, such as Forsaken and Incoming, are not as particular about the performance of the FPU.

If you have a Pentium MMX or Pentium II CPU, you'll want a 3D chip that reaches high absolute results in frame rate and can scale well with the system processor. The best chip in this respect is the RIVA 128 from Nvidia, which is far from its maximum 3D performance even in a Pentium II–300 system. Although the 3Dfx Voodoo chip reaches its absolute 3D performance somewhere between Pentium MMX–233 and Pentium II–300, Voodoo2 opens the graphics floodgates for faster PCs.

If you have a low or midrange system, performance scaling doesn't matter as much as strong performance when working with slower geometry setup. Here, the 3Dfx Voodoo line and the Rendition Verite 2x00 stand out.

15.5 Graphics Tips

As you've seen, video cards contain several components and subsystems, just like the PC itself. It's no wonder that graphics cards can be tweaked, fine tuned, and even updated in some of the same ways as the main system memory, CPU, and even your productivity suite and World Wide Web browser.

This section discusses several ways of improving video card performance, including overclocking the graphics chip, updating the card's specific drivers, updating the video drivers of your operating system itself, and turning off the Flip at Sync setting.

15.5.1 Overclocking the Chip

Some, but not all, 3D boards can improve performance by bumping up the speed of the coprocessor clock. The Voodoo line of chips, for example, can be nudged to higher speeds, thus enabling higher pixel and triangle fill rates. Of course, you run the risk of overheating the chip and violating memory timings, which can lead to failure and possibly component damage.

Proper cooling should be a consideration if you expect to overclock your graphics chip—or any other chip for that matter. You might want to consider replacing your existing power supply with a cooler-running, high-airflow model that will help enhance airflow. If the board you own doesn't have a heat sink mounted on the graphics chip, you can purchase heat sinks, fans, and thermal epoxy to mount on the silicon, thus providing even better protection. Of course, any thermal device will take space, requiring you to keep the expansion slot next to the graphics board open.

In many cases, you may have to create or edit a text configuration file or noodle with the Windows 95 Registry to boost the clock rates. In some cases, however, a useful display utility is provided, as is the case with the Diamond and Creative Voodoo2 boards. However, if you really want to turn up the clock, you'll probably have to resort to text-based edits because the provided utilities limit speeds to a range considered safe by the vendor. Just keep in mind that overclocking can really boost 3D performance but will have little or no impact on 2D and video capability. You'll find instructions for overclocking specific graphics boards at the Tom's Hardware Web site at `www.tomshardware.com`.

15.5.2 Updating Drivers

Graphics drivers are notorious for changing rapidly, whether it's to incorporate new features, fix bugs, or boost performance. Microsoft isn't helping things by releasing new versions of its DirectX APIs every six months or so. You should make a point to check your board vendor's Web site early and often to see if new drivers have been released for your board. Also, when you buy a new board, the first thing you should do is download new drivers because the ones in that shrink-wrapped box are probably months old.

Often, vendors will provide two versions of their drivers: one that is formally tested and approved by Microsoft's Windows Hardware Quality Labs (WHQL) and another that features shortcuts that don't meet Microsoft's approval. The difference is that the uncertified drivers often include a feature called *GDI bypass*, which substitutes optimized code for standard GDI commands. The enhancement speeds graphics performance but can introduce incompatibilities. Sometimes, uncertified drivers may be perfectly compliant but are still awaiting final approval from Microsoft.

15.5.3 Beware of DirectX Driver Updates

Microsoft has a vision of driver compliance that aims to do away with off-the-cuff driver upgrades. In an effort to ensure compatibility, the DirectX installation routine used in most games and titles will check the installed drivers to see if they are Microsoft approved. If not—and many are not because of the time involved in getting approval—the installation will prompt you to replace the existing drivers with generic ones verified by Microsoft.

As a general rule, you should not overwrite your existing drivers unless you've noticed problems. It's quite likely that the approved drivers are a revision or two behind the ones you have, and replacing them will result in lost performance and features. If you do notice problems after the DirectX update, however, you may consider taking Microsoft up on its efforts to see if an approved driver fixes any glitches. The good news: Even if the DirectX installation replaces your original driver set, you can reinstall it quickly from your hard disk because the old drivers are not erased. All you need to do is go to the Display Properties dialog box and click through to the Advanced button to select the latest driver version for your hardware. The previous driver will appear as an option in the drop-down list box.

If you're reasonably sure you're using the latest drivers, you can also avoid the driver switcheroo by simply aborting out of the DirectX auto-install routine. What's more, this can protect you from having an older title trying to install an aged version of DirectX over your newer one.

15.5.4 Turning off Flip at Sync

3D gamers can realize an extra boost by turning off the Flip at Sync setting on their graphics cards. The problem is that 3D performance is sometimes dependent on the refresh rate, where the graphic chip may only draw a new page into the screen buffer memory when a whole picture has been displayed onscreen. Therefore, the lower the refresh rate, the more often the graphic chip must wait until it can push a new picture to screen, thus resulting in lower frame rates. This issue is well known with 3Dfx Voodoo cards, where most users have switched off this feature using the special Glide setting.

To turn off Flip at Sync, you may have to update your `autoexec.bat` file or create a batch file when you start a game. You can find out more about changing this setting for specific boards at the Tom's Hardware Web site (`www.tomshardware.com`).

15.6 Tom's Pick

There are literally hundreds of different graphics boards to choose from, spanning all manners of applications. It's nearly impossible to point to a single product or model line and say that it's the best for all uses. In fact, demanding users will probably have occasion to make use of two or more graphics boards, depending on what they need to do.

15.6.1 3D Graphics

The most demanding and exciting area of graphics technology today is in the area of 3D gaming. If you want to get the most realism and responsiveness out of games such as Quake II and Incoming, you can't do better than a graphics card based on 3Dfx's Voodoo2 graphics chip. This chip provides unparalleled frame rates and visual fidelity, thanks in part to a sophisticated design and the powerful Glide 3D API.

There are numerous boards based on Voodoo2, but the best of the bunch is Diamond Multimedia's Monster 3D II board. Like all Voodoo2 products, it's a PCI-based card that works in conjunction with your existing 2D graphics accelerator. Diamond sells the board with either 8MB or 12MB of fast EDO DRAM memory, thus allowing users to spend a bit more for enhanced realism.

Voodoo2 boards are particularly attractive to serious gamers because they offer a unique upgrade path. Install a pair of Monster 3D II or other Voodoo2 boards in your system, and the two cards work together to provide a feature called *scan line interlacing (SLI)* to double the pixel fill rates of 3D graphics. SLI divvies up the graphics work between the two boards, with one board handling even lines in the display while the other handles the odd lines. By splitting up the display work, the boards provide much higher performance even at extreme resolutions.

Of course, API support is absolutely critical in any board purchase, and the Voodoo2 excels in this respect. The 3Dfx Glide API is used by a large community of programmers, in large part because 3Dfx has done such a good job of supplying powerful, game-oriented silicon to the market. 3Dfx's first Voodoo chip ʳᵉᵐᵒᵛᵉᵈ ___ the most popular gaming graphics chip. Because of this, ___ ls enjoy a large base of compatible applications. Just as ___ performance is very good. The Diamond Monster 3D II ___ top of the pack in Direct3D application testing, even when ___ D-specific silicon such as Nvidia's Riva 128 and Intel's i740 ___

15.6.2 2D Graphics

___ on and developer energy being spent on 3D gaming ___ erlook the importance of 2D performance. However, for ___ isiness users, 3D graphics is still merely a blip on the ___ rtists, software developers, corporate presenters, and even ___ jockeys, a top-notch 2D graphics card is critical.

___ is the venerable Matrox Millennium II. Based on Matrox's ___ chitecture, the Millennium II uses 8MB of fast, dual-ported ___ AM) to provide fast screen refresh rates even at 1600×1200 ___ t cost-cutting graphics boards, Matrox uses an external, ___ o keep screen refresh rates high. Although the Millennium ___ for PC-based gaming, the board does provide a basic set of ___ es.

___ the decision. Matrox provides a powerful suite of display ___ MGA PowerDesk. This enhancement to the basic Win- ___ ls lets you set up virtual screens, manage color output ___ ures such as zoom and bird's-eye view. Perhaps most

Graphics Board Guide

important, Matrox provides stable, effective drivers that cover a variety of operating systems. Windows 3.*x*, Windows 9*x*, Windows NT, OS/2, and Linux are all supported by Matrox's drivers. There's even a Macintosh version of the Millennium II.

Chapter

16

Display Guide

No high performance PC is complete without a serious display. A larger screen can make life easier for harried business users who need to spend less time scrolling around spreadsheets and more time reviewing their data. A large 19- or 21-inch monitor lets these users see much more of the document and can ease eyestrain caused by tiny fonts and graphics. Of course, there's simply no comparing the impact of playing deathmatch *Quake* on a tiny 15-inch monitor with playing the game on a huge 21-inch monitor. (Of course, keep in mind that many games run at fixed resolution, so you won't see more of the landscape when playing, just larger graphics). When it comes to monitors, bigger is definitely better.

There's just one problem: Big monitors cost big bucks. Even though prices have come down a long way, a decent 17-inch monitor still runs $600 or $700. Also, 21-inch monitors start at about $1,200 and go up from there. Even if you can afford a thousand dollars or more for a display, you'll still need to find space for it—larger displays can take up a lot of desk space.

16.1 How CRTs Work

A PC monitor works a lot like a television set. The plastic case holds a large vacuum tube, which is mounted with the wide face toward the front of the unit. The tube tapers at the back into a narrow cylinder, where it interfaces with the monitor's electronics. Mounted inside the tapered portion of the tube are three *electron guns*, which shoot a stream of charged electrons corresponding with red, green, and blue pixels toward the front of the vacuum tube. The electron gun enjoys the busy task of painting the monitor screen many times each second in order to produce visible graphics to the user.

The face of the vacuum tube is coated on the inside with a phosphorescent material (see Figure 16.1). When exposed a specific electrical charges, this material reacts by giving off red, green, or blue light. The electron guns illuminate three closely spaced phosphors with varying levels of red, green, and blue to create the appearance of as many as 16.7 million individual colors. Defining the dots is a *shadow mask* or an *aperture grill*. A shadow mask is a thin layer of perforated steel (usually invar) that filters the electrons to precise points on the screen, whereas an aperture grill consists of very fine wires that present rectangular openings to the phosphor material. In both cases, the intervening layer enables sharp image reproduction and precise color positioning.

Colors are produced by varying the intensity of the three beams used to create red, blue, and green subpixels. If the red beam is set to high intensity but the other two are shut down, the result is a completely red pixel. Varying the charge of each of the three beams can turn one pixel aqua while the next glows magenta, yellow, blue, white, or one any of millions of other colors.

Figure 16.1.

This cutaway of the CRT vacuum tube shows the electron gun pointing at a phosphor-coated screen backed by an aperture grill.

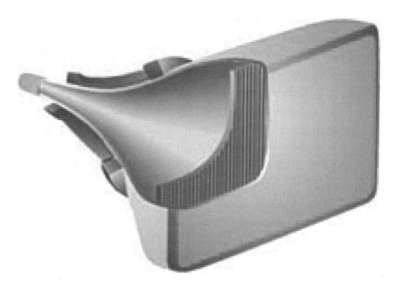

16.1.1 Scanning Screens

The phosphors on the monitor's tube only glow for a brief period of time. Once the electron beam strays from a pixel, it will go dark almost instantly. For this reason, the electron beam must light each pixel on the screen about 70 times or more each second, a process called *refresh*. The number of times each pixel on the screen is lit each second is called the *refresh rate*. This is an important feature of monitor operation. The refresh rate is expressed in hertz; therefore, a 70Hz monitor refreshes 70 times per second.

Monitors will often present over one million pixels. A 17-inch monitor displaying 1,280 pixels horizontally by 1,024 pixels vertically, for example, will display 1,310,720 pixels. At 1600×1200 resolution—a graphics mode common on 21-inch monitors—the number of pixels increases to 1,920,000. In order to provide comfortable viewing, the electron gun must light every one of those pixels 70 times or more each second. That's a lot of work—enough that some monitors cannot keep up the pace at the highest resolutions.

The following list shows exactly how many pixels your monitor must illuminate in each pass as resolutions go up.

- 640×480: 307,200 pixels
- 800×600: 480,000 pixels
- 1024×768: 786,432 pixels
- 1280×1024: 1,310,720 pixels
- 1600×1200: 1,920,000 pixels

Display Guide

Here's how it works: The electron beam sweeps horizontally across the screen, lighting each pixel in the row from left to right. Once the beam reaches the right edge of the screen, the gun switches the beam off and moves down to the left-most point on the next row. The process repeats for each row on the display, with the entire screen being refreshed 70 times or more per second.

The process of scanning each line in order is called *progressive scanning* and marks a major difference in the way your TV works. TVs use *interlaced scanning*, where every other row of the screen is refreshed in one pass. After the last line is drawn, the beam is shut off until the gun refocuses to the top to draw the alternate lines in a second pass. This reduces the strain on the electron gun and electronics—one reason why TVs are so much less expensive than PC monitors is because the gun does not need to track nearly as quickly as it must when scanning progressively.

> **NOTE** Until 1992 or so, many PC monitors used interlaced scanning as a way to cut expense and allow operation at higher resolutions. However, improving electronics and declining costs have since made interlacing an obsolete practice. Interlaced displays are painful to look at close up because of the way pixels behave. As the gun is refreshing even lines on the screen, the phosphors in the odd lines are busy growing dim. As a result, the lines on the screen are alternately bright or fading, a pattern the brain perceives as flicker.

The iron rule of monitor operation is that higher refresh rates are better. Unlike TVs, which display moving images and are viewed from distances of 10 feet and greater, PC monitors display static text and graphics and are viewed from 18 inches (or closer). At this close range, text and graphics appear to jitter when refresh rates fall to 70Hz or lower. This flicker occurs because at these lower rates, your brain is able to perceive the rapid lighting and fading of pixels—some people are more sensitive to it than others. The flickering can result in eyestrain and headaches, making it difficult to work for any period of time.

16.1.2 Moving Magnets

All this furious activity is made possible through the use of magnetic fields inside the monitor that deflect the electron beam to the desired point. In order to generate the energy to fire the beam and to maintain the magnetic fields, a typical display uses a lot of energy. A 17-inch monitor, for example, will consume almost 70 watts of electricity and will produce thousands of volts inside its magnetic coil.

The high voltages make doing any sort of tinkering inside the monitor case a very dangerous proposition. Even unplugged, significant electrical charges can exist in the monitor's coil, inviting potentially fatal electric shock. If you find your monitor is in need of servicing, you should take it to a qualified repair shop.

The presence of focused electron beams and magnetic fields make monitors a hostile environment for magnetic media such as floppy disks. Shielding reduces the amount of electromagnetic frequency (EMF) radiation put out by a display, but you should take care not to place your floppy or Zip disks on or near the monitor chassis all the same. Stray magnetic charges can wipe out your data, particularly if left exposed over time.

16.2 Performance Impact Report

The monitor won't make your applications run any faster, but it can allow you to work much more quickly and efficiently than with a smaller display. Large monitors running at high resolution can eliminate time-consuming scrolling and make navigation of complex documents or multiple applications much easier. Anyone who has gone from working with a tiny 14-inch CRT to a spacious 17-inch model can tell you just how effective the larger screens are when it comes to multitasking and working with complex documents.

Of course, a large high-resolution monitor is critical for desktop publishing, image and video editing, and other creative applications. For these applications, the wide array of interface controls consume a large portion of the available display on smaller monitors, leaving little room to show the actual graphics being worked on. For these applications, 21-inch monitors are often used. Some users actually employ two monitors—one to show the graphics and the other to show the interface. Of course, your software needs to be aware of multiple monitors to provide this feature. Windows 98, for example, adds multiple monitor support (Windows 95 has only single-monitor capability). The same feature is also present in Windows NT 4.0, OS/2, and various forms of Unix.

Gaming, surprisingly, gets mixed benefit from large-screen monitors. Although games such as *Quake II* are able to scale up resolutions to enhance visual impact on larger monitors, most games lack this flexibility. A larger monitor only results in enlarged text and graphics onscreen. Therefore, you won't see more of the *Command & Conquer* battlefield for example. Instead, you'll just see bigger objects. What's more, pushing resolutions on 3D games such as *Quake II* places such a processing strain on the CPU and graphics card that frame rates may plummet, making high-resolution modes much less satisfying than you would think.

Refresh rates can also impact relative performance because perceived screen flicker can result in distracting eyestrain and headaches. Low refresh rates make it extremely difficult to read text or concentrate on the screen for any length of time.

Display Guide

16.3 Currently Available Monitors

The PC monitor landscape is broken down into two major categories: TV-like CRT displays and flat-panel displays used for both notebooks and desktops. CRTs are affordable, produce excellent brightness and contrast, and work with virtually any graphics card. Flat panel displays are compact, lightweight, and energy efficient, but they remain extremely expensive and require specific support from the graphics subsystem to operate. As a result, flat panel displays remain a focus for vertical markets.

16.3.1 Viewable Area

The most recognizable distinction among displays is pretty obvious—screen size. Generally, the size of a monitor is described by the size of the vacuum tube face, as measured diagonally from point to point. Tubes are produced in a number of standard sizes, notably 14-, 15-, 17-, 19-, and 21-inch diagonals. The differences in viewable areas can be significant. A 17-inch display provides about 40 percent more area than does a 15-inch monitor—a major improvement for a scant 2 inches in measure.

The different size tubes appeal to different applications and price ranges. Table 16.1 provides a quick overview of monitor sizes and their uses.

Table 16.1. Larger monitor sizes enable higher resolutions and better viewing for applications.

CRT Size	Comfortable Resolution	Application(s)
14 inch	640×480	Non-GUI text.
15 inch	800×600	Basic windowing, email, word processing, Web browsing, and gaming.
17 inch	1024×768	Enhanced windowing, multitasking, Web browsing, gaming, and low-end graphics.
19 inch	1152×970, 1280×1024	Enhanced windowing, heavy duty multitasking and Web browsing, midrange graphics and Web design, and gaming.

CRT Size	Comfortable Resolution	Application(s)
21 inch+	1280×1024, 1600×1200	High-end gaming as well as high-end graphics and design, including 3D, video, and Web production.

> **NOTE** It's worth noting that the actual usable area of the display is smaller than the tube measurement. Therefore, a 15-inch monitor usually presents about 13.8 to 14 inches of screen area, whereas a 17-inch tube presents 15.9 to 16 inches. The larger the monitor gets, the lower the percentage of "lost" tube area—in part because the bezel surrounding the edges does not need to grab more surface to hold its place around the tube. Monitor makers recently began marketing their products by viewable area, in part due to legal action taken by a number of states.

Monitor prices are largely dependent on tube size because the vacuum tube represents a large portion of the cost of any monitor (and is not subject to the dive-bomber price curve of silicon components). Recently, 17-inch monitors have moved into the value range of the market, thanks in large part to the entry of additional manufacturers and growing economies for 17-inch tube production. A typical 17-inch monitor costs from $600 to $800.

Although 21-inch monitors remain very expensive—starting at $1,200—the recent introduction of 19-inch tubes has created an intriguing market for mainstream computer buyers. Most major system makers now sell systems with 19-inch monitors, either standard or as an option. These tubes present about 50 percent more screen area than those of 17-inch CRTs, while costing about $900 (30 percent less than the least expensive 21-inch display).

Why don't monitor prices drop the way hard disk, CD-ROM, and CPU prices have over the past ten years? The fact is, monitors are a mature technology—manufacturers have been making CRTs for 40 years. In addition, the glass tube itself represents a major part of the product cost, so larger tubes result in higher costs. Finally, 21-inch displays typically require more sophisticated electronics to maintain visual fidelity and high refresh rates than do smaller monitors. The result is higher prices.

16.3.2 Flat Panel Displays Emerge

People have been talking about flat panel displays forever. Certainly, we've seen big gains in the notebook market, where new 14.1-inch screens opened unprecedented vistas for the road weary. Now desktop versions are becoming available. NEC, ViewSonic, and other major display makers have also released new flat panel desktop displays in the last 12 months (see Figure 16.2).

Display Guide

Figure 16.2.
The ViewSonic VPA150 active matrix 15" ViewPanel produces pictures in both portrait and landscape modes.

Flat panel displays are a neat technology, to be sure, but don't expect them to supplant that mammoth CRT you use now. The technology behind flat panels remains expensive. Even optimistic projections place flat panel displays at two to three times the price of similar-sized CRT monitors. That premium grows quickly as you move into larger form factors above 15 diagonal inches.

So who would use a flat panel display? The technology is valuable for anyone who needs to find space for five or six separate monitors in a cramped workspace. Stock brokers, administrators, and security personnel are just a few examples. The technology is also popular among Japanese companies because of the high premium placed on space.

How LCD Technology Works

Flat panel displays work by exciting liquid crystals embedded between two layers of glass. When an electrical charge is applied to the crystal, its structure changes, causing the crystal to refract light that's passed through it. In this respect, flat panel displays are different from CRTs. CRT pixels actually produce colored light, whereas LCD pixels filter light directed from behind the screen in order to show the desired spectrum to the user.

Flat panel displays differ in how the charge is applied, with the majority of desktop displays using the so-called *active-matrix technology*. This approach puts a transistor directly on each pixel. When a pixel is to be lit, the graphics controller charges the transistor and lights the pixel.

Cheaper passive-matrix displays cut costs by arraying transistors along the top edge of each column and the left edge of each row of pixels. The transistors shoot a charge down their respective row and columns, lighting the pixels where charges intersect. The problem with passive displays is that pixel refresh occurs slowly, making them inappropriate for video or animation. Also, the diffused electrical charges result in much less brightness and contrast, limiting readability to an area directly in front of the screen.

LCD Buying Issues

Almost everyone agrees that flat panel displays are a really neat technology. They are slim and light, sip electricity, and have crisp, bright images to boot. However, flat panels are darned expensive. Unless you have a real need for one of these slimline products, you're best off with a good CRT monitor that employs power management to reduce your electricity bills.

In addition, flat panels won't work with every PC. Monitors display output generated by analog video signals coming from your graphics card or adapter. However, flat panels work with their own type of signal format, which means you need a graphics adapter tailored for double duty. Most cards won't send the proper signals to drive an LCD display, so you'll need to make sure you have proper driver software and hardware for the job.

Finally, flat panel displays fail in a way that CRTs do not—individual liquid crystals can become defective and stop reacting to electrical impulses. The result is a tiny—but very noticeable—dead spot on the screen. Enough of these can render a display more annoying than useful. If you buy a new display, you should check it right away for bad pixels and see if you can return the product if any are present.

Display Guide

16.4 Evaluating Monitors

Choosing monitors comes down to a couple of really easy issues and quite a few more subtle ones. The easy stuff is already out of the way. Namely, how big you want your screen and how much you can spend. However, monitors can differ widely in visual quality, brightness, comfort, and controls, as shown in Figure 16.3.

Figure 16.3.
The Mitsubishi Diamond Pro 1000 is a spacious 21-inch monitor that produces sharp graphics and high refresh rates. However, like all 21-inch CRTs, it's too big and expensive for all but the most demanding users.

In addition, new monitors are packing some intriguing nondisplay oriented features. Multimedia monitors, which integrate speakers and microphones into the monitor housing, have been around for several years. Speaker cables run from the monitor to your sound card, whereas volume, bass, treble, and other audio controls are provided on the front bezel of the display.

Although these models save space and clutter by eliminating separate speakers and their attendant power cords, their audio quality leaves a lot to be desired. Most are underpowered and lack effective output at the low end. The one exception is Sony's VAIO monitor, which integrates a subwoofer into the housing, but even that monitor produces only adequate sound compared to better desktop speakers.

More useful for newer PCs are monitors with built-in Universal Serial Bus (USB) connectors. These monitors connect to your PC's USB ports just like any other USB peripheral, and they present one or more USB ports for plugging in compliant mice, keyboards, scanners, and other devices. Not only can a USB monitor add valuable ports, but the placement of these ports are a lot more convenient than those behind the back of your PC's chassis.

16.4.1 Refresh Rates

One critical issue when buying a monitor is refresh rate support. As discussed earlier, the refresh rate defines the number of times each second the monitor's electron gun repaints the screen. In general, a good refresh rate is about 85Hz (or 85 times per second), whereas 75Hz is considered adequate. These are rough figures. As the display gets larger, you'll want higher refresh rates to counteract the growing tendency to perceive flicker. Also, if you tend to read black text against a bright white background, you'll want higher refresh rates because the bright, detailed graphics tend to enhance the perception of flicker.

As you know, flicker is bad. Imagine staring at a low-intensity strobe light about 10 hours a day! Although studies have shown that the perception of flicker usually goes away at about 70 or 75Hz, I wouldn't recommend working at anything below 85Hz. The Video Electronics Standards Association (VESA), an industry consortium governing graphics and display standards, has set 76Hz as its recommended minimum.

Refresh rates vary as you change your resolution. At higher resolutions, many more pixels must be lit on every pass, posing a growing challenge to the monitor electronics. The specification that determines your monitor's refresh capability is called the maximum horizontal frequency, which is expressed in *kilohertz* (or thousands of times per second).

Just because a monitor can theoretically support a given refresh rate doesn't mean it will. When buying a CRT, look for *multisync monitors*, which are able to lock into a wide variety of resolutions and refresh rates. Fixed-rate monitors will lack the flexibility needed to optimize refresh rate performance.

To determine what refresh rate your monitor can support at any resolution, you can do a little math. Multiply the desired refresh rate (say, 75Hz) by the number of rows at a given resolution (say, 768 rows at 1024×768 resolution). Now multiply that number by 1.04, which is a fudge factor that reflects the time it takes for the electron gun to track from one row to the next.

The result (in our example, 59,904 or 59.9KHz) is the horizontal frequency required to achieve 75Hz refresh at 1024×768 resolution—well within the capability of most PC monitors sold today. At 85Hz, that figure rises to 67.9KHz. Things get challenging at 1280×1024 resolution, where 85Hz operation requires a

Display Guide

vertical frequency of 90.5KHz. Most monitors fall into two vertical refresh categories: 82KHz and 120KHz. When buying a monitor, you should make note of the vertical frequency to determine if the display will provide stable viewing at the resolutions you desire.

Of course, you can turn the equation around to determine what refresh rates a given vertical frequency can support. Therefore, if a monitor you're looking at provides 85KHz maximum horizontal frequency, you can determine the refresh rate at 1280×1024 resolution by following these steps:

1. Take 85KHz and divide it by the number of rows (in this case 1024).

2. Divide the result by the fudge factor (1.04).

3. The result is the top refresh rate, in hertz, supported at the resolution you specified. A monitor capable of a maximum horizontal scan rate of 85KHz can deliver a top refresh rate of 80Hz refresh at 1280×1024 resolution.

It's worth noting that more than your monitor is involved here—your graphics board needs to support high refresh operation, too. Therefore, a brand new high-refresh monitor matched with an aged graphics board will flicker like the devil. If you want high-refresh operation for your monitor, look for a graphics card with a 200MHz or faster RAMDAC. (For more information, see Chapter 15, "Graphics Board Guide.")

16.4.2 Shadow Mask Technologies

The shadow mask sits just behind the glass screen, where its many individual holes act as focal points for the pixels on the screen. Each of the three colored dots (red, green, blue) in each pixel is accessed through a tiny space in the shadow mask. Most monitors use an invar shadow mask, which is made of an alloy that resists expansion when heated, as well as oxidation over time. This property is critical because the stream of electrons heats the shadow mask, inviting expansion that can cause the holes to become misshapen.

An alternative to the invar shadow mask is the Sony-developed Trinitron design. Unlike a standard shadow mask, which is a sheet with millions of tiny holes, a Trinitron mask (known in generic terms as an *aperture grill*) consists of a tightly bound grill that creates tall, thin rectangles for the electron beam to shoot through (see Figure 16.4). A pair of stabilizing wires hold the vertical wires in place.

Perfectionists will note that the Trinitron mask produces rectangular, slightly off-shaped pixels, but in reality the effect is nearly unnoticeable. The advantage Trinitron delivers is significant. Trinitron screens are brighter, crisper, and produce more saturated colors than their shadow mask counterparts, making them an excellent choice for graphic designers, multimedia producers, and game players. Unfortunately, you'll pay more for Trinitron or similar technology (Mitsubishi's Diamondtron, for example), with these monitors often costing $200 to $300 more than their shadow mask counterparts.

Figure 16.4.

The Sony GDM-440PS uses an aperture grill Trinitron tube to produce superior brightness on its 19-inch CRT screen.

Also, aperture grill-based tubes do generally carry a drawback in the form of a pair of faint horizontal lines that cross the screen. These two lines, located about halfway up and down from the center point of the screen, are especially visible against a white, stable background and can be a source of annoyance to some users. The lines are created by the shadow of a thin wire used to fix the Trinitron in place so that it doesn't stretch during heating.

The shadow masks used in monitors differ in the level of detail they can produce. The closer together the individual holes (or rectangles) are on the shadow mask, the sharper the images will appear onscreen. The distance between the center of any two dots of the same color is called the *dot pitch*, which is measured in millimeters.

Display Guide

The dot pitch generally varies based on the size of the CRT. The larger the screen, the tighter the dot pitch. This allows monitors to produce sharp, detailed pixels at the high resolutions used on large screens. In general, the smaller the dot pitch number, the better the display. Of course, aperture grill monitors don't use dots. In this case, the distance between openings in the aperture grill is known as the *stripe pitch* and is likewise measured in millimeters.

Table 16.2 provides a list of display sizes and their likely dot pitches.

Table 16.2. Recommended dot pitch by monitor size.

CRT Size	Maximum Recommended Dot Pitch
14 inch	.39mm
15 inch	.28mm
17 inch	.26mm
19 inch and up	.21mm

Note that a typical TV has a dot pitch of something like .40mm because TVs are intended to be viewed from across a room—you simply are not close enough to discern pixel-by-pixel detail. The 31-inch monitor used on Gateway's Destination PCs, as well as on living room–sized displays from vendors such as Princeton Graphics, likewise use a larger dot pitch. Although lower dot pitch becomes critical at close range, fuzziness is visible in these CRTs even at lower display resolutions. The reduced fidelity can cause eyestrain as your brain struggles to focus images. Note that dot pitch is not something you can fix: If the shadow mask dot pitch is too high for effective operation, you are stuck.

16.4.3 Controls

Like a television, PC monitors feature controls for adjusting brightness, contrast, display size and position, and other characteristics. Less expensive monitors provide fewer controls, limiting your ability to correct image imperfections and adjust for differences in ambient lighting. Monitor controls break into three distinct groups:

- Basic controls
- Geometry controls
- Color controls

Basic Controls

At a minimum, virtually all monitors include the basic control set, which includes brightness, contrast, sizing, and positioning features for the display. Unfortunately, this slim set of controls falls short of what you need to keep your display working well.

Geometry Controls

One reason you need more than just basic controls is to counteract flaws that can creep into monitor operation over time—a function served by geometry controls. Table 16.3 shows the geometry adjustments you'll find on most midrange monitors. There's quite a vocabulary to this feature set, which can make choosing a monitor difficult.

Table 16.3. Midrange Monitor Geometry Adjustments.

Control	Function
Convergence	Resolves fuzziness and blooming in pixels by focusing the monitor's electron beam.
Degauss	Realigns the monitor's magnetic field to resolve distortions caused by interference or drift.
Pincushion	Adjusts the display corners to resolve bowing that curves the vertical edges of the image toward the center of the display.
Barrel distortion	Adjusts the display corners to eliminate bowing that curves vertical edges away from the center of the screen
Trapezoid	Adjusts the top and bottom edges of the display so that both are the same width.
Rotation/tilt	Levels the image of the display after it has been tilted by variations in external magnetic fields.

These controls are critical because, unlike most of the other components on your PC, the monitor is an analog device. The electron gun operates in response to the analog video signal sent to it over the 15-pin VGA cable. Magnetic fields are used to channel the beam of electrons to the desired points on the front of the tube. However, these fields can be impaired over time by competing magnetic fields, physical jarring, or simple drift in the controls. Even the earth's magnetic field can impair your monitor's ability to accurately display color.

Display Guide

Magnetic interference is, in fact, a very common cause of display flaws because so many sources of magnetic fields often sit on the desktop. Anything from unshielded speakers and tabletop fans to telephone handsets can throw the magnetic fields in your monitor out of whack. If your monitor has no controls for countervailing distortion, you could end up staring at misshapen graphics all day long.

Color Controls

Higher-end monitors will also include color controls. These features let you fine-tune the color balance of the display, producing whites, reds, yellows, and other colors that are just so. The most prominent color control features are as follows:

- Color temperature
- Color matching

Color temperature refers to the baseline color output of your monitor. By setting the precise level of charge when producing the color white (in essence, the sum of all colors), you're able to dictate the overall output of the monitor. White temperature is expressed in degrees of Kelvin, with higher temperatures producing a bluish-white effect. Ironically, because of the blue tint that creeps in at the highest settings, a high white temperature monitor is said to produce "cool tones."

Color matching is a sophisticated feature that ensures that what you see on your monitor is identical to what comes out of your printer. The problem is that every monitor and printer has its own way of doing things and produces its own distinct color signature. This is exacerbated by the fact that printers produce colors using a subtractive process (they use ink or toner to block the reflection of unwanted spectrums of light to produce specific colors), whereas monitors use an additive process (they use a colored light source to add spectrums together to form color).

The result is that color matching is a tricky and complex science, rife with mathematical theory. At its basic level, color matching consists of a database of device profiles (including your monitor), which allows the software to tell the printer exactly how to match up with the output viewed on your monitor screen. This approach requires vendors to write drivers for the color-matching scheme, so if you plan to use this feature, you should purchase printers and monitors with color-matching compatibility in mind.

More sophisticated schemes actually use a sampling device to scan the monitor screen to determine the precise output. This device can spot poor color settings and help you tune your display to optimum output, while at the same time ensuring that your color-matched monitor and printer are in sync. Again, these features are critical for professional designers but are otherwise of limited usefulness for most buyers.

Digital Versus Analog

Whatever the control set your monitor uses, an important issue is how it works. Monitors can provide either analog controls (those familiar thumb wheels) or digital controls (often pushbuttons). Digital operation carries a number of advantages, not the least of which is the fact that your monitor can remember adjustments and return to a specific, fine-tuned state when you enter a certain graphics mode.

Unfortunately, display controls are notoriously difficult to use. Low-cost monitors shave expense by eliminating most of the front panel controls, instead providing an adjustment control and a button for selecting individual properties. Adjustments are then viewed onscreen, usually by way of a rudimentary and hard-to-navigate onscreen menu. The overall effect makes monitor adjustments difficult, time consuming, and often inaccurate. If you intend to switch among numerous graphics modes and want fine control over your display, look for a monitor that presents distinct controls for both basic and geometry adjustments; otherwise, you may find yourself struggling with a poor onscreen interface.

16.4.4 The New USB Generation

If you intend to get a new monitor, consider getting a model that features USB ports build into the base. USB stands for the Universal Serial Bus, a Plug and Play external bus for everything from keyboards and joysticks to scanners and printers. PCs have been shipping with a pair of USB ports on the back for nearly two years, meaning that most Pentium MMX and Pentium II owners have access to this useful technology. Of course, you'll need to have USB-compliant peripherals to make use of USB, but if you build such a collection, a USB monitor is a good idea.

USB-equipped monitors do several things. One, they can add to the meager two ports found on most PCs, letting you plug in more devices. They also add convenience—the monitor ports are right on your desktop, making it easy to hot-swap USB devices you want to share with other systems or stow away when not in use. Be aware that a monitor must incorporate a USB hub in order to add more than a single pass-through port. Better USB monitors will offer multiple USB connections, and they will provide supplemental electrical power to the ports to allow scanners and other power-drawing devices to run reliably.

The most compelling USB monitors take advantage of USB's data-carrying talents to provide an onscreen user interface. Instead of struggling with inscrutable buttons and knobs, you simply launch a Windows-based monitor utility to fine-tune all the characteristics of your display. You can adjust display size, geometry, brightness, and other settings from a standard Windows application that runs on your PC. The result: Faster and more precise adjustments.

Display Guide

16.4.5 Shielding and Power Management

Advances over the past five years have made shielding and power management a less critical concern. In the past, PC monitors flooded their users with EMF (electromagnetic frequency) that streamed out the front of the screen. With TVs, this wasn't an issue because EMF drops off exponentially as it travels from its source—at six feet or so, virtually none is present. However, at 18 inches, the EMF from a bright, 17-inch display can be high enough to cause concern.

The first standard to address EMF was the MPR-II specification adopted in Sweden. By 1994, most monitors were meeting MPR-II compliance, reducing EMF dramatically. By that time, however, the Swedes had moved on to a stricter standard, called TCO. This standard dropped EMF levels dramatically, all but eliminating any potential health risk due to exposure to electromagnetic radiation. Today, many monitors offer TCO compliance. If you work for long hours in front of a monitor, TCO-level shielding is probably a good thing to have.

Around the same time that EMF became a burning issue, monitor makers were struggling with power consumption. Monitors need a lot of juice to light all those pixels, resulting in steep energy bills. Large companies even face increased air conditioning costs due to the heat all their monitors throw into the air while operating—a double whammy that corporations were anxious to resolve.

Working in conjunction with a compliant graphics card, power management features allow the monitor to be sent into one of three states: active, sleep, and deep sleep. In most cases, you can set your Windows screensaver to kick off these modes at specific intervals. For example, a monitor might go to sleep after five minutes of system inactivity and then slip into a deep power down mode after about 15 minutes of inactivity. This scaled approach allows reasonable energy savings without forcing long restart waits for users.

The sleep mode essentially shuts off the electron beam. This is similar to turning the brightness and contrast all the way down so that the screen shows nothing but blackness. The internal components remain active and heated, and the gun itself remains charged. For this reason, the monitor continues to consume some electricity and produce heat but at a lower level than during active operation. The advantage: The monitor quickly returns to active operation when you hit a keyboard key or move the mouse.

The deep sleep or power down mode realizes big savings by actually switching off power to the electron gun altogether. At this level, power usage can drop to a mere five watts—just enough to keep the electronics active to get the monitor running again. In this mode, monitor components will cool, much the way they do when the display is shut off altogether. For this reason, recovering from deep sleep mode can take up to 30 seconds as the black screen slowly brightens. You'll often hear a crackling sound—again, similar to when the monitor is physically turned on—as the shadow mask and tube expand slightly with heat.

16.4.6 Assessing Image Quality

Ultimately, visual quality determines the value of a monitor. To determine the preciseness of a display, closely examine thin vertical and horizontal lines that appear close to the corners of the display. Monitors have a hard time maintaining straight edges and sharp pixels at the far edges of the display because the electron beam must be bent sharply to reach these regions. Lower quality monitors lack the electronics to maintain round pixel shape at the screen edges.

In addition, not all monitors produce the same amount of brightness and contrast. NEC and Sony Trinitron monitors, for example, tend to produce brighter output, making them excellent for displaying motion video and animation. MAG monitors, on the other hand, do not crank up the brightness, making them more suitable for business applications that demand long hours of onscreen reading.

Other things you can do to assess quality include checking for blooming, which occurs when colors bleed out of the edges of the pixels. To do this, crank the brightness up to full and look closely at the image. Also look closely at the display edges to see if the display area is square. To bring out any flaws in the monitor image, display images with thin vertical lines along the outer edge of the screen.

An excellent tool for assessing and tuning monitor quality is Sonera Technology's DisplayMate utilities (see Figure 16.5). This software steps you through a series of graphics-intensive screens, prompting you to examine the display for specific characteristics. You'll also find useful information for resolving problems.

Figure 16.5.

Sonera's DisplayMate utility is a terrific value if you need to fine-tune the output of your display.

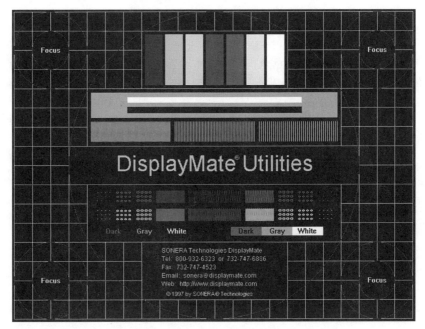

Display Guide

16.5 Monitor Optimization Tips

Want to get the most out of your monitor? This section contains ten tips from the folks at Sonera Technology, the maker of the popular DisplayMate monitor diagnostic software. Used as a critical assessment tool in many magazines' monitor reviews, DisplayMate enables you to see, identify, and resolve many visual imperfections in your display.

Keeping your display in tip-top condition is necessary in order to obtain the best possible image and picture quality, prolong the display's useful life, and get the most from your investment. These important issues are sometimes overlooked.

There's no comparable section on maintaining your video board because, generally, nothing can be done for a video board except return it to the manufacturer for repair. Fortunately, they are extremely reliable, do not deteriorate with age, and seldom break. If they do, however, you'll be glad to know that most come with a long warranty period.

16.5.1 Screen Cleaning

Screen cleaning is the easiest and possibly the most important aspect of regular display maintenance. If you like to point with your fingers on the screen, you may need to do this daily; otherwise, you should clean your screen whenever there's a noticeable accumulation of dust or stains. The faceplate of most CRTs attracts superfine particles suspended in the air that may coat the screen so uniformly that you are unlikely to notice the buildup. In general, it's best to clean your display the first thing every Monday morning. In the absence of specific manufacturer's instructions, ordinary glass cleaner and paper towels should do fine. Spray the liquid onto the paper towel, not the screen, so that the drippings don't seep inside the display or stain the bezel or other plastic parts.

The antiglare coatings on some screens are delicate and may easily scratch or even rub off under excessive pressure. The hardest screens to clean are those with antireflection coatings that absorb oils, particularly form fingerprints, which produce a multicolor iridescent appearance. With those you may need to clean the screen several times before all the streaks disappear. There are also special cleaning kits with antistatic cleaner and soft lint-free cloths. The antistatic liquid may slow down the build up of dirt. Most of the time the kits come with an insufficient number of cloths.

16.5.2 Display Set Up

Adjusting the controls on a display is something you'll also need to do regularly. This is one of the primary functions of DisplayMate for Windows. For example, if the room lighting changes, you'll need to adjust the contrast control. If the change in room lighting is substantial, the brightness control may also require adjustment in order to reset the optimum black level.

The display itself is subject to drift, possibly over a period of hours, often requiring minor adjustments for centering and brightness. The fastest way to readjust the display is to run the DisplayMate Master Test Pattern by double-clicking the Master Test Pattern icon. By adding this icon to your Windows Startup group, you'll obtain the test pattern automatically every time Windows is started.

Use the DisplayMate setup program when you first install your monitor. The best time to use the tune-up program is after you've worked with the monitor for a few days and are thoroughly familiar with it. Thereafter, run through the setup program weekly to check and touch-up settings. Run through the video obstacle course once a month to check and correct for the inevitable aging and drifting. Use the tune-up program when you make any changes to the monitor or video board settings, to the computer system hardware configuration, or to your work area.

16.5.3 Life Expectancy

There are a number of simple things you can do to increase the life of your display. The first is maintaining good ventilation in order to minimize the display's internal temperature. Keep all the ventilation holes and slots free and clear and never place papers or anything else on top of the display. If you notice dirt accumulating on the openings, you should vacuum them clean.

Power line spike and surge protectors should not be necessary for well-designed computer equipment, but they certainly don't hurt. Every once in awhile they may contribute to saving the life of your display or computer; for example, if lightning strikes nearby. If you experience periodic picture shrinkage on your display, you should plug your computer into a power outlet that's controlled by a different circuit breaker or fuse. If you have recurring problems or experience other forms of power line interference, do not rely on a spike or surge protector, but rather have the problem investigated by an electrician or an electronics technician.

If you want to maximize the long-term image quality and life expectancy of your display, avoid repeatedly turning it on and off many times during the course of a day. Every time you turn your display on or off, voltage instabilities and current surges that stress some components may occur as the power ramps up or down. Temperature cycles inside individual components, as well as within the entire piece of equipment may stress and prematurely age some components.

Display Guide

Beginning in 1994, the U.S. government strongly encouraged a reduction in computer energy consumption through the Environmental Protection Agency's Energy Star Program. The government awards an Energy Star label to monitors that use 30 watts or less of power in a standby mode. Most monitors use between 60 and 100 watts during normal operation. A monitor enters a standby mode after the computer is idle for a certain period of time.

Although at first sight our recommendations may appear to conflict with the goals of the Energy Star program, bear in mind that there's a large ecological cost from discarded units that fail or perform unsatisfactorily. Not only is there a considerable waste of resources because the display must be replaced, but monitors are a hazardous, toxic, and bulky waste for landfills. Recycling the CRT and other materials is currently not practical. It's definitely important not to waste electricity, so you should turn the display off when you're not going to use it for an extended period of time.

16.5.4 Stability and Drift

Another reason for not repeatedly turning the display on and off many times during the course of a day is that many monitors take a fair amount of time to warm up and reach their optimum operating point. Most CRT displays will experience their greatest drift when they are first turned on. Many will require at least 30 minutes in order to stabilize completely. During this period, the image centering and black level will often vary the most. Other parameters, such as focus, may not be optimal during warm up. Most of the major manufacturers are implementing the Energy Star program using the DPMS (Display Power Management Signaling) standard developed by VESA, the Video Electronic Standards Association. The DPMS standard has four power levels: On, Standby with 30 Watts or less, Suspend with 4 watts or less, and Off. Because there are two low power states that are implemented by the monitor's own circuitry, some of the electrical and thermal cycling problems identified earlier are reduced, but not eliminated.

16.5.5 Phosphor Efficiency and Burn

All of the phosphors used in displays are subject to burn and to a loss of light-emitting efficiency with time. Phosphor burn is seen as a patterned discoloration on the screen when the display is turned off, often in the form of stripes from recurring text output. The glass in some displays is also subject to discoloration.

A reduction in phosphor efficiency occurs slowly over a period of time and may be noticeable as a pattern of reduced light output on the screen during the screen uniformity test. The loss of light-emitting efficiency is proportional to the beam intensity and to the amount of time it's applied. If you make extensive use of a program that produces a structured output, that pattern also will become embedded in the screen over time. Although color displays are highly resistant to these problems, some long-persistence phosphors used in monochrome displays are more susceptible to burn.

16.5.6 Screensavers

Screensavers have become extremely popular because of their entertainment value. Unfortunately, many screen savers actually accelerate phosphor aging because they continually produce full-color, full-screen graphic images on the display. Because the images move, the accelerated aging is at least uniform, so no particular pattern is embedded on the screen. In principle, the best screen saver is one that keeps most of the screen black most of the time but still alerts you to the fact that the monitor and computer are turned on and possibly in the middle of an important application. The Windows Desktop Control Panel's Starfield Simulation setting is an example of such a screensaver.

16.5.7 Aging

All electronic equipment ages, but the aging process is most easily noticed in video displays where qualitative differences are easily seen. The aging arises from the variation of certain electronic components with time, as well as from a gradual deterioration of the precise mechanical configuration and alignment of certain assemblies in the display. This deterioration process will be accelerated by frequent rough handling in shipment or by frequently turning the display on and off. Some of these effects can be corrected through the user controls. The changes may occur so slowly that you're unlikely to notice them if you frequently adjust the controls.

Screen brightness is also likely to decrease with time, so purchase a screen with a brightness higher than what you really need. In CRT displays, the screen brightness will decrease slowly with time due to a reduction in the efficiency of the cathode (the "C" in CRT) and the light-emitting efficiency of the screen phosphors. In portable computers with LCD displays, another source of aging is the fluorescent tubes that backlight most displays, which also deteriorate slowly with time.

Display Guide

16.6 Tom's Pick

When it comes to monitors, bigger is almost always better. A wide screen can open access to data that would otherwise lie hidden along the edges, forcing you to break your concentration to scroll around documents and Web pages. Games, too, gain a level of impact on larger monitors. Not only can a large screen bring the action closer to you, more advanced games like Quake 2 can actually scale their graphics up to take advantage of the 1280×1024 resolutions possible on 19- and 21-inch screens.

If I could have only one monitor, then, it would be an oversized 21-inch display. Once the exclusive domain of graphics designers and engineering software wizards, 21-inch monitors are threatening to enter the mainstream. And that means that a good 21-inch model is perfect for my system., which is why the **Iiyama VisionMaster Pro 500 MT-9221** graces my desktop.

The VisionMaster Pro 500 does it all. The Trinitron-like Diamondtron tube measures 20 inches in viewable diagonal area, and delivers the saturated colors, sharp contrast, and top brightness that you expect from a high-quality aperture grill tube. Advanced electronics allow for high refresh rates even at 1600×1200 resolution, so you can really crank this monitor up to its potential. Just make sure your graphics board is up to the task!

Graphics artists will appreciate the BNC component connector for delivering optimal graphics at high resolutions and refresh rates, while a standard 15-pin VGA connector preserves convenience. A compact design limits depth to just over 19 inches, helping alleviate at least some of the hassle of such a big screen.

Chapter

17

Sound Card Guide

PC-based audio has come a long way since those first tinny beeps and pops emitted from the cheap speaker of the first IBM PC. Intended initially as a prompt for troubleshooting boot up routines, sound on the PC has long been something of an afterthought. Even after the Macintosh proved the phenomenal entertainment value and utility of digital audio, most PCs didn't ship with built-in sound until 1994 or 1995. For those brave—or stupid—enough to try to add audio to the media mix, the result was often a harrowing string of hardware conflicts and incompatible software.

Times have certainly changed. Today, virtually all PCs ship with some form of audio—either on a separate add-in card or in a chipset soldered to the motherboard. What's more, the quality of that audio has made big strides over the last three or four years. Virtually all new audio subsystems can handle digital audio files that match the fidelity of audio CDs—although you'll find that the actual fidelity of the sound lags far below that produced by consumer audio components. Also included is support for Midi synthesis, a digital music format that plays back music scores based on instructions in a compact file.

Today, PC audio is well on its way toward an important shift that will leave the bad old days of DOS behind. Creative Labs' Sound Blaster standard, long the *de facto* standard in the market, has been usurped in the Windows market by Microsoft's DirectX APIs. The result: Boards are offering a varying level of DirectX and Sound Blaster compliance, as well as causing a lot of buyer confusion in the process.

This chapter will help you make the right decisions when buying digital audio for your high-performance PC. Although audio quality and features are generally the focus, the right audio card can actually enhance PC performance in games and titles that use processor-intensive audio effects. From 3D positional audio to high-fidelity AC-3 Dolby surround sound, audio can have a real impact on your PCs performance.

17.1 Inside Digital Audio

Several varieties of PC-based audio formats and technologies exist that you need to be aware of when buying a soundcard. Here are a few of the major ones:

- Digital audio

- Midi audio

- 3D positional audio

- AC-3 audio

Until recently, the only two technologies that concerned users were digital audio and Midi, but that's changing fast with advances in game software development tools and the introduction of theater-quality Mpeg-2 Video to the PC. Digital audio, also called *wave* or *waveform audio*, is the digital version of sound recordings, whereas Midi is a scheme that lets your PC play back instrument notes based on commands in a Midi file. Both audio types are found on virtually all new PCs, although they serve very different uses.

Positional 3D and AC-3 audio represent a growing class of technologies targeted at entertainment software and titles. The technologies, which often require new hardware to run smoothly, deliver enhanced realism and impact to multimedia titles, digital movies, and other rich content.

17.1.1 Digital Audio Explained

Before you can understand how soundcards work, you have to understand the workings of digital waveform audio. Analog sound is produced by the motion of sound waves through a medium—usually air. The tighter together these waves are, the higher the perceived pitch of the sound; the looser those waves, the lower the pitch of the sound. The perceived volume is created by the relative amplitude of the sound waves—that is, how far up and down the wave extends in its curve.

Digital audio on the PC works with the representation of this waveform to produce sound. To do this, audio files create a digital reproduction of the sound wave by taking snapshots of the wave as it goes by. The more snapshots that are mapped in the digital file, the more closely the PC can re-create the exact amplitude and frequency of the original analog sound. This process is called *sampling*.

Figure 17.1.
*This representa-
tion of analog
audio shows the
waveform that all
sound produces.*

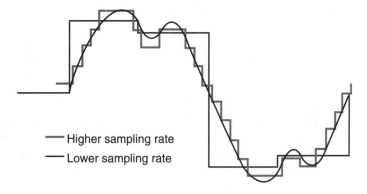

Higher sampling rate

Lower sampling rate

To re-create the unique character of the sampled sound, the PC must store the character of the analog sound in each snapshot it takes (see Figure 17.1). In most cases, audio files will dedicate 8 bits or 16 bits of data to each individual point. Because this type of digital audio re-creates the waveform of analog audio, the digital audio files under Windows are called *wave files* and have the extension .WAV.

The accuracy of wave audio is expressed in terms of the number of samples recorded each second, as well as in the number of bits dedicated to each sample. The more samples that are recorded, the more closely the digital version of the waveform will conform to the analog source. Fewer samples means that portions of the curve are lost, resulting in poor reproduction. Likewise, the amount of data stored in each sample is a critical factor in realistic audio playback.

The benchmark of digital audio precision is the audio CD format. CD-quality sound is sampled 44,100 times per second (or 44.1KHz) at a resolution of 16 bits per sample. At this level of fidelity, the bits pile up fast. One second of CD-quality audio consumes 88,200 bytes, which adds up to about 5MB for one minute of audio. Capture the same clip in stereo format and the numbers double with over 10MB of data required to store one minute of sound.

Because of the huge file sizes, audio clips are often sampled at lower bit depths and sample rates. Table 17.1 shows the relative file sizes for one minute of uncompressed digital audio.

Table 17.1. Uncompressed audio files sizes.

Sample rate	Bit depth	Mono	Stereo
11.025KHz	8 bits	0.6MB	1.3MB
11.025KHz	16 bits	1.3MB	2.5MB
22.05KHz	8 bits	1.3MB	2.5MB
22.05KHz	16 bits	2.5MB	5MB
44.1KHz	8 bits	2.5MB	5MB
44.1KHz	16 bits	5MB	10.1MB

To reduce file sizes, the audio in many games and other multimedia titles is often down-sampled to lower resolutions and sample rates in postproduction. For example, many titles use 22.1KHz, 16-bit audio. In addition, the audio files are compressed using software that can cut file sizes down by a factor of 10 or more. The most common compression scheme is the PCM (pulse code modulation), which comes standard as part of Windows 95.

17.1.2 Understanding Midi

Midi stands for *Musical Instrument Digital Interface* and is a communications standard crafted by the music industry to enable synthesizers and other electronic musical devices to share a common platform. Technically, Midi doesn't need to be used for music at all—its commands can be used to drive pyrotechnics, for example—but the standard is now a critical part of soundboard operation. Midi files contain commands that describe the instrument and notes to be played, as well as how long each note should be attacked, released, and sustained. These commands can then be arranged to form entire musical scores played back by sophisticated arrangements of musical instruments.

Although Midi cannot be used to record voices or sounds, it is very useful for playing and composing musical scores. In fact, Midi-editing software makes it easy to create digital compositions—some software even lets you scan in musical notations and turn them into digital Midi format for immediate playback. More important, even long Midi scores result in files that are only a few kilobytes in size—about 100 times more compact than wave files of similar size.

In order for soundcards to reliably read and output Midi scores, all software and hardware needs to have a common understanding of the Midi instructions. At the core of this compatibility is the General Midi specification, which defines 128 individual instruments. This standard ensures that different instruments—be they soundcards or synthesizers—produce the same output when reading the same file. Therefore, if the Midi score calls for a clarinet to play a C note, both devices will faithfully and reliably respond by playing a clarinet, rather than, say, a trumpet.

Complicating matters is the fact that there are three types of Midi sound synthesis used on soundcards. The different approaches to Midi reproduction provide very different levels of realism. If you want to create and play back original Midi scores, you'll want a board that uses wavetable technology. Gamers, likewise, will want this technology on hand, if only to avoid an aural assault of synth-sounding music that can really drag down the impact of game play. Here are the three Midi synthesizer technologies:

- FM synthesis
- Wavetable synthesis
- Waveguide

FM Synthesis

FM Midi synthesizers were common on early soundcards but provided limited realism during Midi playback. FM synthesizers work by using frequency modulation (thus the moniker *FM*) to alter the frequency of one or more sine waves by other sine waves. Originally developed at Stanford University and later sold to Yamaha, FM synthesis technology provided an inexpensive way to play back Midi scores on soundcards, in large part because no additional memory is needed to store instrument sounds.

Unfortunately, the low-cost implementations found on soundcards produced less-than-terrific results. For one thing, FM synthesis struggles with certain instrument types, including brass and saxophones. For another, the limited synthesis hardware cannot produce realistic scores using a large number of instruments. The overall result is unsatisfying Midi playback.

The advantage of FM synthesis is that it's the least expensive to implement. No additional memory is needed to store or produce instrument sounds, and the approach requires fewer hardware components than other synthesis technologies. Until 1995, when memory prices dropped significantly, FM synthesis was the most common Midi type.

Wavetable Synthesis

The more common Midi technology today is wavetable synthesis, which produces superior sound compared to FM synthesis. Wavetable Midi uses actual recorded samples of instrument sounds to create realistic instrument sounds, particularly for instruments such as saxophones, which FM synthesis cannot accurately render. When the Midi file calls for a clarinet to play an A note, an actual recording of a clarinet is used in the playback. Because the sounds of real instruments are being used, the Midi output generally sounds more authentic than FM synthesis.

In order to bring real instrument sounds to Midi playback, samples must be stored in memory. Until very recently, that meant putting read-only memory (ROM) onto the board, an expensive proposition until just two or three years ago. Most cards use anywhere from 512KB to 4MB of ROM, with more memory allowing for more detailed samples, which result in better playback. Today, some cards use RAM instead of ROM to store sounds or supplement onboard ROM. The advantage? Programs can swap out custom sample sets of instrument sounds to provide custom playback.

Of course, there isn't space for every note of every instrument, so algorithms are used to bend the limited sample set into the desired notes. Therefore, if a C note is stored but an A note is called for, the soundcard produces the desired note by processing the stored C note. Here, the quality of the algorithms—along with the compression used to squeeze samples into limited space—is critical. In other words, although a larger instrument sample set is almost always better, two cards with the same 2MB of ROM might produce Midi instrument sounds of varying quality and accuracy.

Physical Modeling Synthesis

A less common Midi implementation is *physical modeling synthesis*, also best known as *Waveguide Midi*. This technology produces instrument sounds by creating a physical model of the instrument being called for. The technology can provide even greater realism than wavetable Midi, because the variable performance of instruments at different points of play can be reflected.

The processing needed to actually model instruments in realtime is simply too much for current PCs to manage. For this reason, physical modeling is not a common feature on soundcards, although vendors such as Creative Labs provide waveguide capability. Developers can actually program in the distinct characteristics of instruments of different makes, ages, and materials. In the future, we may see this technology become more prevalent.

17.1.3 Understanding 3D Sound

The most dynamic area in the audio market today is with 3D sound, which produces the illusion of surround sound from two or more speakers. This capability is particularly compelling for games because the 3D audio creates an immersive quality to the game play.

There are actually two general classes of 3D audio:

- Positional

- Spatial enhancement

These classes are not the same, so you should make a point of knowing how they differ to avoid buying a soundcard lacking critical features. When buying a soundcard, look for 3D-positional audio support. This technology is used in newer Windows 95–based games and titles to create the illusion of three-dimensional sound on a system with two or more speakers.

Behind 3D positional audio are key Windows standards for developers. The A3D standard from Aureal Semiconductor is currently used by most games and soundboards. A3D consists of a set of algorithms that are used to process digital audio into a form that produces the illusion of immersive sound. Developers work with the A3D application programming interface (API) to include code in their games tailored for A3D. The code tells the software exactly where sounds should be coming from in the 3D space. An A3D-compliant soundboard then processes the audio in realtime so that the sound appears to be coming from around, in front of, or behind the user, as determined by the program.

A3D uses an intriguing scheme called *head-related transfer algorithms*, which produce the illusion of immersive sound by taking into account the size and shape of the user's head, as well as the position and shape of the ears. The room environment is also taken into account—the algorithm factors in rebounding sounds coming from the walls and objects in the room. Unfortunately, the algorithms must make assumptions about your environment, which means that audio will sound less than 3D if you're sitting outside of the so-called *sweet spot* or if you have your speakers misaligned. Also telling, A3D only supports two speakers, limiting performance for those wanting a more immersive experience.

Be aware that 3D audio exacts a price in performance. Less feature-rich soundboards lay more of the processing at the doorstep of your CPU, which can degrade performance. A3D, on the other hand, requires hardware on the soundboard to work—look for soundboards that carry an A3D logo to ensure that this capability is available to you. If A3D hardware is not present, software may switch to DirectSound 3D, which can try to emulate 3D effects using the host CPU; otherwise, you may lose this function altogether. If you want effective 3D gameplay, look for cards that allow hardware acceleration of 3D audio.

It should come as no surprise that Microsoft has jumped into the 3D audio standards market. DirectSound 3D adds 3D positional audio to the already-established DirectSound specification. Although the Microsoft API initially lagged behind A3D in terms of market support, the technology will likely move past A3D because of its open architecture. The proprietary A3D API will be hard pressed to fend off the challenge posed by Microsoft's DirectX 6.0 version.

Understanding Stereo-enhancing Sound

Another spin on audio is *spatial enhancement*. This technology, which vendors sometimes erroneously describe as "3D," adds depth and breadth to stereo sound by extracting out information present in the original master recording. Going by brand names such as SRS and Spatializer, the technologies are specifically tailored for recorded content—as opposed to Midi files or digital sound effects—and can try to add the perception of fullness to the audio.

Be aware that spatial enhancement can be a dodgy business. Broadening the original signal by definition introduces distortion to the sound. SRS and Spatializer typically boost midrange frequencies, for example, which can make music sound shrill. What's more, many devices try to add impact by punching up the bass and volume of the sound, which can be an inconvenience. These technologies tend to be of limited use for games, although music playback can benefit.

17.2 The New Audio Market

With Microsoft's DirectX APIs establishing an industry standard for PC-based audio, the importance of Creative Labs' Sound Blaster standard has been on the wane. Although Sound Blaster compatibility is still important for aging DOS games that support only a limited number of specific soundcards, the situation with Windows is very different. Microsoft's DirectSound API provides a common standard for both applications and audio hardware; therefore, developers do not have to write their code specifically for a certain soundboard (see Figure 17.2).

Figure 17.2.

This schematic shows how the various DirectX audio components interface with the Windows operating system, providing a common standard for devices and software.

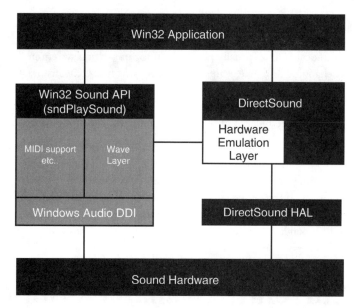

In addition to establishing a universal audio standard, DirectSound enhances the performance of audio playback. The API allows hardware to accelerate audio effects such as reverb, echo, and chorus, as well as to provide deep buffers to ensure timely playback of wave and Midi files.

More important, DirectSound has opened the market to PCI-based soundboards. Sound Blaster compatibility doesn't allow for PCI audio because the standard demands that system resources such as DMA and IRQ settings be static. However, PCI's Plug and Play capability allows for dynamic allocation of these resources, thus violating the specification.

PCI audio has a lot going for it. For one thing, the bus can provide 132MBps of bandwidth, many times that available on the slow ISA bus. The ample bandwidth enables the use of multiple channels of audio, useful for 3D positional audio and rich playback of multiple, simultaneous sounds. Under ISA, no more than two separate channels can be reliably sent over the bus. Newer games and titles, however, rely on the ability to juggle multiple, independent audio channels in order to allow for dynamic playback of music, sound effects, and other audio in response to user input and programmatic updates. Be aware that multichannel audio is distinct from multitrack recording.

17.3 Performance Impact Report

Soundcards don't usually get credited for improving system performance, but that is changing as new features are incorporated into PC software. Positional 3D places a real processing strain on the system, which better soundboards can help relieve. More efficient architectures, PCI bus mastering, and deep memory buffers all serve to reduce CPU overhead and enhance system performance.

PCI audio has a big role to play in enhanced performance. The PCI bus can provide more channels of audio and deliver them more reliably than ISA. Bus mastering on the PCI bus means that audio data continues to be sent even when the CPU is busy, thus reducing delays or cutouts that can occur when the system gets overloaded. At the same time, more efficient PCI bus transfers mean that the CPU spends less time tied up with audio business, thus opening performance in other areas.

17.4 Currently Available Soundcards

The soundcard market is in an era of unprecedented change. Since the introduction of the first scratchy, 8-bit Sound Blaster board, users have become used to rapid-fire advances. Wavetable Midi, growing feature sets, and bundled software have all improved the audio landscape. However, not only are cards currently moving from ISA to PCI, but they are incorporating new features such as 3D positional audio and multichannel capability. The result is a confusing marketplace.

17.4.1 ISA Soundcards

ISA-based soundcards are a fading breed, but they're still the most popular type on the market. Creative Labs' Sound Blaster AWE64 line, for example, is based on the ISA bus (see Figure 17.3). Although these cards generally provide Sound Blaster compatibility of some form, many are also able to work with Microsoft's DirectSound and DirectSound3D APIs. The board vendor simply has to provide DirectSound drivers for the hardware that allows software to access its features. The presence of a fast DSP to accelerate DirectSound operations can help enhance operation. However, ISA soundboards are limited by their slower bus and are unable to support full multichannel audio. When DirectSound calls for multiple channels of audio to be used, the API will have to multiplex (or *mux*) the individual signals into one or two (for stereo) signals. The result is added overhead and lost quality.

Figure 17.3.

The powerful and versatile Creative Labs Sound Blaster AWE64 Gold is among the most popular ISA-based soundcards.

Virtually all ISA soundboards provide CD-quality wave audio (44.1KHz, 16-bit) recording and playback. However, Midi playback may vary depending on the board. Most newer ISA boards include a hardware wavetable Midi synthesizer, and you should consider no less if you want reasonable Midi playback.

If you're considering a new soundboard, an ISA model is probably not your best bet. Support for ISA soundcards in upcoming games and titles will wane, as more and more game makers look to multichannel audio to add realism to their products. ISA soundboards also cannot provide the level of system performance that PCI models can. Any device on the ISA bus will consume a greater portion of system resources than an identical PCI device, due in part to ISA's lack of direct memory access (DMA) capability as well as the longer time that ISA transactions take to happen.

Of course, if you're playing a lot of older games or DOS-based flight simulators (among the last games to move to the new Windows 9*x* regime), an ISA card is definitely for you. PCI soundboards cannot ensure Sound Blaster compatibility because PCI's Plug and Play can dynamically change key settings such as DMA, IRQ, and address port addresses.

17.4.2 PCI Soundcards

PCI soundcards are taking the market by storm (see Figure 17.4). These boards fall into three broad segments:

- Cheap models ($49 or lower) that rely on the host CPU to handle wavetable Midi synthesis and all audio transformations.

- Midrange boards ($99) that provide wavetable synthesis hardware but typically store instrument sounds in system RAM. Acceleration for A3D, DirectSound, and DirecSound 3D is typically absent or limited.

- High-end boards ($200) that provide hardware acceleration for APIs such as A3D, DirectSound, and DirectSound 3D, as well as dedicated wavetable Midi memory.

Figure 17.4.
Diamond's Monster Sound line is among the most successful of the new, low-cost PCI soundcards.

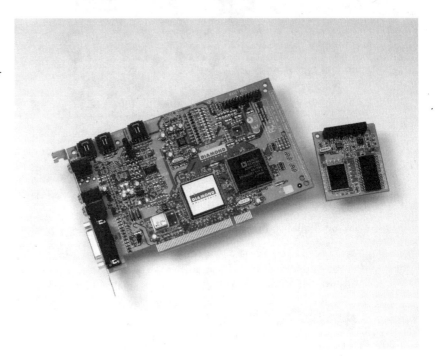

New audio chipsets from Crystal Semiconductor and others are boosting acceleration features. They're also adding the capability to handle more channels of audio (as many as 64 in some cases), which should allow you to take advantage of the most aggressively designed games and titles. These titles will employ distinct channels to provide compelling 3D positional sound, realistic and interactive music and special effects, and better system performance. Higher-end boards also put the wavetable Midi memory and processing back on the soundboard, relieving the CPU of those duties.

Some card vendors are talking about adding support for Dolby Digital, or AC-3 audio, to their soundcards. Designed to play back digital surround sound audio from DVD titles, the Dolby technology provides surround sound output on a true home theater setup with five satellite speakers and a subwoofer. AC-3 allows producers to place specific audio events in discrete channels so that sounds come from specific speakers in order to immerse the listener in sound.

AC-3 audio is output via a S/PIDF jack that splits into the six-component cable needed to handle the various speakers. You may not see many soundcards with AC-3, however, because Dolby Labs charges a licensing fee for its technology and demands that vendors pass rigorous testing in their qualification labs. However, most DVD-ROM kits include a media decoder board that does include the AC-3 decoding capability and S/PIDF jack.

What many soundcards can do is provide down-sampling of the AC-3 signal, so that the AC-3 audio signal may be output to a two- or four-speaker setup. A decoder interpolates the original signal, using 3D positional technology to help bend the sound so that some semblance of the original, immersive content is preserved. Of course, a 5.1 home theatre produces results vastly superior to a two-speaker desktop setup.

Playing back AC-3 audio is a demanding task. Although MMX-enhanced CPUs can do it, your MPEG-2 videos will drop frames, and your games will likewise suffer. If you want AC-3 audio playback, look for a soundcard that includes an AC-3 decoder on board.

> **NOTE** If you have a DVD-ROM upgrade kit in your PC, there's a good chance that an AC-3 decoder is provided on a media board in the PC. Check this first before spending extra money on a soundcard!

17.5 Evaluating Soundcards

With all the changes in the audio market, there are a lot of things to look for in a soundcard. As always, you should buy for your needs. Business users who want to be able to hear the Windows warning sounds really don't have to spend $200 on a card that can decode surround sound audio. Likewise, hardcore gamers and digital movie fans will be sorely disappointed with a $99 PCI board that supports a limited number of audio channels and lacks acceleration features.

17.5.1 Audio Fidelity

Beyond the bits and bites, audio fidelity is a huge concern. Although the 1s and 0s of digital audio are immune to distortion and noise from electromagnetic frequencies (EMF) produced inside the PC case, analog audio is not. In fact, soundcards always produce fidelity that is much lower than that of even inexpensive consumer audio gear because of electrical interference from the PC. The one exception: High-end cards used by sound studios that output signals in digital format using S/PIDF ports.

When buying a soundboard, fidelity should be of concern because games and DVD-ROM movies are providing better and better sound quality. No longer is the quality bottleneck with the tinny and small digital audio files—it has moved to the noisy environment of the PC, which adds unwanted junk to the original sound signal.

Specifications

When talking about fidelity, you can refer to an entire laundry list of specs. Some of the most important ones are described in Table 17.2.

Table 17.2. Key audio specifications defined, as well as comparisons to typical consumer audio results.

Specification	Description
Frequency response	Expressed in decibels, the frequency response measures the deviation from optimal performance along the spectrum of human hearing (from 20Hz to 20KHz).
Signal-to-noise (S/N)	Expressed in decibels, S/N defines the ratio between the audio signal voltage and the noise voltage. A device with a high signal-to-noise ratio means that the signal is clean and has relatively little noise contamination.
Distortion	Expressed as a percentage, distortion measures changes between the original signal and the output. A lower number is better.
Crosstalk	Expressed in decibels, crosstalk measures the leakage of signals from one channel into another. Too much crosstalk will wipe out the impact of a stereo signal. Here, a lower number is better.

In virtually all cases, no soundcard can match or even approach the aural quality of inexpensive consumer audio gear. Again, the PC itself is largely to blame. The CPU, hard disk, CD-ROM drive, RAM, and other components all throw EMF pollution into the shielded interior of the PC case. When digital audio data is changed to audio signals on the soundboard, EMF creeps into the signal, thus destroying its purity.

In addition, soundboard components are often selected for their low cost, not for their fidelity. It doesn't help that soundboard vendors often inflate their specs, or at least base them on best-case scenarios taken from the rosy numbers provided by component suppliers. In general, you should not expect any soundboard to produce audio quality matching that of a decent CD player. Always take comparative claims of audio fidelity with a grain of salt.

Amplification

Many soundboards come equipped with a built-in amplifier, which allows the card to drive sound to unpowered desktop speakers. These amplifiers are quite small, producing no more than 2 or 3 watts, and are often very poor in quality. As a result, the sound produced by the amplified speaker out port is almost always much worse than the sound produced by the unpowered line out.

The reason for the audio degradation is two-fold. One, power is added to the analog signal inside the electrically noisy PC case. This addition of power to the signal amplifies both the original signal and the noise inside it. Second, and more important, soundcard amplifiers are so cheap that they fail to preserve the integrity of the original signal. Because they lack much power, they must often be pushed to produce even moderate sound, further adding distortion.

Where possible, avoid using the speaker out port on your soundcard. Powered desktop speakers include their own higher-quality amplifiers that should be used for producing voluminous sound. In the worst case, users may inadvertently connect their speaker out to an amplified speaker, thus compounding the problem of added distortion because the two amplifiers overdrive the signal. Some soundcards allow you to disable the amplifier to avoid this mistake.

17.5.2 Wave Audio Features

As mentioned earlier, virtually all soundcards—no matter how cheap—can play and record CD-quality audio. With samples rates of 44.1 or even 48KHz, and depths of 16 bits per sample, the audio files contain more information than your ear can discern. However, if you intend to record your own audio, look for a board with 48KHz sampling because this matches the rate of digital audio tape (DAT). If you're only playing back audio, a 44.1KHz board should suit your needs.

Another issue that often gets hidden is the quality of the digital-to-analog and analog-to-digital converters used to move bits in and out of the soundboard. The chips used in these critical functions can determine whether or not the original digital audio file will be reproduced at its intended level of fidelity. Some soundcards provide 16 bits of resolution in their D-to-A and A-to-D operations, whereas others go as high as 18 and even 20 bits. The additional resolution preserves the original source, but it adds cost to the card. For most users, 16-bit resolution is sufficient, but professionals should look for boards with 18- or 20-bit resolution.

With that said, events are afoot that may change all this. The music industry is busy trying to craft a DVD Audio standard that would increase the amount of data used to store sound as defined in the current CD Audio specification. Once

DVD Audio gets its start and music DVDs begin to sell in stores, you can expect that PCs will need to be able to match the enhanced digital format. If you're buying a soundcard in 1999, you should at least keep an eye on this imminent Audio standard.

One feature you should look for is support for full-duplex operation. This feature is critical if you intend to use your soundcard as part of a video conferencing or digital speaker phone arrangement because it allows the card to both receive and output audio simultaneously. Less expensive cards save you money by only allowing audio to move in one direction at a time, which results in cutouts in the audio on the other side. Full-duplex operation also makes it possible to play a music score while recording your voice, for example. This feature is critical for musicians who use the PC to play back certain tracks while recording others.

17.5.3 Midi Support

On the Midi side of the fence, you already know to look for wavetable Midi. In most cases, software-based Midi schemes—which use the CPU and system memory to store and process wavetable Midi scores—are adequate and can save you $50 or so on the price of the soundcard. However, this approach will suck CPU cycles and can lead to skips and delays in playback on an overmatched PC. Also, because software Midi requires the Windows API interface to be present, your DOS-only games will not be able to play Midi using these cards.

My recommendation is to spend the dollars on a hardware-based wavetable Midi card. The extra bucks relieve the system CPU of the processing burden imposed by Midi playback. If your 3D games use Midi files for theme music—and most do—you'll get higher frame rates and better responsiveness if you use hardware Midi.

Soundcards are limited in the number of Midi notes they can play at one time. Most cannot, for example, faithfully reproduce the sound of a 50-person orchestra because only 20 or so Midi notes can be played simultaneously. This capability is expressed in a card's polyphony and multitimbrality, both critical specifications to look for.

In fact, polyphony has entered the marketing game. The Sound Blaster AWE32 gets its name because it can produce 32-voice polyphony, playing 32 separate instrument notes at a time. (Note that its predecessor, the Sound Blaster Pro 16, got its name from the fact that it produces 16-bit wave audio. When it comes to the market, bigger numbers are *always* better.) The Sound Blaster AWE64 is named because it doubles this figure, playing up to 64 simultaneous Midi voices. However, only the first 32 are played in the hardware. To achieve 64-voice polyphony, your CPU must process the last 32 simultaneous instrument notes.

A related specification is *multitimbrality*. This number defines how many different instruments can be sounded at the same time. Multitimbrality is critical for playing back orchestral scores that call for numerous types of instruments to be playing at the same time.

Some cards also allow you to customize Midi instruments. The Sound Blaster AWE64, for example, includes onboard RAM that can be loaded with custom instruments for playback. Creative Labs' SoundFonts technology provides a standard way for creating, editing, and using custom Midi voices. This can be useful for producing low-bandwidth special effects, music scores with unique instruments, and other applications.

Taking custom Midi sounds a step further is the concept of downloadable samples (or DLS). This technology is included in Microsoft's new DirectMusic API that is part of DirectX 6.0. DLS allows wavetable Midi sample sounds to be downloaded into system memory in realtime, thus allowing games and music scores to adapt to changing conditions based on user input or programmatic control.

17.5.4 Multichannel Audio Operation

New to the soundcard spec game is the emergence of *multichannel audio*. You haven't run across this in the past for the simple reason that ISA-based soundcards lack the bandwidth to manage numerous distinct channels of audio at once. New PCI cards, however, have bandwidth to spare. Developers can use this bandwidth to toss around multiple channels of distinct sounds in order to enhance the impact and realism of their games and titles.

Right now, software that takes advantage of multichannel audio is fairly rare, but that should change over the next couple years. Microsoft's new DirectX APIs are piling on the audio features and making them easier to employ in software. The emergence of 3D positional audio as a key feature in gameplay should be a big factor in making multichannel support important.

So how many channels is enough? Many cards today support only a limited number of channels—as few as six—but new audio chipsets are pushing those numbers higher. As a rule, you should look for support for about 20 or 24 channels of audio. This will ensure that your card has enough headroom to handle forthcoming software.

17.5.5 3D Audio Handling

As mentioned earlier, 3D audio is a red-hot area of the audio market. If you buy a new soundboard, you should seriously consider making sure that 3D positional audio support is part of the feature set. Here are the two major 3D audio APIs:

- A3D

- DirectSound 3D

Right now, A3D is the must-have 3D audio feature. Cards that support this technology should bear an A3D logo on the box—Aureal, the company that provides the technology, only allows proven compliant products to display this artwork. A3D enables fully interactive, programmable 3D positional audio. Therefore, when a helicopter flies over you, you will hear the sound travel over your head and behind your back, even on two speakers.

The other major 3D positional audio technology is Microsoft's DirectSound 3D. Although DirectSound 3D works a lot like A3D, developers have complained that it's more difficult to work with (and later to market) than Aureal's technology. With that said, DirectSound 3D does support four speakers, versus A3D's two. What's more, Microsoft has made DirectSound 3D part and parcel of its DirectX package, and most soundboards are compliant with the DirectSound 3D technology. Given Microsoft's tenacity in the standards-setting business, I would be surprised if DirectSound 3D doesn't become a critical element of feature support in the near future.

Another positional technology exists in the form of *Q Sound* from QSound Labs. Like A3D and DirectSound 3D, Q Sound creates the illusion of surround sound from a two-speaker set by processing the audio output. Software makers can programmatically tell Q Sound where individual sounds should come from, thus allowing the application of the Doppler effect as sounds move toward and away from the user.

Q Sound suffers from the problem of being first to market. When it arrived, the computation involved in Q Sound's positional audio made it too challenging for realtime 3D audio and gameplay. Now that the market has moved toward these technologies under Windows 95, A3D and DirectSound 3D have become the leading technology contenders. Although many cards provide Q Sound software for putting 3D audio into presentations, for example, few games make use of the technology. Still, some cards, such as VideoLogic's AudioStorm, actually emulate A3D compliance by using Q Sound to emulate A3D.

17.5.6 Ports

Look on the mounting bracket of any soundcard and you'll see a bunch of ports and plugs. Here's where the business of getting stuff into and out of your PC happens. Most soundcards have the following ports:

- Line in

- Microphone in

- Line out

- Speaker out

- CD audio port

- Midi/game port

- S/PIDF port

Audio Ports

The line-in port is the workhorse connection for your recording operations. If you want to record audio from tape recorders, radios, CD players, and other devices, you plug them into the line-in port. Not all line-in ports are created equal—in fact, most lack enough electrical headroom to comfortably record output from consumer electronics products.

The microphone-in port is likewise used to record sounds to the board, but it's tailored for use with microphones. Used mainly for recording speech, the microphone port includes an amplifier that boosts the lower-powered signal that comes from microphones. Unfortunately, tests of soundboards have shown that the quality of microphone-in connections is often quite poor.

The line-out port is used to send analog audio signals to a speaker or other audio device. The line-out port is unpowered, which means that any amplification of the signal must be done at the receiving component, such as a speaker. As a rule, the line- out port is your best option for getting clean, analog audio out of your soundcard.

The other standard out-bound port is the speaker-out plug. Not found on all soundboards, the speaker-out port outputs a signal that has passed through an amplifier in order to boost sound on its way out of the card. The added step of amplifying the sound inside the PC case invariably adds noise and distortion to the audio, so you should avoid using this port if at all possible. The main use of the speaker-out port is to drive cheap, unpowered desktop speakers.

Finally, the CD audio port connects your CD-ROM drive to your soundcard. Often located along the top edge the soundcard inside the PC case, this wire accepts analog audio played directly from your CD-ROM drive, most often from audio CDs. The direct connection avoids jamming the system bus with digital audio traffic between the CD-ROM drive and the soundboard.

Gaming Port

The Midi/game port is the rectangular plug with several pin holes in it. Originally created to allow game devices such as joysticks to connect to the PC, the

15-pin plug can accept Midi input by using a simple adapter to match the DIN-style connector used by Midi devices. Support for joysticks over the Midi/game port is pretty universal, although older cards may not be able to support the digital operation of joysticks such as Microsoft's Sidewinder 3D Pro.

Joysticks are serious business in the world of gaming performance. An analog joystick—as all have been until just two years ago—requires constant attention from the system CPU. Because there's no intelligence built into the joystick or the game port, the CPU must constantly check in on the analog signals coming from the game port. Even if no activity is occurring, the CPU must stop and check to make sure. During this time, nothing else can happen, thus robbing your PC of valuable CPU cycles.

In a field where every frame packs thousands of texture-mapped polygons, losing 15 percent of the CPU is unacceptable. Digital joysticks eliminate the "cycle sucking" by putting a microprocessor in the joystick itself. This chip reads the position of the stick, throttle, and other controls and sends a digital update to the system whenever a change occurs. Gone are the long processor wait states. These are now replaced by a simple interrupt routine. Unfortunately, not all existing soundcards' game ports are equipped to handle digital joysticks. If you want to buy such a model, you should check on your card's compatibility; otherwise, the stick will drop into analog mode and hog CPU cycles like any analog joystick.

Digital Audio Port

A less common, but growing feature on soundcards is the presence of an S/PDIF (Sony/Philips Digital Interface) port. S/PDIF's main appeal is that it provides digital input and output of audio to and from the soundcard. This feature is required for sending AC-3 audio to a home theater speaker system, for example, but it's still more widely used among recording artists to output audio to digital audio tape (DAT) or to a high-quality digital-to-analog converter.

S/PDIF ports are common on DVD media cards, which contain the decoder hardware for MPEG-2 Video and AC-3 audio. However, with DVD-ROM drives poised to become standard equipment on PCs, the presence of an extra, DVD-dedicated card doesn't make much sense. Therefore, the AC-3 handling is bound for the soundcard, whereas the MPEG-2 decoding is pushed to the graphics card or the system CPU. A soundcard outfitted with a S/PDIF port is able to support AC-3 five-channel audio.

17.6 Speakers

No discussion of soundcards would be complete without talking about speakers. PC speakers are distinct from their consumer audio cousins in two ways. First, they usually incorporate an amplifier to boost the signal for comfortable hearing, whereas stereo speakers rely on an external amplifier. Second, PC speakers are shielded to prevent leakage of magnetic radiation from the housing. These factors inflate the price of PC speakers somewhat.

In addition to being self-powered, most PC speakers are also classified as being near-field monitors. This means that the sound field is very close to the source of the sound. Therefore, unlike typical hi-fi speakers, which are designed to fill a room or other large space, the speakers on your desktop are optimized to produce sound within a couple feet of the speaker itself.

17.6.1 Types of Speakers

When buying speakers, you should definitely look for powered speakers that provide their own amplifier. This will let you avoid using the poor, weak, and noisy amplifier on the soundcard and will provide more power than the card-based amplifier could ever provide. In general, PC speakers should deliver anywhere from 5 to 30 watts of power, depending on your needs. However, trying to choose a self-powered speaker based on wattage is a wasted exercise. Low-wattage amps, such as those found on some Cambridge SoundWorks speakers, can sound much better than the overpowered and overdriven amps built into other speakers.

You'll also want to ask yourself if you need a subwoofer with your speaker set. This separate component drives low-end audio signals to augment bass response. Game players will get a kick out of feeling explosions and engine sounds, whereas both music and video watching gain impact from the bass response (see Figure 17.5). Most subwoofers sit on the floor because the low bass sounds they produce are nondirectional—in other words, the listener cannot pinpoint the source of the sound.

Subwoofers add to the cost of a speaker set, however, so you need to weigh your desire for audio impact with the price of the speaker set. You can buy separate subwoofers from vendors such as Bazooka and Labtech. This enables you to upgrade a speaker system when your budget allows.

You might also consider a new class of speakers that uses the Universal Serial Bus to receive digital audio signals and accept audio settings such as volume, bass, and treble. The advantage of USB speakers is that the digital audio stays digital until it's at the speaker itself, well outside the EMF-polluted PC case. As a result, USB speakers can potentially deliver much better audio quality than is possible from any affordable soundcard.

Another upside to this class of product is the ability to change speaker settings from software using Windows-based controls. That means no more reaching for tiny knobs and buttons. What's more, a much richer control set is available because adding software controls is generally less expensive than adding hardware parts and logic to the speakers themselves.

Figure 17.5.
This Cambridge SoundWorks MicroWorks speaker system includes a subwoofer for enhancing low-frequency output.

Unfortunately, there are several downsides to this intriguing technology. For one thing, some USB speakers only work with Windows 98. The only way to make them work otherwise is to plug them into the line-out port using plain-old analog connections; however, you'll lose all the USB benefits while still paying for the USB circuitry. What's more, virtually none will work with DOS or Windows 3.*x*. Finally, the USB audio scheme, itself, is bandwidth limited, making it a poor choice for demanding multichannel audio applications. If you're a business user looking for useful software controls over your sound, USB speakers may be worth considering. Otherwise, stick with standard speakers and a good soundcard.

17.6.2 Speaker Specs

Speakers share many of the same specifications with soundcards, including signal-to-noise, frequency response, and crosstalk. Also like soundcards, they share the dubious distinction of being marketed based on questionable specs. The problem is that there is no industry standard—as there is in the consumer audio world—for measuring and reporting audio fidelity. That leaves the marketing field wide open to interpretation and inflation.

The most abused speaker specification is wattage, which expresses the relative power of the speaker. When buying, you should look for wattage expressed as "RMS," which stands for *root mean square*. This is an accepted methodology for coming up with wattage output. You should also make sure that the wattage number is based on watts per channel and that the distortion rate for the specified output is at a level of about 0.5 percent.

The problem here is that speaker vendors often publish wattage based on peak power output (also called PPO) operation. Although the output wattage is high, the distortion produced at this level makes the resulting audio all but unusable. You should make a point to avoid—and even shun—any vendor that uses PPO wattage in its marketing.

Beyond wattage games, you can expect speaker specs to be consistently off the mark. Because of this, your best bet is to simply go with a reliable brand name. Fortunately, a number of well-known consumer audio speaker makers have entered the market, and these companies have a vested interest in keeping a consistent level of quality with their consumer products. You're probably best served going with these vendors.

Of course, the only way to pick speakers is to listen to them. Even the most trustworthy vendor can't print specs that accurately describe the aural impact its speakers will have on you.

17.7 Audio Tips

Want to get the best response from your audio? Here are a few tips to enhance performance and quality:

- If you're in the market for a card, go for a PCI model. The higher bandwidth bus allows support for more complex audio handling, including multichannel operation that is critical for upcoming games and titles.

- To enhance the output from your speakers, try turning down the volume a bit. Maxing the volume can strain the amplifier and introduce a lot of distortion into the signal. Also, make sure your powered speakers are not plugged into the speaker-out port because this output produces poorer audio than does the line-out jack.

- If you're playing games using 3D position audio, make sure to position your speakers evenly on either side of the monitor and to sit directly in the center, facing the screen. Positional 3D algorithms must assume that the user is front-and-center at the desk; moving away from that "sweet spot" will destroy the intended 3D effect.

- Protect your data by keeping any and all magnetic disks away from your desktop speakers. Even with shielding, magnetic fields emanate from the speaker housings—particularly from the front—which can wipe data clean from the media.

- To avoid feedback when recording, place your microphone well away from the speakers.

17.8 Tom's Pick

In a confusing market, picking a single product is tough, so here I'll pick two: an ISA-based board that provides ensured compatibility with existing DOS-based games and titles, and a PCI-based board that can handle everything DirectSound and DirectSound 3D are expected to throw at it.

For the top ISA board, go with the Creative Labs Sound Blaster AWE64 Gold. This board offers complete compatibility with your older software and titles, yet provides outstanding audio quality and the ability to play up to 64 Midi voices at one time. The board features gold-plated ports, which improve the electrical connection to speakers and other devices. It also comes with 4MB of Midi ROM for top wavetable Midi playback.

Creative Labs provides a pile of software with its products, including digital audio and Midi editing and creation software packages. You'll also get a voice command and control program as well as a desktop microphone. If you need rock-solid compatibility, the ability to play old DOS games, and advanced Midi features, the Sound Blaster AWE64 Gold is the way to go.

If you're more concerned about advanced musical applications and audio recording than you are about gameplay, you might consider Guillemot International's MaxiSound Home Studio Pro 64 soundcard. This ISA-based board provides a dizzying array of realtime audio effects, as well as the ability to record multitrack audio. Like AWE64 Gold, it provides gold-plated outputs, as well as a digital S/PDIF for connecting to DAT or a Dolby Digital speaker system.

On the PCI side, Diamond Multimedia's Monster Sound MX200 stands out. This PCI board provides full support for DirectSound, DirectSound 3D, and A3D, and it's able to support up to four speakers. The MX200 uses hardware-based wavetable Midi synthesis to cut down on CPU overhead, and it includes 4MB of instrument sounds in onboard ROM. The board can play up to 64 simultaneous Midi voices. MX200 provides gold-plated connectors to enhance signal connections to other devices. Finally, gamers get full versions of the games Incoming and Outlaws, both of which take advantage of 3D positional audio.

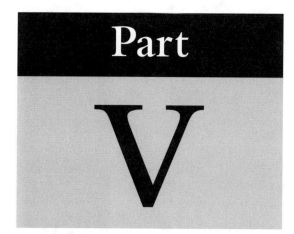

Getting
Connected

Chapter

18

Modem Guide

18.1 Understanding Modems and Adapters

If the wheel enabled modern transportation, then the modem may be considered the crucial innovation of the Internet age. From its humble beginnings as an expensive, balky, 300bps communications device, the PC modem has become a critical bridge that connects individual users with the Internet. Where just five years ago only a fraction of PCs actually shipped with installed modems, today virtually 100 percent of nonnetworked systems feature this communications hardware.

With everyone spending more and more time using the PC to communicate and access remote data and services, the implications for system performance are profound. Even the fastest Pentium II-400 system cannot make the public network go any faster at 7 o'clock on a Friday evening. Downloads that should take a few minutes can take half an hour, an hour, or perhaps never complete at all. Web pages crawl, phone and ISP bills mount, and everyone's temper starts to seethe.

Figure 18.1.

3Com's USR Courier V.Everything is fast, but even it can't unclog delays incurred by heavy Net traffic.

A faster modem or comm adapter can fix some of this. By placing wider and faster pipes connecting your PC to the Internet, you can enjoy noticeable gains in responsiveness. Not only can you save time and enjoy more reliable service, but you'll probably save money in the form of shorter connect times.

Although analog modems remain the most prevalent type of communications devices—particularly among standalone desktops—digital and digital-hybrid technologies are starting to take hold. ISDN, ADSL, satellite, and cable modems are all alternatives to the familiar analog modem. These products are very different from analog devices, but they serve the same application—connecting individual desktops to the larger network. For this reason, all these technologies are covered in this chapter.

18.1.1 How Communications Hardware Works

The word *modem* actually stands for *modulate-demodulate*, which describes the way these devices convert digital bits into sound and back into bits again. On the way out, the modem transforms data on the PC into the screeching sounds you hear on the phone line. At the other end, modems decode the analog audio into digital 1s and 0s. Although the term *modem* strictly addresses only those devices that interface with the analog network, the term has in fact become common for describing digital communications adapters used for ISDN, cable, and ADSL connectivity.

Analog Communication

No matter if the devices in question are digital or analog, they need to be speaking the same language in order to talk to each other. This is the reason why we see such tortured and deliberate standards formation from the International Telecommunications Union (ITU), the worldwide body that sets modem standards. Its v.34 specification standardized 33.6Kbps modem communications, whereas the more recent v.90 spec promises to finally do away with the confusing and incompatible x2 and K56Flex standards.

Analog modems communicate by using a standard set of audio frequencies and modulations to represent digital values to remote PCs. To do this, modems decode bits into waveform audio signals, using a scheme called *phase key modulation*, in which transitions in waveform timings designate a 1 or a 0 value. By managing and accelerating frequency transitions, modems are able to send up to 9600bps.

Adding volume to the mix of variables further increases the density of transmission. The addition of amplitude variations pushed modem speeds to 28.8Kbps and then to 33.6Kbps, more than 100 times faster than the data transfer rates provided by those first 300bps modems conforming to the Bell 103 specification. When 33.6Kbps modems arrived, almost everyone agreed it was the end of the line for analog communications. An axiom called Shannon's Law states that the theoretical maximum transfer rate for two analog modems on the public-switched telephone network (PSTN) is about 35Kbps. The culprit: so-called *quantization noise*, which gets introduced into the analog signal when converting digital bits to sound frequencies.

So how do you explain the arrival of so-called *56K modems*, which can communicate at theoretical speeds of 56Kbps? Simple, they circumvent the law. 56K modems take advantage of the fact that the PSTN is now almost entirely digital, with the exception being the last 100 feet or so leading to your house. These new modems are able to achieve their higher data rates when connecting to a digital source at the other end—such as an ISP or corporate hub that connects to the Internet via T1, T3, ISDN, or other digital line. Because these sources do not produce any analog noise, 56K modems can retrieve information at the higher 56Kbps data rates. However, the digital-to-analog conversion that occurs in modem transitions limits upstream transactions to 33.6Kbps.

However, achieving 56Kbps connections is all but impossible. For one thing, line noise in those last 100 feet of wire pulls data rates down from their optimal point. What's more, the FCC has determined that the voltage levels required to achieve 56Kbps data rates were too high to comply with FCC regulation. As a result, 56K modems operate at lower voltages, limiting their effective maximum data rate to 53Kbps.

Digital Communications

Today, a number of alternatives exist to the analog modem and its reliance on PSTN. Most of these use digital connections entirely, eliminating dial tones, lengthy handshake procedures, and disruptions due to line noise and D-to-A degradation. Among the available technologies today are the following:

- Integrated Services Digital Network (ISDN)
- Satellite
- Digital Subscriber Line services (xDSL)
- Cable modem
- T1

There's more to these technologies than simply exchanging analog tones for digital bits. Most of these devices work on different types of networks than your modem, which uses the public-switched telephone network (PSTN). When you place a modem call, you're handed a dedicated line for the duration of the connection. If no lines are available, other users get a busy signal. ISDN modems and T1 connections work the same way, except they use a digital connection end to end to achieve higher speeds.

However, cable modems and ADSL technology both use packet-based networks, which have a lot more in common with, say, your Ethernet LAN than they do with the phone network. When you make a call, you share space on the network with all the other users. During periods of light traffic, you're likely to enjoy optimal performance, whereas heavy usage times will yield slowdowns as more and more people split the available resources. Only in the most extreme cases would you get the equivalent of a busy signal.

Satellites are a different fish, in that they only work going downstream. Although your upstream communication occurs the same as any analog call, downstream data is received from an orbiting satellite that beams data to your dish. Of course, the satellite doesn't just point at your house—it is beaming to anyone who will listen. Your PC and satellite comm card pick out the intended communications from the "broadcast." Again, as with other digital technologies, perceived satellite throughput will drop if many people are using the service.

18.1.2 Performance Impact Report

Make no mistake, communications hardware makes a big difference in the speed and reliability of connections to the Internet, online services, and email servers. In fact, adding a fast modem or digital connectivity device can save you much more time than upgrading a CPU or RAM, particularly if you spend a lot of time now waiting for Web pages and email documents to download.

The fact is, if your PC is waiting on data coming over the modem, then you're trying to sip a thick milkshake through a tiny straw. Even a relatively minor jump from a v.32 to v.34 modem (28.8Kbps to 33.6Kbps) yields an impressive 17 percent boost in transfer rate. Pushing that upgrade to 56Kbps provides a potential doubling of download speeds.

Unfortunately, there's only so much modems can do. The analog nature of the devices mean that line noise, quantization noise (from the D-to-A operation), and handshaking routines will all rob you of performance. In addition, analog connections typically suffer from poor ping rates—a measure of the responsiveness of your connection—making rapid-fire updates impossible. Depending on the quality of the connection, the modem standard, and the relative quality of the interacting comm hardware, ping rates can vary from a respectable 100ms to an atrocious 500ms. At the higher end of the spectrum, it becomes difficult to play Quake over the Internet, because your PC is receiving updates much more slowly than others who are playing.

Making matters worse for gamers is the fact that games don't do well with compressed packets. As a result, many online games need to be played with communication compression turned off, further limiting the bits available to the software. Combined with poor ping rates, the lack of compression makes it particularly difficult to get acceptable game performance over an analog modem connection.

To enjoy higher data rates and lower ping rates, you have no option but to look at a digital connection of some sort. However, no digital comm adapter enjoys the ubiquitous support of analog modems, meaning that you may have a hard time finding an ISP or other users who are able to talk directly to this hardware.

Modem Guide

With the exception of satellite links, which rely on a modem upstream connection, all these technologies keep your bits in the digital domain. Bandwidth ranges from 128Kbps for ISDN, to a blazing 10Mbps and higher for cable modems. However, like 56K modems, most of your options involve asymmetric technologies that can receive data more quickly than they can send. Only ISDN and T1 lines guarantee equal performance going up and down stream—an important consideration for video conferencing, Web publishing, and remote networking applications.

18.2 Currently Available Modems

As discussed earlier, users face a lot of decisions. Right now, individual users can consider any one of five competing technologies for connecting to the Internet. Unfortunately, a number of these options are in formative stages, meaning that hardware bought now may not be compatible with industry standards that develop later. What's more, availability of digital service for many of the technologies is hard to come by. If you live outside a major metropolitan area (as I do), you may find that your decisions are already made for you.

Here are the relevant technologies to consider:

■ Analog modems

■ ISDN

■ Satellite

■ xDSL

■ Cable modem

One technology that I do not cover in detail here is T1, a digital, always-on leased line that provides 1.44Mbps of bandwidth in both directions. A mainstay among corporate offices seeking to provide Internet access over the LAN, T1s are both expensive to setup ($1,000 to $3,000) and expensive to maintain ($300 to $1,000 per month). Small offices and companies can get a break on the monthly fees by going with a *fractional T1*, which provides a subset of the 1.44Mbps bandwidth at a lower price.

An even faster digital variant is called T3, which is able to transfer 54Mbps. T3 lines are typically used by ISPs to connect to the Internet backbone, or by large order processing centers needing gobs of guaranteed bandwidth. Prices are significantly higher than those for T1.

18.2.1 Analog Modems

Analog modems are defined by the communications protocol they support. The protocol determines how fast the modem can communicate with other modems and is the first thing you should consider in any purchase. Today's 56Kbps modems are standardizing around the v.90 standard from the International Telecommunications Union (ITU). This is a welcome change from six months ago, when two proprietary and incompatible 56K modem technologies—x2 and K56Flex—vied for the market.

Table 18.1 shows the relevant ITU standards and the data rates they support.

Table 18.1. Advancing international standards have ensured that all modems are able to talk to each other.

ITU Standard	Data Rate
v.32	4800 and 9600bps
v.32bis	14.4KBps
v.34	28.8KBps
v.42bis	36.6KBps
v.90	56KBps

Virtually all modems are backward compatible, so a v.90 model is able to fall back to accommodate communications with modems using v.42-bit or v.34 communications. Although this allows for compatibility, it does slow down the speed of the transaction on both sides.

The most critical specification is the new v.90 standard, which moves to replace two proprietary standards: The x2 technology from US Robotics and 3Com, and the K56Flex scheme from Hayes and Lucent Technologies. Although these two interim technologies allow 56Kbps operation, they do not work with each other. That forced users into tough gambles about which approach would gain acceptance among ISPs.

Fortunately, v.90 moots this confusing argument. The one exception: If your ISP has yet to move to v.90-compliant hardware, you'll still need to match up with its selected 56K standard in order to get optimal data rates. Your best bet is to look for v.90 modem that also supports the proprietary technology used by the ISP. The good news: Over the next year, this situation should disappear completely.

Modem Guide

Duplex Modems

A recent innovation has been the introduction of *duplex operation* to boost bandwidth. Duplex modems are actually two modems working across a pair of phone connections to effectively double the data rate available to analog communications. With a typical 56Kbps modem, optimal upstream data rates can go from 33.6Kbps to 67.2Kbps, whereas downstream data rates can go from 53Kbps up to 106Kbps. These figures approach single and dual-channel ISDN transfer rates.

Figure 18.2.

This schematic shows how duplexed modems aggregate bandwidth over a pair of analog phone lines.

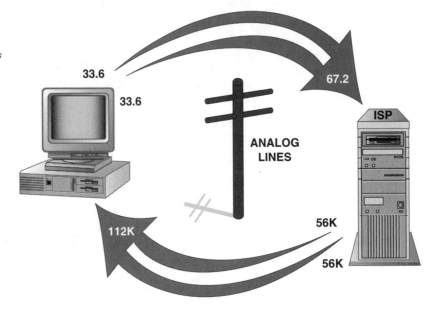

To work optimally, duplexing requires ISP support, because you need to be able to use both lines to download a single file and then have the file reconstituted at your end. Expect to pay a premium for such duplexed ISP accounts. If such support is unavailable, you can get two ISP accounts, but the two modems will not be able to split up file downloads. Still, you'll see a Web browsing boost, because each modem can handle parts of a Web page update, which consists of many files and elements.

The best part about duplexing is the fact that it's available everywhere. If you have two phone lines going into your home or office, you can take advantage of this technology to increase online performance. It's also highly flexible, because you can choose when you want to use both lines; for example, when you're performing large uploads to a Web site or downloading megabytes of Adobe Acrobat files. This flexibility makes duplexing a terrific option for small businesses and home users not willing or able to commit to pricey and still evolving digital services.

Duplexing has its drawbacks though. As mentioned, you're looking at higher costs for ISP access one way or the other, and you'll also bear the cost of two modems. Integrated duplex modems, such as Diamond Multimedia's Shotgun line, can help reduce cost by placing both modems on a single card. Of course, duplexing does nothing for line noise and other modem travails, so ISDN remains a superior option for reliable, network-like access to the Internet and remote computers.

Inside Modems

Inside the modem, you'll find a number of components that work together to handle the flow of digital bits and the conversion of digital signals to analog audio, and vice versa. A brief description of the components comes courtesy of 3Com:

Figure 18.3.
This schematic shows how the subsystems of a modem work together.

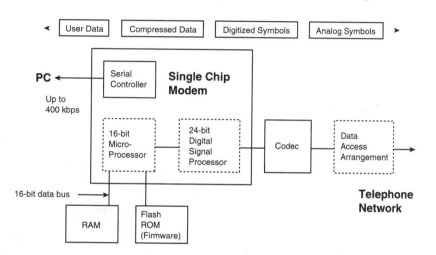

- Processor unit: The modem's microprocessor runs the program that controls such functions as data compression and error correction. It consists of a microcontroller, RAM, and erasable programmable memory (EPROM or EEPROM chips). The microprocessor handles data compression, error correction, AT command processing, and test functions.

- Modem data pump: This component performs the complex processing that converts digital signals to analog signals, and vice versa. The data pump consists of a digital signal processor (or DSP, a specialized math coprocessor), modem code contained in DSP ROM (or external RAM), and a codec (see *Codec* later in this list) to handle the coding and decoding of analog signals.

■ Data access arrangement (DAA): The DAA is an analog/digital hybrid component that acts as an interface to the analog telephone network. The operation of the DAA includes such telephony functions as ring detect, pulse dialing, and off-hook relay. DAA quality is a key variable in connection speeds.

■ Serial controller: A serial controller is required to pass data between the modem processor and the PC. Standard serial chips can support data rates up to 115Kbps. Using a serial controller with intelligent buffer management can improve these speeds to 400Kbps or beyond.

■ Codec: An abbreviation of "coder/decoder." The codec translates between a digitized version of the analog waveform provided by the DSP and a true analog signal, which is then sent to the DAA.

■ Firmware: The firmware is the control program stored in memory. Storing it in EPROM flash memory enables the user to upgrade the program more easily.

ISDN

Integrated Services Digital Network, or ISDN, has not had what you would call a terrific track record. Despite being around for over 10 years, the technology never gained much market share even as demand for bandwidth has skyrocketed. Still, this all-digital version of the public-switched network provides real advantages to telecommuters, remote office, and bandwidth hogs of all stripes.

ISDN delivers a total of 128Kbps of data over two 64Kbps channels, thus providing more than twice the top data rate provided by 56K modems. Perhaps more important, ISDN completely eliminates line noise and quantization noise from the performance equation—bits zip along at their optimum transfer rates unimpeded by the usual potholes in the analog network. As a result, ISDN acts a lot like a standard network connection, without the higher costs and very limited availability of ADSL or even T1.

> **NOTE** If you have an external ISDN modem, you may be selling yourself short. The serial ports used in virtually all PCs only support a top data rate of 115Kbps, about 13Kbps below the 128Kbps transfer rate provided by dual-channel ISDN. If you want to make full use of the hardware—particularly for critical applications such as video conferencing—you'll want to use an internal ISDN adapter.

Figure 18.4.

3Com's Impact IQ provides dual-channel ISDN capability in a convenient form factor.

An ISDN connection actually consists of three separate channels: two bearer (or B) channels that carry the data, and one data (or D) channel that carries connect commands, information, and status traffic. Each B channel is capable of transferring 64Kbps, yielding ISDN's 128Kbps total transfer rate, whereas the D channel adds 16Kbps.

Today, ISDN is the most widely deployed of the digital public networks, yet the technology is on the verge of becoming a footnote. The reason: Telephone companies (telcos) have been slow to deliver ISDN service, have priced it out of the market, and have provided abysmal service and support for the technology. Furthermore, ISDN can only be provided close to a digital telephone switch, at distances no further than 18,000 feet, or just over three miles. That means rural areas are unlikely to have access to ISDN, and the slow pace of switch and line upgrades make the service availability spotty even in metropolitan areas.

Even if you're within the reach of ISDN service, it can prove very difficult to set up. The phone company will probably have to run new lines into your building to support the service. Also, ISDN requires that you understand and master terms such as service provider ID numbers (SPIDs), switching hardware, and NT-1 boxes. Fortunately, newer ISDN terminal adapters use AutoSPID technology and other tricks to cut down on the amount of manual setup. However, the very fact that you need to know who's switch the phone company uses just to get an ISDN modem to work is a prime example of what's wrong with this technology. Making matters worse—the telcos often don't seem to know their own network, dispensing inaccurate or incomplete information.

If you can get ISDN installed and working, you'll enjoy immediate benefits. The 2× to 4× data rate increase will certainly speed downloads, and it makes video conferencing a real application, provided the other party is also on a fast, digital connection. Adding performance to these transfers is STAC compression technol-

Modem Guide

ogy found in the more popular routers used by ISPs. Most important, once time-consuming connection procedures become rapid, quiet affairs, because the all-digital connection does not require tricky handshaking routines. Finally, ISDN connections almost never, ever quit. The reliable, persistent, and speedy connection makes ISDN a terrific option for those needing LAN-like access to remote systems or networks.

18.2.2 Digital Subscriber Line Services (xDSL)

The phone companies have spent years botching ISDN, but the thing that may kill it off is another euphonic acronym that goes by the letters "xDSL." Standing for *digital subscriber line*, xDSL describes a family of all-digital, packet-based, public data network technologies that could emerge as the backbone for mainstream connectivity over the next five years. Like ISDN, xDSL does away with analog noise, D-to-A conversions, and other bandwidth-killing problems. However, unlike its predecessor, xDSL uses a packet-based approach that does away with the line-grabbing practice of switched networks such as ISDN.

The key to xDSL technology is its speed. In most cases, data goes faster heading to the receiving end than it does when transmitted. Although this may pose a problem for Web publishers, remote content creation, and straight-up network access, for the vast majority of users the speed mismatch is not a problem. After all, Web browsing consumes much more bandwidth in the downstream direction than it does going up.

So how fast is xDSL? Well, that depends. Telcos are planning to provide different levels of xDSL performance, targeting both the price and technology thresholds in the market. Initial rollouts have provided 1.5Mbps transfer rates going downstream, with up to 8Mbps possible. Downstream rates vary from 16Kbps to 640Kbps.

In fact, there are a number of xDSL variants, each serving a different segment of the market. ADSL (which stands for *asymmetric digital subscriber line*) is by far the most significant, because its architecture appeals to a broad, low-cost service. These technologies are as follows:

- High bit rate DSL (HDSL): Symmetric, high performance connection over a shorter loop. Requires two or three copper twisted-pair wires.

- Single line DSL (SDLS): Symmetric connection that matches HDSL performance using just a single twisted-pair wire but operates over a shorter loop.

- Very high bit rate DSL (VDSL): Extremely fast downstream and fast upstream but over a very short loop.

- Rate adaptive DSL (R-ADSL): Dynamic connection that adapts to the length and quality of the line.

Figure 18.5.
ADSL and its variants provide outstanding digital bandwidth over existing copper twisted-pair wiring.

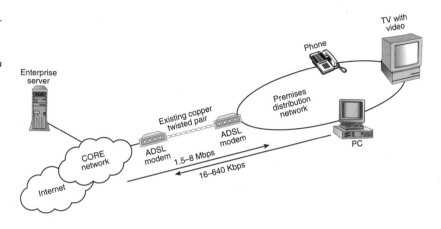

Table 18.2 shows the various xDSL alternatives and their highlights.

Table 18.2. Different flavors of xDSL appeal to WAN applications and high-speed symmetrical link-ups.

Type	Upstream	Downstream	Loop Distance
ADSL	1.5Mbps–8Mbps	16Kbps–64Kbps	12,000–18,000 feet
HDSL	1.544Mbps	1.544Mbps	15,000 feet
SDSL	1.544Mbps	1.544Mbps	10,000feet
VDSL	13–52Mbps	1.5–2.3Mbps	1,000–4,500 feet
RADSL	Varies	Varies	Varies

In virtually all cases, the numbers are significantly higher than even ISDN can provide. A top-of-the-line xDSL connection will deliver about 100 times the downstream bandwidth of a 56K modem, and about 50 times that of an ISDN adapter. Even a low-cost 1.5Mbps connection is more than 10 times faster than ISDN. Of course, the packet-based topology means that performance may degrade during times of heavy use, just as an Ethernet network can bog down during a busy day at the office.

One reason for the excitement over xDSL is the fact that it works over the existing copper twisted-pair wire already laid in most homes and buildings. Where ISDN requires new lines to be installed, xDSL works by plugging into your existing lines. What's more, xDSL allows you to continue to use the line for voice phone calls at the same time as xDSL data transmissions. This is possible because xDSL signals happen at very high frequencies, completely outside the 4KHz band reserved for analog voice operation. In effect, xDSL opens unused lanes on the freeway, dedicating them to data traffic even as the older lanes continue to carry their slower traffic.

The technology isn't without its challenges. For one thing, telcos need to upgrade all their switching hardware to handle the new communications scheme—a pricey and time-consuming proposition. What's more, the copper wire in many older homes may not be up-to-grade even for basic ADSL service, meaning that a significant percentage of users—I've heard numbers as high as 40 percent—may need line upgrades to enable it. Finally, like ISDN, all xDSL variants works in a fairly tight loop, because the digital signals and timing degrade as they get further from the switch. To have access to 1.5Mbps ADSL (also known as *G.Lite*), you need to be located with 18,000 feet—or 3 miles—of an xDSL-capable phone switch. Higher bandwidth operation works in an even shorter loop, between 10,000 and 12,000 feet.

To get xDSL to work, your PC needs an xDSL adapter, sometimes called an *xDSL* or *DSL modem*. This device handles the translation of digital bits into the packet format recognized by the public network and is able to pick out the packets intended for your PC as they pass. In this respect, DSL adapters work very much like network interface cards. Vendors such as 3Com and Cisco are developing or marketing DSL adapters, which are currently being used in technology trials taking place in select markets.

One critical concern for both telcos and modem providers is to eliminate the need for a physical line splitter to separate the voice and data portions of the xDSL service. Although higher speed DSL variants require splitting hardware, the ADSL G.Lite standard allows for modems to provide ADSL and voice service over existing copper wire, without requiring phone company service reps to schlep to every house in America to make ADSL happen. ADSL adapters are expected to cost about $200 to $300 when service begins rolling out in earnest in 1999.

18.2.3 Cable Modems

Even as excitement grows over ADSL, cable companies are winning market share by providing Internet access. Cable providers have bandwidth galore, thanks to the thick coaxial cable that runs to over 62 million homes in the U.S. So much so, in fact, that they can run Internet data next to the existing television programming and still be able to offer transfer rates well in excess of even ADSL.

How much data are we talking about? Well, that depends on a lot of things. Your cable provider's network hardware, the level of service, the type of comm adapter, and even the traffic on the cable network all factor into the equation. However, users can expect downstream data rates of up to 42Mbps and upstream data rates of 10Mbps, based on a growing industry standards called *DOCSIS* (for *Data Over Cable Service Interface Specifications*). Those figures are well in excess of even best-case ADSL service, making cable an extremely attractive technology.

Figure 18.6.
This 3Com internal cable modem adapter includes the telltale coax connector on the back plane. (Photo courtesy of 3Com.)

In fact, DOCSIS could play a critical role in vaulting cable over ADSL as the high-bandwidth option of choice for Internet access. The gating issue for the nascent cable modem market has been the complete lack of standards. Although some 100,000 cable modems were on the market in 1998, most of those would not work with any cable provider other than the one it was installed with. The lack of modem and hardware standards meant that an expensive cable modem purchase could be wasted should you move out of your provider's area. DOCSIS specs out a standard, compatible modem design that uses the Plug and Play USB bus to connect to the PC.

As with ADSL and 56K modems, cable access is asymmetric (although the upstream transfer rates promise to be high enough to make this a minor concern). More of an issue is the fact that up to 90 percent of the existing cable infrastructure lacks the ability to handle upstream data at all, meaning that users must use a separate phone line to connect with the Internet. Therefore, for the time being, cable customers may be able to enjoy multimegabit download speeds, but their uploads will crawl along at the same paltry 33.6Kbps data rate.

Because cable infrastructure is set up in a broadcast scheme, performance will vary greatly depending on the number of users accessing the Internet. Each local service area has a cable *head-end*, from which the individual homes are served. If more and more users access the head-end resources, it leaves less bandwidth for each user. Should a particular area enjoy rapid use of cable modems, transfer rates are certain to fall well below their maximums.

18.2.1 Satellite Services

Today, the most widely available high-bandwidth Internet access option is the one that requires no dedicated lines. The DirecPC direct satellite system (DSS) from Hughes Networks lets you tap into downstream bandwidth from one or more geostationary satellites. The service untethers you from expensive and scarce digital networks by using an 18- or 21-inch satellite dish to collect ku band signals from earth orbit, providing up to 400KBps data rates going down stream.

The main advantage of satellite service is that it can be had in even the most remote locations. All that's required is a phone line, a clear view of the southern sky, and the interfacing hardware, including the satellite dish and comm adapter. This characteristic makes services such as DirectPC a terrific solution for those living outside of metropolitan areas.

Although satellite access benefits rural users, its appeal is blunted by a number of factors. One, the dish and other hardware is expensive and can be difficult (even dangerous, sometimes) to install. Second, satellite lacks any upstream capability—you must connect using a standard land connection for sending commands and data to the Internet. Third, the service remains pricey, with unlimited daytime access priced at nearly $130, although a number of pricing and service options are available to help defray the costs. Finally, the failure of the Galaxy 4 satellite in May, 1998 illustrated the relative fragility of satellite-based access. About 50 percent of DirecPC customers were forced to repoint their dishes in order to gain access—a process that can be very difficult to do without third-party intervention.

DSS access does gain some appeal when bundled with satellite-based broadcast service. The DirecDuo service combines DirecTV and DirecPC into a single package, allowing users to get both services for a fraction of the cost of two separate installations. Although heavy rains can impede the signal, the service actually holds up extremely well in even the most inclement weather.

When you get a dish installed, you still call into your regular ISP using a land line. However, your system's network settings are configured to connect into the Hughes network over the Internet. Commands go to Hughes, out to whatever Web server you're hitting, and then come back to Hughes. From there, the data is beamed up to a satellite and bounced back to earth, where your DirecPC dish receives it. The comm card in the PC recognizes the packets matching your IP address and assembles these into Web pages, images, text, and other useful data.

Although the system can deliver real performance—up to 400KBps—the roundabout path slows down responsiveness. Ping rates for a DirecPC setup can run up to 500ms and higher—about a half-second delay in getting information in. A good ISDN or network connection can experience ping rates of 40ms. The slow response isn't a big deal when browsing through Web pages or downloading the latest version of Netscape Navigator, but it spells certain doom when playing Quake and other online action games.

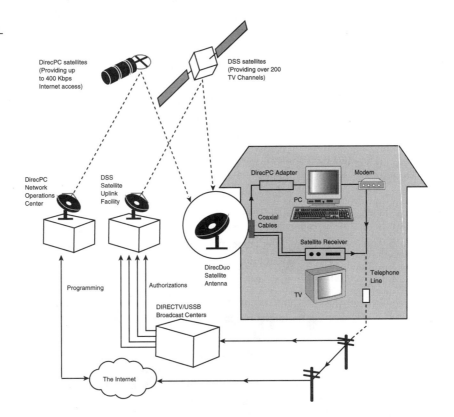

Figure 18.7.
The circuitous path your data must take to be delivered to the high-bandwidth satellite connection.

A final concern: Satellite systems such as DirecPC are limited to TCP/IP communications. If you need to dial directly into a network or another PC, whether via a program such as LapLink or over a remote IPX connection into a Novell network, you may be out of luck: All these transactions will happen over the land line at regular modem speeds.

18.3 Evaluating Communications

With so many emerging alternatives, many of them as yet only half cooked, it's tougher than ever to decide on a communications purchase for remote access. More than just price and performance are at issue here. Availability of service, both in terms of geographic coverage and ISP service and pricing, is a big question. You may also find that support for satellite, cable, and ADSL hardware will be limited under some operating systems, including Windows NT.

18.3.1 Transport Technology

Whether you are using a creaky old 14.4Kbps analog modem or a lightning fast 40Mbps cable modem, many of the same principals apply. Underlying technologies such as error correction and data compression enable and speed communications, whereas issues such as the PC interface and device form factor can impact effective performance. Although modems and ISDN both enjoy a stable platform of standards to ensure interoperability, you'll find that ADSL and cable service are both still very much under construction. Even so, many of the basic principals of operation apply to these technologies.

Compression

Today, all modems rely on data compression to boost performance over the wire. Hardware in the modem looks at groups of bits and compresses them into a more efficient format using shortcuts to represent larger, repeating collections of bits. This compression is similar to that used in PK Zip or hard disk compression, with the compression happening on-the-fly as data passes through the modem. The receiving modem decompresses the data stream so that it can be recognized by your PC.

To make this work, modems need to be speaking the same language. The ITU specifies standard compression schemes—separate from the comm protocols—to ensure market-wide compatibility. Just as important, newer modems must recognize all compression schemes employed by older models. By default, modems will agree upon the most advanced compression scheme available to both. In general, the ITU-established V.42bis protocol is preferred, with the MNP-5 compression protocol serving as a backup.

Compression can yield big gains when moving text, executable, and uncompressed image files (BMP, for example). However, precompressed formats such as GIF and JPG, and video formats such as AVI and MPG will likely not compress at all. In general, the technology is a big boost to moving HTML Web pages, because the text-based format compresses significantly. ISDN users will see an additional benefit from the use of STAC compression on routers used by most ISPs.

Correction

With all the dropouts, line noise, and signal delays involved in modem communications, you'd think the post office was running the Internet. One way to keep your data from being folded, spindled, and mutilated is through the use of error-correction technology, which essentially applies extra bits in the data stream so that the receiving modem can make sure nothing has changed.

Today, two primary error correction standards exist on the market: v.42 and MNP-4. Virtually all modems sold in the last two to three years support these technologies. The ITU-ratified v.42 specification is the primary correction technology, whereas MNP-4 is applied if both modems fail to support the first option.

There are two approaches to catching errors: forward error correction and data-level error correction. The first line of data defense is forward error correction, which uses redundant bits in the data stream to reconstitute corrupted data during transmission. The approach requires a significant amount of redundant data, thus cutting down on efficiency. However, it eliminates time-consuming retransmissions should errors occur.

The second defense is data-level error correction, which uses checksum bits to compare received data against expected results in a small header field. The sending modem segments outbound data into standard-sized blocks, which are book-ended by information about the data itself. At the front of the block—or the header—goes information on the data's order in the transmission so that late arriving data can be stitched back into place on the other end.

On the back end, error-correction bits are applied based on the data that resides inside the block itself. The receiving modem checks these bits, using an agreed-upon error correction algorithm, to determine whether they match the expected result based on the pattern in the block itself. An unexpected result tells the receiving modem to request another transmission of the affected block.

Modem Guide

18.3.2 **Where You Live**

Unlike virtually all other aspects of computing, PC-based communications are very much bound by where you live or work. Reliable and attractive alternatives abound in metropolitan areas such as San Francisco, Seattle, San Jose, Chicago, and Boston. However, work in Vermont or Wyoming, and your options dwindle rapidly.

One reason is the simple economics of market share. Densely populated urban and suburban areas provide a large and ready market of potential subscribers to a new service or technology. Telephone and cable companies can invest in the local infrastructures in these places and feel certain they can reach millions of customers. This is why many technology trials of ADSL service, for example, are happening in key urban market. Often, even a single employer can help move the effort, as is the case with ADSL deployment by U.S. West in the Seattle market, where Microsoft is a major center of economic gravity.

Just as important, these urban areas are densely populated enough that significant portions of the population live and work close to telephone switching stations. Services such as ISDN and all flavors of xDSL generally require that the subscriber be located anywhere from 10,000 to 18,000 feet from the switch (a distance of about 2 to 3.5 miles). Any farther, and degradation in the signal makes reliable service untenable without the use of expensive repeaters or the installation of a new switch.

Of course, competition from cable providers is also a factor in larger areas. If you live near a city, you're much more likely to find an ISP that offers a wide range of connection options, whether its ISDN, ADSL, or cable via a cable provider's service. Table 18.3 shows the relative distribution of communications options available today.

Table 18.3. Availability of digital communications networks vary greatly by location.

Type	Metro areas	Rural
POTS	Universal	Universal
ISDN	Widely deployed	Limited deployment
Cable	Limited deployment	Very limited deployment
ADSL	Trial tests only	Unavailable
Satellite	Widely available	Widely available

If you're uncertain about your options, check with your telephone company about their plans. You should also ask around with local ISPs, who may well have better insight into the local telco's network than the telco itself does. I'm not kidding about this. I've found ISP representatives much easier to reach and more helpful in discussing local connect options than any telephone company.

If you're checking into ISDN or ADSL service, you should have the phone company conduct a loop qualification test. This will determine the quality of your connection, as well as nail down the distance to the switch. Just be aware that you need an active phone number to conduct the loop-quality test on.

18.3.3 Performance Comparisons

Ultimately, choosing a connection technology is about performance. Otherwise we'd all still be using our 9600bps modem instead of worrying about replacing every telephone switch in the country in order to get ADSL service. However, how much of a difference are we talking about really? Well, that depends. Services such as ADSL and cable, for example, come in a variety of tiers and flavors that can yield very different data rates. What's more, most of these new options are asymmetric, which means the download speeds can be many times higher than the upload speeds.

The golden rule of communications is worth keeping in mind: Digital is always better than analog. Although a 56Kbps analog modem can give you nearly all the theoretical downstream performance of a single-channel (unbonded) ISDN link, you'll find that the digital ISDN connection is vastly superior. It won't get thrown by hiccups in the network, degrade due to noise on the line, or otherwise mistreat you. In fact, an ISDN link behaves a lot like a slow LAN connection in that you experience reliable and responsive access to remote hardware. Analog connections, on the other hand, suffer lag times imposed by the modulating/demodulating of audio tones, as well as problems due to poor line quality.

By the numbers, Table 18.4 shows the relative promised transfer rates of these communications options.

Table 18.4. Digital options provide more than just faster speeds—they also deliver quick response.

Type	Upload	Download	Responsiveness
POTS	33.6Kbps	53Kbps	Slow
ISDN	128Kbps	128Kbps	Quick
Cable	33.6Kbps	10–40Mbps	Slow
ADSL	16–640Kbps	1.5–6Mbps	Quick
Satellite	33.6Kbps	400KBps	Dog slow

It's worth noting that many of these numbers are real pie-in-the-sky stuff. Even the best 56K modem will achieve 53Kbps downloads only a tiny fraction of the time—typical transfer rates will range between 40 and 48Kbps. Likewise, satellite downloads will be impinged by weather, your relative position to the satellite, and network traffic. ADSL and cable connections (both packet-based networks) will slow down when traffic is heavy. In fact, the only option that's likely to guarantee consistent performance is ISDN, because it uses a dedicated connection—a switched circuit in network parlance—that does not have to share time with other peoples' work.

Modem Guide

Figure 18.8.

This graph shows the incredible downstream performance of satellite service compared to other widely deployed options, but upstream data rates lag well below those of ISDN.

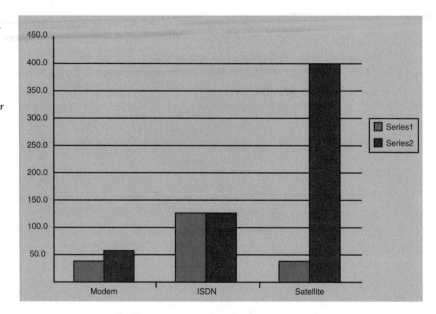

Figure 18.9.

By comparison, the data rates of developing digital systems— including ADSL and cable modems—provide much higher performance. However, asymmetric bandwidth continues to be a concern.

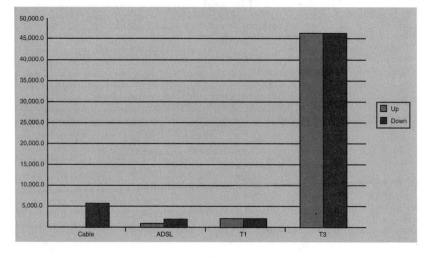

Even then, any communication option will fall victim to the responsiveness of the Web server it's contacting, as well as the entire Internet itself. I run a fast DSS satellite link from my home office in Vermont, which provides instant updates of graphics-heavy Web pages such as ESPN's SportsZone and CNN Interactive. However, when a fiber optic line was cut in the Midwest—a construction accident, I understand—the entire Internet, and my connection, slowed to a crawl.

A critical bottleneck in any connection is your ISP. AOL's travails are well known in the market and should be a stern lesson to anyone looking for reliable and fast service. An overloaded ISP will not be able to fulfill the performance promise of your fast comm hardware. If you're running a modem or ISDN adapter, here are a couple things to inquire about:

- The user-to-modem ratio: This tells you how many subscribers there are for each modem link the ISP has available. If that number goes above 11 to 1, you're almost certainly looking at trouble.

- The primary clientele: Check into the relative proportion of users that keep business or personal accounts. A business-heavy ISP will likely be very busy between 9 a.m. and 6 p.m., whereas a consumer ISP (such as AOL) can fall victim to logjams in the evenings and on weekends.

- The ISP's backbone connection: Does the ISP use a T1 or T3 to connect to the Internet? Or does it use a much faster OC-3 connection? You'll need to balance this information against the number of modems and users in the area you're dialing to.

- ISDN service: If you plan to use an ISP's ISDN service, make sure it offers bonded ISDN capability. Otherwise, you'll be limited to a single channel, which can move only 64Kbps—a real disappointment.

- 56K compliance: For modem users, make sure the ISP supports the 56K technology in your modem, either x2 or K56Flex; otherwise, you'll be operating at 33.6Kbps. Better still, go with a modem and an ISP that's already moved to the ITU v.90 specification.

18.3.4 Internal Versus External

The age-old question applies first and foremost to analog modems, which operate within the limited 115Kbps transfer rate of the modern PC's serial bus. There are a number of reasons to consider an external communications device, among them are the following:

- Independent power: Allows you to reset a modem that has locked up during a transmission. Otherwise, you may have to reboot the PC just to get the confused device to let go of the line.

- Status lights: You can see when send (SD) and receive (RD) activity is occurring, a big help when trying to assess whether a session is hopelessly stalled. ISDN models also offer status about the presence of a working ISDN line, thus helping troubleshoot during initial setup.

Modem Guide

- Resource friendly: External modems use the COM1 or COM2 port on your PC, whereas internal devices need an IRQ line—a precious resource in today's loaded PCs.

- Sharable: You can move an external comm adapter among systems, including notebooks. In the case of ISDN adapters, external devices allow you to connect phones or faxes without having to leave the PC on all the time.

- Spares internal slots: Many Pentium II systems now ship with just one or two ISA slots, a real problem if you have an ISA sound card already installed. External devices can help ease the add-in card crunch.

With that said, there are a lot of advantages to internal cards, including the following:

Figure 18.10.

Diamond Multimedia's internal 56Kbps modem will take up an ISA slot, but requires no external power source.

- Performance: Higher-speed adapters for ISDN and faster access outstrip the PC's serial and even parallel ports, making the port the bottleneck. Older systems may even have serial ports that bog down anything faster than a 14.4Kbps modem, because they lack a 16550 UART chip for fast transfers. Internal models break these bottlenecks.

> **NOTE**   You can get past the serial port bottleneck by installing an I/O upgrade card that uses a faster 16750 UART. The Pacific Commware TurboCard (www.turbocom.com) installs into an ISA slot and provides data rates as high as 972Kbps. The card also includes additional parallel ports, adding value to your system.

- ■ Space savings: Internal models consume no desktop space, nor do they use bulky power blocks that can consume two or more outlet spaces on a typical power strip.

- ■ Cost: You'll save $20 or more on an internal device because of the elimination of the case, indicator lights, and power supply.

18.3.5 Other Features

Communications hardware can provide a lot of other benefits, aside from connecting your PC to the outside network or to other systems. The proper hardware can turn your desktop into a telephone answering machine or even a full-fledged voice mail system. It can also add fax, remote operation, and other useful capabilities to your system.

Simultaneous Voice and Data

If you're connecting over analog phone lines, you should look for modems that provide the ability to handle data and voice at the same time. These modems— known as *DSVD modems*, for *digital simultaneous voice and data*—let you speak to the other party while using the same phone line to download documents, collaborate on a whiteboard, or play games.

Although the facility is attractive for handling voice and data over a single phone line, the feature does not come without its costs. Moving voice through the write robs about 9Kbps of the bandwidth from the digital transaction, thus slowing performance. If you're connecting at a lower data rate due to line noise or other problems, the degradation can become an issue. Also, the compressed audio won't sound quite as good as a normal conversation, although most people will hardly notice.

About three years ago, an alternative technology called *Radish VoiceView* offered a similar capability by quickly switching between data operation and analog voice passthrough. The switching happened so fast that both transactions seemed to occur transparently. This technology has since fallen behind the all-digital DSVD approach, because software and hardware vendors have supported the digital technology.

Of course, the emergence of digital connections and the wildfire popularity of second phone lines have eroded some of DSVD's popularity on the market. Still, the technology can be very useful for many home office users. However, don't expect DSVD to let you pepper your foes with insults as you blow them away in a game of death-match Quake—technology doesn't work that well with games.

Faxing Facts

Once upon a time, faxing was a big deal. Modems with fax capability cost more and were marketed as neat products. Today, virtually all modems can receive and

Modem Guide

transmit faxes at speeds of 14.4Kbps. One reason for this was the inclusion of fax capability directly within Windows 95, making it just another feature in the operating system.

Of course, faxes need standards just like anything else, and a few have risen to enable reliable fax transmission. Most modems now comply with the Class 1 fax specification, which is built into Windows 95's fax software. The one drawback is that Class 1 requires the host CPU to handle the fax processing, which can really slow operation when sending and receiving documents. Newer systems, of course, have much more horsepower to deal with the faxing chores, making this issue much less of a concern.

Class 2 standard fax modems include onboard circuitry and additional modem commands to handle the fax processing. Although a terrific advantage for older systems, Class 2 has failed to take hold due to lack of support in the operating system. Although older boards and fax machines communicate at 9600bps, products sold in the last two years can move data at 14.4Kbps. Considering the costs of long distance faxing, such an upgrade could pay for itself in a few months, if not even weeks.

A Word on Win Modems

If you're in the market for a budget modem, you could consider a "controllerless" modem, also called a *Windows modem* or *Win modem*. These devices shave about $50 off the price by using the system CPU to handle controller functions usually residing in the modem chip. The obvious drawback is that Win modems suck CPU cycles, degrading performance during communications—particularly on older systems. If you use a modem to play demanding 3D games online, for example, a Win modem will drag down your frame rates and make you easy pickings for your better-equipped foes.

Another drawback: Win modems will not work with DOS-only software and games unless drivers have been specifically written for that software, because the DOS software lacks the hardware abstraction layer that lets Windows do the talking to all modems via a standard interface. Because game makers are often busy doing things such as, well, making games, it usually falls to the modem vendor to pick DOS software to support. That's quite a risk if you enjoy multiplayer gaming on popular flight simulators and other titles.

18.4 Tom's Pick

Before you choose a product, you have to decide on a service. In a perfect world, we'd all have our pick of analog, ISDN, xDSL, satellite, and cable services. Unfortunately, all these options are available to only a small subset of users, most of whom live in desirable metropolitan markets, where service providers can efficiently roll out the updated infrastructures needed for the new services.

18.4.1 xDSL

If I had my druthers, I'd go with either cable modem or xDSL technologies—but with significant reservations. The main drawback to consumer DSL services is limited availability. Otherwise, this intriguing digital technology really stands out as the best all-around choice for Internet connectivity. Although consumer-level ADSL (also called G.Lite) is asymmetric, with upstream data rates running slower than downstream rates, it does not require a separate upstream phone connection the way satellite and cable services do. In fact, the "slow" upstream transfer rate actually runs at a healthy 64Kbps, matching the speed of single-channel ISDN access.

Best of all, downstream rates run at an impressive 1.5Mbps. No, this won't match the staggering performance of cable modems, but the rate is about 30 times faster than the downstream rate of 56Kbps modems. ADSL will likely run on your existing phone lines, so you won't face the hassle of a line upgrade. Best of all, you'll be able to make voice and data calls at the same time you use the ADSL service.

The only problem is that ADSL is probably not available where you live. If you can get the service for a reasonable price, do it. Otherwise, you'll be forced to make compromises with other available choices.

Modem Guide

18.4.2 Cable Modems

If you don't have xDSL available to you, cable modems are your next best option. Cable can provide truly blazing downstream transfer rates that reach into the tens of megabits per second. That's good stuff. What's more, cable modem service is actually being deployed in many residential areas, making it the only viable high-speed option in many communities.

Unfortunately, most cable services lack an upstream channel, forcing users to dial into their ISP via a standard analog phone line. With upstream rates limited to the 36.6Kbps transfer rate of the modem, cable modem service suffers from a significant bottleneck. Still, if you need access to Web pages, email, and online documentation, the wildly asymmetric connections won't bother you all that much.

18.4.3 Analog Access

If you're like me, you're stuck with analog service. My solution: Get DirecPC's digital satellite service. The 21-inch dish sits on top of the roof of my house and receives downstream IP data from a geosynchronous satellite at a rate of 400Kbps. Web pages spring up fast and large file downloads cruise right onto the hard disk. Of all the high-speed Internet options available, satellite is the only one that can be had in rural areas.

Satellite service has real drawbacks, however. Like cable, you'll need an analog phone connection to your local ISP to send upstream data. The service is also expensive, requires difficult dish setup, and typically demands an unobstructed south-facing view of the sky in order to "see" the satellite. If you have a cabin in the woods or a condo in the city, clear skies might not be available to you.

If you can't afford high-cost satellite or ISDN service and can't get access to xDSL or cable service, you'll have to go with a standard modem. My pick: The multitalented Courier I-Modem from 3Com. This unit is a combination 56Kbps v.90 modem and ISDN adapter that provides unparalleled versatility. Intriguing security features let you set password access to the modem itself, thus helping prevent unauthorized remote access.

For sheer analog performance, you can do even better with Diamond's Shotgun II modem, which joins the bandwidth of two modems into a single session. You'll need two phone lines to make the separate dialups, and you may even need two ISP accounts or at least a modified account, but the difference is telling. With two 56Kbps v.90-compliant modems sitting on a single card, the Diamond Shotgun II can move 112Kbps of data upstream and 67.6Kbps going down.

Chapter

19

Network Hardware Guide

19.1 Understanding Network Hardware

The Internet has proved in no uncertain terms the enormous value of connecting PCs. From planet-wide email to online publishing and instant access to data and services, the global network has helped vastly enhance the role of personal computers in our society. The same benefits accrue on a private scale when you connect two or more PCs in a local area network (LAN). Whether your PCs are in an office or in the den, there's an immediate and significant benefit to connecting them.

In the office, LANs become the backbone of the digital workplace, enabling employees to work efficiently on projects and files, as well as to share resources such as printers, disk drives, and communications hardware. In the home, a small LAN is a terrific way to put older PCs to work as a communications center or to perform other specific tasks. File, printing, and other device-sharing facilities help you take maximum advantage of your hardware.

Another great network application exists: gaming. Today's Windows 95 games take advantage of DirectX communication facilities to allow two or more players to play the same game. Although many games let you do this over a direct serial cable connection, you'll need the speed and flexibility of an Ethernet connection to do this well. With data rates ranging from 10mbps to 100mbps, a low-cost Ethernet network provides ample performance for rapid updates, quick file transfers, and reliable device sharing.

19.1.1 How They Work

Networks, no matter their technology, share some key characteristics. All enable PCs to share resources and data among themselves, using a standard language—or *protocol*—to ensure that all the PCs on the network can understand each other. The protocol also determines how data is moved through the network to ensure that bits don't get lost and that systems don't get confused by sending bits that crash into each other on the wire.

Of course, a lot of hardware—and software, for that matter—goes into connecting PCs together. Any network is made up of the following components:

- Server and client computers
- Network interface cards (NICs)
- Cabling

- Hubs, switches, and routers

- Network operating system

Servers and Clients

Virtually all larger networks are arranged in what is called a *client/server model*, where many individual desktop computers communicate with a few, powerful server systems to access applications and resources. Centralizing services among a limited number of servers allows Information Systems (IS) management to efficiently set up and manage resources, as well as to ensure security.

In addition to servers, a variety of devices can be accessed directly through the network. Printers, scanners, CD-ROM drives, modems, and other hardware are all common peripherals. In some cases, these devices may be connected directly to a server, whereas in others the devices themselves may act as a node on the network.

Accessing the services dished up by servers are *client PCs*, the individual workstations where people do their work. Client systems can range from so-called *dumb terminals*, which lack even a hard disk, to multiprocessor graphics workstations. The common thread: Clients are systems that access software, files, and services located on servers.

Network Interface Cards

Connecting your client PC to the network is a *network interface card*, or *NIC*. This ISA, EISA, or PCI add-in card includes a port on the back plane for plugging into the network wire and acts as your system's point man in handling network data. The card translates data bound for the network into formatted packets of data that servers and other network cards can understand. The packets are turned into electrical signals and transmitted out onto the cable.

Figure 19.1.

3Com's family of 10 and 100mbps Ethernet cards come in both ISA and PCI flavors.

Incoming network data is also handled by the NIC. The packeted data, received in the form of electrical signals, is decoded on the card. Because network transmissions can encounter delays and other hiccups, the card must also properly arrange the received packets after the fact, creating a sensible data set out of a disordered jumble of packets. Of course, it's also taking attendance, ensuring that all the packets are received, as well as providing error-checking routines to make sure no packets were corrupted in transmission.

Today, NICs are sold primarily for the PCI and ISA bus, although the PCI version of these cards offers a lot of compelling advantages. Plug and Play, guaranteed bandwidth, bus mastering, and other factors all make PCI-based NICs a much more attractive option. Once you get up to 100mbps Ethernet operation, in fact, PCI-based NICs become a necessity, because the throughput of the fast Ethernet network can outstrip ISA's ability to transfer the incoming bits.

Cables and Wires

Of course, a fast network card and supercharged PC won't get very far if there's nothing connecting it to other PCs on the network. Cables provide the critical physical connection among networked PCs, allowing them to zip bits over the wire and communicate at a high rate of speed. A plumbing analogy is apt here, because the electrical charges that form the transmitted data in many ways behave like water running through pipes.

It's no surprise that your pipes need to be tailored for the equipment and applications you're running. In almost all cases, this means working with the telephone-like unshielded twisted-pair (or UTP) cable, which provides the best balance of affordability, performance, and ease of installation. However, a range of other options exist depending on the simplicity or complexity of your network.

Don't underestimate the importance of cabling, particularly if you're wiring a large number of machines or plan to draw the wire through the walls or ceilings of your workspace. Purchase cheap cable for a growing LAN, and you'll find yourself facing a massive rewiring job not far down the road. Go overboard on fiber optic cable, however, and you could blow your entire budget on cable and installation before you've even purchased a single PC.

Here are the most common cable types:

- Unshielded twisted-pair (UTP)

- Shielded twisted-pair

- Coaxial cable

- Fiber optic

In all cases, the cables are used to transmit bits across the network. With the exception of fiber optic, which uses pulses of lights to represent 1 and 0 values over the wire, these choices push electrical signals. Fiber optic's main advantage is that the light signal does not suffer from problems such as reflection, crosstalk, and attenuation, which means it does not degrade even over vast distances. The other cable types, however, vary in ability to maintain the integrity of electrical signals over distances.

Hubs, Switches, and Routers

Hubs, switches, routers, and gateways are used to segment, interconnect, and otherwise manage networks. These devices are needed to handle limitations in cable lengths, the topology of the Ethernet and other network architectures, and the traffic load of larger networks. Although the most simple networks can be put together without any of these devices, their ability to grow and adapt is limited by their simple connections.

The most important piece of the network puzzle—and nearly ubiquitous in any Ethernet network—is the *hub*. This device is the core of almost any Ethernet setup (thinnet cable requires no hub, only terminators at the ends of the cable run). It's used to aggregate client PCs and provide a single, standard connection to a network server. A single cable connects the hub to a network server or another hub, and a number of ports—from as few as four to several dozen—are used to connect client PCs. Hubs are often designed to be stacked atop each other, as shown in Figure 19.2, making it easy for administrators to support growing networks simply by adding inexpensive hubs.

Figure 19.2.

The 3Com SuperStack II 100 hub makes it easy to add clients to a network by simply stacking hubs one atop the other.

Unlike other network components, hubs are fairly stupid beasts. They diligently pass along the bits that move through them, doing no checking of the packets to try to filter down traffic that doesn't need to go out to systems on its section of the network. However, hubs ensure the fidelity of the electrical signal, allowing you to extend the physical reach of your network past the 100-meter limit of UTP cable.

As networks grow, however, the need to conserve the available bandwidth grows with it. Switches are hub-like devices that add useful filtering capabilities for cutting down on unnecessary traffic clogging your network. For example, if a group of five PCs tend to share a lot of huge digital files, using a switch to interface that group to the rest of the network allows you to keep those files from going out to the rest of the company. The switch will look at the IP address embedded in the header of each packet and throw out those not destined for points outside of the segmented group.

Why not use switches like the one shown in Figure 19.3 on all networks? For one, the added intelligence in the switches makes them more expensive than simple hubs. Also, the processing that must occur for each packet does exact a slight performance overhead. If switches were used throughout a network, you could expect some slowing of performance, because every packet is subject to scrutiny at every switch.

Figure 19.3.

The 3Com Office Connect Netbuilder router provides intelligent management of TCP/IP traffic over the Internet or an intranet.

Another option comes in the form of routers (shown in Figure 19.4), which are useful for connecting your networked users to the Internet. These devices let client systems share access to modems, ISDN adapters, or other networks. Because not everybody needs Internet access all the time, a router can save money by cutting down on individual modem installations, as well as eliminating the need for individual ISP accounts for each user. Rather, a router allows your network systems to share access to the same hardware and ISP resources.

Figure 19.4.

One stop shop: The Cisco AS5200 serves as a telecommuting resource for businesses, with routing, switching, communication services, and ISDN and modem capabilities in a single box.

Finally, small office or small home office networks might consider a proxy server instead of a router. Products such as Winproxy let you set up easy Internet access for several networked PCs, using a single modem or ISDN line. These products are also much less expensive than routers.

Network Operating System (NOS)

It's not hardware, but the NOS you run on your network server can really define how your network works. From management tools to directory services, you can't overstate the importance of the NOS in the behavior of the network. Today, most users face two choices:

- Novell NetWare

- Microsoft Windows NT

Both offer ample tools for setting up even large networks of over 1,000 seats, although each has its strengths and weaknesses. Novell NetWare, for example, continues to excel in its facilities for setting up and managing network-based resources and devices. The presence of effective printer services, user directories, and other bread-and-butter facilities are the main reason that many organizations continue to use NetWare as their NOS.

Microsoft's Windows NT, meanwhile, continues to bring pressures on the market by making strides in areas where NT has been deficient. All along, it has enjoyed the enormous advantage of being closely tied with the preferred client OSs of networks—Windows 3.*x*, Windows 95, and Windows NT Workstation. However, Microsoft has worked hard to bring its directory and print management tools up-to-grade with Novell's offering. In addition, the inclusion of built-in TCP/IP and Dynamic Host Configuration Protocol (DHCP) has made NT an excellent NOS for Internet-savvy networks. This is particularly important if you want to set up an intranet with a minimum of configuration hassles.

Of course, your client PCs continue to run standard desktop operating systems, although they will be tweaked for network access. Windows 95, for example, comes with drivers and protocols for the more mainstream networks such as NetWare and NT Server.

Protocols

Hand in hand with the operating systems are the protocols that allow networked PCs to talk to each other. TCP/IP, IPX, and NetBEUI are all popular network transport protocols, and each has its own strengths and weaknesses. Here are the three most common protocols used on PC-based networks:

- TCP/IP

- IPX

- NetBEUI

A *protocol* is software loaded in the operating system that is bound to the network hardware, such as the NIC. Without a protocol, the NIC and system won't be able to make sense of the packets that come across the wire, effectively disabling the hardware. Packet size and architecture, error correction, and other critical standards are defined within the protocol's specification.

TCP/IP

TCP/IP (Transmission Control Protocol/Internet Protocol) was developed by the Department of Defense to allow dissimilar computers to communicate with each other. Today, of course, TCP/IP is the basis for the global Internet network, providing a single, common language for the millions of disparate computers that reside on the Net. Because it must span vast distances and cross networks, TCP/IP is a routable protocol that's able to send bits through a router on its way to a destination. The routing capability makes TCP/IP more cumbersome and less quick than, say, NetBEUI, but it affords tremendous flexibility for networks large and small.

IPX/SPX

Novell's IPX/SPX is tailored for a company's NetWare NOS; however, Microsoft has built compatibility with IPX/SPX into Windows NT and Windows 95. Like TCP/IP, IPX (as it's often called) is a routable protocol that's appropriate for large, multisegmented networks. Better yet, the optimized structure makes it more nimble than the somewhat clumsy TCP/IP technology, allowing for responsive access even over large networks.

IPX has one drawback: It works very slowly over analog phone lines. Unlike TCP/IP, which can open an address channel and stream data to the client, IPX continually checks on the status of the transmission to make sure everything arrives. Over analog phone lines, the process of checking the status consumes a good portion of the available transmission bandwidth, yielding excruciatingly slow remote access. Of course, because TCP/IP blows off the transfer checking, it is much more likely to mess up a transmission than IPX. TCP/IP simply won't notice an error, thus requiring the receiving/processing software to step in to correct things.

NetBEUI

Designed for small LANs, Microsoft's NetBEUI protocol is the fastest network protocol option you'll find, because NetBEUI lacks the addressing overhead found in TCP/IP and IPX, thus reducing processing overhead. However, at the same time, the lack of this data means that information may only be shared within the local network—you cannot use NetBEUI to reach across networks via a router or gateway. Another limitation is the fact that only Microsoft's networking schemes support NetBEUI. However, if all you're doing is connecting three or four Windows 95 workstations, NetBEUI is a fast and efficient option.

19.2 Currently Available Network Hardware

Networking is a big area, so there's no lack of things to talk about when discussing available networking products and technologies. To limit the discussion to a reasonable area, the focus here is on smaller, private networks, with a focus on small and home offices and similar setups.

When looking at networking products and technologies, there are a variety of things to consider, but the question that faces most buyers is the type of NICs and the cabling to be used. I'll discuss each of these issues here, delving into more specific comparative detail in the next section.

19.2.1 Network Interface Cards

The NIC is the critical client-side portion of the network setup, and it can be the ultimate determiner of effective bandwidth. A low-end 10mbps card installed on a system connected to a high-speed network will limit your access to the 10mbps rate. Therefore, you need to match your card purchase with the Ethernet network flavor you're running. Even better, you can give yourself room to grow by buying a fast Ethernet card (100mbps) for a standard Ethernet network (10mbps), making it possible to immediately crank up your bandwidth when you move to faster hubs and wiring.

Today, there are three flavors of Ethernet, each of which demands that you purchase a NIC compatible with its capabilities:

- Ethernet: 10mbps

- Fast Ethernet: 100mbps

- Gigabit Ethernet: 1000mbps (or 1Gbps)

Each of these Ethernet flavors comply with the IEEE 802.3 specification that defines the Ethernet structure and layout. The good news is that faster Ethernet NICs are backward compatible with older Ethernet implementations. So there's no problem installing a 100mbps NIC into your clients on a 10mbps Ethernet network—the card will simply crank along at the lower 10mbps speed. However, should you upgrade your hubs and wiring down the road for fast Ethernet, your client PCs will immediately enjoy the ten-fold performance benefit because their NICs are ready for the updated topology.

> **NOTE** Unlike NICs, many 100mbps hubs will not work at the lower 10mbps speed. If you intend to run slower network cards on a fast Ethernet hub, you need to specifically buy a hub that can operate with 10mbps NICs. Otherwise, you'll need to upgrade all your NICs to 100mbps in order for them to work with the new hardware.

Note that not all hubs are created equal. If you're upgrading, you need to either upgrade *all* the NICs to 100mbps or get hubs that support both 10mbps and 100mbps. Many 100mbps hubs only run at that speed. Most NICs come in two flavors: ISA and PCI. Where possible, you should make a conscious effort to buy PCI-based network cards. As stated earlier, PCI cards enjoy better performance and superior installation capabilities. However, these cards also deliver significant system performance improvement by reducing the amount of time your CPU spends tracking network data transactions. The secret is *bus mastering*, an attractive feature of all PCI 2.1 (and later) bus slots that allows the bus to move data without requiring CPU intervention.

Bus mastering can become critical if you're constantly trading data over the NIC, such as in the case of online applications and data sharing, or if large amounts of data sometimes are transacted. One good example: Network-based video conferencing, which can stream megabits of video data every second. If your CPU is actively involved in these kinds of transactions, obviously there will be less bandwidth available for other operations.

So why would anyone buy ISA cards? For one, they're less expensive than brand name PCI NICs. You can often save $10 or $20 by purchasing an aging ISA-version of a network card. Also, older PCs may either lack PCI slots or have only one or two available, making ISA the more attractive choice in terms of accessibility. Also, some PCI-equipped PCs lack the bus-mastering feature, robbing them of one of PCI's most beneficial features when it comes to network performance.

You'll also find NICs in other shapes and sizes. 3Com's Megahertz unit sells PC Card Ethernet adapters, for example, which allow notebook users to plug into the network. There are also useful combination units that put both a 56Kbps modem and a 10/100mbps Ethernet adapter on a single Type II PC Card module (see Figure 19.5). This is a boon if you only have a single PC Card slot in your notebook PC. Finally, you can buy network adapters that plug into the parallel port, allowing virtually any desktop or notebook PC to be turned into a networked client. The drawback? Parallel port network cards are very slow, and they often impair operation of other parallel port devices, such as printers.

Figure 19.5.

The 3Com Fast EtherLink XL PC Card adapter provides 10 and 100mbps Ethernet capability for notebook PCs.

19.2.2 Cabling

Not to be overlooked is the media that holds all this stuff together: cable. If you include the cost of installation, network wiring is a significant portion of any office networking budget. There are three major types of network cable:

- Unshielded twisted-pair (UTP)

- Shielded twisted-pair

- Coaxial cable

Unshielded Twisted-Pair

Called *UTP* for short, unshielded twisted-pair looks a lot like the telephone wires found in any home or office. The difference is that more wires are inside the insulation, allowing for higher speed transmissions. UTP wire is graded by category, with Category 2 (or CAT 2) wire used in most telephones. Although you can run a 10mbps Ethernet network over CAT 3 wiring, the media conks out at about 16mbps of bandwidth—too low for handling fast Ethernet operation.

For this reason, the vast majority of Ethernet networks use CAT 5 UTP wiring. It's able to handle both 100mbps and even 1000mbps Ethernet operation, positioning even the largest networks for upgrades down the road. Because it's cheap to buy and install, CAT 5 UTP is nearly ubiquitous, with the vast majority of network cards offering a CAT 5 interface, called an *RJ45 port*. CAT is able to push Ethernet signals over 100 meters of wire before requiring an intervening hub or other device to boost the signal.

Network Hardware Guide

Shielded Twisted-Pair

Called *STP*, shielded twisted-pair is functionally identical to the popular UTP cable. It uses the same twisted-pair wires and the same RJ11 or RJ45 jack. However, the shielding allows STP to be laid over slightly longer distances than UTP because it eliminates degradation from outside electromagnetic frequencies (EMF). In addition, shielded twisted-pair is a more secure cabling, with the shielding making it more difficult for snoops to pick up data from the EMF radiation coming off the wire.

STPs drawbacks are enough that the cable is not widely installed. The additional insulation drives up the cost of the cable and also makes it somewhat more difficult to work with (it's not as easy to work around corners, for example). Given that most companies aren't worried enough about security to actually shield the wires connecting their networks, STP is of little used.

One place where STP is of real usefulness is in situations where the wire is exposed to a lot of ambient EMF, say on factory floor settings where there's a lot of heavy-duty electrical equipment. Generators, large fans, moving electrical parts, and transmitters can all flood the wire with unwanted electrical noise—enough to confuse the values being moved over the network. STP wiring is a terrific option in these cases because it matches up with the huge universe of UTP-compliant devices while at the same time managing to limit exposure to outside EMF. What's more, because STP and UTP cable can coexist on the same network, you can choose to lay STP wire only in areas subject to extreme interference. Less expensive UTP can then be used in less harsh environments.

Coaxial Cable

Similar to the thick, black cable used to hook your cable TV box to the incoming cable service, coax was the original Ethernet medium. However, the thick and stiff makeup, combined with higher cost, make coax a little used option in today's offices.

There are actually two flavors of Ethernet-grade coax: thinnet and thicknet. Thinnet can go 185 meters before requiring a hub or other intermediary, nearly twice the distance of UTP. Thicknet stretches the reach even farther, up to 500 meters. Both cable types are found on so-called *backbone Ethernet*, direct network setups in which systems are simply arrayed along a line of coax cable, with no hub present.

Despite its longer reach, thicknet is little used because it's more expensive and tougher to work with than thinnet. Both coax types are significantly more difficult to install into a structure than is the pliable UTB wiring. However, in both cases the shielding is excellent, making the cable terrific for securing against snooping as well as for protecting against unwanted EMF interference.

Fiber Optic

The fastest, longest-reaching, and most capable type of wiring is fiber optic. Made of slender lines of optically enhanced glass, fiber optic wire is able to pass information in the form of pulses of light. Because light does not suffer from signal degradation and interference problems common with electrical signals, fiber optic wire is able to run much longer without intervening hardware. It's also ten times faster than twisted-pair wiring and is immune to both outside EMF noise and snooping efforts.

So why isn't fiber laid in every building, home, and corporate campus? Fiber optic wire is extremely expensive and quite difficult to work with. Although these drawbacks don't prevent the material from being used in long-distance connectivity—such as cross-country Internet backbones—it does make it inappropriate for LANs. Most telling is the fact that the distance and performance advantages of fiber optic wire go unutilized even on a fast gigabit Ethernet LAN—there's almost no benefit to going with the fiber optic media in these instances.

19.2.3 Alternative Network Choices

If you're setting up a small or home network, you actually face a couple other intriguing choices. These new technologies depart from the standard NIC/cable/hub model, rather making use of wireless technology or alternative wiring to deliver bits among PCs. The advantage comes in the form of simpler installations and less invasive wiring setups, but you'll pay a price in performance and sometimes in cost.

Wireless Networks

Wireless networks are intriguing because they untether you from the RJ45 jack coming from the wall. All you need is a power outlet to plug into and the wireless transceivers for your client and server PCs. The network itself looks and acts like standard Ethernet, with the same packet structure and networking protocols in place. However, the bits are transmitted via radio waves rather than through a twisted-pair or coax wire.

Unfortunately, wireless is pricey. Transceivers can cost $200 or more a pop—about twice the price of even a brand name network card. In addition, performance is well below the 10mbps rate you see with standard 10BaseT Ethernet. WebGear's Aviator, for instance, uses the parallel port for moving bits to and from the transceiver. Expect data rates in the range of 1 to 2mbps.

Despite some of its drawbacks, wireless is simply terrific if you're unable or unwilling to rip into walls and ceilings to lay Ethernet cable. Older buildings and homes, for example, are both prime candidates for going wireless. The technology is also a boon if you want the flexibility to move around with a networked notebook computer, for example. In these cases, wireless will actually save you money over pulling Ethernet wire and installing jacks at every possible working point.

Home Networks

So-called *home network* products are those that plug into the existing power or telephone infrastructure to deliver bits. There are two approaches:

- Power grid networks
- Telephone grid networks

Power grid networks actually use your house's power lines as the medium for sending and receiving Ethernet packets. Bits are sent through the power line by modulating a signal from the transceiver. The receiving PC senses the modulation, which it recognizes as digital bits making up standard Ethernet packets.

The most simple power line–based networks, such as X-10, were limited to pokey 60bps data rates and often only allowed one way communication. Today, new implementations allow for data rates of 350Kbps with full two-way capability. Advances are also allowing for less expensive components. The Intelogis PassPort transceiver, for example, costs about $50 for each PC.

Telephone grid networks are another viable alternative in home and small office settings. Although phone jacks are not as ubiquitous as power outlets, they nonetheless abound in many buildings. What's more, these phone-based networks can provide higher data rates, with performance of 1mbps on currently available products (see Figure 19.6). In essence, you trade a level of convenience for about three times the bandwidth.

Tut Systems' HomeRun, shown in Figure 19.7, offers telephone-based networking. Once again, an adapter acts as the custom Ethernet interface to the home wiring—this time, telephone—allowing PCs to send bits to each other. Packets conform to standard Ethernet design, allowing full compatibility with popular applications and protocols. More important, the data communications happen outside the band of voice communications, which means that the phone can be used for normal modem and voice use even while you're sending and receiving network data.

Finally, the USB ports found on most new desktops open intriguing options for connecting them together. Under Windows 98, systems can be connected using USB cables, providing Ethernet networking without the use of any additional hardware. Lack of integrated driver support in Windows 95 and NT means that only Windows 98-based PCs will be "networkable" using simple USB connections.

Figure 19.6.
By pushing network data through existing CAT 2 twisted-pair phone lines, Tut Systems' HomeRun technology can push up to 1mbps of data.

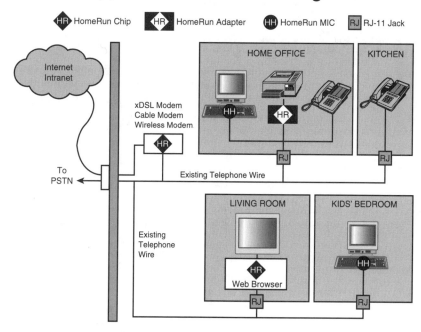

Typical HomeRun Configuration

HR HomeRun Chip   **HR** HomeRun Adapter   **HH** HomeRun MIC   **RJ** RJ-11 Jack

Figure 19.7.
The HomeRun adapter card looks similar to any ISA-based network interface card, but it uses RJ-11 ports instead of the RJ-45 ports found on most Ethernet adapters.

Network Hardware Guide

19.3 Evaluating Network Cards

So you're setting up a network. What hardware do you need to go with? Ultimately, that depends on the size of the network, its applications, as well as your budget and existing equipment. After all, a network of five Pentium MMX PCs trading Excel files and email has very different demands from, say, a rendering farm that links together 100 multiprocessor graphics workstations crunching high-resolution, 3D animations.

This section will help you make smart decisions when buying network cards by setting your priorities in line with the applications you need to run.

19.3.1 Keep It Simple

Fortunately, advances in network interface cards have made the choices easier than ever before. Most important, you should try to stick with PCI-based network cards wherever possible. Not only does PCI offer a faster, more efficient interface to the PC, it also gives you a much better chance of avoiding incompatibilities. A PCI-based NIC is ensured of delivering dynamic resource allocation, for example, allowing Windows 95 to ferret out free IRQ and DMA resources at startup. ISA boards, particularly cheap ones, boast only spotty compliance with PnP, thus inviting a host of problems.

If reliability is your major concern—and it always should be—make a point to standardize all your network card purchases around a single vendor and model type. Better yet, consider going with a name brand vendor who has a known reputation in the market. This can enhance your chances of getting up-to-date drivers, decent service, and reliable product operation. One way to ensure interoperability is to buy a network kit, which consists of 5 to 20 NICs and a hub. Identical drivers, consistent documentation, and a single support contact help take much of the pain out of networking.

The major advantage to limiting network card models is that you can apply driver and other updates across the network without having to juggle a dozen versions of the software. Also, standardizing your hardware can prove a big timesaver in troubleshooting. Once you're familiar with the resource requirements and operating quirks of the cards, you'll be better able to discern and fix problems that do arise—such as a conflict with a sound card, for example.

You'll enjoy even easier maintenance and installations if you apply a similar conformity to your client PCs. By standardizing both the network hardware and the PCs it runs on, you're much better equipped to predict, spot, and resolve conflicts and breakdowns. Of course, not all of us have the option of buying all our client PCs in a single purchase, but trying to standardize the network side of the equation will help.

19.3.2 Bandwidth Is Good

For years, 10mbps Ethernet has been the network standard, and it has served amazingly well. In almost no instance will a small network outstrip the ability of a 10mbps Ethernet setup to deliver bits in a timely fashion. With that said, the simple rule of computing is "the more bandwidth, the more better." With 100mbps NICs now very affordable, it really makes little sense to purchase the slower cards.

If 10mbps is adequate, why buy the faster card type? For the simple reason that software always finds a way to fill the unused capabilities of your hardware. Streaming audio and video, emerging 3D interfaces, and enormous program installations are all applications that can clog even a fast network. More important, networks have a tendency to grow. By populating your machines with 100mbps Ethernet now, you will be able to move to the new standard down the road simply by replacing your hubs—no need to individually install new cards in the client PCs. Of course, 100mbps NICs are compatible with 10mbps networking, so there's no problem running these cards side by side on a lower network.

Coming next is gigabit Ethernet, which can push 1,000mbps. Although gigabit products are available now, the role for this technology is still many years out. Companies with large networks will want to use gigabit Ethernet to join together network segments via a high-speed backbone, thus relieving bottlenecks behind the scenes. However, the Ethernet hardware in the PCs themselves should remain 10mbps or 100mbps for many years to come.

19.4 Tom's Pick

When it comes to picking NICs, speed and name recognition are the names of the game. With prices for 100mbps fast Ethernet cards so low, there's no reason to go with a slower and cheaper 10mbps card. Not only will the faster card likely enjoy longer support in terms of driver development, but you'll gain an immediate upgrade path should your hubs be boosted to 100mbps.

Just don't expect to wait for 1,000mbps gigabit NICs, because these devices cost hundreds of dollars more than their fast Ethernet cousins. What's more, gigabit Ethernet hubs and cabling add hundreds and even thousands of dollars to the cost.

NICs are not sexy devices. They sit in your PC and silently process the millions of packets that make up network communications. However, if you want reliable operation and easy setup, you should consider spending a little more for a name brand model. Intel and 3Com both sell popular, affordable, and reliable NICs. Because both companies enjoy a prominent position in the market, they're likely to be around to provide drivers and support for their hardware in the years to come—something off-name products cannot guarantee.

Also make sure you purchase a PCI network card if at all possible. The fast PCI bus provides plenty of headroom for the most bandwidth-intensive transfers, and it adds several benefits that take the load of your system CPU. PCI bus mastering, for example, allows bits to flow directly from the network card to your hard disk or other subsystem, without requiring constant CPU intervention. Also, PCI's more rigid Plug and Play facility helps reduce setup hassles and IRQ conflicts.

Network Hardware Guide

Part

VI

Completing Your System

Chapter

20

Input
Devices

Buy a high-performance PC and look where your money is going: $1,000 or so for the processor, another $500 to $1,000 toward a 17-inch or 19-inch monitor, and as much as $300 for 64MB of RAM. That's $1,800 to $2,300, and you haven't even gotten to the hard disk, CD-ROM drive, or motherboard. So what's the surprise? The most critical components of your PC don't even figure among these devices.

In fact, the devices you should be paying the most attention to are the most low-tech of all—the keyboard and mouse. You spend most of your day interacting with these lowly peripherals. Every word you type, every command you issue, virtually every interaction you have with the PC involves the use of these two devices.

Most important, the quality and flexibility of your input devices can have a much greater impact on overall performance and productivity than you think. After all, when it comes to moving data in and out of the PC, the single greatest bottleneck is the user. Accomplished typists can input a meager 50 to 70 words per minute, which is the equivalent of about 320 to 400 bytes of data. A typical 32× CD-ROM drive, which is often considered a bottleneck itself, can push 3,600 *kilobytes* of data each *second*. That's 36,864,000 bytes each second, or about 100,000 times the transfer rate of a capable touch typist. You get the idea.

Other issues abound as well. New mouse variants relieve you of tedious sliding around the desktop, whereas wireless, integrated, and ergonomically-designed keyboards and mice all promise to enhance functionality and comfort. Game players have a lot to follow as well—advances such as cheap force-feedback joysticks and all-digital connections are improving both performance and gameplay.

Here's a list of the components covered in this chapter:

- Keyboards

- Pointing devices

- Gaming devices

20.1 Understanding Keyboards

People who buy a new PC tend to overlook two things—the monitor and the keyboard. Yet both are absolutely critical to getting work done quickly and efficiently, and both play a key role in user comfort. In fact, the keyboard is probably the most neglected of all. Bargain hunting buyers often get stuck with cheap, chintzy, rattling keyboards that make typing an unnecessary effort just because they failed to ask any questions before making the purchase.

It doesn't have to be that way. For a few extra bucks, you can get a keyboard that will provide more comfort, superior response, and ergonomic benefits. There are also a variety of programmable, multifunction, and otherwise advanced keyboard designs that can help you break the human bottleneck.

20.1.1 How Keyboards Work

There's not a whole lot of submicron physics going on inside your keyboard, but there is some intelligence in there nonetheless. When you type on the keys, the keyboard detects the activity. A keyboard controller processes the simple information and stores it in an outbound buffer, where the data is aggregated and then sent on to the PC over the keyboard wire.

The detection occurs based on electrical signals produced when the keys are pressed. The keys are mounted on plungers that sit atop an electrical sensor grid. When a key is pressed, it makes contact with the grid and causes a change in the electrical signature. The keyboard processor constantly polls each of the key contacts on the grid, sending signals to each key point from the sides of the grid. When a key is pressed, the processor detects the change in the signal response, which it interprets into the appropriate character.

On the other side, the keyboard processor lets your PC know that input is occurring. It sends a signal to the CPU, in the form of a system interrupt, that tells the system to accept the new data. The keyboard processor conducts this relay thousands of times per second, thus enabling the keyboard to accept input from the fastest typist without problem.

Unlike the CPU and expansion boards, however, the keyboard operates in an open and often hostile environment. Water, food, dust, and soft drinks are all bound at some point to introduce themselves to the keyboard. For this reason, the keyboard keys don't sit directly atop an exposed circuit board. Rather, a plastic surface, called a *shield*, sits between the keys and circuitry with holes in the surface to allow the plungers to make contact.

These holes have raised edges that fit neatly underneath the hollow interior of the keys to form an effective barrier against foreign objects. The shield also prevents heavy-duty typists from banging the life out of the circuitry, because the key edges are designed to strike the protective plastic cover before the plunger is driven into the circuit board.

The physical design of keyboards come in two variations: mechanical and membrane. Virtually all keyboards used on desktop PCs are of a mechanical design, which means that the keypads are mounted on a post and spring. Membrane keyboards do away with the post-and-spring mechanism in favor of a pliable, conductive material that sits beneath the keys. When a key is pressed

Input Devices

down, it makes contact with the membrane, changing its conductivity and alerting the controller that the key was pressed.

Mechanical keyboards have the primary advantage of being cheap, reliable, and easy to maintain—exactly the kinds of characteristics to warm the hearts of PC makers. They also provide a lot of flexibility in terms of the tactile feedback that users perceive when typing, whether it's a "clicky" IBM- or Compaq-style keyboard or the more subdued response from a Microsoft model.

Although membrane keyboards cost a little more, they are popular in industrial settings and areas where fire hazards are an issue. That's because the membrane forms an effective seal that protects the circuit board and controllers as well as eliminates the hard contact between the plunger and the circuit board. The soft contact eliminates the possibility of sparks. Membrane keyboards typically lack the crisp feedback of mechanical models, and they're often described as "mushy."

Most keyboards plug into one of two types of connectors: a DIN5 keyboard connector or a smaller MiniDIN6 keyboard connector. Almost all new systems and keyboards use the MiniDIN6 format—a key advantage because it's the same connector used on notebooks. It's worth noting that USB-based keyboards are already on the market and may be a fine alternative to standard models.

20.1.2 The Many Faces of Keyboards

What Henry Ford said about his Model T—people could buy any color they like as long as it was black—certainly applied to keyboards about 10 years ago. Virtually every keyboard featured 101 keys, plenty of tactile feedback, and function keys arrayed along the left side. Certainly, few vendors dared to vary from the sloped-and-flat keyboard face or took the risk of adding custom keys to the standard set.

Fast forward a few years to the world of choice: You've got 100 channels on cable TV, a nearly infinite selection of Web sites, and now a bevy of keyboards designs to choose from. Where alternative keyboards designs once lurked in a gray underground, they are now proudly bundled with PCs from market-leading system vendors and grace the shelves of CompUSA. What's more, they're nearly as affordable as the putty-colored me-too models that we've all used for so long.

The vast majority of keyboards can be broken into the following categories:

- Standard

- Split face

- Wireless

- Multifunction

Despite their differences, virtually all these products conform to the ubiquitous QWERTY key layout made popular on typewriters. You can find more exotic variants, but not without looking hard. Alternative key orders (such as the Dvorak layout) promise to enhance typing speeds but end up confounding practiced QWERTY typists. More exotic variants include vertical key faces and tiny, one-handed devices.

Standard Keyboards

This familiar workhorse needs no introduction. You'll find 101 keys aligned horizontally in five rows, with a long spacebar running along the bottom. Function keys sit across the top and/or left side, and many models include a numeric keypad at the far right. In most cases, the Return/Enter and Shift keys are enlarged, as is the backspace key in many models.

If you're a conservative user, these models will present you with a familiar and comforting interface. The major difference to look for is in keypad behavior—an area ruled by personal preference. Some users will want the reassuring feedback of heavy, IBM-like "clicky" keyboards, whereas others will prefer the quieter operation and less strenuous action of other models. The only way to tell what suits you is to try them out.

More sophisticated models often include extra macro keys and control buttons for kicking off prerecorded operations or automatically launching Internet browsers or communication software, or, perhaps, turning the PC on and off. Gateway's AnyKey keyboards, for example, have long featured macro capabilities. More recently, the company began including buttons for system power and specific application launches along the top of the keyboard.

Of course, any time you add to the plumbing, you invite more backups, and macro keys are no exception. Gateway keyboards have a long history of being accidentally knocked into program mode, with the undesired result of becoming totally muddled by the unexpected keystrokes that follow. For years, the company put a warning sticker right on the top of the unit, telling readers how to get keyboard control back in the case of an accidental activation.

Split-faced Keyboards

Rapidly growing in popularity are *split-faced keyboards*, with keys that slope up from the edges to provide for a more comfortable hand position. The keyboards are usually split down the center, between the right-hand and left-hand keys on a QWERTY layout keyboard, as shown in Figure 20.1. Examples of these types of ergonomic keyboards include Microsoft's Natural Keyboard Elite and Cirque's Wave Keyboard 2.

Input Devices

Split-faced keyboards have gained popularity because of the enormous increase in repetitive strain injuries (RSIs) suffered by keyboard users in recent years. The problem arises because of the way a user must type on a flat keyboard, with hands close together and palms pushed flat—a position called *pronation*. Pronating one's wrists can bind tendons, restrict circulation, and crimp nerve bundles, thus leading to chronic discomfort and other RSI symptoms.

The sloped keyboard attempts to resolve these problems by allowing users to type with their palms tilted slightly inward—a more natural position that doesn't require any twisting or flexing. The hands are also set wider apart (closer to shoulder width), which is also a more natural position.

These products look different, but they operate on the same principles as any standard keyboard. However, the new orientation will take some getting used to. In fact, so-called *ergonomic* keyboards have been known to cause discomfort in previously healthy workers, as they strain to master the new keyboard layout. You'll find that these keyboards tend to have a larger footprint (that is, they consume more desk space).

Wireless Keyboards

The benefit of a wireless keyboard is self-evident: They have no encumbering wires, allow you to sit where you like, and are excellent for presentations. They are also gaining use in an important new application—TV-based Web browsing. Most models include a separate receiving device, as shown in Figure 20.2, that plugs into the PS/2 keyboard port on the back of your PC. A length of cord lets you place the receiver where you need it.

Figure 20.2.

Sejin's FreeBoard Beamer keyboard uses an infrared beam to communicate with a receiver module installed on your PC. (Photo courtesy of Sejin.)

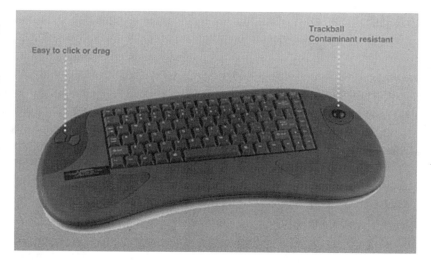

Most wireless keyboards use an infrared beam to communicate with the PC; however, you can also find radio frequency (RF) models. IR is inexpensive, appearing in keyboards costing less than $150, and it doesn't require FCC approval for noninterfering emissions. However, IR models will not operate out of the line of sight, thus limiting your ability to place and move the unit while maintaining contact with the PC. Ranges are typically restricted to about 30 feet, and operation can be impaired by bright sunlight. IR keyboards can be found on "family room" PCs such as Gateway's Destination line.

RF wireless keyboards, on the other hand, let you work from almost anywhere. With ranges of up to 50 feet, you can type in documents from the next room. However, you'll pay as much as $400 for a decent RF keyboard. No matter which type you use, you'll have to stock up on batteries—both need them to power the small transmitter and keyboard controller.

Multifunction

Here's another area that has become very busy. Multifunction keyboards can be as simple as models with a built-in mouse to products as elaborate as a keyboard scanner or keyboard speaker/audio control combination. Not surprisingly, some of the components built into keyboards fail to match the performance of the best standalone peripherals. An integrated black-and-white sheet-fed scanner, shown in Figure 20.3, won't do for high-resolution color work, and keyboard speakers lack the power of their desktop siblings. You might also have to contend with extra wires attached to the keyboard, which can complicate your desk space.

Input Devices

Figure 20.3.
With its integrated sheet-fed scanner along the top of the keyboard, this NMB Technologies keyboard can help turn your desktop PC into a document center. (Photo courtesy of NMB Technologies.)

There are a number of variations on the multifunction theme. Here are some of the components that may be integrated into a keyboard:

- Sheet-fed scanner

- Speakers, microphone, and audio controls

- Pointing device options

- USB bus ports

- Control keys

- Calculator/clock/display

Many of these options are designed to save valuable desktop space and enhance convenience. A keyboard-integrated scanner, for instance, turns your PC into a powerful document center and makes simple work of scanning documents for faxes. Likewise, an integrated trackball or TrackPoint pointing device eliminates the need for a separate mouse and connecting wire.

USB keyboards forego the PS/2 interface and instead plug into the USB ports that have been shipping on PCs for well over a year now. All keyboard data moves along the USB wire. Because USB allows for daisy-chaining of peripherals, USB keyboards can include their own USB ports, making a handy input for USB joysticks, mice, and other devices.

Other keyboards add little extras. Special control buttons can let you do things such as launch your Internet connection and browser, put your PC into sleep mode, or shut down and power up your PC. Others with LCD display panels, as shown in Figure 20.4, can display the time, results from calculations, and other useful data.

Figure 20.4.

The Focus Electronic FK-8200 EZ Pro keyboard includes an LCD display for the built-in clock and calculator.

20.1.3 Choosing a Keyboard

Nifty gimmicks, advanced buses, and bells and whistles are all well and good. However, ultimately choosing a keyboard is about your personal preference and comfort. If you've been typing on a standard flat-faced keyboard for ten years without a problem, switching to a split-faced model could prove to be more traumatic than you think. At the very least, your productivity will plummet for a week or so as you struggle to relocate keys that have moved from their familiar places.

Look and Feel

So what goes into comfort? First up is the age-old debate of "clicky" versus "mushy" keyboard keys. IBM keyboards (now Lexmark) practically turned clicky keyboards into a branding legend. The issue is with the tactile feedback that the user perceives when typing. When you hit a Lexmark keyboard, there's never a question about whether or not the key input took. An audible, physical click greets every press. This feedback was particularly welcome years ago, when users were more familiar with the responsive action of typewriters.

Many other models take a more subtle approach, ranging from a subtle click to almost no audible response at all. The feel of these devices can vary widely as well. Depending on how the springs are set under the keys, you may perceive little direct contact as you type. The advantage of these models is that typing becomes a much quieter activity—an important consideration if you're in a crowded office or type while talking on the phone.

Input Devices

Key travel is also something to look out for. The travel defines how far down a key can be pressed. Longer travel makes some people feel more secure because they perceive greater tactile feedback, whereas for others it can just become tiring. Typically, the key travel on notebook computers is very limited, because it tends to be on small footprint and wireless keyboards.

You might also want to keep an eye on the keys themselves. Are the tops concave, to help lead your finger into the center of each key? Are the key tops slated toward you at a single angle, or do the furthest keys slant a bit more to aid contact? You might also want to look for keys with roughened surfaces, because slick keys can lead to more mistakes when typing. Finally, tiny nubs on the F and J keys can help you find the home row quickly.

Beyond the keys, you should check out the heftiness of the keyboard. If you play a lot of keyboard-based games, a lightweight keyboard will jump around on the desktop as you try to strafe and shoot. Heavier keyboards tend to provide a more stable feel when doing hours of typing; however, if you like to type with the keyboard on your lap, a compact, lightweight model might be preferable.

Key Layout

We already talked about alternative ergonomic designs, but even among these design types, key layouts can vary. In order to fit their keyboards in small spaces or allow for extra keys, vendors may alter the shape and positioning of peripheral keys. Cursor controls, page controls, function keys, and numeric keypads are all subject to plenty of tweaking.

Microsoft's Natural Keyboard Elite, for example, is a broad, expansive keyboard that happens to shrink virtually all the keys that aren't letters or numbers. It also juggles the position of Page Up/Down, Insert, Delete, and other keys, which can lead to plenty of mistakes. The cursor keys are tiny affairs, which can be a real detriment to gameplay.

Perhaps the most critical aspect is the need to be consistent. If you have one type of keyboard at home, try to use the same at work. I tried switching between a Microsoft Natural Elite and a Dell QuietKey keyboard for about three weeks, and I found myself messing up chronically on both. Eventually, I switched back to the standard model, because I had two of those handy.

Multifunction Capabilities

If you're buying a new keyboard, upgrading can get interesting. If you have a PC with USB ports, you might consider a USB keyboard to start off your collection of USB peripherals. As you add new peripherals to your PC, you'll be able to plug them into convenient ports located on the desktop rather than behind your PC.

Be aware that you'll probably need Windows 98 in order for many of these products to work. Many vendors simply are not anxious to tangle with USB drivers and compatibility issues under Windows 95.

An integrated pointing device is certainly worth considering. Mice are terrible wasters of motion and often lead to back and shoulder strain as users reach across to use them. The Cirque Wave Keyboard 2 keyboard puts a trackpad directly on the split-style keyboard, whereas IBM sells a keyboard that has a TrackPoint device positioned in the middle of the keys.

On the multifunction side, you should be cautious. Keyboard-integrated speakers simply won't match the quality and power of traditional desktop-based models. The positioning of the units is also limited to the width of the keyboard, which may throw off some positional 3D audio schemes that assume the speakers are positioned about six inches off either side of your monitor.

Scanners face a few issues as well. In addition to lagging behind the standalone models, keyboard scanners may actually be less convenient than you think. The high profile of keyboard scanners may block your floppy drive bays if you have the PC sitting horizontally on your desk. In this situation, you'll also be unable to scan cardboard stock straight through, because the document will run into the PC or monitor on its way out.

20.1.4 Ergonomic

Keyboards are at ground zero of the ergonomic debate about PCs. IBM and others have lost high-profile lawsuits that say the keyboard was to blame for career-ending injuries. Today, many keyboards come with a warning sticker or at least documentation about ergonomic use. However with people spending 8, 10, even 12 hours at work furiously typing, it's very difficult to fix the problem. After all, keyboards work because they enable rapid repetition; however, rapid repetition is what causes injury.

The problem is that too many people think a sloped keyboard is going to fix things, when it fact it just changes them. As long you work hours on end without breaks, the risk of repetitive strain injury is present. Although the theory behind the ergonomic designs seems sound, there are plenty of stories that indicate that using these keyboards can sometimes cause problems where none previously existed. Ultimately, you need to rely on your own experience and level of comfort when buying a keyboard. Also, make sure you practice good working habits to allow an ergonomic design to work.

20.1.5 Notebook Keyboards

When you buy a notebook computer, you're buying a keyboard as well. In fact, the keyboard layout is a critical purchase decision, because notebook keyboards

Input Devices

almost always incorporate compromises to fit into the cramped area. Here are some items you'll see on notebook keyboards:

- Half-sized function, cursor, and page keys

- Shrunken primary keys

- Nonstandard cursor and page key layouts

- Multiuse keys, activated by holding down a dedicated Fn key

- Limited key travel and thin key tops

- Integrated trackpad or trackball pointing devices

All these compromises make typing on a notebook a bit more difficult than on a standard desktop keyboard. What's more, the notebook doesn't have a tilt to it, and keypads often face straight up instead of being slightly tilted toward the user. With all that said, notebook keyboards differ widely. You should make a point to try out the keyboard before buying a notebook.

20.2 Understanding Mice and Trackballs

Of course, computing today is as much about pointing and clicking as it is about anything else. In fact, HTML-formatted Web pages basically demand that you sling a mouse or some other device to click through the ubiquitous links. You simply won't get far without a mouse, trackball, or other pointing device, and a bad pointing device can almost be as much of a burden as no mouse at all.

As with keyboards, your choices have expanded a lot in the last few years. Alternative designs have emerged to address repetitive strain concerns, add nifty features, and ease operation in tight spaces. There are even 3D mice for navigating VRML and other 3D environments.

20.2.1 How Pointing Devices Work

Each of these devices work in their own specific way, but all share some key traits. For example, they all create a change in electrical impulses to notify the system of a change in the pointer's status. Also, they all map out the position of the onscreen cursor using relative coordinates so that a nudge to the left is interpreted as just that, regardless of where the onscreen cursor or the pointing device happens to be positioned at the time of the motion.

The ubiquitous pointing device is the mouse, which is basically a plastic housing holding a tacky rubber ball. When the mouse is pushed around on a surface, the ball rolls in its socket. A pair of roller bars, positioned perpendicularly to each other, sit up against the sphere so that when it moves, they move. If the mouse moves forward, the vertical (or Y) roller spins with the ball. If the mouse moves left or right, the horizontal (or X) roller spins.

A motion digitizer reads the turning of the two bars, interpreting them as increments of travel (measured in hundredths of an inch). A controller inside the mouse sends the digitized signals to the PC, telling it how to update the onscreen cursor to reflect the movement. As mentioned before, the mouse tracks based on relative position—it has no idea where the cursor is on the screen.

Today, most mice detect motion to a precision of $\frac{1}{400}$th of an inch, four times the resolution provided by desktop rodents about five years ago. Although this is far more resolution that most users will ever require, it's handy to have if you find yourself working with detailed graphics, CAD, or other precise applications that require lots of precise mouse work.

A few mice forego the physical rollers in place of optical sensors, which detect motion based on changes in laser light reflected off a special mouse pad. These mice have no moving parts, which eliminates concern about gummed up mouse balls; however, they do require a special mouse pad that must be kept in clean condition. Dents or nicks in the reflective pad can return spurious positional data, causing cursor fits.

Other devices work on similar principals but vary in the way the actual commands are captured. For example, trackpads sense disruptions in the uniform conductivity of the trackpad surface. When you touch the pad or drag your finger across it, sensors detect the position of the conductivity change, which it can interpret as relative movement. IBM's TrackPoint works like a tiny joystick, with contacts at the bottom of the eraser-like nub sending an electrical signal that the controller can understand.

Of course, no mouse is complete without buttons, and you'll usually find two or three of these on the top of most mice. Like the roller bars, these buttons have sensors that send a signal each time they are pressed or released. Virtually all non-mouse pointing devices include two or more buttons as well.

20.2.2 Types of Pointing Devices

There are several types of pointing devices for PCs, including (in more or less declining order of popularity) the following:

- Mouse

- Trackball

- Trackpad

- IBM TrackPoint

- 3D mouse

Several of these devices are primarily intended for the notebook market, where pointing becomes serious business indeed. However, even these portable pointers—including trackballs, trackpads, and TrackPoint devices—have all been adapted to varying levels of desktop service.

The Mouse

At this point, the mouse has been pretty well introduced already. Overall, it affords the best balance of control and precision, in part because of the wide field of operation (the mouse pad) that these devices enjoy. Although the standard-issue, two-button PS/2 mouse remains very popular, changes have and are occurring.

For one thing, many models now sport curved designs intended to provide support and comfort. Microsoft really kicked things off with its Mouse 2.0, which replaced the original Microsoft Mouse that had gained the moniker "dovebar" for its shape. Mouse 2.0 features a high, rounded rear portion that slopes down to the two buttons at the front. The intent is to support the palm during operation so that users do not strain to keep their wrist clear of the mouse pad. However, southpaws worldwide took issue with the right-hand orientation of the mouse (Microsoft asserts that its design is equally effective for lefties as well).

More useful was the introduction of the Microsoft Intellimouse, shown in Figure 20.5, which adds a small wheel to the two buttons atop the mouse's back. The rubber wheel is used for scrolling through Web pages, spreadsheets, and documents without having to move the cursor over to the vertical scroll bars at the right edge of the application. In addition to in-place scrolling, the button can be pushed to enable access to alternate scroll controls; however, I've found it far too easy to accidentally activate the push control and have long since turned that feature off.

Figure 20.5.

The Microsoft Intellimouse built on the success of the Mouse 2.0 design by adding a scrolling wheel for navigating documents.

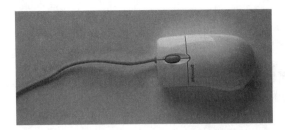

Others have joined in. Logitech's MouseMan Plus includes a scroll wheel similar to the Intellimouse, whereas IBM has incorporated its TrackPoint design into a mouse. Users simply nudge the tiny eraser head forward or back to scroll the page, eliminating the troublesome fingering required to spin the Microsoft mouse wheel.

Trackballs

The most popular mouse alternative, trackballs, are simply mice turned on their backs (see Figure 20.6). Most are designed around the same ball-and-rollers mechanics found in mice—the difference is that the roller ball is sticking halfway out of the top of the device. You simply spin the ball with your thumb, and the rollers inside the trackball sense the action and report it to the PC.

Figure 20.6.
The Logitech TrackMan Marble+ lets you point in place. (Photo courtesy of Logitech.)

Although most trackballs are designed to sit on desktops, smaller ones are found built into some notebooks. There's even a tiny notebook add-on trackball with a ball the size of a BB, allowing you to mouse around without needing a flat surface. For children, Microsoft makes a colorful, oversized trackball designed to appeal to tiny hands. In between, you'll find products such as Logitech's TrackMan Marble, which features a marble-sized ball and three buttons along the right-front edge.

Trackballs have a couple advantages over mice. One, they can reduce repetitive strain injuries by eliminating reaching and stretching from the shoulder. Two, they don't pick up grime from a mouse pad or other surface, thus reducing the need to clean out the innards.

However, there are reasons why people don't use trackballs. The thumb is the least-dexterous finger, which makes it difficult to precisely move the cursor using most trackballs. It's also much more difficult to hold down a button while wagging your thumb back and forth over the ball, making simple actions such as clicking and dragging quite difficult.

As with any input device, personal preference is the overriding factor. If a trackball device feels good to you, then it's probably a good choice. However,

Input Devices

you'll want to consider your applications. Notebook users will want a small trackball that they can hold in one hand, whereas desktops users will want something with a stable base. Useful features include a drag toggle button that lets you select an item and drag it across the desktop without having to keep pressure on a button when rolling the ball.

Trackpads

Trackpads have become standard issue on many notebooks, thanks to their low cost, small footprint, and utter lack of moving parts. These little black squares serve as your finger's mouse pad, letting you literally point with your index finger to move the cursor onscreen.

Although trackpads don't get gummed up with grime, there is a downside: Your finger is a fairly inexact pointing device. TrackPoint driven cursors tend to jump around a bit if you rotate the end of your finger on the pad, and using the pad in conjunction with buttons can get tricky. Still, these devices present the smallest and thinnest footprint of any pointing device, making them perfect companions on the road. You can also find trackpads built directly into keyboards, as shown in Figure 20.7, or sold as a separate device.

Figure 20.7.
By integrating a trackpad into an ergonomic keyboard design, the Cirque Wave Keyboard 2 saves space. (Photo courtesy of Cirque Corporation.)

TrackPoint

Another popular notebook pointing device is the IBM TrackPoint. Essentially an eraser-size nub that sits in the middle of the keyboard, the TrackPoint's main advantage is that it eliminates all the furious wagging and dragging of fingers required by other devices. Rather, you simply apply pressure on the nub, pointing it in the direction you want to go. Resistors at the base are able to sense contact pressure to speed or slow the rate of travel—a useful touch.

TrackPoints are to be found on all IBM ThinkPad notebook PCs, as well as on some IBM keyboards. The company is also integrating its pointer into a scrolling mouse, which could make it a superior design to the popular Microsoft Intellimouse.

3D Mice

Now for something completely different. Diamond Multimedia, Logitech, and other vendors have released so-called *3D mice*, which use a gyroscope to track the presence of the device in the air. Hardly useful for your typical spreadsheet, 3D mice are terrific for everything from VRML browsing environments to delving the corridors of games such as Descent. Unlike other pointing devices, which can go only forward, back, left, and right, 3D mice also enable up and down control, thus providing six degrees of freedom.

The Diamond GyroMouse sits on a base unit, which recognizes pressure in all six directions (left, right, front, back, up, and down). To move up in a 3D environment, just pull the hand unit upward; to move down, press the unit down toward the base. However, keep in mind that these exotic devices make poor substitutes for normal mice and trackballs in standard business applications.

20.3 Gaming Devices

When it comes to controllers, no one cares as passionately as a gamer. The thin line between victory and humiliating defeat can often be drawn straight from your joystick or game controller. Get a stick with the right set of controls, programmable features, and hardy construction, and you'll enjoy an immediate edge over your competition in flight sims, death-match shootouts, street fights, and all other fast-action games.

What's more, times are changing in this market. Microsoft-driven standards are making advanced game controller features affordable and universally supported, whereas USB is paving a digital path to these devices for enhanced performance. Figure 20.8 shows the variety of controllers available by just one company, Thrustmaster.

Figure 20.8.
There's a wide variety of game input devices to suit almost every genre, such as the family of devices from Thrustmaster. (Photo courtesy of Thrustmaster Corp.)

Input Devices

20.3.1 How Game Controllers Work

Game controllers aren't that far removed from pointing devices in the way they work. Whether it's a joystick, a game pad, or a steering column, all these peripherals create electrical variances that are interpreted as positional or command data for PC games and software. In effect, they are glorified pointing devices, crafted in shapes that provide instant access to a wide range of controls as well as resemble the equipment found in jet cockpits or other vehicles.

By far the most pervasive and well-supported game controller is the joystick. Its popularity on the PC got an early boost from the phenomenal and ongoing success of Microsoft's Flight Simulator, and later from a rich field of combat flight sims. Unlike many other games that benefit from dedicated controllers, flight simulators are virtually impossible to play effectively from the keyboard.

Joysticks are pretty simple. You move the stick to initiate motion, and a selection of buttons and other controls let you fire weapons and send game commands. The action happens at the base of the stick, where four resistors make contact with leads on the stick when it's pushed. The further you push forward, the greater the rate of change. Sensors check the resistance and report changes in the attitude of the stick. Driver software turns the signals into program-specific commands for down, up, left, right, and so on.

Until recently, virtually all joysticks plugged into the MIDI/game port found on the back of most sound cards. The CPU constantly polls the game port, interpreting the changes in the analog electrical signals into positional information. Although the connection is simple and universal, the lack of a digital component in the joystick means that the processor must wait on the joystick hand and foot.

It's no surprise that all this hand holding comes at a cost. The time spent polling the game port saps CPU cycles, thus stealing as much as 10 to 15 percent of the processor's performance. That's a huge penalty when your system is already straining to keep up with the demands of a modern 3D flight simulator.

Newer joysticks and game controllers have switched to a digital connection, adding a processor and memory buffer to the mechanisms inside the housing. The internal processor digitizes the electrical input and stores the values in the local buffer, which the device sends to the system over a wire. Because data is being actively sent to the CPU, it no longer needs to waste time waiting for input. Voilà, instant gains in frame rates and responsiveness.

20.3.2 Types of Game Devices

There are a wide variety of game controllers for every flavor of game software. The main problem is the limited usefulness of many of these products. A steering column, for example, is only really useful for car racing games, whereas a joystick really won't help you much when playing Mortal Combat or Quake II. For this reason, it's important to consider what games you enjoy and play the most, and then equip yourself appropriately.

Certainly the most fertile ground for game controller devices is in the area of flight simulation. Joysticks, flight yokes, rudder peddles, and throttle controls are all oriented specifically at flight and combat simulators. The additional controls add substantial realism to game play, as users enjoy the added control, complexity, and realism of manually coordinating rudder movements—something that the software often does for you because most systems are not equipped for the task.

Joysticks

As the quintessential game controller, joysticks have already been pretty well covered and described earlier. However, joysticks, themselves, are changing, and users can find a wide selection of these products on the market. Among the joystick innovations to look for are the following:

- Digital connections over USB or game ports

- Force-feedback interaction

- Programmable features

- Extended controls

Go Digital

Certainly, anyone considering a new joystick needs to make sure they go digital. Cheap analog models will waste CPU cycles and degrade system performance. What's more, these older devices fall victim to drift, requiring periodic recalibration of the sensors in order to maintain precise control. For over a year now, Microsoft, CH Products, Logitech, and others have been selling digital joysticks that run off the standard game/MIDI port. Also, USB versions of the products are starting to come out as well. USB joysticks provide the added benefit of letting you plug into any port, thus allowing you to plug and unplug the hardware without having to manually initialize drivers.

If you intend to buy a digital joystick for your MIDI/game port, you'll want to make sure you don't run into problems. Many PCI audio cards have problems working with digital joysticks. You should check with the soundboard and joystick vendors before you make a purchase to ensure that your existing and new hardware will be compatible.

Input Devices

Feel the Force

Force-feedback technology is a big hit in the gaming market, and no wonder. These joysticks incorporate small motors that activate in response to code in the software, creating tactile response to events such as turbulence, gunfire, aircraft damage, and the like. This compelling technology adds a new dimension to game play, although force feedback capability adds $100 or more to the cost of a joystick. You'll also find these sticks are bulky, heavy, and require a separate power cord (see Figure 20.9).

Of course, force-feedback devices require additional data to be sent between the game and the hardware. In most cases, an additional serial cable is used; however, Microsoft makes use of the MIDI data pin on the game/MIDI port to handle this transaction. The problem is that the Microsoft Force-Feedback Pro will not work with most dedicated game port cards, such as CH's Gamecard III Automatic.

Figure 20.9.

Microsoft's Sidewinder Force-Feedback Pro will put some kick into your games, but you'll have to dig deep into your pockets to afford it.

If you're thinking about buying a force-feedback joystick, consider one that supports Immersion Technologies I-Force 2.0 standard. Microsoft's Sidewinder Force-Feedback Pro provides only limited application support because it uses a proprietary API. Immersion's API is fully compatible with DirectInput, the controller API used in DirectX 5.0 and later. Microsoft has announced that future force-feedback products will support DirectInput.

Programmability and Control

Don't overlook the benefit of extended features with your joystick. You can enjoy enhanced control of complex aircraft by making use of features such as throttle wheels, multiple selection buttons, and a hat control for switching cockpit views. For instance, Advance Gravis Firebird 2 provides four buttons on the handle and another nine on the base.

Better sticks will let you program in behaviors for your specific games, thus allowing you to use the same buttons for weapons selection, for example, no matter which combat flight sim you're using. In addition, many let you use buttons to access multiple commands when used in conjunction with a keyboard Shift or Ctrl key, for example. Better still, look for controllers that let you download configurations to apply to specific games. These devices let you to play immediately by optimizing your controller for your current game without the tedious trial-and-error programming of individual buttons.

Game Pads

Game pads are critical for playing fighting sims, sports games, and arcade-style racers and flight games. The simple yet immediate X-Y disc and accessible action buttons let you invoke complex punch and weapon combinations in an instant. For anyone who has strained to reach far-flung control keys on a keyboard while in the heat of battle, game pads are a terrific solution.

Like joysticks, these devices plug into your game port and are very simple to set up and use. Also, newer models are introducing digital controls to enhance responsiveness, system performance, and precision. Logitech's ThunderPad Digital, shown in Figure 20.10, is a good example.

Figure 20.10.

The Logitech ThunderPad Digital uses a digital connection and all the classic game pad controls to offer rapid-fire command over your games. (Photo courtesy of Logitech.)

Input Devices

Other devices

There are a variety of other input devices, including the following:

- Steering columns

- Flight yokes

- Throttles

- Foot pedals for automobiles and aircraft

- Pistols

Virtually all of these products vie for attention on your soundboard's game/Midi port. Because your game port can support a pair of devices, you're able to mix and match controllers to your specific gaming needs. Therefore, a throttle control might make a perfect match for the force-feedback joystick, or you might ditch the joystick for driving games and go with a combination of a steering column and foot pedals.

Although your game port can support two devices, only a single port is available. You'll need a Y-splitter to allow two devices to plug into the game port. In the case of packaged products—such as Thrustmaster's T2 steering column and foot pedals—the devices come with a splitter built in. If you want to work with a joystick/throttle/pedal combination, you may need to use a keyboard pass-through connector, which enables the third device to send commands to the software via the keyboard.

CH Products and Thrustmaster both offer a broad selection of genre-specific controllers.

Game Input Accessories

Finally, there's a whole class of input accessories for gamers. Many of these products allow you to run multiple input devices at once, rectifying one of the PC's greatest weaknesses—the inability to allow two people to play head to head. CH Products' Y Cable lets you plug two joysticks into the Midi/game port, for example, whereas the Gamecard 3 shown in figure 20.11 puts a pair of game ports on a dedicated ISA card.

In addition to splitter cables and game cards, extension cables increase the reach of your game devices. Finally, multiport switch boxes are useful for selecting among several installed game devices. This is a real benefit if you're a serious gamer, because it eliminates the need to fish around behind your PC every time you switch games.

Figure 20.11.
CH Products' Game Card 3 expands your controller options by adding a pair of game ports to your PC. (Photo courtesy of CH Products.)

20.4 Tom's Pick

Picking a game controller is a profoundly personal decision. As with any input device, user preference and comfort is the driving factor. Certainly, novice players will be intimidated by the complexity (and cost) of the most advanced force-feedback joysticks. By the same token, serious combat sim fans will eschew the Microsoft SideWinder series for the realistic flight stick feel of CH Product's F16 Flight Stick.

Our pick in this area is clear: Microsoft's SideWinder Force-Feedback Pro is the most versatile, general-purpose joystick on the market. The stick is big, heavy, and fairly expensive at $200. However, it offers a decent selection of buttons and controls—including a built-in wheel that can serve as a throttle—and the ability to accept programmed and downloaded button assignments. Microsoft's Profiler utility, while a bit difficult to work with, lets you customize your joystick for each specific game—a big plus when it comes to mastering advanced interfaces.

The SideWinder is both attractive and durable. The optical position sensors don't wear the way traditional electrical contacts do, and the digital system eliminates the annoyance of recalibrating the stick every so often. Of course, digital operation means lower CPU usage and smoother game play. Microsoft uses the existing MIDI/game port to handle the digital force-feedback connection, which eliminates the need for a separate serial cable. However, some dedicated game

Input Devices

cards may lack the circuitry to work with the product—so be careful when shopping.

Perhaps most important, Microsoft is supporting industry standard force-feedback technologies in its joystick. Both Immersion's I-Force and Microsoft's own force-feedback technologies will work with the hardware, thus providing the widest range of game compatibility.

Chapter

21

Cases and Power Supplies

Not everything that goes on in your PC involves high-tech wizardry and submicron engineering. In order to make that 400MHz processor and 16GB hard disk drive go, you need support for the rank and file. Power supplies must provide a steady and reliable stream of electricity to components, even as power demands rise and fall. Backup power and surge protectors ensure that your expensive hardware doesn't get fried in the next summer thunderstorm. Finally, truly mundane items such as system cases ensure adequate cooling, protection from dirt, and elimination of interfering electrical signals.

Here are the three items discussed in this chapter:

- Power supplies
- Backup power and surge protectors
- System cases

Whether you're building your own systems or perhaps upgrading an existing one, these not-so-sexy components play a critical role in completing the PC.

21.1 Power Supplies

Although it's neither high-tech nor sexy, the power supply is critical to the reliable and extended operation of your PC. Unfortunately, many popular systems save a buck by skimping on the power supply. As a result, you may be facing trouble down the road if you decide to add disk drives or other power consuming peripherals (see Figure 21.1).

Figure 21.1.

The Emko JS-200ATX power supply provides 200 watts of power in a shape that should fit any ATX-style motherboard and compliant case.

If you want to add tape drives, DVD-ROM drives, and other hardware to your PC, you should think seriously about improving the power supply in your system. At the very least, you should keep an eye on its specified output to make sure you're not outstripping the supply's capability to keep up with the demands of your onboard components. Remember, not all power supplies work for all systems—you'll need to make sure you find hardware that's compatible with your system.

21.1.1 How Power Supplies Work

A power supply is a relatively simple device that consists of a fan, a magnetic coil, and resistors and capacitors for stepping voltages of incoming electricity. The surrounding metal case protects the insides from dirt, shields electromagnetic frequency (EMF) radiation, and prevents potentially deadly electric shock to the user. Several cables run from the power supply, connecting to the system motherboard and various disk drives as well as other storage peripherals.

The power supply plugs into a standard 110-volt wall outlet from which it draws electricity. The cord is always a three-pronged, grounded wire to ensure that excess electricity is safely drawn off to prevent damage to the power supply and onboard components. The incoming electricity must be processed from 110 or 240 volts to the 5 volts or even 3.3 volts used by your system components. (Many supplies are actually switchable, allowing you to use them in different countries.) Your power supply handles this critical task, stepping down the voltage to match your motherboard's needs.

The process of stepping down voltage produces heat, which the power supply expels out the back of the chassis using a small fan. This fan serves a dual purpose—it provides airflow inside the PC that draws cool outside air through the front bezel of the system and evacuates the warm inside air out the back (refer to Figure 21.2).

Unfortunately, as a constantly moving part exposed to lots of dirt and heat, the fan is often the first part on the power supply to go bad. If you notice that the power supply fan is not working or is making a louder-than-normal noise, you should replace the supply right away. Power supplies are so inexpensive (about $50 for a nice model) and servicing them is dangerous enough that it makes sense to simply replace a failing supply.

Cases and Power Supplies

Figure 21.2.
The large fan outlet is clearly visible on the back of this compact NMB Technologies SPW-1004, a 200-watt power supply designed to fit into slimline NLX-style cases and motherboards.

21.1.2 Buying a Power Supply

Power supplies vary in their output (measured in watts) as well as in their shape, airflow, and noise production. When looking for a power supply, here are some things to consider:

- Power output

- Form factor

- Airflow

- Noise output

- Redundancy

You might not even be considering a new supply, but you could end up facing such a purchase should a problem arise. Here are a few things to consider when buying time approaches:

- First, be on the lookout for trouble. Random reboots, memory glitches, and lockups are all typical symptoms of failing power. If you see these problem arise, you should suspect the power supply.

- Buy more than you need. A larger power supply not only provides headroom for additional peripherals, it runs cooler and better than one running at full tilt. Power supplies actually perform best when run at 25 to 75 percent of their rated capacity.

- To prevent problems with your hard disk drives, consider a power supply with independent regulation and extra cooling.

- Suspect your current OEM supply. PC manufacturers typically skimp on the power supplies, installing under-powered ones in their systems.

Power Output

The most important factor is power output—this determines how much hardware the supply is able to support. When you buy a system, the strength of the supply is often determined by the type of case. Larger cases, such as towers, often feature more powerful supplies to support the large number of drives often found in these types of PCs. Table 21.1 shows the typical power output of supplies found in different types of PCs.

Table 21.1. Typical output of power supplies found in different types of systems.

PC Type	Power Output
Slimline	100 to 150 watts
Standard desktop	150 to 200 watts
Minitower	150 to 250 watts
Full tower	250 to 300 watts

As you can see, a slimline desktop PC may have one-half to one-third the power output capacity of a supply found inside a full-sized tower. Usually, this doesn't pose a problem, because the small, "pizza box" chassis in these PCs simply can't accommodate enough components to outstrip the power supply. However, you can run into trouble if you decide to upgrade your system motherboard or move your components into a new, larger case. In these instances, sticking with the original power supply can invite problems, because you may load up on more internal peripherals than the supply was ever expected to support.

If you're buying a power-oriented system, I suggest you get a supply that can put out at least 250 watts. This is a bit more than the typical 200-watt unit found in many popular midtower PCs, but it affords some valuable headroom for expansion. If you intend to load up a PC with drives and expansion cards, consider stretching for a 250- to 300-watt model.

What happens when you need more wattage than your power supply is designed to deliver? Usually, nothing—at least, not right away. However, the stress placed on this supply will eventually cause it to run hot as it struggles to produce sufficient power for the system. Over time—how much depends on the amount of strain—the overheating supply will lose efficiency and simply fall behind the electrical draw of the components.

When this happens, voltages to your components will lag or fluctuate. All of a sudden, those crisp digital 1s and 0s, which are all based on the presence or absence of a specific voltage threshold, start to get muddied and unclear. Then you'll see all the classic symptoms of a power problem—memory errors, data loss, and random shutdowns, lockups, and reboots. When things get really severe, the system may shut down altogether and fail to start up successfully (for example, it may get through the BIOS bootstrap and POST routines but then fail when the power-hungry disk drives are activated).

In general, compact systems draw less power than tower PCs, because they simply hold fewer drives and add-in cards—components that draw power during operation. Of course, external devices such as monitors, scanners, and printers draw their power independent of the PC, making them a nonfactor in power consumption.

Form Factor

Motherboard space is a valuable commodity, so power supplies must be designed to fit inside the case without blocking or contacting components on the board. For this reason, you need to make sure that the power supply you purchase is designed to fit in your PC. Most new desktop and minitower systems, for example, use the ATX form factor specification. As long as you buy an ATX power supply, you should have no problem mating the supply with your motherboard and case.

Your best bet is to try to match your new power supply to the one that already fits into your PC. Measure the power supply housing in all three dimensions; then see if you can't find products that are a match. Most supplies comply with a handful of size formats, including the following.

- Baby AT format: 8.35"×5.9"×5.9"

- Desktop format: 8.35"×5.5"×3.4"

- ATX or slimline format: 5.9"×5.5"×3.4"

- Tower format: 8.35"×5.9"×5.9"

- Custom format: Varies

If you own a compact desktop system, you may face a challenge. Slimline PCs from vendors such as Hewlett-Packard, Compaq, and IBM often use custom power supplies designed to fit into the tight spaces of these machines. The lack of a standard design means that you may have only one source for a replacement supply—the vendor who built the system. In general, you can expect to pay more for a nonstandard power supply, which is yet another reason to avoid slimline systems.

There is some good news in this area. Intel and others have crafted standard motherboard layouts for compact desktops that are very popular among corporations. The NLX and LPX form factors provide for low-profile desktop designs, including the use of vertical riser cards (in the case of NLX) for holding add-in boards. These specifications also allow for standard power supply form factors, which should ease some of the restrictive issues in this part of the market.

Enhanced Power Supplies

Once you've got a power supply with enough muscle and the proper form factor, your work is done, right? Not necessarily. There are actually a wide variety of supplies designed to handle many different roles. Network servers, for example, might need to guarantee operation even if a power supply should fail outright. Crowded offices might demand extra-quiet operation, whereas high-end PCs might require high air flow to ensure cool operation.

Here's a list of some of the power supply enhancements you might consider:

- Dual or redundant power supplies
- High airflow designs
- Extra-quiet operation
- Line-conditioning supplies

Redundant power supplies are attractive for anyone doing mission critical work, whether it's running a network or Web server, or executing large processes on a desktop workstation. In essence, these products put two power supplies into a single module. If one should fail, the other is at hand and ready to take over. Unlike backup power supplies, which use battery power to give the PC enough time to shut down, redundant power supplies are able to run indefinitely on the second module (refer to Figure 21.3).

Even single desktop PCs can benefit from extra-quiet, high-airflow power supplies. These products will reduce the noise produced by the supply and ensure that proper cooling is provided for your internal components. You'll pay an extra $20 or so for these features, but depending on your work environment, they could be well worth it.

Figure 21.3.

The Two-In-One 500 power supply from PC Power and Cooling puts two 250-watt supplies into a single unit.

Quiet-running models can cut the noise output of a typical power supply significantly. Where a normal unit might produce 45 to 50 decibels of sound during operation, a quiet-running power supply will cut that figure to 35dB. Quiet power supplies are critical for desktop PCs, where the power supply is in your face, as well as for offices with several PCs.

Line-conditioning, finally, is a useful feature found in many power supplies. These units actually monitor and treat the incoming power, smoothing out spikes and sags and otherwise ensuring that the supply does not fall victim to the stress incurred by dirty power. In a sense, these devices provide some of the services found in power backup and surge protection devices.

21.2 Surge Protectors

Surge protectors are an almost universal piece of hardware, used by many for the simple reason that six or more power outlets are now available in proximity to the PC. Unfortunately, most people don't understand that a surge protector plays an absolutely vital role in protecting data and equipment. What's more, the majority of surge protectors being used either lack enough protection or have long since lost their protective abilities, meaning that they are of little use in the case of a power surge.

21.2.1 How Surge Protectors Work

A surge protector plugs into the wall outlet and presents four, six, or more outlets for your components to plug into. The device acts as an electrical weight station, checking the quality and character of incoming electricity and ensuring that too much juice doesn't assault your hardware. Better surge devices offer line-conditioning features, which smooth out sags or dips in the power flow, though most inexpensive products only handle overcharges—called *spikes*.

When an overcharged voltage comes through the wire, a component in the surge protector, metal-oxide varistor (MOV), clamps down on the line and draws away the excess energy. This electricity is immediately dissipated via the ground wire, preventing it from ever reaching your PC's power supply. The MOV component is designed to act at a specific threshold, draining away any electricity in excess of its rated value.

Unfortunately, exposure to electrical surges and spikes degrades the MOV components. Over time, or even after one or two big hits, the surge protector loses its ability to dissipate overcharges, resulting in complete loss of protection. Most protectors, therefore, include an indicator light that indicates when the varistor has been spent. When this happens, you need to replace the surge device in order to regain electrical protection.

21.2.2 Buying a Surge Protector

When buying for a surge protector, you should look for the following features:

- Rated protection (measured in joules)
- Number of outlets
- RJ-11 jacks for phone and modems
- Line-conditioning features
- Bundled insurance for hardware loss
- Audible surge alarm

The most important factor is the rated protection, because some surge protectors are able to stop larger spikes than others. The power rating is expressed in *joules*, a unit of energy measurement, with higher numbers indicating better protection. At a minimum, make sure your suppressor is rated to no less than 240 joules, and buy greater protection if possible.

One nice thing to check for is the presence of a hard cutoff on the surge suppressor. Should a catastrophic spike occur (for example, during a nearby lightning strike), a suppressor with a hard cutoff will be able to physically break the circuit before the spike can arc through the device and destroy your hardware. In these severe cases, a good suppressor lacking this feature will not be able to dissipate all the energy in time.

You'll want to make sure any surge protector has enough receptacles for your needs and that they are spaced to accommodate power blocks that will otherwise block two or three outlets. In addition, some models include RJ-11 jack connectors for protecting your modem, fax machine, and phones from power spikes (see Figure 21.4).

If you live in a building with older wiring or feel that the power flow varies a lot, consider a model that provides limited line-conditioning. Although these products can't supplement the incoming power—they lack their own power source to do this—they can smooth out mild spikes and filter out unwanted noise in the cyclic power signal. These features can help prolong the life of your PC's power supply by eliminating chronic, low-level stress on the components.

Figure 21.4.

The Belkin SurgeMaster II includes ports for your modem or telephone, as well as spaced receptacles for accommodating large power blocks.

Finally, always look for an insurance guarantee when buying a surge protector. Many companies warrant their products with up to $25,000 worth of coverage. Therefore, if a lightning strike or other event results in the loss of your hardware—and the surge protector failed to stop the damage while properly installed—your losses will be covered.

21.3 Uninterruptible Power Supply

Better than a surge protector—and more expensive—is an *uninterruptible power supply (UPS)*. This device not only performs all the tasks of a surge protector, but it also features a built-in battery that provides temporary power to your PC should a blackout occur (see Figure 21.5). This device is a terrific boon for users who value their hard-earned data, because a sudden blackout can result in the loss of hours of work. What's more, these kind of power surprises can disable a system altogether, corrupting system files on the hard disk and even frying the CPU or RAM.

Figure 21.5.

The compact Back-UPS Office from American Power Conversion provides power and telephone surge protection as well as backup power.

21.3.1 How a UPS Works

A UPS is a combination surge protector and backup power supply. Like a surge protector, it sits between your PC and the wall outlet, serving as an intermediary in the electrical circuit running to your PC. The device, itself, is usually a bit larger than a standard surge protector, which allows for the presence of backup batteries and often an informational display. One or more ports may be included that allow the device to communicate with your PC or the network.

Inside, a UPS includes all the components found in a surge protector, including the metal-oxide varistor for dissipating surges through a ground wire. Better backup devices will also include a hard cutoff for disabling the physical circuit in the event of a catastrophic spike from a lightning strike or other event.

Where the UPS gets interesting is in its ability to keep your PC afloat even during prolonged power outages and brownouts. One or more batteries sit in line on the electrical circuit and automatically step in when power drops off. After power comes back on, the drained batteries trickle charge by drawing slightly from the incoming power.

If your UPS is properly matched with the PC, it should provide at least 10 minutes of operation before the batteries run out. That gives you enough time to save your documents and shut down all running applications before turning off the PC. Better models include software that automatically starts the process of shutting everything down whenever the battery is activated. A serial, USB, or network connection provides the digital connection to the PC or server.

The amount of available battery power is expressed in the UPS's voltage-ampere rating, or *VA*. For a typical desktop system, consider 250 VA a good minimum, although you'll want a higher rating for a system with multiple hard disk drives, RAID arrays, and the like.

Many UPSs work even when the power seems to be fine. The device monitors the incoming power, conditioning it to remove unwanted spikes, sags, interruptions, and other problems in the power flow. These problems are common in buildings with older wiring, for example, or when your system is running on the same circuit with an air conditioner, refrigerator, or other appliance that can overdraw the circuit (see Figure 21.6).

Figure 21.6.

The American Power Conversion Back-UPS line provides line-conditioning for a variety of desktop PC requirements.

Line-conditioning makes use of the online battery to augment the current from the outlet when it falls short. In addition, the UPS provides the same noise reduction features found in many surge protectors, squelching unwanted signals in the electrical cycle.

> **WARNING**   When using a UPS, avoid plugging unnecessary peripherals such as laser printers or monitors into it. These power-drawing devices will dramatically decrease the time the batteries can support your PC, thus imperiling your data.

21.3.2 Types of UPS Devices

There are three types of UPS devices that define the way a UPS interacts with the power stream:

- Standby UPS

- Online UPS

- Line-interactive UPS

Standby UPS

The least expensive UPS does little more than provide battery backup. Power flows straight from the wall, through the UPS, and to your system. However, because the battery is not directly involved in the power transfer, standby UPSs take longer than other types to kick in. This delay in getting battery power fed to the PC can be enough to cause some systems to shut down or lose data.

The good news is that most newer systems are able to handle the transition. In fact, many power supplies can hold up to 100ms (a tenth of a second) of power in reserve, more than enough time for this hand off. However, if such transitions happen frequently, they will stress the power supply, possibly shortening its useful life.

Online UPS

Online UPSs actively manage the incoming power, flattening out spikes and sags and eliminating unwanted noise in the signal. When voltage sags, the UPS battery jumps in to make up the difference, something that surge suppressors cannot do. In fact, if your building has unreliable or "dirty" power, a line-conditioning online UPS will extend the life of your system and possibly resolve mysterious crashes and data loss.

The path the electricity takes is a bit different than in standby models—it runs into the battery and out through an inverter, which converts DC power to AC format. Because the battery is already an active component in the power stream, transitions from normal to battery power is nearly instantaneous.

Online UPSs cost a bit more than their standby counterparts, and you'll find that the batteries in these products wear more quickly than on standby models. On some models, if a battery does go dead, you'll find that the UPS will no longer pass power through to your PC. For this reason, you should make sure you get a unit that includes a pass-through feature that lets you take the battery out of the circuit when needed.

Line-Interactive UPS

The most recent UPS innovation provides line-conditioning services without relying on battery power. These line-interactive UPSs cover voltage sags by pulling more electricity from the outlet. Because they don't draw on the battery to make up power shortages, the battery in line-interactive UPSs will last longer than those in online models.

Although line-interactive models cost less than online products, they provide inferior conditioning because of the lack of an active power source. These devices can pull only so much out of the line.

21.3.3 Other Features

There are other features to look out for, including advanced monitoring and communications capabilities. Line-monitoring, for example, provides real-time data on the power stream, keeping a history of voltages and power cleanliness. This can be particularly useful for troubleshooting problems and determining the source and frequency of power problems. You should also look for UPSs that provide a status on battery power so that you know how long the batteries will last before running down.

Connectivity features are particularly useful for IS professionals. Remote management software enables network administrators to track and control UPS activity over a network or modem using standard SNMP capability. Some devices can also send out power status messages, including shutdown notification, via pager, email, and fax. This feature provides critical, time-sensitive warnings to IS managers so that they can react to power outages. Although these features are nice, most small-office or home users can probably do without them.

21.4 System Cases

The final piece of any system is the case—the cover that encloses the system motherboard and other components. The case plays an important role in containing and protecting system components. Of course, the case needs to fit the motherboard and chassis. There are several standard systems sizes (with cases to match):

- Slimline
- Desktop
- Minitower
- Midtower
- Tower

You'll need to check the motherboard documentation and specs to make sure your case will fit (see Figure 21.7).

Figure 21.7.
*This system chassis from Addtronics (*http://www.wco.com/~addtron/*) is designed to fit compact, NLx factor motherboards.*

21.4.1 Functional Duties

The case cover does more than offer aesthetics; it provides important protection against wear and tear on the internal components. Hot-running components such as the CPU get more effective cooling when the case is tightly shut, because fans in the power supply and often in the front grillwork are better able to channel direct airflow over the CPU. In fact, many new cases include plastic scoops to channel air directly onto the heat sink.

An open chassis limits the ability of the case fans to draw in and focus airflow on critical components. In a warm room, the stagnant air around the processor could lead to overheating problems. In fact, some corporate PCs won't even boot without the cover attached.

The case also helps keep dust, dirt, and grime off your internal components. This is particularly a concern for midtower and tower systems sitting on the floor, where the most dust is likely to gather. If dust gathers in the expansion card slots, it can prevent good contact between the leads of the card and the bus slot. Dirt and dust can also gum up fans and trap heat on components such as RAM chips, again inviting thermal problems. A secure case will limit accumulation of particles, although you'll still want to clear the motherboard once in a while with a shot of compressed air.

The case has another function—serving as an EMF shield for your PC. The CPU, RAM, and disk drives all emit a good deal of EMF radiation, which can interfere with radios and TVs. PC cases are shielded to block these signals, thus preventing reception problems. If you have an open PC case and are noticing problems with reception on a nearby radio, it's possible that EMF from the system is the source of the problem. Try sealing the case or moving the radio to see if that alleviates the problem.

Finally, you'll want a case that's good and durable. When looking at a cover, try standing it up by itself. Notice whether the case bends or sags. Also try grasping the ends of the case and twisting it a bit. Does the material give very easily? This is a particular concern for desktops, which are often called upon to bear the weight of a 15- or 17-inch monitor—a load of as much as 40 pounds.

21.4.2 Convenience Features

Better PC cases offer a number of conveniences that can ease upgrades, enhance system access, and even help you avoid injury. Some ATX designs, for example, feature a removable motherboard back that allows you to easily remove and replace the motherboard. Likewise, screwless designs let you loosen the case attachment using a simple thumbscrew or tabs, eliminating the need for tools and the possibility of losing tiny case screws.

Unfortunately, eliminating screws won't ensure that the case is easy to remove. Many cases can prove devilishly difficult to take off. Then, once off, they can be a bear to put back on. You'll want to work with a specific case design, if possible, before making a purchase.

Personally, I like cases that provide a removable panel. That way, I'm able to access the motherboard without having to find space for a large wraparound case. I can lean the siding up against the system chassis or the wall without taking up too much space. Hinged cases provide a similar convenience.

Finally, look for case designs that go the extra distance to eliminate sharp or jagged edges. Case surfaces should roll over the edge to present a rounded corner. This helps you avoid cuts when handling the unit.

21.5 Tom's Pick

There are a lot of things to pick in this chapter, so I'll make it quick.

When it comes to a power supply, more is almost always better. The additional wattage will ensure that you have enough headroom for future drive upgrades, while also ensuring that the unit runs cooler and well within its tolerances. Better still, go with a dual-supply model, which provides built-in redundancy in a single module. Here, the APC Two-in-One is my choice. It provides lots of wattage, two online supplies, and total redundancy.

For protecting my investment, I go right past surge protection and look to a good universal power supply. Specifically, I go with an online model that actively conditions the incoming power using an inline battery module. The online feature costs a bit more, but it allows the unit to step in for voltage sags that would otherwise need to be covered by the power supply. Line-conditioning should add years to the life of the power supply and may help avoid stressing motherboard components.

My choice for backup power? APC's Back-UPS 400, which delivers a 400 VA rating to provide about 10 minutes of shutdown power to a loaded desktop PC. The unit includes online line-conditioning to maintain electrical consistency, as well as a serial port for connecting to the PC. This digital connection lets the Back-UPS log power-related events, send a warning message about a shutdown, and set device settings.

Cases and Power Supplies

Part

VII

Tom's Dream Machine

Chapter

22

Tom's Dream Machine

Okay, we've been up and down the technology flagpole, assessing everything from CPUs and graphics controllers, to lowly keyboards and mice. One thing's for certain: A lot of disparate technologies have to come together cleanly in order for any PC to deliver optimal performance. Although effective industry standards, years of manufacturing experience, and advanced OSs and BIOSs help matters, getting the best of everything remains a challenge.

Why? For one reason, managing hardware bottlenecks can be like chasing chickens around a henhouse. You get your hands on one, and half a dozen others spring lose and start causing all sorts of trouble. In fact, it may not be at all possible to lock down every bottleneck and performance crimp. Even if you have $10,000 or so to spend on the absolute best of everything, you may still face compatibility problems.

For the rest of us, building a dream machine is about managing technology. For example, a hot new bus may boost through-the-roof data rates but might lack any effective disk drives that support it. The result: You're better off sticking with the mundane technology (such as SCSI) rather than chasing promises. The same goes for CPUs and graphics chips. No matter how fast the optimized performance or component clock, what ultimately matters is how much useful performance the part can deliver. This is a prime reason why Intel's Pentium II-400 is a superior choice to Digital's much-faster Alpha 750 CPU.

However, that's enough talk. Let's take a tour of Tom's Dream Machine.

It should come as no surprise that our system is big and rangy, with a large tower chassis that's able to accommodate all the drives and devices that we might ever want to install in there. A big power supply, lots of expansion slots, advanced external ports, and top-notch input devices all support this muscle-bound PC. Because price is no object—at least, to a point—we'll be able to splurge on the best components and peripherals.

We'll break down our examination of Tom's machine into three sections, first discussing the individual components that we chose for the system. After that, we'll look at some important device interactions that affected our decision making and that may be important to you in weighing overall value. Finally, we'll talk applications and software. You'll see what types of uses have the most impact on which subsystems and how you can best manage those challenges.

22.1 The Grand Tour

Here's where the rubber meets the road. From each chapter of this book, we've drawn out the outstanding hardware and applied it to our overall system configuration. From the CPU to the network card, we'll go with the best that current technology has to offer. In an effort to accommodate the rapid pace of change in the computer industry, we'll also look ahead a bit to make sure our picks stay relevant.

So, with no further ado, we'll start our rundown of the best devices you can find.

22.1.1 CPU

It's no surprise that our grand tour starts here. Although the CPU depends on the efficient operation of many other components to work well, it remains the most vital piece of hardware in any PC. Whether you capture full-motion video, play 3D games, calculate spreadsheets, browse the Web, or write simple email and word processing documents—the CPU is the ultimate determiner of performance.

Just as important, the CPU remains one of the most expensive single components in your PC. Even as the relative amount of money spent on the hard disk, system memory, and CD-ROM drive have fallen, CPUs have held steady. In fact, you can expect about one-quarter to one-third of the money you spend on a new system to go toward the CPU. With that kind of cash outlay, as well as the importance of the CPU in staving off obsolescence, users face a real challenge in balancing their needs and their pocketbooks.

With all this in mind, what CPU did we choose to populate our power-minded PC?

Despite plenty of competition in the CPU market, the choice was pretty easy: Intel's fastest **Pentium II** processor simply can't be matched by any competing x86-compatible CPU. It's enviable balance of outstanding integer performance, very strong floating-point capability, and unparalleled MMX processing make it the best all-around performance choice. Although both AMD and Cyrix have managed to squeeze as much—if not more—integer operations per clock tick as Pentium II, neither can come close in the FP and MMX arena. With 3D graphics and video growing more demanding and critical everyday, this critical advantage makes Pentium II a CPU with legs (refer to Figure 21.1).

Figure 22.1.

Pentium II is no shrimp, whether you're talking size or performance.

The secret is in the Pentium II's P6 core, which is highly superscalar and includes three integer pipelines and a single, well-optimized FP/MMX pipeline. Sophisticated prediction and instruction buffering enable Pentium II to crank along on conditional code even as critical brand determining bits work their way into the loop. Although there's a penalty for blowing branch prediction guesses, the Pentium II hits more than it misses, thus reducing performance-draining stalls.

Pentium II excels under Windows 95, yet it's truly optimized under 32-bit OSs such as Windows NT. The P6 legacy is hard at work under 32-bit code using a feature called *out-of-order execution*. In these cases, instructions are actually completely processed despite the fact that earlier operations in the pipeline are still waiting on bits. This feature allows Pentium II to complete about three operations in each clock tick (up from two operations per tick in Pentium and Pentium MMX).

Perhaps most important is Pentium II's enhanced L2 cache design, which pulls the fast store of local memory off the motherboard and onto a fast bus that's half the speed of the CPU. With the cache running at 225MHz on a Pentium II-450 system, the L2 memory clicks along at over three times the speed of that found on most Socket 7 systems (66MHz). When the Pentium II is able to stay within its L2 cache, things can really move along.

AMD's K6-2 gets the nod as the budget-minded selection, beating out Intel's Celeron thanks to its intriguing instruction set extensions, faster clock, and boosted FP and MMX capabilities. Although the integer core is the familiar K6 technology, AMD did a good thing by adding a second FP/MMX pipeline. This addition bolsters K6's weakest side, thus making K6-2 a viable platform for 3D gameplay and multimedia playback.

More problematic is the 3D-Now instruction set extensions, a set of 20 instructions (similar to MMX) that targets 3D graphics operations. AMD has managed to gather fellow CPU competitors Cyrix and IDT under the 3D-Now flag; therefore, products from all three Intel-alternative vendors will use the same instruction set. Although 3D-Now can deliver a welcome boost to 3D graphics, software must be tailored for it. Even with Microsoft incorporating 3D-Now compliance into its DirectX 6.0 APIs—a *big* win for AMD—the development cycle for games means you may have to wait a year or more for this technology to gain full support. What's more, game developers will have to tune their geometry setup routines for DirectX, something that few developers have been willing to do thus far.

22.1.2 Motherboard

Despite Intel's ongoing and deepening domination of the motherboard sector, a lot of good companies continue to put out commendable products. The best of the lot is the **Microstar MS-6119**, a single-processor, 440BX-based motherboard that features a convenient jumperless design and a wide range of features. A versatile motherboard, the MS-6119 runs at 66, 75, 83, 100, and even 133MHz. Although the 133MHz setting provides opportunity for those wanting to tweak up their existing Pentium II–350 or faster CPUs, owners of older Pentium IIs will have to cover the B21 lead to switch off the 66MHz fail-safe Intel has built into its Pentium II line.

Although we had some trouble with this board in our network card compatibility test—it refused to allow network access with any IRQ above 5—the MS-6119 was otherwise as stable a motherboard as we've seen. Add important application and system management features such as Wake-On-LAN and Wake-On-Ring, as well as tweaks such as a CPU fan suspend mode for cutting down noise, and you have yourself one full-featured motherboard. Best of all, the MS-6119 features a jumperless design that allows you to switch the front bus clock and clock multipliers from BIOS setup. (A reset feature allows you to recover should you select a setting that disables the motherboard and makes it impossible to access the BIOS.)

Performance-wise, the latest crop of Pentium II motherboards run true to form. Which is to say, performance varies by a negligible amount among different products—about 3 percent in our last roundup. With that said, the MS-6119 also happens to be the fastest 440BX motherboard we've tested—a nice plus to an already excellent product.

If you don't mind losing the convenience of jumperless operation and the useful "Wake On" features, Asus's P2B impressed us with top-notch reliability. It ran with all sorts of SDRAM variants, proving resilient all the way to 112MHz on the front side bus. Like the MS-6119, it supports the entire clock range from 66MHz to 133MHz. There are also versions with an onboard U2W SCSI and an onboard LAN adapter.

22.1.3 Memory

Although some users are eagerly awaiting the arrival of Rambus DRAM (RDRAM) system memory, the rest of us are doing just fine with 100MHz SDRAM rated at 50ns refresh. Thanks to Intel's masterful (and unhurried) orchestration of the system board bus upgrade from 66MHz to 100MHz, 100MHz SDRAM is in plentiful supply from a wide variety of manufacturers. That means this memory is fast, cheap, and available from reliable manufacturers such as Micron and Samsung.

Better yet, our tests show that many SDRAMs on the market enjoy a nice amount of headroom, allowing efficient operation in system boards pushed to 133MHz. Overclockers will want to keep a close eye on their memory buying

Tom's Dream Machine

decisions, however, to ensure that they get reliable parts that are able to handle the boosted operation. Your best bet: SDRAMs from Micron or Samsung (see Figure 22.2).

Figure 22.2.
Until DDR SDRAM and RDRAM start muddying the waters, 100MHz SDRAM remains the easy memory choice. (Photo courtesy of Crucial Technologies.)

We aren't going to skimp on RAM either. Our dream machine comes loaded with a full 256MB of 100MHz SDRAM to ensure that even the most demanding applications, operating systems, and multitasking mixtures don't have to resort to slow virtual memory to get things done. To fit this into our three-DIMM-equipped MS-6119 motherboard, that means going with a pair of 128MB SDRAM DIMMs.

22.1.4 3D Graphics

There's no question in the 3D graphics arena—no one matches the stunning combination of performance and realism dished out by 3Dfx's Voodoo II chip. So it's no surprise that our top graphics pick—the **Diamond Multimedia Monster 3D II**—is based on this same Voodoo II chip. Although Diamond was a bit late getting to market with Monster 3D II, it has produced a superior product available in enough versions to make any serious gamer happy (refer to Figure 22.3). An attractive software bundle as well as ample opportunities for performance overclocking seal the deal.

Figure 22.3.
Diamond's Monster 3D II is the best of the Voodoo II bunch.

Monster 3D II is a separate PCI-based board that offloads 3D graphics handling from your existing PCI or AGP-based graphics adapter and comes standard with 8MB of EDO RAM. Although the Creative Labs 3D Blaster Voodoo II packs a standard 12MB of memory, our visual and performance benchmarks were unable to show an advantage for the larger memory buffer. However, with 3D games growing more complex by the hour, Diamond did a good thing and now offers a 12MB version of Monster 3D II.

Like other Voodoo II–based boards, Monster 3D II supports scan-line interleaving (SLI) to allow two Voodoo boards to effectively double the fill rate for 3D graphics. The performance of games tailored for 3Dfx's own Glide API is simply breathtaking. Frame rates go through the roof on a Pentium II-300, scaling toward a healthy 90fps as you boost processor power. Just as important, Monster 3D II and Voodoo II–based cards like it finally unseated Nvidia's Riva 128 chip as the best silicon for Direct3D games. It's this admirable versatility that makes the Voodoo II a winning platform for 3D gaming.

So why did we choose Diamond over, say, Creative Labs, Canopus, and other vendors? For one thing, Diamond's Monster 3D II proved the most "overclockable" Voodoo II board, and it includes a simple software interface that lets you crank chip speed to 95MHz. Also, Monster 3D II was the most stable product when clocked beyond 100MHz—a key advantage over 3D Blaster Voodoo II. Other wins include Diamond's generous game bundle (available at the time of this writing), and the company's long track record as a leading graphics card vendor. You can expect enduring driver support from Diamond, whereas smaller or new-to-the-business companies may lack such stalwart backing.

If you aren't willing or able to put a dedicated PCI graphics card into your PC for 3D only, you'll find yourself shopping for one of the many 2D/3D combination cards. Although Intel's 740 chip has made quite the splash on the market, our pick goes to Nvidia's improved Riva 128 ZX graphics chip, with STB's Velocity 128 AGP leading the way among boards outfitted with the silicon. One of the few 3D parts tailored specifically for Microsoft's Direct3D API, the Riva 128 ZX provides some of the highest frame rates in Direct3D games, and it boasts features such as trilinear filtering to produce attractive 3D scenes. Unlike the earlier Velocity 128, which was limited to 4MB of SGRAM, the new ZX-based version can hold up to 8MB of memory, thus improving resolutions to 800×600 at 16-bit color.

22.1.5 2D Graphics

Matrox's Millennium II graphics card has become the gray lady of Windows graphics. It's simply the most enduring graphics brand out there. The 64-bit MGA-2164W chip powering the winning Matrox Millennium II board provides ample data bandwidth, advanced 2D acceleration features, and an interface to

Tom's Dream Machine

outstanding Windows RAM (WRAM) memory (see Figure 22.4). Most important, the stable chip architecture and driver legacy has helped build rock-solid compatibility and stability into the Millennium II—a huge advantage over competing boards.

Figure 22.4.

8MB of dual-ported WRAM and a fast 250MHz RAMDAC make the Millennium II the preeminent 2D graphics choice.

Although Millennium II ships with 4MB, 8MB, or even 16MB of WRAM, our pick is the 8MB version. Affordable at under $260, the 8MB version can display true color at 1600×1200 resolution. More important, Matrox still uses an external RAMDAC, which allows for high-speed operations (250MHz) for enabling fast refresh rates up and down the entire resolution range. In fact, you won't find a faster RAMDAC on a mainstream graphics cards.

Taking advantage of the RAMDAC is the fast, dual-ported WRAM memory type, which includes tweaks for speeding graphics memory calls. Although fast, single-ported memory types get the nod on affordable boards, none can deliver stable refresh at stratospheric resolutions—there's simply too much incoming and outgoing data sharing a single port.

Driver support is outstanding. You'll find Millennium drivers for every OS under the sun—Windows 95, Windows 3.*x*, Windows NT 3.51 and 4.0, as well as OS/2, Linux, and various flavors of Unix. Also, there's a Millennium for every platform. PC versions are available for both PCI and AGP, and a PCI-based Macintosh version of the board can be had as well.

22.1.6 Monitor

What you see is what you get. This phrase rings true when it comes to outfitting our dream machine with a monitor. If we load up on 450MHz processors, buckets of RAM, and ultra-wide SCSI hard disk drives, we better have a monitor that can display all the rocket-fired graphics and information we'll be working with.

In our case, we think big, and the **Iiyama VisionMaster Pro 500 MT-9221** fits the bill. This expansive 21-inch CRT uses a Trinitron-like Diamondtron tube to deliver rich, saturated colors as well as high contrast and terrific brightness. Pixels are sharp and well focused, with no ugly blooming or shape distortion; also, refresh rates stay high (76Hz), even at 1600×1200 resolution. The monitor includes both a standard 15-pin VGA connector and a high-fidelity component BNC connector for retaining image quality at the highest resolutions and refresh rates (see Figure 22.5).

Figure 22.5.

Big, bright, and beautiful, the Iiyama VisionMaster's 20-inch viewable area lets you work efficiently.

The 21-inch diagonal display serves up 20 inches of viewable area—25 percent more area than you get on a typical 17-inch CRT monitor, and nearly 50 percent more than on a 15-inch display. This kind of screen area helps make fast work of space-hungry applications such as spreadsheets, 3D design, and HTML and page layout applications. Best of all, a game of Quake II played at high 1024×768 resolution on a big screen becomes an absolutely mind-blowing experience.

Can't spend $1,500 on a monitor? We're not willing to compromise on this critical area, but you might shop around for one of the intriguing 19-inch models now on the market. A relative newcomer to the CRT scene, 19-inch monitors provide a real improvement over their 17-inch cousins, allowing comfortable viewing even at 1280×1024 resolutions. Although most of these models are affordable at $800 to $900, few make use of Trinitron or other technologies to deliver exceptional sharpness and color saturation. Therefore, you should expect to trade off visual fidelity for greater viewing area.

22.1.7 Hard Disk

When it comes to hard disks, you face the initial IDE versus SCSI choice. Needless to say, IDE drivers are less expensive, more plentiful, and generally more "value minded" than their SCSI counterparts. You can save a cool $200 just by going with the IDE version of the same-capacity SCSI drive. With the advent of ATA-33 interface motherboards and drives, these affordable disks are able to push near-SCSI data rates, topping out at 33MBps.

Despite the welcome advances, SCSI retains its undeniable performance edge. Yes, you'll pay more, but if you need responsive performance, swift file transfers, and uninterrupted capture or playback of streaming media data types, only a SCSI drive will do. Although there are a plethora of excellent SCSI hard disk drives out there, our dream machine comes equipped with two: the **IBM UltraStar 9ZX**.

The 9ZX enjoys the full 40MBps throughput available from the ultra-wide SCSI interface, and it spins at a heady 10,000rpm to enhance throughput and minimize rotational latencies. In fact, you won't find a faster spinning hard drive for your powerhouse desktop PC (see Figure 22.6).

Figure 22.6.
IBM's UltraStar 9ZX is big, fast, and loaded with attractive diagnostic features.

Available in both ultra-wide SCSI and Fibre Channel (up to 200MBps) interfaces, the 9ZX drive can handle the most demanding performance challenges. Average seek time is a blinding 6.7ms (about 20 percent quicker than most desktop hard disk drives), and the fast rotation cuts latency times to 2.9ms. Sustained data transfer rates—not burst, mind you—settle in around 17MBps. Also, a large 1MB onboard cache helps cut out delays in accesses.

You'll also find welcome diagnostic technologies on this drive to ensure that thermal buildup and other operational demands don't imperil your data. Self-Monitoring Analysis and Reporting Technology (SMART) provides real-time diagnostic gathering of drive parameters, producing a log that can help you assess and resolve performance and operational problems. IBM's Predictive Failure Analysis (PFA) detects accumulating bit-level variances, which allows you to see a drive problem before it arrives, and an onboard drive temperature indicator processor keeps tabs on drive temperature.

For cost-cutters, you can't beat IDE hard disk drives with a stick. Today, no one can touch IBM's IDE offerings, which are the only drives available that use Giant Magneto Resistive (GMR) head technology to boost capacities to 16GB. The IBM DeskStar 16 costs just $399 yet provides enough storage to stave off an upgrade for at least another two years. Based on the ATA-33 IDE interface, the drive can burst 33MBps over the IDE bus, using CPU-friendly bus mastering to relieve overall pressure on the system.

22.1.8 CD-ROM/DVD-ROM

There are so many types and flavors of mainstream optical storage that picking a single device is almost impossible. If you want maximum performance and compatibility, a top CD-ROM drive is the best choice. You'll need a DVD-ROM drive to take advantage of new DVD titles and MPEG-2 video, but your CD-ROM playback performance will lag. CD-R and CD-RW, useful recordable and rewritable formats, also come with a performance penalty, cost more than CD-ROM, and generally bring a variety of compromises. Finally, the burgeoning and attractive rewritable DVD formats continue to confound, thanks to protracted standards battles and high costs that limit the audience of compatible reading devices.

So what's our no-compromise solution? Right now, a second-generation DVD-ROM drive offers the broadest range of disc compatibility, reading CD-ROM, CD-R, CD-RW, and DVD-ROM discs. Most important, it lets you play the emerging category of DVD-based games, which incorporate sophisticated MPEG-2 video cut scenes, vast data sets, and convenient single-disc packaging.

The best of the DVD-ROM bunch that we've seen is the **Creative Labs Encore Dxr2** kit, which includes a good selection of titles, including Wing Commander IV, Claw, and Forsaken. The kit includes a second-generation, IDE-based DVD-ROM drive that's compatible with all rewritable CD formats and spins CD discs at 20× spin rates. The included media decoder card uses an analog loopback for dropping video into the RGB graphics stream (eliminating compatibility problems that still plague PCI bus–mastered approaches) as well as a S/PDIF port for outputting digital AC-3 audio signals to compliant hardware (refer to Figure 22.7).

Figure 22.7.

Creative Labs' Encore Dxr2 upgrade kit recognizes all CD formats, comes with compelling DVD-ROM titles, and includes a media decoder card that works around stifling compatibility problems.

The Encore Dxr2 is a good drive kit, but for CD-ROM playback it can't touch the Plextor UltraPleX CD-ROM drive. This 14×–32× SCSI-based CD-ROM drive uses a convenient tray-fed mechanism and includes SCSI auto-termination and auto–ID detection to eliminate two frequent SCSI installation gotchas. Plextor's efficient drivers and mechanism, combined with the SCSI bus, yield some of the lowest CPU utilization rates we've seen. Finally, the UltraPleX supports bootable CD-ROM discs, provided your system includes a bootable SCSI adapter.

If you need to record optical media, your best bet now is a CD-RW drive. CD-R can save you a hundred bucks or so on the purchase, but it lacks CD-RW's terrific versatility to read and write all recordable CD formats. DVD rewritable formats, meanwhile, remain mired in a standards struggle. Our pick for best CD-RW drive is **HP's CD-Writer Plus 7200i**, a 2× record and 6× playback drive that interfaces to the IDE bus and costs $425. Although slower than most CD-R models, it can write to both CD-R and CD-RW discs for maximum flexibility. Also, the lower playback speeds are not an issue if you keep a second read-only drive (which I heartily recommend) in your system. The same drive is available in SCSI and parallel port versions, although the parallel drive will result in markedly poorer performance.

22.1.9 Near-line Storage

Forget Iomega Zip and LS-120. The best near-line storage out there today is **SyQuest's** intriguing **Sparq** format. These little 5.25-inch drives read and write cartridged media that hold a capacious 1GB of data—100 times the capacity of Zip. At $199 for an IDE drive, the price is right in the Zip ballpark (see Figure 22.8). In fact, the Sparq is the first cartridge drive to blur the line between floppy disk successors (Zip, LS-120, HiFD) and traditional near-line storage (MO drives, Iomega Jaz).

Figure 22.8.

The perfect removable format? Sparq is cheap, fast, large, and built by a proven name in the industry.

Most impressive, Sparq drives deliver performance that's vastly superior to the Zip drive. Average access times are a zippy 12ms, whereas sustained data transfer rates start around 3.7MBps (the parallel port version tops out at just 1.25MBps, however). Although the media is a bit pricey at $30 per cartridge, the actual cost per megabyte is among the lowest in its drive class, at just under 3 cents per meg. Add all this to SyQuest's proven record in the removable and near-line storage arena, and Sparq has what it takes to light a fire under your storage needs.

22.1.10 Audio

There's a new sheriff in the PC audio arena, and its name is DirectSound. The emergence of Microsoft's audio API has all but displaced Creative Labs' Sound Blaster standard in the Windows development market, meaning that your next soundboard better be ready to handle the new technology. One thing DirectSound has done is finally nudge sound cards off the troublesome ISA bus, introducing PCI Plug and Play, lower system resource requirements, and the ability to juggle multichannel audio.

Our pick in this arena goes to the **Diamond Multimedia Monster Sound MX200**, a PCI-based soundboard that brings the whole raft of features to the PC. Like excellent soundboards such as Creative Labs' Sound Blaster AWE64, the Monster Sound MX200 plays both CD-quality wave audio and hardware-based wavetable MIDI synthesis (see Figure 22.9). With 2MB of wavetable sounds in onboard ROM, the board is able to produce realistic scores without hitting up your system processor and RAM for valuable resources. With 64 simultaneous MIDI voices supported in the hardware, it provides better performance than the AWE64, which delivers 32 voices in the hardware and the second 32 voices in the software.

Figure 22.9.

The Diamond Monster Sound MX200 does it all—multichannel PCI audio, 3D positional effects, wavetable MIDI, and CD-quality wave audio record and playback.

Where Monster Sound MX200 excels is in Windows 95–based audio. Games produced with Aureal's A3D or Microsoft's DirectSound 3D positional audio technology are able to create the illusion of surround sound in a two speaker environment. Bad guys growl from over your shoulder and enemy planes roar from left to right as they streak across your monitor's view on the world. Also,

Monster Sound's 32 channels of audio mean that developers can pour on the realism, mixing up sound effects, music scores, complex positional elements, and other audio elements without overloading the card.

For speakers, we decided to go with Altec Lansing's USB-powered ACS-395 speaker and subwoofer set. The space-conserving satellite units feature variably angled drivers that help spread the sound, producing a broader effect and enhancing the effectiveness of positional 3D audio. With 10 watts of RMS power, the satellites are more than powerful enough for desktop audio, although anyone doing presentations or other public sound projection will want more strength. The matched subwoofer goes under the table and produces excellent bass sounds, adding that special oomph to low-range sounds. Explosions, bass tones in music, and the low rumble of spacecraft engines all benefit from the subwoofer's impact.

Another key element is the USB capability, which allows you to use onscreen controls to precisely control volume, base, treble, balance, and other speaker characteristics. The intuitive controls are a huge improvement over tiny and hard-to-reach knobs. What's more, the speakers can plug either into a traditional analog line-out port or use the USB port for accepting audio signals. The digital USB connection allows for higher sound fidelity, because the critical digital-to-analog (D-to-A) conversion doesn't happen inside the PC case, where rampant EMF introduces noise to the signal. However, we have serious reservations about USB's ability to deliver multichannel audio for games, so we'll keep it plugged into the analog sound board ports for now.

22.1.11 Communications

Today, the importance of communications hardware can't be stressed enough. After all, the analog or even ISDN modem represents the biggest performance bottleneck in your whole system, forcing you to wait while graphics-heavy pages load in your browser or large files crawl down from an FTP site. For the vast majority of users, the only available choice is an analog modem, and it is clear that a 56KBps model that conforms to the ITU v.90 specification is the only way to go.

So which one do we like for our power system? The **Courier I-Modem** is our choice because it offers all the performance of USR's 56KBps Sportster model yet adds neat features such as remote access and configuration for allowing you to update the modem's Flash ROM BIOS over a network. Built-in security features let you password-protect modem access, adding another layer of confidence, and support for distinctive ring and Caller ID help you get the most out of your analog phone lines.

With that said, we are also intrigued by **Diamond Multimedia's Shotgun II** modem, which incorporates a pair of 56KBps, v.90-compliant modems on a single card. The Shotgun product lets you double your bandwidth by dialing into

Tom's Dream Machine

the same ISP over two separate phone lines, stitching together the separate accesses into a single connection at your PC. ISP support for Shotgun is a factor for getting the most out of this product, but you can still enjoy benefits if you have two separate accounts for dialing into.

For ISDN access, our favorite is the **3Com Impact IQ**. Available in an internal ISA or external parallel port version, this intelligent device does all the heavy lifting for you. An automated wizard guides you through setup, querying the ISDN line to snoop out the telco's switch type, SPID assignments, and other critical information for you. Even if it can't find all the answers—as it successfully did for me—a friendly interface and good documentation will help you puzzle through ISDN's difficult moments.

22.1.12 Networking

When it comes to LAN cards, there's not much to it. PCI-based cards offer rock-solid compatibility and all the bus bandwidth you need to support even 100mbps fast Ethernet networking. Most critical, you need compatibility with NE2000 technology, but that's something you'll find in almost any name brand network interface card (NIC). Our pick, then, is **3Com's Fast EtherLink** family of 10/100mbps fast Ethernet NICs.

Specifically, we like the PCI version of the Fast EtherLink, with its built-in Plug and Play, fast bus support, and lower CPU requirements due to PCI 2.1's built-in bus-mastering facilities. All these cards match up with 10BaseT twisted-pair CAT 5 wiring, which is all but ubiquitous in current network setups. 3Com offers a limited lifetime warranty on its products, and the company's success in the network hub field makes it easy to group your NIC purchase with other network components, further easing maintenance overhead.

22.1.13 Joystick

Make no mistake, gaming is serious business. We spend hundreds of dollars on the hottest 3D graphics accelerators, big monitors, and fast CPUs. However, skimping on a joystick is probably the best way to ensure that you'll meet a quick death at the hands of a foe in an online game of death-match Quake.

The best joystick we've seen is **Microsoft's Sidewinder Force Feedback Pro**. A hulking black monument of a device, the Sidewinder Force Feedback Pro provides fast digital response and compelling tactile feedback when played with games developed with a force-feedback API. Pull Gs in Microsoft Flight Simulator or take fire in a combat flight sim and you'll feel the stick strain and stutter against your hand. A wide range of motions, bumps, grinds, and other effects are supported by the stick, providing different sensations for different actions, weapons, and impacts (refer to Figure 22.10).

Figure 22.10.
All that and looks too! The Microsoft Sidewinder Force Feedback Pro provides tactile response to onscreen action.

The Sidewinder is solidly built and comes with a good selection of buttons and controls, including a throttle wheel (which could use a bit more resistance) and six base-mounted, programmable buttons. The stick uses optical sensors in the base to eliminate drift and degradations that are inevitable with physical, electrical contacts. An IR sensor on the stick itself senses when your hand is on the device so that force-feedback effects are only executed when you're playing.

Although a USB version is due out soon, the Sidewinder we used runs off the standard MIDI/game port. However, an onboard processor and a digital communication workaround eliminates the need for the CPU to conduct performance-sapping polling of the game port. As a result, frame rates go up and joystick responsiveness improves.

22.1.14 Mouse and Keyboard

Once again, Microsoft dominates. The **Microsoft Intellimouse** builds on the winning design of the Mouse 2.0 product (refer to Figure 22.11). The comfortable design supports the palm and wrists, and an oversided #1 button provides easy clicking. The integrated scrolling wheel is really useful for navigating Web pages, spreadsheets, and long documents that too often have you clicking on the vertical scroll bars. IntelliPoint software allows you to adjust the settings, including allowing you to turn off the annoying wheel push option, which too often gets accidentally invoked.

Figure 22.11
*The Microsoft
Intellimouse
eases scrolling
and clicking.*

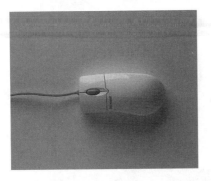

The **Microsoft Natural Keyboard Elite** is the most successful ergonomic keyboard on the market. It's slightly sloped and split-center design eases wrist pronation, allowing you to type with your hands at a gentle angle (see Figure 22.12). Keyboard response is quiet but confident, and the cord is long enough to reach around to the back of midtower systems tucked deep under the desk. Also, a USB version of this keyboard adds another level of convenience.

Figure 22.12.
*The Natural
Elite Keyboard
may frustrate
some, but it's still
the best of the
ergonomic brands.*

With that said, some users may want to stick with a traditional flat-faced keyboard. The split and slope takes time to learn and can really aggravate accomplished typists. Also, in order to save space, Microsoft has shrunk the function, cursor, and page control keys on the Natural Elite, which can lead to a lot of missed keystrokes.

22.2 Wrapping Up

So you've seen everything that goes into making the Dream PC. But how does it look from without? Well, there are a few things to consider. For example, whereas most PCs sold today come in a midtower format, we prefer a rangy tower for our purposes. Granted, this monster may not fit under a desk, but the extra space means we can load up on drives without worrying about running out of space. The big case also makes accessing internal components much easier.

On the back of our system, you'll see the usual, dizzying array of ports and connectors. Critical among them are the two USB ports, which provide access to a growing list of intelligent, Plug and Play external devices. Augmenting our USB ports is a powered USB hub, the **Andromeda** from **CATV, Inc.**, which includes four ports for adding USB-based peripherals. The integrated power supply allows the hub to augment the electrical current in the bus, so we can add USB scanners, modems, video cameras, and other power cordless devices without overloading the bus-powered USB wire.

Our power supply is similarly bulky: With 300 watts of output, it's more than a match for our muscle-bound PC. Whereas most current desktops ship with 200-watt power supplies, our 300-watt unit won't overheat or strain to provide juice to components. We've selected the extra-cooling power of the **Turbo Cool 300** from **PC Power and Cooling**, which provides enhanced airflow inside the chassis. At $119, it's more expensive than other supplies, but the additional cooling and power overhead will help avoid catastrophic heat-related breakdowns later.

When it comes to software, we choose to have a choice of Windows. Our PC dual-boots Windows 98 and Windows NT 4.0, using a shared FAT16 partition that allows us to use the same program installations under both operating systems. This decision loses some nice diagnostic and performance value in NT's NTFS file system, but the downside of separate program installations involved in using separate file systems makes this the best option. Of course, selecting a file system is something you can change on your own.

Tom's Dream Machine

Appendix A

Benchmarking

Almost anyone who has purchased a computer or even a graphics card or printer has had to puzzle through benchmarks. In fact, performance testing is pervasive in the industry, serving as a crucial evaluation, marketing, and evangelism tool for vendors, analysts, and press alike. In all cases, a lot rides on benchmarking, whether it's the fate of a new product or the impact of a magazine review.

There's just one problem. Benchmarks are an utterly imperfect way to assess relative performance. The problem is that even the best benchmark cannot precisely reproduce the individual performance needs of every user. What's more, the way vendors or publications decide to benchmark hardware can have an enormous impact on the results. These kinds of issues make benchmarking a much trickier proposition than the simple integer scores and bar charts would seem to suggest.

A.1 Types of Benchmarks

Benchmarking can vary a lot depending on the particular class of product being reviewed. For example, the benchmarking elements used to test PCs, printers, and soundcards must be very different in order to effectively assess their unique features. A PC review will tend to focus on application performance—that is, the speed with which operations are completed—whereas a soundboard benchmark will most likely focus on audio fidelity. Even within a product category, variations are inevitable. So-called *Network Computers (NCs)*, for example, are typically benchmarked in very different environments than standalone home PCs.

In general, you can break most PC-specific testing into several categories.

- Performance
- Qualitative
- Compatibility
- Usability

A.1.1 Performance Testing

Performance benchmarks are the main focus of this appendix and are by far the most pervasive class of testing procedure. These tests can vary from simple stopwatch-timed application routines, to complex, automated scripts that closely mirror user interaction. Although end results may be reported in a variety of metrics, almost all are based on how quickly the tested hardware performs its tasks. Popular general-purpose performance benchmarks include WinBench and WinMark, SpecMark, SysMark, and PC WorldBench.

A critical area of performance testing is in graphics, particularly 3D graphics acceleration. Here, the primary unit of measure is *frames per second*, with higher values indicating better performance. The point in 3D graphics testing (and video playback testing as well) is to determine how efficiently and quickly the graphics card and system are able to process complex graphics. This involves assembling 3D scenes and then using the graphics card to apply color, shading, and effects, as well as committing the result to the display.

The most common 3D graphics test is probably the Quake II game demo, using the built-in frame counter to determine frame rates. The advantage here is that an actual gaming engine is being used, and the frame counter provides a clear indication of performance. The use of a standard demo is certainly critical, because the results from any game test involving user interaction would, by definition, be affected by variations in the inputs. Other popular 3D gaming benchmarks include Turok Dinosaur Hunter, Rage Incoming, and Psygnosis G-Police. Another popular 3D graphics benchmark is ZD BOp's 3D WinBench 98, a synthetic graphics benchmark.

A.1.2 Qualitative Testing

Second to performance testing is *qualitative benchmarking*, which is used to assess the relative quality of device operation. Most often used to assess device output from printers, scanners, displays, and graphics cards, this kind of testing relies on the personal observations of one or more testers. Often, a jury of experts is called upon to make assessments, thus enabling the tester to take into account variations in personal perception.

In fact, qualitative testing is a very tricky business. The variety of 3D graphics APIs, for example, make it difficult to set a level playing field to assess the visual output of cards. However, other product areas face challenges as well. Monitor output testing needs to be conducted in a very controlled environment; otherwise, testers might make their judgments based on the lighting conditions surrounding a particular monitor rather than on the quality of the display itself. This need to control the testing environment takes resources—space, proper lighting, intelligent placement, and careful configuration—that smaller organizations simply might not have available. Of course, these tests need to be conducted blindly so that testers do not color their perception with preconceived notions about particular monitor makes or models.

Other tests that involve so-called *taste tests* include video playback, printer output, scanner input, and digital camera output. In all cases, performance only tells a small part of the story, because visual quality is often the primary focus (so to speak) of the technology. However, once again, qualitative testing requires vigorous controls, a well-selected jury pool, and a rock-solid methodology.

A.1.3 Compatibility Testing

Compatibility benchmarking is perhaps the most difficult—and less common—of all testing procedures. This kind of testing seeks to establish the relative stability and reliability of a hardware platform by exposing it to challenging, but controlled, hardware and software interactions. Most such tests consist of a number of pass-fail operations, intended to let users tell which products are most likely to work reliably with a broad range of products.

The problem with this kind of benchmarking—and the reason you don't see it more often—is that it's nearly impossible to cover the full range of compatibility issues. The staggering variety of motherboards, add-in cards, external peripherals, and attendant drivers and applications means that any compatibility test is based on a very limited sample. What's more, even simple compatibility testing is a rigorous, time-consuming exercise that must be constantly monitored to make sure that perceived incompatibilities are being caused by the controlled environment and not some X factor.

Is compatibility testing useful? Yes and no. Personally, I think it plays a critical role in assessing the relative value of any hardware platform. However, readers and reviewers need to be on guard and remember that compatibility testing results cannot be taken as statistically significant. A motherboard that chokes with one particular soundcard, for instance, may run flawlessly—and in fact, better than all its competitors—with all other types of hardware. In essence, it could flunk a compatibility test because it happened to be tested in its single area of weakness. Yet, that same board could, in fact, be more compatible than any other. Buyer (and reviewer) beware.

A.1.4 Usability Testing

Usability benchmarking has gained a lot of attention over the last several years as publishers have sought to tailor their coverage to the growing base of PC users. Half benchmark and half focus group, usability testing draws conclusions from observing actual users asked to conduct specific operations in a controlled, repeatable environment. Often, the point here is to see how quickly, efficiently, and effectively a given task or tasks can be accomplished, whether it's formatting a document or setting up a new PC. Although results may include time-based measurements to express how quickly tasks were performed—a reasonable measure of efficiency—many elements of usability testing rely on field observations and general analysis of user behavior.

Once again, usability benchmarking is a very difficult, detail-oriented, and expensive business. As with qualitative benchmarking, the testing environment must be rigorously controlled to ensure that test subjects are perceiving the same things as they run through their scripts. For example, you simply cannot accept any results gained when one person performs a hardware upgrade in a 70-degree room while a second does it in a steamy 90-degree room. The temperature is probably playing a greater role in the test than any amount of documentation, product design, and software utilities.

In addition, your users are part of the environment. Testers must be carefully selected to match the profile of your benchmarking—and even then, there's no guarantee of what you will get. In general, the only way to ensure proper results is to use a lot of testers, an approach that will consume inordinate amounts of time and money.

Finally, usability results interpretation is probably the most dangerous of all. Scores are usually based on a combination of careful observation, post-testing interviews with subjects, and time-based measurements. With the exception of the timing, all elements of this testing are subject to personal interpretation.

A.1.5 Types of Performance Benchmarks

Although performance benchmarks vary widely, they fall into two major classifications: application-based benchmarks and synthetic benchmarks. Application benchmarks use actual shipping applications and software to perform real-world tasks. Typically, some sort of internal or external script is used to drive the benchmark actions, thus ensuring rapid and repeatable execution of the test. The script is used to measure the time it takes to launch applications, open files, print files, and conduct other time-consuming, frequent tasks under the application.

Synthetic benchmarks, by contrast, consist of self-contained executable code that's designed to mimic the demands placed on the hardware by shipping applications. To create their tests, benchmark designers closely profile the behavior of typical applications when used by their audience, measuring how much time it takes for applications make API calls (as well as how often). This kind of low-level profiling can be incredibly useful but can also lead designers way off the mark when trying to decide exactly where to stress their benchmark measurements.

Available Application Benchmarks

There are a number of popular application-based benchmarks. Among them are the following:

- ZD WinStone 98
- PC WorldBench 98
- BAPCo SysMark

The Ziff-Davis Benchmark Operation WinMark 98 benchmark is the most popular application-based benchmark on the market. Used in conjunction with

Benchmarking

the ZD WinBench synthetic test suite, it's half of the most comprehensive benchmark product available to users today. Here are the component applications of WinMark 98:

- Netscape Navigator

- CorelDRAW! 7

- Microsoft PowerPoint 97

- Microsoft Access 97

- Microsoft Excel 97

- Lotus 1-2-3 97

- Corel Quattro Pro 7

- Microsoft Word 97

- Corel WordPerfect 7

In addition, WinStone offers a companion test for NT systems called the *High-End Winstone*. This test focuses on demanding applications such as 3D graphics design and visualization and programming environments.

PC WorldBench, like WinMark 98, uses business-class applications to test system performance. Here are the component applications:

- Microsoft Word 97

- Microsoft Excel 97

- Lotus 1-2-3 97

- Lotus WordPro 97

- Borland Paradox 8.0

- Picture Publisher 7.0

Unlike the previous two benchmarks, the BAPCo test is produced by an independent industry association. Dues-paying members, which are mainly hardware and software vendors, bankroll the development effort. BAPCo publishes a variety of application-based benchmarks that span environments such as Windows 95, Windows NT, and Java. The BAPCo SysMark/32 suite includes the following applications:

- Microsoft Word 7.0

- Lotus WordPro

- Microsoft Excel 7.0

- Borland Paradox 7.0

- CorelDRAW 6.0

- Lotus Freelance Graphics 96

- Microsoft PowerPoint 97

- Adobe PageMaker 6.0

Available Synthetic Benchmarks

On the other side of the testing coin are so-called *synthetic benchmarks*. You'll find even more of these types of tests in the marketplace, if only for the simple reason that there are a lot of device-specific benchmarks that use programmatic code to achieve results. In fact, synthetic benchmarks are able to test subsystems that application-driven tests often cannot reach, thus providing valuable insight into device behaviors and interaction.

The most well-known synthetic benchmark is ZDBop's ZD WinBench 98. This system-wide test takes stock of a broad range of system components, returning results specific to the CPU, hard disk, memory, graphics subsystem, and the like. Although ZD WinBench produces a single, overall score, the real value of the test comes in the rich detail of component results. The components of ZD WinBench 98 include the following:

- ZD Graphics WinMark 98

- ZD High-End Graphics WinMark 98

- ZD Disk WinMark 98

- ZD High-End Disk WinMark 98

- ZD CPUmark32

- ZD CD-ROM WinMark 98

In addition, WinBench adds a video playback test, scaling video clips and reporting the frame rate of the playback. The test uses videos compressed using Cinepak, Indeo 3.2, Indeo 4.*x*, and MPEG-1.

Other examples of synthetic tests include the following:

- Threadmark: Hard disks

- CD Stone and DVD Stone: CD-ROM and DVD-ROM drives

- Indy3D: OpenGL 3D graphics

- TPC: Web server test suite

A.1.6 Benchmark Characteristics

Every benchmark, be it synthetic or application driven, needs time to run. A benchmark that completes in five seconds, for example, is too short to produce verifiable results, whereas one that takes three days to run will not be used either. The relative size and range of benchmark operations likewise have an impact on how well the test will be accepted. In fact, benchmark designers must often trade off precision—achieved with large, long-running tests—for ease of use, distribution, and other factors.

Here are some of the critical issues in benchmark development:

- Distribution
- Product size
- Range of operations
- Runtime

Distribution

In many ways, benchmarks are really functional beauty contests, with publishers and vendors positioning their tests as much for their ability to be publicly distributed as for their precision and accuracy. In this respect, synthetic benchmarks enjoy a vast advantage over their application-based counterparts, which often require the presence of working applications to produce results. Synthetic benchmarks, by contrast, can deliver the effective execution load of actual applications at a small fraction of the file size.

Public distribution brings a lot of benefits to a benchmark. For one, it allows the end user community to compare published results against their own hardware and configurations, thus enhancing the perceived value of both the benchmark and the publication using it. It also creates a terrific PR vehicle, further enhancing the benchmark's perceived value. Creating an active community of benchmark users also helps the publisher produce better benchmarks down the road by taking advantage of input from the user community.

Application-based benchmarks, by contrast, are very difficult to distribute. Although you can easily distribute the scripts—particularly if they're written within a program's macro language—you generally have to rely on users having the correct versions of the applications you run in your tests. Some application benchmarks take a different approach by actually including crippled versions of their applications on a CD-ROM. The problem is that this approach takes a lot of work to secure proper licensing from vendors and requires a CD-ROM for distribution, thus adding considerable expense over online distribution.

Runtime

Another critical area is benchmark runtime, or the amount of time it takes for the test to produce complete results. As a general rule, the broader and more precise your benchmark, the longer the required runtime, because you need to produce a lot of individual behaviors in order to get insight into them all. What's more, better benchmarks properly weigh operations to reflect their user base, which adds time because some operations may need to be conducted many times more than less frequent ones.

Runtime, of course, is very hardware dependent. A diverse user base can run everything from 486DX-based systems to Pentium II-400s. For a benchmark to appeal to all these parties, it would have to be short enough to not take all day to execute on older PCs, while being long enough to still deliver reproducible results. Because of this, many benchmarks only appeal to a limited machine set.

Once again, synthetic benchmarks enjoy a big advantage. These benchmarks are able to strip away unwanted or unimportant operations in order to spend time only on critical tasks. For example, developers are able to mimic application machine states very quickly, instead of waiting for program code to get to that point. Because of these advantage, synthetic benchmarks are able to produce scores in a very short time.

Results

Performance benchmarks generally work by timing the execution of tasks. However, the results that users see can vary significantly. Some report a whole slew of statistics, including time to execute, CPU load, memory and disk activity, and a wide variety of other items. More often, benchmarks spit out a single, easily quotable number that can then be expanded upon.

In this respect, synthetic benchmarks are once again superior, because the programmatic scripts lend themselves to isolating specific subsystems and operations, which again allows them to produce scores. Application benchmarks, by contrast, are not as easy to focus. In fact, attempting to provide detailed subsystem analysis in an application benchmark can distort the relevance of the test.

A.2 Benchmarking Lessons

Benchmarking is an exacting, tricky business. Unfortunately, way too many individuals and publications take a devil-may-care attitude, failing to ensure that their results are valid and repeatable. What's more, vendors are constantly hard at work trying to optimize their products for benchmark tests, sometimes even crossing the line into unscrupulous behavior.

Whether you're running benchmarks yourself or relying on information from other testing, you need to be aware of the critical role that methodology plays in the process. Benchmark numbers that are presented without complete information about tested hardware and conditions are indistinguishable from fiction. In order for tests to provide any value, you need to exercise due diligence. This section will help you learn what to look for.

A.2.1 Benchmarking Methodology

Whether you use a synthetic or an application benchmark (or both), you need to plan properly to get results worth waiting for. Careless testing will only yield questionable results that could lead to you wasting money on poor purchases. If you're testing multiple systems and devices, for example, you need to make sure the hardware and software configurations are adequately comparable. Although it may be impossible to get everything identical between the various PCs, for example, you can make sure they are configured as similarly as possible. Better yet, you can configure the systems as you would generally use them.

Another major issue is ensuring repeatability of results. That is to say, your benchmarks should be able to produce close to the same score on multiple runs. Executing a test once and assuming that the result is valid is one of the most common mistakes made by users and organizations. There's simply no way to tell from a single run whether the numbers you're seeing are valid. Your next run could be off by 5 percent or 45 percent. Until you run the test again, you won't know.

In general, a good approach is to run a benchmark at least three times before considering the results. What's more, you should make sure to always benchmark hardware from a clean state. Reboot your test systems between passes to ensure that all your tests are being run on the same track. Disk caches, memory leakage, Windows heap resources, and any number of other variables can cause your results to skew badly if you don't take the time to reset the platform between runs.

If you see any unusual variances in the scores, you need to investigate. Check the screen resolution and color depth and make sure these remain consistent. Look for possible problems in caching mechanisms or perhaps system startup applications. Also, make sure the hardware is in a secure place during runtime so that mice or keyboards don't get accidentally bumped, possibly altering the scores.

A.2.2 Cheating Benchmarks

If you rely on synthetic benchmarks to assess performance, be on guard. Peripheral and system vendors live and die by published results in popular benchmark tests, often basing multimillion dollar ad campaigns on their results. With the stakes so high, it's no surprise that some vendors are willing to go to extreme lengths to ensure that their products do well in these tests.

In this respect, application-based benchmarks are vastly superior, because they rely on program code to test system performance. Speed up the benchmark, and you'll generally speed up the entire program, delivering a real benefit to users. However, hardware optimized for synthetic benchmarks often fail to deliver any corresponding performance enhancement. In fact, the extra processing that goes into detecting and enhancing a synthetic benchmark operation can actually create a drag on performance.

How do vendors optimize their products? In some cases, they'll embed code in the device drivers that detect and act on known benchmark behaviors. It might be a matter of detecting text strings or a pattern of rapid screen updates, for example. The code would then instruct the device to skip processing that would normally occur, thus producing highly accelerated performance in the optimized portion of the test.

Fortunately, publishers have gotten better at spoofing would-be benchmark cheaters. For example, ZD's Graphics WinMark tests check to make sure the graphics card is not cutting out display operations in order to boost system response. It also does away with easy-to-detect text strings and bitmaps that in the past have been a signal to graphics drivers to shortcut operations.

A.2.3 3D Benchmarking

Perhaps no area of performance benchmarking is more difficult and challenging than 3D graphics. The problem isn't so much with creating a benchmark. Heck, any decent game demo script and frame counter can yield reproducible results. The real challenge is with the torrid pace of 3D graphics technology development, which constantly redefines the performance playing field.

API Confusion

The main challenge comes from the variety of 3D APIs on the market, with chips tailored to one API or the other. However, to effectively benchmark, you need to pick a consistent platform. So what do most folks do? They test under Microsoft's Direct3D API, of course, and expect all products to perform at equal efficiency. That's a big mistake, unless all your audience does is run Direct3D-based titles and games.

Consider the analogy of a car race. In this scenario, let's say that Direct3D is the equivalent of circular race track, whereas 3Dfx's Glide API is a hilly, back road course (this is not to imply any characterization of the nature of the APIs themselves, by the way). If we pit a Porsche 911 against a U.S. Army Humvee on the Direct3D track, it's fairly obvious that the Porsche is going to win this race going away. If you happen to always drive on such a track, you'll be happy with the results you base your decisions on. However, switch to the 3Dfx Glide course, and the Porsche won't even be able to finish the race, much less compete. If you tend to drive through mud and dirt roads, obviously the Humvee is a better choice.

So when benchmarks results from WinBench 3D get tossed around, it becomes a very difficult situation. After all, most titles today are tailored to a chip's specific API, rather than to Direct3D alone. Yet, most buyers are being led by results from tests run under Direct3D—at best a matter of misinformation. In order to attain reasonable results, you need to be willing to run tests under multiple APIs, as well as to run test group subsets that allow you to compare graphics cards that share primary API support. This way you're comparing your Humvee with sport utility vehicles, whereas your Porsche is run again fellow sports cars.

Sometimes, the API thing can get downright questionable, as we found with Intel's i740 chip running on the 3D WinBench 98 test. Our tests showed the Real3D Starfighter board—one of the first with the i740—to be much faster than any Nvidia Riva 128 board and the equal of 3Dfx Voodoo II-based boards. Yet, when we ran game-based benchmarks, we found that frame rates for the i740 were consistently 30 percent or more below these chips.

It gets better. Tests of ATI's Rage Pro Turbo chip using a new driver turned up an astonishing 40 percent improvement under 3D WinBench 98. Bear in mind that no change to hardware occurred—only the software driver was updated. What was going on here? A good question, because when the same board was run under Quake II, Turok, Incoming, and other game benchmarks, frame rates either stayed unchanged or dropped by as much as 25 percent. That's right, the new driver scored better in 3D WinBench 98, but in all the real-world applications we tested, it either ran the same or worse than the original.

The problem, really, is with 3D WinBench 98's enormous market impact and popularity. Vendors can't afford to let Direct3D performance slide, even if few of their target users and applications actually use the API, because poor scores under 3D WinBench 98 translate into poor reviews and weak marketing. In other words, doom.

For users, the issue is clear. You need to look beyond support for Microsoft's API when assessing graphics boards, because it's simply not as critical as many would like to believe. Editors and users alike crave clear answers and simple solutions, and running a single benchmark under a single API can do that. However, the answers you get will be wrong unless you take the time and effort to run each card on its own track.

Visual Quality

3D benchmarking has another critical component—visual quality. Any graphics board can make 3D games play at astronomical frame rates if they're willing to throw out all the complex visual information that makes handling the scenes difficult. The real challenge is to deliver visual quality and smooth action in the form of high frame rates.

However, once again, the discussion gets bogged down in issues of API support. That's because the specific graphics technology used by a game and graphics chip defines the visual feature set. Until recently, for example, critical features such as alpha blending, bilinear and trilinear filtering, and advanced lighting and texture-mapping routines were not universally supported in all APIs. Advances in Direct3D with DirectX 5.0—and soon DirectX 6.0—is finally helping to even out feature variability.

As a result, a game that looks only so-so under Direct3D might look absolutely gorgeous when the API-specific version is run on the board instead. Or, visual quality may be on par, but the Direct3D-based test will run more slowly because the underlying hardware is tuned for its own API. Once again, users and publishers need to take the time and effort to run individual boards under their optimized APIs to allow these boards to show off their stuff. The problem is, the same games are not available under all APIs, making direct comparisons very difficult.

What can you do? Unfortunately, until a single API serves as the development target for the entire hardware and software market, there will be no way to make absolute apples-to-apples comparisons in quality. However, close observation of application behavior, research into API feature support, and a thorough benchmarking approach can go a long way toward enhancing the quality of benchmark data.

A.2.4 Video Benchmarking

Another somewhat tricky performance area is *video playback*. Once again, the name of the game is frames per second, with better systems and boards pouring out more frames each second. However, compared to the challenge of testing 3D performance and quality, video benchmarking is a walk in the park. The reason: Video under Windows 95/98 is handled almost exclusively by Microsoft's built-in DirectDraw and ActiveMovie technologies. That provides a critical, common technology base upon which various boards can be tested.

Also, video performance is not the feature wildcard that 3D tends to be. The main points of video acceleration boil down to three primary features—pixel interpolation, color space conversion, and motion estimation. Beyond that, it's really a matter of CPU power (including MMX support) and throughput.

Benchmarking

Not to say that video is easy to test. Getting consistent frame rates is fairly easy, but the visual quality of the video must be assessed in order to yield usable results. Two cards may provide identical playback frame rates, but the one that offers sophisticated pixel interpolation will produce a much more pleasing image than one with only basic image-stretching support. Interpolation is critical because video is often doubled up in size to make up for the low encoding resolutions used to conserve space.

To assess video quality, it's important for testers to look closely at the video clip as it plays, watching for blockiness, jagged lines, and smeared colors. Better cards will apply more silicon to the task of averaging out pixel color values when resolutions are multiplied, thus yielding smoother images with reduced blockiness. However, not all are equal, and the differences may be enough to make a board with slightly lower frame rates worth considering over one that produces less-than-pleasing images.

Appendix

B

Future
Casting

Living with computer hardware is a bit like playing the stock market. Your decisions and anxieties are projected on events that are expected to occur months, if not years, down the road. Just as brokerages are likely to slam dunk stock prices when they expect interest rates to rise in the next quarter, users will base their hardware and software purchases on what's coming as much as on what's already here.

With PC technology, what's coming is always a major concern. New standards can wipe out hundreds or even thousands of dollars of investment in "legacy" platforms. Bloated, performance-hogging software can swamp an affordable midrange CPU within months of a purchase. Also, explosive changes in computing models, such as the emergence of the Internet, can have you scrambling to stock up on modems, Web browsers, and HTML editing software.

However, the march of technology cuts both ways. After all, overblown expectations can lead to disastrous purchases of failed technologies and products. Beta-format VCR buyers know all too well the anxiety facing those considering a DVD-RAM drive purchase, for example. Also, anyone who's still waiting for USB—after more than two years—to take over their external devices knows what I'm talking about.

The dangers are many, but it's important still to keep a sharp eye on the horizon when purchasing your equipment. Will Intel's IA-64 make a joke out of that 500MHz Willamette processor? Are Iomega Zip drives really bound to become the next floppy disk, or are they already being surpassed by gigabyte-range formats from SyQuest and Castlewood Systems? I'll take a look at the future of computing hardware to try to help you hedge your bets.

So what will your future PC look and act like? There's no telling for sure, of course, but the research that should shape your future computing hardware is already in the works. From flat-panel desktop displays to multimegabit Internet connections, you can expect the rapid-fire improvements in performance, features, and capabilities to continue. Of course, many of these will arrive initially at a heavy premium, meaning that it could take years for mainstream PCs (those in the $2,000 range) to adopt these new technologies. What's more, enhancements in existing products will force people to make tough decisions between today's refined technologies and tomorrow's innovations.

B.1 Mainboard Components

Driven primarily by Intel, the motherboard of future PCs will look and act quite differently from today's PCs. Wider and faster buses will pour data to all corners of your system, and ever-climbing clock rates will thrill marketers and buyers alike. Critical market choices loom, however, as Intel plans to move us all to new memory technologies and faster motherboards, as well as not one, but two new CPU connectors.

Of course, we'll need new system chipsets and technologies to support the emerging processors. Intel already has a pretty detailed road map laid out (see Figure B.1), whereas AMD has plans for transitioning to a whole new CPU connector design. Alongside these innovations are critical improvements to the system's main memory, opening data rates to keep pace with future 200MHz system buses and fast AGP 4× graphics cards. For Cyrix and AMD, the challenge will be a stiff one. Although Cyrix enjoys licensing of at least the Intel Slot 1 technology, AMD will have to go it alone with its own Slot A approach. However, their efforts to keep pace with Intel will be challenged by new bus types, emerging memories, and yet another increase in the system front bus clock.

Figure B.1.

Intel CPU roadmap to the end of 1999.

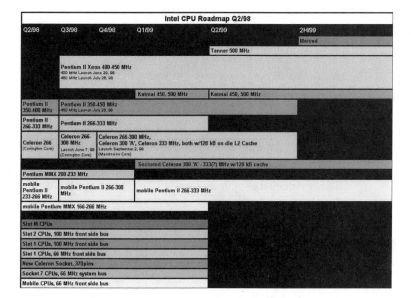

B.1.1 CPU

It wasn't more than a year ago that both scientists and the press were fretting about the imminent demise of Moore's Law, the statement that predicted the more-or-less doubling of CPU power every 18 months. The cause for concern: Limitations in the current CPU manufacturing infrastructure, which relies on light-driven photolithography to lay down intricate submicron patterns in silicon that form the circuitry inside CPUs. As manufacturing processes shrank from .35 microns to .25 microns and .18 microns, the width of the circuits were closing in on the physical limits of the technology.

As circuits get smaller, electronics traveling their microscopic paths start to misbehave in quantum ways. Charges jump their gates, bleed through intervening material, and randomly change their states. In order to maintain a semblance of order in their tiny data engines, CPU manufacturers needed to move to new processes and new materials, a transition that entails a catastrophically costly shift in manufacturing infrastructure.

IBM Microelectronics helped save the day when it figured out how to get semiconductive silicon to coexist with copper, a metal that helps reduce internal resistance, thus ensuring rising clock speeds and smaller circuits for at least another two or three CPU generations to come. At the same time, advances in the photolithographic process have helped stave off the dreaded switch to a narrower pattern source, ultraviolet (UV) light.

These combined advances lay a clear road map to faster and smaller CPUs, with clock speeds expected to hit 1,000MHz by the year 2000. Circuits on these fast chips will measure a meager .13 microns in width, about one-half the size of today's most advanced CPUs. The smaller circuitry will also enable lower voltages, dropping from 2.8 volts to as low as 1.8 volts over the next three years. The reductions will cut down heat dissipation and enable advanced CPU designs to migrate into notebooks.

1999

1999 will be a busy year in the CPU world. In the second half, Intel will roll out its long anticipated Merced processor, the first in its IA-64 workstation-class CPUs, developed conjointly with HP. This 64-bit processor can address hundreds of gigabytes of main memory and will provide performance that's an order of magnitude better—or more—than the fastest Pentium IIs available today. Initial clock speeds are expected to be 800MHz running on top of a 200MHz front side bus. Clock rates will increase quickly after that, pushing to 1,000MHz and beyond in 2000.

IA-64 will plug into a new, enlarged Slot M connector and will provide *explicit parallelism*, which results in several parallel machine codes after compilation of the source code. Merced will offer 128 integer and 128 floating-point registers and multiple integer and floating point units, which can all work in parallel. IA32, by contrast, is only capable of *implicit parallelism*, resulting in one machine code after compilation. IA32 offers only 8-32 integer and 8-32 floating-point registers and has only two integer and floating-point units.

Initial IA-64 production will be strictly for high-end workstation graphics and servers and will be priced well out of the desktop market. For mainstream users, Intel will continue plying the divergent paths of its Pentium II core technology, with bargain buyers perhaps enjoying the greatest enhancements.

Look for the Celeron family to grow up in a big way in 1999, as a cache-equipped version of this chip (code-named *Mendocino*) running at 333MHz provides big performance gains just before the year starts. The 128KB L2 cache will be built directly into the CPU silicon—not on a separate backside bus as Pentium II does today—allowing it to run at CPU speed. Even more intriguing, Intel plans to integrate its 2D/3D i740 graphics core into the Celeron CPU to provide system-in-a-chip functionality. Code-named *Whitney*, the integrated part is due out in late 1999.

Intel has also discussed its intention to integrate the i740 core into the north bridge of its popular system chipsets. Although the graphics core will run at a lower clock rate than that of CPU-integrated cores, the design should enable cheap and powerful 3D graphics on systems costing well under $1,000.

Pentium II gets an improvement early in 1999 with the roll out of the Katmai processor. Armed with 70 3D graphics-specific instructions (Katmai NI) with double-precision floating-point SIMD (single instruction multiple data) facilities, Katmai will run at 450MHz and, later, at 500MHz. An enlarged L1 cache is a likely probability, thus further enhancing performance.

Around the same time, Intel will also massage the upper end of its P6 line with the Tanner processor. This improvement on the original Xeon processor will run on the Slot 2 connector and will offer the Katmai instruction set extensions for 3D graphics. Details are sketchy, but Tanner could provide some Merced technologies as well.

By 1999, AMD and Cyrix will both have turned up the heat as well. AMD will leave behind the Socket 7 form factor for its K7 CPU, moving to a Slot A connector. Based on the bus used for Digital's Alpha CPU, Slot A is the same size as Intel's Slot 1 but uses a different signaling. K7 will include the 3D-Now instruction set extensions introduced in the K6-2 CPU.

Cyrix's Jalapeño, meanwhile, will most likely find a home on the Intel Slot 1 connector, thanks to licensing agreements held by Cyrix's parent company—National Semiconductor. Cyrix hasn't released any specific information on its next-generation CPU at the time of its writing, but one thing to consider is the success of the company's integrated system-on-a-chip technologies.

2000

Things get fuzzier as we push further out. In 2000, Intel will release the Willamette processor, a next-generation 32-bit CPU with a core that can be considered a P7. Built on a .18-micron process and running at 800MHz at its roll out, Willamette will be up to 50 percent faster than Katmai. It will likely run on a

Future Casting

200MHz system bus. The presence of IA-64 Merced at the high end should allow Willamette to play on the power desktop market. Merced will continue to improve as well, with the 1,000MHz version likely making its debut this year. Cyrix is also slated to enhance its Jalapeño CPU.

2001

Call it the year of the die shrink. Intel expect to transition its high-end products to a .13-micron process in 2001, allowing for significant gains in both performance and mainstream availability. Look for Willamette to play in the low end of the market, with the Katmai NI/Katmai instruction set extensions propagated throughout the mainstream market. An integrated, on-chip L2 cache of perhaps 256KB is likely to help maximize performance.

The .13-micron Merced CPU should finally make IA-64 an option for desktop power users, although prices will likely remain quite high. At the server end, Merced's follow on, McKinley, will continue to push clock rates and enhance the 64-bit processor core.

Other Happenings

Beyond 2001, it's tough to say what will come next. Intel is planning to push its manufacturing processes down to .10 microns, and that should happen in 2003. At this point, Merced looks to be a mainstream CPU, with IA-64 becoming the platform of choice for personal computing. However, future gains will be tough to come by, as circuit sizes begin to reach levels that invite quantum irregularities and require the use of specialized, ultraviolet processes.

One area that will continue to confound is notebook computing. High-end CPUs continue to post a challenge for engineers trying to fit the technology into the limited thermal and power envelopes of notebook computers. Intel's Geyserville technology provides a solution by automatically throttling back the CPU when the notebook is running on batteries. Plug into an AC outlet, and the system logic pushes CPU speed back up. However, some form of active cooling—most likely a heat-activated fan—will probably be needed, thus adding weight and power draw.

In general, expect notebook CPU releases to lag behind significantly. The gating factor: Intel must shrink the die of the original desktop version by at least one manufacturing step to make it work inside the limited resources of portables.

B.1.2 System Chipsets

With all those new CPUs coming out, Intel will be rolling out chipsets to support them. It all begins at the end of 1998 with the 450NX chipset for Slot 2 servers, which offers four-way or even eight-way SMP support, up to 4GB of main memory addressing, and a 66MHz fast PCI bus. Also, the front bus will run at 100MHz. This release follows closely that of the 440GX, the less-sophisticated Slot 2 chipset that should be released by the time you read this. Designed for more affordable Slot 2 systems, the 440GX supports 2GB of main memory and is otherwise similar to the Slot 1–based 440BX.

Things get interesting in 1999 with the introduction of the Camino chipset, which will support the upcoming Katmai CPU. The first chipset to support Direct Rambus (Direct RDRAM) memory, Camino's front-side bus will actually run at an enhanced 133MHz, 33 percent faster than previous chipsets. Also integrated into the chipset is support for AGP 4×, the ATA-66 IDE interface, and the AC '97 digital audio codec for enabling high-fidelity USB and PCI-based audio.

Finally, 450NX will be succeeded by the Carmel chipset, designed for servers and workstations and the Tanner CPU. A server version of Camino, Carmel includes AGP 4×, Direct RDRAM, ATA66, and integrated AC '97. As a server platform, it also adds the wide 66MHz PCI bus.

B.1.3 System Memory

As you can see, Intel has definite plans to wean the user base off dynamic RAM technologies. The introduction of direct RDRAM in 1999 should provide a compelling performance advance, provided Intel's implementations are efficient enough to take advantage of the swift, serialized memory interface. At the same time, the introduction of double data rate (DDR) SDRAM will nearly double the effective throughput of today's platform. In other words, Intel has its work cut out.

RDRAM is a big change because, unlike current SDRAM memory, it doesn't depend on an ever-widening connection to push more bits per second. In fact, RDRAM's critical advantage is that its narrow 8-bit bus can be clocked to astronomical speeds, starting at 400MHz. Because it's much easier to boost the clock on a simple serial bus than it is to add more signals to a fast parallel bus, RDRAM presents plenty of potential performance headroom.

In fact, RDRAM will constitute a system bus all its own on the motherboard when it's introduced in 1999. A separate RDRAM controller will handle timings and accesses along the serial connection, thus enabling efficient flow of data from the RDRAM subsystem to the system chipset. Coupled with AGP 4× and the upcoming 200MHz system bus, RDRAM should play a critical role in scaling overall system performance along with advanced CPU architectures.

Future Casting

At the same time, DDR SDRAM could extend existing motherboard designs. By allowing access on the rising and falling edges of the clock, DDR SDRAM doubles the effective data rate of the memory. The scheme requires new components, updated memory, and compliant chipsets, but it should work within the existing electrical structure of the system board. DDR SDRAM could play a critical role in extending the Super 7 motherboard market.

B.2 Peripherals

Big things are afoot off the board as well. Mass storage is in the midst of major changes as a crucial capacity limit looms on the near horizon. Unfortunately, this could also invite yet another glut of incompatible standards, which have always plagued this segment of the industry. Meanwhile, graphics technology continues to push the realism of 3D to new heights, whereas displays make a slow transition to flat panel screens. Perhaps most exciting is the emergence of advanced connectivity options for your PC, from smart external buses to cheap home networks. The Internet has proven that PCs want and need to be connected. Now the technology is coming that will do just that for every PC in your home, without requiring new wiring, hubs, network cards, and software.

B.2.1 Storage

Believe it or not, the storage picture looks to be very revolutionary, even more so than CPUs. In fact, PC-based storage could be looking at enormous gains over the next five years or so, as intriguing technologies arrive to solve imminent capacity bottlenecks in magnetic and optical mass storage. Two major technology breakthroughs are driving the market:

- Near-field recording (NFR)
- Optically assisted Winchester (OAW) technology

The new technologies are being developed to stave off something called the *superparamagnetic limit*. This ominous sounding term essentially spells the end of growing hard disk capacities, due to the limitations of the magnetic storing properties of the media. Over the past ten years, disk makers have made a living by cramming more and more bits into the same amount of space, pushing the so-called *area density* of the media to new limits. Today's disks hold about 3 gigabits per square inch (GBpsi), whereas the superparamagnetic limit is thought to lie somewhere between 10 and 20GBpsi.

When you hit these densities, bad things start happening to your data. The individual magnetic charges become so packed together that even the weakest coherent charges begin to overlap into each others' space. The pattern of 1s and 0s degrades into a hard-to-detect fog of tiny blooming charges, making reliable storage impossible. Moving the read/write head closer to the media to better detect the charges is not an option, because the overlapping fields pollute the entire magnetic structure. Weakening the charges further is no longer an option, because doing so makes them susceptible to random polarity changes, again destroying data.

Near-Field Recording

Developed at Stanford University and marketed by Terastor, *near-field recording* (NFR) overcomes the superparamagnetic limit by bringing light into the picture. Like today's hard disk drives, NFR uses a flying head to travel over the rotating media. However, where current drives rely strictly on magnetic fields to read and write data using a magneto-resistive head, NFR augments the process with an optical lens, called a *solid-immersion lens*.

The optical lens sits between the magnetic coil and the media and serves to focus a laser beam at a pinpoint target on the media. Once heated, the magnetic coil is able to set the state of the underlying point on the media. Because only the heated point on the media is able to change states, there's no problem with contaminating adjacent bits with the magnetic field.

To achieve extremely high area densities, a technique called *crescent recording* is used, where the tiny data spots are actually overlapped.

Terastore says that its process can pack areal densities of 40GBpsi, making it four to eight times more efficient than the best existing disk drive technology. Terastore expects to continue to refine its process, thus enabling even greater gains beyond the year 2000. Expect initial NFR hard disk media to hold 20GB to 40GB, with removable cartridged media based on the technology emerging as well. The first NFR drives should arrive in late 1998 or 1999.

Optically Assisted Winchester

Another solution to the superparamagnetic limit is in the works over at Seagate's recently acquired Quinta division. Called *Optically Assisted Winchester* technology, this approach is similar to NFR in that it introduces a laser to the magnetic-only read/write head assembly of the hard disk drive.

A fiber optic wire is used to carry light pulses from an optical switching module in the drive housing to the read/write head. Here, tiny micromirrors are positioned and focused to project the red laser pulse onto a specific point of the media below, heating it to its Curie point. Once heated, the amorphous media is susceptible to charge state changes, which are executed by the magnetic coil in the flying read/write head.

Future Casting

To read data, a low-power laser pulse is projected onto the surface point. The magnetic charge of the underlying bit is detected by the rotation of the polarization of the reflected laser light. Seagate expects OAW drives to pack 20GBpsi and even 40GBpsi, similar to the areal densities projected by Terastor for its NFR technology.

Farther Out

For a few years now, researchers have pinned their hopes on so-called *holographic memory* as a viable technology for storing terabytes of data in a tiny space. Although these efforts continue—and enjoy some success—the emergence of NFR and OAW technologies will most likely mean that rotating mass storage media will serve quite adequately for another ten years to come.

Rather than riding a read/write head above a spinning platter, holographic media is accessed by shining lasers into an optically doped structure. Specific bits are read or written by intersecting two lasers at a target point within the media. When reading data, the device detects the reflected light from the intersecting lasers, which it interprets as a digital 1 or 0 based on its state. To write data, higher-powered lasers are focused to switch the optical state of the targeted bit.

Holographic memory has some enormous advantages over any spinning media type. Perhaps most important are the potential low access and seek times implied by the solid-state holographic technology. Because the mechanism does not have to move across physical distances and wait for the targeted point of the media to rotate under it, the time needed to access data can be cut significantly. Just as important, holographic memory is capable of parallel execution. By operating multiple laser pairs, disparate bits can be fetched from all over the three-dimensional media structure simultaneously, vastly enhancing noncontiguous data access.

Unlike any current mass storage medium, holographic technology brings the enormous capacity advantage of being three-dimensional. A cubical structure one centimeter to a side—smaller than a sugar cube—could store gigabytes of information. However, don't go putting off any drive purchases for the new technology just yet.

B.2.2 Displays

The future of display technology is clearly in the realm of flat panels. Advancing manufacturing processes and dropping prices should make 17-inch active-matrix TFT and plasma-based flat panel screens a reality for mainstream desktops. Already this year we've seen surprising drops in prices. However, continued reductions in CRT monitor prices will ensure that flat panels will continue to sell at a hefty premium of five to ten times the CRT cost.

Still, the advantages are many. LCDs are many times smaller and lighter than their CRT cousins—a huge advantage, in particular, for corporate, medical, and other professional environments. They also draw much less power and throw off a lot less heat than CRTs, providing cost savings in the form of reduced electrical bills.

For mainstream users, one ray of hope exists in the form of advanced passive-matrix technology, called dual supertwist nematic, which is often used in budget notebooks. Sharp's High-Contrast Addressing (HCA) technology boosts the marginal contrast of passive technology to that approaching TFT displays, thus eliminating problems with ghosting and readability. Responsiveness is also enhanced, although it still lags behind TFT.

All this may be a moot point, however, as CRT monitors continue to improve. Perhaps the most mature technology in your PC, CRT displays will get larger, less expensive, and easier to tune. Nineteen-inch monitors are already making a splash at the high end of the mainstream market, providing tube sizes just two inches shy of the true professional graphics market. As non-Japanese tube manufacturers transition over to the larger CRT form factors, expect even 21-inch monitors to drop in price from their current $1,500 to $2,500 range.

One major problem with large CRTs is the prodigious amount of space they consume. The issue is with the vacuum tube, which must taper back to a narrow column that holds the electron gun. If the gun sits too close to the monitor glass, the angle created to fire its beam to the edges of the screen becomes too extreme to maintain the round pixel shape. However, vendors are employing advanced magnetic fields to guide and adjust the beam when swept to extreme angles, allowing for shortened chassis depth. This same technology also lets engineers flatten out the curve in the monitor's front glass, producing a truly flat screen.

In the area of controls, expect a USB wire to connect to any monitor you buy, whether it's an LCD, plasma, or CRT display. The digital connection will allow you to send software-based configuration commands to the hardware, so you can set display position, geometry, size, and color-matching settings without fiddling with knobs or onscreen controls. Built-in USB ports on the monitor house itself will also let you plug desktop devices into convenient ports on your desktop.

Future Casting

B.2.3 Graphics

The 3D graphics world continues to plow forward with innovations both incremental and dramatic. The first, best step will probably come in the form of Microsoft's DirectX 6.0, which should include a well-improved implementation of the Direct3D API. After years of frustrating promise, however, Direct3D may finally get on track.

Behind the optimism is a highly streamlined architecture that will shrink the current set of DLLs from 3.5MB to a svelte 880KB. Developers will gain incentive to write to Direct3D thanks to a more intuitive programming model. The inclusion of vertex buffers should allow developers to get away from clumsy execute buffer model programming and instead use DrawPrimitive in their code. Finally, new features such as bump mapping and stencil buffering will further enhance the realism and efficiency of 3D graphics in games and titles. Nvidia's Riva 128 TNT chip will be first to market with support for bump mapping and stencil buffering.

Further down the road, Microsoft will join up with Silicon Graphics to begin work on a unified 3D graphics API that will merge Direct3D and OpenGL. Called *Fahrenheit*, the new API is expected to be backward compatible with Direct3D software while providing the features and resources of OpenGL. The intended result: To provide a single API target for both consumer 3D games and applications as well as for precision-driven engineering and design software.

On the hardware front, AGP 4× will invite system memory to deliver texture data to the tune of one gigabyte per second, whereas truly optimized AGP-compliant chips will eliminate latencies that currently plague direct memory execution (DIME) operation. At the same time, falling memory prices will put 16MB of RAM onto most game 3D cards, enough that the visual benefit of going to slower main memory becomes a real question.

Ultimately, graphics will be addressed in the CPU. Intel's Whitney project puts the i740 graphics core directly into its Celeron product, completely eliminating the AGP or PCI bus from the access equation. Cyrix has similar plans with its Media MXi CPU, the follow up to its successful Media GX line. Graphics chips will also get an enormous boost from improved geometry and setup performance in the CPU as 3D-Now and Katmai/Katmai NI instruction set extensions address the weakest link in the 3D graphics chain.

Putting pressure on the 3D graphics market is Intel, which plans to introduce its Portola follow up to the i740 in the second half of 1999. Expected to provide five times the 3D performance of i740, Intel calls it a "Katmai processor balanced solution." Portola will support TV-out and video capture, but it will only use AGP 2×. Portola is targeted to the performance PC market segment.

B.2.4 Connectivity

PC buses will continue to grow, merge, adapt, and die. By 2001, expect ISA to be a goner, as system vendors finally move on to PCI as the workhorse system bus of choice. Although PCI will click along at its familiar 33MHz and 32-bit data path, fast and wide PCI variants will proliferate in the server and other vertical application arenas. Meanwhile, AGP will all but take over the graphics market by 2000, particularly as improved AGP implementations allow vendors to lay AGP graphics chips on the motherboard without forcing users to forego the possibility of future card-based upgrades. Also expect AGP to get enhanced in 1999, with the AGP 4× specification being trotted out for high-end graphics and imaging applications.

The back of your PC will start looking a bit less chaotic, as vendors trade a bunch of dumb ports for fewer smart ones. After three years of virtual stasis, USB will finally catch on as system vendors begin shipping USB versions of scanners, monitor-top cameras, and, later, keyboards and mice with their systems. The new bus should help ease the IRQ bottleneck facing many new system owners.

Joining USB around 2001 will be Firewire, the fast IEEE 1394 bus originally founded by Apple. It's high 400MBps data rates (with plans for 1GBps and beyond) and Plug and Play operation make it a perfect match for video capture, removable data storage, and Plug and Play networking. Firewire will also figure prominently into products such as Gateway's Destination PC line, which aims to join your PC with your home electronics. Another big Firewire application: Interfaces with digital video cameras that use CCDs to capture video to magnetic tape.

Home networks will explode, but don't expect this to happen with NICs and Ethernet hubs. Rather, users will plug USB adapters into their home phone jacks or electrical outlets and ride data across the networks that are already installed. Data rates will be lower—about 350KBps to 1MBps—but should be more than enough for consumer use. Wireless radio also looks to be an option, but the expense of transceivers, coupled with the need to plug into a power supply anyway, will limit their appeal.

Future Casting

B.3 Tom's Vision

The continued advances in PC technology will allow for smaller, faster, smarter, and better connected computing at lower price points than ever before. Sub-$1,000 PCs will cease to be a joke and will become a dynamic marketplace of devices able to take on a plethora of tasks. However, the maturation of instruction sets, advanced graphics APIs, and rich interfaces will continue to drive the market for more expensive PCs.

Games, in particular, will lead the charge. API support for bump mapping and other visual features will vastly enhance the realism of real-time gaming, whereas the integration of geometry-savvy features into both CPUs and graphics chips should whittle away at the last remaining bottleneck in the graphics pipeline. Empowered by sophisticated APIs and wide-and-smart graphics acceleration, advanced games will continue to put pressure on mainstream computing hardware.

The ultimate fruition of computing advances will come in communications. The ubiquity of IP communications, coupled with DirectX and other standards, will help finally stomp out the ridiculous complexity of PC-based communications. ADSL, bi-directional cable modems, and wireless communications will all benefit from open standards development. Before long, the dial tone will be out of the picture, providing "click once" connectivity that offers instantaneous response, ample bandwidth, and a LAN-like feel.

No, the future of high-performance computing will not be a hand-held device or even a sub-$1,000 box. The integration these devices require will always force buyers to forego performance and capabilities needed to enjoy the most-advanced software. The same holds true for notebooks, where the growing need to preserve battery life and reduce thermal output will prevent these products from closing the performance gap with desktops.

The good news is that $2,000 or $3,000 will buy a heckuva lot of computer. 3D games will present realism that rivals prerendered content such as Pixar's Toy Story movie, whereas application and OS interfaces will grow to sop up the incredible bandwidth dished out by top CPUs and buses. Web content, in particular, will drive high-end PCs. Microsoft's Chrome initiative promises to make 3D processing a much-valued feature for Web browsing.

Ultimately, the future of computing will be ruled by the organic process of evolution. Uneven standards development, unexpected applications, and the vagaries of the technology market will all conspire to make the next five to ten years well worth experiencing. One thing is for sure: Your dollar will go much farther then than it does now.

Index

C

H

S

X

Y

Z